FINANCING
METROPOLITAN
GOVERNMENTS
in DEVELOPING
COUNTRIES

FINANCING METROPOLITAN GOVERNMENTS *in* DEVELOPING COUNTRIES

Edited by

ROY W. BAHL
JOHANNES F. LINN
DEBORAH L. WETZEL

LINCOLN INSTITUTE
OF LAND POLICY
CAMBRIDGE, MASSACHUSETTS

© 2013 by the Lincoln Institute of Land Policy

All rights reserved.

Library of Congress Cataloging-in-Publication Data

Financing metropolitan governments in developing countries / edited by Roy W. Bahl, Johannes F. Linn, Deborah L. Wetzel.

     pages cm
  Includes index.
  ISBN 978-1-55844-254-2 (alk. paper)
  1. Municipal finance—Developing countries. 2. Finance, Public—Developing countries. 3. Local taxation—Developing countries. 4. Municipal government—Developing countries. 5. Municipal finance—Developing countries—Case studies. 6. Finance, Public—Developing countries—Case studies. 7. Local taxation—Developing countries—Case studies. 8. Municipal government—Developing countries—Case studies. I. Bahl, Roy W. II. Linn, Johannes F. III. Wetzel, Deborah L.
  HJ9695.F663 2013
   352.4'216091724—dc23   2013001063

Designed by Westchester Publishing Services

Composed in 10.5/13 Minion, by Westchester Publishing Services in Danbury, Connecticut.
Printed and bound by Puritan Press Inc., in Hollis, New Hampshire.

The paper is Rolland Enviro100, an acid-free, 100 percent PCW recycled sheet.

MANUFACTURED IN THE UNITED STATES OF AMERICA

Contents

ILLUSTRATIONS

BOXES

FOREWORD

One of the several things I did to prepare to write this foreword was review the original volume of Bahl and Linn, which came out in April of 1992, titled *Urban Public Finance in Developing Countries*, including the foreword that I prepared for that volume. In the foreword I stated, "When the World Bank initiated this research program on urban public finance in the early 1970s, Roy, Johannes, and I found it difficult to raise much interest in the topic." Fortunately, over the years, much of the work by Bahl and Linn on urban public finance in developing countries has reached wide audiences in academia and developing countries. Their book distilled the lessons learned during many years of work by themselves and a growing cadre of others who were prompted by the funding of the World Bank's initial research projects and fieldwork during that early period. As a result, our main objective of providing the basis on which further research and operational work could build was largely achieved.

Now, more than 20 years down the road, the audiences have expanded, and the knowledge base has been greatly extended, deepened, broadened, and, perhaps most impressive, pushed into several new dimensions of importance. For example, 20 years ago we could not have produced a chapter on the role of metropolitan cities in national economies (Shahid Yusuf); on their place in the national fiscal structure (Paul Smoke); on institutions and politics (Inder Sud); or on infrastructure and capital markets (Greg Ingram et al.).

Further, a large core of a new generation of specialists—drawing on the initial and continuing work of Bahl, Linn, Richard Bird, Charles McLure, and others—has continued to grow up around the world, and the ability to administer modern revenue systems is in place in many locations. There has been some improvement in governance and finances of metropolitan areas, including better expenditure assignments, the implementation of buoyant revenue systems in some places, borrowing to finance urban infrastructure, and, most of all, more elected representation in many regions.

Metropolitan planning has become a reality in most large urban areas, even though the planning agencies are ineffective in moving things forward and generally in linking their plans with the fiscal and financial aspects of metropolitan government. There are also a growing number of success stories in metropolitan finance and management that, together with the now accumulated experience and proper efforts and support, could be extended to an even broader array of forward-looking programs to address the growing public service needs of metropolitan-area populations.

Nevertheless, an honest look at what use has been made of the now very substantial knowledge base reveals that the response has not been heartening. As documented in this volume, sweeping metropolitan-area fiscal reforms have been few and far between; the urban policy reform agenda is still a long one; and there is a reasonable prospect that closing "knowledge gaps"—the gaps between what we know how to do and what is actually being done—will continue to be difficult and slow. The following are some of the most worrisome areas where such gaps exist, judging by the evidence presented in this volume.

We have not developed the ability to govern effectively the metropolitan regions that have become the most important concentrations of people on Earth. National and state (or provincial) governments shackle city and metropolitan governments and/or neglect their problems. Add to this frequent conflict, or at least a lack of co-ordination, among the many different authorities. Gross inefficiencies continue to plague delivery of most services in most metro areas. Metropolitan revenues remain gravely insufficient despite rapidly burgeoning needs and a growing tax base. Appropriate transfer systems that reflect the differences between metros and other local governments have, in general, not yet been implemented. Huge infrastructure deficiencies persist or, in developed countries, have emerged; and there are few signs they might be addressed on anything approaching sufficient scale anytime soon.

The same is true of basic social services. Some countries and cities are scrambling to address these problems, but often outside any context of a metropolitan fiscal strategy. Perhaps of greatest concern, the data that might help elucidate these and related problems so that more appropriate or politically palatable solutions might be designed remain largely absent or inadequate.

One must ask why the going has been so slow for so long. This is a matter we pondered, to little effect, in 1992 and again in this volume. Now, after the wholly worthwhile investment of so much more time, effort, and money, it would be a grave error to be again naively hopeful about the future or to fall back on the excuse that development takes time, though of course this is true. So, though it may be presumptuous, I suggest that we contemplate a serious investigation of this "failure on the action front," along the following lines.

Quite a few thoughts about what has held things back emerge from these chapters. A complex set of government weaknesses, a lack of democratic participation, and the nature of politics have played important parts. One important aspect is the urban versus rural struggle, both for political power and influence and for the resources to meet respective needs. In addition, higher-level (federal and state or provincial) government officials fear that they might lose control of things if too much autonomy is given to (sometimes capable and ambitious) metropolitan mayors.

However, by far the dominant reason for lack of progress is that the central importance of cities, of urban agglomerations, remains far too imperfectly understood by most people, including many extremely well-meaning people: advocates of alleviating rural poverty; many environmentalists; and, above all, most of the influential policy makers who might be able to get the ball rolling. As a result, though the interest in urban matters has tended to cycle up and down, it has seldom been and has never remained a top priority. Substantial progress has been made on certain aspects of the urban "problematique," including municipal and metropolitan finances. However, sustained progress on a broad front toward smarter growth, creating more sustainable cities, and alleviating grave pollution problems—including global warming—has been lacking, as has progress toward reforming municipal and metropolitan finances so that the resources might become available to deal with these and other important matters.

In view of these obstacles, it would be putting the cart before the horse to insist that solutions to this host of problems should start with the emendation of municipal and metro finances. Rather, I believe, the search for a way forward will need to start with a better understanding of the overall urban dilemma and that it cannot be successfully addressed on an item-by-item basis. Cities, especially large metropolitan areas, are where our greatest economic and social opportunities lie and where our most threatening economic and social problems manifest, the former underexploited and the latter aggravated by inadequate and counterproductive policies and actions.

Fortunately, there has been substantial progress in urban research since the early 1990s. This has been admirably summarized by perhaps the single greatest contributor to this progress, Edward Glaeser, in his outstanding book *Triumph of the City* (2011). In this very readable book, Glaeser comprehensively treats the (limited) nature of cities' "triumph": in spite of the many obstacles, people will come to cities and become "richer, smarter, greener, healthier, and happier" as a result. He also demonstrates the many contributing reasons for this triumph over adversity, emphasizing that, at its core, the indomitable strength of cities is due to the education, knowledge, and skills of its residents (importantly, including those added via immigration) and the cities' functions in bringing these residents together most productively. He suggests the elements of what can be the path toward a future where the triumph of the city might no longer be limited—if we will have the sense, and can mobilize the will, to take it.

Some influential opinion makers have come to understand the issue at hand. In an op-ed in the *New York Times* on December 5, 2012, titled, "How Cities Can Save China," Henry M. Paulson Jr., former chairman of Goldman Sachs, former U.S. treasury secretary, former chairman and still an important force in the Nature Conservancy, wrote: "A flawed system of municipal finance is driving debt . . . while unsustainable urban planning has yielded polluted cities that are destroying China's ecosystems. . . . Cities can, however, be part of the solution." And what he says is true not merely about China (though it is surely nowhere else demonstrated in bolder relief), but everywhere. It is around such an appreciation as this that a successful approach might be organized.

What seems to me the only realistic path out of the current dilemma, not just for metropolitan and city finance but for the urban problematique, is for there to emerge—to be encouraged to emerge—a powerful urban coalition that can begin to force change and to evolve a strategy to interest and eventually involve the requisite actors. Perhaps this could begin with the C40 Cities Climate Leadership Group, currently chaired by Michael Bloomberg, particularly if it could adopt a more comprehensive view of the problem and its agenda. And perhaps such a group, abetted by the international development banks and a number of other organizations, might prevail upon the G20 to make these concerns central in its agenda. Success along such lines would greatly strengthen the demand for action on the metropolitan and municipal finances front.

At the same time, a push could come from the supply side of ideas, with research started now, building on the chapters in this volume, that could lead to the publication of another volume in the future. The new agenda could include, among other things, research focused on urban institutions, management, and political issues and on more effectively accessing capital markets. Additionally, the agenda could cover case studies on positive trends and developments, including factors that have impeded or disrupted progress in metropolitan management and finance. Such a comprehensive program, presumably under U.N. auspices, could at last confidently build the database to support research on these and other critical urban problems.

And, finally, a serious effort might be made to persuade the World Bank to partner with the relevant regional development banks and perhaps other institutions to initiate a large pilot program on metro finance reform in a promising metropolitan region. Such a partnership might undertake the arduous task of discovering a region that appears to meet most of the several exacting preconditions for success, or work with the relevant actors in the region and at the national level until the groundwork for potential success can be laid down.

DOUGLAS H. KEARE
Former Visiting Fellow
Lincoln Institute of Land Policy

Governing and Financing Metropolitan Areas in the Developing World

ROY W. BAHL, JOHANNES F. LINN, AND DEBORAH L. WETZEL

The economic activity that drives growth in developing countries is heavily concentrated in urban areas.[1] Catchphrases such as "metropolitan areas are the engines that pull the national economy" turn out to be fairly accurate.[2] But the same comparative advantages of metropolitan areas that draw investment also draw migrants who need jobs and housing, lead to demands for better infrastructure and social services, and result in increased congestion, environmental harm, and social problems. The challenges to metropolitan public finances are to capture a share of the economic growth that is adequate to finance the new and growing expenditure needs and to organize governance so that services can be delivered in a cost-effective way, giving the local population an adequate voice in fiscal decision making. At the same time, care must be taken to avoid overregulation and overtaxation, which will hamper the now quite mobile economic engine of private investment and entrepreneurial initiative.

This book identifies the current issues of importance in metropolitan governance and finance in developing countries, describes the practice, explores the gap between practice and what theory suggests should be done, and lays out the reform paths that might be considered. Part of the solution will rest in rethinking expenditure assignments and instruments of finance. But this will need to be done in a context of how government is structured, the characteristics of the local economy, the infrastructure gap, the concentration of poverty and slums, environmental

---

[1] This chapter uses, for simplicity's sake, the traditional terminology distinguishing between developing countries and industrial countries, following the World Bank in its World Development Indicators (World Bank 2012): the former are referred to as *low* and *middle income countries*, and the latter, as *high income countries*. Although the line between low- and middle-income countries is becoming increasingly blurred, the grouping remains broadly relevant.

[2] All broad generalizations are bound to have exceptions. For example, economies that rely heavily on primary exports such as natural resources may be driven primarily by commodity prices.

concerns, and the external financing options. The "right" approach also will depend on the flexibility of political leaders to relinquish some control in order to find a better solution to the metropolitan finance problem.

This chapter reviews the main lessons that have been learned about each of these issues, by drawing on the existing literature and on the research reported in the 14 chapters that follow.

URBANIZATION TRENDS AND ECONOMIC GROWTH

The rate of urbanization in developing countries is projected to reach the 50 percent mark in the 2010s (United Nations 2008). According to current estimates, the world population will likely grow from approximately 7 billion in 2012 to more than 9 billion by 2050 (U.S. Census Bureau 2012), and virtually all of the population increment will be absorbed by urban areas in developing countries (figure 1.1).

The number of megacities (populations > 10 million) is projected to increase from 19 in 2007 to 27 in 2025, when about 10 percent of the world's urban population will reside in these cities. Of the projected 27 megacities, 21 will be in less developed countries. By 2025, 48 cities will have populations from 5 to 10 million, and three-fourths of these will be in developing countries (United Nations 2008).

FIGURE 1.1

Rural and urban population by major regions, 1950, 2010, and 2050

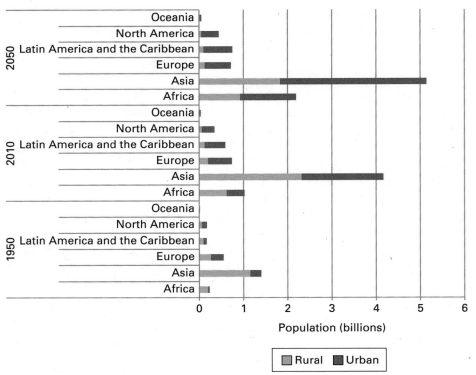

SOURCE: United Nations (2012).

It is not uncommon for individual metropolitan areas to account for more than one-fourth of national gross domestic product (GDP) in Organisation for Economic Co-operation and Development (OECD) member countries (OECD 2006).[3] The same is also true in developing countries, for example, 27 percent in Istanbul and 52 percent in Buenos Aires (Braun and Webb forthcoming; OECD 2008a). The benefits and costs of this degree of economic primacy are not limited to the largest cities. The positive trickle-down effects will include growth in firms that supply metropolitan-area industries and generation of tax revenues that are redistributed to local governments in the rest of the country. But there also are negatives, such as the brain drain from other regions to metropolitan areas, as the most talented workers move to cities to seek better opportunities, and the political friction that metropolitan-area dominance sometimes causes (see Smoke, chapter 3; Sud and Yilmaz, chapter 5).

The size of metropolitan areas can be an economic blessing or a curse, depending on how they are managed. But there is no question that big challenges lie ahead.

- Not only will an increasing number of cities be megasized (10 million and greater), but also they will be clustered in multimetro regions/corridors. Regional planning will be imperative.
- Rising mobility with greatly expanded car ownership will result in declining urban densities and will create challenges for infrastructure, environment, and agricultural land use. Effective land use regulation can help address this challenge.
- With globalization, metro economies are highly integrated in the global economy and will need to be more competitive. In particular, the growth of the largely unregulated and mobile service sector in these metro economies requires "smart growth" strategies by cities. The development of information technology services will be a key factor.
- The delivery of adequate services in metropolitan areas should be viewed as part of the smart growth strategy and will be especially challenged by the large populations living in slums.
- Metropolitan areas will need to be at the forefront of the response to climate change and green growth opportunities (see Wetzel, chapter 12).

In chapter 2, Yusuf summarizes key factors that can drive strong and sustainable metropolitan income and employment growth: (1) an economic base that is competitive in domestic and global markets; (2) strong information technology and transportation linkages; (3) a concentration of human capital skills; and (4) quality governance that supports metropolitan growth and captures the opportunities upon which urban growth thrives. Glaeser and Gottlieb (2009) also link metropolitan growth to the transfer of information.

---

[3] This chapter uses the term *metropolitan area* to refer to the built-up space covered by large cities, including their suburban areas. This is similar to the definition used by the United Nations (2008, 13) of *urban agglomeration*, which includes the population "contained within the contours of a contiguous territory inhabited at urban density levels without regard to administrative boundaries."

The poster children of smart-growth metro areas among the developing countries are Shanghai and Bangalore (Bengaluru).[4] But in many developing countries, the metropolitan areas have not developed a globally competitive economic base. African cities such as Kinshasa and Dar es Salaam have experienced significant population growth but mostly because of conflict and worsening conditions in rural areas. In chapter 2, Yusuf cites Karachi, São Paulo, Cairo, Manila, and Johannesburg as examples of cities that are growing but not generating exports or importing new technologies.

GOVERNING METROPOLITAN AREAS

Typically, the responsibility for governance and service delivery in a metropolitan area is vertically fragmented among central, provincial/state, and local governments. They are horizontally fragmented among municipalities, areawide general-purpose local governments, special-purpose districts, and public enterprises. Rarely is there enough coordination among these governments (Rojas 2008).

Theory

There is a strong case for metropolitan-wide governance, and the case grows stronger as metropolitan areas grow. But "thinking metropolitan" is much easier than restructuring government or coordinating service delivery for the entire urban area. The metropolitan area is an economic concept, with boundaries that change as the economy changes. In practice, it is mostly used for planning purposes. These plans usually are not fully implemented, and even if they are, they tend to be limited in their coverage of the area and the functions considered. Local governments, in contrast, are elected (or appointed) entities and are defined by political boundaries that fragment the metropolitan area (see Bahl, chapter 4). The idea of metropolitan governance across political boundaries has not been easy to sell.[5]

The decentralization choice that so perplexes central governments in developing countries can also be applied to the question of governance within metropolitan areas (see chapter 4). The fiscal decentralization theorem gives a norm that all services should be delivered at the lowest level of government, consistent with efficiency considerations (Oates 1972). So, if there were no economies of scale in service provision and no externalities, and if only economic efficiency was considered, the best governance for the metropolitan area would be a large number of small municipalities with relatively homogeneous populations. But there are scale economies, externalities, and political factors to consider, and preferences for strong local autonomy vary across regions. So, how metropolitan governance is finally structured

---

[4] Hong Kong and Singapore also demonstrate that it is possible to turn troubled cities into thriving metropolises in a few decades. While these two cities are atypical in that they are city-states, they also faced many of the same challenges and grasped many of the opportunities that the large metropolitan areas in the rest of the developing world are facing today.

[5] For a discussion of the difficult political economy issues involved in moving toward metropolitan governance in Toronto, see Slack (2000). For a discussion in the developing country context, see OECD (2008b).

depends on the relative strength of the demand for home rule versus the demand for more efficiency in service delivery.[6]

The Practice

The practice of metropolitan governance varies considerably. Any taxonomy of the various models used is likely to oversimplify things, but this section classifies governance systems according to the horizontal (intrametropolitan) and vertical (federal-provincial-local division) arrangements for service delivery and taxation.[7]

HORIZONTAL ARRANGEMENTS

The structure of governance within metropolitan areas is usually a mixture of the three basic strategies: jurisdictional fragmentation (autonomous municipalities within a metropolitan area), functional fragmentation (single-purpose public enterprises), and metropolitan-wide government (Bahl and Linn 1992). The way in which countries mix these strategies depends on politics and how they value local autonomy, on the one hand, and technical efficiency, on the other. At one extreme are São Paulo, which includes 39 autonomous municipalities, and the Mexico City metropolitan area, where services are delivered by two states, a federal district, and more than 50 local level governments. Johannesburg and Cape Town, at the other end of the spectrum, are metropolitan governments that deliver their assigned services on an areawide basis with little autonomy at the submetropolitan level. Lying between are all sorts of arrangements. Manila's 17 cities and municipalities are overlaid by a metropolitan government with some areawide responsibilities, and metropolitan Mumbai relies on central- and state-owned parastatals (public companies) for metrowide service delivery.

The great variation in practice that exists among developing countries suggests that almost any arrangement can work, if "work" means that local services do not collapse. The questions are whether a stronger set of services could have been delivered under a different government structure, and whether economic development would have progressed as a result. Unfortunately, there is no good evidence to prove the better results from one system than from another, and of course, "better" also depends on what local voters want from their government. This is mostly because so many other factors are important.

There is much for developing countries to learn from the experience with metropolitan governance in industrial countries about how they have handled the tensions from demands for local control versus areawide government and how they have financed this growth.[8] This experience can help identify the governance choices that are feasible when constraints on revenue mobilization and service delivery capacity are relaxed. It supports a hypothesis that time and economic growth will lead metropolitan governance practices in developing countries toward workable

---

[6] Here *home rule* means the extent to which governance of a local jurisdiction is in the hands of the local population.

[7] While the taxonomy originally developed in Bahl and Linn (1992) is followed here, an alternative is suggested by Shah in chapter 9.

[8] The experience with fiscal decentralization in industrial countries is reviewed in Bahl (2011) and Slack (2007).

decentralized structures. But in the short run, the choices in developing countries are much more limited because of rapid population growth and scarce resources, and movement away from fiscal centralization is proving to be difficult. It will be a long time before governance in a metropolitan area such as Mumbai or Mexico City settles into a structure like those adopted by Toronto or Copenhagen.

VERTICAL ARRANGEMENTS

The defining feature of public finance and governance in most developing countries is centralization. In chapter 5, Sud and Yilmaz point out that only a handful of developing countries specifically recognize local governments in the constitution. Central governments raise most of the tax money, spend the largest share of the public budget, and make the rules about how subnational governments operate (e.g., expenditure assignment, taxing powers, and the borrowing framework). The road to better metropolitan governance and fiscal outcomes in metropolitan areas begins with the national government (and with the state government in some large federal countries). Virtually all enabling legislation for metropolitan-area governance requires a central or state government initiative.

To a large extent, the success of metropolitan-area public finances depends on how vertical intergovernmental relations are structured (see chapter 3). In particular, three issues are of great importance. The first is whether metropolitan cities will be treated the same as other local governments in the country or be given a differential fiscal treatment. In some countries, local governments in metropolitan areas are not treated differently (see Bird and Slack, chapter 6). In others, there is differential treatment (see chapter 3), usually taking one of the following forms: (1) provincial city status (see box 1.1); (2) special expenditure assignment and taxing arrangements for cities of different sizes; (3) special arrangements under the intergovernmental transfer system (Bahl 2011); or (4) special status for national capital cities.

The second issue is the direct delivery of services within metropolitan areas by higher-level governments: the so-called vertical programs of the central (or state) government. The policy question is whether and how service delivery by local governments and higher-level governments will be coordinated within the urban area.

Third, there is the issue of the degree to which the actions of metropolitan local governments will be tightly regulated by higher-level government ministries. A ministry of local government or a ministry of interior often provides general control to ensure compliance with laws and regulations, but regulations that are too stringent can undermine local authority and create obstacles to good performance (see chapter 3). Arguably, more problematic are the controls imposed by sector ministries (e.g., in infrastructure, education, and health), which can significantly limit local government expenditure discretion, as has been the case in Colombia and Peru (see Bird forthcoming; Martinez-Vazquez forthcoming; see also chapter 3).

REFORM OPTIONS

On balance, stronger metrowide governance approaches, supported by local coordination and accountability mechanisms, are appropriate and ultimately unavoidable. Continuing rapid urbanization has overtaken present metropolitan gover-

BOX 1.1

Provincial-level cities

Historically, city-states have been among the most successful jurisdictions in producing rapid economic growth and effective urban growth. Medieval Venice and the cities of the Hanseatic League in Northern Europe are early examples. Hong Kong and Singapore are the contemporary counterparts. Interesting questions are whether there are lessons to be learned for metropolitan governance and finance from the experience of the city-states, and whether there is a way to pattern metropolitan governance at least partially after that model. In larger countries, this could take the form of provincial cities, where the metropolitan-area local government has both provincial and local status. For example, in China, the four largest cities are treated as provinces and have the powers of both provincial government and local government.

There are some clear advantages to this approach. It allows for areawide governance that can internalize potential external effects but also allows for significant autonomy in making budgetary decisions. It becomes much like a state in a federation but usually with more manageable boundaries and without the understructure of local governments to deal with. A further advantage is that its boundaries can be large enough to allow regional taxation, and perhaps to adopt a broad-based tax. Finally, its borrowing powers can be enhanced because it can oversee and regulate larger public enterprises and because its revenue base can support debt better than if it were a city government within a metropolitan area or subject to provincial oversight.

There also are disadvantages. For one, the metropolitan area may have already spread across jurisdiction boundaries so that the city-province status is assigned to the core city. In this case, the areawide governance advantage is lost. This is the case of Buenos Aires. Another disadvantage is the hinterland problem; for example, if Mumbai were made a state in India (an appealing prospect), it would leave the present state of Maharashtra without its most important revenue generator. A third disadvantage is that city-states are ad hoc arrangements, created as special cases by the central government. How does one draw the line for deciding if there will be more of them, and how will the provincial city be made to fit within the existing local government code or budget law? Finally, a city-state may be politically strong, with a governor or mayor who might be considered a rival by the central government and the legislature. This can lead to some degree of discrimination against the metropolitan area in terms of its treatment within the metropolitan area.

---

nance structures in terms of the ability to coordinate services, provide infrastructure, and make use of regional financing tools. There is no single magic bullet for reform that is right for all countries, because the taste for fiscal decentralization within metropolitan areas varies from location to location. However, the reform process must begin with the central government (or state government) taking a metropolitan (vs. a submetropolitan local-government) view of reform choices. One likely result of this reform direction is that some measure of home rule below the metropolitan level will be lost.

If the potential loss in home rule from areawide governance is thought to be too great, and history suggests this to be the case in many metropolitan areas, a second-best solution is to institute coordination mechanisms. Vertical coordination, if the case of Mumbai is any indication, is a very difficult matter (see chapter 10). In practice, the experience with this approach has been one of mixed success, especially when coordination and consultation are voluntary rather than mandatory. A good case in point is the São Paulo metropolitan area, where the autonomy of the 39 municipalities is guaranteed by the constitution, leaving each with veto power over coordination programs for service delivery (see chapter 12). In response, São Paulo and other Brazilian metro areas have begun to experiment with metropolitan councils and other such coordination mechanisms that bring all the stakeholders together to find solutions.

PUBLIC EXPENDITURE CHALLENGES

The pressure on expenditure budgets to support metropolitan services is not likely to lessen in the coming decades, though the severity of the problem will vary from city to city. The demand for services will remain high, costs are rising, backlogs are severe, management is problematic, and the special problems of slums are overwhelming.

Expenditure Demands

The factors that will pressure increases in public expenditures in urban areas include (1) population growth; (2) growing per capita incomes; (3) business demands to upgrade the infrastructure and to upgrade the public amenities necessary to attract and retain a strong labor force; (4) the negative externalities that accompany urbanization, such as pollution (solid waste collection) and congestion (transportation); and (5) the special needs of a heavy concentration of poor and badly housed families, often in sprawling slums, that call for major public investments by metropolitan governments. The magnitude of the slum problem is staggering. One estimate is that about $60 billion per year will need to be spent on slum improvement and prevention for the next 15 years (see Freire, chapter 14).

Supply-side factors also drive up unit costs of service provision disproportionately in the urban areas. Some of these are due to diseconomies of size. Examples are the costs of handling refuse collection and solid waste disposal, managing traffic congestion, dealing with pollution, and supplying such resources as potable water. Metropolitan labor and land costs also are higher than in smaller cities and rural areas.

A tension in urban budget decisions arises from the pressure to invest in new physical and social infrastructure versus the pressure to maintain and improve existing assets. Metropolitan economic growth is often associated with heavy investment in transportation: mass transit and freeways to reduce congestion, as well as seaports and airports (see chapter 2). Infrastructure to support new residential developments is in step with strengthening the amenity attractions of cities, while infrastructure to support industrial parks is in keeping with the goals of capturing agglomeration economies. Modern hospitals and an emphasis on education curriculum that supports the new economy are also aligned with the strategy. Innovations in governance, such as e-governance, are signs of progress with which most political leaders would like to be associated. And in all of this, there is the political appeal of being associated with modernity and all the visibility this produces.

The competing strategy is to concentrate more on fixing what already exists, and what in many cases is woefully inadequate. For example, basic water and sewer systems may need major repair and upgrading, roads and streets are often in disrepair, and solid waste disposal may be surviving on a temporary solution. The delivery of social services is often outdated, for example, overcrowded school classes, improperly staffed or supplied health clinics, and unenforced environmental regulations. As necessary as they are, expenditures to address the backlog can, at the margin, be viewed as crowding out expenditures that attract new investment (Glaeser 2011).

Managing Service Delivery

The poor record of service delivery by local governments in developing countries has long been used as the justification for keeping public expenditure management centralized (see Bahl and Linn 1992). In various countries, the problem is linked to a combination of weak staffing, inadequate management systems, inability to capture economies of scale, expenditure mandates imposed by higher-level governments, and an inadequate revenue base. In chapter 5, Sud and Yilmaz argue that the institutional weaknesses of local governments that stand in the way of the provision of good services are an even bigger problem than the shortage of resources. A major reason for lack of capacity at the local level is the inadequacy of the civil service system, which often accords local government officials a lower status, including lower salaries and fewer chances for advancement, and generally a system that does not encourage professionalism.

The view that local governments have little capacity to deliver services (or collect revenues) is, however, too broad a generalization. A review by the World Bank (2009) of 190 of its municipal development projects, covering about 3,000 municipalities, reports significant improvements in urban public management. And the quality of public services delivered in metropolitan cities is far better than that provided in the rest of the country (see chapter 6). The coverage of basic water and sewer services is higher, health clinics are more accessible, and the scope of services provided is broader. This has been explicitly recognized in countries such as Colombia, where the large cities have been given more expenditure responsibility and autonomy.

An important route to further strengthening public management in metropolitan areas is to give local governments more discretion in making decisions about service delivery and about managing their budgets. The kinds of central controls that might be relaxed are the appointment of chief local officers; decisions about hiring, firing, and promoting employees; employee compensation; budget allocations; and the selection and design of capital projects (see chapters 3, 5, and 6).

Another key element of improved urban management is increased accountability of the service providers to their ultimate clients: voters and businesses in the cities. How exactly such accountability is established, through political oversight by elected officials and local councils, community and business advisory councils, citizens report cards, contractual obligations, and so forth, will vary with the political and administrative system and culture. But without such accountability, public and private providers will have few incentives to improve the management and delivery of metropolitan services.

Reform Directions

Those who believe that the problem of efficiency in service delivery is mostly poor management have an oversimplified viewpoint. The following are five areas where structural and management changes could benefit service delivery in urban areas.

1. Clear up the often murky division of responsibilities across central, state, and metropolitan local governments. The action needed here is to review and revise the local government code or budget law and to make explicit provision for the metropolitan level of government.
2. Improve the capacity of local employees to deliver services. Achieving this goal involves undoing a multitude of policy sins, including freeing up local governments to make budgetary decisions (including personnel decisions), upgrading the status of local government employees in the civil service system, and improving management techniques.
3. Increase resources available so that more efficient infrastructure can be put in place and properly maintained.
4. Better capture economies of scale in service delivery by addressing external effects stemming from local government budget decisions in metropolitan areas. This might involve more effective coordination of service delivery among local governments or, preferably, internalizing the externalities by creating areawide governance and service delivery.
5. Increase accountability of local officials for the quality of service delivery by instituting various accountability mechanisms and by moving away from the practice of higher-level governments appointing local officials.

TAXES AND CHARGES

The low level of revenues raised by subnational governments in developing countries is often cited as a failing of the intergovernmental fiscal system (see chapters 4, 6, 8, and 13). However, implementing a strategy to increase local revenue mobilization will be difficult. Subnational governments often have only limited taxing power, and they often underuse the taxing power that they do have. Central (state) governments are loathe to give up their control over the tax base for fear that their own revenue mobilization efforts will be harmed by the competition, and elected local government leaders are not always eager to have the accountability that comes with increased taxing powers. There also is a pure political dimension: increased local taxing power may enhance the success and hence visibility of local politicians, who may be present or future political rivals. Add to this the limited assignment of expenditure responsibilities given to subnational governments in many developing countries. The result is that subnational government taxes in developing countries account for 2.3 percent of GDP, compared with 6.4 percent in industrialized countries (see table 1.1).

Theory

In chapter 8, Martinez-Vazquez points out that no unified theory of revenue assignment will identify the best division of taxes between local and higher levels of

TABLE 1.1

Fiscal decentralization: International comparisons for the 2000s

Region	Subnational government expenditures		Subnational government taxes	
	Percentage of total government expenditures	Percentage of GDP	Percentage of total taxes	Percentage of GDP
Developing countries	18.8	5.1	11.4	2.3
	($n = 16$)	($n = 20$)	($n = 16$)	($n = 20$)
Industrial countries	27.8	13.9	22.7	6.4
	($n = 26$)	($n = 26$)	($n = 24$)	($n = 25$)

Data reported are unweighted averages for the 2000s for years in which data are reported. Numbers in parentheses are numbers of countries included.

SOURCE: Calculations based on data from the International Monetary Fund (various years) and estimates drawn from the case studies by Roy Bahl.

government. However, he argues that the principles of benefit taxation and optimal taxation can provide useful guidance.[9] The benefit approach to subnational government taxation emphasizes vertical balance in the system; that is, metropolitan-area governments should have enough taxing power to cover the portion of assigned expenditure responsibilities that confers local benefits. In practice, few, if any, metropolitan areas in developing countries achieve this level of vertical balance, and by this rule, almost all are overly dependent on transfers. When the cost of raising funds is introduced as a consideration, the theoretical vertical imbalance is smaller.

Practice

No reliable, comparable data allow a comprehensive international comparison of how metropolitan-area public services are financed (see box 1.2). In chapter 8, Martinez-Vazquez uses country case studies to survey the practice. He points out two systemic weaknesses related to the failure of local governments to use their taxing potential: the limited assignment of revenue-raising powers to subnational governments, and the bad design of the local tax instruments that are assigned. These weaknesses may be attributed to political economy constraints; the frequent incompatibility of metropolitan government structure with regionwide taxation; the fact that the usual candidates, user charges and property taxes, cannot be levied at high enough rates to cover the expenditures of large urban governments; and the failure of central governments to design intergovernmental transfers to provide incentives for increased local government revenue mobilization.

---

[9] In chapter 8, Martinez-Vazquez notes that from optimal taxation, the optimal solution to the revenue assignment problem is characterized by an identical marginal cost of public funds for all government units. The marginal cost of public funds captures the economic losses to society associated with raising additional revenues to finance government spending, including the excess burdens of taxes, political costs, and administrative and compliance costs.

BOX 1.2
Data limitations

Very few comparable data are available to describe or track the fiscal performance of metropolitan-area local governments. Neither of the two major sources of fiscal information, the International Monetary Fund and the OECD series, report data for individual local governments or attempt to aggregate the finances of these local governments to a metropolitan-area standard. To the extent that data for individual local governments are available at all, it is for individual countries. And even here, many countries do not bother to report this information on a comparable basis.[1]

If the chapters in this book identify a constraint to understanding the fiscal performance of metropolitan-area fiscal systems, it is the absence of comparative information. And, given the expected explosion of urban population that will continue until mid-century, it is crucial to know more about public finances. It is not possible to benchmark important indicators such as tax effort, infrastructure spending, or fiscal disparities or how the metropolitan areas fit within the transfer equalization system. Such data would also be invaluable for evaluating fiscal decentralization strategies, assessing borrowing capacities, and researching the determinants of successful practice.

Why has such a data set not emerged? One answer is that there has not been much interest in local finances in general and in metropolitan-area finances in particular. Another is that it would be a costly exercise and would require country cooperation. But it could be done, probably best by an international agency. The International Monetary Fund would be a good choice because of its interest in revenue mobilization and because much of the national tax base lies in metropolitan areas. The World Bank would be a good choice because of its extensive urban operations and its interest in the financial solvency of subnational governments. The job itself could start with a sample of perhaps the 50 largest governments and would entail defining the database, working out the method of aggregation to a metropolitan-area basis, and assembling the data on a comparable basis. The resulting annual compendium could be of enormous value.

---

[1] South Africa and Indonesia do report local government finance data on a comparable basis for individual local governments.

PROPERTY TAXATION

The property tax has most of the characteristics of a good local tax, including the potential to match tax burdens approximately with expenditure benefits, to make relatively little interference with market decisions, and to avoid imposing heavy burdens on poor families.[10] It is a particularly good fit for metropolitan areas, even where government structure is fragmented. The assignment of expenditure responsibilities to local governments may be limited to property-related services such as police and fire protection, parks, refuse collection, local roads, and primary schools. Since these functions have relatively limited spillover effects, the case for financing by a property tax (and user charges) is a strong one (Bahl and Linn 1992).

In practice, the property tax is a relatively minor source of revenue in most developing countries (Bahl and Martinez-Vazquez 2008). Data are not readily available to compare property tax collections in individual metropolitan areas of developing countries, but a survey of 30 large metropolitan areas carried out by McCluskey and Franzsen in chapter 7 provides some basis for inference about recent revenue performance. Two conclusions stand out in this survey. First, most property tax revenue is collected in metropolitan areas. For example, metropolitan Manila local

---

[10] In chapter 6, Bird and Slack caution that the burden of nonresidential property taxes might be exported and therefore might not offer the efficiency advantages that residential property taxes offer.

governments account for 20 percent of the Philippine population but for nearly half of all property tax collections. Second, recent revenue performance varies widely, with some large cities showing growth and others experiencing real per capita declines. It is difficult to generalize about why some cities do better than others.

One explanation for the weak revenue performance of the property tax is its unpopularity with voters and local political leaders. Property taxes are visible; they are levied on a subjective, judgmental basis; and they tax unrealized increases in wealth. The result is that most local governments are unwilling to impose the tax at a meaningful effective rate. Exemptions and preferential treatments narrow the tax base, sometimes dramatically; collection rates are low in many metropolitan areas; and aggressive enforcement measures have little support.

Another explanation for the weak revenue performance of the property tax is that intergovernmental transfers have grown along with the economies in many countries (see Shah, chapter 9). This has allowed metropolitan local governments to avoid raising property tax rates or issuing new valuation rolls. Another possible explanation for slow growth in property tax revenues is that successful nonproperty tax revenues such as the sales tax on services in Brazilian cities have crowded out the use of property taxes. Finally, for many large metropolitan areas, especially those with significant slums, property tax collections are limited by the absence of legal title to property.

Administration is a major constraint to property tax revenue mobilization, though significant improvements have been made in many metropolitan areas in recent years. The use of technology and the improved quality of staff have led to a more comprehensive coverage of parcels and to better recordkeeping (see chapter 7). But some metro cities are still tied to the paper-based systems, and the property tax rolls are incomplete. Furthermore, property valuation presents major administrative problems. While it has become easier to identify properties and keep track of improvements with computerization and such tools as satellite photography and geocoding of data, reliable information on market values are rarely available. Hence, properties are assessed infrequently and at a rate that is well below market value. Finally, legal constraints such as rent control in Mumbai have held back revenue mobilization (see chapter 10).

Governments in developing countries have not been standing still on property tax policy, and many different approaches to defining the tax base have been tried. In chapter 7, McCluskey and Franzsen note a trend suggesting that governments are moving toward capital value systems where the tax is levied on both land and improvements and away from rental systems and site value systems. In recent years, there has been increased interest in area-based systems where the tax is levied on the physical characteristics of properties rather than on its assessed value.

The property value base might be reached with several other forms of taxation. Such taxes include property transfer taxes, capital gains taxes on land, various kinds of special assessments, and the sale of government land. In principle, these revenue instruments can increase the total return from the property value base. However, the size of the revenue yield on these taxes varies significantly from place to place, as does the quality of the administration (see box 1.3).

BOX 1.3

Property transfer taxes

The property transfer tax is levied at the time of a sale of real property, usually against a legal base of the total market value of the property as stated in the sales contract. However, the taxed base in developing countries is almost always lower than the actual sales proceeds because of under-reporting in the value of sales contracts (see chapter 7). Moreover, the property transfer tax is sometimes a state or central government tax, and the revenues do not flow to local governments in the metropolitan area where the transaction takes place.

Some analysts have argued that the transfer tax is an inefficient and badly administered sales tax whose elimination is overdue. Another view is that with appropriate reforms it has good potential as a revenue instrument and could be used to strengthen the annual property tax (Bahl and Wallace 2010). If there were a joint administration with the property tax, local governments would be in a position to upgrade the property and transfer tax administration and valuation simultaneously, based on a roll of market values for all properties that sold in the metropolitan area in a given period of time.

An alternative to the property transfer tax, and arguably a superior tax instrument, is a capital gains tax on real property. By taxing property value increases, governments could recoup some of the gains associated with public investment in the metropolitan area. The drawback to capital gains taxes on land is the administrative difficulty, particularly with setting a base value and with making adjustments for inflation and investments in new improvements.

USER CHARGES AND BENEFIT CHARGES

Researchers of local government finance have long discussed the significant potential for user charges and benefit charges, including charges for water and sanitation, electricity, solid waste disposal, urban transport infrastructure, and mass transit services (see Bahl and Linn 1992; see also chapter 6). The charges can be directly related to the use of a service (e.g., the consumption of water), or they can be levied on the value or physical attributes of the property that is serviced to capture some of the benefits that result from public investments in metropolitan areas. The so-called betterment levies, special assessments, or development charges may be structured to cover the cost of construction of new infrastructure or to capture a part of the land value increase resulting from new infrastructure. Various forms of betterment levies are used in the financing of general infrastructure and even slum upgrading projects (Bahl and Linn 1992; see chapters 13 and 14).

There is ample evidence that user and benefit charges can be structured to support cost recovery, especially in the case of transportation and public utilities. User charges have formed the backbone of financing for public enterprises that deliver urban services on an areawide basis. But some analysts argue that metropolitan local governments have not used such charges to the extent they could have (see chapters 8 and 13), and when they have made use of public service pricing regimes, they often have done it badly (see chapters 6 and 10).

The primary reason for the poor experience with user charges is the politics of raising the price of services that are often considered as necessities and hence the concern that user charges are highly regressive. More likely, the resistance is from those who use the services most heavily, who usually are not poor, and who basically object to the removal of a subsidy that they have enjoyed (Bahl and Linn 1992; see chapter 6). Moreover, users resist paying higher charges when services are of low quality or only intermittently provided, which is often the case in cities in low-income countries.

NONPROPERTY TAXES

It is not likely that even well-administered property tax and user charge systems will generate enough revenue to meet the financing needs of metropolitan local governments; therefore, other broad-based taxes will be necessary if revenue self-sufficiency is to be enhanced (Bahl and Linn 1992; see chapter 6). One might also argue that, structured correctly, such alternative taxes could approximately pass the benefits test; that is, a local sales tax or a local income tax could be viewed as a benefit levy on those living, shopping, or working in the city.[11]

Though several types of nonproperty taxes can meet the revenue test and can satisfy efficiency norms to a reasonable extent, these options are not widely used in developing countries.[12] This said, it should be noted that some metropolitan-area local governments in developing countries have adopted broad-based taxes (see chapter 8). Where metropolitan local governments have provincial status, sales and payroll taxes have been easier to assign. The local business tax accounts for one-third of city and provincial revenues in China (see Wong, chapter 11), and the gross receipts tax accounts for 70 percent of revenues in the capital district of Buenos Aires. Various forms of local sales tax have also done well in Bogotá and São Paulo, where they account for about one-third of revenues.

In practice, however, these taxes are often badly designed. For example, Buenos Aires and Bogotá make use of distortionary gross receipts taxes, and the state governments and the national capital district in the Mexico City metropolitan area impose a tax on payrolls by place of work, with no recognition of commuting patterns.[13] Metropolitan Mumbai still relies heavily on revenues from the *octroi*, a kind of import duty on goods entering the city, which distorts trade flows and is poorly administered (see chapter 11).

Motor vehicles are an attractive target for financing metropolitan services (Bahl and Linn 1992) but are generally underutilized. Motor vehicle taxes can take the form of licenses to operate; a tax on the estimated value of the vehicle; a sales tax on motor fuel, tolls, or parking; and restricted permit charges. Aside from the potential to raise substantial amounts of revenues, higher motor vehicle taxes might lead to beneficial economic and environmental benefits. One of the formidable obstacles to more use of motor vehicle taxes to finance metropolitan-area services is the fragmented nature of local governance. Vehicle owners in a system such as Manila, with 17 local governments, could simply shop for the lowest rate, and enforcement by the losing local governments would not be cost-effective. The same would be the case

---

[11] In chapter 8, Martinez-Vazquez makes the good argument that taxes on public utility use, such as telephone service and electricity, can fit the benefit principle well because consumption of these services tends to be a good proxy for the use of local public services by households and businesses.

[12] By contrast, subnational governments in industrial countries make relatively heavy use of broad-based taxes (see chapter 8).

[13] Technically, the industry and commerce tax in Bogotá is better described as a business tax, though its base is primarily gross receipts.

for motor fuel taxes. For governments that have a regionwide jurisdiction boundary, or for regional taxing districts, this problem would largely disappear.[14]

Reform Options

Allowing local governments to set the tax rates and user charge rates so that the cost of local services is more nearly covered is an efficient strategy and reduces the claims of large cities on the national budget. Certainly there are instruments of non-property taxation that can lead to a significant revenue increase. One is to finance a greater share of expenditures assigned to metropolitan governments with region-wide taxes on sales, income, or motor vehicles. If the metropolitan government structure is fragmented, the direct levy of a broad-based tax may not be feasible. In this case, the options are to use intergovernmental transfers more heavily or to make use of a regional taxing district and then allocate the revenues by formula among the eligible local governments in the metropolitan area. Such horizontal sharing arrangements are used in industrial countries and a few developing countries.

There is an especially strong case for metropolitan-area taxation of automobile ownership and use, including motor fuel taxation. The technical difficulty to be overcome is how to assess the tax on a destination basis, either by fuel taxation at the pump or by requiring recordkeeping by distributors.

Metropolitan local governments need to look especially hard at the policies for making more and better use of user and benefit charges. Here there are many good options, ranging from a recapture of land value benefits resulting from public infrastructure investment, to removal of subsidy elements in the present system of user charges (see chapters 13 and 14), to user charges levied at cost recovery levels.

The property tax has not played the dominant role in big city finances that many had hoped. But reformers have not given up, and sizable investments continue to be made in making the tax more productive and fair. Investment is concentrated mostly on administration, particularly on the identification of taxable properties and on valuation. To some extent, such improvements will naturally evolve in metropolitan areas because of economies of scale in administration and because of their ability to attract and retain higher-quality staff and to make more extensive use of private valuers. The ability to absorb modern technology has also led to an upgrade in property tax administration (see chapter 7).

Valuation remains key to a more productive and fair property tax. Some countries have begun to experiment with computerized mass appraisal, but the jury is still out on whether this is an appropriate technology for developing countries. Otherwise, better sales value data, as might be obtained through a better administered property transfer tax, and three-year revaluation cycles are the most obvious steps to be taken.

In many countries, changes in the property tax structure are a prerequisite to improving property tax revenue performance. Reforms in broadening the tax base by eliminating exemptions and preferential treatments can lead to a significant

---

[14] In the United States, some local governments raise substantial amounts of tax revenue from taxes on automobiles registered in their jurisdictions.

increase in revenue productivity and can improve horizontal equity. The potential returns from such actions are great but require taking on some powerful special interests. This political resistance is often the deal breaker in property tax reform.

Many urban areas could benefit from a comprehensive review of their property tax system. Among the important questions that can be answered in such a review are how to divide administrative responsibilities when government structure is fragmented, how best to capture economies of scale in assessment and collections, how to set up an areawide system for monitoring outcomes, how to coordinate the administration of the various property related taxes, and how to involve higher-level governments in the administration of the property tax.

INTERGOVERNMENTAL TRANSFERS

The amounts spent for public services provided in most metropolitan areas are much larger than own-source revenues of local governments, which means that much of the job of financing local services is left to the intergovernmental transfer system and to vertical programs. Some policy analysts see this as an inevitable outcome in developing countries and stress the need to sharpen the structure of transfers so that they can better match the goals that have been set for them (see chapter 9).

Theory

Grants can be justified to fill the gap between expenditure assignments and revenue-raising powers, to compensate for external benefits of metropolitan government spending beyond the city boundaries, and to equalize revenues across jurisdictions. These objectives tell us that grants will play a significant role in metropolitan finances in developing countries (see chapter 9).

However, there is a good case for an asymmetrical transfer system in terms of how metropolitan local governments are treated compared with all other local governments. Their stronger economic base and hence higher local revenue mobilization capacity suggest that they will require fewer transfers than other jurisdictions and will not participate in equalization grants. However, rapid and sustained metropolitan growth also generates needs and expectations for rapid expansion and improvements in physical and social infrastructure services; hence, revenue needs are greater (see chapter 6). Another asymmetry stems from different choices made about governance in metropolitan areas. For example, a fragmented local government structure will require more financing from transfers (or through vertical programs), all else being equal, than an areawide structure, because externalities and disparities must be accommodated and because the possibilities for regional taxation are more limited (see chapters 4 and 9). In cases where metro areas combine state/provincial and local government responsibility, as is often the case for capital cities, they will be entitled to a larger transfer share.

The Practice

The extent to which metropolitan local governments depend on transfers varies greatly across cities. On the one end of the spectrum, central cities like Buenos Aires have been assigned significant taxing powers and finance nearly 70 percent of their budget from own-source revenues. The same is true for the metropolitan areas in South Africa. But most large urban areas appear to depend much more on intergovernmental transfers (see chapter 9). More self-financing might be a favorite recommendation of policy analysts, but it has been less embraced by elected politicians. Indeed, control of transfers and direct spending in metropolitan areas is a tool often used by central authorities to encourage the "good behavior" and/or policy alignment of key metropolitan areas.

The reasons behind this are not hard to understand. Metropolitan areas in many developing countries raise much of the national revenue.[15] By keeping metropolitan-area local governments more dependent on transfers (vs. local taxes), the competition for the metropolitan tax base can be minimized. If the central government can give itself a near monopoly in taxing urban economic activity, by denying subnational government's access to the more productive tax bases, it will be in a position to use the tax/transfer system to draw funds away from the metropolitan area to use for equalization grants and for its own direct expenditures. Moreover, elected subnational government officials are not anxious for more power to impose politically unpopular taxes and often would rather lobby the national parliament for discretionary grants. With the increased urban population in most countries, and increased representation in national and state congresses, their chances at success with discretionary grants have increased. Finally, in chapter 8 Martinez-Vazquez notes that the structure of broad-based taxes that most subnational governments levy is highly distortionary.

Many countries do not provide for a differential structure of transfers for metropolitan vs. nonmetropolitan local governments (see chapter 9). The large urban governments may get less on a per capita basis, for example, in South Africa, but all local governments are covered under the same transfer formula. Some countries use an asymmetric treatment but usually owing to special governance structure arrangements such as provincial-level cities or national capital districts (see box 1.1). Asymmetric treatments are more likely to favor metropolitan areas by recognizing their special needs, while uniform-formula systems are more likely to discriminate against them with provisions for equalization. The other route to a differential treatment is conditional grants, usually for capital projects, which are given on an ad hoc basis and may be earmarked for urban infrastructure, as has been the case in India.

Reform Options

It is not uncommon for developing countries to restructure their intergovernmental transfer systems. But reforms rarely focus on developing a metropolitan strategy. If they did, the strategy for restructuring transfer regimes for big cities might include two reform components.

---

[15] For example, metropolitan Bogotá accounts for about 20 percent of Colombia's population but for nearly one-half of total value added tax collections (Klink 2008).

The first would focus on weaning the metropolitan local governments from transfers while ensuring that they have sufficient authority to tax and impose user charges. A hard budget constraint with no "back door" for financing deficits would be part of this strategy. The financing of infrastructure investment would be shifted from transfers toward debt finance, where the borrowing is supported by locally raised revenues. Transfers will never disappear entirely as a financing source, because there will always be externalities to reckon with, but in many metros, grants can be reduced dramatically.

A second, complementary component of the strategy would be to redesign the transfer system to be asymmetric, with metro local governments treated under a different regime than other local governments. The vertical-share entitlement of metropolitan-area governments would be lower because of their greater taxable capacity. The resulting revenue loss to metropolitan local governments would be compensated by increased taxing powers. With a separate regime, it will be possible for the central government to accommodate differences in metropolitan government structure (more reliance on grants where local government is more fragmented), provide incentives for regional taxes and greater tax effort, and address intrametropolitan fiscal disparities. The latter could be accomplished with the transfer formula for central (state) grants, with horizontal transfers from rich to poorer local governments within the metropolitan area and with earmarked grants, such as for slum improvement programs.

INFRASTRUCTURE PROVISION AND FINANCING

The success of metropolitan areas in attracting the investment necessary to sustain economic growth, offering the amenities to attract and retain high-quality human capital, and providing minimum acceptable levels of public services to the population will depend to a large extent on the quality of the metropolitan-area public infrastructure. Better infrastructure can attract investment that leads to new revenue streams and can draw private investors, foreign capital, and donor support, thereby increasing the pool of available resources. But the provision of infrastructure in large urban areas is beset with an enormous backlog and with new demands generated by rapid population and income growth.

Expenditure Needs

No comparative data set will allow an international comparison of infrastructure expenditure needs in developing countries. In chapter 15, Kharas and Linn project annual global urban public infrastructure investment requirements amounting to $120 billion, based on estimates for Asian cities by the Asian Development Bank. Another recent model based on country data estimates annual expenditure needs to be about 3 percent of GDP for new infrastructure plus another 2 percent for maintenance (see Ingram, Liu, and Brandt, chapter 13). By comparison, subnational government taxes in developing countries average only 2.4 percent of GDP (see table 1.1).

Case studies of metropolitan areas provide evidence on the magnitude of unmet infrastructure needs. For example, in chapter 12 Wetzel reports that the city of São

Paulo has maintained capital spending levels at 8–10 percent of current expenditures, which is well below investment needs. Mumbai metropolitan local governments could cover only one-tenth of infrastructure needs, even if borrowing were at full capacity (see chapter 10).

Quality of Services

The responsibility for providing infrastructure services within the metro areas is often shared among several local governments, and there usually are coordination problems among them. This is the case in both Mexico City and São Paulo. An alternative is for the service to be the responsibility of a metropolitan public enterprise (or several public enterprises) or of a higher-level government, but in this case, local control over planning and service delivery will be diminished, as in the case of Mumbai (see chapter 10).

Other arrangements have the potential to produce a more satisfying result. One possibility is a metropolitan local government with areawide responsibility for a range of infrastructure services. Under this arrangement, some degree of home rule for the underlying municipalities and even neighborhoods can be preserved; service delivery can be coordinated, and planning can be more efficient. This is the case in Johannesburg, Cape Town, and Toronto.

An arrangement that might work effectively is one where the general-purpose metropolitan government plans and authorizes the infrastructure investments but the management and financing are accomplished through a special district: a single-purpose local government such as a school district or an urban development district. This approach has been taken in some metropolitan areas in China (see chapter 11).

Irrespective of the governmental responsibility for planning and management, infrastructure service provision is often weakened by inappropriate public policies. These include poor incentive frameworks such as soft budget constraints, subsidies, poor maintenance, and bureaucratic inefficiencies (see chapter 13).

Financing

Infrastructure needs on the order of 5 percent of GDP are well beyond the financial reach of most metropolitan areas in developing countries. However, there is space to increase significantly the resource base for infrastructure finance. The focus might be in four areas: (1) increased revenue mobilization from own-source revenues; (2) debt financing; (3) transfers; and (4) funding from public-private partnerships (PPPs).

Own-Source Revenue

Buenos Aires, São Paulo, and Bogotá are examples of metropolitan areas that have done quite well with additional revenue mobilization. But in most developing countries, local governments are less successful. Own-source revenues of all subnational governments in developing countries are equivalent to less than 3 percent of GDP.

The overall contribution to infrastructure finance has been well below what is needed. In fact, however, there are plenty of viable revenue options, including improved property taxation, selective use of nonproperty taxes, and user and benefit charges (see chapters 6–8).

Chinese metropolitan governments have been particularly innovative and have engaged heavily in land sales (long-term leases) as a method of mobilizing resources for infrastructure finances. For all local governments in China, land leases now account for about 30 percent of revenues (see chapter 11). Land sales have great advantages: revenue potential and low political cost. But even in a unique setting like China, there are drawbacks, including sensitivity of land revenues to the real estate cycle; riskiness of land value collateral for loans; the temptation of "easy money" leading to overspending in local government budgets; underestimating opportunity costs of converting land to urban use; and the exhaustible nature of government-owned land as a resource (see chapter 11).

INTERGOVERNMENTAL TRANSFERS

In countries that decentralize revenue raising to a lesser extent, capital transfers may be used directly to fund infrastructure projects. These are usually ad hoc grants that are earmarked for specific capital purposes, as is done, for example, in São Paulo (see chapter 12). Direct transfers earmarked for infrastructure are also used in India (see chapter 10). South Africa makes use of a more formal municipal infrastructure grant, designed primarily to improve services in poor neighborhoods, and about 24 percent of the allocations go to metropolitan-area local governments (van Ryneveld 2007). Another approach is to dedicate a share of intergovernmental transfers to debt repayment, as has been done in Mexico.

BORROWING

Borrowing is arguably the most efficient way to pay for public assets that have a long life. By matching payment for the infrastructure with the time pattern of benefits received, governments can capture the returns from infrastructure investments while deferring the payment. Larger urban governments often are in a good position to make use of debt markets to fund long-lived public assets. Their economic bases are stronger and more diversified; there is an unmet demand and some willingness to pay for better services, and metropolitan areas (sometimes) have access to a strong base of own-source financing. In functionally fragmented systems, enterprises operating on a metropolitan-area basis can support debt with properly structured user charges.

But there can be problems with borrowing by metropolitan-area governments, as some researchers of metropolitan finances have argued (Prud'homme 1995; Tanzi 1996). The revenue stream of local government revenues may not be large enough to sustain repayment, but borrowing may go forward anyway in anticipation of some form of bailout. This has led to overborrowing and to some form of bailout in such metropolitan cities as Buenos Aires, São Paulo, and Johannesburg, and more recently in China (see chapter 11). Many countries attempt to control for overborrowing with various forms of fiscal responsibility legislation (Liu and Webb 2011), though these programs have met with varying degrees of success. Another problem is that the capacity of subnational governments to manage, plan, and deliver local services may be limited, and this may compromise both the quality of the services provided and the repayment plan (see chapter 10).

Intergovernmental arrangement may be a further complicating factor in metropolitan areas with fragmented government structures. In these cases, the best possibilities for debt finance will involve enterprises that operate on a regionwide basis but are independent of the underlying municipal governments.

The practice of borrowing by metropolitan local governments in developing countries and the success with debt finance vary widely among large urban governments. South African metropolitan governments borrow from a government-owned bank and through a privately owned intermediary but without a repayment guarantee from the central government (van Ryneveld 2007). At the other extreme are Chinese local governments, which could not borrow but created a backdoor route with special-purpose urban investment companies that borrowed on behalf of the municipal government and were supported by assets pledged by the municipal government (see chapter 11).

Governments might consider the following guidelines in forming policies to strengthen the use of debt finance for improved metropolitan infrastructure services.

- Provide local governments with more autonomy on both the revenue and expenditure sides of the budgets. If infrastructure is to be maintained, and if the debt obligations are to be met, local governments need to be able to control their level of budgetary resources. Even a well-structured borrowing framework cannot substitute for repayment capacity of the local government.
- Limit debt finance to capital projects with a long life.
- Impose a hard budget constraint on borrowers, with no possibility of a "costless" bailout by higher-level governments if the underlying problem is that the local government was imprudent in incurring the debt obligations. Put a central-government-mandated borrowing framework in place with clear rules about who can borrow, how much, for what purpose, from whom, with what instruments, and with what restrictions. Compliance with the framework should be carefully monitored.

PUBLIC-PRIVATE PARTNERSHIP

During the 1990s and early 2000s, the hope was that private involvement would increase the efficiency of service provision and provide badly needed resources to support urban infrastructure investment. In fact, PPP has added relatively little to urban capital financing in developing countries in the 1990s and 2000s (Annez 2007; Alm 2010). Less than 10 percent of investment has been in the high-priority water/sewer sector, and an even smaller share has been in the form of full or partial privatization (Menard forthcoming). To the extent that PPP has been used, it has focused more on the energy, telecommunications, and transport sectors.

Annez, Huet, and Peterson (2008); Annez (2007); and Ingram, Liu, and Brandt in chapter 13 all argue that the inherent riskiness of urban investments is the main constraint to increasing the flow of private capital. There is a weak record of full cost recovery and often an unwillingness of local governments to stand behind the kinds of tariff levels and regulatory arrangements needed to attract private investors, especially for longer-term contracts. In chapter 10, Pethe describes the failure to use PPP arrangements in Mumbai as being due to a "trust deficit" between the public and private sectors. There also is weak institutional capacity for dealing with PPP.

For the public sector, there is the risk that services provided may not be what the public wants. There is also the risk that the private partner will fail and the public sector will have to take on the obligation in full. How successful such arrangements are from the perspective of either partner depends very much on the details of exactly how the contractual arrangements are structured and how the risks are shared.[16] Given the weak institutional capacity of subnational governments in many developing countries, it seems unlikely that they will have a strong hand in negotiating such contracts. The Indian High Powered Commission on Urban Infrastructure (High Powered Expert Committee 2011, 101) puts it well: "Weak governments cannot rely on private agents to overcome their weaknesses nor can they expect to make the best possible bargains for the public they represent."

Financing Slum Improvement

Slums are a pervasive feature of most cities in developing countries. Poor people, both city born and immigrants, live in overcrowded and unhealthy conditions, with little access to clean water and sanitation; no tenure security; limited access to jobs, education, and health services; and restrictions on their ability to engage in basic entrepreneurship, except in informal activities that fall below the radar of municipal authorities.

According to estimates of the United Nations, about 1 billion slum dwellers lived in the cities of developing countries in the mid-2000s, a number that is projected to double by 2030. The largest concentrations of slums are then expected to be in Africa and South Asia (see chapter 14). The total amount in investment required to meet the backlog in services and the demands of the growing urban poor population is huge: one estimate puts the total cost at $900 billion over 15 years. This would require a sixfold increase over what is currently being spent.

Five key elements are needed to address the problem: (1) basic services, including water, sanitation, transport, education, and health; (2) improved shelter (housing); (3) security of tenure; (4) an absence of obstacles for the poor to engage in formal-sector employment and entrepreneurial activity; and (5) improved security to deal with the pervasive threat of crime and violence, especially in Latin America.

---

[16] For detailed exploration of the appropriate way to structure PPP arrangements when this approach seems appropriate, see Engel, Fischer, and Galetovic (2010). For a skeptical view of the range of opportunities to exploit such possibilities, see Menard (forthcoming).

The good news is that, among these problems, only basic services, shelter, and crime control place significant demands on the national and metropolitan authorities' fiscal resources. Creating security of tenure and a supportive business environment, in contrast, mainly requires political readiness to take on established interests that benefit from the status quo and resist the regularization of tenure and a supportive approach to low-income entrepreneurial activity. Indeed, by providing tenure security and by drawing the poor into the formal economy, the metropolitan authorities will be able to turn some slum dwellers into urban citizens who can share in financing the costs that metro governments incur on their behalf. Protection from crime and violence requires not only better policing, which does cost money, but also more jobs, reduced corruption, and more community engagement.

In terms of financing instruments, it helps to distinguish between service and shelter provision (Bahl and Linn 1992; see chapter 14). Metropolitan infrastructure services for slum areas, such as water, sanitation, solid waste collection, and transport, usually involve a combination of public and private provision, and their operating costs can in principle be funded by user charges; however, the capital costs need to be covered from cross-subsidies (with better-off users funding the poorer ones), from general municipal revenues, or from higher-level government grants. Education and health services usually also involve a combination of public and private providers, but if metro governments wish to upgrade these services for slum dwellers in the interest of a better-educated and healthier work force, they will have to find the resources in their municipal budgets or partner with national or state level ministries.

The situation differs for shelter construction. Slum dwellers generally create for themselves a minimum amount of shelter, without any public financial support, by investing their own limited resources and labor in incremental improvements over time. The question, then, is how public and private engagement can support and enhance this process of shelter construction. Traditional mortgage finance mechanisms are usually out of reach of slum dwellers. However, credit is potentially important, and one avenue is the development of microcredit schemes. These are often initiated by nongovernmental, not-for-profit organization without direct government funding, but they need a supportive regulatory framework and can be helped by limited public grant funding, especially to overcome start-up hurdles. Other mechanisms involve grants that allow slum dwellers to purchase building materials or help them improve specific components of their houses (e.g., pouring a cement floor, such as the *piso firme* program in Mexico that was supported by a large private company). Public housing programs that involve the large-scale construction of multistory housing for slum dwellers are generally financially unaffordable in low-income countries, and even in middle-income countries they are difficult to finance and manage, the successful experience of Hong Kong and Singapore notwithstanding (see chapter 14).[17]

---

[17] In chapter 14, Freire reports that in some developing countries public housing subsidies are sizable, up to 4 percent of GDP; however, they are usually not effectively targeted at poor families living in slums; rather, they tend to benefit the better off. One option for governments therefore is to reduce such housing subsidies and put the

Addressing the challenge of slum improvement in the large cities of developing countries is complicated by the geographic fragmentation of metropolitan jurisdictions and by murky intergovernmental fiscal relations. Metropolitan fragmentation means that poor and rich municipalities coexist in metro cities, making it very difficult to plan and implement comprehensive slum improvement programs and to cross-subsidize from better-off to poorer neighborhoods, even though all would benefit if the prevalence and severity of slums were reduced. The problem is compounded where responsibility for metropolitan slum improvement is divided or unclear among national, state, and metro agencies, as is generally the case, and where revenue authority at metropolitan and municipal levels is constrained. Establishing a metrowide authority to address slum improvement and giving it clear planning, implementation, and financing mechanisms, as was the case in Hong Kong and Singapore, would go a long way toward overcoming the challenges that slums pose to modern metro management and financing.

THE ROLE OF INTERNATIONAL AID

As in other areas of development, international development assistance can and does provide support in filling domestic resource gaps for urban investments.

Current Practice

Many donors are involved in providing such aid, with the World Bank by far the largest, followed by Japan and then the regional development banks (see chapter 15). But aid flows to urban areas have been stagnant in recent decades and undersized relative to urban investment needs, despite frequent calls by urban experts in and out of aid agencies for greater support. Aid in urban areas has often been confined to single sectors, such as roads or sanitation, without addressing broader, cross-cutting issues of management that might strengthen the sustainability of those interventions that do exist. Africa's urban investment needs, in particular, have seen neglect by donors. Donor agencies have prepared urban strategy documents; these have called for greater engagement in supporting urban development, but implementation of the strategies generally has fallen short of the stated goals.

This underinvestment in urban aid occurred even though evaluations show that such investments on average tend to have greater development impact than does aid to other sectors. To make matters worse, engagement of donors at country and city levels has generally lacked a long-term strategic perspective and hence has been one-off, fragmented, and uncoordinated rather than systematically sequencing and scaling up successful interventions.

A key constraint to the sustainability and scaling up of donor-supported programs has been the lack of development of local financing capacity for maintaining

---

money to better targeted use in supporting urban infrastructure development and schemes that directly help slum dwellers improve their shelter conditions.

and building on the aid-financed initiative, once donor support ceases. This, in turn, can be traced back to either a lack of focus by donors on the fiscal capacity of urban governments or, where donors did focus on this important dimension, a lack of impact in actually enhancing local revenue-raising capacity. In addition, donors generally do not focus on the question of how to rationalize intergovernmental transfers, which provides a critical part of local government resources. And while there have been some examples where donors systematically tried to help strengthen the borrowing capacity and institutional and policy framework for city governments, in general such interventions showed little impact. Finally, donors have not paid adequate attention to the special financing needs and capacities of metropolitan areas compared with other urban areas (see chapter 10). This is in part because donors are obliged to work with national-level government entities and metropolitan areas are often not a formal level of government, in contrast to state or city levels.

Reform Directions

Aid donors need to go beyond broad statements of strategy and focus more systematically on the financing needs and the need to build the institutional capacity of urban governments. Experience shows that donors could effectively channel at least some of their resources through municipal development funds (also known as urban investment funds), which are national-level agencies that provide funding and technical support to urban governments for meeting their investment needs. But such funds, and the financial and technical support that donors provide, have to be carefully tailored to country conditions, for example, credits in middle-income countries and grants in low-income countries (Annez, Huet, and Peterson 2008; see chapter 15).

Donors could also form better partnerships with one another and pool their resources for comprehensive and longer-term engagement in support of urban and metropolitan investments, institution building, and policy reform. To do so effectively, they would need to better support the preparation of in-depth analytical reviews of metropolitan socioeconomic conditions and investment needs, assess the institutional capacities and stakeholder interests, and help develop and implement longer-term metropolitan development strategies. In doing so, special attention should be paid to the urban finance dimension, that is, supporting the development of (1) local financial revenue mobilization and management capacity; (2) effective intergovernmental transfer schemes; and (3) effective metropolitan debt management frameworks.

THE WAY FORWARD

Building and sustaining metropolitan economic competitiveness and providing adequate services will be as essential as it is difficult, given the existing backlogs and the expected high rate of urbanization. The relative prosperity in urban areas has also drawn poor migrants, and large slums have grown up, with attendant social problems. The urban poor have little taxpaying power and many needs. A competing claim on resources is the infrastructure and social services needed to support the economic growth sectors. Both face significant financing gaps.

There are different scenarios for where all of this might lead. No doubt, different countries will make different choices. The following three considerations might usefully inform these choices: the metropolitan strategy; the relation of finance, function, and governance; and political economy.

Developing a Metropolitan Strategy

In most developing countries, metropolitan finance and governance seem to have been on the back burner, with higher-level governments more often reacting to problems brought by urbanization than addressing the more fundamental issues. The reasons for this are not difficult to understand. The quality of services is already much better in metropolitan areas, and metropolitan local governments tend to finance a greater share of their budgets from their own resources than do other local governments. Metropolitan local governments also typically serve a more educated electorate than do those in the rest of the country, and the accountability process probably works better. Why spend central reform efforts and political capital on something that seems to be working? Moreover, mayors and governors might be future political rivals, and strong ones at that, so it is understandable that the sitting central government might not want to address metropolitan governance and finances.

But the continued growth of urban populations and urban economies and the challenges of global competition will change all of that, at least for some metropolitan areas. Many countries will come to recognize the need for a metropolitan strategy. They will amend their approach to fiscal decentralization by developing a separate model for spending, taxing, and borrowing in the large metropolitan areas. The efficient provision of public services, and their financing, has outgrown the jurisdictional boundaries of the central cities; hence, a new approach needs to be designed to cover these metropolitan-wide governance and finance challenges. The new mix of service provision and financing should include regional taxes, delivery of at least some services on a regional basis, and a revenue model for metropolitan areas that focuses more on self-sufficiency.

Finance Follows Function Follows Governance

Many metropolitan areas comprise numerous local governments. The boundaries of these jurisdictions do not change often or easily. To a large extent, the assignment of expenditure responsibilities to local governments conforms to these boundaries, as does the financing. Most of the fragmented local government structures in metropolitan areas are highly dependent on intergovernmental transfers or on vertical program spending by higher-level governments.

Metropolitan-wide government, on the other hand, allows externalities for many public services to be internalized and a broader range of services to be assigned to the metro-level agencies. Financing of a metropolitan city government will include property tax and user charges, but other taxes, often those reserved for state-level authorities, should be considered in the mix, while intergovernmental transfers will become less dominant in the revenue structure.

The lesson here is that discussions of innovative financing of metropolitan-area local services must begin with a recognition of the limits placed by the existing governance structure and an assessment of how it might be changed to accommodate service delivery on an areawide basis, and hence regional taxation. Efforts to build metropolitan councils and to draw on new e-technologies for accountability and transparency may also help to support more effective management of metro areas, when it may be politically difficult to alter formal governance structures.

Political Economy

Good economics and good public management objectives may point toward metropolitan strategies that are not in step with the political realities in the cities concerned. In the end, political solutions usually win out. Most developing countries have a long history of fiscal centralization, and the centralists are particularly resistant to giving subnational governments more power to tax the broad bases of income and consumption. Borrowing by subnational governments is another fear, and rigid local borrowing frameworks are now the rule in many countries. On the question of expenditure assignment to metropolitan local governments, centralists will resist giving up control over matters such as employee compensation policy and will hesitate to relax some mandates for local spending.

But for many cities of the developing world, circumstances may now be more in favor of a metropolitan strategy. With the increase in urban population, the metropolitan-area constituency is growing in political power and may be in a better position to sway politicians. Moreover, the opportunities and the challenges of metropolitan cities are likely to become great enough to force themselves onto the policy agenda of governments around the world.

REFERENCES

Alm, James. 2010. Municipal financing of urban infrastructure: Knowns and unknowns. Working Paper No. 19. Washington, DC: Wolfensohn Center for Development, Brookings Institution.

Annez, Patricia Clarke. 2007. Urban infrastructure finance from private operators: What have we learned from recent experience? In *Financing cities*, ed. George Peterson and Patricia Clarke Annez, 307–338. Washington, DC/Los Angeles: World Bank/Sage.

Annez, Patricia Clarke, Gwenaelle Huet, and George E. Peterson. 2008. *Lessons for the urban century: Decentralized infrastructure finance in the World Bank*. Washington, DC: World Bank.

Bahl, Roy. 2011. Financing metropolitan cities. In *Local government finance: The challenges of the 21st century*, ed. United Cities and Local Governments. Barcelona: United Cities and Local Governments.

Bahl, Roy W., and Johannes F. Linn. 1992. *Urban public finance in developing countries*. New York: Oxford University Press.

Bahl, Roy, and Jorge Martinez-Vazquez. 2008. The property tax in developing countries: Current practice and prospects. In *Making the property tax work: Experiences in developing and transitional countries*, ed. Roy Bahl, Jorge Martinez-Vazquez, and Joan Youngman. Cambridge, MA: Lincoln Institute of Land Policy.

Bahl, Roy, and Sally Wallace. 2010. A new paradigm for property taxation in developing countries. In *Challenging the conventional wisdom about the property tax*, ed. Roy Bahl, Jorge Martinez-Vazquez, and Joan Youngman. Cambridge, MA: Lincoln Institute of Land Policy.

Bird, Richard. Forthcoming. Fiscal decentralization in Colombia: A work (still) in progress. In *Fiscal federalism in Latin America: Argentina, Colombia, Mexico and Peru*, ed. Roy Bahl and Geeta Sethi. Washington, DC: World Bank.

Braun, Miguel, and Steven Webb. Forthcoming. Fiscal federalism in Argentina: Recent trends and future challenges. In *Fiscal federalism in Latin America: Argentina, Colombia, Mexico and Peru*, ed. Roy Bahl and Geeta Sethi. Washington, DC: World Bank.

Engel, Eduardo, Ronald Fischer, and Alexander Galetovic. 2010. The economics of infrastructure finance: Public-private partnerships versus public provision. *EIB Papers* 15(1):40–69. Santiago, Chile: University of Chile.

Glaeser, Edward. 2011. *The triumph of the city: How our greatest invention makes us richer, smarter, greener, healthier, and happier.* New York: Penguin.

Glaeser, Edward, and Joshua Gottlieb. 2009. The wealth of cities: Agglomeration economies and spatial equilibrium in the United States. *Journal of Economic Literature* 47(4):983–1028.

High Powered Expert Committee. 2011. *Report on Indian urban infrastructure and services.* Delhi: Ministry of Urban Development, Government of India.

International Monetary Fund. 2009. Government finance statistics. Washington, DC.

Klink, Jeroen. 2008. Recent perspectives on metropolitan organization, functions and governance. In *Governing the metropolis: Principles and cases*, ed. Eduardo Rojas, Juan Cuadrado-Roura, and Jose Miguel Fernandez Guell, 77–136. Washington, DC: Inter-American Development Bank and Rockefeller Center for Latin American Studies.

Liu, Lili, and Steven B. Webb. 2011. *Laws for fiscal responsibility for subnational discipline: International experience.* Policy Research Working Paper No. 5587. Washington, DC: World Bank.

Martinez-Vazquez, Jorge. Forthcoming. Fiscal decentralization in Peru: A perspective on recent developments and future challenges. In *Fiscal federalism in Latin America: Argentina, Colombia, Mexico and Peru*, ed. Roy Bahl and Geeta Sethi. Washington, DC: World Bank.

Menard, Claude. Forthcoming. Is public-private partnership obsolete? In *Assessing the obstacles and shortcomings of PPP*, ed. Piet De Vries and Etienne Yehoue. London: Routledge.

Oates, Wallace. 1972. *Fiscal federalism.* New York: Harcourt Brace Jovanovich.

OECD. 2006. OECD territorial reviews: Competitive cities in the global economy. Paris: Organisation for Economic Co-operation and Development.

———. 2008a. OECD territorial reviews: Istanbul, Turkey. Paris: Organisation for Economic Co-operation and Development.

———. 2008b. OECD territorial reviews: Cape Town, South Africa. Paris: Organisation for Economic Co-operation and Development.

Prud'homme, Remy. 1995. On the dangers of decentralization. *World Bank Research Observer* 10(2):210–226.

Rojas, Eduardo. 2008. The metropolitan regions of Latin America: Problems of governance and development. In *Governing the metropolis*, ed. Eduardo Rojas, Juan R. Cuadrado-Roura, and Jose Miguel Fernandez Guell. Washington, DC: Inter-American Development Bank and David Rockefeller Center for Latin American Studies, Harvard University.

Slack, Enid. 2000. A preliminary assessment of the new city of Toronto. *Canadian Journal of Regional Science* 23(1):13–29.

———. 2007. Managing the coordination of service delivery in metropolitan cities: The role of metropolitan governance. Policy Research Working Paper No. 4317. Washington, DC: World Bank.

Tanzi, Vito. 1996. Fiscal federalism and decentralization: A review of some efficiency and macroeconomic aspects. In *Annual World Bank conference on development economics*, ed. Michael Bruno and Boris Pleskovic, 295–316. Washington, DC: World Bank.

United Nations. 2008. *World urbanization prospects: The 2007 revision, economic and social affairs.* New York.

———. 2012. World urbanization prospects: The 2011 revision [CD-ROM]. POP/DB/WUP/Rev. 2011. New York: United Nations, Department of Economic and Social Affairs, Population Division.

U.S. Census Bureau. 2012. World population: 1950–2050. (August 28). www.census.gov/population/international/data/idb/worldpopgraph.php

Van Ryneveld, Philip. 2007. Fiscal decentralization and financing of urban infrastructure in South Africa. In *Financing cities,* ed. George Peterson and Patricia Clarke Annez, 183–204. Washington, DC/Los Angeles: World Bank/Sage.

World Bank. 2009. Improving municipal management for cities to succeed: An IEG special study. Washington, DC.

———. 2012. World development indicators 2012. Washington, DC.

METROPOLITAN CITIES

Their Rise, Role, and Future

SHAHID YUSUF

2

The world's population crossed the 7 billion people mark in 2011, more than half of whom make their homes in cities. Each week, the ranks of urban residents increase by 1 million, and on every single day some 20,000 new dwellings and 160 miles of road are added to the existing stock. China alone constructs 2 billion square meters of floor space each year, approximately half of the global total. Looking toward the middle of the century, demographers project a global population of close to 9 billion, barring unexpected changes in fertility trends and unforeseen calamities, and urbanists assume that 70 percent of this vast number will live in cities. More people and more cities are an inescapable part of the future. Should urban densities continue declining at about 2 percent per annum, as they have through much of the twentieth century, the built-up area will expand at a far faster rate than the urban population. By one estimate, the urban population in developing countries could double by 2030, whereas the built-up area encompassed by cities would triple. Clearly, future generations are in for exciting times.

METROPOLITAN CHALLENGES

Research on urbanization since the 1960s shows that it closely correlates with industrialization and with rising incomes because of the higher productivity of average urban workers relative to their rural counterparts.[1] But too many cities in advanced and developing countries are failing to exploit the "urban advantage" and in fact are

I am greatly indebted to Lopamudra Chakraborti for assistance with the research for this paper. I owe a special thanks to the editors and the participants of the Brookings workshop for their many valuable comments and suggestions that have helped improve content and presentation.

[1] However, industry does not appear to cause urbanization in the sense proposed by Clive Granger (1969 as it arguably did from 1850 to 1960 (see Henderson 2010). Granger devised tests for determining whether one time series data could forecast another thereby demonstrating a measure of causality.

31

struggling to cope with the physical and financial pressures resulting from growing populations and the associated crowding, pollution, vehicular traffic, shortages
of housing and services, increasing poverty and inequality, spread of slums, and
environmental degradation.[2] Very few cities in developing countries are fortunate
enough to steadily generate enough jobs for the growing workforce and to address
endemic problems of unemployment. Where economic performance falters and/or
revenue effort is weak, urban services suffer, which affects business activity and the
quality of life, especially for the poor. With vehicle ownership mushrooming, cities
confront an equally daunting task of financing, building, and maintaining needed
infrastructure. Soaring automobility is exacerbating the problem of carbon and
other emissions associated with urbanization. In fact, most cities have barely begun to tackle the physical and institutional changes required to contain greenhouse gasses and to engineer the resilience demanded by the threat of climatic
extremes.[3]

For an expanding global economy, energy and resource scarcities will be mount-
ing concerns requiring a change in urban design, in modes of transport, and in soft
and hard infrastructures. And climatic change will expose cities to pressures and
shocks rarely experienced before. Few cities will be spared, and many coastal and
semiarid locations may continue to remain habitable only through major injections
of capital.[4]

Inevitably, no infallible recipe or sufficient conditions will assure successful urban
development. However, the collective experience of scores of urban centers, many of
which have embarked upon innovative policies, strengthened their finances, and
introduced new technologies, provides reliable pointers on creating a dynamic
metropolitan region that would provide most inhabitants with jobs and a decent
quality of life.[5]

Starting with the reasons underlying rapid urbanization in recent decades and
its likely continuation through the first half of the century, this chapter first examines the rise of the metropolitan region and the advantages stemming from agglomeration. It then details the factors determining the pace and characteristics of
urbanization, focusing on national policies, economic structure, financing issues,
physical characteristics and infrastructure, the implications of "smartness," governance, and sustainability.

---

[2] That too many cities in advanced and developing countries are failing to exploit the "urban advantage" is emphasized by the U.N. Human Settlements Programme (UN-HABITAT 2008). Inequality is greatest in African cities (Gini coefficients of 0.58), but it is rising most rapidly in Asia (UN-HABITAT 2008). Although the percentage of
those living in urban slums is estimated to have declined from 39 percent to 32 percent from 2000 to 2010, the
absolute numbers have risen. On current trends, there will be almost 900 million slum dwellers by 2020 (UN-
HABITAT 2008). According to other estimates, up to 2 billion people will be living in informal settlements by 2030.

[3] Cities account for 80 percent of all greenhouse gas emissions, with the top 50 cities releasing 2.6 trillion tons
of greenhouse gases per year (Oxford Analytica 2011). The topic of urban resilience has brought forth a considerable literature (see, e.g., International Council for Local Environmental Initiatives 2012; Newman, Beatley, and
Boyer 2009; World Bank 2008).

[4] In a number of instances, these injections of capital will include expenditures on infrastructure to augment
the water supply with the help of transfers from other parts of the country, as in China, and through desalination
of seawater.

[5] An increasing number of innovations are targeting the vast army of low-income slum dwellers (see Smith
2011).

URBANIZATION: FROM CANTER TO GALLOP

Five factors account for accelerating urbanization and its structural characteristics, and their persistence determines the dynamics, challenges, and policy implications of urbanization discussed throughout this chapter.

First, the demographic transition caused by a sharp decline in infant mortality, increasing life expectancies, and a much more gradual reduction in fertility has resulted in ballooning populations in developing nations. This increase in population has caused cities to grow and has also led to in situ urbanization with small towns and villages mushrooming into cities in China (see Zhu et al. 2009), Pakistan, and Brazil, for example, with Brazil having achieved European rates of urbanization by 2000.[6] Greater rural population densities have pushed people to migrate, and higher incomes and greater amenities in cities have exerted a parallel pull.[7] With population pressures rising, cities are seen as beacons of opportunity as economic prospects are diminishing in rural areas. Urbanization is correlated with rising living standards, even as the transfer of populations has led to increased poverty in cities (Ravallion 2007). The share of the population in urban areas living on the equivalent of less than a dollar a day rose from 19 percent to 24 percent from 1993 to 2002; over the same period, the urban share of the population as a whole rose from 38 percent to 42 percent. The urbanization of poverty was most rapid in Latin America, with a rise in proportion of the poor living in urban areas from 50 percent in 1993 to 60 percent in 2002. By contrast, less than 10 percent of East Asia's poor live in urban areas, largely because absolute poverty in China is overwhelmingly rural.

Second, agricultural production is becoming less labor intensive, with machinery, chemicals, and energy serving as substitutes.[8] Fewer hands are needed on farms, and if the impressively productive agricultural systems in advanced economies are harbingers of what developing economies can expect, the share of the agricultural labor force in low- and middle-income countries will drop from an average of about 25 percent of the national total in 2007 to less than 10 percent. Furthermore, dispersed small-scale rural industry, which tends to be inefficient and polluting, is fighting a losing battle with urban producers, which enjoy manifold advantages compounded by declining costs of surface transport and increasing efficiencies in distribution and marketing technologies.

Third, technological advances and the evolving income elasticity of demand are responsible for structural changes that have enlarged the role of services. A stream of innovations have raised the productivity of manufacturing, contributing to growth but also resulting in declining relative prices of manufactures and reduced employment in industry, which explains why the share of manufacturing has fallen from 1980 to 2008. Thus, the share of manufacturing is a shrinking proportion of gross domestic product (GDP) in the larger cities, although it remains high for some smaller cities with industrial specializations. Meanwhile, rising demand for urban services and much slower gains in productivity have increased the share of

---

[6] Brazil's urban population rose from 36 percent in 1950 to 75 percent in 1990. http://www.citymayors.com/statistics/urban-population-intro.html; and World Bank, World Development Indicators 2011.

[7] This income gradient is the so-called Harris-Todaro effect of higher urban incomes (see Fields 2007).

[8] On the energy (and nitrogen fertilizer) intensity of modern agriculture, see Smil (2008; 2011).

urban services in GDP and employment. With the exception of China, services now dominate GDP everywhere, and in most cities in advanced countries, services provide the majority of jobs and generate more than half of the income.[9] In fact, with industry pushed to the margins of some urban economies, services are the economy. A fraction of services are tradable, but the bulk of urban services in developing countries are nontradable, and services comprise a small share of the exports of low- and middle-income countries, tourism being the largest contributor.[10] This has long-term implications for the number and type of jobs the urban economy is likely to create, for growth, and for exports to balance the city's trade accounts, because to be viable over the longer term, cities, much like countries, must have something to sell, with any shortfall being offset through capital transfers. Until a few decades ago, all growing cities were industrial cities with export potential. This has ceased to be the rule with the rise of services, both formal and informal.[11]

Fourth, cities enable firms to specialize and realize scale advantages. These so-called localization economies are an important asset for midsize industrial cities and a source of productivity gains from labor markets, technological spillovers, and the benefits of clustering of other producers and suppliers of services. For larger urban centers, urbanization economies are more prominent. These are the economies arising from the multiplicity of industry and services that open the door to diversification and induce the entry of new firms. Together, these lead to significant productivity gains and higher average incomes. Currid (2007, 460) notes that "agglomeration may be even more important to maintaining the social mechanisms by which the cultural economy sustains itself [through nonmarket transactions]." A vast literature, mostly on cities in developed countries, has attempted to estimate the gains from agglomeration, whether from localization or urbanization or from scale economies (Gill and Goh 2009; Glaeser and Gottlieb 2009; Rosenthal and Strange 2004; World Bank 2009).[12] Researchers differ on which type of agglomeration matters more; however, all agree that agglomeration pays, although how much productivity can be traced to size and diversity varies from 3 percent to 12 percent.[13] A meta-analysis of elasticities drawn from 34 studies cautions that the gains from largeness should not be exaggerated (see Melo, Graham, and Noland 2009), but little or no evidence indicates that growth is disadvantageous for cities. However, casual empiricism suggests that as cities grow larger and more complex, management and service provision become difficult and congestion, pollution, and crime diminish the quality of life, as, for instance, in Bangalore (Bengaluru), São Paulo,

---

[9] From 1977 to 2007, the share of services in global GDP rose from 55 percent to 70 percent, and to 75 percent in Organisation for Economic Co-operation and Development member countries (Francois and Hoekman 2010).

[10] See Eichengreen and Gupta (2009; 2011) on the role of services with reference to India, Ghani (2010) on how growth in India could continue to be propelled by services, and Spence and Hlatshwayo (2011) on the contribution of nontradable services to the bulk of the employment created in the United States since 1990.

[11] In 2007, the global value of cross-border trade in services amounted to $3.3 trillion, or about a fifth of total trade. However, the share is closer to 50 percent when measured by value added, both direct and indirect (Francois and Hoekman 2010). The growth of cross-border trade is impeded by regulatory restrictions and by the greater protection accorded to services.

[12] Physicist Geoffrey West compares large cites to big animals whose size is a source of scale economies; when a city doubles in size, the resources required to sustain it grow by 85 percent (see Lehrer 2010).

[13] Rosenthal and Strange (2004) note that a doubling of city size can lead to an increase in productivity of 3–8 percent.

Lagos, Karachi, and many booming Chinese cities in the Pearl River Delta. Whether these collectively erode the productivity-enhancing advantages of size is debatable.[14]

The fifth and final factor contributing to the vigor of urbanization is the role of cities in sparking ideas, stimulating social change by inculcating new values, and encouraging innovation in every sphere of life. Johnson (2010, 16, 162) compares cities in all their variegated complexity to coral reefs "powerfully suited to the creation, diffusion and adoption of good ideas. . . . [T]hey cultivate specialized skills and interests, and they create a liquid network where information can leak out of those subcultures and influence their neighbors in surprising ways. This is one reason for superlinear scaling in urban creativity."[15] Such innovation has buoyed productivity; equally, it has enhanced human capabilities and raised the quality of life. Looking ahead, as cities in developing countries attempt to come to grips with increasing size, complexity, and pressures arising from climate change, their innovative potential will become ever more important and the basis not just of survival but also of prosperity.[16]

While continued urbanization appears to be a given, urban development is likely to evolve in different directions, with implications for growth and quality of life. From the perspective of this volume, the interesting issues pertain to the potential of the metropolitan model of urban development and how creatively metropolitan centers address the many different challenges they will face.

THE METROPOLITAN POWERHOUSE

Megacities, with populations of 10 million and more, have increased in number from 9 in 1985 to 23 in 2010, and they account for almost half of the world's wealth.[17] Moreover, some of the megacities in East Asia and South Asia account for a third or more of the national GDP. A striking characteristic of the urbanizing tendencies in the United States, Latin America, and East Asia is the emergence of metropolitan regions or metropolitan corridors composed of a cluster of cities, which may or may not include a megacity. Seoul, Jogjakarta, São Paulo, and Bangkok are examples of metropolitan economies with a core primate city that has brought (or created) a number of dormitory, secondary, and edge cities into its orbit. The Pearl River Delta comprises another vast metropolitan corridor extending from Hong Kong to Guangzhou that arose with great rapidity once China adopted the Open Door Policy in 1979 and industry began transferring from Hong Kong.[18] A metropolitan

[14] Inskeep (2011) vividly describes the combustible nature of life in Karachi. Cohen (2004) presents some data underlining the unstoppable increase in average city size over the past two centuries: the largest 100 cities in the world had an average population of 200,000 in 1800, which rose to 5 million by 1990. Beijing was the only city with 1 million inhabitants at the beginning of the nineteenth century; 100 years later only 16 cities were of this size, but by 1950 their numbers had swelled to 86.

[15] *Superlinear scaling* refers to a faster than exponential rate of increase. Thus, as cities grow, according to physicist Geoffrey West and his coworkers at the Santa Fe Institute, such superlinearity is evident in telecommunication traffic, patenting, and pedestrian speed (see Andris et al. 2009).

[16] How cities can induce innovation is compactly summarized in Atkinson (2012).

[17] The 2010 U.N. State of the World Cities report (UN-HABITAT 2008) points to the emergence of the megaregion: an endless city. However, the bulk of the urban population resides in midsize and small cities.

[18] See McGee et al. (2007) on the rise of the Hong Kong–Guangzhou region and Berger and Lester (1997) on the transfer of industry from Hong Kong to emerging cities in the Pearl River Delta.

corridor is also taking shape in Pakistan, connecting the cities of Lahore and Rawalpindi. There are a number of reasons that the metro region might be the form that urbanization will take in the future, with isolated cities becoming an endangered species.[19]

The need to economize on energy use and on the cost of providing urban infrastructure makes the compactly designed metropolitan model a more viable proposition than the relatively isolated city that lacks the connectedness to a multiplicity of other conurbations (Glaeser 2011). The metropolis can also internalize urbanization and localization economies by combining a portfolio of cities in a single urban domain. The core city, with diverse services and advanced emerging industries that draw oxygen from proximity to centers of research, can be the primary source of urbanization economies (or Jacobs economies), while smaller peripheral specialized cities can serve as sites for industrial activities requiring cheaper land for factories and lower-rent accommodation for workers.[20] By yoking these different kinds of cities together with an efficient multimodal transport system that tempers the reliance on private cars, the metropolitan region can maximize the gains from agglomeration and market size economies. By expanding in the vertical plane, it can also squeeze many more people into a place with proven locational advantages, for example, a coastal or riverine plain location amply supplied with potable water, and capitalize on an existing foundational infrastructure and possibly a brand name.

A broad economic base and a large urban market make it easier for a metropolitan region to meet its financing needs and minimize fluctuations in revenue streams while keeping tax rates at moderate and competitive levels. Revenue adequacy underwrites industrial capabilities and provides the means for a city to adapt and change as circumstances change, calling for displacing of older industries by newer ones and a renewal of infrastructure and buildings so as to incorporate the latest technologies and accommodate changing lifestyles.[21] No metropolitan region ever optimizes on all these fronts, and when there are many adjacent municipal jurisdictions, coordinating infrastructure development, revenue-raising arrangements, and financial burden sharing can be severely challenging. By failing to arrive at coherent and mutually advantageous outcomes through negotiated give-and-take, multijurisdictional metropolitan entities are squandering the benefits of agglomeration, both economic and financial.

BUILDING THE METROPOLITAN ENGINE

Size and agglomeration economies can influence urban fortunes through productivity, but there are too many examples of metropolitan regions that are not

---

[19] Eventually, some of these isolated cities will either shrink drastically or end up as ghost towns once younger people migrate, revenues decline, services atrophy, and infrastructures deteriorate.

[20] Jacobs (1970) emphasized the advantages of innovation and stimulation of new activity that cities derive from diverse industries, hence the term *Jacobs economies*, which larger cities are more likely to benefit from than are smaller cities with a narrower base of activities.

[21] An example of recent technologies is the incorporation of information and communication technologies and new green technologies, which enable buildings to economize on water and energy. Smaller household size, increasing numbers of older people, and the explosion in relational networking are among the factors influencing lifestyles and demands on urban infrastructures and services.

realizing their potential. In some megacities the development of industry and tradable services is creeping along or in retreat, growth is stagnating, unemployment is widespread, and the supply of housing and public services is struggling to keep up with the demand because the productive economic base and revenue effort are both weak. Karachi, São Paulo, Cairo, Manila, and Johannesburg belong to this category of cities that are deriving few advantages from size and suffer instead from the diseconomies of unbridled agglomeration and sprawl. What differentiates these cities from metropolitan regions that are dynamic economically and registering high growth rates? For low- and middle-income countries, with lagging urban development in the face of rising urbanization, the missing ingredient is exploding business activity represented by the entry and growth of firms producing tradables (either manufactured products or services), creating good jobs, generating exports, and serving as a channel for new technologies absorbed from overseas and supplemented by their own adaptation and innovation.[22] Shenzhen, Bangkok, and Bangalore owe their dynamism to the continual value-adding and growth-enhancing churning of the business scene, with new (domestic and foreign) firms serving as a conveyor belt for investment and technology and competitive pressures sharpened by exposure to global markets, continually weeding out the laggards.

Entry of firms and growth of the most entrepreneurial ones are the lifeblood of the metropolitan region.[23] The dynamic cities not only benefit from high rates of entry but also, as in Beijing or Dongguan, encourage the formation of clusters that give rise to technological spillovers, stimulate productivity, and create conditions conducive to the formation of new firms.[24] Entry, cluster formation, and growth of the more productive firms can promote exports that in turn further stimulate economic expansion.[25] In fact, urban industrialization in the current context, and for all but the largest countries, is inseparable from participation in the international market.[26] This broadens market opportunities for the venturesome firms—a minority everywhere, but an important one—and spurs productivity and growth. Firms with the greatest managerial, organizational, and technical capabilities grow, and in both East Asia and Latin America, participation in international value chains has provided firms with technology and growth ladders. The Taiwanese experience, in particular, highlights this process of urban industrialization through a proliferation of small and midsize enterprises, their entry into trade, their proactive technology absorption and reverse engineering aided by public research institutes,

---

[22] All those who pour into cities are looking for "good jobs," if not for themselves then for their children (Banerjee and Duflo 2011).

[23] Firms develop and test their competitiveness by selling in the domestic market, frequently sheltered by tariffs, transport costs, local regulations, cultural predispositions of consumers, and complexities of marketing and logistics that foreign firms have difficulty mastering. Lenovo, the Chinese personal computer manufacturer, and Haier, the producer of white goods, have established and maintained a lead in the domestic market by catering more effectively to local preferences and effectively using domestic marketing channels.

[24] See McGee et al. (2007) on the globally oriented industrialization of Dongguan and Yusuf, Nabeshima, and Yamashita (2008) on the international experience with clusters.

[25] Larger, capital-intensive, and productive firms are more likely to venture into the export market (see Bernard et al. 2007). On the relationship between trade and growth, see the survey by Lopez (2005).

[26] Some evidence suggests that successful small and midsize businesses begin orienting toward global markets from the very outset (see Lloyd-Reason and Sear 2007).

and their emergence as globally competitive entities that drive the economies of Taiwan's cities and the national growth rate.

Once urban development takes off, the large metropolitan region has several advantages that can help to both build and sustain momentum. The medium-size peripheral cities are likely to be a fast-growing worldwide trend, with a large, youthful population that can provide entrepreneurial dividends and with lower-priced land to encourage new starts, especially in manufacturing. The core city, with a concentration of services and unskilled workers, offers a different range of opportunities, with many more niches for new startups and easier access to financing for existing firms or clusters of firms and for small and midsize enterprises.[27] The core city is better supplied with business development services, which can be valuable for new starts. The core city is also the focus of academic and cultural activities. Together, the concentration of universities, research and consulting services, and recreational facilities provides opportunities for knowledge workers with diverse skills to exchange and breed new ideas, some of which are enriched by combining two or more disciplines.

The metropolitan region, combining the advantages of midsize and large cities, has strong economic potential; however, its full development is realized when certain other criteria are met, in whole or in part:

- National policies.
- Industrial composition and clustering.
- Financing of urban development.
- Smart urbanization and governance.
- Connectedness.
- Sustainability.

These criteria or attributes were not uppermost in the minds of national policy makers when metropolitan cities were taking shape in the twentieth century. At the time, the financing of infrastructure and services was viewed as largely being the responsibility of the state; fuel was cheap; land for development seemed abundant; pollution and population pressures were less obtrusive; and sprawling low-rise cities seemed appropriate for the foreseeable modes of economic activity and lifestyles. Few, if any, city authorities and their allies among the developer communities seriously considered adopting a holistic long-term approach, which is warranted from the vantage point of current knowledge. But looking ahead, to succeed in attracting resources and talent and to maintain adequate growth rates, metropolitan cities, which have acquired more autonomy, will need to monitor progress with reference to the above, moving further along some axes than others, depending upon circumstances, without neglecting any one of them. Moreover, metropolitan cities will need to mobilize their political capital and to play a more active role in shaping national policies, something that cities such as Karachi have not done.

---

[27] Much depends upon the availability of affordable accommodations for small firms and their employees. In cities such as New York, London, and Paris and the cities in Silicon Valley, such space is becoming hard to find, which is squeezing out the most dynamic elements of the urban economy.

Wealth of Cities Derives from National Policies

If cities are truly the drivers of economic growth, how closely is that performance keyed to the national policy and overall national economic conditions? In other words, can cities forge ahead by dint of good urban policies more or less independent of events at the national level? Singapore surely fits this description, being a city-state, but other cities, even the largest and most prosperous, such as Tokyo, Seoul, São Paulo, Bangkok, Hong Kong–Guangzhou, and Shanghai, depend upon the enabling matrix of national-level trade, investment (domestic and foreign), fiscal, education, innovation, and other policies to provide the springboard for their own development.[28]

Even though decentralization and localization have transferred more administrative and fiscal discretion and policy initiative to subnational governments, and even though cities are at the leading edge of development, fundamental national policies define policy parameters, incentives, and the degrees of freedom available to city managers and, crucially, determine the fiscal and financial resources they can mobilize. The industrialization of Seoul and Shanghai was enabled by planning and day-to-day decision making conducted by city authorities and by a host of local regulations, rules, standards, and licensing requirements, but the opportunities for the cities were delineated and circumscribed by the investment, exchange rate, trade, industrial, labor, education, and technology policies of the central government. Both cities successfully groomed highly competitive export industries, which generated economic momentum and employment and catalyzed the development of other sectors of the urban economy. In particular, export-oriented industrial growth was paced by the expansion of transport and energy infrastructures financed partly through central government budget allocations and partly through loans from state owned (or controlled) banks.

From the mid-1990s, Seoul took a lead in establishing a world-class infrastructure to harness the potential of information and communication technologies (ICT), with Shanghai now close behind. Weak leadership and an incoherent national policy environment have hobbled cities in South Asia, Latin America, and Africa, a malaise now spreading to "developed" countries. In East Asia, these measures initiated the process of modernization and integration with the global economy. The end result as of 2012 is two metropolitan economies that rank among the most vibrant in the world.

However, in both instances (and these examples can be multiplied), urban outcomes were prompted and shaped by national policies. The Korean government, once it embraced export-oriented industrialization, viewed Seoul as the engine of the economy, and urban development complemented other policies, more recently, policies to develop an ICT-supported knowledge and cultural economy.[29] It is the

---

[28] Foreign direct investment is an important source of capital and technology transfer for industrializing countries and is likely to remain a vital conduit. Singapore was the leading urban recipient of foreign direct investment projects in 2009, followed by Shanghai, London, and Dubai. In Latin America, São Paulo, Bogotá, and Mexico City led the field. See FDI Intelligence (2011).

[29] Even though the Korean government was painfully aware of Seoul's vulnerability to an attack from the north, given that it was just 30 miles from the demilitarized zone, it acknowledged and exploited the city's strategic location and long-standing role in the national economy.

industrialization of the Seoul metro region that propelled the Korean economy during the high-growth era starting in the mid-1960s and continues to do so as Korea enters a postindustrial stage. Seoul has served not only as the seat of government and the nation's cultural hub but also as home to several of Korea's leading export industries, including textiles, machinery, electronics, and now the creative industries.[30]

Once China set its sights on reform and catching up with the leading East Asian economies and designated Shanghai as the head of the Dragon because of its location at the mouth of the Yangtze delta and its role in leading the economy of the Yangtze region, the city authorities had the green light to pursue an ambitious urban industrial strategy, which was amply supported by the central government and banks, as in the case of Seoul, and supplemented by the leasing of land to developers and by foreign direct investment induced through central policies reinforced by municipal incentives.[31] Shanghai's development since the early 1990s is the stuff of legend, and it owes much to the vision and energy of a succession of local officials, but it was the central government that loosened the rules binding Shanghai, encouraged the local authorities to raise their sights, and created the policy environment that allowed the city to more fully exploit its resource base, harness its vast latent capabilities, and bid for capital from elsewhere in China and from abroad.[32]

It is the central government that sets the stage and, to a greater or lesser extent, through policies and other interventions, choreographs urban development, in either positive or negative directions. Where central governments are missing in action, passive, or obstructive and predatory, urbanization may continue as it has in sub-Saharan Africa and in South Asia, but the urban economic, infrastructural, and institutional development that results in growth, exports, and jobs may be slow to materialize, if at all. Some cities in Africa, such as Kinshasa and Dar es Salaam, have become more populous during the 2000s but have not developed. Urbanization in Zimbabwe and the Congo is the direct outcome of conflict and worsening conditions in rural areas. Development has gone into reverse because the states have faltered or are failing (see World Bank 2011). Thus, the policy-making and administrative capabilities of the state and its urban strategy broadly define the opportunities for urban development. Some cities, especially capitals, are favored over others, and they have a head start; however, with the rules of the game as points of reference, it is up to the municipal authorities and other stakeholders to derive maximum mileage from the urban assets at their disposal, to enhance competitive advantage in profitable directions, to augment the local resource base, and to encourage investment that can maximize long-run growth.

---

[30] The creative industries include online video games, multimedia, moviemaking, and publishing (see Organisation for Economic Co-operation and Development 2005; World Bank 2008; Yusuf and Nabeshima 2006).

[31] Its past history made Shanghai a logical choice as a principal Dragonhead (see Yusuf and Nabeshima 2006; 2010; Yusuf and Wu 1997).

[32] Some of the mayors who contributed to Shanghai's resurgence were Wang Daohan (mayor 1981–1985); his protégé and successor, Jiang Zemin (1985–1989, later party chief and president of China); and Zhu Rongji (1989–1991).

The Matrix of Industry and Services

It is appropriate to start with industrial composition because this is of immediate relevance for growth, employment, and exports, and the current mix foreshadows future options for a metropolis. The competitiveness of activities dominating the metropolitan economy determines growth prospects through sales in domestic and foreign markets and the gains to be derived from productivity through innovation or technological catch-up. Industrial composition also points to employment elasticities and the types of skills likely to be in demand. When firms cluster in ways that promote spillovers, the productivity bonus can be larger. The information technology (IT)–enabled service sector in Bangalore and in Gurgaon, the second largest city in the state of Haryana, located about 30 km south of New Delhi, are clusters of proven competitiveness and export success employing highly skilled workers and diversifying into more complex services offering larger rewards.[33] IT and similar industries, with good long-term potential and significant local linkages, are assets for the metropolis, not least because they have low entry barriers, which encourages the proliferation of businesses in societies where demonstration effects can uncork pent-up entrepreneurial energies.

Dongguan, one of the fastest-growing metro cities in China, is the center of manufacturing, covering a spectrum ranging from textiles to electronics.[34] These industries provide jobs to skilled and unskilled workers, and the diversity is fertile soil for new businesses. Manufacturing activities in Dongguan target foreign markets, and major multinational corporations (MNCs) such as Foxconn and Nike have located their main manufacturing assets in the city. This further enriches the industrial ecology of the city because large factories owned by MNCs exploit scale economies and buy inputs from or subcontract with thousands of specialized suppliers.[35] The MNCs nourish the ecosystem with capital and production technologies and boost the development of local research, standard setting, and testing facilities.[36] No less important from the productivity angle are the managerial, design, and marketing techniques and the multifaceted, incremental innovations that the MNCs introduce. That manufacturing productivity is increasing by 10 percent or more in cities such as Dongguan testifies to the speed at which technologies are being disseminated, and this helps to absorb rising wages while maintaining healthy profit margins.[37]

Bangkok is yet another example of a dynamic industrial metropolis. The core city is richly supplied with services, and around it have sprung several secondary cities crowded with manufacturing firms that rely on the providers of IT, finance,

---

[33] See Heitzman (2004) on the development of Bangalore.

[34] With a population of almost 7 million in 2008, including nearly 5 million migrants, Dongguan is ranked fourth in China in exports.

[35] As of 2012, Chongqing is attempting to create a similar ecosystem, having induced Hewlett-Packard and Foxconn to establish production facilities for computers and peripherals in the city, with the promise that the city would work with them to attract suppliers to the inland metropolis. Together, the two companies will be investing $3 billion (Song 2009).

[36] MNCs account for 87 percent of China's exports of electronic devices and 88 percent of the exports of telecommunications equipment (Moran 2011).

[37] Despite rising wages, new entry and export growth continued in the Pearl River Delta during 2009–2010.

management, marketing, logistics, and human resource management services located in Bangkok city.[38] The metropolitan economies and the advantages accruing from the presence of the central government are such that efforts to disperse economic activities to the central and northern parts of Thailand have made limited headway. Other cities, such as Cairo, Rio de Janeiro, and Johannesburg, with a modest suite of tradable activities, pay a price. Cairo's manufacturing sector is smaller, mainly low tech, and low also in the scale of competitiveness. Services cater mostly to domestic demand and tourism. This constrains productivity gains, technological change, diversification, and growth. São Paulo and Rio de Janeiro are in a similar predicament, having deindustrialized and failed to adequately substitute departing industries with tradable services.[39] Rio, for all its natural beauty, is a city without the leading export and research-intensive sectors that can deliver high rates of growth and employment and lessen the city's dependence on budgetary transfers from the center.[40]

Johannesburg also suffers from slow growth, largely because of the decline of mining and affiliated engineering industries as ore bodies have been depleted and producers have begun shifting their operations to other countries. Engineering industries, which tend to be skill intensive, have created few jobs for South Africa's legions of unemployed, youthful, unskilled workers. Growth prospects of the Johannesburg–Gauteng region look increasingly dim over a longer horizon unless industrial trends are reversed.

What is learned from Chinese and some Southeast Asian metropolitan centers is that, for low- and middle-income countries, a broad manufacturing base, complemented as in Bangkok, Taipei, and Shanghai by the densification of service industries, promises growth and the scope for diversification. Analysis using the Hausmann-Rodrik-Hidalgo product space-mapping technique indicates that production systems lying on the periphery of the product space without many linkages to other product categories, as in the case of Johannesburg and Rio de Janeiro, face difficulty in acquiring the richly networked core activities that contribute to a deepening of industrial capabilities with better longer-term growth prospects.[41] A broadening industrial base and the complementary deepening of business services are the vital sources of local financing: cities that are able to draw upon such financing can support services that underpin continuing development; without resource mobilization, development is quickly imperiled.

---

[38] Government investment in port and highway infrastructure and incentives for developers contributed to the growth of these cities and the transfer of some of the auto, electronic, machinery, and other industries from the core city areas (see Yusuf and Nabeshima 2010).

[39] A software industry serves the domestic market in São Paulo and Rio de Janeiro, but the cities lack the large firms that account for the performance of Indian IT centers. Cape Town is in a similar predicament: the software/IT industry caters mostly to the domestic finance and insurance industry, which constrains its growth prospects.

[40] The discovery of huge offshore pre-salt oil deposits will increase the revenues accruing to the state, depending, of course, upon the terms negotiated with the center. Whether this leads to the emergence of firms serving the oil exploration, drilling, and downstream activities or instead inflicts damage on the metro economy (so-called Dutch disease) remains to be seen.

[41] See the discussion of the product space and core periphery issues in Hidalgo et al. (2007) where it is explained how various products are related with respect to technologies and sophistication and how closeness facilitates transition from one product group to another.

Financing Urban Development

Urban development assumes the provision of an array of services for businesses and households. If these dip below minimum standards of adequacy, development is impeded and the urban economy begins to stall and unravel. Infrastructure services, public health, education, and police/security services are among the basics. Scarcity of water, for example, can seriously constrain urban development, and poor sewage, waste disposal, and sanitation compromise the health and living conditions of the majority.

Whether a metropolitan region can build and maintain the physical infrastructure, provide basic services, supply affordable housing, and offer recreational amenities is ultimately a function of finances. Transfers from central and provincial level governments (both general and specific) are a source of revenues, but these are on a declining trend as a share of metropolitan revenues in most countries, with the spread of fiscal decentralization and fiscal constraints impinging on central governments. In the interest of sustainability, transfers should constitute a relatively modest source of revenue, and the local tax base should be the primary source of revenues. For a city to be broadly revenue self-sufficient, at least five criteria need to be satisfied.

First, as noted above, revenue generation is a function of the scale of economic activity and how this translates into earnings of residents, the distribution of incomes, and the values of taxable assets. Thus, metropolitan policies to promote business activities, which include fiscal policies and service delivery, are important determinants of the revenue base.

Second, the revenue actually raised depends upon the degree of local tax autonomy and taxes assigned to local authorities. Other fees collected by municipalities supplement taxes, but income and real property taxes generally constitute the bulk of local revenues. To meet expenditure assignments, subnational governments often look to central governments to bridge any gaps, but a sustainable metropolis should in principle be self-sufficient (see Bird 2011). Self-sufficiency also should not be tied to the leasing of land that is providing short-term revenue windfalls for many cities in China (40 percent of revenues on average) and Vietnam but is a rapidly depleting source of municipal income.

Third, the selection and use of tax instruments need to be efficient and to derive the maximum advantage by maintaining incentives for businesses and households to remain in the jurisdiction (see Inman 2007). Moreover, local authorities need to be able to enforce and collect the taxes, especially property/real estate taxes, and regularly assess properties and adjust rates.

Fourth, a metropolis spanning multiple jurisdictions must be able to coordinate regional development to optimize the provision of infrastructures and internalize scale economies where these exist. Equally important is the coordination of tax instruments and rates to avoid distorting incentives and inducing tax arbitrage and Tiebout shopping.[42]

---

[42] Philadelphia has suffered from a lack of coordination on taxation, land use, and transport development among the 238 municipalities comprising the greater metro area (see Pugh O'Mara 2002). Municipalities offer a

Fifth, fiscal responsibility laws can serve to underscore local responsibilities, minimize moral hazard, and induce fiscally prudent behavior.[43] Furthermore, local government fiscal performance and service delivery can be bolstered by procedures for evaluating performance. Bangkok, much like other metropolitan centers in developing countries, relies on a mix of transfers and locally sourced revenues, but efficiency is compromised by the large number of local government organizations and an inability to effectively analyze the data collected so as to improve monitoring and performance.

Tax revenues can partially finance infrastructure; however, most long-lived capital-intensive facilities call for additional financing, which can come from development grants provided by the center or can be raised by issuing bonds that are guaranteed by the center or provincial governments until such time as a city has established a track record and financial credentials.

Whether via tax revenues or financing through public-private partnerships or the financial market, sustainability first and foremost assumes that industrial development is on track and that the trends are pointing in the right direction. Where the development impetus is weak or failing, financial sustainability can prove elusive. Financial health can also be imperiled by a failure of governance mechanisms, central and local. This includes corruption and malfeasance, which are rife in Karachi and Mumbai, as well as legislative logrolling, when legislators avoid the risk of policy gridlock by indiscriminatingly voting for all new initiatives and, in the process, store up vast problems of indebtedness, as in Brazil, for instance.[44]

The Smarter Metropolis: Harnessing Intelligence and Improving Governance

The globally connected metropolis, which is a "smart city," like Seoul, Singapore, San Francisco, or San Jose, is doubly advantaged because it has the capabilities to exploit the opportunities arising from globalization. There is no precise definition of the smart city. Being "smart" is associated with a number of attributes, including a large percentage of the population with college degrees, state-of-the-art ICT infrastructure, and the early adoption of environmentally friendly and green technologies.[45] However, for our purposes, urban "smarts" or intelligence derives from a concentration of skills and the quality of governance. In other words, being smart has to do with the brainpower a city can marshal to manage and accelerate its development with the help of innovation at many different levels. Alongside depth and quality of human capital, these cities require institutional mechanisms and

---

bundle of services, amenities, and tax rates, and in principle, the mobile and well-informed individual can choose among competing priced options a la Tiebout (1956).

[43] The bailouts of Rio de Janeiro and São Paulo highlight this problem. Discouraging cities from using long-term debt to finance current expenditures is a key objective. For a review of international experience of fiscal responsibility laws, see Liu and Webb (2011).

[44] Inman (2007) cites a study of U.S. cities showing that a doubling in the size of a city council results in a 20 percent increase in spending per city resident.

[45] Cisco, IBM, and Siemens are among the companies working to create smart networked cities, where computer monitoring and control of activities will increase the efficiency of everything from transport systems to energy and water use. For a description of Cisco's Connected Urban Development approach and how it affects the workplace, transport, energy consumption, and businesses using IT, see Villa and Mitchell (2010).

basic research for generating ideas and avenues of debating, testing, and perfecting these ideas.

The smart city can achieve rapid and sustainable growth of industry by bringing together and fully mobilizing four forms of intelligence: (1) the human intelligence inherent in local knowledge networks enriched by in-migration of people with diverse talents; (2) the collective intelligence of institutions that support innovation through a variety of channels and serve to urbanize technologies, shaping them to suit the environment and making them easily available to users; (3) the production intelligence of its industrial base; and (4) the collective intelligence that can be derived from the effective use of digital networks and online services, a kind of involuntary crowd sourcing that contributes to problem solving and a progressive upgrading of the urban environment (Komninos 2008).[46] Cities positioning themselves to become innovative hotspots (e.g., Singapore and, more distantly, Bangalore) are open to ideas and thrive on the heterogeneity of knowledge workers drawn from all over the country and the world. Moreover, such cities are closely integrated with other global centers of research and technology development (they are a part of the global innovation system), and their teaching and research institutions must compete with the best for talent and to validate their own ideas. Last but not least, because smart cities are at the leading edge of the knowledge economy, their design, physical assets, attributes, and governance need to reflect their advantage over others.

Industrial cities can become innovative cities, and in fact, a strong manufacturing base can be an asset, as it is for Tokyo, Stuttgart, Munich, Seoul, Seattle, and Toulouse. But industry is not a necessary condition: Cambridge (U.K.), Helsinki, San Francisco, and Kyoto are not industrial cities; they are innovative cities that have acquired significant production capabilities that are high tech or Information-tech. As long as a city is part of a metro region or adjacent to one, size can be a secondary consideration and overridden by the advantages of livability. Medium-size industrial cities, by exploiting localization economies, can promote the formation of vibrant industrial clusters. And because they tend to be less congested, medium-size cities can appeal to younger age groups concerned about the cost of living and environmental quality, as well as to members of the creative class who place a high premium on the quality of life, all of which ranks cities with respect to quality of life and creativity and highlights the lead enjoyed by medium-size cities.[47] Of course, only a subset of midsize cities are potential winners, but those that exploit their location and strategically develop the assets that contribute to long-term prosperity can equal or exceed the innovation and productivity advantages of the most dynamic large cities.[48]

A city with an abundance of skills is better positioned to maintain industrial competitiveness, to move up the value chain by assimilating technologies and reinforcing catch up with innovations, and to diversify into more profitable activities as existing ones enter the stage in their life cycle when commoditization lowers entry

---

[46] The presence of major universities is likely to attract these four forms of intelligence (see Winters 2011).

[47] Depending on the type of industry and environmental regulations, midsize cities can be more or less polluted.

[48] The relationship between size and innovation is analyzed in Carlino, Chatterjee, and Hunt (2007).

barriers, pares profit margins, and triggers migration to lower-cost locations. Glaeser (2005) singles out Boston as a skilled city that has flourished because its world-class universities and urban ambience have made it unusually "sticky" for talented people.[49] The wide base of skills has nurtured entrepreneurs and has led to the proliferation of firms, supported by local venture capitalists and angel financiers, offering jobs for skilled workers. In addition, with the universities generating so many ideas, Boston has recovered from downturns and bouts of deindustrialization by pursuing new technological opportunities using its unique labor pool and financing these with the help of highly experienced, locally based venture capitalists. Boston is not alone— other cities, such as Taipei, Beijing, Singapore, and Bangalore, aided by national policies, are adopting similar models of development to good effect.

The leading smart cities have not only deep pools of skills but also the highest-caliber skill qualities. Growth regressions have uncovered a robust relationship between the quality of schooling as captured by test scores of middle school students and increases in GDP (Hanushek 2010; Hanushek and Woessmann 2010). These results are supported by related findings highlighting the significance of the numbers of students in the upper tail of the distribution of test scores (see Pritchett and Viarengo 2010). A country or city with many students with science and math scores in the highest percentiles has the strongest growth prospects. Singapore, which is top ranked by test scores, also has impressive competitiveness and innovation capacity rankings. It has successfully diversified and sustained an average growth rate of 5 percent since 1995. Shanghai, which topped the Organisation for Economic Co-operation and Development's Programme for International Student Assessment results in 2009, is on its way to becoming a smart metropolis the equal of Seoul and Tokyo. Shanghai is a magnet for talent from throughout China, and this inflow augments its own base of high-quality skills. As traditional light manufacturing industries transfer to cities in Shanghai's hinterland or to the interior, new and more skill-intensive activities are enabling Shanghai to expand in fresh directions appropriate for a city with a per capita GDP that is five times the average for China. Mexico City and São Paulo trail Shanghai's performance, and their prospects are less bright because they have not set their sights on becoming smart cities with human capabilities as the prime source of growth.

Governing the Metropolitan Center

A metropolis will struggle to accumulate and retain talent and create new business lines if urban planning, management, and financing do not provide the necessary preconditions for development. That is, smart urban governance complements other forms of urban intelligence. The topic of urban governance and management is covered elsewhere in this volume. Suffice it to say that the selection and empowerment of city managers are requisites. Smart cities plan ahead, establish realistic monitorable targets, and place a premium on rapid and efficient implementation of policies.[50] Cities such as Singapore, Seoul, and Tokyo draw their governance capa-

---

[49] On city stickiness, see Markusen (1996).

[50] The grave weaknesses of governments in industrializing countries are not so much in the making of policies as in their implementation.

bilities from the quality of a well-paid municipal workforce and an institutional infrastructure that evolves with changing developmental imperatives and is quick to incorporate IT as well as other technologies to enforce accountability and improve service delivery. The enduring characteristic of smart cities is the awareness of competition and the commitment to incremental progress through benchmarking and learning from other cities. Smart cities, such as Singapore, are not caught unawares by the hollowing out of traditional industries and seek to anticipate and avert or neutralize trends that can lead to the entrenching of slums and environmental decay, both physical and social. Rio de Janeiro, Karachi, and Cape Town have sacrificed many of the advantages that could be derived from producing and concentrating skills because the environment in both cities is rendered perilous by widespread unemployment, serious security concerns, and the obtrusiveness of slums, whether in the core city areas or on the outskirts.

Being smart is all about defining ambitious but achievable development objectives, mobilizing resources using a frequently sharpened set of incentives to deliver results, thinking ahead so as to minimize the risk of being caught unawares, and solving problems expeditiously. Smart cities can raise their game by making full use of technological opportunities as they arise and by inculcating a culture of innovation. However, high-tech and IT intensity is not the answer for most cities, or, at best, is it a partial answer. Smart urban development in Karachi and Cairo would be low-tech yet innovative at the outset while aiming for longer-term growth based on skills and technological capabilities that would narrow the vast gaps in productivity between these cities and some of their competitors in East Asia.

Connectivity

A highly connected metropolitan region enhances productivity and maximizes the benefits from increased trade and capital flows, the circulation of talented people, and the collaborative efforts of researchers in different countries. There are several facets to connectedness, but the two that deserve the most attention are the quality of the ICT and the transport infrastructures and the linkages they help create.

A wealth of research has pieced together evidence mainly from developed countries showing that the cross-sectoral applications of ICT in myriad activities has raised productivity and induced innovation. Erik Brynjolfsson, who is a professor at the MIT School of Digital Business and co-author with Saunders (2010) of "Wired for Innovation," believes that ICT is changing the innovation process itself. He claims that ICT "is setting off a revolution on four dimensions simultaneously: measurement, experimentation, sharing, and replication. They reinforce and magnify each other" and permit the rapid scaling up of innovations (quoted in Hopkins 2010, 52). The United States has been the leader in this regard, although European countries have also benefited, and some developing countries are catching up.

The point to be noted is that the use of ICT for industrial, commercial, or social purposes is to a great extent an urban phenomenon, and because frequency of exchanges via electronic media also increases face-to-face encounters (Leamer and Storper 2001), a metro region well furnished with ICT infrastructure and recreational amenities is the ideal setting for circulating information, testing ideas, and developing innovation.

Seoul is a classic example of a city with state-of-the-art ICT infrastructure providing locals with unparalleled access to the Internet and the latest advances in mobile telecommunications. Seoul's edge over most other cities derives from the government's ambitious plans to wire the nation, launched in 1995 in enlightened anticipation of a tectonic shift in communications and in the use of media (see Farivar 2011; Lee 2005), and its subsequent initiatives to develop IT-based activities, including the Digital Media City, to support the growth of the digital content industry, a major source of high-value-adding jobs in the metro area.

Productivity gains aside, the large strides made in weaving ICT into the fabric of Korean urban life has spurred innovation, as evidenced by increasing patent output and, more important, the rise in international collaboration between Korean and foreign researchers. Domestic connectivity strengthened urban civil society and energized social and intellectual activities. International connectivity is tightening the linkages that Korea needs to sustain its competitiveness.

Singapore is another example of a city that has leveraged ICT to maximize gains from globalization and has made its business environment the envy of other countries in the region and beyond. Singapore is a leader in technologies to expedite the operations of its busy container port and its world-class airport.[51] It has also used time of day electronic pricing of autos using downtown streets to smooth traffic flows and to minimize congestion. Singapore's e-government platform is the benchmark for other cities, and the government is continuously searching for ways of further pruning transaction costs. Through these investments in ICT, as well as others in education and in health care, Singapore has strengthened connectivity, attracted investment in productive activities, and raised total factor productivity. Other cities, taking note of the benefits accruing to Seoul and Singapore, have begun investing in infrastructure and training, but what they frequently neglect is a comprehensive approach encompassing financing, which is the key to mutually reinforcing gains from several interlocking activities.

A major metropolis seeking greater connectivity must also look to its airport and, if it is a coastal city, its port facilities. An urban economy reliant on trade—and the foremost metropolitan regions depend upon trade to boost domestic sources of demand by a few percentage points—must enlarge and grease the channels through which trade flows.[52] The economic significance of ports has long been recognized. A busy port has a large footprint, employing tens of thousands, and consumes a wide assortment of locally produced services.[53] The contribution of a major international airport equals and may exceed that of a port. By value, close to one-third of global trade is now shipped by air.[54] This includes high-value electronic

---

[51] On Singapore's Portnet IT-based business-to-business system, see Portnet.com (n.d.).

[52] São Paulo's Port of Santos has long been a bottleneck, even though the cost and the roots of its inefficiency are well known (see Doctor 2002).

[53] Cities with major ports are coming to recognize the air and water pollution caused by shipping but have been slow to take remedial action, although some are preparing to offer docked ships power sources to run their systems.

[54] On the importance of air cargo services, especially for high-value goods, see Leinbach and Bowen (2004).

products and pharmaceuticals, cut flowers, and meat and other farm products requiring a cold chain, and the percentages are rising as the cost of air transport declines in relative terms with the introduction of larger fuel-efficient aircraft. In addition, airports serve as the gateways for the export of tourism and business travel services that cities such as Cape Town, Rio de Janeiro, Cairo, and Bangkok depend upon for the large slice of their earnings from trade. As air transport has increased its share of trade, major airports with space around them are becoming the foci of industrial, agricultural, and service clusters, as in the case of Dubai.[55] A classic example is Dulles International Airport, which serves the area in Washington, DC, that is the axis of IT, telecommunications, and defense industry clusters and the growth driver for the metropolitan region.[56] Other cities are also discovering that airports can stimulate clustered industrial activities through connectivity and induced employment. Songdo, a city that is sprouting IT activities adjacent to Incheon International Airport in Seoul, is one example (see Songdo IBD 2012); Bangkok's new Suvarnabhumi International Airport is another. Both cities see these airports as hubs for new activities with a high trade component.

The Sustainability Imperative

A metropolis that is deemed smart and successful must also meet the test of sustainability. Metropolitan economies in low- and middle-income countries, after decades of growth in the 5–8 percent range, must strive to generate enough employment, raise living standards of the vast majority to socially acceptable levels, and find the resources to address legacy problems and upcoming challenges, not to mention environmental and economic shocks.

Today's metropolitan regions emerged in most instances with a minimum of planning and without much attention given to resource constraints or long-term environmental considerations. Low energy prices, transport subsidies, cheap land, low property taxes, the lure of automobility, and the emergence of powerful lobbies composed of real estate developers and auto manufacturers together led to horizontal, sprawling urban development. Unfortunately, urban planning as actually practiced remains frozen in time, and one can see the dead hand of the past in industrializing economies such as China, Malaysia, Indonesia, Nigeria, and South Africa, and also in North America, which provided the model of the sprawling metropolitan region.[57] This form of development, while it surely gives city dwellers more living space, requires costly investment in transport, water, sewage, and energy infrastructures and greatly increases dependence on private automobiles.[58]

---

[55] The greenhouse-based cut flower business around Addis Ababa also depends on air transport to ship flowers to markets in Dubai and The Netherlands. Looking a decade into the future, rising fuel costs could put a damper on air shipment, absent major gains in productivity.

[56] This clustering has given rise to Internet Alley in a four-square-mile area named Tyson's Corner, a short drive from Dulles International (see Ceruzzi 2008).

[57] In China and Vietnam, the dependence of municipalities on revenue from land leasing (40 percent on average) makes a retreat from sprawl even harder. North America is the model also of the sprawling industrial and science parks that have proliferated in developing countries (O'Mara 2007).

[58] It also imposes a heavy burden on the poor living on the fringes of the city who must engage daily in long and costly commutes, as in, for instance, Johannesburg and Rio de Janeiro.

Sprawl also goes hand in hand with eating and exercise habits that are injurious to health (Frumkin, Frank, and Jackson 2004).

The sprawling metropolis, with its low densities (see Seto et al. 2011) and its emptiness, poses a huge challenge for sustainable development.[59] Sustainability is predicated on energy and resource conservation and on the building of robust and resilient infrastructures. The model of a resource-frugal city is compact and vertical, with high population densities that permit the efficient utilization of public transport.[60] This model, attractive to efficiency- and resource-conscious planners, may be coming into vogue, but it should not take the form of the "tower in the park" model so popular in China, which is much more energy intensive and isolating than the mixed-use neighborhoods it is displacing.

A doubling of urban populations demands a rethinking of how people can be accommodated, especially if there is a growing need to conserve energy and the fertile farmland adjacent to cities. The need to invest in facilities to protect the more vulnerable cities from the consequences of climate change is another factor that will be harder to realize given the declining trend in global savings linked to aging populations in the developed world, as well as in some industrializing countries. The imminence and seriousness of each of these can be debated. Legacy housing, transport and public utility infrastructures, and inertia arising from habit persistence and entrenched lifestyles are huge obstacles to changing the pattern of urban development that cannot be ignored, but retrofitting these cities will be unavoidable. Resistance to increasing energy and water prices, to pricing the externalities arising from unchecked private automobile use, to raising and collecting real property taxes, and to modifying zoning and floor area regulations affecting land use (Mumbai is a frequently cited example) is fierce in all countries.[61] The political economy of urban development in virtually all countries favors endless delay. This is because politicians with short time horizons have few incentives to champion radical policies; interest groups with a stake in the status quo forcefully oppose actions that would jeopardize the rents they gain from existing arrangements; and households reflexively oppose higher taxes and prices. Even severe fiscal crises, the threat of spiraling energy prices, and the increasing frequency of severe weather events seem unable to persuade metropolitan residents in advanced and developing countries that delay is fast becoming an unaffordable luxury.

The issue of urban sustainability is here to stay, and with each passing year it will only become more pressing. In different ways, sometimes obliquely, sometimes directly, it is being debated in crisis-ridden advanced countries in a state of political paralysis, such as the United States; in industrializing countries currently with deep

---

[59] The architect Rem Koolhaas remarks that "there are city centers around the world in which no one seems to be a full time resident" (quoted in Heathcote 2010, 4).

[60] This point is strongly championed by Glaeser (2011). Interestingly, although Manhattan is compact and densely populated, the New York metro area covers 3,000 square miles (Greater London is 600 square miles; Paris, 1,000 square miles), and it is significantly less dense than Los Angeles, the supposed epitome of a sprawling metropolis (with 7,738 residents per square mile vs. 5,728 per square mile for New York). But for all its density, Los Angeles is not a walkable city (Rybczynski 2011). Metropolitan São Paulo covers 8,000 square kilometers, while the Cape Town city region stretches almost 100km from end to end (UN-HABITAT 2008).

[61] Regarding automobile use, the vision of "mobility on demand" offered by the MIT Media Lab is alluring, and bit by bit some elements of this are taking shape. Whether it or something like it is a part of the metropolitan future, and not in just a few enlightened cities but worldwide, remains to be seen.

pockets where urbanization is approaching a midpoint, such as China; and in low-income countries in the crosshairs of climate change, such as Pakistan, struggling with acute resource scarcities, limited organizational capabilities, and dysfunctional governance. Reluctantly, and later rather than sooner, the great metropolitan centers throughout the developing world will translate the concept of sustainable urbanization into practice through a physical redesign of cities and the widespread incorporation of green technologies and resource-frugal ways of living. Legacy infrastructures cannot be wished away overnight; however, through a process of deconstruction, retrofitting, adaptation, and new construction based on green templates, cities will be transformed if they are to remain livable and economically dynamic. It may be too late to maintain atmospheric carbon dioxide concentrations below the desired 450 ppm; mankind will need to adapt to the 550-ppm atmosphere toward which the planet is heading.

Concluding Observations on the Metropolitan Future

Continuing urbanization and global warming are among the few trends about which there can be little doubt. But no one can claim with reasonable certainty that an increasing number of metropolitan regions will adopt the coherent long-term strategies that will lead to smart, IT-enabled, compact, vertical, mixed-use, green, and sustainable development, including in Beijing, Karachi, and São Paulo, to take just three very dissimilar metro regions.[62] Although many initiatives abound, with cities forming alliances and eagerly sharing experiences, the organizational capabilities underpinned by political consensus and the mechanisms for formulating long-term strategies and mobilizing resources seem far too elusive from the current perspective. City managers have internalized few lessons on effectively planning and financing urban development or in promoting tradable activities that can be a source of jobs, and too many cities remain vulnerable to financial crises. Despite recurrent fiscal debacles, local politicians and city managers are unable to learn enduring lessons, and the accumulating research on urban fiscal policies has failed to substantially improve urban tax systems worldwide.

The advantages, and also the drawbacks, of the compact city have been aired for many years, but the fast-growing metro regions in emerging economies have ignored these. The technologies, hard and soft, that can make a city "greener" have been taking shape and are being tested piecemeal, but little has been achieved to date. Not one of the tiny experimental green cities currently under construction has been put to the test and its carbon neutrality convincingly established.[63] The livability of compact and green cities and how they would accommodate diverse industrial activities are also unknowns. The technologies coming off the drawing boards, and some being commercialized, are perhaps decades away from wide-

---

[62] For example, the World Bank (2009) notes that in China the fragmentation of land on the fringes of cities is growing worse, land use is not being coordinated with the development of urban transport, and floor area ratios are increasing much too slowly. In fact, the gross floor area ratios of Chinese cities are far lower than in Seoul or Tokyo and much lower than in Manhattan.

[63] Some incredible specimens of the green city are taking shape in Abu Dhabi (Masdar), in Tianjin, in Shanghai, and in Seoul–Incheon, but their economic and social viability and carbon neutrality remain to be established (see also Kahn 2010).

spread application once they have been debugged and made more affordable. However, building sustainability cannot wait. Karachi, Dhaka, Cairo, Shenzhen, and São Paulo are daily pouring more concrete into the ground, accommodating more people, and building more roads. Instead of densifying, urban densities are declining. Bangkok's urbanized area grew 16-fold from 1944 to 2002; that of Accra, by 153 percent from 1985 to 2000.

These are frightening trends and missed opportunities. Left unchecked, they will make rationalization of urban development far more difficult. Some economists are of the view that price adjustments reflecting energy and water scarcities, increased vulnerability of cities near rivers to flooding and coastal locations to rising sea levels, and inland areas to droughts and firestorms will bring about the redistribution of the population, force a refashioning of the urban landscape, and demand the building of passive and active coastal defenses, as in The Netherlands (see Kahn 2010).[64] Economists rightly underscore the strength of market mechanisms but are apt to minimize its failings, as evidenced by the devastating financial crisis of 2008 and 2009 and the many real estate bubbles.

From the perspective of urban sustainability and green development, market-induced changes might be too slow, too myopic, and too piecemeal, and the market might not promote the kind of fast-paced innovation that is urgently needed or provide the insurance required by inhabitants of vulnerable cities in developing countries.

On the current trajectories, Karachi and Lagos could become the world's two largest cities by mid-century, assuming that the availability of water (fresh, desalinated, and recycled) permits such growth. A doubling of populations with no change in the layout will lead to metropolitan regions that suffer from agglomeration diseconomies and are ungovernable.

Advanced countries may have the resources to indulge in wasteful sprawling urban regions, and they may even endure deindustrialization for several decades by living off their accumulated fat. But industrializing countries need to learn quickly and avoid the costly decisions made when energy, land, and water were relatively cheap, green technologies were unknown, and global warming was a scientific curiosity. Low-income countries have even less room to maneuver because they lack the growth momentum of the leading middle-income nations, as well as the technological capabilities and resources, and in addition, they must cope with rapidly expanding populations.

With so much urbanization still lying ahead and the stakes rising, the design and implementation of forward-looking urban development strategies are taking on a heightened importance. Whether countries make rapid strides on the economic front will depend upon one or a small handful of metropolitan centers. And whether these are smart, sustainable, economically dynamic, and livable will also depend on how cities develop organizational and technical skills, assure revenue autonomy, create agile infrastructures (soft and hard), and make the best use of evolving practical ideas and technologies to take existing and budding metropolitan regions boldly into an uncertain future.

---

[64] See Jha et al. (2011) on both the magnitude of the problems and remedial measures.

REFERENCES

Andris, Clio, Assaf Biderman, Francesco Calabrese, Nashid Nabian, and Carlo Ratti. 2009. City gravity: Visualizing telecommunications traffic across the US reveals surprising patterns of innovation and urban growth. *Seed* (February):24–26. www.carloratti.com/publications/on _us/20090101SeedMagazine.pdf

Atkinson, Robert D. 2012. *Innovation in cities and innovation by cities.* Washington, DC: Information Technology and Innovation Foundation (February).

Banerjee, Abhijit, and Esther Duflo. 2011. *Poor economics: A radical rethinking of the ways to fight global poverty.* New York: PublicAffairs.

Berger, Suzanne, and Lester Richard. 1997. *Made by Hong Kong.* New York: Oxford University Press.

Bernard Andrew, J. Bradford Jensen, Stephen J. Redding, and Peter K. Schott. 2007. Firms in international trade. *Journal of Economic Perspectives* 21(3):105–130.

Bird, Richard M. 2011. Subnational taxation in developing countries: A review of the literature. *Journal of International Commerce, Economics and Policy* 2(1):139–161.

Bosker, Maarten, and Eltjo Buringh. 2010. City seeds. Geography and the origins of the European city system. CEPR Discussion Paper No. 8066. London: Centre for Economic Policy Research.

Bosker, Maarten, Eltjo Buringh, and Jan Luiten van Zanden. 2008. From Baghdad to London: The dynamics of urban growth in Europe and the Arab world, 800–1800. CEPR Discussion Paper No. 6833. London: Centre for Economic Policy Research.

Brynjolfsson, Erik, and Adam Saunders. 2010. *Wired for innovation: How information technology is reshaping the economy.* Cambridge, MA: MIT Press.

Carlino, Gerald, A. Satayajit Chatterjee, and Robert M. Hunt. 2007. Urban density and the rate of innovation. *Journal of Urban Economics* 61:389–419.

Ceruzzi, Paul E. 2008. *Internet alley: High technology in Tysons Corner, 1945–2005.* Cambridge, MA: MIT Press.

Cohen, Barney. 2004. Urban growth in developing countries: A review of current trends and caution regarding existing forecasts. *World Development* 32(1):23–51.

Currid, Elizabeth. 2007. How art and culture happen in New York. *Journal of the American Planning Association* 73(4):454–467.

Doctor, Mahrukh. 2002. Business and delays in port reform in Brazil. *Brazilian Journal of Political Economy* 22(2):79–101. www.rep.org.br/pdf/86-5.pdf

Eichengreen, Barry, and Poonam Gupta. 2009. The two waves of service sector growth. NBER Working Paper No. 14968. Cambridge, MA: National Bureau of Economic Research.

———. 2011. The services sector as India's road to economic growth. NBER Working Paper No. 16757. Cambridge, MA: National Bureau of Economic Research.

Farivar, Cyrus. 2011. *The Internet of elsewhere.* Piscataway, NJ: Rutgers University Press.

FDI Intelligence. 2011. *Manufacturing makes a comeback: FDI global outlook report 2011.* London: Financial Times Business (April/May).

Fields, Gary S. 2007. The Harris-Todaro model. Working Paper No. 21. Ithaca, NY: Cornell University. http://digitalcommons.ilr.cornell.edu/workingpapers/21

Francois, Joseph, and Bernard Hoekman. 2010. Services trade and policy. *Journal of Economic Literature* 48(3):662–692.

Frumkin, Howard, Lawrence D. Frank, and Richard Jackson. 2004. *Urban sprawl and public health: Designing, planning, and building for healthy communities.* Washington, DC: Island Press.

Galama, Titus J., and James Hosek. 2007. Perspectives on U.S. competitiveness in science and technology. Santa Monica, CA: RAND Corporation.

Ghani, Ejaz, ed. 2010. *The service revolution in South Asia.* New Delhi: Oxford University Press.

Gill, Indermit S., and Chor-cheng Goh. 2009. Scale economies and cities. *World Bank Research Observer* 25(2):235–262.

Glaeser, Edward, L. 2005. Reinventing Boston 1630–2003. *Journal of Economic Geography,* 5(2):119–153.

———. 2011. *Triumph of the city.* New York: Penguin Press.

Glaeser, Edward L., and Joshua D. Gottleib. 2009. The wealth of cities: Agglomeration economies and spatial equilibrium in the United States. *Journal of Economic Literature* 47(4):983–1028.

Granger, Clive W. J. 1969. Investigating causal relationships by econometric models and cross-spectral methods. *Econometrica,* 37(3):424–438.

Hanushek, Eric A. 2010. The high cost of low educational performance: The long-run impact of improving PISA outcomes. Paris: Programme for International Student Assessment, Organisation for Economic Co-operation and Development.

Hanushek, Eric A., and Ludger Woessmann. 2010. Education and economic growth. In *Economics of education,* ed. Dominic J. Brewer and Patrick J. McEwan, 60–67. Amsterdam: Elsevier, 2010.

Heathcote, Edwin. 2010. Urban evolution. *Financial Times,* September 8.

Heitzman, James. 2004. *Network city: Planning the information society in Bangalore.* New York: Oxford University Press.

Henderson, J. Vernon. 2010. Cities and development. *Journal of Regional Science* 50(1):515–540.

Hidalgo, Cesar A., Bailey Klinger, Albert-Laszlo Barabási, and Ricardo Hausmann. 2007. The product space conditions the development of nations. *Science* 317(5837):482–487.

Hopkins, Michael S. 2010. The four ways IT is revolutionizing innovation. *MIT Sloan Management Review,* (May 21).

Inman, Robert P. 2007. Financing cities. In *A companion to urban economics,* ed. R. J. Arnott and D. P. McMillen. Oxford: Blackwell.

Inskeep, Steve. 2011. *Instant city: Life and death in Karachi.* New York: Penguin Press.

International Council for Local Environmental Initiatives. 2012. Resilient cities series. http://resilient-cities.iclei.org/bonn2011/about/

Jacobs, Jane. 1970. *The Economy of cities.* New York: Vintage Press.

Jha, Abhas, Jessica Lamond, Robin Bloch, Namrata Bhattacharya, Ana Lopez, Nikolaos Papachristodoulou, Alan Bird, David Proverbs, John Davies, Robert Barker. 2011. Five feet high and rising: Cities and flooding in the 21st century. Policy Research Working Paper No. 5648. New York: World Bank.

Johnson, Steve. 2010. *Where good ideas come from.* New York: Penguin Press.

Kahn, Matthew. 2010. *Climatopolis.* New York: Basic Books.

Komninos, Nicos. 2008. *Intelligent cities and the globalization of innovation networks.* New York: Routledge.

Leamer, Edward E., and Michael Storper. 2001. The economic geography of the Internet age. NBER Working Paper No. 8450. Cambridge, MA: National Bureau of Economic Research.

Lee, Byoung Nam. 2005. Korean government-driven ICT policy: IT 839 strategy. Paper presented at the Regional Seminar on Costs and Tariffs for the TAS Group Member Countries, Cyberjaya, Malaysia (May 31–June 3). www.itu.int/ITU-D/finance/work-cost-tariffs/events/tariff-seminars/kuala-lumpur-05/presentation-lee.PDF

Lehrer, Jonah. 2010. A physicist solves the city. *New York Times,* (December 17). www.nytimes.com/2010/12/19/magazine/19Urban_West-t.html

Leinbach, Thomas R., and John T. Bowen, Jr. 2004. Air cargo services and the electronics industry in Southeast Asia. *Journal of Economic Geography* 4:299–321.

Liu, Lili, and Steven B. Webb. 2011. Laws for fiscal responsibility for subnational discipline. Policy Research Working Paper No. 5587. New York: World Bank.

Lloyd-Reason, Lester, and Leigh Sear, eds. 2007. *Trading places: SMEs in the global economy: A critical research handbook.* Cheltenham, U.K.: Edward Elgar.

Lopez, Ricardo, A. 2005. Trade and growth: Reconciling the macroeconomic and microeconomic evidence. *Journal of Economic Surveys* 19(4):623–648.

Markusen, Ann. 1996. Sticky places in slippery space: A typology of industrial districts. *Economic Geography* 72(3):293–313.

McGee, Terry, George C. S. Lin, Mark Wang, and Andrew Marton. 2007. *China's urban space: Development under market socialism.* New York: Routledge.

Melo, Patricia C., Daniel. J. Graham, and Robert. B. Noland. 2009. A meta-analysis of estimates of urban agglomeration economies. *Regional Science and Urban Economics*, 39:332–342.

Moran, Theodore H. 2011. *Foreign direct investment and development*. Washington, DC: Peterson Institute of International Economics.

Newman, Peter, Timothy Beatley, and Heather Boyer. 2009. *Resilient cities: Responding to peak oil and climate change*. Washington, DC: Island Press.

O'Mara, Margaret. 2007. Landscapes of knowledge: History and the evolving geography of high technology. *Places* 19:1.

Organisation for Economic Co-operation and Development. 2005. Territorial Review: Seoul, Korea. Paris: Organisation for Economic Co-operation and Development.

Oxford Analytica. 2011. Cities spearhead climate initiatives. www.oxan.com/display.aspx?ItemID=ES167025

Portnet.com. n.d. Home page. www.portnet.com/WWWPublic/pdt_portnet.html

Pugh O'Mara, Margaret. 2002. Learning from history: How state and local policy choices have shaped Philadelphia's growth. *Greater Philadelphia Regional Review* (March).

Pritchett, Lant, and Martina Viarengo. 2010. Producing superstars for the economic mundial: The Mexican predicament with quality of education. Cambridge, MA: Harvard University Press. www.hks.harvard.edu/fs/lpritch/Education - docs/ED - Econ Growth, impact/Mexico Economic Mundial.pdf

Rai, Saritha. 2006. Is the next Silicon Valley taking root in Bangalore? *New York Times*, March 20. www.nytimes.com/2006/03/20/business/worldbusiness/20bangalore.html?ex=1300510800&en=993a11e65908ab91&ei=5088

Ravallion, Martin. 2007. Urban poverty. *Finance and Development* 44(3). www.imf.org/external/pubs/ft/fandd/2007/09/ravalli.htm

Rosenthal, Stuart S., and William Strange. 2004. Evidence on the nature and sources of agglomeration economies. In *The handbook of urban and regional economics*, ed. Vernon Henderson and Jacques Thisse, 4:2119–2172. Amsterdam: Elsevier.

———. 2007. The micro-empirics of agglomeration economies. In *A companion to urban economics*, ed. R. J. Arnott and D. P. McMillen. Oxford: Blackwell.

Rybczynski, Witold. 2011. Dense, denser, densest. *Wilson Quarterly* (Spring).

Seto, Karen C., M. Fragkias, B. Guneralp, and M. K. Reilly. 2011. A meta analysis of global urban land expansion. *PLoS ONE* 6(8):e23777. www.plosone.org/article/info:doi/10.1371/journal.pone.0023777

Smil, Vaclav. 2002. Nitrogen and food production: Proteins for human diets. *Ambio* 31(2).

———. 2008. *Energy in nature and society: General energetics of complex systems*. Cambridge, MA: MIT Press.

———. 2011. Nitrogen cycle and world food production. *World Agriculture* 2:9–13. www.vaclavsmil.com/wp-content/uploads/docs/smil-article-worldagriculture.pdf

Smith, Cynthia, ed. 2011. *Design with the other 90%: Cities*. New York: Smithsonian.

Song, Jingli. 2009. HP, Foxconn to build laptop manufacturing hub in Chongqing. *China Daily*, August 5. www.chinadaily.com.cn/business/2009-08/05/content_8528616.htm

Songdo IBD. 2012. Master plan. Gale International LLC. www.songdo.com/songdo-international-business-district/the-city/master-plan.aspx

Spence, Michael, and Sandile Hlatshwayo. 2011. Evolving structure of the American economy and the employment challenge. Working Paper. Washington, DC: Council on Foreign Relations.

Tiebout, Charles. 1956. A pure theory of local expenditure. *Journal of Political Economy*, 69(5):416–429.

UN-HABITAT. 2008. *State of the world's cities 2010/2011—cities for all: Bridging the urban divide*. New York: U.N. Human Settlements Programme.

Urban and Regional Innovation Research Unit. 2010. Innovative cities and regions. Thessaloniki, Greece: Department of Urban and Regional Planning and Development in the Faculty of Engineering, Aristotle University of Thessaloniki.

Vanderbilt, Tom. 2011. Long live the industrial city. *Wilson Quarterly* (Spring).

van Pottelsberghe, Bruno. 2008. Europe's R&D: Missing the wrong targets? Bruegel Policy Brief No. 2008/03. Brussels: Bruegel (February).

Villa, Nicola, and Shane Mitchell. 2010. Connecting cities: Achieving sustainability through innovation. Paper presented at the Fifth Urban Research Symposium 2009, Connected Urban Development Cisco Systems, Internet Business Solutions Group.

Wikipedia. 2011a. Garment District, Manhattan. (June 7).

———. 2011b. World's most livable cities. (June 14).

Winters, John V. 2011. Why are smart cities growing? Who moves and who stays. *Journal of Regional Science* 51(2):253–270.

World Bank. 2008. *Climate resilient cities: 2008 primer.* Washington, DC. http://siteresources .worldbank.org/EASTASIAPACIFICEXT/Resources/climatecities_fullreport.pdf

———. 2009. World development report 2009: Spatial disparities and development policy. Washington, DC.

———. 2011. World development report 2011: Conflict, security and development. Washington, DC.

Yusuf, Shahid, and Kaoru Nabeshima. 2006. *Post-industrial East Asian cities.* Palo Alto, CA: Stanford University Press.

———. 2010. Two dragonheads: Contrasting development paths for Beijing and Shanghai. Washington, DC: World Bank.

Yusuf, Shahid, Kaoru Nabeshima, and Shoichi Yamashita. 2008. Growing industrial clusters in Asia. Washington, DC: World Bank.

Yusuf, Shahid, and Weiping Wu. 1997. *The dynamics of urban growth in three Chinese cities.* New York: Oxford University Press.

Zhu, Yu, Xinhua Qi, Huaiyou Shao, and Kaijing He. 2009. The evolution of China's *in situ* urbanization and its planning and environmental implications: Case studies from Quanzhou municipality. In *Urban population-environment dynamics in the developing world: Case studies and lessons learned,* ed. A. de Sherbinin, A. Rahman, A. Barbieri, J.-C. Fotso, and Y. Zhu. Paris: Committee for International Cooperation in National Research in Demography. www.ciesin.columbia.edu/repository/pern/papers/urban_pde_zhu_etal.pdf

Metropolitan Cities in the National Fiscal and Institutional Structure

3

PAUL SMOKE

An important yet neglected issue in the study of urban public finance in developing countries is how urban and metropolitan governments are situated in the broader national fiscal, institutional, and political framework. The details and dynamics of this framework affect the ability of urban governments to operate with legitimacy and to perform effectively. This is particularly critical at a time when urban governments are being called on to play greater roles in promoting economic development, addressing environmental problems, and dealing with other growing challenges (see, e.g., United Cities and Local Governments (2010), Birch and Wachter 2011).

The multifaceted national framework for urban government has likely been underexplored because its diverse, complex, and evolving nature creates challenges for both single-country and comparative analysis. Factors that affect urban performance, such as the number of government levels and their respective functions, are shaped by context-specific historical dynamics that may limit or complicate policy reform options.

Despite these challenges, there is potential value in broad-based assessment of national frameworks. Much fiscal analysis of urban governments has been too centered on normative diagnostics that are limited in scope and inadequately consider key factors that can affect fiscal performance. The best intergovernmental fiscal systems, for example, are unlikely to be effective without appropriate institutional structures and accountability mechanisms in place, and politics always influence reforms.

Normative principles of fiscal federalism, local democracy, local accountability, and other aspects of intergovernmental frameworks are well known and have

Research assistance was provided by Dave Algoso, Gundula Loffler, Jenna Magee, and Alberto Orozco-Ochoa. Particularly valuable comments were provided by Roy Bahl, Blane Lewis, Vito Tanzi, Philip van Ryneveld, Khaled Amin, and David Gomez-Alvarez.

received considerable attention, including elsewhere in this volume. Rather than exhaustively cover these principles or present a comprehensive diagnostic, this chapter provides a broad synopsis of fiscal and institutional structures and intergovernmental relationships that do or could affect the ability of local governments to meet critical objectives.[1] To illustrate variations and how they may influence fiscal performance, a selective set of countries is considered, with reference to additional experiences where relevant.

The next section outlines basic facts about the countries being examined. This is followed by a review of their overarching institutional, fiscal, and governance frameworks and other aspects of their intergovernmental systems. The chapter concludes with a summary of the case for better understanding national frameworks as part of the process of selecting pragmatic policy choices to promote local and metropolitan fiscal performance.

THE COUNTRIES AND SOME BASIC FACTS

The countries examined in this chapter are not scientifically representative, but they do include an array of developing and middle-income countries located in Africa, Asia, Latin America, and the Middle East (table 3.1).[2] The countries range from primarily rural (Cambodia, Uganda) to primarily urban (Brazil, Mexico, South Africa), with several countries in between (Egypt, Ghana, India, Indonesia, Philippines).[3] Some of the less urbanized countries (Cambodia, Uganda, Ghana) are urbanizing rapidly.

India has 46 urban areas with more than 1 million inhabitants, while Brazil, Mexico, Indonesia, and South Africa have 21, 12, 8, and 7, respectively. Smaller countries (Cambodia, Ghana, Uganda) have only one or two urban areas of this size. Even

---

[1] A number of broad-based or comparative references include Ahmad and Tanzi (2002), Cheema and Rondinelli (2007), Connerly, Eaton, and Smoke (2010), Slack (2007; 2010), Slack and Chattopadhyay (2009), Steytler (2005), and Wilson (2011).

[2] A number of comparative (global or regional) references were used to derive information for multiple countries reviewed here, including Burki, Perry, and Dillinger (1999), Crawford and Hartmann (2008), Ichimura and Bahl (2009), Martinez-Vazquez and Vaillancourt (2011), Ndegwa and Levy (2003), Peterson and Annez (2007), Sahasranaman (2009), Smoke, Gomez, and Peterson (2006), Stren and Cameron (2005), United Cities and Local Governments (2010), World Bank (2005), and Wunsch and Olowu (2003).

[3] Information on Cambodia is drawn largely from the review in Smoke and Morrison (2011) and the website of the National Committee for Subnational Democratic Development (http://www.ncdd.gov.kh). Information on Uganda is drawn largely from Ahmad, Brosio, and Gonzalez (2006), Smoke, Muhumuza, and Ssewankambo (2011), and the Uganda Local Government Finance Commission website (http:/www.lgfc.go.ug). Information on Brazil is drawn largely from Alfonso and Araujo (2006), de Mello (2007), Rezende and Garson (2006), and Souza (2003). Information on Mexico is drawn largely from Grindle (2007), Guigale (2000), Moreno (2003), Revilla (2012), and informal sources provided in other notes. Information on South Africa is drawn largely from Bahl and Smoke (2003), Republic of South Africa (2008), van Ryneveld (2007), and the National Treasury (Intergovernmental Fiscal Affairs Division) and Department of Cooperative Governance and Traditional Affairs (formerly the Department of Provincial and Local Government) websites (http://www.treasury.gov.za/publications/igfr/default.aspx and http://www.cogta.gov.za). Information on Egypt is drawn largely from Algoso and Magee (2011) and Ebel and Amin (2006). Information on Ghana is drawn from Awortwi (2010), Hoffman and Metzroth (2010), and Kuusi (2009). Information on India is drawn largely from Garg (2007), Government of India (2009), Rao and Bird (2010), and the websites of the India Finance Commission (http://www.fincomindia.nic.in/), the India Planning Commission (http://planningcommission.nic.in/), the Union Public Service Commission (http://www.upsc.gov.in/), and National Institute of Public Finance and Policy (http://www.nipfp.org.in/). Information on Indonesia is drawn largely from Alm, Martinez-Vazquez, and Indrawati (2004), World Bank (2005), Republic of Indonesia, Ministry of Finance (2011), and Indonesian Decentralization Support Facility (2012). Information on the Philippines is drawn largely from Manasan (2004), Nasehi and Rangwala (2011), World Bank (2005), and Yilmaz and Venugopa (2010).

TABLE 3.1

Basic urban and institutional profiles

Country	Region	Total population, in millions (percent urban), 2010	Urban growth rate, 2005–2010	No. urban areas with populations >1 million, 2010	Type of national government	Political competition
Brazil	Latin America	198.9 (86.5)	1.52	21	Federal	Multiparty competitive
Cambodia	Asia (Southeast)	15.3 (20.1)	3.03	1	Unitary	Multiparty; one dominant
Egypt	Middle East (North Africa)	79.5 (43.4)	1.99	2	Unitary	Single party until 2011 (disbanded); reforms under way
Ghana	Africa (West)	24.9 (51.5)	3.59	2	Unitary	Multiparty; recent historic peaceful electoral transition
India	Asia (South)	1220.1 (30)	2.31	46	Federal	Multiparty competitive
Indonesia	Asia (Southeast)	239.6 (44.3)	1.74	8	Unitary	Multiparty competitive after long one-party dominance
Mexico	Latin America	110.3 (77.8)	1.38	12	Federal	Multiparty competitive
Philippines	Asia (Southeast)	93 (48.9)	2.14	2	Unitary	Multiparty competitive
South Africa	Africa (Southern)	49.3 (61.7)	1.78	7	Unitary	Multiparty; one dominant
Uganda	Africa (East)	34 (13.3)	4.43	1	Unitary	Newly multiparty; one dominant

SOURCE: All urban data are taken from the U.N. Department for Social and Economic Affairs (2009), although recent sources suggest that these figures may understate urban growth in Indonesia. Other data are from country-specific sources in notes 2 and 3.

some larger countries only have a few, for example, two each in Egypt and the Philippines.

Most of the countries are unitary systems, but Brazil, India, and Mexico are federal. All of the countries are at least nominally multiparty democracies, but some have competitive elections, while single parties dominate others (Cambodia, South Africa, Uganda), and one (Egypt) is undergoing a dramatic political and institutional transition.

These country characteristics are often indicative, although not neatly deterministic, of how subnational governments are treated in the intergovernmental system. Intergovernmental relations differ in unitary systems relative to federal systems, although not always in obvious ways. Strong local governments can be established in the former, and local governments can be constrained by state governments in the latter.

Larger urban governments tend to have more independence through formal design or, more typically, by virtue of their greater size, functions, and revenue capacity. That does not, however, necessarily protect them from higher-level interference and problematic intrajurisdictional dynamics. Such relationships can be complicated even in federal systems where states have strong constitutional authority or where different political parties control national/state (provincial) and urban/metropolitan governments.

THE OVERARCHING POLICY FRAMEWORK

This section reviews the constitutional and legal framework for subnational government, noting (if known) whether urban or metropolitan areas are differentially treated. The focus is on basic institutional structures and major legal/policy provisions.

Intergovernmental Institutional Structure

All countries considered here have multiple subnational levels (table 3.2), ranging from two (Brazil, Mexico, South Africa) to five (Egypt, Uganda). Some countries have semiautonomous local governments that substantially answer to their constituents (devolution), such as South Africa. In others, subnational jurisdictions have greater accountability to the central government (deconcentration), as in Ghana, where one level (the region) is purely administrative.

The treatment of urban areas varies across countries. It is not uncommon to adopt a special designation for the capital city (Brazil, Cambodia, India, Indonesia, Mexico, Philippines, and Uganda). In some cases, the capital is legally equivalent to a higher government tier. For example, the city of Kampala has the legal status of a district, and Jakarta functions much like a provincial government. Mexico City has characteristics of both a state and a municipality, but it has a unique legal status. Cairo has no special status, but it is governed differently than other urban areas in Egypt.

There are also other asymmetries in the treatment of urban governments. In Cambodia, the three largest municipalities after the capital Phnom Penh have provincial status, and metropolitan divisions in Ghana (districts) have the same

TABLE 3.2

Levels of government and administration

Country	Levels
Brazil (two levels)	• States (26) and Federal district (Brasilia) • Municipalities (5,564)
Cambodia (three levels)	• Provinces (23, including 3 municipal) and capital • Districts (159) and municipalities (26) • Communes and *sangkat* (municipal communes) (1,621) divided into villages
Egypt (five levels)	• Governorates (29) • *Markaz* (regions) and city administrations (232) • Districts (smallest entity in urban governorates) • Villages (in mixed urban/rural governorates) • No special provisions for the capital, but new legislation planned
Ghana (three levels)	• Regions (administrative) (10) • Districts (170), including 40 municipal and 6 metropolitan districts • Town/area councils/others under districts (>16,000)
India (three levels)	• States (28) • Union territories (7), including the federal district • Local bodies—urban local bodies: municipal corporations (138), municipal councils (1,595), town councils (2,108); rural local bodies (*panchayati raj*): *zilla* (593), *samities* (6,087), *gram*/village (239,432)
Indonesia (three levels)	• Provinces (33), special regions (2), and capital city • Local governments: *kota* (cities, 98) and *kabupaten* (districts, 410) • *Desa* (villages)—very limited role (69,249)
Mexico (two levels)	• States (31) and the federal district (Mexico City) • Municipalities (2,456)
Philippines (four levels)	• Provinces (79) • Cities (112) • Municipalities (1,496) • *Barangays*/villages (41,944)
South Africa (two levels)	• Provinces (9) • Municipalities: metropolitan (8), districts (44), and local (231); the latter are "wall to wall" within districts
Uganda (five levels with one primary)	• Districts and the city of Kampala (112) (primary) • Counties (162) plus 22 municipal councils and 5 city divisions • Subcounties (1,147 plus 64 municipal divisions and 165 town councils) • Parishes (7,771 including city wards) • Villages (66,579)

SOURCE: Urban data are taken from U.N. Department for Social and Economic Affairs (2009). Other data from country-specific sources summarized in notes 2 and 3.

status as rural district governments. In Indonesia, cities (*kota*) are legally identical to districts (*kabupaten*), and South Africa has three categories of municipal government: metropolitan or metro areas, districts, and local areas.

Decentralization and Subnational Government Policy

Countries take different approaches to decentralization and subnational government policy (table 3.3). Egypt is the only country here that has not formally empowered local governments, although minor decentralization was piloted prior to the fall of President Mubarak in 2011, and the new constitution (2012) suggests that decentralization is likely to be important in the future, but many details need to be developed in future laws.

Devolution tends to be stronger in federal countries (Brazil, India, Mexico) than in the unitary countries, but the former usually give states considerable control over local (and urban) governments. Brazil empowers and finances municipalities

TABLE 3.3
Decentralization and subnational government policy

Country	Policy
Brazil	Strong devolution, with three levels of government and considerable relative independence of third tier from second tier.
Cambodia	Long centralized system with minor decentralization to communes (2001). Reforms have been mandated for provinces, municipalities, and districts (2008) but not fully implemented.
Egypt	Highly centralized system with limited experimentation with decentralization. System will change after uprising of January 2011, with some form of decentralization likely.
Ghana	Deconcentration with nominal devolution. Lack of resources at subnational levels severely constrains district autonomy.
India	Federal system with strong states. Lower tiers are dependent on states, but larger urban areas have more independence. There is some policy discussion about pushing states to empower local tiers more significantly.
Indonesia	Focus on devolution to cities and districts in 2001, replacing former emphasis on deconcentration to provinces. More recent reforms have marginally increased the role of higher levels.
Mexico	Federal system with strong states. Lower tiers are dependent on states, but there are new efforts to empower municipalities and promote cooperation in metropolitan areas.
Philippines	Focus on devolution to subprovincial units since early 1990s, but national agencies and provinces still play a significant role.
South Africa	National/provincial/local framed as three distinct but interdependent (not hierarchical) spheres of government. Municipalities (especially metropolitan) are more independent than provinces. Recently, powers of metropolitan and large urban governments have increased, and there has been some discussion of restructuring weak municipalities.
Uganda	Focus on decentralization of responsibilities to devolved district councils with four tiers below, but considerable recentralization in recent years.

SOURCE: Information from country-specific sources summarized in notes 2 and 3.

directly, although over time the federal government has increased constraints on municipalities.

A number of unitary states (Indonesia, South Africa, Philippines, Uganda) give considerable powers to subnational governments, sometimes differentially to certain levels or urban jurisdictions. Indonesia and the Philippines empower the local tier more than the intermediate (provincial) tier. Uganda has no provincial or state governments (due to geographic ethnic identification and association with traditional kingdoms that modernizers wanted to marginalize), and Ghana has administrative regions without elected councils. South Africa does not use the terms *tier* or *level* in its framework; it has three distinct, nonhierarchical *spheres* (national, provincial, municipal).

Another noteworthy issue is how decentralization is rolled out and sequenced.[4] Reforms often focus simultaneously on all levels, or first on larger urban areas, but there are exceptions. In Cambodia, for example, decentralization started at lower rural levels, not in urban areas (due to strong rural support for the ruling party). Only more recently have higher levels been included, including conferring special status on Phnom Penh.

Decentralization policy may change over time. Uganda has rolled back key local (including urban) powers, while South Africa has increased metropolitan powers through sectoral laws, including in transport and housing (and is also considering consolidation of small/low capacity municipalities). The Indian and Mexican governments have proposed or taken steps to increase lower-level powers because states have not. Such shifts generally result from evolving political dynamics and/or performance concerns (see Eaton, Kaiser, and Smoke 2011).

Formal Basis for Decentralization

Countries establish and define subnational governments through constitutional, legal, or administrative provisions (table 3.4), with the former generally considered stronger and more durable. In the Philippines and South Africa, reform was initiated with constitutional provisions followed by clarifying laws. In Ghana, Indonesia, and Uganda, laws established the framework, which was then at least partly codified in a constitutional amendment or new constitution. The recently replaced Egyptian Constitution provided for local administration, with subsequent laws both supporting and limiting local powers. The 2012 constitution outlines the broad contours of a decentralized system but leaves the details to further legislation. Cambodia is the only country here that has no constitutional basis for decentralization (except to establish levels of administration).

Constitutional and legal provisions are usually general, such that additional legal or administrative action is required. In Cambodia and Indonesia, follow-up has been insufficient to establish functional clarity. In some unitary systems and under certain political conditions (Philippines and Uganda), it has been possible to ignore or rescind, formally or informally, constitutional and legal provisions without a strong challenge (see Smoke, Muhumuza, and Ssewankambo 2011; World Bank

---

[4] The issue of sequencing is reviewed in Smoke (2010).

TABLE 3.4
Decentralization frameworks

Country	Framework
Brazil (constitutional and legal)	The constitution (1988) gives considerable powers to state and municipal governments. The Fiscal Responsibility Law (2000) outlines additional regulation and oversight, and various specific laws apply.
Cambodia (legal and administrative)	The Law on Commune/*Sangkat* Administrative Management (2001) and Election Law (2001) established elected commune councils. The Law on Administrative Management of Capital, Provinces, Municipalities, Districts and *Khan* (2008) extends powers to other levels. Details are to be provided in laws or decrees.
Egypt (legal and administrative)	Law 124 (1960) created a hierarchy of local councils. Law 52 (1975) increased powers of local elected councils. Law 43 (1979) removed some powers. A new system is outlined in general terms under the 2012 constitution.
Ghana (legal basis/ constitutional codification)	The Local Government Law (1988) established a new system with district assemblies as the key institutions. The constitution (1992) further codified this system. The Local Government Act (1993) assigned general responsibilities to districts.
India (constitutional and legal)	The federal system is outlined in the 1949 constitution; some amendments, including the 73rd and 74th (1992), strengthen substate institutions and governance, but these are subject to state government legislation and regulation.
Indonesia (legal basis/constitutional amendment)	Law 22 on Regional Government (1999) amended as Law 32 (2004), Law 25 on Fiscal Balance (1999) amended as Law 33 (2004), and Law 34 on Regional Taxes/Levies (2000) amended as Law 28 (2009) provide the basic framework. A constitutional amendment (2000) strengthens the basis for decentralization.
Mexico (constitutional and legal)	The constitution (1917) lays the foundation for state and municipal governments, with additional details outlined in the Law on Fiscal Coordination (1980) and amendments. New legislation is intended to strengthen municipalities.
Philippines (legal and constitutional)	The constitution (1987) provides for local government autonomy. The Local Government Code (1991) and various laws (pre- and post-Marcos) define aspects of the system.
South Africa (constitutional and legal)	The constitution (1996) and the Municipal Structures Act (1998) established three spheres of government and defined functions/powers. Additional laws include the Municipal Systems Act (2000), Municipal Finance Management Act (2003), Municipal Fiscal Powers and Functions Act (2007), and some sectoral legislation, including the 2009 National Land Transport Act.
Uganda (constitutional and legal)	The Local Governments (Resistance Councils) Statute (1993) reinforced political authority of existing local councils. The constitution (1995) outlined functions and finances of local councils. The Local Government Act (1997) defined expenditure assignments in more detail.

SOURCE: Information from country-specific sources summarized in notes 2 and 3.

2005). States in federal systems (India and Mexico) tend to retain substantial control over lower tiers. In Mexico, the central government recently acted to empower municipalities. In India, the 13th National Finance Commission increased resources for local bodies (although still channeled through the states), and there is talk of further pro-local-government reform.

Finally, even if they establish urban and metropolitan governments, few constitutional and legal provisions differentially empower them with specificity. For example, Article 197 of the Ugandan Constitution states: "Urban authorities shall have autonomy over their financial and planning matters in relation to the district councils as Parliament may by law provide." The Ghana Local Government Law (1988) provides for metropolitan and municipal districts where the population meets certain thresholds but without asymmetric empowerment. South Africa, on the other hand, allows for differentially empowered metropolitan municipalities. Similarly, the Indian framework enables creation of municipal corporations with more robust powers (subject to state variation) in large urban areas. National laws may provide for overarching governance structures where there is jurisdictional fragmentation, for example, the Metropolitan Manila Development Authority.[5]

FISCAL POWERS AND FUNCTIONS

Any level of government, urban or otherwise, is assigned fiscal powers (functions, revenues, transfers, and borrowing authority). Some frameworks are specific about and differentially empower urban areas, but more often detailed assignments are left to subsequent laws and regulations. Where there is lack of clarity, service delivery gaps, redundancies, or inefficiencies are more likely. Problems can arise in metropolitan areas where functions are fragmented across separate jurisdictions.

Distributing Functions Among Levels of Government

There is considerable variation in functional assignments and public spending shares across levels (table 3.5). Brazil has extensive cosharing, with only limited exclusive municipal assignments. In other cases, subnational levels receive more functions than the center, including Indonesia, the Philippines, and Uganda. In Cambodia and Ghana, functions remain more centralized or are subject to strong central control and/or require follow-up legislation. In Egypt, most functions are centralized, and subnational actors largely follow national directives. South Africa splits major functional responsibilities between levels: provinces have more responsibility for education, health, and social welfare, while municipalities provide roads and basic utilities, although there is considerable concurrency that complicates service delivery.[6] In federal countries, such as India and Mexico, state governments have discretion over functional assignment to municipal and rural governments as well as how and at what pace to devolve.

Formal provisions assigning differential functions to urban/metropolitan areas appear uncommon, with a few exceptions. South Africa provides for differential

---

[5] See the discussion of the Metropolitan Manila Development Authority in Nasehi and Rangwala (2011).
[6] For recent thinking on this, see Steytler and Fessha (2011).

TABLE 3.5

Local functional assignments and expenditure shares

Country	Subnational functions	Subnational share of total expenditures*
Brazil	Most functions are shared. Preschool and primary education, preventive health care, and historic/cultural preservation are primarily local. Only public transport (inner city) and land use are purely local.	26.3% (2007) by municipal governments.
Cambodia	Provinces dominate subnational service delivery but remain under national line ministries until 2009 legislation is further defined and implemented. Communes have discretion but few mandatory functions and resources. Legal provisions are in place for eventual transfer of more functions.	Around 20% overall (2007), but only 2–3% at the commune level, with the rest mostly deconcentrated until new reforms occur.
Egypt	Major public services (education, health, housing, etc.) are primarily delivered by national line ministry departments/agencies at the governorate level. Funding is available for limited local functions through the Ministry of Local Development.	11.2% (2007) by all subnational levels, mostly deconcentrated expenditures made as per central directives.
Ghana	National ministries provide education, health, and agriculture services. Districts provide water/electricity and have authority for other sectors but lack resources.	10% (2006) local, including metropolitan areas and districts.
India	The constitution (12th Schedule) allows 18 municipal functions, but each state determines specifics. States differentiate (variably) in practice, generally favoring large urban areas. Around 60% of local government spending is on "core functions" (mostly urban), including water, street lighting, sanitation, and roads.	Around 66% subnational (2004), nearly evenly divided between states and lower tiers, with higher expenditures in urban areas.
Indonesia	Obligatory local functions include health, education, environment, and infrastructure. Provinces were originally assigned coordination and gap-filling roles. Law 32/2004 increases their role and raises concern about lack of functional clarity.	Around 35% (2007) by all subnational levels, with about 80% of that by districts and cities.
Mexico	Many functions shared across levels. Local functions include fire, housing, planning, refuse collection, parks, leisure, aspects of transport, and public utilities.	Around 45% in total, of which around 6% is municipal (2007).
Philippines	Substantial functions are devolved to subnational governments, particularly health, social services, environment, agriculture, public works, education, tourism, telecommunications, and housing.	25% at the subnational level (2006), with about 55% of that by cities, municipalities, and barangays.
South Africa	Provinces are responsible for primary/secondary education, health care, and social welfare. Municipal governments are responsible for water/sanitation, roads, and electricity. Actual responsibility varies by region and municipal government capacity. There is an ongoing shift of built environment functions to metros.	56.3% of total public expenditures (2007) occur at the subnational level, and 22.1% municipal, with metros accounting for 57.5% of all municipal spending.
Uganda	Districts and urban governments are responsible for most functions but are increasingly governed by national mandates and conditional transfers. Urban areas have larger revenue bases and more de facto discretion.	23% of total public expenditures occur at the local government level.

*Separate data for intermediate and local levels are provided where relevant and available.

SOURCE: Information from country-specific sources summarized in notes 2 and 3.

treatment of metropolitan municipalities in the constitution and in some laws (see table 3.4). The 2009 National Land Transport Act, for example, specifically empowers metros. With or without explicit legal mandates, however, metropolitan and large urban areas tend to provide a greater range of services than other local governments, often with greater de facto autonomy.[7] In South Africa, eight metro municipalities accounted for nearly 60 percent of total spending by the 238 municipalities in 2007 (for details, see Republic of South Africa 2008).

Subnational Revenues: Own-Source Revenues and Sharing of Specific Higher-Level Revenues

Subnational own-source revenue and tax-sharing provisions are diverse (table 3.6). Local sources are limited in Cambodia, Egypt, and Uganda and more extensive in Brazil and the Philippines (see also chapters 6, 7, and 8). Full local autonomy over any tax is rare, but there is often some discretion over the rate, at least within a range. Pricing of major services, such as water, is typically subject to regulation, but there is often some flexibility on setting local user charges. In Indonesia and Uganda, postdecentralization constraints have been placed on local revenue generation. In Indonesia, however, these restrictions were intended to reduce the use of problematic taxes that emerged after decentralization (for details, see Lewis 2003; 2005).

With respect to tax sharing, a few countries, for example, Brazil and Indonesia, provide substantial sharing of revenues from a number of individual higher-level taxes. In most cases, however, revenue sharing is primarily accomplished through formula-based transfers (see next section and table 3.7) that allocate a block of nationally raised revenues.

Local governments not uncommonly collect 10 percent or less of their revenues. This might be expected in Cambodia, Egypt, and Uganda, but it is also true in more devolved countries, such as India and Indonesia. However, this must be interpreted in context. Indian subnational governments, for example, receive significant shared revenues and transfers, which may reduce their incentive to tax locally. The Indonesian property tax has been a national tax shared with lower levels, although it is now being devolved.

There can be considerable variation in vertical imbalance within countries. In federal systems, this partly results from differential state policies, but it is substantially due to the superior revenue bases and capacity of major urban areas relative to smaller urban and rural jurisdictions.[8] In South Africa, for example, metropolitan municipalities are much more fiscally independent than other local governments, and they are seeking the implementation of a new local business tax.

Intergovernmental Transfers

Intergovernmental transfers often heavily supplement subnational resources, but they can also constrain local autonomy and discourage revenue generation (see also chapter 9). Their use, in terms of importance, objectives, distribution across

---

[7] This is the general sense that emerges from the various case materials.
[8] This is the general sense that emerges from the various case materials.

TABLE 3.6
Subnational revenues: Local/municipal own-source revenues and shared taxes

Country	Own-source revenues	Shared sources*
Brazil	Municipalities are allowed to collect tax on services (most important in major cities), urban property tax, real estate transfer tax, and fines and public utilities fees. Municipalities collect about 20% (2007) of their revenues from own-source revenues, more in larger cities.	The federal level shares rural property tax (50%), industrial tax (25%), and gold financial operations tax (70%). Municipalities get 25% of state value added tax and 50% of vehicle registration.
Cambodia	No major own-source revenues are collected. Communes are legally allowed to collect administrative fees, land and property tax, and user charges, but this authority remains mostly unimplemented. Authority to higher levels under 2009 legislation is also not implemented.	Most revenue sharing occurs through line-ministry allocations to provinces and transfers to communes (see table 3.7).
Egypt	Only minor local own-source revenues are permitted. The only notable exception is the Local Services and Development Account, which allows local administrations to charge fees for ad hoc activities, but it rarely raises more than a small portion of local revenues.	Local entities share tax (entertainment, property) and nontax (drivers license and various fees) sources, but rates are fixed.
Ghana	Local governments collect more than 50 mostly minor taxes, licenses, fees, and charges. They can set the tax rate but not the base, and collect fees but not taxes. Revenue generation is subject to central approval.	Central revenue sharing to local governments occurs through a pool of general resources (see table 3.7).
India	Municipal bodies can levy/collect taxes allowed by states from a list in the constitution (7th Schedule): • Property taxes (highest own urban revenue). • *Octroi* (on goods entering a locality), once a major source but now abolished in all but one state. • Minor fees/charges (dominate rural own-source revenue). There is major vertical imbalance: local bodies account for 33% of public spending but only 3% of revenues, ≥10% of own-source revenue, and >90% from urban areas.	Federal and state revenues are mostly shared with lower tiers through formula-based transfers (see table 3.7). The government is proposing a destination-based goods and services tax, with sharing details under discussion.
Indonesia	Subject to some central control: • Provincial (substantially shared with local level): motor vehicles, fuel, groundwater taxes. • City/district: electricity, hotel/restaurant, entertainment, advertisement, mineral exploitation, parking taxes, various others. • User fees and charges at both levels. Local governments collect around 15% of their revenues (2008), more in cities; provinces collect around 45%.	Main sharing is via formula transfers (see table 3.7). Select taxes/state enterprise revenues are shared, including property tax (being devolved), natural resources revenues, and personal income tax. Revenue sharing has been expanded.

TABLE 3.6

(continued)

Country	Own-source revenues	Shared sources*
Mexico	Municipalities receive revenues from urban property taxes, vehicle registration, and fees that vary by states. Municipalities collect 15.6% (2007) of their total revenues, but this can be higher in major urban areas.	Main sharing occurs through intergovernmental transfers (see table 3.7); 20% of oil production revenues from states are shared with municipalities.
Philippines	Subject to regulation, subnational sources include • taxes on real property/property transfer, local business turnover, quarries, amusement, public enterprise proceeds; and • many types of user fees and charges Cities can impose the full set of subnational taxes, with fewer allowed in provinces and municipalities. Cities and provinces must share many revenues with municipalities and barangays. Subnational governments collect about 30% of their revenues (2006) but less (20%) by provinces and can be much higher (≥60%) in cities.	Central revenue sharing occurs mostly through intergovernmental transfers (see table 3.7). National wealth composite (based on a specific set of national revenues) and the tobacco excise tax are shared with subnational governments.
South Africa	Major municipal revenue sources include • property rates; • service fees (water, sanitation, electricity); and • a Regional Services Council Levy until abolished in 2006 and replaced in metros with an origin based share of the national fuel levy. The metros are seeking approval for a new local business tax. Municipalities in the aggregate collect about 75% (2007) of their revenue but there is considerable diversity, from near fiscal independence in metros to near full dependence in smaller urban/rural areas.	Revenue sharing is done primarily through the intergovernmental transfer system (see table 3.7).
Uganda	Primary local revenue sources include • property rates; • a range of fees and charges; and • a graduated personal tax that was the main source outside Kampala until suspended in 2006. Local governments were partly compensated, and service/hotel taxes instituted, but with uneven benefits. Local governments collect <10% of revenues, although this can be higher in urban areas.	Central revenue sharing is done entirely through transfers (table 3.7). No individual taxes are specifically shared; this may change with the discovery of oil and gas and the possibility of shared taxation of these resources.

*The focus is on municipal/local sources unless provincial/state resources are shared with lower levels.
SOURCE: Information from country-specific sources summarized in notes 2 and 3.

levels of government, and degree of discretion in their use, varies substantially (table 3.7).

In some cases, fixed percentages of specific taxes (Brazil) or national revenues (Cambodia, Ghana, Indonesia, Mexico, Philippines) are transferred, mostly by formula but sometimes in part on derivation (Mexico). In a few cases, the pool is decided in the annual budget process (South Africa and Uganda) or fixed for a period (e.g., five years in India as per the National Finance Commission recommendations). Transferred resources dominate in Egypt but through a nontransparent budgeting process (see Algoso and Magee 2011; Ebel and Amin 2006).

Some countries have only a few transfer programs with a dominant unconditional formula-based transfer (Indonesia, South Africa, Philippines). In other cases, multiple transfers are important or use of general revenue sharing is restricted (Brazil, Ghana, Uganda). In Ghana, this was intentional from the start, but in Brazil and Uganda earmarking increased over time because of service delivery concerns. India has a complex set of transfers framed by national planning and finance commissions and further defined by state finance commissions. This includes a variable (across states) mix of unconditional and conditional transfers, some not transparently allocated. In India and Mexico, states have an important role in determining transfers to municipal and other substate levels.

Few transfers are specifically dedicated to large urban or metropolitan areas. Examples include the Jawaharlal Nehru National Urban Renewal Mission for urban infrastructure in India (see Government of India 2009) and the Municipal Development Fund in the Philippines (which also executes infrastructure loans; see below). Major urban areas, however, are often considerably less dependent on transfers in both aggregate and per capita terms because of their superior revenue capacity and, in cases, ability to borrow for capital investment.

The impact of transfers on urban areas can shift over time. In South Africa, for example, metros are increasingly dependent on transfers because of an influx of poor residents (the Equitable Share transfer formula is based on the cost of providing certain basic services to citizens living below the poverty line), devolution of expensive functions (especially public transport), and the abolition in 2006 of the Regional Services Council levy, a combination payroll levy and turnover tax that heavily benefited larger municipalities (for details, see Republic of South Africa 2008).

Subnational Government Borrowing

All countries reviewed here except Cambodia have constitutional and/or legal provisions for subnational borrowing (table 3.8). In Ghana, Egypt, and Uganda, there is little or none in practice. In Indonesia, borrowing has at times been significant (mostly from public sector mechanisms), but poor repayment and lack of an adequate borrowing framework have led to a decline relative to infrastructure investment needs (see Lewis 2007 and Indonesian Decentralization Support Facility 2012).

A number of more advanced economies with some creditworthy subnational governments have moderate or extensive borrowing, including Brazil, India, Mexico, the Philippines, and South Africa. In federal systems, a large share of subnational

TABLE 3.7

Intergovernmental transfers

Country	Unconditional transfers	Conditional transfers
Brazil	Federal equalization transfer to the municipalities funded with a 22.5% share of the federal value added tax and income tax revenues; 10% goes to the state capital and 90% to other municipalities by formulas.	Some earmarked and discretionary transfers are partly funded from revenue sharing (e.g., primary education and health) and partly from special sources (e.g., education tax on payroll and the National Fund for Social Assistance).
Cambodia	Communes receive unconditional formula-based transfers financed by a fixed percentage of national revenues (currently 3%) allocated to the Commune *Sangkat* Fund. Transfers for provinces, municipalities and districts are to be determined.	Provinces and districts rely mostly on line-ministry allocations, not transfers. Decentralization laws allow for conditional transfers to communes, and multiple kinds of transfers to higher levels as further decentralization mandated in 2009 proceeds.
Egypt	There are only minor unconditional transfers; most funds are allocated through the national budget by sectors.	Conditional transfers dominate in the form of nontransparent budget allocations; there are few formal allocation criteria or formulas.
Ghana	The District Assembly Common Fund, which receives 7.5% of national revenues, is by law permitted to be unconditional but is usually earmarked.	The District Assembly Common Fund finances an average of 80–90% of each district's revenues; these funds are typically earmarked by the central government for capital projects.
India	Indian transfers are complex. There are substantial formula-allocated transfers. National finance commissions constituted every five years determine the revenue-sharing pool and formula and the planning commissions provide development grants. State finance commissions share state revenues with lower tiers. Minor federal transfers for lower tiers pass through states.	There is a large and growing number of conditional transfers, mostly through individual ministries. Allocation criteria vary greatly in terms of clarity. A key urban infrastructure program is the Jawaharlal Nehru Urban Renewal Mission. Recent finance commissions, especially the 13th Commission (2010–2015), have adopted performance-based grants for specific purposes.
Indonesia	Formula-driven Dana Alokasi Umum revenue sharing accounts by law for at least 26% of domestic revenues. Horizontal shares are based substantially on salaries and partly on a fiscal gap measure. Criteria change periodically.	Special-purpose transfers (Dana Alokasi Khusus) were initially limited, grew in importance for several years, and then stabilized in 2007. There is a 10% subnational matching requirement under Law 33 (2004) and recent limited experience with performance-based transfers.
Mexico	Twenty percent of the state share in federal revenues is shared with municipalities; 1% of federal revenues are shared on a derivation basis with municipalities.	Not highly conditional, but 20% of federal government investment grants (*Fondo de Compensación*) go to the 10 poorest states for use by their municipalities.
Philippines	The Internal Revenue Allotment allocates by formula 40% of internal revenues, distributed as 23% each to provinces and cities, 34% to municipalities, and 20% to barangays. The allotment dominates transfers (94% in 2006).	There is a modest level of categorical but not highly conditional grants, including the Municipal Development Fund, the Local Government Empowerment Fund, and the Calamity Fund.
South Africa	There is no fixed pool for the Equitable Share (unconditional) transfer, which accounts for almost 20% of aggregate local revenue (2007) but much less in metros and much more in rural municipalities (pro-poor formula).	Conditional transfers are growing; their importance varies over time, but in 2007 they constituted only about 15% of provincial transfers and about 30% of municipal transfers.
Uganda	No fixed pool is shared with local governments. Only about 10% of transfers are unconditional (2008). A small equalization grant authorized by the constitution has been shrinking and is almost inconsequential.	Almost 90% of total transfers are conditional recurrent grants earmarked for sector-specific activities, and about 20% of total transfers are development grants; these used to be mostly unconditional and are now mostly conditional.

SOURCE: Information from country-specific sources summarized in notes 2 and 3.

TABLE 3.8

Local government borrowing frameworks

Country	Framework
Brazil	Subnational borrowing is allowed by the constitution but subject to a regulatory framework developed in response to problematic state borrowing. Some critics argue that fiscal restraints imposed in the wake of the subnational debt crisis in the 1990s have constrained municipal access to capital markets.
Cambodia	Subnational government borrowing is prohibited by law.
Egypt	Subnational governments are allowed to finance debt up to an amount equal to 20% of shared tax and nontax revenues. In practice, they only borrow from Egyptian government sources and with approval from the Ministry of Local Development.
Ghana	Subnational borrowing is allowed by law but is virtually nonexistent in practice.
India	Subnational government borrowing is allowed and increasingly accessed from multiple sources, including bonds. Local borrowing is subject to state guarantee, although not always in practice. Urban governments dominate local borrowing; indications are that loans are increasingly used to finance operating deficits.
Indonesia	Subnational government borrowing from public and private sources is allowed by law, but most has been from the central government or international agencies through central government on-lending, which has diminished in importance.
Mexico	Local government borrowing is permitted subject to regulation but was long underutilized. Until 2002 much municipal borrowing came through the federal government. There has been an increase in state and municipal borrowing and some recent innovations to promote borrowing, including at the state level.
Philippines	Local government borrowing is allowed by law but relatively limited in practice. Much of it comes through government or quasi-government mechanisms, but some municipalities issue bonds or borrow from private sources.
South Africa	Subnational government borrowing is allowed by constitutional and legislative provisions. It is increasingly important (13% annual growth rate from 2004 to 2008), especially for metros, and Johannesburg and Cape Town have issued bonds.
Uganda	Subnational government borrowing is allowed by the constitution with central government approval but is rare in practice.

SOURCE: Information from country-specific sources summarized in notes 2 and 3.

debt is assumed by states. Brazil and South Africa have robust fiscal responsibility and borrowing frameworks. In Brazil, however, critics argue that the framework, a response to a 1990s subnational debt crisis, unduly constrains municipal borrowing (see Rezende and Garson 2006).

Allowable sources and mechanisms of credit for subnational governments vary. In the Philippines, much borrowing occurs through dedicated mechanisms: the Municipal Development Fund, a public agency that mixes grant and loan finance, and the Local Government Unit Guarantee Corporation, a private entity promoted by the Development Bank of the Philippines. A range of finance options is available in South Africa, but nearly 70 percent of municipal borrowing occurs through the Development Bank of Southern Africa (a public agency) and the Infrastructure Finance Corporation (a private corporation that issues bonds to lend for municipal infrastructure) (see Republic of South Africa 2008). Cape Town and Johannesburg have issued bonds, and other urban municipalities access private credit.

The Ahmedabad Municipal Corporation was the first urban local body in India to directly access capital markets in 1998. Since then, municipal corporations have raised considerable resources through both taxable and tax-free municipal bonds, some without state guarantees. In recent years, both the Tamil Nadu Urban Development Fund and the Greater Bangalore Water and Sanitation Project have raised funds through pooled financing that allows municipalities to jointly access the capital market (see Government of India 2009). Mexico has also adopted innovative finance mechanisms, including future flow securitization and pooled finance schemes, which are making municipal credit more readily available (see Guigale, Korobow, and Webb 2000; Leigland and Mandri-Perrot 2008; U.S. Agency for International Development 2010).

There are no special legal provisions for borrowing by urban and metropolitan governments, but they tend to be among the more creditworthy local governments. In Brazil, three large municipalities recently accounted for 70 percent of local borrowing (see de Mello 2007). Indian municipal corporations have also incurred a large share of local borrowing. Loans financed about a third of South African municipal capital expenditures in 2007, but only 26 of 283 municipalities have borrowed, with the metros dominating the field (see Republic of South Africa 2008).

OVERSIGHT, GOVERNANCE, AND ACCOUNTABILITY

Beyond the fiscal powers discussed above, other key aspects of the overarching national framework can affect subnational government performance, some of which are discussed in more detail in chapters 4 and 5.[9] These include a variety of higher-level oversight, governance, and accountability measures.

Higher-Level Regulation and Monitoring

Unitary states commonly have ministries or departments with a general mandate to regulate, monitor, and support local governments: local administration (Egypt), local government (Ghana, Uganda), interior (Cambodia), interior and local government (Philippines), provincial and local government (South Africa), and home affairs (Indonesia). In some cases they have considerable control, while in others they largely ensure that substantially autonomous local governments meet legal requirements. Specific formal provisions for metropolitan governments are rare, but they may be treated differently because of their higher profiles, greater roles, and resource significance.

Central or state agencies with a specific cross-sectoral mandate (finance, planning, civil service, etc.) generally have some regulatory and monitoring control over local governments or policies that govern them (see Connerly, Eaton, and Smoke 2010). The framework for subnational public financial management, procurement, audit, and so forth, is particularly critical.[10] Unitary states tend to have standardized public financial management systems, while variations among states may exist in federal systems. Standardized systems and strong fiscal responsibility

---

[9] A framework for assessing local accountability is outlined in Yilmaz, Beris, and Serrano-Berthet (2010).

[10] Fedelino and Smoke (2013) review public financial management and fiscal decentralization linkages.

frameworks, as in South Africa, Brazil, and Uganda, can promote transparency and consistency.

Sectoral ministries (health, education, public works, etc.) also play a key role in subnational service delivery in most countries. In some cases, they primarily develop and monitor standards, while in other cases they heavily control local government spending, for example, through how they manage sector-specific conditional fiscal transfers.

Although these regulatory and oversight functions are essential for an effective public sector, they can create obstacles to good performance if they are too stringent, not appropriately followed, or inconsistently applied. Public financial management provisions, for example, can undermine local autonomy if they highly limit local expenditure discretion, as in Uganda, or if procurement is managed or must be approved by a higher level, as in Cambodia and Egypt. Thus, higher-level agencies have a legitimate oversight role, but they can also interfere in ways that may undermine local government performance.

Subnational Elections and Assemblies

In all countries under review, subnational elections are held regularly except at purely administrative levels, such as the county and parish in Uganda (table 3.9). How elections are conducted affects the role that representative bodies can play in realizing the expected benefits of fiscal decentralization.

In some cases, elections are multiparty and competitive (Brazil, India, Indonesia, Mexico, Philippines). In other cases, multiple parties exist but one or two dominate (Cambodia, Ghana, South Africa). In still other countries, there has been a recent transition to multiparty democracy (Uganda) or a major transition is under way (Egypt). Choice in municipal elections is, of course, a key aspect of accountability.

Mayors or local assembly heads are directly elected in Brazil, Indonesia, Mexico, Philippines, and Uganda, but this is of mixed significance. In Mexico, mayors can serve only one three-year term. In other cases, the significance of direct elections is partly neutralized by the appointment of an influential local representative of the center (Uganda) or the chief executive to elected councils (Cambodia, Ghana), potentially reinforcing upward accountability.

In a few countries, there is a lack of clarity on the relationships among subnational levels of government. These include local and district municipalities in South Africa, the *panchayati raj* institutions in India, districts and communes in Cambodia, and the multiple subdistrict councils in Uganda (including city and municipal divisions). The use of multiple tiers with unclear mandates can complicate developing consistent mechanisms for service delivery and accountability relationships between the electorate and the main local governments. On the other hand, if properly structured with appropriate functions and financing (e.g., with major network functions at the higher tier), multitier arrangements can enhance local political connectivity while promoting efficient areawide delivery of major services.

TABLE 3.9

Subnational elections and assemblies

Brazil	Elections are held at both state and municipal levels every four years. Municipal councils and mayors are directly elected. There is considerable political competition.
Cambodia	Representative bodies are elected through universal suffrage only at the commune level. District and provincial councils are elected indirectly by the next lower council. Political competition is limited, with dominance by the Cambodia People's Party.
Egypt	Local people's councils were elected at governorate and *markaz* levels. Under Mubarak the former ruling National Democratic Party dominated. Local elections are provided for in the 2012 constitution, but the details need to be determined.
Ghana	District (including metropolitan) assemblies have four-year terms. They comprise 70% elected members and 30% presidential appointees. The district chief executive, who serves like a mayor, is appointed by the president, and a presiding officer is elected by the members of the assembly.
India	Elections are held at the state (some bicameral) level and various substate levels (three-tier *panchayati raj* system in states with > 2 million population), including the municipal level. There is considerable political competition and diversity, and the system is very complex.
Indonesia	Regional people's assemblies are elected at local and provincial levels every five years. Since 2005, provincial governors and local mayors are directly elected.
Mexico	State and municipal assemblies are elected, every six years at the state level (in line with federal elections) and every three years in municipalities. Direct election of municipal mayors is relatively new, and those elected can serve only one term.
Philippines	Directly elected bodies exist at all subnational levels, with the assembly size depending on status (province, city, municipality, barangay) and population. Provincial governors, municipal mayors, and barangay captains are directly elected.
South Africa	Each province and municipality elects a unicameral legislature every five years. Provinces use party-list proportional representation. The legislature elects a premier from members, and the premier appoints an executive council. Municipal elections use proportional representation and a ward system. The council elects a mayor from its ranks, and the mayor appoints a mayoral committee with executive powers.
Uganda	Three of the five subnational government levels (district, sub-county and village) have an elected council with direct election of a chairman and vice chairman (the other two levels are administrative). Adoption of multiparty democracy (abandoning the "no party" National Resistance Movement) increased political competition.

SOURCE: Information from country-specific sources summarized in notes 2 and 3.

Subnational Autonomy in Budgetary and Staffing Decisions

Local governments prepare their own budgets except in Egypt and at higher levels (until recent legally mandated reforms are implemented) in Cambodia (table 3.10). Various factors, however, constrain local discretion, and some countries allow more flexibility than others. Local governments in the Philippines and South Africa have considerable autonomy (and receive mostly unconditional transfers) in spending and hiring. Higher-level governments review budgets in the Philippines but only to ensure regulatory compliance.

TABLE 3.10

Subnational budgeting and staffing discretion

Country	Framework
Brazil	State and municipal governments have independent budgets and hire staff. Autonomy has been somewhat constrained by earmarked transfers, but there is still considerable flexibility, and municipal budgets do not require state approval.
Cambodia	Commune governments have their own budgets, whereas provincial and district budgets remain embedded in the national budget until reforms proceed.
Egypt	Local autonomy is highly limited by the complex and fragmented national budgeting process. The many budget authorities are not coordinated within, much less across, sectors. All public hiring is subject to central guidelines and review.
Ghana	District assemblies prepare and approve their own budgets subject to earmarks, and personnel decisions are made jointly by local and national government. The president appoints chief executives of districts, with approval from district assemblies.
India	State governments have considerable autonomy. Urban and rural local bodies fall under state jurisdiction, and levels of local autonomy vary across states, with different transfer and supervisory policies.
Indonesia	Subnational governments initially had complete budget autonomy, with legality review by the next-higher level. National civil service regulations allowed a reasonable degree of subnational discretion. Law 32 of 2004 expanded higher-level control over budgeting review and civil service decisions.
Mexico	State budgets are coordinated with federal allocations by sector and through a codified fiscal negotiation process. Municipal budgeting also includes joint negotiations with state governors and the federal government for resources beyond revenue-sharing allocations. Municipal budgets and borrowing must be approved by state legislatures. Municipalities hire staff subject to state laws.
Philippines	Subnational governments prepare budgets with legality review by the next-higher level. National civil service regulations allow subnational discretion.
South Africa	Municipalities develop their own budgets for approval by the municipal council, but budgets and hiring must follow relevant laws and regulations.
Uganda	Local governments have little budgetary autonomy. Most revenue is in the form of conditional transfers. Unconditional transfers are mostly consumed by fixed administrative costs. Local governments had significant hiring autonomy, but with central approval, and some local positions have been recentralized.

SOURCE: Information from country-specific sources summarized in notes 2 and 3.

At the other end of the spectrum, local budgeting and hiring in Egypt are almost fully controlled by national agencies. Cambodia's communes have budgets and unconditional transfers subject only to legality control, but they are small. Provincial, municipal, and district budgets are still embedded in the national budget. The center controls civil servants at all levels, with line department staff accountable to the parent ministry. The budgeting situation may change as reform proceeds, but continued central control of the civil service seems likely (see Smoke and Morrison 2011). In Ghana, district (including metropolitan) assemblies pass budgets but subject to heavily conditional resources and the appointment of their chief executives by the president. Other hiring seems to involve joint central-local processes (see Awortwi 2010; Hoffman and Metzroth 2010; Kuusi 2009).

Between extremes is a range of experience. Among unitary countries, Ugandan local governments have legal autonomy in budgeting and hiring, but the 2001 fiscal decentralization strategy imposed a budget template of conditional transfers. Local own-source revenues have been declining, and recent laws increase the central government role in local hiring and place a central representative in every district. Larger urban areas seem to enjoy more de facto discretion, but this is not well documented. Like Uganda, Indonesia's local governments have legal autonomy, but with some restrictions imposed in recent years. Budgets require higher-level approval, and there is more central control over local personnel decisions than there was under the initial decentralization policy. Indonesia is still more devolved than Uganda (transfers are mostly unconditional, and the relatively productive property tax is being devolved), but there has been some modest rollback of local autonomy.[11]

The federal cases are more complicated. Brazilian municipalities have considerable independence from states in budgeting and hiring, and they receive generous revenue shares. At the same time, the federal government has increasingly earmarked shared revenues. In Mexico, municipal budgets are partly negotiated (for resources above statutorily allocated shares) through a formalized fiscal coordination process, making municipal mayors dependent on state governors. Municipal budgets must be approved by state legislatures, and staff decisions are subject to state civil service legislation. Indian states also regulate budgeting and hiring processes for local, including urban, bodies. As with all things in India, there is much complexity. A periodic national pay commission outlines terms of service guidelines, and some individual states form a pay commission. Each state has a public service commission, but their exact functions differ across states.

Metropolitan-Area Coordination Frameworks

Fragmented metropolitan governance is a well-known challenge in major urban areas around the world (see, e.g., Slack 2007; 2010; Slack and Chattopadhyay 2009). This topic is covered more fully in chapter 4, but it is important to note here that coordination mechanisms can be part of the national framework. The Philippine government, for example, created the Metropolitan Manila Development Authority to help coordinate metropolitan-wide planning and service delivery among the 16 cities and one municipality located in the Manila metropolitan region. The authority is not considered to be very effective, however, in part because it is seen as a national agency (dating to the Marcos era), but also because it is financially dependent on the center and creates few incentives or accountability mechanisms to induce individual mayors to work beyond their own constituencies for the larger metropolitan good.[12]

---

[11] For further details on Uganda, see Ahmad, Brosio, and Gonzalez (2006) and Smoke, Muhumuza, and Ssewankambo (2011). On Indonesia, see Indonesia Decentralization Support Facility (2012).

[12] For further details on Manila, see Nasehi and Rangwala (2011).

Greater Cairo incorporates five governorates and eight new cities (see Algoso and Magee 2011). The latter were created to attract people from the Nile Delta and operate outside the regular intergovernmental system under the New Urban Communities Authority of the Ministry of Housing, Utilities and Urban Development. Governorates face poorly coordinated planning and budgeting by central agencies. Governors in the Cairo region formed a steering committee to create a strategic metropolitan plan that includes the new cities with support from the General Organization for Physical Planning of MHUUD. How this will play out in the evolving political environment remains to be seen.

Another promising development is offered by recent policy reforms in Mexico.[13] Recognizing the negative effects of metropolitan fragmentation, new federal legislation is creating incentives and funding for municipal-state coordination of development and public investment among municipalities in metropolitan areas. New laws in the states of Monterrey and Guadalajara are creating additional mechanisms. In general, there is often room for improvements in metropolitan coordination in developing countries, and national frameworks and policies can play a key role if properly conceived and implemented.

Transparency and Civic Engagement Frameworks

Access to information and mechanisms that allow citizens to engage with local governments beyond elections are critical for accountability. Most countries covered here have made efforts on these fronts. Some countries have passed national legislation, such as South Africa's Promotion of Access to Information Act (2000), Mexico's Federal Law of Transparency and Access to Public Government Information (2002), India's Right to Information Act (2005), Uganda's Access to Information Act (2006), and Indonesia's Freedom of Information Act (2009). Brazil also recently passed legislation after many failed attempts, but the Philippines and Ghana failed to enact similar bills in 2010. Cambodia and Egypt have no such legislation. In some cases, such as Indonesia and Uganda, the implementation of the transparency laws has been criticized as lacking.

Civic participation is also critical to promoting good local governance, especially in developing countries, where local governments often lack political credibility. All countries here except Egypt have formal frameworks, some of which were initially piloted by international donors. In Cambodia, for example, participatory mechanisms developed for a donor program took root in the communes but have not yet expanded into higher levels or urban areas (see Smoke and Morrison 2011). In contrast, participatory mechanisms broadly promoted by the Ministry of Local Government in Uganda are criticized as mechanical and have not been deeply embraced (see Smoke, Muhumuza, and Ssewankambo 2011). In a few cases, such mechanisms emerged organically from specific local political contexts, through formal government action (e.g., participatory budgeting in Brazil) or civil society channels (as in parts of India).[14] National enabling frameworks for civil society

---

[13] This discussion is based on personal communications with David Gomez-Alvarez and Alberto Orozco-Ochoa in May and June of 2011.

[14] A critical overview of participatory budgeting is provided in Wampler (2007).

organizations are also critical. Some governments (Brazil, several Indian states, Philippines, South Africa) enable or promote civil society. Support in other countries, such as Cambodia, Ghana, and Indonesia, has been more muted.

Finally, it is important to recognize that citizen engagement can be affected by how intrametropolitan governments and governance are organized. The elected councils and administrations of large municipalities can be distant from constituents. Size may help local governments to achieve scale economies and internalize externalities, but it may also reduce political connectivity to constituents. The above-noted resistance of individual jurisdictions to metropolitan coordination is partly rooted in the desire of smaller councils to respond primarily to their specific electorate rather than attend to the broader needs of the larger metropolitan area. Some balance, however, may be achieved in larger jurisdictions by leaving limited local functions to subjurisdictions. Uganda, as noted above, has multiple levels in district and municipal structures, with most powers at the higher level, and in the Philippines the barangays can enhance political connectivity by providing minor local services while leaving major functions to the larger municipalities.

International Development Assistance Frameworks

International development agencies often play a major role in supporting urban development and local government, as discussed more fully in chapter 15. Such support, however, is often fragmented and may push the intergovernmental system and individual urban governments in conflicting directions, particularly where aid must be channeled through national ministries (see Eaton, Kaiser, and Smoke 2011). For example, donors commonly support local government development and capacity building through a ministry of local government or the equivalent. The same or other donors may simultaneously support public financial management or civil service reforms through a ministry of finance or civil service commission in a way that weakens decentralization. Still others may support service delivery through individual line ministries in ways that are inconsistent with other public sector reforms or limit local autonomy. Fragmented, competing donors may even reinforce counterproductive dynamics among government agencies. Such problems have occurred in a number of countries, including Cambodia, Indonesia, and Uganda.

These issues are generally less relevant in higher-capacity countries that depend less on or more selectively seek foreign aid, or where national development assistance coordination is robust. Donors themselves, however, acknowledge their weakly harmonized and ineffective use of resources for local governance programs in some countries (see Donor Partner Working Group on Decentralization and Local Governance 2011). Where donor fragmentation occurs, the risks need to be recognized and addressed.

IMPLICATIONS FOR SUBNATIONAL GOVERNMENT PERFORMANCE

The national fiscal and institutional frameworks in which local and metropolitan governments operate can decisively affect their performance. Evaluating the nature and effects of these frameworks, however, is not a simple exercise.

The diversity of even the small number of developing and middle-income countries considered here is great. Although they face a number of common issues, there is much variation in historical context, intergovernmental systems, the degree of authority and autonomy granted to local and metropolitan governments, and the nature and quality of accountability mechanisms, among others. The observed variations do not seem particularly systematic, even across countries with some similar characteristics. Equally diverse are the multiple factors that influence how systems are framed and function, including political economy considerations, which may constrain the feasibility of desired reforms and affect the nature of suitable strategies to implement them (see, e.g., Smoke 2007; 2010). In this complex landscape, generalization about improving national frameworks is difficult beyond a few well-known normative principles.

The most fundamental step in evaluating metropolitan fiscal performance is to diagnose in a broad-based and well-grounded way the match between the features of the national institutional and fiscal framework and a country's objectives for metropolitan government and development. A number of considerations are important in this regard.

First, the powers and functions of metropolitan governments must be understood in the context of the overall structure of the public sector. This requires documenting what they do and how they are funded relative to the central government and other types of subnational governments, including any cosharing of functions and any special metropolitan status or considerations. Metropolitan governments may be territorially isolated or contiguous to independent jurisdictions with which they should ideally work to deliver services, raise revenue, and promote development. Inadequate functional clarity and insufficient vertical and horizontal interjurisdictional cooperation can nontrivially compromise performance.

Second, it is important to understand how components of the fiscal system interact. Proper functional assignments for metropolitan areas are important, but implementation can suffer if funds are poorly matched to responsibilities, unpredictable, or subject to rigid conditions or problematic manipulation. Unconditional development grants, for example, are often recommended to finance devolved infrastructure, but they may have limited impact if metropolitan governments have insufficient access to and/or control over the resources needed to operate and maintain new infrastructure. Similarly, responsible borrowing is considered desirable, but metropolitan governments may have weak incentives or capacity to take loans if they have easy access to development transfers or inadequate recurrent resources to service debt. Such inconsistencies and weaknesses in the fiscal architecture can impede good performance.

Third, recognizing how aspects of the accountability framework fit together is critical. Reasonable national (and in federal systems, state) standards and oversight for metropolitan and other local governments are legitimate, and collection and analysis of performance data help higher levels to allocate resources and provide useful information to voters. Strong downward accountability mechanisms (beyond competitive elections) are also needed to realize the expected benefits of decentralized decision making. Yet central and/or state regulatory overreach is common, even for capable and well-resourced metropolitan governments, and downward accountability (through the structure of metropolitan government and the means for citizen engagement) is also often neglected. Together, these realities may complicate local accountability and tend to skew it too far to the upward side of the spectrum.

The relevance of these institutional, fiscal, and accountability framework issues will vary across countries, as will the reasons these frameworks have evolved in a particular way and the prospects for improving on the status quo. Documenting the facts is needed in each case if pragmatic remedial action is to be crafted.

Three different approaches can be used to help overcome the effects of observed framework limitations. First, national policy measures (institutional reform, incentives for local actors, asymmetric treatment of metropolitan governments, etc.) can, if properly structured, help to correct common systemic problems, such as revenue-expenditure mismatches, inappropriate assignment of responsibilities, and functional or jurisdictional fragmentation that undermines good governance and service delivery efficiency.

Second, governmental actors in metropolitan areas can independently take formal or informal steps within the existing national framework to alleviate fiscal and governance problems that undermine good performance. Such measures include improving cooperation in making fiscal decisions and raising funds, as well as adopting mechanisms to improve transparency and appropriately increase citizen engagement.

Third, civil society actors in metropolitan areas can put pressure on government officials to change their behavior. This can be accomplished through more robust use of electoral and participatory mechanisms, collective action taken by business and industry associations, and the adoption of civil society organization driven citizen report cards, among others.

Although each can play an independent role, the relationships among these actors and levels of action needs to be considered. Focusing on larger fiscal and institutional issues independently of how metropolitan areas are governed internally and the extent to which their governments are credibly connected to their constituents is not sufficient. For example, the desirability of additional revenue generation in many countries is well recognized. But national policies to increase revenue autonomy may have little impact if local governance is weak and citizens and businesses resist paying taxes because they lack faith in their metropolitan government. What matters for realizing potential benefits from empowered metropolitan governments is how intergovernmental structures, local governance mechanisms, and political connectivity to local taxpayers work together.

If meaningful change is to occur, at least some of the actors involved in this challenging arena must be motivated to act. Productive action requires sufficiently understanding the structures of metropolitan governments, the challenges they face, and the factors underlying both. This chapter provides a preliminary sense of why such analysis is important and how to approach it. The relative dearth of work on the topic, however, should inspire researchers and practitioners to deepen our understanding of how metropolitan governments are being and could be better supported by the national fiscal and institutional framework to meet their critical responsibilities and priority goals.

REFERENCES

Ahmad, Ehtisham, Giorgio Brosio, and Maria Gonzalez. 2006. Uganda: Managing more effective decentralization. Working Paper No. 06/279. Washington, DC: International Monetary Fund.

Ahmad, Ehtisham, and Vito Tanzi. 2002. *Managing fiscal decentralization.* Oxford: Routledge.

Alfonso, Jose Roberto, and Erika Amorim Araujo. 2006. Municipal organization and finance: Brazil. In *Local governance in developing countries,* ed. Anwar Shah. Washington, DC: World Bank.

Algoso, David, and Jenna Magee. 2011. Structures of metropolitan governance and finance: A case study of Cairo, Egypt. Working Paper. Cambridge, MA: Lincoln Institute of Land Policy.

Alm, James, Jorge Martinez-Vazquez, and Sri Mulyani Indrawati. 2004. *Reforming intergovernmental fiscal relations and the rebuilding of Indonesia.* Cheltenham, U.K.: Edward Elgar.

Awortwi, Nicolas. 2010. The past, present, and future of decentralization in Africa: A comparative case study of local government development trajectories of Ghana and Uganda. *International Journal of Public Administration* 33(12):620–634.

Bahl, Roy, and Paul Smoke, eds. 2003. *Restructuring local government finance in developing countries: Lessons from South Africa.* Cheltenham, U.K.: Edward Elgar.

Birch, Eugenie, and Susan Wachter, eds. 2011. *Global urbanization.* Philadelphia: University of Pennsylvania Press.

Burki, Shahid Javed, Guillermo Perry, and William Dillinger. 1999. *Beyond the center: Decentralizing the state.* Washington, DC: World Bank.

Cheema, G. Shabbir, and Dennis Rondinelli, eds. 2007. *Decentralized governance: Emerging concepts and practices.* Washington, DC: Brookings Institution.

Connerly, Ed, Kent Eaton, and Paul Smoke, eds. 2010. *Making decentralization work: Democracy, development and security.* Boulder, CO: Lynne Rienner.

Crawford, Gordon, and Christof Hartmann. 2008. *Decentralization in Africa: A pathway out of poverty and conflict.* Amsterdam: Amsterdam University Press.

de Mello, Luiz. 2007. Fiscal responsibility legislation and fiscal adjustment: The case of Brazilian local governments. In *Financing cities: Fiscal responsibility and urban infrastructure in Brazil, China, India, Poland and South Africa,* ed. George Peterson and Patricia Clarke Annez, 40–73. Los Angeles: Sage.

Donor Partner Working Group on Decentralization and Local Governance. 2011. *Busan and beyond: Localizing Paris principles for more effective support to decentralization and local governance reforms.* Bonn: Gesellschaft fur Internationale Zusaamenarbeit.

Eaton, Kent, Kai Kaiser, and Paul Smoke. 2011. *The political economy of decentralization reform: Implications for aid effectiveness.* Washington, DC: World Bank.

Ebel, Robert, and Khaled Amin. 2006. Egyptian intergovernmental relations and fiscal decentralization. Washington, DC: World Bank.

Fedelino, Annalisa, and Paul Smoke. 2013. Public financial management and fiscal decentralization: Opportunities and challenges. In *Public financial management and its emerging architecture,* ed. Marco Cangiano, Teresa Curristine, and Michel Lazare. Washington, DC: International Monetary Fund.

Garg, Subhash Chandra. 2007. Overview of urban infrastructure finance in India. In *Financing cities: Fiscal responsibility and urban infrastructure in Brazil, China, India, Poland and South Africa,* ed. George Peterson and Patricia Clarke Annez, 108–157. Los Angeles: Sage.

Government of India. 2009. Report of the 13th Finance Commission: 2010–2015. New Delhi.

Grindle, Merilee. 2007. *Going local: Decentralization, democratization and the promise of good governance.* Princeton, NJ: Princeton University Press.

Guigale, Marcelo. 2000. Achievements and challenges of fiscal decentralization: Lessons from Mexico. Washington, DC: World Bank.

Guigale, Marcelo, Adam Korobow, and Steven Webb. 2000. A new model for market-based regulation of subnational borrowing: The Mexican approach. Washington, DC: World Bank.

Hoffman, Barak, and Katherine Metzroth. 2010. The political economy of decentralization in Ghana. Washington, DC: Center for Democracy and Civil Society, Georgetown University.

Ichimura, Shinichi, and Roy Bahl, eds. 2009. *Decentralization policies in Asian development.* Singapore: World Scientific.

Indonesian Decentralization Support Facility. 2012. *Proceedings of the international conference: Alternative visions for decentralization in Indonesia.* Jakarta: World Bank.

Kuusi, Suvi. 2009. Aspects of local self government: Ghana. Helsinki: Finnish Association of Local Authorities.

Leigland, James, and Cledan Mandri-Perrott. 2008. Enhancing the creditworthiness of municipal bonds: Innovations from Mexico. *Gridlines* 39 (August).

Lewis, Blane. 2003. Tax and charge creation by regional governments under fiscal decentralization. *Bulletin of Indonesian Economic Studies* 39(2):177–192.

———. 2005. Indonesian local government spending, taxing and saving: An explanation of pre- and post-decentralization fiscal outcomes. *Asian Economic Journal* 19(3):291–317.

———. 2007. On-lending in Indonesia: Past performance and future prospects. *Bulletin of Indonesia Economic Studies* 43(1):35–58.

Manasan, Rosario. 2004. Local public finance in the Philippines: In search of autonomy with accountability. Discussion paper. Manila: Philippine Institute for Development Studies.

Martinez-Vazquez, Jorge, and Francois Vaillancourt, eds. 2011. *Decentralization in difficult environments.* Cheltenham, U.K.: Edward Elgar.

Moreno, Carlos. 2003. Fiscal performance of local governments in Mexico: The role of federal transfers. Mexico City: Centro de Investigación y Docencia Económicas.

Nasehi, Carly, and Rahil Rangwala. 2011. Structures of metropolitan governance and finance: A case study on Manila, Philippines. Working Paper. Cambridge, MA: Lincoln Institute of Land Policy.

Ndegwa, Stephen, and Brian Levy. 2003. The politics of decentralization in Africa: A comparative analysis. Washington, DC: World Bank.

Peterson, George, and Patricia Clarke Annez, eds. 2007. *Financing cities: Fiscal responsibility and urban infrastructure in Brazil, China, India, Poland and South Africa.* Los Angeles: Sage.

Rao, M. Govinda, and Richard Bird. 2010. *Urban governance and finance in India.* New Delhi: National Institute of Public Finance and Policy.

Republic of Indonesia, Ministry of Finance. 2011. *Fiscal decentralization in Indonesia a decade after Big Bang.* Jakarta: University of Indonesia Press.

Republic of South Africa. 2008. *Local government budgets and expenditure review: 2003/04–2009/10.* Pretoria: National Treasury.

Revilla, Ernesto. 2012. Mexico's fiscal federalism. Draft Paper. Washington, DC: World Bank.

Rezende, Fernando, and Sol Garson. 2006. Financing metropolitan areas in Brazil: Political, institutional and legal obstacles and the emergence of new proposals for improving coordination. *Revista de Economia Contemporânea* 10(1):5–34.

Sahasranaman, Anand. 2009. *Pragmatic municipal finance reform: Lessons from policy in South Africa, Brazil and select experiences in India.* Chennai: Institute for Financial Management Trust.

Slack, Enid. 2007. Managing the coordination of service delivery in metropolitan cities: The role of metropolitan governance. Policy Research Working Paper No. 4317. Washington, DC: World Bank.

———. 2010. Financing large cities and metropolitan areas. Toronto: Institute on Municipal Finance and Governance, Munk School, University of Toronto.

Slack, Enid, and Rupak Chattopadhyay. 2009. *Finance and governance of capital cities in federal systems.* Montreal: McGill-Queens University Press.

Smoke, Paul. 2007. Fiscal decentralization and intergovernmental relations in developing countries: Navigating a viable path to reform. In *Decentralized governance: Emerging concepts and practices*, ed. G. Shabbir Cheema and Dennis Rondinelli, 131–155. Washington, DC: Brookings Institution.

———. 2010. The imperative of strategic implementation. In *Making decentralization work: Democracy, development and security,* ed. Ed Connerly, Kent Eaton, and Paul Smoke, 191–217. Boulder, CO: Lynne Rienner.

Smoke, Paul, Eduardo Gomez, and George Peterson, eds. 2006. *Decentralization in Asia and Latin America: Towards a comparative interdisciplinary perspective.* Cheltenham, U.K.: Edward Elgar.

Smoke, Paul, and Joanne Morrison. 2011. Decentralization in Cambodia: Consolidating central power or building accountability from below? In *Decentralization in difficult environments,* ed. Jorge Martinez-Vazquez and Francois Vaillancourt, 313–342. Cheltenham, U.K.: Edward Elgar.

Smoke, Paul, William Muhumuza, and Emmanuel Ssewankambo. 2011. Comparative assessment of decentralization in Africa: Uganda. Washington, DC: U.S. Agency for International Development.

Souza, Celine. 2003. Brazil's system of local government, local finance and intergovernmental relations. Birmingham, U.K.: University of Birmingham, International Development Department.

Steytler, Nico. 2005. The place and role of local government in federal systems. Johannesburg: Konrad-Adenauer Stiftung.

Steytler, Nico. and Yonaton Fessha. 2011. Defining provincial and local government powers and functions: The management of concurrency. Bellville, South Africa: Community Law Center, University of the Western Cape.

Stren, Richard, and Robert Cameron, eds. 2005. Special issue on metropolitan governance reform. *Public Administration and Development* 24(4):275–364.

U.N. Department for Social and Economic Affairs. 2009. World urbanization prospects. New York.

United Cities and Local Governments. 2010. Financing local government: The challenges of the 21st century. Second GOLD Report. Barcelona: United Cities and Local Governments.

U.S. Agency for International Development. 2010. Subnational government finance in Mexico. www.usaid.gov/mx/financeeng.html

van Ryneveld, Philip. 2007. Fiscal decentralization and the financing of urban infrastructure in South Africa. In *Financing cities: Fiscal responsibility and urban infrastructure in Brazil, China, India, Poland and South Africa,* ed. George Peterson and Patricia Clarke Annez, 183–204. Los Angeles: Sage.

Wampler, Brian. 2007. *Participatory budgeting in Brazil: Contestation, cooperation, and accountability.* University Park, PA: Penn State University Press.

Wilson, Robert. 2011. Metropolitan development: Does governance matter? Washington, DC: Woodrow Wilson International Center for Scholars.

World Bank. 2005. East Asia decentralizes: Making local government work. Washington, DC.

Wunsch, James, and Dele Olowu, eds. 2003. *Local governance in Africa: The challenge of democratic decentralization.* Boulder, CO: Lynne Rienner.

Yilmaz, Serdar, Yakup Beris, and Rodrigo Serrano-Berthet. 2010. Linking local government discretion and accountability in decentralization. *Development Policy Review* 28(3):259–293.

Yilmaz, Serdar, and Varsha Venugopa. 2010. Local government discretion and accountability in Philippines. *Journal of International Development,* doi: 10.1002/jid.1687.

The Decentralization of Governance in Metropolitan Areas

4

ROY W. BAHL

The theory and practice of providing government services in metropolitan areas are subjects that have attracted a great deal of attention in the industrial countries but have been largely ignored in low- and middle-income countries.[1] With urbanization and the growth of megacities, time is running short for these countries to develop a workable approach to governance and finance in metropolitan areas with several million persons.

This chapter assesses whether the fiscal decentralization model that has been so instrumental in decisions about structuring governance on a nationwide basis can be applied successfully in metropolitan areas. The first section considers the theoretical underpinnings for choosing among the various possible metropolitan governance structures. Next is a review of some of the urban governance models used around the world and a discussion of their advantages and disadvantages. The chapter concludes with a discussion of the range of policy reform options that would appear to be feasible.

Unfortunately, there are no comparable data on metropolitan-area governance and public finances, so there is little empirical evidence on the impacts of various forms of decentralized governance on economic performance.[2] This chapter adopts the less ambitious goal of describing and analyzing the governance practices in a nonrandom sample of metropolitan areas in both industrial and developing countries. The choice of the sample is based on availability of information rather than any formal attempt at "representative" coverage. This chapter draws on the experience in industrial countries to demonstrate the kind of governance choices that are possible at higher levels of economic development.

---

[1] Mohanty et al. (2007, 139) conclude an intensive study of urban government finances in India by noting that local governments are yet to be put "on the public finance map of the country."

[2] For discussion of the link between decentralization and economic performance, see Martinez-Vazquez and McNab (2001) and OECD (2006a).

Theory and Metropolitan Governance

There is no single "best" way to structure governance in metropolitan areas; it depends on which objectives the government most wants to achieve and the costs it most wants to avoid. Most researchers on this subject start with economic efficiency criteria. The core argument is the now-familiar decentralization theorem, which holds to a basic rule of assigning each function to the lowest level of government consistent with its efficient performance (Bahl 2011; Bahl and Linn 1992; Bird and Slack 2004; Oates 1972). The apt phrase is that "people get what they want." When this rule is followed, the overall public welfare is enhanced. The assignment that finally results involves a balancing act where expenditures characterized by economies of scale, or those generating external costs or benefits, are assigned to higher-level governments, and everything else stays local.

Can this same thinking be applied to assigning expenditure responsibilities within metropolitan areas? If so, such issues as the extent to which smaller local governments in a fragmented metropolitan governance system should drive expenditure decisions, whether a metropolitan government is necessary for managing and financing areawide services, what physical area the regional government should encompass, and how important state/federal vertical programs should be, can begin to be answered.[3]

Preferences and Home Rule

A major factor driving expenditure assignments in metropolitan areas is the demand for home rule. The smaller the population of a government, the greater the influence of an individual voter on budget choices. The larger the local government, the less likely it is that local voters will see their preferences matched by budget outcomes. Unless preferences are uniform, the welfare losses will rise as the population of the city government increases. Loss of local control and, even more so, loss of direct involvement of higher-level governments in urban service delivery are major criticisms of metropolitan-area-wide government. In places where budgetary decisions are in the hands of areawide governments or a higher-level government, lower-level units sometimes have been created either to give autonomy to neighborhood units or to get their advice for purposes of inputs to fiscal planning.[4]

Where this thinking leads is that, all else being equal, the stronger the push for direct local involvement in governance and fiscal decisions, the smaller the "optimally sized" local government. If sentiments about home rule are strong, a jurisdictionally fragmented system, or a two-tier metropolitan government structure with a strong bottom tier, is more likely than a dominant metropolitan government.

---

[3] A *vertical program* is one where the service is delivered in the metropolitan area by a provincial or central level government, and the funds do not pass through the budget of any local government budget.

[4] An example from industrial countries is the 21 districts within the city of Madrid that have been delegated administrative functions in such areas as urban parks, health, and licensing. In 2007, these districts managed about 12 percent of the city budget. The district councils include both appointed and elected members. A similar arrangement to encourage local participation is in place in The Netherlands, in the form of elected district councils that operate at a level below the elected municipal councils.

Economies of Scale and Externalities

A justification for assigning expenditure and financing responsibility to a higher tier of government is the welfare gains that come from economies of scale in the delivery of a service. To translate this guideline to practice, it is necessary to identify those public services that are characterized by economies of scale. Intuition and some empirical evidence tell us that some public services are characterized by economies of scale, for example, capital-intensive infrastructure such as public utilities, solid waste disposal, sewerage, and mass transit. Some social services may also qualify, and not much is known about the relationship between unit cost and government size for functions such as education, health, and welfare services. Unfortunately, much of the empirical research on this question has been undertaken in industrialized countries, and even there the findings are mixed (Fox and Gurley 2006). Most studies conclude that separating out all other variables (e.g., the quality of the service offered and the setting in which the question is asked) makes it difficult to come to a single, defensible answer about the optimally sized city.[5]

The presence of externalities will also push up the optimal size of government. For those public services assigned to them, lower-tier governments will underspend (or overspend) because they will account only for local benefits and costs in making their budgetary decisions. The problem is multiplied in a metropolitan area because there often are so many local governments operating in close proximity to one another. Almost every government's decisions affect someone else.

There are many examples of this. Suburban jurisdictions might underspend on hospitals and clinics, causing their residents to commute to the central city to take advantage of better health care services. Central city governments might underspend on the infrastructure necessary to control pollution, with the result that the environmental conditions in other jurisdictions in the area are harmed. Moreover, if services such as mass transit are not coordinated, the resulting congestion will harm all consumers, and the cost of providing any given level of services might be higher. In all of these cases, the provision of such services by a metropolitan-areawide government would internalize these externalities.

As in the case of economies of scale, it is difficult to translate theory into practice. Spillover effects are known to cause economic losses, and often the public service areas that are most challenged can be identified (e.g., transportation and solid waste disposal). But in most cases, the welfare loss due to underspending or overspending by the local government can only be guessed. Nor is it usually known how large the service boundaries should be in order to internalize these external effects.

GOVERNMENT STRUCTURE IN METROPOLITAN AREAS

Policy leaders have used these considerations, and politics, to decide on a governance arrangement for service delivery in metropolitan areas. Some have created very fragmented structures with strong decentralization of responsibility and power,

---

[5] An interesting review of the evidence for other Organisation for Economic Co-operation and Development (OECD) member countries comes to a similar conclusion (OECD 2006a).

whereas others have taken a more regional approach to service delivery. Almost all have tried to strike some balance between capturing the efficiencies of areawide government and maintaining local control. If there is a general conclusion that can be drawn about the choices actually made, it would seem to be that the sentiments for local control have largely held off the formation of metropolitan governments.

Bahl and Linn (1992) considered three basic approaches to metropolitan governance: jurisdictional fragmentation, which emphasizes home rule; functional fragmentation, which emphasizes technical efficiency; and metropolitan government, which emphasizes coordination and internalizing externalities. In practice, the advantages and disadvantages of various forms of metropolitan governance almost always play out in a compromise that attempts to capture the benefits of a favored approach while minimizing some of its costs. The result is mixed models of metropolitan governance.

Jurisdictional Fragmentation

Under a jurisdictional fragmentation approach, many general-purpose local governments operate in the same metropolitan area with some degree of independence in choosing their package of public services and their tax, user charge, and debt financing arrangements. In some cases, there also is an overlying metropolitan government, or regionwide special district, but the emphasis in service delivery is on the role of the lower-tier governments.

The advantage of the jurisdictional fragmentation model is that it keeps government close to the people. That is, the population of the fiscal decision-making unit is smaller than it would be if governance were areawide (as in the case of a metropolitan government). It also protects the position of the local government bureaucracy and local politicians by making them accountable to a relatively small constituency to whom they are known. However, the welfare gains from this home rule model will come at some cost: a failure to capture economies of scale, and operating within a set of boundaries that are arguably too small to internalize important external effects or to allow coordinated service delivery. Jurisdictional fragmentation also can lead to large fiscal disparities among local governments in the metropolitan area, since constituent local governments almost surely will have different expenditure needs and different financing and service delivery capacity.

INDUSTRIAL COUNTRIES

The jurisdictional fragmentation model best characterizes governance in most industrial countries. The traditions of home rule are particularly strong in the United States. Most urban services are delivered by municipalities, counties, and single-function special districts, that is, by the lower-level local governments. Regional planning is commonplace in the United States, but regional governance seems to have hit a dead end.

Strong traditions of home rule are also found in western Europe (Lotz 2006; OECD 2009a). The Copenhagen metropolitan region is an example of a jurisdictionally fragmented structure. Its 2.4 million population is governed by 45 municipalities, which are the dominant tier in terms of service delivery and taxation, and the national capital region. The capital region is an elected areawide government that has health services as its primary responsibility, but it has no taxing powers.

The population of the city of Paris is about 2 million, but another 6 million people live in the inner suburbs. Local governance in this agglomeration is by eighty municipalities, three departments, and numerous companies that provide public services. The Stockholm metropolitan region includes sixty-five municipalities and five counties (OECD 2006b). The Randstad (Holland) metropolitan region contains 50 municipalities (OECD 2007b).

MIDDLE- AND LOW-INCOME COUNTRIES

The local government code in the Philippines, enacted in the 1990s, reassigned expenditures among the central, provincial, and local governments in a manner "consistent with the decentralization theorem" (Manasan 2009, 338). In metropolitan Manila, the eleven cities and six municipalities are responsible for those services whose benefits are thought to not spill over local boundaries.[6] The Metropolitan Manila Development Authority, the overlapping areawide government, is responsible for planning and for delivering or coordinating services with a metrowide impact, such as transportation, flood control, sewerage, urban renewal, zoning, health, sanitation, and public safety.

The Mexico City metropolitan area is perhaps the textbook example of jurisdictional fragmentation. The metropolitan area is overlapped by the Federal District and its 16 municipal-like subunits, the states of Mexico and Hidalgo with their 59 municipalities, and the federal government. The Federal District has most of the fiscal functions of states and an elected assembly. It has no constitution and is directly subordinate to the federal government. All of the lower-tier local units in the two states have elected governments, but the boroughs within the Federal District have no taxing powers. The service delivery emphasis is with the states and the Federal District. There is very little coordination of service delivery within the metropolitan area and virtually no planning (OECD 2004a).

The Kolkata metropolitan area is governed by three municipal corporations (including Kolkata), thirty-eight municipalities, and twenty-four rural local governments. The municipal governments are dominant in terms of service provision and revenue raising. The Kolkata Metropolitan Development Authority, an areawide government, has responsibility for planning and carrying out major infrastructure development in the metropolitan area. The authority is a state agency, though some elected local representatives are on its board. It is financed by grants from the federal and state governments.

The São Paulo metropolitan region, with a population of about 18 million, comprises 39 municipal governments with no overlapping metropolitan government. Coordination among the local units is attempted by agreement or compact among these municipalities, by a number of agencies and councils, and by the state government. The core city in the metropolitan area more or less drives the fiscal health

---

[6] The major departure from the textbook assignment is elementary and secondary education, which remains with the central government (though the responsibility for construction of school buildings was assigned to the local government units).

of the region. In the first half of the 2000s, the municipality of São Paulo faced a fiscal crisis that limited the ability of the larger metropolitan area to deal with over-all problems (World Bank 2007). This reflects an important concern with jurisdictional fragmentation.

Functional Fragmentation

A second approach to metropolitan governance is functional fragmentation. Under this model, the delivery of a single function (or a related grouping of functions) is placed under the control of either a public company or a special district government. In fact, some degree of functional fragmentation exists in almost all metropolitan areas, but the structures vary widely, as does the degree of emphasis placed on the use of public companies.

A main advantage of functional fragmentation is that the autonomous agency is likely to be more technically efficient because it is specialized. Moreover, if the salary schedule is outside the normal civil service, the company may be able to attract and retain higher-quality workers. It also may be more efficient in its operations because it has a large enough area of coverage to capture economies of scale. Because it is usually the only entity in the urban area responsible for the function, the problems of coordination for that function are considerably less than under a jurisdictionally fragmented model. Finally, a public company or a special district government may have access to a dedicated revenue stream (e.g., an earmarked tax, a compulsory transfer from the city government, or user charges), and if well run, it has arguably a greater potential for debt finance than would a general-purpose local government.

The major drawback to this approach is that it is usually under less direct control of local voters than, for example, an elected municipal council. The extent of this disadvantage depends on how the board and the management of the autonomous agency are determined. Under one version of this approach, the city council(s) may have some membership on the board of the autonomous body, or even some ownership of the company. Under another model, the public service company might have an appointed independent board with no local government membership. A third approach would have the autonomous body function as an arm of the state or national government, with operational but not political autonomy. Neither of the latter two models protects accountability to a local constituency.

INDUSTRIAL COUNTRIES

Regional transportation is often provided by a separate agency that may or may not be linked to the municipal governments in the area. In the case of bus transit in Copenhagen, the coordinating body is a joint regional government/municipal government company. But in the New York metropolitan region the transportation authorities function more as state agencies than as local entities (Benjamin and Nathan 2001).

Another version of functional fragmentation assigns several areawide functions to a single government or agency. Sometimes these are related functions, such as transportation services and transportation planning, but sometimes they have only their regional coverage in common. The Greater Vancouver Regional District consolidated all functions provided previously by special districts, most notably hospitals, water and sewer, capital expenditures, and solid waste management. Finances are primarily from user charges (Bird and Slack 2004). The governing board of the regional district is elected municipal government officials, but municipalities can opt out of many of the district functions.

The water boards in the Randstad region in The Netherlands, with responsibility for flood control, water quality, and wastewater treatment, are local, independent public authorities that are democratically elected (OECD 2007b). The 11 boards do not have administrative boundaries that are coterminous with municipalities but do have taxing powers, including a water board charge and a pollution levy.

Functional fragmentation opens a number of new doors in terms of financing metropolitan services. Since the services delivered are often amenable to pricing (e.g., public transportation and garbage collection), user charges provide a base level of revenues. In other cases, the services are partially financed by compulsory transfers from the city budget, or they might be profitable enough to subsidize the city budget. In Stockholm, a holding company was organized to manage several city-owned companies that provide services such as public housing, real estate management, port operations, and water utilities. These public companies are in a surplus position and have been paying dividends to the city budget. The same is true in the case of two energy companies in which the city of Oslo holds equity. The city of Lausanne has fully incorporated the electricity company into its budget, and the company maintained a surplus position during the late 2000s.

In other cases, the local government subsidizes the public company. The city of Paris participates (or is part owner) in several enterprises that provide services ranging from transportation to social services. These are financed by user charges and by compulsory transfers from the city budget. The city of Madrid makes compulsory transfers to the two public companies that provide transportation services. In several Italian metropolitan cities, transfers to the companies providing transportation, waste collection and disposal, and water treatment services account for about 25 percent of total metropolitan city government expenditures.

MIDDLE- AND LOW-INCOME COUNTRIES

Special-purpose agencies can be especially important in managing and financing public service delivery in countries that are not industrialized. Because the special district status helps to separate the service delivery function from politics at the local government level, it can make management easier and arguably more professional, and it can be a route to a dedicated revenue stream and debt finance. Moreover, separation from the general-purpose local governments enhances the possibility for full cost recovery in providing the service. Probably the most important reason is that it provides for more efficient delivery of the service than under a fragmented assignment of expenditure responsibilities. The institutional arrangements vary greatly, from public companies with some local control to central and state government enterprises that operate within the metropolitan area.

One area where public companies can play an especially important role is in the provision of metropolitan transportation services. In metropolitan Mexico

City and in Rio de Janeiro, mass transit is the responsibility of many providers, and there is relatively little coordination on routes or fares. In metropolitan Bogotá, however, a public company was created to implement a comprehensive transportation plan that included the regulation of private providers of bus services. The transit operations are fully financed from user charges and a surcharge on the gasoline tax.

In some cases, special-purpose agencies can become a dominant player in local government finance. Webster (2000) points out that more than 65 percent of urban infrastructure expenditures in metropolitan Bangkok are by state enterprises, compared with approximately 25 percent by the national government and less than 10 percent by the city government. India makes use of parastatals, which are public companies operated by various departments within the state government. The functions of these agencies range from planning to roads to housing and slum redevelopment. The 21 parastatals operating within Mumbai account for a large share of total infrastructure spending in the metropolitan area. A joint venture company owned by the city of Buenos Aires and the province of Buenos Aires is responsible for the disposal of solid waste.

Public companies also are important in delivering services in the metropolitan areas in transition countries. For example, the city of Riga provides services through 42 companies in which it holds ownership or has an equity stake. Most of these companies are self-supporting, but the transport enterprise claims about 10 percent of the operating budget of the city. In Zagreb, most capital spending (and some current spending) is the responsibility of a holding company that was created following the merger of 22 municipal companies. The city of Zagreb uses more than 15 percent of its budget for subsidy payments to the holding company. In other eastern European metropolitan cities, such as Sofia, Budapest, and Odessa, it is often more a matter of the city supporting the loss-making activity of a single company, notably transportation.

Metropolitan Government

Under the metropolitan government model, most general services are provided by an areawide metropolitan government.[7] In theory, the metropolitan government would be elected and would have significant powers to regulate service delivery and financing. In practice, most areawide governments share fiscal powers with lower tiers of government or publicly owned companies.

The significant advantage of the pure metropolitan government approach is built-in coordination in the delivery of functions. This has the potential for better resource allocation compared with dividing responsibility for local services among multiple municipalities and special-purpose governments. The metropolitan government form also offers greater potential for equalization because the quality of local services is not tied to the wealth of each local jurisdiction, as it is with jurisdictional fragmentation. Finally, because factors are less mobile across than within metropolitan areas, there are more choices for efficient taxation (Bahl and Bird, 2008).

---

[7] For discussions of metropolitan-area governance, see Bahl and Linn (1992), Bird and Slack (2004), Jouve and Lefevre (2002), OECD (2006a), and Slack (2007).

On the other hand, the metropolitan form of governance diminishes the power of local voters to influence the local budget. In effect, the election of the local council is replaced by election of local representatives to the more distant metropolitan council. A second drawback is that metropolitan governance often brings intergovernmental conflict. If lower-tier local governments exist under a metropolitan arrangement, they may resist the leadership (and especially the dominance) of the metropolitan government. When a function is shared between the metropolitan government and a higher-level state (province) or federal government, as is often the case, another set of conflicts may arise.

Another drawback is that the boundaries of the metropolitan government may not be large enough to fully capture the benefits of areawide governance. In this situation, one of the most significant advantages of metropolitan government may be substantially diminished. This problem might be resolved by annexations or consolidations or by appointing a commission to redraw jurisdictional boundaries, as was done in South Africa (Ahmad 2003; Cameron 2005).

INDUSTRIAL COUNTRIES

Toronto comes close to being a true metropolitan government. The former two-tier metropolitan government was replaced with a single-tier metropolitan city in 1998 (OECD 2009b; Slack 2000). All local government functions, including those previously invested in special districts and underlying municipalities, rest with the new metropolitan government. Following the amalgamation, the provincial government established the Greater Toronto Services Board to oversee regional transit. This board has no legislative authority.

There are other examples of areawide governments in Organisation for Economic Co-operation and Development (OECD) member countries. In Madrid, the dominant local government in the metropolitan area is the Community of Madrid, which is seen by some as being about the same size as the functional urban region of Madrid (OECD 2007a). Underneath the community are 179 municipalities, including the city of Madrid, which account for about half of the population of the metropolitan area. The functions of the community, however, are considerably broader than those of the municipalities.

The Tokyo metropolitan government has responsibility for service provision to a population of about 12 million persons (Togo 1995; Tokyo Metropolitan Government 2012). It has prefecture (state) status in Japan's intergovernmental fiscal system. Below the metropolitan government are twenty-three special wards in the core area, in addition to twenty-six cities, five towns, and one village. All have elected assemblies. The special wards carry out service delivery for designated functions on behalf of the metropolitan government, while the municipalities are general-purpose local governments.

The Greater London Authority was created in 1999 as a senior level of government in metropolitan London, with provision to elect a mayor and, separately, an assembly. The authority has responsibility for a number of functions, including transport, economic development, land use planning, environmental protection, and police. About 80 percent of expenditures are made for transport and police. It is financed by central government grants (63 percent), user charges (20 percent), and property taxes (10 percent) (Bird and Slack 2004). In part because resources are so limited, it would be inaccurate to classify London as a strong metropolitan government. The underlying 23 boroughs are independent of the authority and provide basic urban services such as education, housing, social services, street cleaning, and roads. There is a clear separation of expenditure responsibilities between the higher and lower tiers of government in the metropolitan area.

MIDDLE- AND LOW-INCOME COUNTRIES

Before 1994, Cape Town comprised 61 local government entities. This number was reduced to six general-purpose governments and a metropolitan authority in 1996, and finally to a single local authority, the "unicity" of Cape Town, in 2000 (OECD 2008a). The gross inequity in services provided and the need for local input and coordination of areawide services were driving forces behind the consolidation. The present expenditure assignments mostly square with what theory would suggest: functions with large external effects and fixed costs are assigned to the center and the provinces; services with a smaller benefit zone are assigned to the local governments. When Cape Town became a metropolitan city with no lower-tier governments, it inherited all local government functions. In practice, most city expenditures are made for water, sewerage and drainage, and administration. Social services are a shared function with the province.

A different model was adopted in Manila, where the Metropolitan Manila Development Authority exists to manage areawide functions, while the local government units are responsible for local functions. The local government units (cities and municipalities) are governed by elected councils, while the chair of the authority is appointed by the president and its membership is prescribed by law. The formation of the authority (and its predecessor bodies) was a result of the concern for delivery of areawide services and the perception of government that the well-being of metropolitan Manila is a national priority. The history of metropolitan governance in Manila has been one of a struggle for power between the metropolitan government and the lower-level local governments.

Istanbul is a special case because the metropolitan area has both a provincial and a metropolitan city government. Beneath the metropolitan municipality are 73 local-level municipalities. The general pattern of assignment is much like that in other countries: higher-level governments plan and deliver services that are thought to have large external effects, while local (metropolitan) governments deliver services that are thought to have a smaller benefit zone. The result in Istanbul is a highly centralized system, with central ministries and their provincial arms accounting for about 90 percent of public spending in the metropolitan area (OECD 2008b).

Despite the checkered history of success with metropolitan governance, one might make the case that there are some prospects for its success in low- and middle-income countries. One reason is just inertia: in some cases, areawide governments were in place and their boundaries simply grew with their populations. Another reason is that, in many countries, democratically elected local government is relatively new, home rule traditions are much less entrenched, and the opposition to metropolitan government is less unyielding. Finally, the weak level of infrastructure in place and the strains placed on city finances by migration may make areawide government an easier sell.

COSTS AND BENEFITS OF VARIOUS GOVERNMENT STRUCTURES

Most of the normative discussion about government structure in metropolitan areas centers on how various forms of governance and fiscal structures match up with the economic efficiency criteria. But there are other issues to consider, including equity, coordination, and, in some models, the cost of providing services under different structures. There also is more to be said about issues of local autonomy and about the political economy of choosing a metropolitan government structure.

The Cost of Service Delivery

Advocates of metropolitan government often try to make the case that some combination of scale economies and elimination of duplication will lead to a lower cost of government. This was a principal argument made in selling the metropolitan government in Toronto in the late 1990s. In fact, however, there is no convincing evidence that one form of government is more costly than another.

There are several reasons that one might expect a fragmented governance model to be a more costly way to deliver services. This governmental arrangement usually does not capture scale economies, and it leads to costly duplication of services and bureaucracy. For example, in the case of public management, each government must establish a general services staff, support an elected council, and provide facilities for the delivery of services. In theory, governance on an areawide basis could eliminate much of this duplication. Slack (2000) reports such results in the creation of the new metropolitan government in Toronto. The number of departments in the new city was reduced from fifty-two (in the seven former municipalities) to six; the number of divisions, from 206 to 37; the number of executive positions, from 381 to 154; and the number of management positions, from 1,837 to 1,204.

On the other hand, there also is good reason to think that an areawide approach to governance will be a higher-cost solution. Metropolitan government may lead to an equalization of service levels within the region but possibly at a level near the best that was provided prior to the consolidation. It is not clear that the reduction in duplicated efforts due to consolidation will offset the cost of "leveling up." Toronto is a case of consolidation where the harmonization of wages and salaries, as well as the harmonization of service levels, resulted in a cost increase rather than a cost reduction (Slack 2007). This pattern also was observed in the aftermath of government consolidations in the United States in the 1960s and 1970s (Bahl and Campbell 1976). Public companies also may drive up costs if they are able to attract higher-quality (and more expensive) personnel, though this higher cost may lead to better-quality services. Finally, areawide governments are monopolists and miss out on the cost-cutting advantages that might come from competition in a fragmented government setting.

Interjurisdiction Equity

Fiscal disparities within a metropolitan area are likely to be most pronounced in a jurisdictionally fragmented system. A metropolitan government would seem more conducive to the goals of uniformity of service levels. As is discussed below, however, the path to removing fiscal disparities is much more complicated than this.

INDUSTRIAL COUNTRIES

The existence of a metropolitan government would eliminate jurisdiction boundaries. The result should be uniformity in service levels. But will this occur? The political process that often protects the politically powerful under a fragmented system may continue to work under a metropolitan government, and some neighborhoods will continue to be better serviced than others. If the form of metropolitan governance chosen is the weaker version, a jurisdictional fragmentation with an overlying metropolitan government, then equalization possibilities will be limited to those services provided on an areawide basis or through vertical programs.

Areawide government is not the only route to reducing fiscal disparities. In countries that have stayed with the jurisdictional fragmentation model, equalization has been pursued with intrametropolitan transfers from richer to poorer jurisdictions. For example, intermunicipal transfers of tax revenues are required in Copenhagen (OECD 2009a), Stockholm (OECD 2006b), and Madrid (OECD 2007a). In Tokyo, metropolitan government tax collections are allocated among the 23 special wards in the core city according to the difference between their revenue-raising potential and their estimated expenditure needs. The metropolitan city in Busan, Korea, allocates a portion of its tax revenues (on a judgmental basis) to subunits in order to reduce disparities in their fiscal base (OECD 2004b).

Another strategy for equalization of fiscal capacity is through national- or provincial-level fiscal equalization transfers. The U.S. states use this approach to equalization with differential transfers to rich and poor school districts. The Netherlands and Norway accomplish a similar equalization outcome by giving local governments little power to tax, thereby reducing the fiscal advantage of higher-income jurisdictions.

MIDDLE- AND LOW-INCOME COUNTRIES

Klink (2008) points out significant disparities between richer municipalities in the core and those on the outskirts of metropolitan Buenos Aires and São Paulo. He argues that these disparities will continue to grow because the poorer local governments lack sufficient voice to capture a greater share of funds for themselves. A striking example of extremes of fiscal disparities within metropolitan areas is the case of Abidjan, where the average per capita expenditure of the three wealthiest of the ten communes was 49 times the average for the three poorest communes (Stren 2007).

The metropolitan government approach to reducing disparities seems to have been effective in Cape Town. Before 1994, the Cape Town local government comprised 19 white local authorities, six white rural councils, 29 colored management committees, and seven black local authorities. By 2000, this fragmented system, which had delivered a highly unequal level of services, was replaced by a single metropolitan government. The new unicity government produced a rationalization plan in order to create uniform standards of services across the new metropolitan region (OECD 2008a). At the same time, the metropolitan government invested capital to extend water distribution, electrification, and sanitation to disadvantaged areas. Still, equity has been only slowly gained, and significant fiscal- and service-level disparities still exist within the metropolitan region (Jaglin 2004).

Interjurisdictional fiscal disparities were not the primary reason for the creation of a metropolitan layer of government in Manila (Manasan and Mercado 1999). In fact, this may be one of the rare cases where metropolitan government exacerbated disparities. The Metropolitan Manila Development Authority established during the Marcos regime had broad powers to establish and administer programs and provide services. It was an appointed body, but it had legislative powers. It could levy taxes, it received a share of the national government transfer program to local governments (the Internal Revenue Allotment), and it received a 45 percent share of property tax collections by local governments within the metropolitan area. In addition, local governments were required to contribute 20 percent of their regular income to the metropolitan authority. In effect, the first version of metropolitan governance in metro Manila emasculated the local governments. Moreover, a fixed-percentage contribution from each local government, and a fixed-percentage claim on property taxes collected in each jurisdiction, almost guaranteed that the new system would increase fiscal disparities. Later reforms shifted the balance of power back toward the cities and municipalities, but the driving factor appears to be more politics than the desire for more equalization.

Lower-level governments in Istanbul must transfer 35 percent of their revenues to the Istanbul metropolitan municipality to finance services provided by the metropolitan government. Of the remainder, an additional 10 percent of local resources must be transferred to metropolitan Istanbul for transportation investments.

There are significant fiscal disparities between the Federal District of Mexico and the other local governments operating within the Mexico City metropolitan area (OECD 2004a). Per capita spending in the federal district is 75 percent higher than that in Hidalgo state and 42 percent higher than that in Mexico state. The reasons for this disparity are the higher level of economic development of the Federal District and the significantly greater taxing capacity that it has. Since there is no metropolitan government, fiscal equalization is left to the federal and state governments. The intergovernmental transfer system in Mexico, however, has no equalization transfers. A similar situation holds in Buenos Aires, where the capital district spends 40 percent more for education on a per student basis than do the surrounding suburban jurisdictions. The corresponding city-suburb disparity in per capita total expenditures in Mumbai is 60 percent.

Coordination

Public service delivery programs are not well coordinated in many metropolitan areas (Bahl 2011; OECD 2006a; Slack 2007). Even adjacent local jurisdictions may have different ideas about the right level of services to be delivered (e.g., fire protection or policing); traffic and mass transit may not be synched, and ideas about good land use may vary greatly. One reason may be competition among local governments, which can lead to efficiency gains (Tiebout 1956) but also to higher costs, because some economies of size are forgone, as well as to uncompensated spillover costs and irritated consumers who must use these uncoordinated services. Vertical coordination between the higher-level metropolitan government and the lower-tier municipalities also can be very difficult. Sector ministries of higher-level governments deliver services within the urban area and often take little account of local government plans and practices.

The approaches taken to dealing with this issue include establishment of areawide governments, assumption of expenditure responsibility by higher-level governments, voluntary or mandatory cooperation schemes, and simply ignoring the problem.

INDUSTRIAL COUNTRIES

In some U.S. cities, various voluntary schemes have been tried in an attempt to improve service coordination. These include informal arrangements such as joint planning committees and interlocal agreements to cover such functions as police patrols and fire protection services (Chen and Thurmaier 2009). Where areawide government has been tried in the United States, it is usually in the form of single-function special districts.

Some Canadian metropolitan areas have maintained an emphasis on home rule by local jurisdictions but have introduced a mechanism for coordination of service delivery. Metropolitan Vancouver includes 21 municipalities and a population of about 2 million and has a strong tradition of local government autonomy. In 1967 the Greater Vancouver Regional District was created by local initiative to coordinate the delivery of services with regionwide benefits, including water and sewer, capital spending, and solid waste management. It is governed by its member municipalities, which can freely reject its recommendations and even decline to be involved in district functions. Some have argued that it is not likely to succeed in coordinating services in the long run (Smith 2009).

Stockholm authorizes several instruments for interlocal cooperation, ranging from contracting for services to forming a "federation" for joint provision of services and a regional development council for coordination of regional development work and infrastructure planning (OECD 2006b). Denmark replaced a voluntary scheme for coordinating metropolitan services among municipalities in Copenhagen with a directly elected regional government that has the mandate to do comprehensive planning. The regional government has no taxing powers and limited service delivery responsibilities, and it covers an area that is less than the functional metropolitan area. Nevertheless, OECD (2009a) sees the capital region as becoming the vehicle for coordination in metropolitan Copenhagen.

The metropolitan government arrangement in Toronto offers the greatest potential for coordination of services provided in the metropolitan area because a bottom tier of local government is no longer in place. Still, the problem of coordinating service delivery with the provincial government remains. Moreover, the metropolitan government does not cover all local governments in the functional metropolitan area, and as Sanction (2009, 236) puts it, "In short, all the difficult issues associated with metropolitan growth were taking place outside the new city's borders."

MIDDLE- AND LOW-INCOME COUNTRIES

In general, the governance in most developing and transition countries is more centralized than that in industrialized countries. Thus, it is not surprising that the most problematic coordination issue is conflict between governments in the metropolitan area, which take a local view, and sector ministries, which are more bound by national objectives. In the case of Manila, for example, some have argued that the ministries in charge are more concerned with their sectoral priorities than with serving the needs of the metropolis per se (Manasan and Mercado 1999).

The general approach to resolving conflicts between levels of government is some sort of intergovernmental arrangement where the various levels negotiate to resolve the issues. For example, in Cape Town, the law provides a framework for dispute resolution. Still, important unresolved conflicts remain regarding responsibilities for certain functions of government, particularly transportation, infrastructure, housing, land use planning, and policy implementation (OECD 2008a).

In Mexico City, the coordination problem is complicated by the number of layers of government involved, the number of local governments, and the presence of two states and a national capital district. It is further complicated by disagreements among the subnational governments about the uncompensated costs they impose on one another and by the strong presence of political parties with different views (Bird and Slack 2004). The response has been the creation of a number of coordinating and planning bodies, regional trusts, and federal programs. OECD (2004a) argues that the results so far have not led to much coordination.

The metropolitan municipality of Istanbul does have lower-tier membership on its council, but there are 73 participating lower-tier governments. In this situation, dialogue with any single local government and reaching a general consensus become very difficult.

Arguably, the most important vehicle for coordination among governments on matters of service delivery is a metropolitan government. But even this can be a problematic solution. The metropolitan government in Cape Town carries out a five-year management plan that links the municipal budget to the sector plans for transportation and other infrastructure. However, the metropolitan government has no jurisdiction over parastatals or sectoral programs of higher-level government ministries.

Home Rule

Local voter influence is strongest under a jurisdictionally fragmented system. The problem becomes how to maintain some degree of local (even neighborhood) involvement in fiscal decision making while expanding jurisdiction boundaries to capture economies of scale and deal with externalities.

INDUSTRIAL COUNTRIES

Amalgamation to an areawide government will lessen the influence of local voters over local budgets. It also may result in some voters being alienated from government. In the case of Toronto's metropolitan government, the heretofore lower-tier municipality budgets simply disappeared, and voters from smaller municipalities were right in feeling that they had less voice. Slack (2000) reports that for one municipality in what is now metropolitan Toronto, the elected representation changed from 7,300 people per councilor before the reform to 54,214 afterward. The corresponding numbers for the city of Toronto were from 41,850 to 54,214.

This said, various fixes for decentralization in metropolitan governance can be used to claw back some home rule features. The Vancouver arrangement of lower-tier control of the regional government is one example. A two-tier structure of governance as in Montreal is another approach. The election of decentralized districts within the larger urban government, as in Madrid, Amsterdam, and Tokyo, is another.

MIDDLE- AND LOW-INCOME COUNTRIES

In some poor countries, home rule is a luxury that might not be affordable. Government structure in the large cities is driven more by technical efficiency and possibilities for cost recovery and more effective maintenance of the asset stock. These objectives point toward metropolitan governance, special districts or public companies, or central government responsibility as the best arrangements for delivering services.

To make some provision for local voice, arrangements have been institutionalized for community inputs on budget decisions. In Cape Town, there are no political jurisdictions below the metropolitan government level, but 23 subcouncils have been established and empowered to present development plans. This deconcentration approach allows the metropolitan city to demonstrate that it recognizes the need for decentralized decision making without giving up much power.

In the Philippines, elected local government units remain as a lower layer in the metropolitan structure. Beneath the local government level there is a provision for a *barangay* government with some fiscal powers, thereby providing another layer of decentralization.

Political Economy Considerations

Important political agendas and bureaucratic politics must be addressed in designing the structure of service delivery and finance in metropolitan areas. Political economy considerations are often the determining factor on metropolitan government structure. The stronger the local government units in urban areas and the more wedded they are to home rule, the more difficult it will be to create and sustain a strong metropolitan government. And, the more dominant the central and state governments, the weaker will be both the local and the metropolitan-area governments.

INDUSTRIAL COUNTRIES

In the case of Toronto, the metropolitan government was put in place by a provincial act. It was hotly opposed by some citizen groups, mostly on grounds of losses in home rule (Slack 2000). To gain some favor with voters, there also was a promise that the amalgamation proposed would save money by eliminating many "duplicate" local government jobs. Elsewhere in Canada, however, the strength of sentiment for home rule was not overcome, even with provincial involvement in enacting the legislation. In fact, the provincial government in British Columbia went to some lengths to make the point that restructuring Vancouver was not about creating a new level of government (Sanction 2009). The concept of the Greater Vancouver Regional District was sold as a vehicle for better coordination of services. The Quebec legislature established metropolitan communities for Montreal and Quebec City. The Montreal community is made up of the councils of Montreal and Longueuil and 61 other municipalities.

Politics also has led to the dismantling of metropolitan governments. Grimaldos and Ferrer (1999) cite the conflict between the socialist majority in the metropolitan government and the autonomous government of Catalonia as leading to the abolition of the Barcelona metropolitan government. Politics have deadlocked the discussion in Italy to a point where even agencies for intermunicipal cooperation have failed.

The United States represents perhaps the extreme case of opposition to metropolitan government. Hundreds of proposals for governmental consolidation have reached the referendum stage over the past 20 years, but only 34 had succeeded as of 2008 (Hall 2009; Leland and Thurmaier 2005). Boundary changes and changes in the distribution of political power are a tough sell in the United States.

MIDDLE- AND LOW-INCOME COUNTRIES

Governance and finance in low- and middle-income countries are more centralized in general, but this pattern has been challenged by democratization and the growing voice of elected metropolitan-area political leaders. Another consideration is that the post of mayor or governor of a large metropolitan area is high profile and can be a good platform for some who aspire to national office. Especially when the local leader is from an opposition political party, the turmoil can spill over into counterproductive intergovernmental conflicts.

In Mexico City, a political tug-of-war is played out between the federal government and the state governors within the metropolitan area. Matters have become more complicated with the end of one-party rule.

The history in Manila has been a clash between the municipal government units and the appointed metropolitan government. During the Marcos period, the metropolitan government was stronger in terms of its regulatory powers and even held a claim on a significant part of the revenues of the local government units. In the post-Marcos period, the balance of power has swung back toward the local governments in terms of both service delivery autonomy and the claim on revenues (Laquian 2002).

CONCLUSIONS: HOW TO MOVE FORWARD?

Removing the constraints to providing an adequate level of public services in metropolitan areas is a subject that will continue to demand more attention from policy makers, particularly those in middle- and low-income countries. The population growth of urban areas, their importance in the national economy, and the large unmet demand for public services will force this. But reform in this area will not be for the politically faint-hearted. Addressing these issues will require considering whether metropolitan-area governance and finance should be structured differently from the rest of the country.

The Problem

Part of the problem with metropolitan governance is the limited resources available to invest in expanding and maintaining the infrastructure and to support basic social services. This might lead to increased revenue mobilization by local governments, which might be better done under an areawide governance arrangement. But the problem can also be helped by reducing some of the costs of service delivery. This would lead to reforms that address the economies of scale that go uncaptured in many fragmented metropolitan areas and to reforms that can reduce burdensome spillover costs, such as traffic congestion and pollution.

The solution to this problem, or at least part of it, might be to organize metropolitan governance in a more efficient way, that is, to move toward an areawide governance model. But this model would move governance another step away from local control and would impose an efficiency cost on the local population. The dilemma facing those who would change government structures is the trade-off between benefits inherent in metropolitan governance and the loss in home rule this would bring.

The underlying problem in metropolitan governance and finance is the unrealistic goal of marrying two very different spatial units. The functional economic region has boundaries that are informal and always changing, as one would expect of a labor market area. The "champion" of making the region a government entity is the planner who sees great efficiency and equity gains from some form of regional service delivery. The other spatial unit, the local government, has fixed boundaries. The champions of local government are elected officials and voters, both of whom want to maintain control over services provided in the local area. It seems unlikely that these two very different actors will come together easily in support of a general-purpose regionwide government. The issue is even more complicated by the technocratic goals of special districts or public companies whose service boundaries may not be coterminous with either the metropolitan area (labor market area) or the general-purpose local governments. It will take participation by a higher-level government to get around these special interests, though higher-level governments will themselves have vested interests.

The public policy solution lies in finding a way to deliver some services with a degree of local control and financing, while delivering others on a regionwide basis and with a broader finance base. All governments will likely identify with a model that produces better prospects for long-run economic growth and better infrastructure services. Local governments can be moved by strategies that give them some voice and a promise to hold down taxes. But none of these arguments seems to be convincing when it comes to moving basic services away from the local government level or, more drastic yet, abolishing local units of government. The practice shows that governance and finance in some metropolitan areas have moved toward this solution, but almost no one would declare that the delivery of regional services is properly coordinated.

How to Design a Reform

The reform of metropolitan governance and finance in low- and middle-income countries is a relatively new frontier in policy analysis. Economics, politics, history, and culture all play an important role in deciding on the best arrangement for metropolitan governance and finance, so it is not surprising that many different versions are in practice. Theory would have us think of governments and perhaps voters sitting down to decide who should do what, as if the game had just begun. In fact, the game began long ago, and many subnational governments are locked into expenditure assignment and financing "entitlements." These entitlements are not easily discarded just because an urban area has grown rapidly, because two urban areas have grown together to become a single labor market area, or because the current structure of government has become unwieldy. However, the time for wholesale rethinking may be close at hand in many low-income countries.

The place to begin the reform process is with a comprehensive fiscal review for the metropolitan area. This will be new ground for many metropolitan regions, where the status quo on governance is accepted and where there is often a willingness to stray only so far, such as appointing regional advisory commissions. Mostly, there is a willingness to live within the fiscal regime set by the central or state government.

This comprehensive review might include the following:

- A rethinking of the structure of government that will deliver services. While this seems a daunting undertaking, one might point to the experiences in Toronto and Cape Town, where exactly this was done.
- An analysis of options for the division of expenditure assignments among the tiers of government.
- A review of revenue-raising choices, including local and areawide taxes and user charges and intergovernmental transfers.
- Consideration of borrowing powers of metropolitan local governments, and perhaps a separate regulatory framework for these governments.
- Integration of alternative fiscal structures for the comprehensive development plan and land use plan for the metropolitan area.

The committee that develops this plan must include the important stakeholders in the metropolitan area. Without the local government's inputs and eventually approval at some level, fiscal reform cannot move forward. However, most low- and middle-income countries are centralized, so the fiscal review and action plan would have to be led by the central government (or perhaps state government in the case of some federations). It is quite possible that the recommendation will be to enact a completely different fiscal regime than exists for other local governments in the country.

REFERENCES

Ahmad, Junaid. 2003. Creating incentives for fiscal discipline in the new South Africa. In *Fiscal decentralization and the challenge of hard budget constraints*, ed. Jonathan Rodden, Gunnar Eskeland, and Jennie Litvack, 325–352. Cambridge, MA: MIT Press.

Bahl, Roy. 2011. Financing metropolitan cities. In *Local government finance: The challenges of the 21st century*. Barcelona: United Cities and Local Governments.

Bahl, Roy, and Richard Bird. 2008. Subnational taxes in developing countries: The way forward. *Public Budgeting and Finance* 28(4):1–25.

Bahl, Roy, and Alan Campbell. 1976. The implications of local government reform: Efficiency, equity and administrative dimensions. In *State and local government: The political economy of reform*, ed. Alan Campbell and Roy Bahl. New York: Free Press.

Bahl, Roy, and Johannes Linn. 1992. *Urban public finance in developing countries*. New York: Oxford University Press.

Benjamin, Gerald, and Richard P. Nathan. 2001. *Regionalism and realism: A study of governments in the New York metropolitan area*. Washington, DC: Brookings Institution.

Bird, Richard, and Enid Slack. 2004. Fiscal aspects of metropolitan governance. ITP Paper No. 0401. Toronto: Joseph T. Rotman School of Management, University of Toronto.

Cameron, Robert. 2005. Metropolitan restructuring (and more restructuring) in South Africa. *Public Administration and Development* 25:329–339.

Chen, Yu-Che, and Kurt Thurmaier. 2009. Interlocal agreements as collaborations: An empirical investigation of impetuses, norms, and success. *American Review of Public Administration* 39(5):536–552.

Fox, William F., and Tami Gurley. 2006. Will consolidation improve sub-national governments? Policy Research Working Paper No. 3913. Washington, DC: World Bank.

Grimaldos, Angel Simón, and Conxa Aguirre Ferrer. 1999. The Barcelona metropolitan area. In *The government of world cities: The future of the metro model*, ed. Laurence J. Sharpe, 33–56. Chichester, U.K.: John Wiley and Sons.

Hall, John Stuart. 2009. Who will govern American metropolitan regions, and how? In *Governing metropolitan regions in the 21st century*, ed. Don Phares, 54–78. London: Sharpe.

Jaglin, Sylvy. 2004. Water delivery and metropolitan institution building in Cape Town: The problems of urban integration. *Urban Forum* 15(3):231–249.

Jouve, Bernard, and Christian Lefevre, eds. 2002. *Local power, territory and institutions in European metropolitan regions*. London: Frank Cass.

Klink, Jeroen. 2008. Recent perspectives on metropolitan organization, functions and governance. In *Governing the metropolis: Principles and cases*, ed. Eduardo Rojas, Juan Cuadrado-Roura, and Jose Miguel Fernandez Guell, 77–136. Washington, DC: Inter-American Development Bank and Rockefeller Center for Latin American Studies.

Laquian, Aprodicio. 2002. Metro Manila: Peoples participation and social inclusion in a city of villages. In *Urban governance around the world*, ed. Blair Ruble, Richard Stren, Joseph Tulchin, and Diana Varat. Washington, DC: Woodrow Wilson International Center for Scholars.

Leland, Susan, and Kurt Thurmaier. 2005. When efficiency is unbelievable: Normative lessons from 30 years of city-county consolidations. *Public Administration Review* 65(4):475–489.

Lotz, Jorgen. 2006. Local government organization and finance: Nordic countries. In *Local governance in industrial countries*, ed. Anwar Shah, 223–264. Washington, DC: World Bank.

Manasan, Rosario. 2009. Local public finance in the Philippines—Balancing autonomy and accountability. In *Decentralization policies in Asian development*, ed. Shinichi Ichimura and Roy Bahl, 333–388. Singapore: World Scientific Press.

Manasan, Rosario, and Ruben Mercado. 1999. Governance and urban development: Case study of metro Manila. Discussion Paper No. 99-03. Manila: Philippine Institute for Development Studies.

Martinez-Vazquez, Jorge, and Robert McNab. 2001. Cross-country evidence on the relationship between fiscal decentralization, inflation, and growth. In *Proceedings of the ninety-third annual conference on taxation*, 42–47. Baltimore, MD: National Tax Association.

Mohanty, P. K., B. M. Misra, Rajan Goyal, and P. D. Jeromi. 2007. Municipal finance in India: An assessment. Study No. 28. Mumbai: Development Research Group, Department of Economic Analysis and Policy, Reserve Bank of India.

Oates, Wallace. 1972. *Fiscal federalism.* New York: Harcourt Brace Jovanovich.

OECD. 2004a. OECD territorial reviews: Mexico City. Paris.

———. 2004b. OECD territorial reviews: Busan. Paris.

———. 2006a. OECD territorial reviews: Competitive cities in the global economy. Paris.

———. 2006b. OECD territorial reviews: Stockholm, Sweden. Paris.

———. 2007a. OECD territorial reviews: Madrid, Spain. Paris.

———. 2007b. OECD territorial reviews: Randstadt Holland, Netherlands. Paris.

———. 2008a. OECD territorial reviews: Cape Town, South Africa. Paris.

———. 2008b. OECD territorial reviews: Istanbul, Turkey. Paris.

———. 2009a. Copenhagen, Denmark, OECD Territorial Reviews. Paris.

———. 2009b. OECD territorial reviews: Toronto, Canada. Paris.

Sanction, Andrew. 2009. A review of Canadian metropolitan regions: Governance and government. In *Governing metropolitan regions in the 21st century*, ed. Don Phares, 221–236. London: Sharpe.

Slack, Enid. 2000. A preliminary assessment of the new city of Toronto. *Canadian Journal of Regional Science* 23(1):13–29.

———. 2007. Managing the coordination of service delivery in metropolitan cities: The role of metropolitan governance. Policy Research Working Paper No. 4317. Washington, DC: World Bank.

Smith, Patrick J. 2009. Even greater Vancouver: Metropolitan morphing in Canada's third-largest city region. In *Governing metropolitan regions in the 21st century*, ed. Don Phares, 237–263. London: Sharpe.

Stren, Richard. 2007. Urban governance in developing countries: Experiences and challenges. In *Governing cities in a global era: Urban innovation, competition and democratic reform*, ed. Robin Hambleton and Jill Gross, 57–69. New York: Palgrave Macmillan.

Tiebout, Charles. 1956. A pure theory of local expenditures. *Journal of Political Economy* 64(5):416–424.

Togo, Hisatake. 1995. The metropolitan strategies of Tokyo: Toward the restoration of balanced growth. In *The government of world cities: The future of the metro model*, ed. Laurence J. Sharpe, 177–202. Chichester, U.K.: Wiley.

Tokyo Metropolitan Government. 2012. Tokyo—city profile and government. www.metro.tokyo.jp/ENGLISH/PROFILE/index.htm

Webster, D. 2000. Financing city building: The Bangkok case discussion paper. Palo Alto, CA: Asia Pacific Research Center, Institute for International Studies, Stanford University.

World Bank. 2007. Brazil São Paulo: Inputs for a sustainable competitive city strategy. Report No. 37324-BR. Washington, DC: World Bank.

INSTITUTIONS AND POLITICS OF METROPOLITAN MANAGEMENT $\qquad$ 5

INDER SUD AND SERDAR YILMAZ

As discussed in chapter 2, metropolitan cities play a vital role in economic development. In most Organisation of Economic Co-operation and Development member countries and in the dynamic emerging economies, they account for a significant share of gross domestic product and jobs and have higher labor productivity, economic growth rates, and incomes compared with national averages. Metropolitan cities benefit from a diversified economic base, strong innovative capacity, and a high level of skill among residents. While agglomeration economies may initially drive the growth of metropolitan cities, sustaining the comparative advantage of cities as the engines of growth requires that they provide adequate infrastructure and a business-friendly regulatory environment to maintain their competitiveness as attractive destinations for private investment. In an era of growing mobility of skilled and specialized workers, both within and across national borders, the metropolitan cities must also provide a good quality of life that attracts an educated and skilled workforce. Finally, metropolitan cities must deal with problems of exclusion and poverty that tend to accompany growth.

However, few cities in the developing world are able to discharge all these functions effectively. Infrastructure deficiencies are evident in most of the metropolitan cities, and few have been able to deal with the issues of social equity as evidenced by the continued prevalence and even growth of slums and squatter settlements (see chapter 14).

A lack of financial resources is cited by most city managers in developing countries as the principal cause of the unsatisfactory state of affairs, and this is certainly an important factor, as discussed elsewhere in this book. However, inadequate finance is only a part of the story. An even more important factor is weakness in metropolitan institutions that are unable to mobilize the necessary resources or to plan and deliver services effectively to the growing population.

In many countries, the institutional weaknesses of local governments, including those of high-population metropolitan cities, stem from the legal/regulatory environment. Only a handful of countries specifically recognize local governments in their constitutions as organs of governance, and even there, how they should function has not been specified.[1] In most cases, the local governance structure has developed by trial and error, largely through laws and regulations passed by the higher levels of government. Several developing countries have also undertaken reforms in recent years aimed at defining the functions and powers of local governments. While many such efforts emphasize efficiency as the ultimate goal, the increasing voice of the people is becoming an equally important objective in most countries. This chapter draws on the experiences of 11 large metropolitan cities to suggest possible directions in the development of metropolitan institutions in developing countries.

The institutional design for effective metropolitan management rests on three interrelated and mutually reinforcing pillars: autonomy of action; accountability for performance; and capacity to perform the functions. The autonomy of action is largely determined by a city government's charter that defines its powers vis-à-vis the higher level(s) of government. Capacity of the city government is determined by its legislative and management structure and how the two are related. Accountability is determined by the nature of the city-central relations (upward accountability) and the voice the citizens have in the functioning of the city and in demanding performance (downward accountability).

CENTRAL-CITY RELATIONSHIP: HOW MUCH AUTONOMY?

There is wide agreement that cities can perform their functions effectively only if they are given substantial autonomy in managing their affairs: planning, mobilizing, and allocating resources and procuring goods and services. This is based on the theory that the closer the government is to the people, the better it works (Stigler 1957). This assertion has been increasingly borne out by experiences in many industrialized countries, where local governments now enjoy substantial autonomy, albeit with considerable variation in the specific functions assigned to the local government, the financing mechanisms for services, and the legal framework underpinning roles and responsibilities (Shah 2006a).

In terms of functions, cities in virtually all industrialized countries are responsible for providing what Shah (2006b) terms "property-oriented" services, such as water, drainage, transport, garbage collection, environment protection, and land use planning. In many industrialized countries (e.g., Nordic countries, Canada, and the United States), cities also provide many people-oriented services, such as education, health, and social welfare, even though funding sources can vary, with largely local funding at one extreme (Nordic countries), virtually totally central government funding at the other (Australia), and a mixture of local and state/federal in between (Canada, the United Kingdom, and the United States). However, cities are allowed considerable leeway in revenue mobilization from local sources to meet

---

[1] South Africa and Turkey are notable exceptions among developing countries.

their assigned functions. As noted in chapter 6, cities in industrialized countries meet on average about 70 percent of their expenditure needs from local taxes and fees.

In terms of the legal framework underpinning the assignment of powers and responsibilities to cities, in the industrialized countries cities enjoy a large degree of autonomy in managing their affairs. However, variations derive from national constitutions (Denmark, France, Germany, The Netherlands) or national legislation (New Zealand, United Kingdom) in unitary states and from state constitutions (United States, Australia, Switzerland) or state legislation (Canada) in federal states. Although legal frameworks specify the regulatory and oversight roles of the higher levels of government, there are periodic disputes regarding authority of higher-level government in local affairs, particularly in what the local governments consider unfunded mandates.

However, city governments in many developing countries still play a relatively small role in people's lives. The assignment of functions to local governments in most developing countries is still limited, with many essential functions performed de facto or de jure by national/state governments. Lack of capacity, both financial and managerial, is often the reason cited for this limited assignment, although as discussed later, weak capacity is just as much linked to the limited assignment of functions and powers. Table 5.1 presents an overview of assignment of functions in the 11 large metropolitan cities in developing countries selected for this chapter.

In terms of raising revenues, there are relatively few areas where local governments are allowed to operate autonomously. They are generally allowed quite limited autonomy in mobilizing revenues. Higher-level government often decides not only the types of permissible local taxes (which is appropriate for reasons of economic efficiency) but also the rates, levels, and collection methods. The expenditure authority of local governments is similarly highly circumscribed: they are often required to seek approval from higher levels for most contracting of any significant value.

Intergovernmental transfers, the main source of local government revenue, invariably take the form of conditional earmarked grants rather than budget transfers over which local governments have planning and expenditure jurisdiction. Table 5.2 presents an overview of revenue and expenditure autonomy for the same 11 large metropolitan cities.

Other forms of central control commonly include approval of senior staff appointments; reserving senior positions in the city government for appointees from the central government; setting salary levels for city governments; budgets; land use plans; performance standards; and external audit. While many such requirements are justifiable to minimize the risk to public resources, the issues are often the degree of control, the manner in which they are exercised, and whether the control function is within the capacity of the higher level of government itself. For example, central approval of budgets in Kenya can take time, sometimes many months, and sometimes are given only after the end of the financial year (Lewa and Devas 2004). In Ghana, central appointment of the district chief executive is often a cause of political conflict and undermines local accountability. Centrally appointed staff

TABLE 5.1
Service delivery responsibilities of select metropolitan city governments

Function	City										
	Istanbul	Jakarta	Manila	São Paulo	Buenos Aires	Bogotá	Mumbai*	Addis Ababa	Dar es Salaam	Kampala	Johannesburg**
Transportation											
Roads: arterials	M	M	N, M	M, C	N, M	S, M	P, R, C	R, Z, C	M	N, M	C
Roads: streets	C	M	C	M, C	M, C	M, C	C	R, Z, C	M, C	M	C
Public transportation	M	N, M	private	M, C	M	M	N, P, C	M	M	M	C
City services											
Water and sewerage	M	M	private	M, C	M, C	M, C	C, RP	M	M	M	C
Waste collection and disposal	M, C	M	M, C	M, C	M, C	M, C	P, C	M	N, M	M	C
Electricity distribution	private	N	private	N/A	private	N/A	P, C, private	R, Z, C	N/A	M	C
Social services											
Primary education	N	M	N	M, C	C	C	C, private	M	M	M	P, N
Secondary education	N	M	N	P	C	C	C, private	R	N, M	M	P, N
Housing	N/A	N, M	N, C	P, M, C	C	C	P, RP, private	R, Z, C	M	N/A	C
Public health	N	N, M	N	P, M	C	M, C	C, P	R, Z, C	N, M	M	C
Hospitals	N	N, M	N, C	P, M	C	M, C	C, private	R, Z	N, M	N, M	P, N
Social welfare	N	N, M	N	P, M, C	N, C	N/A	C, P	R, Z, C	N, M	M	C
Other services											
Fire protection	M	M	C	M, C	C	M, C	C	M	M	M	C
Police	N	N, R, M	N	P	N, C	M	P	N, R	N, M	M	C, N

Abbreviations: C, city government; M, metropolitan government; N, national government; N/A, not applicable; P, provincial/state government (for federal countries); R, regional government; Z, zone (for Ethiopia).

*In Mumbai, metropolitan-wide bodies and parastatals undertake major service functions, but these are essentially arms of the state government. There is no metro-regional government concept.

**Johannesburg has a single-tier local government for the metropolitan area. The constitution defines several functions as shared among different levels, responsibilities as they exist in practice are depicted here.

often becomes a point of contention with the local elected officials, as in Kenya and India, because they are seen as serving not local interests but those of politicians in the center. There is an inherent tension between local autonomy and central control, and a reasonable balance must be struck between local autonomy and the need for supervision. What is often overlooked in rule making is the limited capacity of the central government to supervise, resulting in a web of rules and regulations that are ineffective in practice or, worse, obstacles to good local governance. The absence of a well-conceived legal framework that governs the central-local relationship adds uncertainty in the relationship and is another factor inhibiting local initiative.

Recent years have seen some progress at least in middle-income countries in devolving greater powers to city governments. Brazil and Argentina had been moving toward increasing decentralization as a part of their transition to democracy in the 1980s and 1990s, but the fiscal autonomy of local governments was curtailed considerably in the late 1990s with the onset of the financial crisis. China devolved functions very aggressively, particularly to the larger cities that it considered drivers of economic growth, at the beginning of its economic reform and the opening up of the economy; however, fiscal autonomy still remains weak. South Africa has been undertaking a major realignment in the functions among its three "spheres" of government that places much greater emphasis on municipalities. India adopted a constitutional amendment in 1994 requiring the states to devolve powers to local urban governments, although in practice the states have generally been very slow to implement the amendment. Indonesia embarked on far-reaching reforms under the new constitution adopted in 2001 whereby cities were granted significant leeway in local taxation and expenditure autonomy both for own-source revenues and for transfers from the central government.

CITY GOVERNMENT INSTITUTIONS

All city governments have three constituent parts: the legislature, most commonly referred to as the city council; the executive responsible for the day-to-day running of city functions; and the bureaucracy. However, the division of functions and relationships among these three parts vary among major cities in the world and define different forms of city government. The variations result from history, tradition, and the system of government at the national level.

The City Council

Most major cities have a council composed of representatives elected by the people. City councils have always been considered an important part of representative democracy, but their importance has grown even more in recent years as the government "closest to citizens." Most theories of representative democracy emphasize the role of elected laymen both in the representation of citizens and in the decision-making process (Berg and Rao 2005). The extent and type of elected representatives' involvement in local affairs depend on the design of the electoral system and the form of government chosen, which in turn defines the relationship between the council and the executive.

TABLE 5.2

Local government revenue and expenditure autonomy in select metropolitan cities

	Istanbul			Jakarta*			Manila			São Paulo			Buenos Aires		
Revenue Mobilization Authority of LG (1)															
Control over:	R	B	C	R	B	C	R	B	C	R	B	C	R	B	C
Property tax	O	⊙	●	⊙	O	⊙	●	●	●	●	●	●	●	●	●
Taxes on vehicles	O	O	O	●	●	●	O	O	O	⊙	⊙	⊙	●	●	●
Fees	●	●	●	●	●	●	●	●	●	●	●	●	●	●	●
User charges for services	●	●	●	●	●	●	●	●	●	●	●	●	●	●	●
Expenditure Authority															
Control over expenditures from own revenue (2)	●			●			●			●			●		
Control over expenditures from intergovernmental transfers	●			⊙			●			●			●		
Intergovernmental Transfers															
Distributable pool (3)	F			F			F			F			F		
Distribution across local governments (4)	F			F			F			F			F		
Purpose of transfers (5)	UCBG			UCBG, CEG			UCBG			UCBG			UCBG		
Management of transfer system (6)	O			O			O			O			O		
Do local governments have discretion to borrow? (7)	International:O Domestic: ●			⊙			●***			⊙			⊙		

Abbreviations: AH, ad hoc; B, base setting; C, collection; CEG, conditional earmarked grant; F, formula based; R, rate setting; UCBG, unconditional block grant.
Symbols indicate control: ● = Full control of the local government O = No control of the local government ⊙ = Partial control.

*The property tax is in the process of devolution to the local government level in Jakarta, which will have full authority over base setting, collection, and, up to a limit, the rate-setting discretion to borrow. Bond issuance is currently being piloting.

**In theory, Mumbai has control over setting rates, but in practice the state exercises considerable control through its approval powers.

***Local government units have the power to undertake loans and borrowing subject to a statutory debt limit (annual debt service cannot exceed 20 percent of income)

There are two main forms of election of councilors: proportional representation and majoritarian or first-past-the-post systems. In the proportional representation family of electoral systems, seats are shared in rough proportion with votes gained by each party, whereas a majoritarian electoral system is based on a "winner-take-all" principle. The proportional representation system favors small and marginalized groups being represented in the council.[2] In majoritarian systems with single-

---

[2] In other words, the objective of a proportional representational system is to form a legislative assembly with each group of voters represented, in proportion to their number in the polity at large, by a party or person who shares their ideology.

	Bogotá			Mumbai**			Addis Ababa			Dar es Salaam			Kampala			Johannesburg		
	R	B	C	R	B	C	R	B	C	R	B	C	R	B	C	R	B	C
	●	●	●	◉	◉	●	●	●	●	◉	○	◉	◉	○	●	●	○	●
	●	●	●	○	○	◉	○	○	○	◉	○	○	○	○	○	○	○	●
	●	●	●	◉	◉	●	●	●	●	◉	○	◉	◉	○	●	●	●	●
	●	●	●	◉	●	●	●	●	●	◉	○	◉	◉	○	●	●	●	●
	●			●			●			◉			◉			●		
	●			◉			◉			◉			◉			●		
	F			F, AH			F			F			F, AH			F		
	F			AH			F			F			F, AH			F		
	UCBG			UCBG, CEG			CEG, UCBG			CEG, UCBG			CEG, UCBG			UCBG		
	○			○			◉			◉			◉			◉		
	◉			◉			◉			◉			◉			●***		

member districts, only two parties will emerge as major parties. That is why the majoritarian system is also sometimes called the *two-party system*. Table 5.3 describes different electoral arrangements and presents country examples.

Some countries have tried to take politics out of local elections in order to improve their efficiency. They require local elections to be nonpartisan on the theory that party politics are more appropriate for national/state level issues and not relevant to the local needs. However, in many cases this restriction is impossible to enforce, as in Kerala, India, where independent candidates for local bodies in practice tend to have a known party affiliation (Venugopal and Yilmaz 2009). Similarly, in Ghana, although district assembly elections are supposed to be nonpartisan, in reality local governments are not free from partisan politics (Yilmaz 2009).

In other countries, party affiliation is integral to the system of government at all levels. In these cases, national politics tend to intrude into local elections, thus diffusing the focus away from local governance. In South Africa, for example, the hegemonic African National Congress controls local politics and local politicians.

TABLE 5.3

Institutional electoral arrangements for local council

Electoral arrangement	Main characteristics	Benefits	Risks	Example countries
Proportional representation	Voters generally vote for a party rather than a specific candidate. Electoral districts have multiple representatives. The share of votes received by a party is translated by a fixed formula into the number of seats to be held by that party.	This system is more inclusive of minorities and women candidates compared with majoritarian systems.	Independent candidates with no political affiliation can become marginalized. Accountability can be compromised for representation.	South Africa, Indonesia, Turkey, Germany, Sweden, Burkina Faso, Ethiopia, Guinea
Majoritarian (first-past-the-post)	Election through single-member districts through plurality votes. The person with the highest number of votes is declared the councilor, representing his or her ward.	Voters have clearer understanding of the individual they are voting for, which leads to better accountability.	Minority candidates may not be electorally represented.	United Kingdom, Canada, United States, Uganda, Tanzania, Pakistan
Mixed systems	Mixture of proportional representation and nomination of district representatives.	This system may guarantee territorial representation. It creates a transition between the other two established systems (proportional representation and majoritarian).	This system may create confusion in representation of district candidates.	Rwanda, Angola

SOURCE: World Bank (2009).

The City Executive

Most cities have a mayor or equivalent, elected either directly by the citizens or from within the city council, who leads the executive branch of the government. But the extent of the mayor's power and influence, and thus role in running the city, varies widely depending on the different institutional arrangements for, and the extent of, the separation of powers between the council and the executive. This in turn determines the relationship of the two branches of government with the citizens. For example, if the executive is also the chairman of the city council, the division of authority is blurred. This is usually the case in parliamentary systems, as opposed to presidential systems, where the executive branch is completely independent of the legislative branch. In a parliamentary system, the extent of authority of the council chairman relative to the council determines, to a significant extent, the responsiveness and representation of the local government. Similarly, if the executive is appointed rather than elected, the political representativeness and responsiveness are compromised.

There are at least four models of city governance practiced around the world, ranging from the council exercising the most powers at one end of the spectrum and the all-powerful mayor at the other, with shared functions between the two. Table 5.4 provides an overview of the four models, their strengths and weaknesses, and examples of some countries that follow each particular model.

COUNCIL AS EXECUTIVE

Sometimes referred to as the "weak mayor" or "strong council" form of government, this is the earliest form of city government. The council elects a mayor from among their ranks, but only as the nominal chief executive. The city council (and, in some U.S. cities, other elected officials such as the city clerk or city auditor) also hold substantial power. The council designates specific members and/or committees of members to run and oversee specific city functions. The council performs all executive functions, including administration and budgeting. The role of the mayor is largely ceremonial and limited to presiding over the meetings of the council and, in some cases, being the "face of the city government" to outsiders.

This model has evolved from the earliest days of postimperial/postcolonial governments when small communities organized themselves to run their affairs. A great premium was placed on local control, in part as a reaction against centralized power. As the representatives of the people, the executives were considered as having the most intimate knowledge of the needs of the citizens to whom they were responsible and accountable. The system works reasonably well in small, homogeneous cities where people are in general agreement and do not expect a lot from the government. But the system comes under strain as cities grow in size. The informal, personal contacts that underlie the council-executive model no longer function in big cities, where social relations tend to be formal and impersonal. City growth also brings bigger and more complex problems that require much more technical expertise than the council typically possesses and that a leaderless, fragmented government is not best equipped to provide. Governance of larger cities also needs more formal checks and balances that the model does not provide. More generally,

TABLE 5.4

Topologies of city governance models

Institutional mechanism	Main characteristics	Benefits	Risks	Example countries
Council as the executive form	The election of a mayor by the council, usually from council members.	District council can have sanction power in case of misconduct.	Local governments cannot implement sound policy decisions.	Rwanda, Guinea, Burkina Faso, Angola, India (Kerala), Tanzania, Indonesia
Council-city manager	The council appoints and contracts with a politically neutral administrator to run and manage the city.	The strong political leadership of elected officials is combined with the strong managerial experience of an appointed administrator. Such an arrangement can preclude politically motivated patronage.	High-level capacity is required among members of government to institute such a mechanism.	Canada, Australia, The Netherlands, New Zealand
Leader and council cabinet (parliamentary system)	The commissioners are both legislators and department chairs.	All have equal powers, even though one commissioner may have the title of mayor.	The system may violate the principle of separation of powers.	United Kingdom, India
Mayor as executive	The mayor decides public policy and has a strong symbolic role in representing the locality.	The mayor can undertake swift public policy measures.	Local councils are often marginalized.	Cote d'Ivoire, Uganda (until 2008), Pakistan, Philippines, Ethiopia

SOURCE: World Bank (2009).

councils can often be "debating chambers," which are not able to implement sound policy decisions (Lankina 2008).

For all these reasons, the council-executive form of government is not well suited to managing metropolitan cities, and most industrialized countries have moved away from it in recent years. Denmark, however, stands out as an exception to this trend and has actually been moving back to the model, even for its largest city, Copenhagen. The Danish approach is driven by the goal of weakening the position and influence of political leaders and increasing the power of the councils that it considers much more representative of, and responsive to, the needs of the citizens (Berg 2005).

COUNCIL-CITY MANAGER FORM

One of the early reforms of city governments was to infuse greater professionalism in the management of various city functions. There was a recognition that the business of local government is to provide basic services of a technical nature and should therefore not be political. This led many cities to adopt the council-city manager form of government. Under this system, the political element of the system, the city council, appoints a qualified individual as the city manager, who is responsible for all day-to-day functions of running the city and exercises most executive powers, with the council providing policy guidance and supervision. As in the council-as-executive model, the mayor is normally elected from among the members of the council (in the United Kingdom the mayor can be elected) and has limited powers, similar to the council-as-executive form of government. The model is akin to a private corporation, with the council being analogous to the board of directors and the city manager the chief executive.

The principal advantage of the model is that a professional manager runs the city in a business-like manner, something that is necessary given the premium on making the best use of limited city financial resources. Such an institutional arrangement can preclude politically motivated patronage (Montjoy and Watson 1995). Since city managers are ostensibly guided more by actual effectiveness and efficiency than by short-term electoral considerations and pressure-group demands, as is the case with elected political executives, they are more likely to pursue policy innovations (Montjoy and Watson 1995). In addition, city managers are not subject to frequent turnover and thus are more likely to ensure policy continuity and to have credible commitments to other actors in local development (Clingermayer and Feiock 1997). In the United States, where the model is quite prevalent (in the majority of small and medium-size cities, but less so in the larger cities), there is a well-recognized cadre of competent city managers who are in high demand.

The criticism of the model is that it undervalues the importance of political leadership that is critical in the running of a city. The city manager may be just a transitory stranger in charge of city affairs (many U.S. cities prefer to hire an outsider who is not immersed in local politics), using the city as a rung on her or his career ladder. In addition, despite the intention of city managers being apolitical, experience from the United States indicates that in practice they view themselves as having substantial influence, often higher than the mayor or the city council

(Svara 2005). In fact, few countries outside the United States have adopted the model to a significant extent; in the United Kingdom, where the local government reform law of 2000 allowed this option, only one local authority, Stoke-on-Trent, has adopted it (Chandler 2009).

The model has also not been much used in developing countries, except where it has implicitly evolved because of higher levels of government maintaining the power to appoint the heads of local governments from among the ranks of national/ state civil servants (e.g., India). While technically a council-manager form, it is in practice more of a mechanism for higher-level government to keep a tight grip on city governments and thus is not really an appropriate practice for effective city management. Metropolitan cities in South Africa use a blend of strong executive and city manager approach by having the mayor as the chief executive who is unambiguously the leader and the city manager as a professional working under him.

LEADER AND COUNCIL CABINET FORM

Most prominent in countries with a parliamentary tradition of government, this form has the leader elected from among the council members (normally the leader of the majority party) serving as the mayor, who in turn appoints up to a prescribed maximum number (three to ten in the United Kingdom) of the council members to serve as his or her cabinet. Individual members of the cabinet can be given responsibility for specific services and/or cross-cutting themes, with delegated authority to make decisions. The council performs the oversight function and may set up committees for specific subjects/themes. However, this arrangement has been criticized for violating the division of powers (Montjoy and Watson 1995). The council is responsible for agreeing on the policy framework and the budget for the city, normally but not necessarily on the proposal of the executive.

A variation of the model is for the people to elect the mayor directly, who then forms the cabinet in the same manner from among the council members. This variation makes the mayor more visible and potentially more powerful than a mayor who is the leader of the council.

The model attempts to strike a balance between the need for clear executive powers and legislative oversight. Keeping the executive leadership within the council, it ensures that the council as the representative of the people is fully engaged in the running of the city. The main disadvantage of the model is that, like parliamentary systems, it can result in an unstable government that is at the mercy of potential changes from votes of no confidence in situations where national party politics are closely divided. While this may well be an appropriate system for national/state level politics, it is not well suited for city government, which requires more stability in order to deliver service effectively. In order to overcome this problem, the U.K. legislation requires a supermajority of a council to remove a mayor or is without the power to remove a mayor that is directly elected. Another disadvantage cited by some is the passive role played by the members of the majority party in the council who are not members of the cabinet (the "back benchers" in the United Kingdom) since they are expected to vote on party lines (Chandler 2009).

MAYOR AS EXECUTIVE

Also sometimes referred to as the "strong mayor" form of government, this model has the mayor (generally) elected directly in citywide polling. The election of the mayor can be at the same time and for the same term as the council, but some cities have chosen to stagger both the timing and the term to draw a clearer distinction between the legislative and executive functions and to provide greater continuity in city governance. The councils normally cannot remove the mayor through no-confidence votes, but some cities provide for the citizens to force a recall election by petition signed by a specified number of voters.

The executive power is entirely vested in the mayor, with the council playing only the oversight role. The city bureaucracy is directly under the control of the mayor, who also may have the powers to appoint (or dismiss) the heads of the various departments. The council may be granted appointment powers for certain positions (e.g., city clerk, auditor, inspector general) that are closer to its role of ensuring accountability in city functions. The mayor presides over the council meetings and sets its agenda. The mayor also has the powers to prepare the budget for council consideration, administer it after approval, and veto acts of council, which the council can override only with significant majority, and generally acts as the leader of the city for all practical purposes.

Despite its increasing prevalence, there is considerable disagreement about the strong mayor model. The proponents of the model see it as offering clarity of leadership and streamlined functioning of the city government, which helps improve efficiency. It also allows the voters to see the mayor clearly as whom they should hold accountable for the performance of the city government. Finally, it clearly separates the oversight responsibility of the council, which tends to be diluted when the council also takes on executive functions. A review of the German experience with directly elected executive mayors seems to confirm these views (Wollman 2005).

The main criticism of the strong mayor model is that it concentrates too much power in one individual, to the detriment of having truly participatory and democratic governance. Critics believe that leadership that relies on formal power to forge coalitions among divergent views and interests common in any city is not necessarily responsive, particularly to those outside the ruling coalition (Blodgett 1999). Citing successful examples of San Antonio, Texas, and Charlotte, North Carolina, Blodgett (1999) argues that it is possible for the mayor to use powers of persuasion and consensus building in a council-leader form of government to bring together different factions to support important initiatives.

Blodgett (1999, 354–355) also dismisses the notion that the council-manager form means "leaderless" government, which cannot take hard decisions because of the problem of "too many hands on the tiller," arguing: "Do we really want a mayor's leadership tools to comprise trading votes for services? Political leadership should not be confused with reactive, demand-responsive leadership. Too often, the political leadership in strong mayor governments encourages conflict among elected officials, which, in turn, produces political gridlock and a reliance on short-term coalition building."

A second criticism of the model is that it marginalizes the role of the councils to essentially rubber-stamping the preferences of the mayor and thus risks weakening the horizontal and vertical accountability linkages between the council and the executive and between the council and the citizens (Lankina 2008). In Côte d'Ivoire and Uganda, use of the strong mayor system has led to mayoral domination of local councils and lack of accountability of councils (Crook and Manor 1998; Wunsch 2001). Surveys of council members in U.S. cities with strong mayors show a growing disaffection among council members, the representatives of the citizens, in their influence in key decisions (Svara 2005).

Despite the differing views, the strong mayor form of government has become increasingly popular, and many countries, developed and developing, have adopted this as the model. France, Germany, and Spain in western Europe are the most prominent examples of directly elected strong mayors, although it has also gained increased prominence in England following the local government reforms of 2000. Most of the largest U.S. cities have directly elected mayors.

The Bureaucracy

Like any other function, cities require managers and staff at all levels who have the necessary expertise, tools, and resources to carry out their assigned functions. The growing complexity of metropolitan cities requires high-caliber staff, or at least staff members who are no less qualified than those who serve in state or national governments. This, however, is not the norm in many developing countries. Local government staff are invariably of lower caliber and command less respect. This contributes to the commonly held view of a lack of capacity in the local governments, which is one of the main inhibiting factors for greater devolution to local government cited by higher-level governments.

In practice, the lack of capacity is not due to lack of availability of qualified people, at least in the metropolitan cities that generally offer amenities (e.g., schools, housing, culture) valued by civil servants. Rather, the main reason is the inadequacy in the civil service system governing local governments that often accords local government officials a lower status, including lower salaries, fewer chances of advancement (when higher-level positions are filled by transitory appointees from the national government), insufficient value assigned to local government functions, and does not encourage professionalism.

Poor governance in the cities is also detrimental to bureaucratic functions. Many local politicians use government jobs as patronage. High levels of political corruption inevitably seep into the ranks of the civil servants, who then become the "enablers" for the politicians. Low salaries and a lack of proper systems of accountability serve as incentives for petty corruption, which is felt most directly by the citizens.

The net result of these factors is that the local government staff are held in low esteem. Citizens generally see them as inefficient, unresponsive, and corrupt. This is quite in contrast with industrialized countries, where local government staff members receive generally positive ratings from citizens, at times even higher than those for the higher levels of government. This reflects the fact that citizens in industrialized countries value the importance of local services on which they exercise much more direct control through their elected representatives.

City governments need significant autonomy over civil service and employment policies in order to address these issues. Ideally, it should include pay policy autonomy (setting overall wage rates); budget transparency (paying staff from one's own budget); budget and establishment control (controlling staff numbers and authority to remove surplus staff); recruitment autonomy (recognition as formal employer); career management control (vertical and horizontal mobility, including transfers to other units within the local government system); and performance management (directing and supervising activities and tasks, conducting evaluations, and exercising the ability to discipline and fire) (Evans 2004). Discretion over these functions allows the local government to hold staff accountable and to allocate staff efficiently by aligning their skills with local activities while managing financial resources. For example, pay policy autonomy and performance management not only enhance the accountability of the local staff to the local government but also give the local government authority over managing fiscal resources. In other words, if the local governments are not in control of each of the above-mentioned functions, the structures of accountability remain misaligned.

In practice, local governments in most developing countries have hardly any authority to make decisions on employment policies, because central governments participate in every aspect of the employment management, including budget payroll, recruitment, setting up standards, and even performance management. As a result, civil service rarely enters the decision calculus of institutional design and is not recognized as essential to good governance. Table 5.5 presents an overview of local government power over different functions in select developing countries.

DEMOCRATIC GOVERNANCE: AUTONOMY WITH ACCOUNTABILITY

Devolving discretion or autonomy to local governments to improve performance needs to be accompanied by strong measures of accountability. As argued above, effective metropolitan management requires local government to have substantial autonomy in carrying out its functions, managing its finances, and managing the personnel or functionaries, the essential "three Fs" of autonomy. Such discretionary power should be accompanied by safeguards against its abuse. In the absence of such safeguards, autonomy alone may actually leave the door open for misuse and abuse of new powers. Public officials could be influenced and captured by elite groups due to a lack of checks and balances for discretionary power. In addition to safeguarding from abuse, accountability mechanisms should create incentives for performance. Devolution without addressing accountability at the same time has been a major reason for the lack of success of decentralization (World Bank 2009).

The traditional approach to accountability of local governments has relied on supply-side or public-sector accountability instruments, which is the hallmark of, and a sine qua non for, good governance (Bovens 2005). It is the obligation of public authorities (governments, elected representatives, and corporate and other governing bodies) to explain publicly, fully, and fairly how they are conducting responsibilities that affect the public. Public accountability focuses on public-sector managers who spend public money, exercise public authority, and manage a corporate body

TABLE 5.5

Discretion over civil service and employment

Function	Angola	Burkina Faso	Ethiopia	Guinea	Kerala, India	Philippines	Punjab, Pakistan	Tanzania	Uganda
Budget payroll									
Authority to dismiss surplus staff	○	◉	◉	○	●	●	◉	◉	◉
Determine the wage envelope	○	○	○	○	◉	◉	◉	○	○
Establishment control									
Control of overall staff numbers	○	○	◉	○	◉	●	◉	○	◉
Control of staff numbers in individual local offices and facilities	○	◉	◉	○	◉	●	◉	○	◉
Recruitment									
Recognized as a formal employer	◉	●	◉	○	◉	◉	◉	◉	◉
Authority to hire	○	●	◉	○	◉	●	◉	◉	◉
Independent merit-based recruitment mechanism	◉	◉	◉	○	◉	◉	◉	◉	◉
Career management									
Promotion	●	◉	◉	○	◉	●	◉	◉	◉
Horizontal mobility within the local government	●	NP	◉	○	◉	◉	◉	○	○
Transfers within the local government	●	●	◉	○	◉	◉	◉	○	○
Performance management									
Direct and supervise activities and tasks	●	●	●	○	◉	◉	◉	◉	◉
Conduct evaluations	●	●	◉	○	◉	◉	◉	○	◉
Offer financial rewards	◉	NP	○	○	○	◉	◉	◉	◉
Discipline and fire underperforming staff	●	◉	○	○	●	◉	◉	◉	◉
Set pay policy	○	○	○	○	○	◉	◉	○	○
Set overall wage rates	◉	○	○	○	○	◉	◉	○	○
Set local incentives/salary top-ups	○	●	○	○	○	◉	◉	◉	○

Abbreviations and symbols: ○, total control of the local government; ◉, partial control of the central government; ●, complete control of the central government; NP, not prescribed.
SOURCE: World Bank (2009).

under public law. The predominant focus is on compliance requirements of public-sector managers for how they exercise public authority, spend public funds, and manage a corporate body under public law. For local governments, institutionalized systems and procedures, upward reporting, prior approvals, public disclosure, and independent audits are the most common instruments of accountability. These have been the areas of focus of many donor initiatives for institution building.

Elections of councilors and the mayor are opportunities for citizens to enforce accountability, and indeed, most developing countries now have some sort of elections at the local level consistent with the trends toward democratization at the national level. However, essential as they are, in practice electoral accountability has been weak because of voter apathy, which can be due to a lack of adequate information on performance or a lack of confidence among the citizens that they have an influence in changing things. As discussed later, electoral arrangements can also influence voter interest and participation in the elections.

Increasingly, however, both practitioners and academics recognize the critical role of the demand side in contributing to accountability. Also referred to as social accountability, the demand side refers to an approach to building accountability that relies on civic engagement, in which ordinary citizens and/or civil-society organizations demand accountability. Recognizing the limitations of both electoral and public accountability mechanisms, demand-side/social accountability approaches require concerted civic education efforts and an expansion in the repertoire of instruments through which citizens can hold the state to account, beyond voting.

Social accountability requires active involvement of citizens in the affairs of the government. Citizen participation at the local level is seen as the foundation of the development of democratic governance that many countries now seek. Indeed, in the industrialized countries, this objective has become the central goal of increasing decentralization, equal to or even more important than the efficiency goal. Citizen involvement can also ensure more effective oversight of governmental functions, something that is particularly necessary at the local government level with the historic concerns about poor performance and malfeasance.

Electoral Systems

Direct election of councilors and the mayor has now become increasingly common and provides the most fundamental form of citizen participation. However, measures can be taken that encourage voter interest and turnout. Of course, fair and open elections are critical. Election of the mayor on a citywide basis has generally drawn greater voter interest because it gives citizens a clear choice of one person they can look to for leadership. Election of councilors on an area basis is important to link citizens to their representative on the council. However, the large population of metropolitan cities and the limits on the total numbers of councilors from the point of view of effectiveness mean that a large number of people are represented by one person (e.g., with a city population of 10 million and council size of 50, one councilor represents 200,000 people, or 40,000–50,000 households). This dilutes citizen voice in the metropolitan cities.

Exogenous factors can negatively affect the effectiveness of the electoral system. In many cases, informal power structure outside of the electoral system influences representation and electoral accountability. Voters in many local settings cast their votes based on their affiliation with the traditional leaders/tribal chiefs. They might be obliged to make their vote public, which prevents them from making their choices in a democratic manner. More important, informal power structures restrict the entry of candidates into the electoral space as those currently in power stifle dissent to exclude certain groups and maintain strict hierarchies. In Punjab, Pakistan, for example, the majority of the candidates who contested local elections previously belonged to the landed elite class of their communities and were related to the politicians at the national and provincial levels (Aslam and Yilmaz 2011). Similarly, in Burkina Faso, traditional chiefs frequently intercede with the deconcentrated or decentralized authorities, especially in rural areas (Mahieu and Yilmaz 2010). In Ethiopia, the de jure multiparty electoral competition is dominated by the ruling party (Yilmaz and Venugopal 2010). Table 5.6 presents such examples from other countries and emphasizes the detrimental effect that certain political factors can have on electoral competition and, consequently, on including citizens in the political process.

Many U.S. cities try to overcome representation and participation problems by having citizens serve on various advisory commissions, neighborhood councils, and so forth. India has created "ward committees" with representation from trade organizations, nongovernmental organizations, and so on, that provide inputs to the councilor (Baud and de Wit 2008). Unfortunately, the ward committees have been captured by elite or special interests in many cities, but they have been effective when they truly comprise grassroots-level representatives and the political leaders show commitment to their success (e.g., Kolkata, India). New Delhi, India, has tried neighborhood committees that are given responsibility for specific functions (e.g., parks, cleanliness), but experience shows that they have been more effective in middle- and upper-class communities and not in the poorer neighborhoods. Greater citizen involvement remains a continuing challenge in urban governance in most cities. In the Philippines, for instance, the local government code mandates that all provincial, municipal, and *barangay* (village/district) governments establish a local development council to set the direction of economic and social development and review local governments' budgets. One-quarter of the council members should come from nongovernmental organizations and community-based organizations (Estrella and Iszatt 2004).

Some countries (e.g., most U.S. states) have made local government elections nonpartisan on the theory that for local-level government it is better to focus on the qualifications and work of the individual rather than promises of political parties. Experience in the United States generally validates this assumption. In contrast, experience in some other countries suggests that partisan elections actually increase voter turnout.

Empowering Citizens

Building a civil society is a long evolutionary process, as witnessed in industrialized countries. The mechanisms by which they develop, or the events that trigger them,

TABLE 5.6

Local electoral accountability: Select examples

Country	De jure	De facto		Local governance outcome
		Good practices	Malpractices	
Kerala, India (election year 2006)	A term of five years is legally mandated for the local elected officials. A no-confidence motion* by the members of the *panchayat* can remove the president and vice president. Independent candidates can run in local elections.	The State Election Commission, which oversees local elections, is well functioning.	Independent candidates for *gram* panchayats and other local panchayat elections tend to a have a party affiliation.	Elections helped strengthen the institutions and mechanisms of decentralization and reduced the role of state members in legislative assemblies in local governance.
Ethiopia (election year 2008)	Political parties have been allowed to register for local election.	The election process was broad-casted daily on radio in several languages.	No political space for opposition parties. Members of the National Election Board are selected by the ruling party.	Although Ethiopia has a multiparty system, the political landscape is almost entirely dominated by the ruling party.
Guinea (election year 2005)	Both urban and rural councils are directly elected by proportional representation, for a term of four years.	The Autonomous National Electoral Commission, composed of representatives from most parties and civil society, is in charge of administering elections. Opposition parties were given access to state their positions on state radio broadcasts.	At the grassroots levels (village and cell), the ballot is not secret by law.	Lack of privacy prevents free and fair expression of voter suffrage and choice. Tribal chiefs affect the outcome of elections.
Pakistan (Punjab) (election year 2001)	The executive is subject to council oversight by law.	Councils have been successful in making decisions independent of the executive.	District mayors are traditional and informal power holders in the area and use their political influence over union councilors.	Elite capture of electoral discretion results in strengthening of central officials.
Tanzania (election year 2005)	Recall provisions are provided at the village, *kitongoji*, and *mtaa* council levels. The election is organized by National Election Committee.	Citizen grievances with the election process can be lodged through petitions in the courts, which have the authority to hear and determine the outcomes.	The minister responsible for local governments continues to supervise the local elections. Only affiliates of national parties refer to recall measures.	Central control of local elections limits political discretionary powers of the local governments and creates ambiguities in accountability structures.

*A no-confidence motion is traditionally put before a parliament by the opposition or citizen's quorum in the hope of defeating or embarrassing a government. Similarly, at the *gram sabha* level, a citizen's quorum can decide to remove the president. SOURCE: World Bank (2009).

are not entirely clear, so the best course is to put in place instruments conducive to civic involvement and participation. Examples of such instruments follow.

GENERIC LEGISLATION THAT EMPOWERS CITIZENS TO DEMAND LOCAL ACCOUNTABILITY

Specific measures can be enshrined in legislation governing local bodies that empower citizens for grievance redress or with the right to request explanations regarding municipal legislation. The following are some examples.

- *Public hearings and consultations.* These are probably the most common instrument of dialogue between citizens and the local government. In most cases the hearings are consultative and nonbinding. They make the government answerable to its constituency, but they lack the enforcement dimension of an accountability relationship.
- *The right to demand a public hearing.* As part of the process of adopting normative acts, the municipality must hold a public hearing on the proposed act if it is requested by at least a minimum number of persons or an association having a minimum membership.
- *Public petitions.* Any person or organization may petition the municipality to adopt, amend, or repeal a normative act, and the petition must be reviewed and responded to in writing.
- *Administrative complaints.* The municipality must go beyond the minimal provisions of the country's administrative appeals law by giving complainants an opportunity to be heard and by shifting the burden of justification to the government to prove that they followed rules and processes, as opposed to the complainant having to show that the government failed to do so.
- *The right to initiate a recall or referendum.* The local government code in the Philippines establishes the mechanism of recall as an immediate accountability mechanism for elected local officials. Their tenure may be terminated by popular vote under a special recall election that can be initiated by a petition. The code also guarantees citizens the right to pass key legislation directly or oppose proposed legislation with the instrument of referendum.

SPECIFIC BODIES AND PROCESSES FOR CITIZEN OVERSIGHT

Citizen oversight bodies are institutional structures that citizens form to provide a direct channel for citizen oversight over local government's work. In Bolivia, for example, the 1994 Law of Popular Participation created local vigilance committees to monitor activities of elected local government bodies and to participate in local planning and budget creation. In Japan, in response to widespread perception of local government corruption, a civic movement began establishing citizen ombudsmen in several municipalities. This initiative spread throughout the country and led to formation of the National Citizen Ombudsmen Liaison Council and recognition of the mechanism in government statutes. In addition, the national council developed a survey to rank the level of transparency of local governments, which was used as an additional source of pressure over local government to improve its performance.

INFORMATION PROVISION AS THE BASIS FOR CITIZEN MONITORING

Improved information flows to citizens reduce opportunism by political leaders and improves resource allocation (Besley, Pande, and Rao 2004). In India, a small Indian nongovernmental organization in Rajasthan initially introduced public hearings in 1994 to stop fraud at the local level. This initiative led to the Every Citizen Has the Right to Information Campaign, which led to India's Right to Information Act of 2005. The act provides that, on payment of a small fee, every citizen can demand and receive details of expenditures on the work done over the last five years in his or her village. In many countries, the right to information does not exist for many administrative activities, and citizen groups have to establish their own networks to make information public. In Uganda, for example, the Uganda Debt Network established local monitoring committees in order to track local public expenditures.

MONITORING PROCUREMENT AND IMPLEMENTATION OF
LOCAL GOVERNMENT CONTRACTS

Procurement, including contracting and implementation of public works and services, is a major source of corruption and mismanagement. A typical source of local government corruption and collusion involves drafting tender documents in ways that unfairly benefit one contractor over others. In the Philippines, the local government code wrestles with this risk by assigning a seat to accredited nongovernmental and community-based organizations in the prequalification, bid, and award committees for local contracts. In many countries, such as El Salvador, Nicaragua, and India, the beneficiaries of public investment projects form a social audit committee to monitor the physical construction process, from the receipt and quality of the materials to their proper use.

MONITORING LOCAL SERVICE PROVISION

Citizens have used a number of strategies to oversee service quality around the world. Some strategies rely on participatory assessments and feedback surveys and are often accompanied by agreements on expected standards of services. Others rely more on public representation in service-specific institutions that channel citizens' complaints and allow them regular oversight. One of the main innovations that drew attention to the potential of the social accountability approach was the experience of citizen report cards, which are participatory surveys that solicit user feedback on performance of public services. They are used in situations where there are no demand-side data, such as user perceptions of quality and satisfaction with public services. Citizens' report cards are instrumental especially in gathering demand-side data about state-owned monopolies, many of which lack incentives to be responsive to their clients. The report card process relies on extensive media coverage and civil society advocacy to achieve greater accountability. The initial experiment of citizen report cards in the municipality of Bangalore proved that, by collecting citizen feedback about the performance of local services in a structured way and using that assessment as a yardstick against which to measure future improvements, the report card approach was a powerful way to improve local government services (Paul 2002). This basic concept has led to a proliferation of initiatives. In Uganda, for instance, Kampala conducted its first citizen report card in early 2005. It provided the city council and other basic public service providers with feedback on water and sanitation, health, education, roads and public transport, solid waste management, public toilets, the management of the city environment, maintenance of law and order, and management of city infrastructure. A complementary strategy has been to develop citizen charters. These are pacts between the community and service providers, spelling out expectations and roles, enabling citizens to interact more effectively with the municipality. They specify the expected standards of services, identify who is responsible, and outline the procedures for redress of complaints. For example, the Citizens' Charter in the municipality of Mumbai, India, covers detailed public services for each municipal department.

RECOMMENDATIONS FOR DEVELOPING COUNTRIES

In considering the appropriate models of urban institutions for developing countries, three important points should be kept in mind. First, there is wide diversity in the structure and functioning of metropolitan institutions both across countries and often within the same country. No single model can be considered as the best model to follow. For every model discussed here, positive experiences have been reported in some cities and negative ones in others.[3] Second, institutional change is a long and slow process, brought about not just by legislation but by cultural changes and adjustments in the perceptions and attitudes of actors implementing the change. Third, getting the right institutions in place is an evolutionary process requiring constant adjustments with changing circumstances. In most industrialized countries, laws governing metropolitan governance have been undergoing change for decades, and in many cases there are still ongoing debates about the right structures (Berg and Rao 2005; Chandler 2009; Sancton and Young 2009).[4]

With these considerations in mind, it is neither feasible nor desirable to set out a single best institutional model for governance of metropolitan cities in developing countries. The structure must be sui generis in each country. With rapidly growing population of their metropolitan cities and their critical role in the economy, developing countries do not have the luxury of the gradual evolutionary approach that typifies metropolitan governance in developed countries.[5] There is now sufficient experience to allow us to draw some key principles of metropolitan governance, as outlined in the following.

A Legal Framework Should Underpin Metropolitan Governance

Local governments are clearly one of the fundamental democratic institutions of a country. Inclusive and effective democratic processes can most readily be achieved at the local level through participatory, transparent management of public resources.

---

[3] See Berg and Rao (2005) for a useful discussion of experiences in a number of countries in Europe and the United States.

[4] The case of the United Kingdom is typical: the first local government act in the United Kingdom was enacted in 1888, and the most recent one in 2000, with several intervening revisions, and there is still ongoing debate about whether certain provisions need to be further amended.

[5] Thirteen of the 20 most populated cities today are in the developing world.

In this process, the roles, responsibilities, authority, and accountability of local governments, including metropolitan cities, should be formalized in an appropriate legal governing framework. Legal frameworks are laws and policies at multiple levels, national, regional, and local, that operate interdependently and together can be considered to constitute an overall legal framework within which citizen and government actions take place. National laws and constitutions provide a backdrop by establishing rights, freedoms, and entitlements of local governments. They should also spell out the fiscal and administrative relationship between the metropolitan city and the national/state government. This provides the citizens a basis on which they can hold metropolitan government accountable by pursuing remedies in the court of public opinion and law.

Central/State Governments Should Delegate Significant Autonomy to Metropolitan Local Governments

This autonomy should include on the expenditure side, (1) full control on at least all property-related services; and (2) implementation of people-related programs (basic education and health) even when the financing may be provided by higher levels; and on the revenue side, (1) autonomy to determine levels of taxes that are clearly property-related; (2) transparency in the share due to metropolitan governments from taxes that are collected by the higher levels; and (3) flexibility in setting rates for their share of the shared taxes.

Metropolitan Governments Must Be Given Full Autonomy in the Three Fs

As mentioned above, the three Fs in metropolitan government refers to functions, finances, and functionaries (personnel). In this regard, the role of higher-level government should be limited to (1) setting the broad legal framework under which local governments are expected to operate, particularly in managing their finances; (2) monitoring compliance with people-oriented programs funded by higher levels; and (3) monitoring the performance of local governments but assigning power for any remedial action to only the legislature at the national/state levels and not to civil servants at higher levels. Higher-level government should not intervene in day-to-day functioning, leaving the oversight of such functions to duly elected local representatives and citizens. The legislative framework should clearly spell out these roles of the national/state levels.

Improve the Quality of Civil Service to Improve Metropolitan Governance

This should start with a clear policy that all city government staff belong to the city and are to be recruited by the local government and not seconded from higher levels of government. Staff appointments and administration should be within a well-defined civil service system that is comparable to the system at the higher levels. There is no reason for salaries at local levels to be lower than those at the state or national levels except for any location cost differences. The system should be administered transparently with all selections done on merit. Although difficult to administer, the system should also provide for merit-based promotions and mechanisms for termination for poor performance. These are not easy measures to undertake, but interestingly, developing countries (e.g., South Africa, Indonesia) are deciding to grant the authority to set civil service conditions to each local government. On the other hand, European countries have moved toward uniformity between national and local levels, preferring to avoid unnecessary political complications from having multiple systems. Some other countries provide national/state guidelines within which the local civil service conditions are set.

Make Strong Executive Leadership Visible to the Citizens to Promote Accountability

A legislature at the city level is essential for overseeing the executive, promoting citizen interest, and encouraging citizen participation. Separation of the executive from legislative functions is also an essential part of maintaining checks and balances for good governance, and various models are possible to achieve this within the political traditions of a country. Nevertheless, it is important that a clear leader is seen as being responsible for the functioning of the city and can be held directly responsible by citizens for delivering results. There is much to recommend for a strong mayor system.

Establish Mechanisms for Downward Accountability

A major impediment to granting greater autonomy to local governments in most developing countries has been the concern about malfeasance, whether in the form of lack of performance or misappropriation of public funds. While mechanisms need to be in place for some oversight by higher levels of government, the most critical accountability is the one that is exercised by the citizens. A representative electoral system with wide participation and the necessary checks and balances is the most critical element. But this should be accompanied by proactive mechanisms for citizen input enshrined in the city charter. Reporting on key city functions by independent bodies in a timely manner and with the widest reach should be another important requirement.

Several developing countries have in the last few years been attempting to carry out reforms of local governments. In Asia, the Philippines and Indonesia have undertaken significant decentralization of functions and resources to local levels. They have also been actively promoting greater participation of citizens in the governance of cities, although there have been concerns that the powerful and the influential still dominate local politics (Hadiz 2010; Laquian 2005). Cities in Brazil, Colombia, and Argentina in Latin America have traditionally enjoyed greater autonomy but have yet to address effectively the problem of multijurisdiction metropolitan governance (Rodriguez-Acosta and Rosenbaum 2005). Similarly, there has been piecemeal progress in some African countries. But few developing countries are yet to implement the fully integrated framework for metropolitan institutions and governance discussed here.

Two notable exceptions, Turkey and South Africa, have implemented reforms for different reasons: Turkey in its quest to join the European Union, and South Africa in taking advantage of the need to move the cities away from the apartheid system that had fragmented cities into enclaves.

Both countries have promoted democratic governance, empowerment, and accountability at the municipal level. In both, the constitution and subsequent local government laws recognize municipalities as organs of local development and make a distinction between different types of municipalities. The South African Constitution (1996) is one of the rare examples from developing countries that explicitly recognize the importance of municipal governments for promoting economic and social development of the cities. It defines local governments as one of the three "spheres" of government (the other two being national and provincial) rather than the conventional "tiers" or "layers" in most federal structures, thereby denoting unique roles, responsibilities, and authority for each. The constitution is also unique in specifically recognizing the importance of some cities (the eight largest cities categorized as "category A" or metropolitan municipalities) and accords them power to exercise "exclusive municipal executive and legislative authority in its area." The constitution also explicitly directs higher levels of government to support and not hinder municipal development. Turkey has been successful in creating a two-tier municipal system in large cities with representative government at both levels, a clear delineation of responsibilities between the two, and effective mechanisms for coordination. But the process of improving metropolitan governance even in these countries is still evolving. In South Africa, there has been concern that the law prescribes too intrusive a role for citizens, which has seriously overburdened municipal administrations and detracted from their core functions of service delivery (Cameron 2005). Nevertheless, both countries can serve as broadly appropriate models for developing countries to follow, albeit with changes to suit their specific circumstances.

REFERENCES

Aslam, Ghazia, and Serdar Yilmaz. 2011. Impact of decentralization reforms in Pakistan on service delivery. *Public Administration and Development* 31:159–171.

Baud, Isabelle Suzanne Antoinette, and Jan de Wit, eds. 2008. *New forms of urban governance in India: Shifts, models, networks and contestations.* New Delhi: Sage.

Berg, Rikke. 2005. From cabinets to committees: The Danish experience. In *Transforming local political leadership*, ed. Rikke Berg and Nirmala Rao, 85–100. New York: Palgrave Macmillan.

Berg, Rikke, and Nirmala Rao, eds. 2005. *Transforming local political leadership.* New York: Palgrave Macmillan.

Besley, Tim, Rohini Pande, and Vijayendra Rao. 2004. *Political selection and the quality of government: Evidence from South India.* Washington, DC: World Bank.

Blodgett, Terrell. 1999. Beware of the lure of the strong mayor. In *Forms of local government: A handbook on city, county and regional options*, ed. Roger L. Kemp, 353–357. Jefferson NC: McFarland.

Bovens, Mark. 2005. Public accountability. In *The Oxford handbook of public management*, ed. Ewan Ferlie, Laurence E. Lynn, and Christopher Pollitt, 182–208. New York: Oxford University Press.

Cameron, Robert. 2005. Metropolitan restructuring (and more restructuring) in South Africa. *Public Administration and Development* 25:329–339.

Chandler, Jim A. 2009. *Local government today.* Manchester, U.K.: Manchester University Press.

Clingermayer, James C., and Richard C. Feiock. 1997. Leadership turnover, transaction costs, and external city service delivery. *Public Administration Review* 57:231–239.

Crook, Richard, and James Manor. 1998. *Democracy and decentralization in South-east Asia and West Africa: Participation, accountability, and performance.* Cambridge, U.K.: Cambridge University Press.

Estrella, Marisol, and Nina Iszatt. 2004. *Beyond good governance: Participatory democracy in the Philippines.* Quezon City, Philippines: Institute for Popular Democracy.

Evans, Anne. 2004. A framework for decentralizing civil servants. PREM Workshop on Decentralizing Civil Servants. Washington, DC: World Bank.

Hadiz, Vedi R. 2010. *Localising power in post-authoritarian Indonesia: A Southeast Asia perspective.* Stanford, CA: Stanford University Press.

Lankina, Tomila. 2008. Cross-cutting literature review on the drivers of local council accountability and performance. Social Development Working Paper No. 112. Washington, DC: World Bank.

Laquian, Aprodicio A. 2005. Metropolitan governance reforms in Asia. *Public Administration and Development* 25:307–315.

Lewa, Peter M., and Nick Devas. 2004. *Building municipal capacity for finance and budgeting in Kenya.* Birmingham, U.K.: International Development Department, University of Birmingham.

Mahieu, Sylvie, and Serdar Yilmaz. 2010. Local government discretion and accountability in Burkina Faso. *Public Administration and Development* 30:329–344.

Montjoy, Robert S., and Douglas J. Watson. 1995. A case for reinterpreted dichotomy of politics and administration as a professional standard in council-manager government. *Public Administration Review* 55:231–239.

Paul, Samuel. 2002. *Holding the state to account: Citizen monitoring in action.* Bangalore: Books for Change.

Rodriguez-Acosta, Cristina A., and Allan Rosenbaum. 2005. Local government and the governance of metropolitan areas in Latin America. *Public Administration and Development* 25(4):295–306.

Sancton, Andrew, and Robert Young, eds. 2009. *Foundations of governance: Municipal government in Canada's provinces.* Toronto: University of Toronto Press.

Shah, Anwar, ed. 2006a. *Local governance in industrial countries.* Washington, DC: World Bank.

Shah, Anwar. 2006b. A comparative institutional framework for responsive, responsible, and accountable local governance. In *Local governance in industrial countries,* ed. Anwar Shah, 1–40. Washington, DC: World Bank.

Stigler, George. 1957. The tenable range of functions of local government. In *Federal expenditure policy for economic growth and stability,* U.S. Congress, Joint Economic Committee. Washington, DC.

Svara, James H. 2005. Institutional form and political leadership in American city government. In *Transforming local political leadership,* edited by Rikke Berg and Nirmala Rao, 131–149. New York: Pelgrave Macmillan.

Venugopal, Varsha, and Serdar Yilmaz. 2009. Decentralization in Kerala: Panchayat government discretion and accountability. *Public Administration and Development* 29:316–329.

Wollman, Hellmut. 2005. The directly elected executive mayor in German local government. In *Transforming local political leadership,* edited by Rikke Berg and Nirmala Rao, 29–41. New York: Pelgrave Macmillan.

World Bank. 2009. Local government discretion and accountability: Application of a local governance framework. Report No. 46059-GLB. Washington, DC.

Wunsch, James. 2001. Decentralisation, local governance and "recentralization" in Africa. *Public Administration and Development* 21:277–288.

Yilmaz, Serdar. 2009. Decentralization in Ghana: Local government discretion and accountability. *Regional Development Studies* 13:62–83.

Yilmaz, Serdar, and Varsha Venugopal. 2010. Obstacles to decentralization in Ethiopia: Political control versus discretion and accountability. In *Decentralization in developing countries: Global perspectives on the obstacles to fiscal devolution,* ed. Jorge Martinez-Vazquez and Francois Vaillancourt, 321–352. Cheltenham, U.K.: Edward Elgar.

METROPOLITAN PUBLIC FINANCE

6

An Overview

RICHARD M. BIRD AND ENID SLACK

> Let me tell you about the very rich. They are different from you and me.
> —F. Scott Fitzgerald, "The Rich Boy"

Not all big cities are very rich.[1] But they are all, by definition, big, and most of them are also rich relative to smaller cities, towns, and rural areas in the countries in which they are located. These differences have substantial implications for metropolitan public finance. The most obvious reason that big cities are different is because they have a much larger population. They also have a population that is both more concentrated and more heterogeneous in terms of social and economic circumstances, often with a higher proportion of immigrants and in-migrants. Moreover, big cities are important generators of employment, wealth, and productivity growth and are often the major economic engines of countries. In the emerging global knowledge-based economy in which innovation is increasingly seen as the key to prosperity, most innovation occurs in large cities and metropolitan areas in which people can reap the benefits of close proximity, often referred to as agglomeration economies (Slack, Bourne, and Gertler 2003).[2] Big cities also serve as regional hubs for people from adjacent communities who come to work, shop, and use public services that are not available in their own communities. All these factors have significant implications for the magnitude and complexity of metropolitan public finance.

---

[1] For simplicity, this chapter follows Angel (2011) in using *city* or *big city* interchangeably with *metropolitan area*. Studies of metropolitan areas frequently employ such different terms as *metropolitan cities, metropolitan regions, city-regions,* and *urban regions.* As Stren and Cameron (2005) discuss, these terms are used in different countries to refer to much the same concept: areas in which there is a large urban core (the "city") plus adjacent urban and rural areas that are integrated socially and economically (if not legally) with the core. Unfortunately, at present, the great differences not only in definition but also in the structures, functions, and finances of metropolitan areas across (and even to some extent within) countries make it impossible to provide comparable cross-country data.

[2] As Glaeser and Gottlieb (2009) note, *agglomeration economies* are simply a way of saying that productivity rises with population, as indeed the evidence suggests. However, since productivity and population size are determined simultaneously, the precise magnitude and nature of such economies remain elusive, although, on the whole, as Glaeser and Gottlieb (2009, 1023) conclude, "the largest body of evidence supports the view that cities succeed by spurring the transfer of information."

Although in most countries large cities and metropolitan areas are seldom treated very differently than other local governments (Bahl 2011), in practice their expenditures are often both much higher and different in nature. Moreover, in part because of their greater ability to pay, big cities should generally have more "fiscal autonomy" than other areas in the sense of being more responsible for delivering local services and for levying and collecting the revenues to pay for such services.[3] One reason that such issues are not adequately addressed is that there seldom is a single "metropolitan government." Instead, a variety of governments and public agencies provide local services and raise revenues within the metropolitan region. Because the political boundaries of governments in metropolitan areas rarely coincide with the boundaries of the metropolitan economic region, problems arise in coordinating efficient service delivery and sharing costs appropriately across the region.[4] Such problems are often exacerbated by overlapping special-purpose districts that are responsible for delivering specific services, such as water or electricity, but within boundaries that are not coterminous with either local or regional governments. Although finance and governance are closely intertwined, the issue of metropolitan governance is not discussed further in this chapter.[5]

Instead, this chapter considers the following questions: Do big cities spend more and differently than smaller cities? Do big cities have more fiscal capacity to finance such spending? How should metropolitan regional finance be structured? The chapter then considers which revenue sources are appropriate for metropolitan cities and concludes with some reflections on how best to deal with the challenges facing metropolitan public finances in developing countries.

DO BIG CITIES SPEND MORE?

Local government expenditures are generally high in per capita terms in large metropolitan areas (Chernick and Reschovsky 2006; Freire 2001). Higher population density often implies a high concentration of problems as well as people. Urban poverty in close proximity to concentrated urban wealth may result in higher crime rates and more expenditure on policing. The higher concentration of special needs and public health problems may call for greater spending on social services. The different physical characteristics often associated with high density also incur costs: taller buildings require more specialized training and equipment for fire fighters, and the need to move large numbers of people around generally makes a good public transit system essential to the effective functioning of the metropolitan area. Moreover, since large cities around the world must increasingly compete on the international stage, they need to provide not only adequate "hard" services such as transportation, water, and sewers, but also, to be competitive in attracting and retain-

---

[3] This argument is further developed with respect to Latin America in Bird and Slack (2007).

[4] There are a very few exceptions, such as Cape Town, where the Municipal Demarcation Board set the geographic boundary of the city to coincide with the economic region.

[5] For further discussion of metropolitan governance and finance, see Bahl (2011), Bird and Slack (2007), Rojas, Cuadrado-Roura, and Fernandez Guell (2008), and Slack (2007a).

ing the knowledge workers on whom their prosperity often rests, such "soft" services as parks, recreational facilities, and cultural institutions (Florida 2002). All this costs a lot, and such costs are especially difficult to finance in rapidly urbanizing developing countries.[6]

For all these reasons, expenditures in the metros of South Africa, for example, are considerably higher than in other municipalities in the country. The six South African metros account for only 34 percent of the population but 59 percent of total local government expenditures in 2007–2008 (Steytler 2013).

Per capita local government expenditures not only are higher in large metropolitan areas but also are particularly high in the central cities within such areas. For example, municipal expenditures in the central city of São Paulo in 2009, with a population that is more than half of the metropolitan region, were twice as much as all of the suburban municipalities combined (Arretche 2013). This difference reflects higher expenditures in the central city on transportation, urban development, housing, and pensions for municipal employees.

Although metropolitan expenditures may be high, there may also be opportunities to take advantage of economies of scale in service provision.[7] However, the evidence on the existence of economies of scale is mixed, varying both with the service in question and the unit of measurement (e.g., jurisdiction size or size of the facility).[8]

Although scale economies are often achievable with respect to central administrative and governance functions, as well as for services with large capital inputs such as public transportation and water and sewage systems, it is less clear that there are economies of scale for "people-related" (soft) services such as education.[9] Moreover, the literature also suggests that diseconomies of scale may exist when cities become too large to deliver services efficiently. Bigness may have many virtues, but lowering the per capita costs of providing local public services is not one of them.

---

[6]Concerns with urbanization costs are not new. Earlier literature (e.g., Linn 1982; Richardson 1987) explored the possible impact of financing such costs on the economy in general and especially the possibly adverse impact on the nonurban population. The more recent literature, however, follows Glaeser (2011) in viewing such costs less as something to be minimized in order to free resources for more productive investment and more as a potentially productive investment in national economic growth.

[7]Cost differences are not the same as spending differences. Spending differences include not only differences in costs (based on factors beyond the control of the local government) but also differences arising from both local preferences for public services and waste or inefficiency.

[8]See, for example, Chernick and Rechovsky (2006), Fox and Gurley (2006), and Hermann et al. (1999). Many measurement problems have been identified in such cost studies. For example, population is commonly used as a proxy for output, and expenditures as a proxy for costs. But population is not a good measure of output: two municipalities with the same population might have very different outputs for a particular service because of demographic differences. Nor are expenditures a good measure of costs, in part because the pattern of expenditures may reflect differences in local government wealth. Since the local government fiscal base is likely correlated with population size, larger expenditures do not necessarily mean that costs are higher.

[9]Of course, expenditure patterns differ sharply from country to country, reflecting the governance structure and the distribution of functions. In Brazil, for example, by far the most important expenditure in São Paulo and Belo Horizonte is social protection (more than one-third of total metro outlays), followed by education (about one-quarter). In Cape Town, on the other hand, the most important metropolitan expenditures are on environment and electricity (about one-quarter each) (Slack and Chattopadhyay 2013).

DO BIG CITIES HAVE GREATER FISCAL CAPACITY?

Revenue patterns differ in metropolitan regions, reflecting both the different nature and level of services they provide and their greater ability to levy taxes. Larger cities usually have a larger per capita property tax base because of higher property values that reflect the extent to which urban public services are at least partly capitalized into land values. Not only do larger cities have above average commercial and industrial tax bases, but they also have higher agglomeration "rents" and can impose relatively higher taxes on such properties without losing tax base to competitive localities (Jofre-Monseny and Solé-Ollé 2008).[10] Similarly, simply because of their higher level of economic activity, big cities are also more able to levy income and sales taxes, if they are allowed to do so. Sales taxes may be particularly attractive when substantial numbers of commuters and visitors from neighboring areas visit the city to work, shop, or enjoy cultural or recreational facilities. The broader the geographic area covered by the metropolitan government, the easier it is to impose such taxes.

Revenue levels in central cities are often higher than in the suburbs. In the case of São Paulo, for example, per capita revenues in the central city are approximately twice what they are in the suburbs, comparable to the difference in expenditures noted above (Arretche 2013). Both property taxes and local sales taxes are higher in per capita terms in the city than in the surrounding suburban municipalities. Of course, the fact that big cities may be legally and economically able to impose higher taxes than their smaller neighbors does not mean they will always do so. Big city mayors are no keener to tax their constituents than are their counterparts elsewhere when there is a politically less painful way to raise revenue, such as transfers.

ARE BIG CITIES TREATED DIFFERENTLY?

Bahl (2011) notes three broad ways in which countries may treat large metropolitan areas differently: city-state status, special taxing powers, and special intergovernmental transfers. Tokyo and the Special District of Bogotá are examples of city-states in which the metropolitan government has both city and regional (state) status and, as a result, has greater taxing powers than other municipal governments. Germany also gives broader responsibilities to three city-states, Berlin, Bremen, and Hamburg, which have both state responsibilities, such as education, security, and social policy, and local government functions, such as transportation, housing, and day care (Zimmermann 2009). German city-states collect both state and local revenues.

Even without city-state status, big cities are sometimes granted additional taxing powers. For example, Toronto is allowed to impose a number of taxes that other municipalities in the province cannot, such as a vehicle registration fee, a land transfer tax, and a billboard tax, although it has done little to exploit this additional taxing

---

[10]Big cities must, of course, be careful not to push this argument too far. In Colombia, for example, where the largest city, Bogotá, both has more taxing power and utilizes that power more extensively than the municipalities surrounding the metropolitan district, there is some evidence that industry has to some extent migrated beyond the district boundary in response (Vazquez-Caro and Childress 2010).

power. New York City can similarly levy a wider range of taxes than most U.S. cities and gets significant revenue from corporate income and business taxes. Large U.S. cities rely less on property taxes and more on sales and income taxes, and they also depend more on own-source revenues than do smaller municipalities. In South Africa, metro governments, but not other local governments, were recently given access to fuel taxes.

Although one might expect that large metropolitan governments elsewhere would also depend less heavily on intergovernmental transfers than do other local governments, the reality is mixed. In Europe, for example, some do (e.g., Stockholm, Paris, Madrid, and Lausanne) and some do not (e.g., in Switzerland and in Eastern Europe) (Bahl 2011). In some capital cities (e.g., Berlin, Bern, and Brussels), the national government provides grants for specific services such as transportation, parks, or cultural facilities, although this appears uncommon. In Brazil and South Africa, as in Spain, large cities receive more grants than do smaller municipalities, apparently in recognition of the presumed higher costs of service provision in such areas.

Examples from less developed countries are also mixed in terms of dependence on intergovernmental transfers by large metropolitan areas compared with other cities. Cape Town derived 30 percent of its revenues from operating and capital transfers in 2008–2009 (Steytler 2013). Because the major transfer is an equalizing transfer, the metros receive a much smaller per capita grant than do smaller cities (Bahl 2011). The Federal District of Mexico also receives significantly less in transfers than do other states in Mexico (Bahl 2011), as does the Special District of Bogotá (Bird 2012). Metropolitan areas in Brazil similarly rely more on own-source revenues than do other municipalities in the country; São Paulo, for example, receives nearly half of its revenues from self-generated taxes (Arretche 2013). On the other hand, Istanbul receives more transfers than smaller municipalities in Turkey because the main transfer is a revenue-sharing grant that is distributed on a derivation basis (Bahl 2011).

FINANCING METROPOLITAN CITIES

An important rule of sound fiscal decentralization is that finances should follow functions (Bahl 2002). Local governments need access to adequate revenue sources to finance the public services they are mandated to provide. How urban public expenditures are financed is a key issue in urban planning and development. Since every city is different, no single approach will suit all. The appropriate strategy for any city will differ depending upon a variety of factors, such as its size, economic conditions, the composition of various population groups within the city, and the extent of urbanization.

As the European Charter of Local Self-Government (Article 9, paragraph 2) puts it, "Local authorities' financial resources shall be commensurate with the responsibilities provided for by the constitution and the law." Those that spend the most, usually the largest cities, obviously need more to spend. For the most part, however, they also have the most to tax. It follows that they should be largely responsible for raising the necessary funds themselves. However, the traditional theory of fiscal federalism prescribes a very limited tax base for local governments.[11] The only good taxes are said to be those that are easy to administer locally, are imposed mainly on local residents, and do not raise problems of harmonization or competition either horizontally (between local governments) or vertically (between local and central governments). Such prescriptions appear to impose severe limits on the revenue instruments likely to be open to big cities. These instruments fall under three headings: (1) own-source revenues: current revenues that are to a significant extent under direct local control; (2) transfers from other levels of government; and (3) sources of capital finance.

Own-Source Revenues

A truly local revenue source might be defined as one whose base is determined by local governments, that is levied at rates decided by local governments, and that is collected by local governments (Bird 2006). In the real world, however, many taxes possess only one or two of these characteristics, and the "ownership" of a particular levy in these terms is often unclear. In some countries, for example, a tax may be called a *local tax*, and part or all of its proceeds may accrue to a city, but the rate and base of the tax are determined by a central or provincial/state government. Such taxes are best thought of as central or provincial/state government taxes that are allocated to cities through a form of transfer. This interpretation is particularly plausible when there is little connection between the amount transferred and the amount collected locally. In appraising local taxes, names and appearances can be deceiving.[12]

USER CHARGES

Consider first the obvious point that local governments should, wherever possible, charge directly for services (Bird 2001). Appropriately designed user fees allow residents and businesses to know how much they are paying for the services they receive from local governments. When proper prices are charged, governments can make efficient decisions about how much to provide, and citizens can make efficient decisions about how much to consume. All too often, however, a vicious circle exists in which the low quality of local public services makes it difficult to collect user charges, with the result being further deterioration in the service levels.

This circle needs to be broken, and not just to obtain the revenues needed to improve services. User charges are also an important way to provide signals, both to consumers of the scarcity value of services and to providers about the demands that need to be met through service provision. Establishing a strong link between demand and supply by forcing both sides to face the real opportunity costs of service provision helps to generate resources for services that people really want and are willing to pay for and also to ensure efficiency in production and accountability in service delivery. User charges are especially appropriate for services such as

---

[11]For a critical review of the traditional theory, see Bird (2009).

[12]This issue and the degree to which revenue sources are under local control vary from country to country, as discussed further in Ebel and Yilmaz (2003) and OECD (1999).

water and public transit, where most direct benefits are confined largely to individual consumers.

Charges are especially important in large metropolitan areas because they not only result in more efficient use of services but also encourage more efficient land use. When marginal cost prices are charged, consumers who are far away from existing services and hence more costly to serve will pay more, and those closer will pay less. The distributional impact of such pricing obviously depends on who lives where and is hence very context specific; with respect to water pricing, for instance, the poor may live higher up (as in Cali) or lower down (as in Nairobi). On the other hand, uniform pricing of urban services, while often politically appealing, is usually economically inefficient. Studies in Chile, for instance, show that underpricing and distortions in water and sewer pricing have resulted in severe locational distortions (Daniere and Gomez-Ibañez 2002). An additional important benefit of more appropriate pricing of urban services is to reduce pressure on urban finances by reducing the apparent need for more investment in underpriced infrastructure. If something costs users nothing, they will generally want more of it, but this does not mean that cities should continue to give it to them for nothing.

All this has been known for years (Bahl and Linn 1992). However, not much has been done along these lines anywhere, essentially for political reasons. Despite the clear (if not always simple) economic advice available on how to design and implement charges and some evidence that people accept the benefit principle at least to some extent, urban user charges appear in most cases to be neither popular nor particularly well designed anywhere.[13] A common reaction to suggestions to increase reliance on user charge financing, for example, is that the results are simply too regressive to contemplate. In reality, almost the opposite is true in most large urban areas: those who benefit most from underpricing services are those who make the most use of them, and the poor are not well represented in this group (Bird and Miller 1989). Relatively simple pricing systems such as low initial "lifeline" charges for the first block of service use often can deal adequately with any remaining perceived inequity from introducing more adequate pricing systems.

The political economy problems of user charge pricing are much deeper than simple concerns with perceived regressivity. Imposing prices on services that were previously provided for free or increasing prices on heavily subsidized services inevitably arouses substantial opposition, particularly when, as is usually the case, those who must pay receive (and perceive) no offsetting benefit for doing so. The politics of user charges are perhaps more difficult in large cities than in smaller communities owing to lower visibility of the direct connection between the amount people pay and the amount of services they receive. On the other hand, getting one's neighbors to accept charges for services is not necessarily easy, even (or perhaps especially) when everyone knows everyone else in the neighborhood.

A possible way of balancing some of these considerations may be for some city functions to be carried out, and the revenues to pay them obtained, at the

---

[13]The sorry state of most user charges in urban North America is set out in such early studies as Bird (1976), Meltsner (1972), and Mushkin (1972). No changes for the better were evident 25 years later (Bird and Tsiopoulos 1997), or now.

neighborhood level, as is done, for example, with a form of land value increment tax in Colombia. Another way to reduce the political pressure on local governments may be to turn over the provision of "chargeable" services like public transit and water supply to a public or even private enterprise. This approach may not increase the likelihood of a sensible charge policy, but it may at least make it easier to finance and provide such services in a metropolitan service area that is fragmented among a number of different governments.

PROPERTY TAX

The property tax is appropriate for financing local services for at least two reasons. First, real property is immovable: it cannot move away when it is taxed. Second, to the extent that there is a visible connection between the types of services funded at the local level and the benefit to property values, the accountability of local governments to local residents may be substantially improved. If a property tax (whether levied on a unit-value or market-value basis) roughly approximates the benefits property taxpayers receive from local services, it is like a tax on the capitalized value of those benefits. Residential property taxes are particularly appropriate to fund local governments because they are borne by local residents.[14] From this "generalized user charge" perspective, residential property taxes may thus again be seen as a way to ensure that those who enjoy the benefits of local services are required to pay for them.

The nonresidential portion of the property tax, generally the most important part of the tax in many countries, while equally appropriate for financing cost-reducing services provided to businesses, is less appropriate for financing local government expenditures directly benefiting residents (Slack 2011).[15] Because taxes on business may be partially exported to residents of other jurisdictions who are consumers of the products or services produced in those properties, there is less accountability. Those who bear the burden of the tax are not those who enjoy the benefits. To the extent such taxes are exported to residents of other jurisdictions, restrictions on local tax autonomy may be needed, such as a maximum rate or perhaps even a requirement that a uniform rate be levied on residential and nonresidential property. Even if agglomeration rents permit metropolitan governments to impose higher rates on business property than do other governments, restrictions may still be needed in metropolitan areas to prevent excessive tax exporting to consumers outside the metropolitan area.

Despite their many virtues as a source of local revenues, relying solely on property taxes for metropolitan revenue substantially reduces the scope of services the big cities are able to provide from their own resources. No country seems able to raise more than 10 percent of total tax revenues from the property tax (OECD 2006), in part because the property tax is relatively costly and difficult to administer properly. The difficulty in pushing for revenues from this source is exacerbated as the size of the tax burden increases.

In some instances, simplified procedures, for example, area-based assessments in such cities as Bangalore (Bengaluru) and the introduction of self-assessment in

---

[14] For a fuller discussion of property tax incidence, see Bird and Slack (1993).

[15] In Poland, for example, 85 percent of property tax revenues come from business property (Swianiewicz 2011).

such cities as Bogotá, have led to significant immediate increases in property tax revenues.[16] However, any gains are likely largely transitory in nature, reflecting more the failings of the preexisting system than any particular virtues of these approaches to property tax administration. Such reforms may serve a useful interim purpose both by increasing revenues and by creating the essential administrative framework and making the tax more acceptable, paving the way over time to a "gold standard" property tax: a well-administered tax based on current market values.[17]

In any case, even a well-administered local property tax is unlikely to be able to finance major social expenditures (education, health, social assistance). Local governments financed primarily by property taxes must either confine their activities to providing such purely local services as street cleaning and refuse removal or remain heavily dependent on transfers from senior levels of government.

Furthermore, property tax revenues respond less quickly to changes in the economy than do taxes on income or sales because economic growth is not fully capitalized into real estate investment and land ownership. Even if property values do increase, tax revenues are unlikely to increase proportionately because assessed values are seldom updated on a regular basis (Bird and Slack 2004). On the other hand, as part of a balanced revenue portfolio, there is much to be said for the relative stability of property tax revenues, as has recently been demonstrated in countries in which land transfer taxes and other revenue sources were substantially expanded by a boom in housing prices, only to decline sharply when prices fell.

INCOME TAX

In principle, a strong case can be made for a local income tax to supplement property taxes for large metropolitan governments that are increasingly being called upon to address issues of poverty, crime, land use planning, regional transportation, and other regionwide needs (Nowlan 1994). To the extent that large metropolitan areas are required to provide social services, an income tax is a more appropriate revenue source than a property tax because it is more closely related to ability to pay. Furthermore, since mobility across jurisdictions in response to tax differentials is less the larger the geographic area, large metropolitan areas are more able than other local governments to take advantage of income taxes. Even within the largest metropolitan areas, however, it is probably desirable to "piggyback" onto higher-level income taxes (i.e., to levy the tax as a supplement to a central or provincial/state income tax) rather than to impose independent local taxes. However, this may be too much of a stretch in developing countries in which even the central government income tax is often a weak and limited source of revenue (Bird and Zolt 2005).

A quite different justification for income taxes for large metropolitan areas might be on grounds of benefits received. Since the residential property tax is tied to the consumption of housing rather than the consumption of public goods, even

---

[16] For discussion of the Bangalore and Bogotá cases, see, respectively, Rao and Bird (2010) and Acosta and Bird (2005).

[17] See Bahl (2009) on paths to property tax reform in developing and transitional countries. Connolly and Bell (2010) provide an interesting comparison of the relative merits and effects of area-based and value-based property taxes in Lithuania.

this portion of the property tax is a benefit tax only to the extent that housing consumption and local goods consumption are highly correlated across different households (Thirsk 1982). In large metropolitan areas with a heterogeneous population, in all likelihood incomes are more highly correlated with consumption of public services than are property values.

Finally, because income taxes increase or decrease in response to changes in wages and salaries, local revenues will increase more quickly in economic expansions. Of course, the other side of this coin is that they will also decrease more quickly in an economic downturn, so even cities with income taxes need more stable property taxes in their revenue portfolio.

GENERAL SALES TAX

General sales taxes are seldom levied by even the largest local governments outside of a number of U.S. states, except in the highly undesirable form of a gross receipts tax. In Brazil, however, the major source of municipal taxation is the service tax (*imposto sobre servicos*, ISS), which is imposed on all services except communications and interstate and intercity public transportation, which are taxed by the states. Generally, the ISS is imposed on retail sales at a minimum rate of 2 percent, with maximum rates that differ by the type of service, the usual maximum being 5 percent of gross revenue. More presumptive methods of assessment are used in some cases. Most analysts in Brazil think that this cascading tax is not desirable and suggest that it should be abolished and services incorporated more fully into a comprehensive value-added tax (Werneck 2007). Much the same has been said at times about the industry and commerce (*industria y comercio*) tax in Colombia, a classified gross receipts tax on a wider range of businesses at lower rates that is both the most revenue-elastic form of local taxation in Colombia and often the largest source of revenue in the largest cities (Bird 2012). However, critics of such "bad" taxes have paid little attention to the need to provide local governments, particularly those in large urban areas, with an elastic source of revenue that is within their control.

The ISS and industry and commerce taxes, like other local sales taxes that are really gross receipts taxes (e.g., China's local business tax), apply to all sales in the taxed sector, including all sales to other businesses. Unlike true value added taxes, businesses do not receive credits for taxes already paid on purchased inputs. Such taxes, particularly when applied not just to services, as in Brazil (and, for the most part, China), but to both goods and services, as in Colombia, may in principle have a very broad base (much broader than gross domestic product, which equals final sales or value added), so they may generate a lot of revenue for a relatively low tax rate. They are also relatively simple to implement, since doing so does not require the government either to determine whether sales are to households or businesses (since all sales are taxable) or to keep track of taxes paid by businesses on their purchased inputs (since these taxes are not deductible from a company's own tax liability). The major problem with gross receipts taxes is that they take a flaw found in most retail sales taxes, the taxation of business inputs, and elevate it to their defining characteristic. The result is substantial tax cascading with consequent distortion to the organization of production in order to reduce tax liabilities.

Nonetheless, even if the only local sales tax is a bad one, a case can be made for it as addressing some of the externalities in municipal services when some beneficiaries of services, such as commuters and visitors, do not otherwise have to pay for them. Sales taxes would both give big cities more choices in determining their own tax structure and allow them to benefit more directly from growth in local economic activity than would a property tax, while at the same time discouraging savings and growth less than an income tax. However, since evasion both is economically distorting and erodes the tax base, large rate differentials between neighboring jurisdictions are unlikely to be sustainable over long periods of time. Piggybacking onto the central or provincial/state tax system with an additional city sales tax of 1 or 2 percent, however, would avoid many of the problems associated with a local sales tax, including high administrative and compliance costs.[18]

SELECTIVE SALES TAXES

As Bahl and Linn (1992) emphasized, taxes and charges on automobiles such as fuel taxes, vehicle registration levies, parking fees, and tolls on major roads are doubly useful: they both discourage road use and produce revenues. The message is powerful, and the logic is persuasive, at least to most economists. As in the case of user charges more generally, however, almost no one (outside of Singapore) seems to have been listening. The most important tax on automobiles from a revenue perspective is the fuel tax, which is also the simplest and cheapest from an administrative perspective. While difficult to levy locally, fuel taxes can generally be levied at a regional level, including in a metropolitan region, although regions would probably not be able to differ much from the rates imposed by their neighbors, given the mobility of the tax base.[19] Cities that levy a fuel tax generally piggyback onto state/provincial fuel taxes, principally because the administrative costs of levying their own taxes would be prohibitive. The revenues generated from such taxes are often earmarked for local roads and transit services. In South Africa, for example, the National Treasury introduced sharing of the national fuel tax levy, for metros only, starting in October 2009. Fuel tax sharing is being phased in, and the metros receive 50 percent of the fuel tax levy share as of November 2010 (Steytler 2013).

However, if automotive taxation is intended to price either externalities (congestion and pollution) or the use of publicly provided services, fuel taxes are at best a crude instrument. Tolls and an appropriate set of annual automobile and driver license fees are preferable. For example, vehicle fees might be based on such features as age and engine size (older and larger cars generally contribute more to pollution), location of the vehicle (cars in cities add more to pollution and congestion), and axle weight (heavier vehicles do exponentially more damage to roads and require roads that are more costly to build). Road tolls and congestion charges, together with appropriate regulatory policies, have been used successfully, for example, in Singapore and London. However, while the merits of this approach from both

---

[18] Such piggybacked sales taxes can work well at the regional level even in countries in which the central sales tax takes the form of a value added tax (Bird and Gendron 2001). However, the only value added taxes that now exist anywhere at the local level appear to take the quite different form discussed below in the section on business taxes.

[19] Such local fuel taxes currently exist in at least eight U.S. states (American Petroleum Institute 2012).

the developmental and the revenue perspective have frequently been pointed out (Bird 2005), countries have proved extremely reluctant to follow this politically unpopular road, even though it leads not just to better urban finance but also to less sprawl and a more efficient pattern of urban development (Slack 2002).

Finally, parking fees in major metropolitan cities may potentially generate substantial revenues. The main rationales for levying parking fees are to reduce congestion of vehicles on the roads and to generate resources to construct parking spaces. At first glance, these two objectives may seem contradictory since increasing parking spaces in itself might seem more likely to induce rather than reduce road congestion. However, in most big cities in developing countries, the poor quality of the public transportation system combined with inadequate provision of parking spaces for vehicles and poor enforcement of street parking regulations results in large-scale traffic congestion on roads. With sharp increases in household incomes and the emergence of a large middle class in countries such as India, the number of vehicles is going to increase sharply in the coming years. Introducing a more comprehensive policy of charging parking fees in accordance with the scarcity value of open spaces in cities as part of a more rational road and urban policy should reduce congestion problems. While such a policy may also generate revenues to construct multistoried parking places, a strong case can be made for letting the private sector deal with the business of providing (taxable) parking facilities, with the public sector concentrating on its proper task of enforcing street parking regulations (Barter 2010).[20]

BUSINESS TAXES

Many countries have regional and local business taxes in the form of corporate income taxes, capital taxes, nonresidential property taxes, transit taxes (*octroi*), license fees (*patente*), and various forms of industry and commerce taxes (Bird 2003). Most of these taxes would not score highly on most reasonable criteria. In India, for example, in most big cities the most important revenue source is often octroi, an archaic local levy on goods entering the city, which a few years ago was reported to account for 70 percent of urban tax revenue in the country as a whole, compared with only 20 percent for property taxes (Rao and Singh 2005). Economists as a rule dislike octroi (essentially a local import duty) as an inefficient, distortionary tax that is often administered very corruptly. Although some states have abolished this tax, in some instances it has been replaced with an "entry tax" with similar characteristics. In most cases, when states abolished octroi, they provided no alternative source of revenue and simply increased the size of the unfunded mandates confronting municipal governments (Rao and Bird 2010).[21]

Few such crude local business taxes are equitable. Almost none are neutral. Most accentuate the disparities between localities, giving most to those who have

---

[20] Creating better parking infrastructure in the central business district of major cities may be an appropriate area in which to explore the public-private partnership approach to capital finance, discussed below.

[21] As Pethe (2011) discusses, Maharastra state recognized its inability to provide adequate offsetting transfers to Mumbai for the loss of octroi revenues and decided, while abolishing the levy in general, to leave it in place in Mumbai, a curious example of one of the developing world's most dynamic and expanding cities relying to a surprising extent on one of the oldest (and least economically efficient) forms of local revenue.

most, though this may, of course, make them especially attractive to metropolitan areas. Most such taxes also lend themselves to tax exporting, thereby violating the correspondence principle that those who pay should be those who benefit. Such taxes are sometimes costly to administer.

Despite such defects, city governments often impose various taxes on local business. Such taxes are popular with officials and citizens for several reasons. They produce substantial revenue and are more responsive to economic growth than are property taxes. Moreover, cities often have more discretion over the rate, base, and application of such taxes than for any other form of taxation. In Colombia, for example, the industry and commerce tax has often been the major source of revenue growth for Bogotá and other such large cities as Cali and Medellín (Bird 2012). Since no one is quite sure of the incidence of such taxes, it is easy to claim that they are paid by someone other than local residents, which makes them more politically palatable, though less accountable, than other taxes such as the property tax.

In addition, a good economic case can sometimes be made for local business taxation as a form of generalized benefit tax. Ideally, specific public services benefiting specific businesses should be paid for by appropriate user charges; however, when for some reason, technical or political, such user charges are not feasible, some form of broadly based, general levy on business activity may be warranted. This argument suggests that a broadly based levy neutral to factor mix, such as a tax on value added, is likely the best form of local business tax (Bird 2003). Such a tax was introduced in 1998 in Italy and was adopted in 2004 in Japan and in 2010 in France.[22] However, considerable attention must be paid to the details of both design and implementation if such local business taxes are not to create a major barrier to the formalization of small and new businesses (World Bank 2007).

A PORTFOLIO OF TAXES

None of the potential sources of metropolitan revenue discussed briefly above is perfect, though, curiously, the one that comes closest in economic terms (user charges) is perhaps the least (and worst) used of all those listed, for reasons that have been discussed elsewhere (Bird 2001). Perhaps the best approach is to provide metropolitan cities with access to a portfolio of taxes adequate to provide both enough stability (through the property tax) to provide a stable source of local government finance and enough elasticity (through good income, sales, or business taxes) to finance the expanding services almost certain to be needed by large and rapidly expanding urban areas in developing countries.

Intergovernmental Transfers

Big cities are more able to levy and collect their own revenues than are smaller cities. They thus need to rely less on grants from senior levels of government.[23] Even though

---

[22]See Bordignon, Gianni, and Panteghini (2001) on Italy and Gilbert (2010) on France. The Japanese system is described in Ministry of Internal Affairs and Communications (2012).

[23]Although there are at least as many problems in classifying transfers as there are in classifying the degree of autonomy with respect to local taxation (Kim, Lotz, and Mau 2010), this subject is not discussed further in this chapter.

their expenditure levels are also generally higher, on the whole big cities should receive less in grants on a per capita basis than do smaller and rural municipalities. The relatively higher costs of services and the greater need for services in big cities than in other urban areas seem unlikely to outweigh the much greater potential tax base.[24] An alternative way to achieve equity may be to design the governing structure to cover the entire metropolitan area. By combining rich communities and poor communities, equalization can take place at least within the metropolitan area. Such equity concerns were, for example, the main reason that the one-tier governance model was adopted in 2000 in Cape Town, South Africa (van Ryneveld and Parker 2002).

In some instances, however, when big cities provide services whose benefits spill over municipal boundaries, intergovernmental transfers, horizontal or vertical, are required to ensure allocative efficiency (Slack 2007b). In large metropolitan areas, some externalities can be internalized within the jurisdiction if boundaries are extended to include all of the users of the service. Nonetheless, for services that generate externalities beyond the borders of the metropolitan area, such as "hub" or nodal services for national transportation or other networks or clear contributions to national competitiveness in the international economic arena, some transfers may still be appropriate.

On the whole, however, in both principle and practice, transfers are less important for large metropolitan areas than for other local governments. Indeed, in countries with wide regional economic disparities, there seems to be little reason that the wealthiest regions (including big cities) should not be able to raise and spend most of their budgets themselves, although even they seem likely to remain to some extent transfer dependent when it comes to financing expensive services with substantial national implications, such as health and especially education. To achieve this goal and to reduce their present dependence on intergovernmental transfers, large metropolitan areas need not only an appropriate governing structure but also more and different revenue sources than other local governments.

Sources of Capital Finance

Good physical and social infrastructure is essential to the economic, social, and environmental health of cities. Cities not only have to provide roads, transit, water, sewers, and other hard services but also have to provide soft services that enhance the quality of life in their communities, such as parks, libraries, social housing, and recreational facilities. Metropolitan infrastructure, like metropolitan spending in general, should usually be financed locally. Often, the most sensible way to do so is to borrow. Other sound ways to pay for infrastructure in particular cases may include such instruments as development charges and PPPs (public-private partnerships).[25]

---

[24] The costs of services in remote areas tend to be even higher than in large metropolitan areas, owing to higher transportation costs (greater distances), higher heating costs (climatic conditions), and so on (Kitchen and Slack 2006). However, particularly in small countries (e.g., Switzerland), these factors may be offset by those resulting in higher costs in more urbanized areas.

[25] A case can be made for "capital grants" from national or state governments when a given infrastructure activity is expected to yield substantial external benefits that will "spill over" to other areas. Such grants are sometimes disguised as loans (that are subsequently forgiven or not repaid) or subsidized loans (from public-sector

BORROWING

Borrowing is generally a perfectly appropriate way to pay for capital expenditures. Where the benefits of a capital investment (e.g., the construction of a water treatment plant) are enjoyed over a long period of time, say, 25 years, it is both fair and efficient to pay for the project at least in part by borrowing so that the stream of benefits matches the stream of costs through the payment of debt charges. On the whole, big cities tend both to have greater access to bond markets than do smaller municipalities and tend to pay lower servicing costs.

Borrowing allows a municipality to enjoy the immediate benefit from the capital improvement, which is not always possible when relying on current revenues (taxes and user fees), which are in any case seldom sufficient to fund large expenditures on a pay-as-you-go basis. Since the pattern of capital expenditures is lumpy, a city may need substantial funds to finance an infrastructure project in one year and then much less for the next few years. Borrowing allows municipalities to avoid large year-to-year fluctuations in tax rates.

The main disadvantage of borrowing from a local perspective is that loans not only have to be repaid at some point but also generate interest obligations that must be serviced annually. Revenues dedicated to debt repayment cannot be used to meet other current expenditures. The costs of the capital project are spread over time, but the need to service the debts constrains local fiscal flexibility. This problem may be particularly important when local revenue streams are volatile. Cities that have less debt and hence lower debt service obligations obviously have more flexibility to respond to unanticipated future events.

Local governments in many developing countries are restricted from borrowing.[26] In some countries, such as China, local governments have found a way around these restrictions. They have created independent, wholly owned companies whose activities are "extrabudgetary" (Wong and Bird 2008). These companies are used to provide funding for development projects and, in particular, infrastructure. They are permitted to borrow on the capital market and are backed by assets (e.g., land) transferred to them by the municipality or the revenue stream from their projects. Because of their extrabudgetary status, however, they do not use standardized accounting and reporting systems and do not face the same level of public scrutiny.

DEVELOPMENT CHARGES

A development charge is a one-time levy imposed on developers to finance growth-related capital costs associated with new development (or, in some cases, redevelopment). These charges are levied for works constructed by the city, and the funds collected are used to pay for the infrastructure made necessary by the development. The rationale for charging developers for such costs is in part one of equity, that growth should pay for itself and not be a burden on existing taxpayers, and in part simply to

---

financial institutions). The "grant" element may vary substantially from case to case. For a discussion of the many different ways that urban infrastructure is financed around the world, see Annez (2010).

   [26]Even when localities can borrow, they are often not eager to do so. In Canada, for example, even the largest cities, with relatively unrestricted access to capital markets, borrow much less than seems optimal (Bird and Tassonyi 2001). On the other hand, smaller municipalities often have little direct access to capital markets unless their debt obligations are guaranteed or "pooled" by higher levels of government.

expand the capacity of local government to carry out infrastructure development without incurring new debt or requiring taxpayers in general to pay higher taxes.[27]

Although development charges are widely used in North American jurisdictions to pay for infrastructure costs that are external to the development (e.g., major roads and trunk sewer lines), only charges for internal infrastructure are common in less developed countries (Peterson 2009). One exception is Santiago, Chile, where development charges are levied to cover the costs of major roadways necessitated by development.

Who ultimately pays development charges (the new buyer, developers, or predevelopment landowners) depends largely upon the demand and supply conditions in the market for new housing or commercial or industrial buildings (Slack and Bird 1991). Over the long term, however, it seems likely that in most circumstances charges imposed for new developments are borne by buyers. If properly implemented, such development charges act, in effect, as a form of marginal cost pricing and hence induce more efficient development patterns and discourage urban sprawl (Slack 2002). For this to be true, however, development charges generally need to be differentiated by location to reflect the different infrastructure costs. In practice, this seldom appears to be the case in North America, at least, although some of the experience in Latin America with land-based charges appears to have induced more efficient land use (Peterson 2009).[28]

PUBLIC-PRIVATE PARTNERSHIPS

Public-private partnerships (also known as P3s) are partnerships between a government body and a private-sector party under which the private sector provides infrastructure or services that have traditionally been delivered by the public sector. PPPs do not necessarily mean full privatization; the government body retains ownership of the assets and sets the policies and level of service. These partnerships are widely used in Europe and Australia, reflecting the expectation of an improvement in the efficiency and effectiveness of local public service delivery and, in some instances, the desire to reduce the public-sector financial obligations connected with such projects.

---

[27] Many other levies are sometimes imposed on developers: land dedications that require the developer to set aside land for roadways, other public works, school sites, or environmental purposes; parkland dedications that require a portion of the land used for development to be set aside for parkland or that a cash payment in lieu of parkland be made; density bonusing, under which developers are granted higher densities than permitted in return for meeting conditions such as providing day care, preserving an historic building, and so on; connection fees to permit developers to buy into existing capacity of water and sewer facilities; and oversizing provisions (sometimes called front-end financing) that require developers to provide more infrastructure than is strictly required for their development.

[28] See also the recent discussion of "betterment levies" in Colombia in Borero Ochoa (2011) for an example of an unusually successful use of taxes on estimated land value increments to finance local public works. Interestingly, although the Colombian experience has been noted and praised for many years (Rhoads and Bird 1967), and superficially similar legislation exists in a number of other Latin American countries (Macón and Mañón 1977), no other country in Latin America has made such successful use of it, and indeed, only a few cities in Colombia itself have consistently done so. The keys to success appear to be a capable and credible local administration that establishes a clear link between benefits and taxes and delivers "value for money." Of course, much the same could likely be said about any effective and sustainable system of local finance.

One of the main advantages of PPPs for local governments is that, by relieving municipalities of the financial responsibility for up-front capital costs, they may enable infrastructure to be built at times when government funding is constrained (Tassonyi 1997). PPPs offer a way to get facilities built without incurring highly visible government debt. The operation of facilities and programs by private operators also reduces municipal operating expenditures and may enable additional revenue to be collected. Ancillary uses such as retail can be accommodated within facilities to provide another source of revenue. Finally, the public sector can draw on private-sector experience and skill.

On the other hand, potential risks are also associated with PPPs (Tassonyi 1997). For the private sector, there are risks that the regulatory framework could change and cause delays in the project. For the public sector, there is the risk that the nature of the public services provided will not be what the public wants. There may also be the risk that the private partner will fail and the public sector will have to take on the obligation in full, as has sometimes happened, for example, with respect to sports facilities. As with any partnership, how successful such arrangements are from the perspective of either partner depends very much on the exact details of the contractual arrangements regarding structure and risk-sharing.[29]

CHALLENGES AND ISSUES FACED BY METROPOLITAN AREAS

Even this brief outline of metropolitan public finance in practice and theory makes it clear that many challenges and issues face big cities around the world, and especially those in developing countries. One common problem, for example, is that the division of expenditure responsibilities is either not clear or simply wrong, as is arguably the case with respect to the extensive downloading of social financing on local governments that took place in the 1990s in a number of Eastern European countries (Bird, Ebel, and Wallich 1996). Similarly, in China local governments are responsible for such significant expenditures as pensions, unemployment insurance, disability, and minimum income support (Wong and Bird 2008).

Even clarity in expenditure assignment and assigning the "right" expenditures to the right government are not enough to ensure good results. There must also be both accountability, in terms of democratic accountability to the local population, and authority, in terms of the ability to manage expenditures and to determine (within limits) revenues. Both financial honesty and political accountability require that municipal budgeting, financial reporting, and auditing be not only comprehensive, comprehensible, comparable, and verifiable but also transparently public. In Brazil, for example, and increasingly in other countries, more and more local budgets and financial accounts are freely accessible on the Internet, and in some instances residents are actively encouraged to participate to some extent in developing the expenditure plans for their areas.[30]

---

[29] For detailed exploration of ways to structure PPP arrangements when this approach seems appropriate, see Engel, Fischer, and Galetovic (2010).

[30] Participatory budgeting is the practice of including citizens in decisions on how the budget is formulated. Porto Alegre, Brazil, introduced the practice in 1989. It is now used by 180 municipalities in Brazil and many

A strong central hand may be needed not only, as Glaeser (2011) emphasizes, to provide such urban basics as safe streets and safe water but also to ensure that good rules are in place and are complied with, both for urban public finance and for such essentially private-sector activities as construction and vehicle use. For example, higher-level governments might establish a model "framework" local budget law and financial reporting system and require adequate external audit. Improving the local budgeting and financial system along these lines will satisfy two essential requirements of good government: (1) establish the basis for financial control; and (2) provide reasonably accurate, uniform, and timely financial information.

Improving local finance information is not a small matter. Improved accountability may be the key to improved public-sector performance, but improved information is the key to accountability. The systematic collection, analysis, and reporting of information that can be used to verify compliance with goals and to assist future decisions are critical to successful urban development. Such information is essential to informed local participation through the political process and to the monitoring of local activity by the central agencies responsible for supervising and (sometimes) financing such activity. Unless local "publics" are aware of what is done, how well it is done, how much it cost, and who paid for it, no local constituency for effective government can be created. Similarly, unless central agencies can monitor and evaluate local performance, there can be no assurance that functions of national importance will be adequately performed once they have been decentralized. Perhaps paradoxically, an important accompaniment of any successful program to strengthen urban local bodies must therefore be an improvement in national evaluation capacity. Decentralization and improved central evaluation and assessment of local activities are not substitutes; they are complements.

Another common problem is that cities have inadequate revenue tools to meet expenditure requirements. In India, as mentioned earlier, some states have at times simply abolished local taxes without providing adequate substitute sources of revenue to municipalities, as when Rajasthan and Haryana simply abolished the property tax without even consulting urban local governments. Similarly, Punjab, again with no consultation, raised the threshold for the property tax so high that almost two-thirds of the properties are exempt (Rao and Bird 2010).

Cities are often further encumbered by unfunded edicts and mandates issued by higher-level governments. In China, for instance, where local governments have substantial social expenditure responsibilities, they cannot set tax rates, change the bases of collection, or introduce new taxes. On the other hand, they often control substantial assets such as land, enterprises, and sometimes natural resources. In these circumstances, it is not surprising that China's cities (and other local governments) have at times responded to fiscal pressures in a variety of undesirable ways. One is to accumulate arrears in wage payments to teachers and other employees,

---

countries in Latin America and elsewhere. Participatory budgeting was introduced, in part, as a way to address severe inequalities in services (especially water and sanitation) and quality of life (Abers 2001). However, experience suggests that such innovations work best when there is a good public financial system in place; they cannot replace such a system.

pension and unemployment insurance payments, and debt payments to suppliers such as utilities. Another is to exact fairly arbitrary payments under a variety of guises (fees, charges, and levies) from local businesses and residents.

Some countries have the opposite problem: instead of being required to spend money they do not have, local governments may be overdependent on intergovernmental transfers that are sometimes poorly designed (incentive perverse) and often, even worse from a local fiscal perspective, unreliable. As mentioned earlier, for example, when some Indian states abolished the local octroi, they promised to replace lost local revenues by state transfers. Unfortunately for local finances, the amount and timing of this transfer in most cases turned out to be more a matter of whim, it seemed, than of law.

Of course, not all problems of city finance are attributable to other governments. Some are definitely the fault of the local government. Both higher levels of government and outside observers have frequently, and critically, commented on the extent to which local governments fail to utilize adequately even those tax and fee powers that they have, in particular by failing to put forth an adequate collection effort. The "fiscal laziness" of subnational governments has been, for example, a common theme in the ongoing discussion of fiscal decentralization in Colombia, as well as in some other Latin American countries, although the empirical evidence of the existence and importance of this phenomenon is far from clear (Bird 2012).

The fragmentation of the governmental structure of metropolitan areas in many countries gives rise to other problems. For example, it is often both technically and politically difficult to make appropriate decisions on expenditures when benefits/costs spill over municipal boundaries, as has been the case with respect to some major aspects of urban development projects in Mexico City (Raich 2008). It can be equally difficult to provide local services in a coordinated and adequate fashion when higher-level governments persist in interfering in such detailed local issues as bus routes and the design of council buildings. How to share costs fairly within the metropolitan area is always and everywhere a controversial issue.

Different models of voluntary cooperation and special-purpose bodies have been used to address the fragmentation of governmental structure. In São Paulo, for example, the Inter-municipal Consortium of the Greater ABC Region was created in 1990 to coordinate economic development policies that had spillover effects across municipal boundaries (Arretche 2013). The Metropolitan Manila Development Authority was created in 1995 to perform planning, monitoring, and coordinating functions for the metropolitan area (but only if they do not diminish the autonomy of local governments on local matters) (Laquian 2002). These attempts at coordination have met with mixed success (Slack 2007a).

Sometimes, however, despite such problems, cities have managed to improve themselves. In Bangalore, for example, the local property tax was substantially reformed by revising the area-based values, introducing a self-assessment system, and improving the technology of the payments system with the result that revenue more than doubled in two years (Rao and Bird 2010). Properties were classified into different zones based on the guidance rental values per square foot set for each zone on the basis of type and quality of construction and age of the buildings. These values were then made available online so that any property owners could compute their tax liabilities simply by plugging in the location, type of construction, and area of the property; they could then also pay their taxes online.[31] The Bangalore experience suggests that such reforms work best when the system is simple and transparent enough to be easily understood by the general public and when there is both clarity in the reform process and thorough public discussion and debate when the reform is adopted. Online payment of the tax was also essential so that the tax-payer did not have to go to the tax department and face numerous hassles simply in order to pay the tax. Furthermore, by matching the properties paying the tax with those in the Geographical Information System (GIS), the government was able to identify and pursue many who were not paying the tax.

Finally, it is critically important to consider metropolitan finance in the context of the whole public policy system with respect to both metropolitan areas versus other municipalities and the relationship between the metropolitan city and the metropolitan region. As Burki, Perry, and Dillinger (1999, 24) put it, "A structure that fails to distinguish between major metropolitan areas and small villages makes it difficult to clearly define the functional responsibilities of local government." The standard economic theory of local governments does not distinguish among large metropolitan areas, intermediate-size cities, or towns and villages. If all local governments are assigned the same responsibilities, either the assignment reflects what the smallest municipalities can provide or, more likely, those municipalities are unable to fulfill their assigned responsibilities. From any economic perspective, it is clear that different types of municipalities should be distinguished in terms of expenditure assignment: big cities can and should do more.

Government structure should adequately encompass the relevant metropolitan region. In addition, appropriate fiscal relationships are needed both between the metropolitan region and the rest of the country and within the region itself. It is important both to avoid unduly subsidizing (or taxing) large urban areas and to price scarce public resources (especially the use of space and public services) properly within such areas.

Metropolitan cities should be given more access to fiscal bases such as property and vehicle taxes and a good local business tax, as well as some access to other tax bases (income and sales taxes) when they are expected to play significant roles in financing expensive and expanding soft services such as health and education. Most important, because metropolitan regions should be essentially self-financing, they should generally have greater fiscal autonomy than other urban or rural areas in terms of both greater responsibility for local services and greater ability to levy their own taxes and charges.

---

[31] A major weakness of this system is the need to revise the unit values periodically in keeping with changes in prices. In the absence of periodic revision, revenues will not respond to changes in the values of properties, and the buoyancy of the tax will depend only upon the addition of new properties. As a rule, it is politically difficult to change the values periodically. One way to overcome this problem might be to link these values automatically to an index of property values, as is done in Colombia, for example.

REFERENCES

Abers, Rebecca. 2001. Learning democratic practice: Distributing government resources through popular participation in Porto Alegre, Brazil. In *The challenge of urban government: Policies and practices*, ed. Mila Freire and Richard E. Stren, 129–143. Washington, DC: World Bank.

Acosta, Olga L., and Richard M. Bird. 2005. The dilemma of decentralization in Colombia. In *Fiscal reform in Colombia: Problems and prospects*, ed. Richard M. Bird, James M. Poterba, and Joel Slemrod, 247–286. Cambridge, MA: MIT Press.

American Petroleum Institute. 2012. Notes to state motor fuel excise and other taxes. www.api .org/statistics/fueltaxes/upload/State_Motor_Fuel_Excise_Tax_Update.pdf

Angel, Shlomo. 2011. Making room for a planet of cities. Policy Focus Report. Cambridge, MA: Lincoln Institute of Land Policy.

Annez, Patricia. 2010. Financing Indian cities: Opportunities and constraints in an nth best world. Policy Research Working Paper No. WPS5474. Washington, DC: World Bank.

Arretche, Marta. 2013. Governance and finance in two Brazilian metropolitan areas. In *Finance and governance of metropolitan areas in federal systems*, ed. Enid Slack and Rupak Chatto-padhyay. Toronto: Oxford University Press.

Bahl, Roy. 2002. Implementable rules of fiscal decentralization. In *Development, poverty and fiscal policy*, ed. M. Govinda Rao, 253–277. New Delhi: Oxford University Press.

———. 2009. *Property tax reform in developing and transition countries*. Washington, DC: U.S. Agency for International Development.

———. 2011. Financing metropolitan cities. In *Local government finance: The challenges of the 21st century*, ed. United Cities and Local Governments. Barcelona: United Cities and Local Governments.

Bahl, Roy, and Johannes Linn. 1992. *Urban public finance in developing countries*. New York: Oxford University Press.

Barter, Paul. 2010. Parking policy in Asian cities. Paper No. Lkyspp: 10–15. Singapore: Lee Kuan Yew School of Public Policy, National University of Singapore.

Bird, Richard M. 1976. *Charging for public services: A new look at an old idea*. Toronto: Canadian Tax Foundation.

———. 2001. User charges in local government finance. In *The challenge of urban government: Policies and practices*, ed. Mila Freire and Richard E. Stren, 171–182. Washington, DC: World Bank.

———. 2003. A new look at local business taxes. *Tax Notes International* 30(7):695–711.

———. 2005. Getting it right: Financing urban development in China. *Asia-Pacific Tax Bulletin* 11(2):107–117.

———. 2006. Local and regional revenues: Realities and prospects. In *Perspectives on fiscal federalism*, ed. Richard M. Bird and François Vaillancourt, 177–96. WBI Learning Resources Series. Washington, DC: World Bank.

———. 2009. Tax assignment revisited. In *Tax reform in the 21st century*, ed. John G. Head and Richard E. Krever, 441–470. New York: Wolters Kluwer.

———. 2012. Fiscal decentralization in Colombia: A work (still) in progress. Washington, DC: World Bank.

Bird, Richard M., Robert D. Ebel, and Christine Wallich. 1996. *Decentralization of the socialist state: Intergovernmental finance in transition economies*. Aldershot, U.K.: Avebury.

Bird, Richard M., and Pierre-Pascal Gendron. 2001. Vats in federal countries: International experience and emerging possibilities. *Bulletin for International Fiscal Documentation* 55(7):293–309.

Bird, Richard M., and Barbara D. Miller. 1989. Taxes, pricing and the poor. In *Government policy and the poor in developing countries*, ed. Richard M. Bird and Susan Horton. Toronto: University of Toronto Press.

Bird, Richard M., and Enid Slack. 1993. *Urban public finance in Canada*. Toronto: John Wiley and Sons.

———. 2004. *International handbook on land and property taxation*. Cheltenham, U.K.: Edward Elgar.

———. 2007. An approach to metropolitan governance and finance. *Environment and Planning C: Government and Policy* 25(5):729–755.

Bird, Richard M., and Almos Tassonyi. 2001. Constraints on provincial and municipal borrowing in Canada: Markets, rules, and norms. *Canadian Public Administration* 44(1):84–109.

Bird, Richard M., and Thomas Tsiopoulos. 1997. User charges for public services: Potentials and problems. *Canadian Tax Journal* 45(1):25–86.

Bird, Richard M., and Eric M. Zolt. 2005. Redistribution via taxation: The limited role of the personal income tax in developing countries. *UCLA Law Review* 52(6):1627–1695.

Bordignon, Massimo, Silvia Gianni, and Paolo Panteghini. 2001. Reforming business taxation: Lessons from Italy? *International Tax and Public Finance* 8:191–210.

Borero Ochoa, Oscar. 2011. Betterment levy in Colombia: Relevance, procedures, and social acceptability. *Land Lines* (April):14–19.

Burki, Shahid J., Guillermo E. Perry, and William R. Dillinger. 1999. *Beyond the center: Decentralizing the state*. Washington, DC: World Bank.

Chernick, Howard, and Andrew Reschovsky. 2006. Local public finance: Issues for metropolitan regions. In *Competitive cities in the global economy*, 417–432. OECD Territorial Reviews. Paris: Organisation for Economic Co-operation and Development.

Connolly, Katrina, and Michael E. Bell. 2010. Financing urban government in transition countries: Assessment uniformity and the property tax. *Environment and Planning C: Government and Policy* 28(6):978–991.

Daniere, Amrita G., and Jose A. Gomez-Ibañez. 2002. Environmental and communications infrastructure in Chile. In *Chile: Political economy of urban development*, ed. Edward L. Glaeser and John R. Meyer. Cambridge, MA: John F. Kennedy School of Government, Harvard University.

Ebel, Robert D., and Serdar Yilmaz. 2003. On the measurement and impact of fiscal decentralization. In *Public finance in developing and transitional countries*, ed. Jorge Martinez-Vazquez and James Alm. Cheltenham, U.K.: Edward Elgar.

Engel, Eduardo, Ronald Fischer, and Alexander Galetovic. 2010. The economics of infrastructure finance: Public-private partnerships versus public provision. *EIB Papers* 15(1): 40–69. Santiago, Chile: University of Chile.

Florida, Richard. 2002. *The rise of the creative class*. New York: Basic Books.

Fox, William F., and Tami Gurley. 2006. *Will consolidation improve sub-national governments?* Washington, DC: World Bank.

Freire, Mila. 2001. Introduction. In *The challenge of urban government: Policies and practices*, ed. Mila Freire and Richard E. Stren. Washington, DC: World Bank.

Gilbert, Guy. 2010. Beyond inter-municipal partnerships towards two-tier municipalities? Presentation at the 6th Symposium on Fiscal Federalism, Barcelona (June).

Glaeser, Edward L. 2011. *The triumph of the city*. New York: Penguin.

Glaeser, Edward L., and Joshua D. Gottlieb. 2009. The wealth of cities: Agglomeration economies and spatial equilibrium in the United States. *Journal of Economic Literature* 47(4):983–1028.

Hermann, Zoltán, Tamás M. Horváth, Gábor Péteri, and Gábor Ungvári. 1999. *Allocation of local government functions: Criteria and conditions—analysis and policy proposals for Hungary*. Washington, DC: Fiscal Decentralization Initiative for Central and Eastern Europe.

Jofre-Monseny, Jordi, and Albert Solé-Ollé. 2008. Which communities should be afraid of mobility? The effects of agglomeration economies on the sensitivity of firm location to local taxes. CESifo Working Paper No. 2311. Munich: Ifo Institute, Center for Economic Studies, and CESifo GmbH (May).

Kim, Junghun, Jorgen Lotz, and Niels J. Mau. 2010. *General grants versus earmarked grants: Theory and practice*. Copenhagen: Korea Institute of Public Finance and Danish Ministry of Interior and Health.

Kitchen, Harry M., and Enid Slack. 2006. Providing services to remote areas. In *Perspectives on fiscal federalism*, ed. Richard M. Bird and François Vaillancourt. WBI Learning Resources Series. Washington, DC: World Bank.

Laquian, Aprodicio. 2002. Metro Manila: People's participation and social inclusion in a city of villages. In *Urban governance around the world*, ed. Blair A. Ruble, Richard E. Stren, Joseph S. Tulchin, and Diana H. Varat, 74–110. Washington, DC: Woodrow Wilson International Center for Scholars.

Linn, Johannes. 1982. The costs of urbanization in developing countries. *Economic Development and Cultural Change* 30(3):625–648.

Macón, Jorge, and José M. Mañón. 1977. *Financing urban and rural development through betterment levies: The Latin America experience*. Westport, CT: Praeger.

Meltsner, Arnold J. 1972. *The politics of city revenue*. Berkeley: University of California Press.

Ministry of Internal Affairs and Communications. *Local government finance in Japan* (2012). www.soumu.go.jp/english/pdf/lpfij.pdf

Mushkin, Selma J., ed. 1972. *Public prices for public products*. Washington, DC: Urban Institute.

Nowlan, David M. 1994. Local taxation as an instrument of policy. In *The changing Canadian metropolis: A public policy perspective*, vol. 2, ed. F. Frisken. Berkeley: Institute of Governmental Studies Press, University of California.

OECD. 1999. *Taxing powers of state and local governments*. Paris.

———. 2006. *Competitive cities in the global economy*. Paris.

Peterson, George E. 2009. *Unlocking land values to finance urban infrastructure*. Trends and Policy Options No. 7. Washington, DC: World Bank.

Pethe, Abhay. 2011. Metropolitan public finances—the case of Mumbai. Unpublished manuscript.

Raich, Uri. 2008. *Unequal development—decentralization and metropolitan finance in Mexico City*. Saarbrücken: VDM Verlag.

Rao, M. Govinda, and Richard M. Bird. 2010. Urban governance and finance in India. Working Paper No. 2010–68. New Delhi: National Institute of Public Finance and Policy (April).

Rao, M. Govinda, and Nirvikar Singh. 2005. *The political economy of federalism in India*. New Delhi: Oxford University Press.

Rhoads, William G., and Richard M. Bird. 1967. Financing urbanization in developing countries by benefit taxation: Case study of Colombia. *Land Economics* 42(4):403–412.

Richardson, Harry W. 1987. The costs of urbanization: A four-country comparison. *Economic Development and Cultural Change* 35(3):561–580.

Rojas, Eduardo, Juan R. Cuadrado-Roura, and Jose M. Fernandez Guell, eds. 2008. *Governing the metropolis: Principles and causes*. Washington: DC: Inter-American Development Bank.

Slack, Enid. 2002. *Municipal finance and the pattern of urban growth*. Toronto: C. D. Howe Institute.

———. (2007a). *Managing the coordination of service delivery in metropolitan cities: The role of metropolitan governance*. Washington, DC: World Bank.

———. (2007b). Grants to large cities and metropolitan areas. In *Intergovernmental fiscal transfers, principles and practice*, ed. Robin Boadway and Anwar Shah, 453–481. Washington, DC: World Bank.

———. 2011. The property tax . . . in theory and practice. In *IEB's world report on fiscal federalism '10*, 24–34. Barcelona: Institut d'Economia de Barcelona.

Slack, Enid, and Richard M. Bird. 1991. Financing urban growth through development charges. *Canadian Tax Journal* 39(5):1288–1304.

Slack, Enid, Larry S. Bourne, and Meric S. Gertler. 2003. *Vibrant cities and city-regions: Responding to emerging challenges*. Toronto: Panel on the Role of Government.

Slack, Enid, and R. Chattopadhyay, ed. 2013. *Finance and governance of metropolitan areas in federal systems*. Toronto: Oxford University Press.

Steytler, Nico. 2013. Governance and finance of two South African metropolitan areas. In *Finance and governance of metropolitan areas in federal systems*, ed. Enid Slack and Rupak Chattopadhyay. Toronto: Oxford University Press.

Stren, Richard E., and Robert Cameron. 2005. Metropolitan governance reform: An introduction. *Public Administration and Development* 25(4): 275–284.

Swianiewicz, Paul. 2011. Tax sharing, grants and fiscal decentralisation in Poland. Presentation to OECD Technical Workshop on Taxonomy of Grants and Measures of Decentralisation, Paris (March).

Tassonyi, Almos. 1997. Financing municipal infrastructure in Canada's city-regions. In *Urban governance and finance: A question of who does what*, ed. Paul A.R. Hobson and France St-Hilaire. Montreal: Institute for Research on Public Policy.

Thirsk, Wayne. 1982. Political sensitivity vs. economic sensibility: A tale of two property taxes. In *Tax policy options in the 1980s*, ed. Wayne Thirsk and John Whalley, 384–407. Toronto: Canadian Tax Foundation.

Van Ryneveld, Philip, and Michael Parker. 2002. Property tax reform in Cape Town. In *Property taxes in South Africa: Challenges in the post-apartheid era*, ed. Michael E. Bell and John H. Bowman, 157–173. Cambridge, MA: Lincoln Institute of Land Policy.

Vazquez-Caro, J., and M. Childress. 2010. Urban renewal-urban decay in Colombia. Presentation to World Bank, Washington, DC (July).

Werneck, Rogério L.F. 2007. Tax reform in Brazil: An evaluation at the crossroads. Rio de Janeiro: Catholic University of Rio de Janeiro (December).

Wong, Christine C.P., and Richard M. Bird. 2008. China's fiscal system: A work in progress. In *China's great transformation: Origins, mechanisms, and consequences of the post-reform economic boom*, ed. Loren Brandt and Thomas G. Rawski, 429–466. Cambridge: Cambridge University Press.

World Bank. 2007. *Designing a tax system for micro and small businesses: Guide for practitioners.* Washington, DC: World Bank.

Zimmermann, Horst. 2009. Berlin, Germany. In *Finance and governance of capital cities in federal systems*, ed. Enid Slack and Rupak Chattopadhyay, 102–125. Montreal: McGill-Queen's University Press.

Property Taxes in Metropolitan Cities

WILLIAM J. MCCLUSKEY AND RIËL C. D. FRANZSEN

This chapter reviews the practice of property taxation with the focus on metropolitan cities in developing and transition countries.[1] Since there are no comparative data to rely on, this chapter presents a database constructed from a sample of metros. Using this sample as illustrative, some important questions about the practice are examined:

- What is the revenue performance of the property tax?
- Is there a pattern to the practice of property taxation among large urban local governments, that is, in the choice of a tax base, the structure of rates, or preferential treatments?
- What choices have metros made about administration of the metro property tax, for example, identification of properties, valuation, billing, collection, and enforcement? To what extent do metros utilize economies of scale to drive efficiencies in the administration of the property tax?
- Do metros have different powers in property taxation compared with other local governments in the country?
- What are the main obstacles to overcome if the effective rate of property tax is to be increased in metros?

REVENUE MOBILIZATION

The importance of property taxation in mobilizing revenues in metros is not surprising (table 7.1), because the concentration of property wealth in metropolitan areas gives a substantial base for taxation. In most cities in this sample, it accounts for 20 percent or more of total revenues (including transfers) and is the dominant

---

[1]The term *metro* is used to refer to large cities.

TABLE 7.1

Importance of the property tax in select metropolitan cities

Metro/city	Percentage of total city revenue		Percentage of local tax revenue	
	2005	2010	2005	2010
Belo Horizonte	No data	No data	36.1	31.2
Cape Town	22.6	20.5	33.1	41.1
Durban (eThekwini)	27.9	21.6	40.5	55.3
Hong Kong	6.9	3.78	8.77	5.10
Johannesburg	19.9	16.3	30.0	43.8
Kampala	3.2	10.7 (2008)	20.2	40.6 (2008)
Kuala Lumpur	68.4	44.9	92.0	93.0
Makati City (metro Manila)	39.0	34.0 (2009)	47.0	41.0 (2009)
Manila (metro Manila)	27.0	28.0 (2009)	43.0	54.0 (2009)
Muntinlupa City (metro Manila)	27.0	28.0 (2009)	52.0	49.0 (2009)
Quezon City (metro Manila)	31.0	21.0 (2009)	44.0	33.0 (2009)
Pretoria (Tshwane)	20.4	19.4	28.4	42.8
Rio de Janeiro	21.8	17.5	34.5	25.0
São Paulo	27.2	24.8	35.0	31.0
Singapore	6.12	5.80	6.90	6.30

sources: Data obtained from various city or country reporters.

local tax. However, revenues from the property tax have declined in their relative importance in recent years in this sample. One explanation for this is the rapid growth of intergovernmental transfers during the economic expansion in the 2000s and the failure of assessed property values to keep up with rising property values (see table 7.1).[2]

Another feature of the property tax to note is its revenue concentration in large cities. For example, Accra, Ghana, contributed more than 50 percent of the country total in 2007 (see table 7.2). In Kenya (Nairobi, Mombassa), the Philippines (Manila), South Africa (Cape Town, Durban), and Tanzania (Dar es Salaam), the property tax is much more important in the metros than in secondary cities and smaller local municipalities. In 2004–2005, property tax collections in the six South African metros (namely, Cape Town, Ekurhuleni, eThekwini, Johannesburg, Nelson Mandela Bay and Tshwane) accounted for 70.3 percent of the country total, but the total metro population accounted for only approximately 42 percent of the national population. Although the property tax generally performs better at the metro than at the country level, a review of revenue growth in real terms over a three-year period (2006–2009) in a number of metros reveals that it has made significant progress in only a few cities (see table 7.3). Interestingly, the greater success with property tax collections in Belgrade, Belo Horizonte, Bengaluru, Cape Town, and

---

[2]Dar es Salaam (Mukhandi 2012) and Kampala (Olima 2010) are outliers in showing a significant increase in reliance on the property tax in overall city revenue, but this could at least partly be explained by the abolition of poll taxes in Tanzania and Uganda.

TABLE 7.2

Importance of metropolitan property tax in select developing counties

Metro	Population Country (million)	Population Metro (million)	Population Metro percentage total	Property tax Country total	Property tax Metro	Property tax Metro percentage of total
Accra	25.2	3.9	15.48	3.73 (2007)	1.93	51.74
Belgrade	7.3	1.7	23.29	16.832 (2009)	4.793	28.48
Cape Town	48.9	3.0	6.13	26.492 (2009)	3.241	12.23
Dar es Salaam	43.6	2.7	6.19	7.580 (2010)	4.212	55.57
Durban (eThekwini)	48.9	3.5	7.16	26.492 (2009)	3.912	14.77
Johannesburg	48.9	7.5	15.34	26.492 (2009)	3.331	12.57
Kampala	35.9	1.7	4.74	43.30 (2008)	4.98	11.5
Kingston, Jamaica	2.9	0.7	24.14	1,395 (2009)	384	27.53
Manila	103.8	21.3	20.52	30.185 (2009)	13.779	45.65
Pretoria (Tshwane)	48.9	2.5	5.11	26.492 (2009)	2.257	8.52

SOURCES: Data obtained from various city or country reporters.

TABLE 7.3

Real growth in per capita property tax revenues in select metros (US$)

City	2006 Property tax (millions)	2006 Population (millions)	2006 Property tax per capita	2009 Property tax (millions)	2009 Population (millions)	2009 Property tax per capita
Belgrade	42.34	1.6	26.46	66.85	2.0	33.43
Belo Horizonte	115.91	4.0	28.98	127.14	4.2	30.27
Bengaluru	56.95	6.8	8.38	137.31	8.0	17.16
Cape Town	285.76	3.2	89.30	319.94	3.4	94.10
Dar es Salaam	2.62	3.2	0.82	3.06	3.6	0.85
Durban (eThekwini)	359.00	3.3	108.79	383.69	3.5	109.63
Johannesburg	364.13	3.7	98.41	321.52	4.0	80.38
Kampala	1.33	1.4	0.95	3.51	1.5	2.34
Kingston, Jamaica	7.28	0.66	11.03	4.12	0.68	6.06
Kuala Lumpur	174.74	6.9	25.32	178.38	7.1	25.12
Manila metro	317.60	14.8	21.46	288.71	16.3	17.71
Porto Alegre	61.82	2.8	22.08	71.83	3.7	19.41
Pretoria (Tshwane)	202.62	2.2	92.10	222.62	2.4	92.76
Rio de Janeiro	430.66	10.8	39.88	395.42	12.0	32.95
São Paulo	1,087.81	17.7	61.46	997.64	18.8	53.07

The year 2006 was used as the base year, and all local currencies were converted to U.S. dollars using the average exchange rate for 2006. The World Development Report consumer price indices (World Bank 2011) were used to determine the real growth in terms of 2006 U.S. dollars for each city. Population figures for 2006 and 2009 are rough estimates.

SOURCES: Data obtained from various city or country reporters.

Kampala can be ascribed to structural reforms in the property tax and/or improved administration.

TYPES OF PROPERTY TAX

The definition of the tax base is a decision usually taken at the national level in unitary countries, or at the state/provincial level in federal countries. The choice of the tax base defines the revenue potential of the property tax. In some countries (Australia, Kenya, Malaysia, New Zealand), legislation explicitly allows cities to select an appropriate tax base from two or more options. In a number of countries, different tax bases are prescribed for different property-use categories (Côte d'Ivoire, Niger, United Kingdom). In most cases, however, a single tax base is prescribed by law (Brazil, Estonia, Indonesia, Philippines, South Africa).

A variety of tax bases are presently utilized in different jurisdictions (Franzsen and McCluskey 2013), ranging from simple or calibrated area-based taxes (Freetown, Dar es Salaam, Kinshasa) to value-based taxes. Regarding the latter, there are examples of land-value or site-value taxes (Kingston, Nairobi, Tallinn), annual or rental-value taxes (Accra, Cairo, Bangkok, Hong Kong, Kampala, Kuala Lumpur, Singapore), and capital-improved (market-value) taxes (Bogotá, Cape Town, Lagos, Rio de Janeiro, Yaoundé).

Area-Based Systems

Area-based systems are used in many cities to get around some of the difficulties of valuation, but there are questions over its fairness and revenue buoyancy of the tax base.[3] For example, in Kinshasa, properties are categorized by neighborhood and taxed accordingly. In Sierra Leone, the law prescribes an annual value-based system, but Freetown, in the absence of a formal market and sufficient valuation skills, presently still utilizes an area-based system (Jibao 2009).

Cities in Tanzania utilize both an area-based and a value-based system. In Dar es Salaam, some adjustments to the area base are made for use, size, and location. This might add fairness to the system, but the administration seems overly complex for a tax with such a low revenue yield. Ahmedabad introduced a "calibrated" area-based system (Rao 2008) that indexes each property according to location, building size, usage, age, and occupancy. There are no clear provisions on how these factors could be calibrated or amended in the future, so there is little buoyancy in the system, apart from the increase in property numbers (Cornia 2008), and revenues have been decreasing.

Bengaluru (Bangalore) has a rather unique system, which can best be described as a hybrid between an area-based system and a value-based system. In 2000, property tax reforms were initiated with the introduction of the self-assessment scheme where property owners declared the physical characteristics of their property. The process was transparent, public meetings were held, and most important, it was backed by politicians and the media. More than 60 percent of taxpayers filed their

---

[3] An area-based system is one where tax liability is related directly to the physical characteristics of the property, especially the size of the land and/or buildings.

declarations within the prescribed 45-day period. In 2008, a unit-area-value taxation system was introduced. This tax is determined with reference to the average rate of expected returns from a property per square foot per month, depending on the location and use of the property. The municipal corporation was classified into value zones based on published guidance values produced by the Department of Stamps and Registration, which are adjusted regularly. Over a three-year cycle, the value increase must be at least 15 percent, resulting in steadily increasing property tax revenues.

Annual Value Systems

A number of countries, especially former British (Ghana, Hong Kong, Malaysia, Singapore, Uganda) and French (Côte d'Ivoire, Niger) colonies, utilize an annual value property tax system (Franzsen and McCluskey 2013). Singapore and Hong Kong operate vibrant, state-of-the-art rental value systems with properties being revalued annually. Although a number of large cities in India have abandoned their outdated annual value systems (Rao 2008), Mumbai still uses the annual value system under somewhat adverse circumstances. Rental values have been fixed indefinitely, due to strict rent control legislation. Given static values over an extended period, the tax rate exceeds 200 percent. As approximately 65 percent of properties in Mumbai are rented, there is severe resistance to implementing a more appropriate property tax system or significantly reforming the current system.

In Abidjan, an annual value system is used for developed parcels, whereas a capital value system is used for undeveloped parcels. In Uganda, an annual value system was retained when the new property tax law was enacted in 2005, despite the shortage of qualified valuers in the country. From 2003 to 2005, a new valuation roll consisting of approximately 110,500 properties was prepared for Kampala. Why an annual value system was retained, given the paucity of valuation skills in the country, is a question that must be asked.

Capital Value Systems

UNIMPROVED LAND VALUE OR SITE VALUE SYSTEMS

Systems based on unimproved land values or site values are presently used in some cities in Australia and New Zealand, such as Sydney, Brisbane, and Christchurch. In developing and transition countries, it is encountered in Kingston, Harare, Nairobi, Suva, and Tallinn. Until 2008, site value taxation was also used in Pretoria (now the City of Tshwane) and Johannesburg. However, new property tax legislation in South Africa mandated that all cities migrate to a capital improved value system. Various studies have been undertaken in Jamaica to research the feasibility of a system based on improved values. In the context of the country, the recommendations have consistently been to retain the system of unimproved land value (Franzsen and McCluskey 2008). In Nairobi, the system is under pressure because the most recent valuation roll could not be implemented. Rates are still determined annually with reference to the 1982 valuation roll. Estonia introduced a land value tax in 1993, and coverage is excellent.

CAPITAL IMPROVED VALUE

The majority of metros studied use some form of capital improved value system. However, systems vary rather significantly in terms of what is taxed and how it must be assessed. South African cities tax the "market value" of the property, but in Dar es Salaam buildings are valued on a depreciated replacement cost basis, with land excluded from the base.

The Manila metro cities value land and buildings separately. Land assessments are based on market transactions, whereas the assessment of buildings and other improvements is based on depreciated replacement cost. This approach is also used in most Latin American cities and is to some extent a solution to the problem of scarcity of valuers/assessors. However, in some cities, such as Bogotá, the assessment process has become more driven by market prices.

Jakarta uses a rather simplified system of assessment for both land and buildings. Land is categorized into approximately 100 value zones according to use and location, whereas buildings are categorized into 40 classes, with each class having a prescribed unit price per square meter. Therefore, individual properties are not separately valued but, rather, assessed according to the prescribed land zone rate per square meter and building class rate per square meter.

SELECTION OF TAX BASE

Why a city uses a particular basis for its property tax can often be traced to the historical British or French rental value approach. However, with the passing of time, property markets in cities evolve, often creating a disjoint with the current practice and the status of the property market. For example, the "old" rental value approach failed in India because rent control had reduced market evidence to the point that a value-based approach was untenable. In South Africa, the lack of reliable transaction evidence significantly weakened the case for a site value base. This can lead to a nationally or locally driven policy to change the system, as in South Africa and several Indian metros. The absence of reliable data on market value of transactions is a major issue in the debate about the most appropriate base for the property tax. Where this is the case and valuation expertise is limited, there has been a tendency to look to area-based approaches. This has raised the question of whether a value-based system is necessarily the best option. An outdated and/or incomplete system relying on discrete values may indeed be more inequitable than a pragmatic, simplistic alternative based on simple or adjusted areas or on value bands.

Infrequent revaluation is a major issue in many cities, such as Rio de Janeiro and Accra. There are exceptions, but dynamic and progressive cities are in some instances held back by national government. Examples of this can be seen in Nairobi (1982 roll), Kuala Lumpur (1992 roll), metro Manila (1993), Rio de Janeiro (1999), and São Paulo (2000), where revaluations are dated not because of the lack of capacity, but because of political interference. With the exception of Bengaluru and Bogotá (Bird 2004), where city-specific property taxation applies, all the other metros reviewed are subject to national (or state) laws pertaining to the property tax.

Size of Tax Base

An important question is whether the property tax rolls have been expanded to keep up with population growth and rapid urbanization. In Accra, Dar es Salaam, and Kampala, valuers have been unable to keep valuation rolls current on existing properties, much less cover the new properties created as a result of the rapid growth in these cities. However, in Bengaluru and Bogotá, where the property tax is linked to and underpinned by a comprehensive Geographic Information System (GIS) database, comprehensive coverage is more attainable.

General revaluations and basic maintenance of the valuation roll are major undertakings, as illustrated by the property counts shown in table 7.4. The city of Cape Town, for example, has nearly 800,000 parcels, of which about 80 percent are residential.

TABLE 7.4

The importance of residential properties in the tax base

| City | Number of properties in the tax base (current valuation roll) | Residential properties | | | Average residential 2010 tax bill (US$) |
		Percentage of total number	Percentage of total value	Percentage of revenue	
Belo Horizonte	698,603 (2009)	74	66	58	437
Bengaluru	1,158,000 (2011)	71	40	No data	No data
Bogotá	1,788,229 (2004)	81	61	No data	208
Buenos Aires	1,610,901 (2003)	69	64	No data	105
Cape Town	792,356 (2011)	80	68	41	429
Dar es Salaam	476,667 (2011)	85	76	No data	12
Durban (eThekwini)	509,641 (2011)	87	64	39	459
Hong Kong	2,350,445 (2010)	75	41	No data	676
Johannesburg	812,275 (2008)	82	68	44	624
Kingston	109,011 (2010)	72	60	No data	73
Kuala Lumpur	463,033 (2010)	75	39	No data	189
Makati (metro Manila)	134,983 (2010)	78	27	No data	263
Muntinlupa (metro Manila)	107,086 (2010)	77	28	No data	100
Navotas (metro Manila)	29,384 (2010)	78	28	No data	20
Pretoria (Tshwane)	522,388 (2011)	87	72	39	750
Porto Alegre	538,296 (2011)	76	50	No data	233
Rio de Janeiro	1,630,225 (1999) 2,000,000 (2010 estimate)	78 (1999)	63	40 (1999)	153 (1999)
São Paulo	2,762,843 (2005) 3,000,000 (2010 estimate)	No data	No data	No data	273

sources: Data obtained from various city or country reports and/or reporters.

Taxpayer

The taxpayer is usually the owner or the occupier of the taxable property and in some instances can be both. Regarding area-based and capital value systems, generally the owner is principally liable for the tax; however, if the owner cannot be found, the occupier may be liable (Bengaluru). In the case of annual rental value systems, the occupier is usually the principal taxpayer, although there are exceptions. In Abidjan, Bangkok, and Niamey, the owner of residential property is taxed, although the tax is only levied on properties that are not occupied by the owner. In Bangkok, this presents tax administration with challenges in identifying taxpayers (Varanyuwatana 1999).

Tax Rates

Because of differences in valuation methods and legal tax bases, comparisons of nominal tax rates are not meaningful. And, because data on real market value or gross domestic product are rarely available by metro, comparisons of effective tax rates are not possible. However, city governments have different levels of discretion to determine their tax rates and use this discretion in different ways.

In a number of cities (Cairo, Jakarta, Kigali, Yaoundé) tax rates are fixed by the central government. Other cities (in metro Manila, Kuala Lumpur, Dar es Salaam, Kampala, Lagos) have some discretion in making adjustments to their tax rates, but this power is rarely used. For example, in Lagos, rates have not changed since 2003, even though the valuation rolls are badly outdated. The result is a decline in revenue receipts. By contrast, the Hong Kong tax rate has not changed for many years either, but revenues have been buoyed by annual revaluations.

Where metros have the power to set the rate, the variations are very large, usually depending on revenue targets for the property tax. Nairobi sets very high nominal rates, because of the site value tax base and the outdated 1982 valuation roll. South African metros have set rates that range from 0.5 to 0.9 percent of market value for residential properties and from 1.0 to 2.5 percent for commercial properties. In contrast, the tax rate on capital value in Yaoundé and Douala in Cameroon is 0.11 percent (of which only 0.01 percent is assigned to the cities).

PROPERTY TAX ADMINISTRATION

The property tax is difficult to administer (Martinez-Vazquez 2011). However, the administrative costs may be less in the metros, where they can often take advantage of economies of scale and develop synergies and advantageous linkages between various in-city departments. Such benefits may not be available to smaller cities. However, not all metros approach property tax administration in the same way, and some are more efficient than others. Administrative arrangements and outcomes are often effected by metropolitan government structure, for example, in the unified metros such as Cape Town, Johannesburg, Jakarta, and Bogotá, as opposed to fragmented metros such as Manila, Mexico City, Rio de Janeiro, Dar es Salaam, and, as far as collection is concerned, Kampala.

Can it therefore be postulated that metros have a distinct advantage in administering the property tax? This question is addressed in the following sections, which examine the four key administrative features of the property tax:

1. Identification of property, occupancy, and ownership.
2. Inventory management.
3. Assessment.
4. Billing, collection, and enforcement.

Identification of Property, Occupancy, and Ownership

The fairness and revenue mobilization goals of the property tax require full coverage of the base; that is, all property parcels have been identified and given a unique reference number; inventory on land and improvements has been gathered; and the taxpayers have been identified. This is one of the most resource-intensive administrative aspects of property tax administration and, consequently, one of the most expensive. Metros with integrated management functions can achieve efficiencies and reduce costs, particularly where, for example, building control, physical planning, and land use departments are electronically linked to the valuation department, as is the case in Kuala Lumpur and South African metros. Where these functions are not within the control of the metros, issues of information flow, accessibility, and data timeliness create severe problems (Accra, Dar es Salaam, Manila).

Crucial in this respect is the cadastral map, which should identify parcels and their boundaries. In this regard, donor agencies have been extremely active over the last 20–30 years in funding projects aimed at land titling and registration. Land administration and management projects in Jamaica, the Philippines, and Thailand have been making significant progress in creating titles for unregistered land and providing "owners" with formal ownership documents. In Kingston, approximately 85 percent of all parcels have a registered title. Prior to the creation of the National Land Agency in Jamaica in 2000, it took 70 days to produce a new certificate of title. Ten years later, in 2010, the average is 30 days.

GIS is the internationally recognized environment upon which digital mapping and land titling is being based. Latin American and South African cities have their cadastres within a GIS framework. Such technologies as satellite imagery, aerial photography, and Google Maps have made significant contributions to improving property tax coverage. Clearly, some metros have the financial capacity to do this, as is evident from the practice in South Africa. Conversely, the use of such technology in, for example, Manila is restricted to the larger cities in the metropolitan region (Makati and Quezon). In several cities, it is estimated that coverage is now almost 100 percent (Kuala Lumpur, Hong Kong, South African metros, Bogotá, Bengaluru). In some Latin American cities, in contrast, informal and illegal constructions are generally not recorded, and the coverage is therefore around 75 percent (De Cesare 2004). The experience is less satisfactory in poorer cities; for example, in 2002 coverage in Dar es Salaam was approximately 30 percent (McCluskey and Franzsen 2005). Difficulties have arisen for other metros when they have no control over the cadastre (Dar es Salaam, Kingston) or when they have no resources to create their own GIS (e.g., Accra, Kampala, and smaller cities in metro Manila).

Metros tend to have a real advantage in this area because they need to create effective land use planning, and in this respect GIS is a principal tool. Bogotá is a good example of a metro that has been given the devolved power to manage and maintain its part of the national cadastre, which resulted in a significant increase in the coverage and, ultimately, in assessed value (Bustamante and Gaviria 2004).

Another example of progress in this area is Bengaluru. This city commenced a GIS project in 2008. An important feature was the allocation of unique property identity numbers, which links property location with property tax data (i.e., location, size, use, ownership, tax liability, and tax payment).

The three Baltic countries of Estonia, Latvia, and Lithuania are interesting in terms of how their property taxes have developed since their independence in the early 1990s. Fundamental to the process was the development of a real property cadastre linked to a land registration system (Malme and Youngman 2008). Each country adopted a centralized approach and created national bodies to develop and maintain these systems. The development of the cadastre utilizing GIS technology has resulted in almost 100 percent property base coverage. GIS and mass valuation approaches have been extensively used in all three counties, permitting the annual updating of values. In Lithuania, for example, some 3 million parcels of land and buildings are revalued each year (Aleksiene and Bagdonavicius 2008).

Self-declaration by way of returns that provide information on the owner's property is widely used as a means of updating the property inventory. This is the case in Bengaluru, Hong Kong, and Kuala Lumpur, as well as many cities in francophone Africa (Abidjan, Kigali, Kinshasa, Niamey). Indian cities, such as Ahmedabad, Chennai, and Delhi, also use self-declaration (even though it is referred to as self-assessment; Rao 2008). Self-declaration of transactions is used in Manila. Pure self-assessment is uncommon; however, Bogotá has successfully used this approach since 1993.

Inventory Management

The assessment department should be the central hub for the property tax system because of its electronic data-sharing systems and protocols with cadastral offices, land registry, and planning and building control departments, as well as the finance and revenue departments. In Jamaica, the creation of the National Land Agency has brought previously separate government departments dealing with property together under one agency (valuation, mapping, titles, and estate management).

With the developments in information technology, the storage and manipulation of data have become more accessible and affordable. A property tax inventory can be massive; for example, if a city has 1 million properties and for each property there are 15 pieces of information, then the database will contain 15 million bits of information, all of which must be maintained in some coherent, logical manner. How the city manages this information is crucial. Property taxes that incorporate improvements into the tax base tend to be more resource intensive compared with land value and area-based approaches. Therefore, the former involves greater administrative costs in maintaining the inventory for existing properties and new properties. The level of computerization and integrated data-sharing systems should create economies and reduce costs. While comparative evidence is difficult to find, it is possible to draw some inferences from the total number of taxable properties and the number of assessors/valuers. In cities that have highly computerized functions, the average number of properties per valuer ranges from 17,000 to 21,000 (Pretoria, Hong Kong, Kuala Lumpur), whereas for those cities using more manual/paper-based approaches, the average ranges from 5,000 to 7,000 (Manila).

In most of the cities, the inventory management is fully computerized. In some cases (Kuala Lumpur, Hong Kong, the larger metro Manila cities, and the South African metros), the assessment department receives weekly/monthly electronic downloads from other departments indicating changes to properties and transaction information.

Transaction evidence can be particularly problematic with respect to two issues: (1) how sales are recorded and notified to the various local and central government departments, such as stamp duty, title registration, and assessor offices; and (2) the reliability of the recorded transaction price. In this case, metros tend to suffer from the same limitations as other smaller jurisdictions: they are at the mercy of archaic paper-based systems that are inefficient and time intensive. Developments in electronic and online delivery of documentation are improving the flow of information.

Assessment

VALUATION CYCLES AND REVALUATIONS

With the passage of time, property values change across geographic space and by property type. General revaluation of the entire jurisdiction is the mechanism to "correct" assessed values and bring them back in line. However, revaluation is one of the most difficult aspects of the property tax in terms of resources, administration, and, ultimately, political approval. In many cases, actual revaluation frequency does not correlate with the legislative prescribed frequency. The practice varies widely: Hong Kong, Jakarta, and Vilnius revalue on an annual basis; South African metros are on a three- to four-year cycle, which appears to be sustainable; several cities with legislated three- to five-year revaluation cycles rarely meet this requirement (Accra, Buenos Aires, Kampala, Rio de Janeiro, Tallinn); in other cites, such as Dar es Salaam, Kuala Lumpur, Manila, Nairobi, Porto Alegre, and Kingston, have serious issues with the age of the current valuation roll.

Revaluations are beset by two problems: enormity of the task and the contentious results that will follow the revaluation. With respect to the first, metros that revalue regularly can build up experience in terms of processes, procedures, and ultimately delivery (Cape Town, Jakarta, Bogotá, Hong Kong). The large numbers of properties to be valued within metros do not necessarily imply greater problems. On the contrary, use of automated valuation methods has greatly reduced the overall cost of revaluations (Cape Town, Hong Kong). However, even metros with adequate in-house resources have problems when revaluations are delayed and postponed over long periods (Kuala Lumpur, Manila, Kingston, Accra).

The second aspect, and potentially the more important and politically sensitive, results from the fact that some (perhaps most) taxpayers will see an increase in their assessed values, and the perception that "higher assessed values mean higher taxes." In practical terms, the tax rate is often rolled back to compensate for the general increases in assessments, a revenue-neutral position in relation to the year prior to the revaluation, but is contrary to the revenue-raising goals of the revaluation. A mechanism to cushion the impact is to have a scheme of transitional relief. Although not widely used, it can be effective in providing some protection against abnormal tax increases. South Africa's new property tax legislation provides, among other things, a phasing in of tax for newly taxable property.

Many metro valuation/assessment departments have sufficient qualified and experienced valuers/assessors to maintain the valuation roll (Bogotá, Hong Kong, some South African metros). However, in some cities the paucity of skills still remains critical (Accra, Dar es Salaam, Freetown, Kampala). Possibly as a response, when revaluations do occur, the private sector plays an increasingly important role (Accra, Kampala, Kingston, Cape Town).

Given the large numbers of properties within metros, it is surprising that segmental reassessment has not been considered to any great extent. This is a procedure by which a specified fraction of real property parcels is reassessed each year, moving through the jurisdiction in sequence. Thus, if a three-year cycle is used, one-third of the properties in the area would be reassessed each year, with all properties being reassessed every three years. This approach can be less resource intensive and make the revaluation task achievable. It could be a more balanced approach and may be the most realistic cycle for large metro jurisdictions. The problems with this approach are that it can produce temporary inequities at a time of significant changes in market values and where uniform rates are applied across the whole metropolitan area.

If general revaluation is not an option, then an alternative presently used in São Paulo and Bogotá is the application of indices to uplift assessed values to reflect property value increases. Indices for each property category can be determined, and all properties within that category receive the same adjustment. This approach is unpopular, particularly if the base valuation is dated, because it results in inequities being further exacerbated. Indices are blunt instruments, and much of the argument in favor of their use has to do with revenue mobilization. However, as an interim measure to reflect increasing property values, it can be a viable option.

In some cases, the political pressure to deal with inequitable assessments is to undertake piecemeal adjustments. In Buenos Aires, the replacement costs for buildings have remained unchanged for more than 20 years, but the city, in trying to achieve greater fairness, made arbitrary adjustments to land value zones (Lafuente 2009). In Manila, increasing land values resulted in many of the cities updating those assessments at various intervals while holding constant the assessed value of the improvements.

Preparation for a general revaluation requires quite extensive data collection and analysis. Irrespective of the basis of the property tax, the assessment department needs to have robust procedures in place to collect information on all forms of transactions, such as sales and lettings, as well as information on building costs. This involves having a legislative system to ensure that transaction evidence is recorded in an appropriate manner. This should be less of a problem in a formal market with appropriate land titling and registration than in a market where many transactions occur informally. In Hong Kong, Kuala Lumpur, and Bogotá, the legislation allows for the assessment department to ask owners to complete questionnaires to gather information on their property, rents, and leases. In Manila, when a property is sold, the owner must complete a tax declaration, a copy of which must be lodged with the assessor's office.

A comparison of revaluation costs across metros and, indeed, countries is quite difficult. However, cities that revalue regularly will have developed cost-effective systems and be able to drive down the cost per parcel. For example, Hong Kong revalues annually, and the cost for the 2010 revaluation (annual values) of the 2.36 million parcels was approximately US$1.5 per parcel. In Dar es Salaam, the 2001 valuation of approximately 18,000 properties cost on average US$17.00 per property (McCluskey and Franzsen 2005). In Bogotá, in 2009 updating property information on 1.2 million properties cost on average US$6.46 (Ruiz and Vallejo 2010), whereas in Jamaica, the estimated cost for the 2012 revaluation (site values) of 790,000 parcels is US$3.43 per parcel.

ANNUAL MAINTENANCE OF VALUATION ROLLS

The maintenance of the valuation roll between revaluations requires that procedures be put in place to capture the alterations made to existing property and changes in ownership and to value new properties. Most cities allow for such changes to the main roll through annual supplementary rolls; for example, in some South African cities, more than one supplementary valuation is done per year. However, in some cities, the lack of resources often precludes this mode of updating the tax base (Dar es Salaam, Accra, Manila).

VALUATION METHODS

The principle valuation methods used for determining property tax assessments on all property types include comparative sales, income (or expenditure and receipts), and cost (often depreciated replacement cost) methods. The majority of property tax systems are based around the concept of market value and attempt to derive objective estimates of value based on market transaction evidence. While there are active property markets in the metros of developing countries, there are not good comparative sales data (Baraquero 1999). However, where this evidence is scarce or unreliable, jurisdictions have had recourse to cost-based approaches such as those used in metro Manila cities, Accra, Dar es Salaam, and several Latin American cities. In these cities, land values are normally estimated with reference to comparable land sales. The use of construction costs without any direct comparison to market values can lead to major problems with assessment levels; for example, the average assessment level was 30 percent in Porto Alegre (De Cesare 2004) and 35 percent in Buenos Aires (Lafuente 2009). This correlates with a study done in India that highlights the lack of market value evidence but suggests assessment ratios of approximately 30 percent for a number of cities, including Nagpur and Kolkata (Mathur et al. 2009).

The need to develop simplified automated valuation processes has been one of the major developments within property assessment during the 1980s, 1990s, and 2000s. Computer-assisted mass appraisal (CAMA) has become the primary tool to assist valuers/assessors, particularly during general revaluations (Eckert 2008).

In developed Western cities, CAMA is used extensively, and the evidence would suggest that significant cost savings can be achieved through the application of automated valuation approaches. The development of mass appraisal solutions for residential property is important for cities in developing countries, given the relatively large number of those properties (see table 7.4). But the development of such automated valuation processes has been held back by the lack of reliable data on market transactions. Jakarta, Hong Kong, and South Africa's metros have been developing automated valuation systems for their bulk class properties: residential, homogeneous office, retail, and industrial. Metros with lengthy revaluation intervals (Accra, Dar es Salaam, Kuala Lumpur, Manila's cities) have not invested in these techniques to the same degree. Whereas CAMA can bring assessment efficiencies (Eckert 2008), its use within many metros is limited due to data constraints.

The application of GIS in identifying the value influence of location is becoming embedded within a number of cities, including Cape Town, several Latin American metros, and Bengaluru. However, a more widespread application of GIS is for identifying parcels and supporting land titling projects. Those metros using GIS have developed innovative tools to maximize the potential of this technique to support valuation and to assist in quality assurance and ratio studies.

QUALITY OF PROFESSIONAL STAFF

It has often been stated that one of the key problems with the ad valorem property tax is the lack of qualified experienced valuers/assessors to provide effective and efficient assessments. Although this is certainly the case in many places, it is notable that in several of the metros reviewed, sufficient qualified staff is becoming much less of a problem. Evidence would indicate that the city valuation departments in Kuala Lumpur, Manila, and South African metros are staffed adequately with professionally qualified personnel. Metros tend to have the capacity to recruit, train, and maintain a professional appraisal workforce. In some cases, valuation responsibility has been assumed by centralized government departments, for example, in Lagos (Ipaye 2007), Kingston, and Jakarta. These departments have greater capability in utilizing CAMA and other automated valuation techniques.

A factor that possibly has contributed to the improvement in staffing levels is the introduction of university-level courses in real estate and valuation (Dar es Salaam, Kingston, Kuala Lumpur, Manila). It is clear that most of the city valuation departments are actively engaged in providing in-house training and workshops to develop the necessary skills. Although the private sector will always be attractive to experienced valuers, they are becoming more heavily involved in property tax assessments in collaboration with city and government valuation departments (Jamaica, Malaysia, South Africa, Brazil, Colombia), as suggested by improved assessment coverage and GIS integration in Bogotá, Bengaluru, Cape Town, Dar es Salaam, and Kingston.

ASSESSMENT QUALITY, OBJECTION, AND APPEAL

Although revaluation quality control may be sparse, many of the metros have built up sufficient valuation/assessment experience to develop valuation manuals and standardized procedures (Kingston, the larger metros in South Africa, Kuala Lumpur, Hong Kong).

The quality of the assessments on the new valuation roll can be subjected to both internal and external validation. The International Association of Assessing Officers provides benchmarks against which an internal audit can be based.[4] A number of cities that undertake fairly regular revaluations publish the results of their internal benchmarking audit (Cape Town, Hong Kong). Some metros opt for external validation (Kingston and Cape Town), but many other metros do not (Cairo, Johannesburg, metro Manila). There is almost no assessment quality validation in the Latin American cities. Assessment ratio studies are rarely undertaken in any of the sample metros due to insufficient market-related data (Mathur et al. 2009).

An approach used in metro Manila prior to implementing the revaluation is to publish a schedule of market values for land, buildings, and machinery and depreciation rates for public consultation (Guevara 2004). After this exercise, the schedule is incorporated into an ordinance. The objective is to instill acceptance of the new values while trying to minimize objections.

In 2007, at the time of its migration from a site-value system to capital improved values, Johannesburg published a draft valuation roll and likely tax rates and followed it up in 2008 with the formal valuation roll and actual tax rates. The objective was to ensure that the new valuation system was better understood by taxpayers.

In jurisdictions with a value-based system, property owners are generally allowed to object and appeal the property value as determined by the assessor. In South African metros, payment of tax is not deferred until the objection or appeal has been finalized. In Lagos, 50 percent of the tax must be paid before an appeal can be filed. This is controversial and could be construed as a violation of a taxpayer's constitutional right to access to the courts and/or a fair trial.

Billing, Collection, and Payment

In some metros, much of the billing is still done manually (Accra, Dar es Salaam, Lagos, Lilongwe) because of data problems (e.g., properties cannot be identified, poor postal services, and/or the lack of street names). In 2002 in Dar es Salaam, municipal valuers were used for billing because of their intimate knowledge of neighborhoods (McCluskey and Franzsen 2005). Some metros bill annually (Accra), some biannually (Istanbul), and others more regularly (e.g., monthly in South African metros).

A few cities have outsourced collection to the private sector (Accra, Kampala). In 2008, the Tanzanian government outsourced collection of the property tax in Dar es Salaam to the Tanzania Revenue Authority. The authority's commission amounts to 20–25 percent of the amount collected, whereas the private collectors in Kampala receive 10 percent (Olima 2010). It is not clear how successful these steps were for these metros. Oversight is problematic when private tax collectors are used.

In Dar es Salaam, collection levels are estimated at less than 50 percent, and in Accra in 2009, it was estimated at 35 percent (Yeboah and Johansson 2010). In contrast, collection levels in South Africa's metros generally exceed 90 percent, whereas

---

[4] The principal international benchmarks include the coefficient of dispersion and price-related differential.

TABLE 7.5

Property tax performance in select cities

Metro	Estimated collection rate (of amount billed) for 2009 (percent)
Accra	35
Bengaluru	80–85
Cape Town	90–95
Dar es Salaam	45–55
Johannesburg	85–90
Kingston	55–60
Manila	55–90

SOURCE: Mathur et al. (2009), Yeboah and Johansson (2010), and various country reporters.

for cities within metro Manila, in 2009 it ranged from 18.6 percent to 125.4 percent (see table 7.5).

Lower compliance costs may partly explain higher collection levels. South African metropolitan taxpayers can pay bills at municipal offices, post offices, and large retail stores; online; or by direct debit. In Accra and Freetown, taxpayers are expected to make payments at the tax offices. Some metros (Belo Horizonte, Bengaluru, Lagos, Nairobi) provide discounts for early payment. In Bengaluru, 80 percent of taxpayers paid within the prescribed period, largely due to conveniently located "help centers" spread across city wards. In 2011, about 60,000 taxpayers paid tax online.

ENFORCEMENT

Although the legislation in most countries reviewed contains adequate enforcement measures, in practice some of these measures are seldom (if ever) used. A reason provided in many countries is the lack of political will and support from local councilors and/or national politicians. In some cities in Tanzania, officials reported poor property and taxpayer data as reasons that tax collectors were reluctant to enforce against delinquent taxpayers. In some instances, the cost of enforcement (e.g., civil action in a municipal or tax court) exceeds the annual property tax, making it a nonviable option.

A measure commonly found in legislation, but only used in practice in a few cities (Jakarta, South African metros), is seizure of the property and its sale in execution. In some metros, this can happen only after three years (South African metros, Dar es Salaam); in others, after only a few months (Freetown, Bangkok). However, the political and public support for this enforcement measure is generally absent.

South African metros withhold services (e.g., electricity) in response to nonpayment of the property tax. Furthermore, Nairobi and South African metros also use "clearance certificates" with property transfers to claim unpaid taxes: before the transfer can be registered in the deeds office, the municipality must issue a clearance certificate that all outstanding taxes and charges have been paid.

TAX RELIEF

Tax relief is granted directly and indirectly through tax base exclusions, preferential assessments, exemptions, and other forms of relief. Property tax bases are in some instances eroded through narrow definitions of property. Exemptions are encountered in all metros and almost always include properties used wholly or mainly for charitable, education, and public worship purposes.

Achieving some progressivity by excluding the first tranche of value from the tax base or by exempting low-value properties from the property tax is encountered in Kingston and Bengaluru, where a flat amount or minimum levy is payable, respectively. In Cairo and South African metros, a national, statutory value threshold applies.

Preferential assessment and rebates are utilized extensively. In many metros, owner-occupied residential properties receive preferential treatment. In Accra, the assessed value for owner-occupied buildings may not exceed 50 percent of replacement cost. In Bengaluru, owner-occupied residential and nonresidential properties receive a 50 percent tax rebate. This is also the case in Ahmedabad, Chennai, Delhi, and Mumbai. In other metros, for example, Abidjan, Bangkok, and Kampala, owner-occupied residential property is completely exempt. In some metros (Cape Town, Johannesburg), rebates are granted to categories of owners rather than use (e.g., on the basis of age and income).

GOVERNMENT PROPERTY AND UTILITIES

In many metros, property owned by higher-tier governments is excluded from the tax base (Brazilian metros) or exempt from local property taxes, and the revenue loss can be considerable (Bahl 2009). One of the issues is whether lower-tier governments have the legal authority to tax this property, but legislation sometimes allows for payments in lieu of taxes. If these payments are based on the assessed value (which is seldom the case in practice), the tax sacrifice can be recovered by the local government (Bird and Slack 2002). The tax treatment of exempt government property is especially important in metros, where government operations are usually headquartered. Often, branches of government occupy some of the most valuable, modern, and well-located buildings within city centers.

The actual practice varies. Government property is exempt in some developing countries. However, in some of these countries (e.g., Côte d'Ivoire, Hong Kong, Ghana, Niger, Sierra Leone, Tanzania), government does not pay any amounts in lieu of taxes. In a number of metros, however, government property is indeed taxed (Bengaluru, Kampala, Lilongwe, Mbabane, South African metros). In Nairobi, Lilongwe, Cape Town, and Kampala, government is often one of the major defaulters, and some cities find it politically difficult to collect arrears. Interestingly, Mbabane and Pretoria tax government property at rates higher than for other properties.

Some metros are able to account for the tax expenditures due to exemption of government properties. In the Kingston metro area, all government property is valued even though it is exempt. The estimated loss due to the exemption is equivalent to about 5 percent of total property tax collections.

In Kuala Lumpur, government properties are subject to a contribution in lieu of taxes that is negotiated based on local government expenditures on such services as fire protection, street lighting, water supply, and refuse disposal (Choong 1998). In 2010, government properties in Kuala Lumpur were about 5.6 percent of the total number, and the revenue contribution from these properties was approximately 3.3 percent of the total.

In Bengaluru, government properties pay only 25 percent of the rate for non-residential properties, unless the property is used for commercial purposes, in which case the standard tax rate applies. Cape Town and Durban also differentiate on the basis of use for government-owned properties.

VACANT LAND AND UNOCCUPIED BUILDINGS

Often the taxation of vacant land is related to achieving other nonfiscal benefits, such as reducing land speculation (Porto Alegre), ensuring optimal urban development and densification, and ensuring that the owners of such land and buildings contribute to the cost of services (Johannesburg and Pretoria). It is an especially important issue in large metropolitan areas. However, the empirical evidence on whether a vacant land tax brings forward the timing of development is inconclusive (Skaburskis and Tomalty 1997).

The practice varies quite widely across metros (table 7.6). An exemption for vacant property is generally associated with systems where the occupier rather than the owner is taxed, as under some rental value systems. In other metros, vacant parcels are taxed at significantly higher rates than developed parcels. In metros using land value systems, all land, whether vacant or not, is valued and, in principle, taxed. In Kingston and Nairobi, a uniform tax rate is applied with no differentiation as to use or occupancy.

In metro Manila, the cities have discretion to levy the idle land tax up to a maximum surcharge of 5 percent.[5] Only recently has this tax become "popular," and it is now levied by most cities. For example, in Quezon City the tax rate applied to idle land located adjacent to national roads is 3 percent over and above the existing property tax. The existing tax rates for 2009–2010 are 1.5 percent on the assessed value of residential property and 2 percent for commercial, industrial, and special properties; for other locations, the surcharge is 1 percent.

PROPERTY TRANSFER TAXES

Property transfer taxes, levied either as a stamp duty or as a transfer tax, are encountered in most countries. It has been suggested (Bahl 2004; Powers 2008; Ruiz

---

[5] The idle land tax is levied on unused agricultural land of more than one hectare, nonagricultural vacant land greater than 1,000 m² , and approved residential subdivisions.

TABLE 7.6

Treatment of vacant/unoccupied properties

Treatment	Metro
Exclude or exempt	Bangkok, Cairo, Dar es Salaam (vacant land), Karachi
Exempt on application for unoccupied buildings	Accra (although a minimum tax applies), Dar es Salaam
Tax vacant and unoccupied properties at the same rate as developed properties	Jakarta, Kingston, Nairobi, São Paulo
Tax vacant land at slightly higher rates than developed properties	Bengaluru (limited), Kuala Lumpur (residential property)
Tax vacant land at significantly higher rate than developed properties	Belo Horizonte, Bogotá, Buenos Aires, Cape Town, Durban, Gaborone, Johannesburg, Manila, Mexico City, Porto Alegre, Pretoria, Rio de Janeiro,* Windhoek

*However, impact is negated because it is coupled with a high value reduction and favorable assessment.
SOURCES: Data obtained from legislation, by-laws, and various city or country reporters.

and Vallejo 2010) that high real estate transfer taxes can be a contributing factor to the poor performance of the property tax in some countries because it discourages owners from transacting in an open transparent market and from truthfully recording market values of property.

In some countries, such as Jamaica (Bahl 2004), as well as elsewhere in the Caribbean, both taxes are levied on real estate transfers. These taxes are quite easy to collect, as the title or deed registration system can effectively be used as an audit for payment. In Indonesia, the land and building transfer tax became a local tax in 2011, with Jakarta being able to determine its own tax rate up to a maximum of 5 percent. It is noteworthy that tax rates are high in a number of jurisdictions, especially in India, Jamaica, and South Africa. In India and Jamaica, however, rates have been decreasing in recent years.

REFORM ISSUES AND TRENDS

Property tax reform never seems to get off the policy agenda in the metros of developing countries. In some cases, this is because reform just does not happen, but in others it is because of the increased property tax capacity that comes with urbanization and economic development. In some metros, there has been reform, but the directions taken do not seem to follow a general pattern.

To the extent that some sort of polarization occurs, it involves the choice of property tax basis. Movement toward the use of capital improved value is clearly evident in the recent reforms in South Africa, Northern Ireland, New Zealand, Hungary, Slovenia, and several states in Australia. Lagos has migrated from an annual value base to improved capital value, whereas the rest of Nigeria retained the rental value approach. But in South Africa, a national uniform basis for the property tax was implemented (capital improved value).[6] To be sure, in some metros

---

[6] Part of this section builds on Martinez-Vazquez (2008).

capital value systems (Bogotá, Cape Town, Durban) or annual value systems (Hong Kong, Kuala Lumpur), a pragmatic approach to the political and market realities, seem to be working well, and the lack or shortage of skilled assessment staff suggests that unique alternatives may indeed be appropriate in some jurisdictions. Bengaluru is a case in point: this city has seemingly overcome the buoyancy problem generally associated with calibrated area or simplified value systems, by regularly updating the use area values. In fact, several Indian metros have replaced a rental value system by one based on property size. It is interesting, however, that the land or site value tax that has been under pressure in several countries is retaining its status in Queensland, Australia, where the 2011 reform brought a shift from "unimproved" value to "site" value, and in Jamaica, Kenya, and Estonia. In fact, in 2011, Harare replaced its split-rate property tax system with a site value tax (Chakasikwa 2011).

In some cases, the need for reform has been ignored. The retention of annual values in Kampala and of capital values in Dar es Salaam, given poor base coverage and the serious paucity of assessment skills, could be questioned. More simplistic and pragmatic approaches, such as calibrated area system or even a U.K.-styled value-banding approach (McCluskey, Plimmer, and Connellan 2002), may in the medium term provide more revenue and a property tax that performs the primary function of generating revenue.

Property categorization according to use, size, and/or location is commonplace and seems to be on the increase (Bird and Slack 2002; Franzsen and McCluskey 2008). All metros in South Africa utilize classified rates. However, these differentiations complicate the administrative tasks and may harm the fairness of the system.

Conclusions

Notwithstanding the difficulties in administering the property tax, it is clearly evident that it remains one of the key revenue tools for metros across the developing world. Though supporting data are weak, this chapter argues that many metros are able to handle the administrative demands of the property tax and to do a better job of realizing its revenue potential than are other local governments. On the one hand, there tends to be a stronger tax base and more human resource skills within metropolitan areas; on the other hand, there are many more properties, more construction, and greater changes in property values to be dealt with. Moreover, many metros have shown an ability to absorb much of the new technology in property tax administration. But the ability to improve property tax administration does not hold everywhere, as can be seen from the practice in such metros as Accra, Nairobi, metro Manila, and Rio de Janeiro.

The revenue mobilization of the property tax in metros continues to be held back by several factors, even in the strongest of these jurisdictions. First, revaluations tend to be problematic in part because of data limitations but mostly because of political interventions. Second, there is need to verify the fairness of the valuation process. The use of the private sector in undertaking the valuation function, in whole or in part, is becoming much more widespread (Bogotá, Cape Town, Dar es Salaam, Jakarta, Kingston). However, in some cases, monitoring the quality of such externally provided valuations by the city is lacking. What is required is more formal oversight to ensure that legislative and technical procedures have been followed.

Third, despite an abundance of literature (Franzsen and McCluskey 2005; Kelly 1995) suggesting that a "collection-led" rather than a "valuation-pushed" reform of the property tax constitutes a more prudent approach, reforms in many low-income developing countries still seem to focus primarily on assessment, for example, Sierra Leone (Freetown), Tanzania (Dar es Salaam), and Uganda (Kampala).

It is probably fair to say that within low-income countries in particular, the metros and cities tend to be holding their own regarding property tax administration. However, outside of the cities, assessment and property tax administration present significant problems. A system that works relatively well in metros or large cities may only have limited applicability in smaller urban and rural jurisdictions, particularly where there is no central administrative support as a backup. Even where such backup is potentially available, the actual reality can be quite different (Malaysia, Philippines, South Africa).

REFERENCES

Aleksiene, Albina, and Arvydas Bagdonavicius. 2008. Value-based property taxes in Lithuania. In *Making the property tax work: Experiences in developing and transitional countries*, ed. Roy Bahl, Jorge Martinez-Vazquez, and Joan Youngman, 411–435. Cambridge, MA: Lincoln Institute of Land Policy.

Bahl, Roy W. 2004. Property transfer tax and stamp duty. ISP Working Paper No. 04–27. Atlanta: Andrew Young School of Policy Studies, Georgia State University.

———. 2009. *Property tax reform in developing countries*. Washington, DC: U.S. Agency for International Development.

Baraquero, Oscar. 1999. Decentralizing property taxation: The Philippine perspective. In *Comparative property tax systems: An international comparative review*, ed. William J. McCluskey, 248–265. Aldershot, U.K.: Avebury.

Bird, Richard M. 2004. Land taxes in Colombia. In *International handbook of land and property taxation*, ed. Richard M. Bird and Enid Slack. Cheltenham, U.K.: Edward Elgar.

Bird, Richard M., and Enid Slack. 2002. Land and property taxation around the world: A review. *Journal of Property Tax Assessment and Administration* 7(3):31–80.

Bustamante, Liliana, and Nestor Gaviria. 2004. The Bogota cadastre—an example of a multipurpose cadastre. *Land Lines* 16(April):3–4.

Chakasikwa, John. 2011. *Property taxation in Zimbabwe: Challenges and opportunities*. M.Ph. diss., University of Pretoria.

Choong, Fong K. 1998. Contribution in aid of rates and its related problems. In *Monograph on rating*, 91–110. Kuala Lumpur, Malaysia: National Institute of Valuation.

Cornia, Gary C. 2008. Commentary. In *Making the property tax work: Experiences in developing and transitional countries*, ed. Roy Bahl, Jorge Martinez-Vazquez, and Joan Youngman, 307–312. Cambridge, MA: Lincoln Institute of Land Policy.

De Cesare, Claudia M. 2004. General characteristics of property tax systems in Latin America. Paper presented at the 7th annual conference of the International Property Tax Institute, Guadalajara, Mexico (September).

Eckert, Joseph. 2008. Computer assisted mass appraisal options for transition and developing countries. In *Making the property tax work: Experiences in developing and transitional countries*, ed. Roy Bahl, Jorge Martinez-Vazquez, and Joan Youngman. Cambridge, MA: Lincoln Institute of Land Policy.

Franzsen, Riël C. D., and Willaim J. McCluskey. 2005. An exploratory overview of property taxation in the Commonwealth of Nations. Working Paper No. WP05RF1a. Cambridge, MA: Lincoln Institute of Land Policy.

——. 2008. The feasibility of site value taxation. In *Making the property tax work: Experiences in developing and transitional countries*, ed. Roy Bahl, Jorge Martinez-Vazquez, and Joan Youngman, 268–306. Cambridge, MA: Lincoln Institute of Land Policy.

——. 2013. Value-based approaches to property taxation. In *A primer on property tax: Administration and policy* eds. William J. McCluskey, Gary C. Cornia, and Lawrance C. Walters, 41–68. West Sussex, U.K.: Wiley-Blackwell.

Guevara, Milwida. 2004. Real property taxation in the Philippines. In *International handbook of land and property taxation*, ed. Richard M. Bird and Enid Slack, 152–158. Cheltenham, U.K.: Edward Elgar.

Ipaye, Ade. 2007. Property taxation and revenue generation in Nigeria. CITN Practice Series No. 27. Lagos, Nigeria: Chartered Institute of Taxation of Nigeria.

Jibao, Samuel. 2009. Property taxation in anglophone West Africa: Regional overview Sierra Leone. Working Paper No. WP09AWA1. Cambridge, MA: Lincoln Institute of Land Policy.

Kelly, Roy. 1995. Property tax reform in Southeast Asia: A comparative analysis of Indonesia, the Philippines and Thailand. *Journal of Property Tax Assessment and Administration* 2(1):60–81.

Lafuente, Mariano. 2009. Public management reforms and property tax revenue improvements: Lessons from Buenos Aires. Working Paper No. 0209. Washington, DC: World Bank.

Malme, Jane H., and Joan M. Youngman. 2008. Developments in value based property. *Land Lines* (October):8–13.

Martinez-Vazquez, Jorge. 2008. Revenue assignments in the practice of fiscal federalism, fiscal federalism and political decentralization. In *Fiscal federalism and political decentralization*, ed. Nuria Bosh and Jose M. Duran. Cheltenham, U.K.: Edward Elgar.

——. 2011. Municipal finances in Latin America: Features, issues, and prospects. International Studies Program Working Paper No. 11-07. Atlanta: Andrew Young School of Policy Studies, Georgia State University.

Mathur, Om P., Roy Bahl, Debdulal Thakur, and Nilesh Rajadhyasksha. 2009. *Urban property tax potential in India*. New Delhi: National Institute of Public Finance and Policy.

McCluskey, William J., Michael E. Bell, and Lay C. Lim. 2010. Rental value versus capital value: Alternative bases for the property tax. In *Challenging the conventional wisdom on the property tax*, ed. Roy Bahl, Jorge Martinez-Vazquez, and Joan Youngman, 119–157. Cambridge, MA: Lincoln Institute of Land Policy.

McCluskey, William J., and Riël C. D. Franzsen. 2005. An evaluation of the property tax in Tanzania: An untapped fiscal resource or administrative headache. *Property Management* 23(1):43–69.

McCluskey, William J., Frances Plimmer, and Owen Connellan. 2002. Property tax banding: A solution for developing countries. *Assessment Journal* (March/April):37–47.

Mukhandi, Shomari. 2012. Local government authorities' own source revenues. Presentation at Gesellschaft für Internationale Zusammenarbeit workshop, Dar es Salaam (February 15).

Olima, Washington H. A. 2010. Property taxation in anglophone East Africa: Case study of Uganda. Working Paper No. WP10NEA8. Cambridge, MA: Lincoln Institute of Land Policy.

Powers, Sally. 2008. Collection and enforcement of the property tax. In *Making the property tax work: Experiences in developing and transitional countries*, ed. Roy Bahl, Jorge Martinez-Vazquez, and Joan Youngman, 372–386. Cambridge, MA: Lincoln Institute of Land Policy.

Rao, Vasanth. 2008. Is area-based assessment an alternative, an intermediate step or an impediment to value based taxation in India? In *Making the property tax work: Experiences in developing and transitional countries*, ed. Roy Bahl, Jorge Martinez-Vazquez, and Joan Youngman, 241–267. Cambridge, MA: Lincoln Institute of Land Policy.

Ruiz, Francisco, and Gabriel Vallejo. 2010. Using land registration as a tool to generate municipal revenue: Lessons from Bogotá. Annual Bank Conference on Land Policy and Administration, Washington, DC: World Bank. http://siteresources.worldbank.org/EXTARD/Re sources/336681-1236436879081/5893311-1271205116054/RuizVallejoPaper.pdf

Skaburskis, Andrejs, and Ray Tomalty. 1997. Land value taxation and development activity: The reaction of Toronto and Ottawa developers, planners, and municipal finance officials. *Canadian Journal of Regional Science* 10(3):401–417.

Varanyuwatana, Sakon. 1999. Property tax in Thailand. In *Comparative property tax systems: An international comparative review*, ed. William J. McCluskey, 148–162. Aldershot, U.K.: Avebury.

World Bank. 2011. World development report 2011: Conflict, security, and development. http://wdronline.worldbank.org/worldbank/a/c.html/world_development_report_2011/abstract/WB.978-0-8213-8439-8.abstract

Yeboah, Kofi, and Linda Johansson. 2010. Urban Management Land Information System UMLIS: Facing urban challenges through efficient revenue collection. Paper presented at the Fédération Internationale des Géomètres (FIG) Conference, Sydney (April 11–16).

LOCAL NONPROPERTY REVENUES | 8

JORGE MARTINEZ-VAZQUEZ

This chapter focuses on the current theory and practice of nonproperty tax assignments to local urban governments in developing and developed countries. Bahl and Linn (1992) concluded that if urban government revenues were to be viable for financing urban public service delivery, broad-based taxes other than the property tax would be needed in the revenue assignment mix. How good a prediction has this been?

Although the theoretical rationale is clear for the presence of a basket of tax instruments, since the marginal resource costs are increasing for any single source, and many urban governments rely on a variety of revenue sources other than property taxation and transfers, the international experience in both developing and developed countries, as described in this chapter, is mixed and uneven. While a few urban governments have introduced economically attractive tax sources other than the property tax, a vast majority of urban governments in developing countries, and also in many developed countries, still struggle with the imperative of revenue adequacy to cover their growing expenditure needs and obligations. The good news is that examples of best practices are not scarce; the bad news is that there is still an extended failure in applying those best practices in the vast majority of urban governments around the world.

This chapter is organized as follows. First the theoretical foundations for the use of taxes other than the property tax in local governments are reviewed. The discussion includes the kind of guidance provided by optimal tax theory and the issues to be considered in making tax administration choices (e.g., central vs. local). Next, actual practices in tax assignments are surveyed; special attention is paid to political

I am grateful to Gustavo Canavire-Bacarreza and Violeta Vulovic for helping organize the data collection and to Krishanu Karmakar, Gabriel Leonardo, and Janet Porras for participating in the data collection. I am also grateful to Charles McLure, Robert Ebel, Roy Bahl, Johannes Linn, and Deborah Wetzel for helpful comments.

economy and institutional capacity issues as potential drivers for the observed differences between an optimal metropolitan revenue system and those that are actually observed. The chapter concludes by extracting lessons from the global experience with nonproperty tax revenue sources and exploring reform directions for urban finance in developing and developed countries.

THEORETICAL FOUNDATIONS OF SUBNATIONAL REVENUE ASSIGNMENTS

Although over the last several decades there have been significant advances in the development of a theoretical framework for tax assignments to subnational governments, a complete general framework is still lacking.

The Relevance of Revenue Assignments

The fundamental promise of fiscal decentralization is that public spending will become more efficient because decentralized governments will be not only more informed (Hayek 1945) but also more responsive and accountable to citizens' needs and preferences (Oates 1972). At the same time, there is general agreement among experts in decentralization that increased accountability is best assured when subnational governments have an adequate level of autonomy and discretion in raising their own-source revenues.

Thus, if effective fiscal decentralization requires meaningful revenue autonomy at the subnational level, which taxes should be allocated at these levels? How much revenue autonomy is needed? This is what is known as the "tax assignment problem" (see, e.g., Bird 2000b; Martinez-Vazquez, McLure, and Vaillancourt 2006; McLure 1998).[1]

The basic role of revenue assignments is to provide adequate financing to subnational governments so they can implement the functions they have been assigned. However, revenue adequacy per se is not a guide for tax assignments because adequate financing can be obtained from many different tax assignments or even without them through intergovernmental transfers.

The "Benefit Principle": How Far Does It Take Us?

To answer the question of how to tax at the local level, the public finance literature has used the "benefit principle" (Lindahl 1919; Musgrave 1938): those that use the service should pay for its costs. If it could be fully used, there is no other approach to urban local finance with the same potential to organize the financial architecture of local governments. The benefit principle tells us how services should be priced, who should pay for them, and how much of the service should be provided. However, the power and simplicity of the benefit principle are diminished by a series of factors.

First, within the complexity of institutional arrangements in many urban settings, it is not always necessarily obvious who should be paid because it is unclear

---

[1]Part of this section builds on Martinez-Vazquez (2008).

which governmental organization is in charge of providing particular services.[2] Second, it is not always easy to identify those that are using the service, unless it is possible to employ user charges and fees and exclude from the service those that do not pay. Third, it is difficult to target users with alternative revenue-raising instruments. Some taxes, such as the property tax, can fit the benefit principle well by targeting taxpayers that directly benefit from an array of services. Other taxes can be used, such as individual income taxes or sales levies, even though they can be hard to design, but in the best of cases the link between benefits from services and tax payments tends to be diluted and even lost, depending on the final economic incidence of the tax.

There are some other limitations to the practical application of the benefit principle, including equity issues, the presence of service externalities into other jurisdictions, and the presence of tax externalities where the actions of some jurisdictions may affect the tax bases of other local governments. All these cases may require different types of corrective transfers from upper-level governments.[3]

However, the benefit principle can offer very useful guidance for the direction in which institutional reforms should move. Those jurisdictions and entities providing the services should be paid by those individuals using the services, regardless of where they reside. The place of residence still can be used as shorthand for approximating where individuals consume most their public services, but the assignment of revenue sources cannot be restricted to the universal use of that proxy (the place of residence). However, there is also little question that, in order to make the benefit principle operational, governments must face the challenge of finding those taxes (when direct use of fees and services is not feasible) that would best approximate a direct payment by users and that, at the same time, would meet other desirable economic properties, or at least avoid undesirable ones.[4]

In Search of a General Theory of Revenue Assignments

Since the application of the pure benefit principle is not possible, a theory of tax assignments is still needed. Significant progress has been made in laying out the desirable economic properties of taxes to be assigned at the subnational level, but up to now a complete theory of tax assignments at the subnational level is still lacking.

---

[2]The issues are complex in this context because of the potential of extensive tax exporting, the presence of special districts and public enterprises with managers that are not elected and thus lack direct accountability mechanisms, and boundaries of elected governments that may not be clearly delineated. As Bahl (2011) points out, tax assignment in metropolitan areas is not independent of how those jurisdictions are structured. And metropolitan areas show diverse and often complex organization structures. For example, Bird and Slack (2004a) identify four models of governance structure for metropolitan areas: (1) one-tier governance, with a single government providing all the local services within the area (e.g., Toronto, Bogotá, Quito); (2) two-tier governance, with one upper-tier government (metropolitan unit) providing some regionwide public services and lower-tier municipalities providing public services of a more localized nature (London, Santiago de Chile); (3) voluntary cooperation, with the existing units of governments creating formal or informal cooperation mechanisms to provide certain services and retaining full autonomy for other services (e.g., Vancouver, São Paulo); and (4) special-purpose districts, created for the purpose of providing a single public service in the area and with all other services provided separately by the existing jurisdictions (e.g., special districts in the United States, Buenos Aires). All these types in reality show a wide array of financing combinations involving user charges, own taxes, and transfers.

[3]Ideally, a benefit tax may reflect the different types of externalities.

[4]See Ebel and Taliercio (2005) for a discussion of the broader interpretation of the benefit principle, including general taxes.

Before examining these issues, note first that the pure application of the benefit principle, utilizing user charges to finance public services, delivers two important things: (1) establishing the right amount of public services demanded by local residents; and (2) efficiently financing those public services with user charges: prices. When moving from user charges to taxes, substitute arrangements must be found for these two issues: (1) how to assure the efficient level of service provision; and (2) how to use alternative tax sources to finance those services, which exhibit different marginal resource costs.

The public finance literature reflects two fairly unconnected strands, each separately addressing one of the sets of issues that needs to be addressed by a theory of tax assignments. The first strand of the literature, grounded on the tradition of Musgrave (1959) and Oates (1972), focuses on the desirable attributes of taxation to foster optimal expenditure decisions, emphasizing the importance of tax autonomy to bring accountability among subnational decision makers. From this perspective, accountability is key to having public officials provide the level and mix of public services desired by taxpayers. This happens automatically when user charges can be used but generally can be lost when moving to use of taxes, with financing decisions being divorced from public service delivery decisions. Under this category are a number of useful and widely accepted rules. First is McLure's (2000) rule that subnational governments require tax autonomy at the margin to fulfill the allocation function efficiently, even though "inframarginal" expenditures can be financed with transfers or other sources. A second widely accepted rule is that the accountability of government officials, and of public expenditure efficiency, increases with the share of own-source revenue collections in the subnational budgets, and thus tax autonomy should be high enough to finance all, or most, expenditure needs of the wealthiest subnational governments. Increasing the share of expenditures that is financed with own taxes also has the benefit of increasing fiscal responsibility by subnational officials, avoiding overspending by making them face the full costs of their decisions. Thus, this strand of the literature can also include those contributions that have emphasized the importance of a "hard" budget constraint to control the "tragedy of the commons" and inefficient expenditure decisions at the subnational level (Rodden, Eskel, and Litvack 2003).

The second strand of the literature, based on optimal taxation theory, has focused on deriving the optimal conditions for an efficient assignment of subnational revenue sources (Dahlby 2009; Dahlby and Wilson 1996; Smart 1998). These use the concept of the marginal cost of funds to characterize optimal distribution of equalization transfers among subnational governments.

In all, the first strand of the literature delivers useful principles and rules for tax assignments, but it falls short of fully informing the choice of optimal subnational tax structure. The second strand of research provides interesting insights about the optimal subnational revenue structure, but it does not directly discuss the tax assignment problem. Martinez-Vazquez and Sepulveda (2011) build on those two strands of the literature in an attempt to develop an integrated theory of tax assignments. For optimal taxation, the optimal solution to the revenue assignment problem is characterized by an identical marginal cost of public funds for all government units. In particular, the optimal mix of revenue sources can be seen as the solution to a classic multiplant problem, where the government uses several revenue sources, or "plants," in order to "produce" a certain amount of revenue at minimal cost. All revenue sources must be used, up to the point where the optimal marginal cost of public funds is reached.[5]

This framework allows the analysis of optimal revenue composition beyond own taxes to include nontax instruments, such as revenue sharing and other intergovernmental transfers. The role of each revenue type depends on its distinctive marginal cost function. Own-source revenues are costly for government authorities, so when their cost is equal to the optimal marginal cost of funds, this allows efficient autonomous decisions about the amounts of public services to deliver. In contrast, intergovernmental transfers (including revenue-sharing schemes) have, in principle, a negligible marginal cost for the local authorities. For this reason, they do not provide the information required for efficient expenditure decisions. However, they can play the important role of "shifting" the marginal cost function to the position at which the government authorities are faced with the optimal marginal cost of public funds when making decisions. For example, equalization grants (reducing fiscal disparities in expenditure needs and fiscal capacity) can help achieve not only a fairer but also a more efficient solution for public good provision. Martinez-Vazquez and Sepulveda (2011) also show that the gains in efficiency due to greater accountability justify a more intensive use of own-source revenues, and thus also a greater marginal cost of public funds.

Why, in Reality, Do Levels of Tax Autonomy Tend to Be Low?

Although decentralized systems in some developed countries have high levels of tax autonomy, in reality, especially among developing countries, significant taxing powers are rarely devolved to subnational governments at the onset of decentralization. From a political economic perspective, low subnational tax autonomy is an equilibrium outcome desired by the two main players involved. Central governments are reluctant to devolve taxing powers for fear of having to compete with local governments for the same tax bases and/or fear of losing control of fiscal policy. At the same time, subnational governments are reluctant to take on the responsibility of making politically unpopular decisions to raise their own taxes. Thus, using intergovernmental transfers to finance subnational government functions is most often the preferred solution for all the parties concerned.

Technical issues may also play a role. Low levels of revenue autonomy may be associated with low levels of administrative capacity in some subnational governments. Uneven administrative capacities could in theory be addressed via asymmetric tax assignments: providing more tax autonomy to larger subnational governments and letting smaller ones "grow into this role" over time. Because of their higher expenditure needs and generally higher administrative capacity, a good case

---

[5]The marginal cost of public funds captures the economic losses to society associated with raising additional revenues to finance government spending (Dahlby 2008). The concept of marginal costs of public funds includes the excess burdens of taxes, and it can be adapted to consider a wide range of possible determinants of revenue collections, such as political costs (as in Hettich and Winer 1984), administrative and compliance costs (as in Slemrod and Yitzhaki 1996), and mobility (as in Wildasin 1998). Thus it provides a great deal of generality to model both the normative and positive aspects of revenue collections.

can be made for an asymmetric assignment of tax sources to metropolitan areas. Asymmetric decentralization design is the exception rather than the rule, and more so in terms of tax authority.[6]

Implementing Revenue Assignments: What Form of Tax Autonomy?

Regardless of actual practice, it is unquestionable that a goal for revenue assignments should remain the granting of a high level of tax autonomy to subnational governments. In practice, the implementation of tax autonomy requires addressing two questions: (1) what type of revenue autonomy is desirable; and (2) what kind of tax instruments should be used to provide tax autonomy.

With respect to the form of tax autonomy, four dimensions have been identified in the literature: (1) who selects the taxes; (2) whether tax bases should be exclusive to each level of government or used by several levels; (3) which level of government should legislate on tax base and tax rate; and (4) what level of government should administer the tax (see Bird 2000b; Boadway 1997; McLure 1998; 2000; Musgrave 1983; Norregard 1997).

With respect to the selection of taxes, there are good reasons for some limits to the ability of subnational governments to introduce certain types of levies, such as in the case of the prohibition of internal tariffs for domestic trade in the U.S. Constitution. Two general approaches are followed: subnational governments can choose from either an open list of taxes, with general limits and restrictions, or a closed list of allowable taxes, determined at the national level. Even though a closed-list approach is more restrictive in terms of autonomy, it may be preferable because it can avoid the introduction of highly distortionary taxes, nuisance levies, and so on. The choice of approach is often specified in the constitution. Closed lists are used more frequently in unitary systems of government. Open lists are used in some federal systems, although a number of federal countries (e.g., India, Pakistan, and Switzerland) clearly delineate what taxes can be used at different levels of government.[7]

The second step is whether the base of specific taxes should be used exclusively by one level of government or simultaneously by several levels of government. Cohabitation has the advantage of providing subnational governments with more choices and meaningful sources of revenue, which may otherwise be monopolized by the central government. It has the disadvantage of introducing vertical tax externalities because one level will not typically take into account the impact its policies may have on the tax base and revenues of the other level of government (see Boadway, Marchand, and Vigneault 1998; Dahlby and Wilson 1996; 2003; Keen 1998). These externalities can be only partially addressed by intergovernmental grants or even by increasing the number of subnational governments (see, e.g., Boadway, Marchand, and Vigneault 1998; Dahlby 1996; Flowers 1988; Keen 1998). In the

---

[6] See Bird and Ebel (2007) for the possibilities and problems associated with asymmetric fiscal decentralization design in a large number of countries.

[7] Where those choices have not been updated in many decades, such as in India and Pakistan, where the federal governments can tax services but only subnational governments can tax goods, this has led to significant difficulties in the implementation of functional value added taxes (VATs).

international experience, when an open-list approach is chosen, generally cohabitation of bases is allowed. In contrast, the selection of a closed list is often made precisely to eliminate cohabitation of tax bases. All things considered, it appears that a hybrid approach with a closed list allowing for the cohabitation of tax bases and using intergovernmental transfers to correct for vertical externalities may capture most advantages and avoid most problems.

The third step in the design of tax autonomy is to assign authority to legislate over the structure of the tax bases and tax rate levels. In general, autonomy to define tax bases is less desirable than autonomy to set tax rates.[8] Variations in the definition of the tax base, either exclusions, deductions, or credits, can lead to more complexity and higher compliance costs across jurisdictions. Autonomy to set tax rates is generally simpler to deal with for taxpayers and administrators in multijurisdiction settings. It is also more transparent in inducing political accountability of subnational officials.

One last dimension of tax autonomy considers which level of government should be charged with administering the various taxes. Although it has been often overlooked, this dimension is quite relevant to autonomy and accountability.

Tax Administration: Administrative Efficiency Versus Added Accountability

What is the most appropriate approach to organizing the vertical structure of tax administration? That a particular tax has been assigned at the local level does not necessarily mean that it should be administered at that level; under some circumstances, it may be more advantageous to have that tax centrally administered, with the subnational government still making the policy decisions of setting tax rates, and so forth.

What are the determinant factors that may make an approach (centralized versus decentralized) more or less optimal for any particular tax?[9] The international experience shows a variety of approaches to the organization and degree of decentralization in tax administration. Countries with considerable decentralized revenue authority may have highly centralized tax administration (e.g., Scandinavian countries), and countries with little decentralized tax autonomy may have highly decentralized tax administration (e.g., Germany). Outside those polar cases are situations with separate tax administrations (each level of government administers its own taxes) or mixed models (the central government administers some local taxes, and much less frequently, local governments administer some central taxes).

From a technical perspective, several factors affect the choice of centralized versus decentralized structure, including (1) economies of scale and scope, informational

---

[8] Autonomy can of course lead to tax competition among subnational governments (Wilson 1999), with both positive consequences, offering more choice to taxpayers and increasing accountability, and negative consequences, a "race to the bottom" and inefficiently low services. Tax competition can also lead to "horizontal" fiscal externalities, whereby the tax policies of one jurisdiction can affect the tax bases and revenues of other jurisdictions. These externalities can be corrected via intergovernmental grants (Arnott and Grieson 1981; Gordon 1983; Wildasin 1983; 1989).

[9] The literature on this issue is not large. See Ebel and Taliercio (2005), Martinez-Vazquez and Timofeev (2010), Mikesell (2007), and Vehorn and Ahmad (1997). Some of the discussion in this section builds on Martinez-Vazquez and Timofeev (2010).

externalities, and so on; (2) compliance costs due to nonuniformity of tax procedures; and (3) accountability to the residents. Political economy factors, such as opportunities for corruption and the creation or control of public employment, can also become relevant.

A supposed primary advantage of centralized tax administrations is the ability to operate with lower costs through a more efficient use of inputs because of economies of scale in production, greater specialization of staff, and more sophisticated uses of capital inputs, especially information technology systems. Nevertheless, some subnational jurisdictions may be large enough to realize at least some of the advantages related to economies of scale, and new developments in hardware and software have reduced the previous advantage of centralized information and processing systems. Unfortunately, so far, the available empirical evidence is still very scarce.[10]

Taxpayer compliance costs generally can be reduced more via centralized tax administration because of fewer offices to visit, less information to process, and so forth. However, decentralization may provide more proximity to subnational offices. Here again, the empirical evidence is scarce and fragmented, although some issues are rather apparent.[11]

On the other side of the balance, there is the basic question of whether a separate local tax administration regime can enhance the accountability of local officials to residents and taxpayers (Mikesell 2007) beyond the accountability that may exist when decentralized local taxes are collected by the central authorities but local government have an appropriate degree of policy discretion, in particular, control over tax rates (e.g., Bird, Burki, and Perry 2000). The particular mechanics of collection and enforcement of each tax are likely to make a big difference in this respect.

From a political economy perspective, subnational officials are sure to care about other issues, such as control of taxes and enforcement levels, assurance of the cash flow, obtaining and leveraging information on tax bases and collections, power over employment decisions, and opportunities to receive bribes or use this power for other kinds of self-benefit.[12] And there is the important question of incentives to collect the taxes of other administrations.[13]

Because of the different objectives that can be pursued, which can be weighted in different ways by decision makers, and because of the variety of political economy issues at play, a large variety of organizational models for tax administration in decentralized systems can be expected. This conjecture is fulfilled in reality. The

---

[10] Overall, that central tax administrations are always able to operate more efficiently should not be assumed. For example, Ebel and Taliercio (2005) report subnational tax administrations in East Asia that operate quite efficiently.

[11] As Vehorn and Ahmad (1997) point out, in the United States a big corporation typically has to file as many as 15,000 sales tax returns in any given year.

[12] This is highlighted in Casanegra de Jantscher's (1990) well-known dictum, "Tax administration *is* tax policy." There is some empirical evidence that the budget situation does affect tax administration effort (Esteller-Moré 2005; Toma and Toma 1986). There is evidence that more centralized collections can delay the flow of cash to local authorities (Bird, Wallich, and Peteri 1995; Mikesell 2007).

[13] Dillinger (1991, 29), for example, argues that the choice between centralized and decentralized tax administration was a choice between "indifference and incompetence."

international experience in the vertical organization of tax administration shows a large variety of models and practices.[14]

Although there is always some arbitrariness about which countries fall into each category, the international experience suggests four main models for the vertical structure of tax administration found in practice: (1) a single centralized tax authority enforcing all national and subnational taxes, which is the experience of Scandinavian countries and other countries, such as Russia and Belgium, and also common in more centralized unitary countries; (2) independent tax authorities at different levels of government, with varying degrees of cooperation, which is common in large federal countries, including Brazil and the United States; (3) fully decentralized tax authorities, with all taxes, both national and subnational, collected at the subnational level, which in practice is the rarest, with examples in Germany and Laos, and historically in the Soviet Union and China before 1994; and (4) mixed models of tax administration featuring variations of centralized and decentralized characteristics, which can be found in Canada, Spain, and Switzerland.

Which model fits better is likely to depend on the specific tax assignment in a country. Separate tax administrations, for example, will not be needed in the case of revenue sharing and piggyback arrangements.[15] Overall, there is a need for flexibility in setting an approach since the desirable level of decentralized administration will vary from tax to tax.[16]

From a purely administrative perspective, because of information externalities, cost structures, and skill levels required, such taxes as income taxes, a destination value added tax (VAT), customs duties, some natural resource taxes, and social security taxes may be more efficiently administered by central tax administrations, while excise taxes, property taxes, user charges, taxes on common natural resources, and so on, may be more efficiently administered at the subnational level (Rubinfeld 1983). A complementary way to arrive at this conclusion is that decentralized tax administration will tend to be more efficient, the less important cross-border transactions are in the tax base (Boadway, Roberts, and Shah 1994). In multilevel tax administration settings, there is ample room for coordination, especially in the areas of taxpayer information and audits. However, generally, less coordination takes place than is desirable (for a review, see Martinez-Vazquez and Timofeev 2010).

What Tax Instruments Are Best Suited for Subnational Governments?

Beyond financing the provision of public services, taxes can also be used as policy instruments to achieve other government objectives, such as income redistribution or macroeconomic stability. Since Musgrave's (1959) seminal contribution, there is

---

[14]The information on individual country cases is drawn from Martinez-Vazquez and Timofeev (2005), Mikesell (2007), and Vehorn and Ahmad (1997), as well as other sources cited throughout this section.

[15]There are examples of upward collection of shared taxes, but in most cases they represent a response to political circumstances rather than of technical nature, such as separatist threats and historical rights in Italy and Spain; constitutional tax sovereignty in Canada, Germany, and Switzerland; and political transformations in China and Russia. In all cases, there have been important incentive issues. But the international experience also shows that the centralized administration of shared taxes is not free from incentive, information sharing, or cash flow issues.

[16]A good example of flexibility in the vertical structure of tax administration is presented by Canada's Revenue Agency, which collects some provincial and territorial sales, corporate income, and individual income taxes, but not for all provinces and not necessarily in the same way for a given tax in all provinces.

wide consensus that these other objectives are better pursued by central governments alone. At the subnational level, the focus needs to be on allocative efficiency (how to best use the resources available to provide goods and services assigned to local governments) in attempting to apply the benefit principle.[17]

Besides the suitability of particular taxes to approximate the benefit principle, there are several properties for all taxes that are also desirable at the subnational level: (1) buoyancy, with revenues changing roughly in proportion to the economic base; (2) horizontal equity, providing equal treatment to taxpayers in similar circumstances; (3) relative efficiency, causing low distortions in economic activity; (4) relatively low administration and compliance costs; and (5) political acceptability.

In addition, several other properties are desirable for subnational taxes, which make them more adaptable to the benefit principle (see, e.g., McLure 1998). They should be geographically neutral in the sense of not distorting the location of economic activity, not interfering with domestic or international commerce, and not being exportable so that the burden is not borne by residents of other jurisdictions, unless matched by benefits to nonresidents.[18] They should also have tax bases that are evenly distributed across jurisdictions, relatively immobile, and relatively stable over the business cycle; be highly visible and transparent to increase accountability; and be administratively feasible.

The typically fragmented structure of metro areas may impose additional constraints in the assignment of revenue sources. For one, tax base competition among the different jurisdictions in the metro area is likely to limit the choices of taxes (on capital and labor income) with highly mobile bases within the metro area. However, quite different equilibriums are possible in tax competition, and some of those taxes may be used, although at rates that are lower and more uniform than may be optimal. Nevertheless, differences in rates and taxes may be expected within fragmented metropolitan areas if jurisdictions can justify them to taxpayers as benefit taxes. For this reason, a more intense utilization of well-defined user charges and fees within fragmented metropolitan areas is expected.

Selecting Tax Instruments for Assignment at the Subnational Level

Few revenue sources fulfill all the desirable properties, and a compromise is generally needed. The criteria reviewed above, at the least, allow us to select among better local tax assignments.

Charges and Fees

There is ample consensus that user charges and fees are the most appropriate source of revenue for local governments, fitting perfectly within the benefit principle

---

[17] But as Bahl and Linn (1992) argued, the distributive impact of local taxes (and expenditures), of course, still would need to be explicitly considered as part of the overall assessment of the distributive impact of the public sector and in the national fiscal policy design.

[18] Tax exporting is generally undesirable because it can lead to an overexpansion of the public sector and to inequities in the distribution of tax burdens. In contrast, the expansion effect may help compensate for the underprovision of public services from several causes, including the lack of good tax handles, tax competition across jurisdictions, public goods problems, or deficits where user charges are used for financing.

(Musgrave 1983; Oates 1972). A considerable array of services are amenable to being financed with user charges and fees, including water and sewerage, electricity, parking, garbage collection, urban transportation and road use, kindergarten and residential care for the elderly, museums, parks, and sport facilities. Other services, such as health and education, can be partially financed with user fees. In addition, user fees can be charged to cover the public costs of registration and monitoring for a wide range of activities, including business establishment, real estate titling and registration, and driving permits. Betterment levies, paid up front by developers and owners for local infrastructure improvements, such as sidewalks, lighting, additional road construction, and water and sewerage access, can be considered a variation of user fees.

Besides the economic efficiency advantages of benefit charges, from a political economy perspective they also offer the advantage of not directly competing for any tax base with central governments, so central authorities tend to be much more generous in granting autonomy to subnational governments to set charges and fees.[19] One disadvantage is that they may be perceived as unfair to the poorer groups, and on this basis, often fees and charges for excludable services, such as water and sewerage, in developing countries are set below full cost recovery for service provision. However, in essence, to consider user charges regressive is tantamount to considering food prices or other private commodities regressive. Income redistribution and equity are, of course, important objectives of any public finance system, but they are better pursued by other levels of government through more appropriately targeted policies. Maintaining user prices at too low a level leads to waste of the resources and unnecessary subsidies for higher-income residents and squanders one of the few good sources of revenue for local governments.

User charges and fees tend to represent significant shares of total revenues in the city budgets of developed countries.[20] However, they tend to represent a much smaller share of total city revenues in developing countries. However, there are some important exceptions; for example, user charges and fees represent more than one-third of total revenues in Cape Town.

However, it is not generally feasible to finance all local services with user charges. Sometimes it is not possible to identify the users; other times it becomes too

---

[19]With price or benefit charges, which exclude from consumption those that do not pay, local government providers can set the charge at the marginal cost of provision. Given that there is a "voluntary exchange," users will utilize the service to the point where their marginal willingness to pay for the service is equal to the price or benefit charge. Direct pricing of these services allows local authorities to get the necessary information on supply capacity at the same time it rations user demand for the services. Besides using the marginal cost of provision, which can be hard to quantify and can lead to financial losses when marginal costs are below average costs, there are several other pricing options. These include average cost pricing, going-rate charges adapting to the user's demand elasticity, and multipart tariffs consisting, for example, of a fixed charge to cover fixed infrastructure costs and an additional charge for using the facility. The choice of pricing method depends on the nature of the service and the type of infrastructure that is needed to deliver the service, and the administrative feasibility of the different pricing options. This latter can be significantly affected by technological innovations; for example, nowadays it is entirely feasible to charge electronically varying fees for the use of highways, depending on the degree of road congestion during the day. Even though the pricing of many public services is generally not complicated, in some circumstances it can become a difficult issue. See Bos (1987) and Weare and Friedman (1998) for further discussion of the issues.

[20]In the United States, local user fees and charges represent one-fourth of own-source revenues (35 percent when local public utilities are included). Canadian local governments similarly raise one-fourth of their own-source revenues from user fees and charges (Fox and Slack 2010). See also Bahl (2011).

expensive to charge the fee or to exclude those that do not pay from using the service.[21] In these cases, services need to be financed through taxes. And ideally, many of these taxes are "benefit taxes," designed so that those that pay are the same as those receiving the benefits from the public services. For example, the value or size of a residential property may be seen as a proxy for the benefits received by residents from street improvements; in this case, a property tax acts as a user charge.

Better Choices of Local Taxes

PROPERTY TAXES AND BETTERMENT LEVIES

There is ample consensus in the public finance literature that property taxes and betterment levies are closest to being benefit taxes, entirely appropriate for local government financing. Because property taxes are analyzed in chapter 7, they are not further addressed here.

VEHICLE AND TRANSPORTATION TAXES

These are generally an attractive form of local taxation because of the strong link between the ownership of vehicles, on the one hand, and the use of local services and infrastructure (particularly roads), on the other. In addition, vehicle and transportation taxes offer the advantage of being "green" taxes, with the double dividend of reducing negative externalities associated with traffic congestion and air pollution in the local area. These are also revenue elastic, relatively stable, and nonexportable taxes.[22] On the down side, owners will tend to register their cars where it is cheapest, and generally it may be difficult to prevent this from happening through ordinary enforcement measures. Motor vehicle taxes remain underutilized relative to the potential and the "goodness" of a tax handle that they represent, especially in developing countries.

LOCAL BUSINESS TAXES

Business taxes and business license fees are justified levies at the subnational level as an indirect but administratively easier way to tax income of business owners but acting as a benefit tax for the services and infrastructure provided by subnational governments.[23]

These levies range from several forms of broad-based taxes to operation licenses and charges. Broad-based levies that are neutral toward the factor mix in production are most desirable, as in the case of the origin-based business value tax (BVT) discussed in Bird (2003).[24] The closest example to a BVT in practice was Italy's

---

[21] In fact, service charges are often collected more like a tax than a market price; for example, charges for garbage collection are collected through the property tax.

[22] Some of those properties also make them attractive to central governments; in some developing countries, vehicle taxes are wrongly assigned at the central level.

[23] The term *business tax* may be confusing because businesses are also taxed with more general taxes on income and profits and on sales. The term is typically used in the more restricted sense of rough or approximated taxes on business entities.

[24] The base of the BVT would resemble that of the VAT, although, in contrast to the destination-based VAT, the BVT would be origin based, therefore taxing exports (and not imports). This better serves as proxy for the benefits businesses receive from subnational government services accruing at the place of production (not consumption).

regional business tax (*imposta regionala sulle activita produttive*, known as the IRAP) prior to the elimination of payroll from the tax base in 2003.[25] More often, different types of business license levies vary by type, size, or location of the business. For example, some South American countries have used taxes on "industry and commerce," and Nairobi and other local governments in Kenya have used a form of this tax, the single business permit, since 1999.

EXCISES AND SALES TAXES

Subject to the constraints imposed by the size of the jurisdiction and cross-border trade and smuggling, excise taxes have potential as piggyback taxes or special taxes at the subnational level. The extent to which excise piggyback surtaxes can be used at the local level depends on the size of the jurisdiction, the technology of product distribution, and points of sales. Excises tend to be more politically acceptable, can be easily administered in coordination with national wholesalers as withholding agents, and allow for rates differentiated by jurisdiction. Moreover, the benefit principle accords well with the assignment of (destination-based) excises on alcohol and tobacco to the subnational level (to the extent that the latter is responsible for health care) and on vehicles and fuel (to the extent of subnational government involvement in road construction and maintenance).

Another attractive form of excise at the subnational level is taxation of public utility services. There is significant revenue potential in some of these services, as in the case of electricity and phone services. Excises on public utility services can fit the benefit principle well because electricity and phone service consumption tend to be good proxies for local public services use by households and businesses. Compared with other commodities, taxation of public utilities would be associated with relatively low distortions because of low price elasticity of demand. Their relatively high income elasticity tends to yield revenue buoyancy and some elements of progressivity (Linn 1983).

Final retail sales taxes can also provide an elastic and high-yield source of revenue for local governments. However, final retail taxes, as opposed to the distortionary general turnover sales taxes, which are not recommendable, can be difficult to implement. More generally, local retail sales taxes can conflict and complicate the operation of the central VAT, which with some few exceptions most countries in the world have adopted.

FLAT-RATE PIGGYBACK INCOME TAXES AND OTHER INCOME TAXES

There is wide consensus that progressive income taxes are best assigned at the central level, because given the mobility of taxpayers, the goal of income redistribution is best pursued by the central government. Another reason for this assignment is

---

Also, in contrast to the typical VAT calculated by the credit method (the tax on gross receipts minus the tax paid on intermediate goods and services), the BVT would be calculated by adding payroll, interest, rents, and net profits on the basis of annual accounts.

[25] The IRAP was origin based and was actually calculated by a subtraction method (sales minus the sum of material purchases and depreciation). It is centrally administered, and the regions have discretion on rates. Despite its many good features, this has proven to be quite unpopular with taxpayers. See Keen (2003).

that progressive income taxes tend to act as automatic economic stabilizers, and macroeconomic stabilization should primarily be a responsibility of the central government.

However, there are several possibilities for the taxation of individual income by subnational governments. The most commonly used form of subnational income taxation internationally is a flat-rate income tax as a surtax or "piggyback" tax on the base (not the tax liability) of the central government individual income tax. This type of tax is almost always collected by the central government administration and the revenues allocated to subnational governments on a derivation basis.[26] To enhance revenue autonomy, local governments are allowed discretion in setting the flat rate, often between centrally legislated minimum and maximum rates.[27] A flat rate local piggyback income tax easily satisfies the benefit principle, and being quite visible, it promotes political responsibility and accountability at the subnational level. This is also an elastic source of revenue.

Another form of income taxation is a payroll tax, as in the case of Mexico City, or, in a wider form, a tax on labor income. However, payroll taxes have the drawback of being potentially more distortionary. Subnational payroll taxes can yield high revenues even at low rates and are not difficult to administer. In particular, payroll taxes may be easier to administer and enforce than general income piggyback taxes in some developing countries with less advanced tax administrations. However, they tend to distort optimal factor composition in production and also discourage employment in the formal sector, an issue of high importance in most developing countries. The tax base of payroll taxes can be quite mobile, especially if they are not applied in a metrowide area. This is also a tax base carefully protected and already highly taxed by most central governments in the form of social security taxes (see Bird 2000a).

NATURAL RESOURCE TAXES (WHEN RESOURCES ARE EVENLY DISTRIBUTED)

There is at least a partial link between taxes on natural resource extraction and the benefit principle at the local level.[28] Extraction activities use local infrastructure (e.g., roads), place stress on other local infrastructure (temporary worker camps, health facilities, etc.), and pollute the environment. But there are also arguments against the local taxation of natural resources. When economically significant resources (e.g., petroleum) are geographically concentrated, which is usually the case, local taxation could cause extensive horizontal fiscal imbalances, inefficient population migration and location of businesses, and internal conflict. Also, given the high volatility of world commodity prices, the yield of natural resource

---

[26] Generally speaking, a local income tax should be levied at the place of residence because that is where most taxpayers consume subnational government services. However, because of administrative convenience, subnational piggyback taxes are often withheld at the place of work by employees. Despite this, it is often quite feasible to distribute the funds according to where workers reside.

[27] Other, less desirable, forms of tax autonomy are practiced, such as modifying tax bases by providing additional deductions, exemptions, and so on.

[28] There has been growing interest in the fiscal decentralization literature in the pros and cons of the assignment of natural resource revenues to subnational governments. See, for example, Bahl and Tumennasan (2004) and McLure (1996).

taxes can be highly unstable and thus not appropriate for local governments.[29] Overall, however, natural resource taxes are generally less relevant to metropolitan areas.

More Controversial Choices for Subnational Taxes

As noted above, the theory of tax assignment is also helpful in identifying those taxes that will not be good choices for assignment at the subnational level. As just remarked, a progressive individual income tax is not recommendable at the subnational level. Another tax that is ill-equipped for application at the subnational level is the corporate income tax or profit tax. Some of the reasons, for example, its role in income redistribution and macroeconomic stabilization, are identical to those of the progressive individual income tax. In addition, it is unlikely that incorporated businesses benefit more from public services than unincorporated ones or that the benefits received vary with profits. At an operational level, it is extremely difficult to apportion the profits of enterprises across subnational jurisdictions where they operate.[30]

The VAT is also generally thought to be a poor choice for assignment to the subnational level. Since the debiting and crediting of the VAT are likely to take place in different jurisdictions, the apportionment of revenues is arbitrary, generally favoring the location of headquarters. The problem has been thought to be that there is no good way to handle the issue of interjurisdictional trade. These difficulties may be aggravated with autonomy to introduce differentiated tax rates.[31] Nevertheless, more recently, developments at the theoretical level and in practice have demonstrated that subnational VATs on a destination basis using the invoice-credit method are feasible, provided the central government levies a VAT.[32]

There are also some directly outright bad choices of taxes. This list would include the *octroi*, a local border tax still used in Mumbai, and general turnover sales taxes, as in the case of Bogotá and Manila. Because these taxes tend to produce significant revenues, they are very difficult to eliminate once they are introduced. This may explain the endurance of the octroi in India despite all the economists' lamentations on their impact on the local economies.

---

[29] In Peru, the "canon," a local sharing in natural resource taxes, is a sharp example of this type of issue; similar situations exist in Indonesia, Nigeria, and Russia.

[30] To this end, some countries use apportionment formulas, for example, a weighted index combining the geographical location of workers, assets, or sales. At the end, the allocation of profits remains somewhat arbitrary. In some cases, if not correctly performed, the apportionment of taxes tends to benefit the jurisdiction where the business headquarters are located.

[31] However, it is perfectly feasible to share VAT revenues with subnational jurisdictions using a formula; for example, the VAT can be shared on the basis of population (as in Germany and Belarus) or on the basis of the regional shares in aggregate consumption (as in Canada's maritime provinces, Japan, or Spain). But, of course, tax sharing does not allow revenue autonomy among subnational governments. The Canadian harmonized sales tax may no longer deserve to be called tax sharing, because since 2010 individual provinces can choose their tax rate.

[32] See Bahl et al. (2005), Bird and Gendron (1998; 2001), Keen (2000), Keen and Smith (1996), McLure (2006; 2010), and Varsano (1995; 1999). See also Martinez-Vazquez (2008) for a discussion of this literature and the experiences of Brazil, Canada, and India with subnational VATs.

THE PRACTICE WITH URBAN NONPROPERTY TAXES ON A GLOBAL SCALE

The international experience with revenue assignments shows great diversity of approaches.

Tax Assignments for Capital Cities

In the practice of tax assignments, it is interesting to note that, in general, capital cities get no special taxes for their special status. If there is any special financial treatment, it is generally in the form of transfers. However, the important exception is for those capital cities that also enjoy the status of regional (intermediate) level of government (e.g., Beijing, Moscow, Tokyo, and Seoul), in which case the tax assignments to regional/provincial governments also apply to the cities.[33]

Actual Practice with (Nonproperty) Tax Assignment in Large Cities

Very little systematic information is available on the actual assignment of (nonproperty) taxes in urban areas around the globe. The information reported here was gathered on a piecemeal basis from a very long list of diverse sources. The review of practices focused on big urban areas and large cities in a large number of developing and developed countries. Table 8.1 lists the large urban areas surveyed, classified as belonging to high-, middle-, and low-income countries. Table 8.2 lists examples of cities in large metropolitan areas, in developing and developed countries, that use the different taxes, both good and more problematic choices, discussed above. On the list of "good choice taxes" are numerous examples in developing and developed countries. However, the particular structure of these taxes can often fail to be desirable. For example, in some cases sales taxes take the form of gross receipt cascading taxes (e.g., Buenos Aires); in other cases, instead of individual income taxes, potentially distorting payroll taxes are used (e.g., Mexico City).

The category of "business tax" is frequently used and takes a variety of forms, such as business licenses to operate and levies based on turnover (e.g., gross receipts), or net income, and they receive a variety of names. In the case of Chinese cities, there is both a local business levy, in the form of a gross receipts tax, and a corporate income tax on locally owned enterprises. In the case of German cities, the business tax is called the *trade tax* and is determined by deducting a tax-exempt amount from trading profits and multiplying it by a tax assessment figure, which is usually 5 percent and fixed by a federal law. This amount, known as the tax assessment amount, is then multiplied by the respective municipal tax rate, which has been slowly growing and is close to 500 percent. In the case of Budapest, the business tax is based on sales revenue net of the cost of goods sold, including

---

[33] Sometimes it becomes difficult to differentiate between metropolitan/city governments and regional governments because both take the same name, as in the case of Madrid or Moscow. But while there is no difference between the city and regional government in the case of Moscow, in the case of Madrid they are entirely disconnected, with the regional government providing services to many other municipalities in the region besides the city of Madrid.

TABLE 8.1

Metropolitan areas surveyed, by income level

Category*	Cities reviewed
High income	Barcelona
	Berlin
	Birmingham (U.K.)
	Chicago
	Frankfurt
	London
	Los Angeles
	Madrid
	Montreal
	New York
	Paris
	Rome
	Seoul
	Tokyo
	Toronto
	Vancouver
Middle income	Bangkok
	Beijing
	Bogotá
	Buenos Aires
	Cape Town
	Guangzhou
	Istanbul
	Johannesburg
	Lima
	Mexico City
	Moscow
	Rio de Janeiro
	Santiago de Chile
	São Paulo
	Shanghai
Low income	Cairo
	Dar es Salaam
	Delhi
	Jakarta
	Kiev
	Kolkata
	Lagos
	Manila
	Mumbai
	Nairobi

*The high-income group corresponds to the high-income Organisation of Economic Co-operation and Development member and nonmember countries. Middle income corresponds to the upper-middle-income classification. Low income corresponds to lower-middle- and low-income groups from the World Bank country classification.

TABLE 8.2

Main types of taxes, with example cities by income level

Tax	High income	Middle income	Low income
Good tax choices			
Business tax	Berlin, Chicago, Frankfurt[1] Los Angeles, Lyon, New York, Seoul, Tokyo	Bangkok, Beijing[2] Budapest, Guangzhou, Shanghai	Dar es Salaam
Individual income and payroll taxes	Cleveland, Copenhagen, Milan, New York, Paris, Rome, Stockholm, Zagreb	Beijing, Bucharest, Budapest, Guangzhou, Mexico City[3] Moscow, Riga, Shanghai	Dar es Salaam, Lagos
Sales tax	Barcelona, Chicago, Los Angeles, Madrid, New York	Bogotá, Buenos Aires, Rio de Janeiro, São Paulo[4]	Manila[5]
Vehicle tax	Barcelona, Chicago, Los Angeles, Madrid, New York, Seoul, Tokyo, Toronto	Bangkok, Beijing, Bogotá, Budapest, Buenos Aires, Guanzhou, Lima, Mexico City, Santiago, Shanghai	Delhi
Transportation tax	Chicago, New York, Paris, Rome, Seoul		Cairo, Jakarta
Excise taxes			
Alcohol tax	Frankfurt		
Electricity tax	Chicago, Los Angeles, Milan, Rome	Cape Town, Istanbul, Johannesburg	Delhi, Jakarta
General excise tax	Berlin, Chicago, New York, Seoul, Tokyo	Bangkok, Beijing, Guangzhou, Moscow, Shanghai	Dar es Salaam, Jakarta
Gasoline tax	Chicago, Montreal, New York, Lyon, Tokyo	Istanbul[6] Lima, Rio de Janeiro, São Paulo	
Green tax	New York, Paris, Seoul		
Telecommunications tax	Chicago		

Possibly bad choices

Corporate income tax	Geneva,[7] Lisbon, New York, St. Louis, Tokyo[8]	Moscow[9]	Cairo, Jakarta
VAT	Seoul[10]	Bangkok, Moscow[11]	Jakarta, Kiev, Manila

Miscellaneous[12]

Amusement tax	Chicago, New York, Seoul, Tokyo	Istanbul, Lima	
Advertisement tax		Bangkok, Istanbul	
Financial tax[13]	New York[14]		
Fire insurance tax		Istanbul	
Gambling tax	Chicago, New York	Bangkok, Lima	
Construction tax	Barcelona, Madrid, Milan, Montreal	Beijing, Bogotá, Buenos Aires (metro)	
Natural resource tax	Seoul	Beijing, Guanzhou, Shanghai	Manila[15]
Slaughter tax		Bangkok, Beijing, Guanzhou, Shanghai	
Stamp tax		Beijing, Budapest, Guangzhou, Shanghai	
Inheritance and wealth tax	Paris	Beijing, Guangzhou, Shanghai	

The high-income group corresponds to the high-income Organisation of Economic Co-operation and Development member and nonmember countries. Middle income corresponds to upper-middle-income classification. Low income corresponds to lower-middle- and low-income groups from the World Bank country classification.

[1] In Germany this is called the trade tax. [2] Chinese cities levy local business taxes in the form of gross receipts taxes and corporate income taxes on any locally owned enterprise. [3] This is a payroll (wage) tax. [4] For both Brazilian cities it is a tax on services (ISS). [5] For Bogotá and Manila these are gross receipts taxes. [6] Istanbul charges the "environmental sanitation tax" as a sales tax on gasoline. [7] New York City has revenue and administration autonomy over its budget, but all tax laws are passed at the state level. The corporate enterprise tax is levied as a "corporate inhabitant tax" on corporations having offices or business establishments located within the Tokyo metropolitan prefecture. Both Geneva and Lisbon have a surcharge on the central corporate income tax. [8] The Corporate Enterprise tax is levied as a "corporate inhabitant tax" on corporations having offices or business establishments located within the Tokyo Metropolitan Prefecture. [9] Moscow acts as city and regional government (subject of the federation). [10] Seoul charges a surtax on top of the national VAT. [11] Moscow has a VAT surcharge because it is also a regional government and is allowed to set a surtax on the corporate income tax. [12] Some of these taxes, such as the stamp tax, could also be classified among the "bad "taxes above. [13] In Lagos there is a withholding tax on interest generated by savings. In New York City, however, this is an additional business tax on banks operating within the city. A bank pays an extra percentage of taxes on profits earned while operating in New York City. [14] New York City levies separately a business tax on insurance companies of 2 percent. [15] Tax on sand, gravel, and other quarry resources: tax is levied on extractors of listed resources within the territory of jurisdiction, with a limit of 10 percent of fair market value in the locality per cubic meter of resource. The revenue has to be shared with *barangays* (the equivalent of boroughs) where the resource is extracted (at 40 percent).

SOURCE: Compiled by the authors from various data sources listed in the references.

the costs of materials. The business tax in Seoul is based on the size of real estate property and number of employees, and in Tokyo it varies by the type of business.

Individual income taxes are also present as assigned sources of revenues in a number of cities in both developed and developing countries, but it is not as common as may be desirable. Sometimes this tax takes the form of a surcharge (piggyback) on state or national taxes. New York City, for example, charges a percentage above the existing state income tax being collected from the residents of the five New York City boroughs; Rome and Milan charge an extra 5 percent onto the national personal income tax. Similar taxes are uses in Moscow and Lagos. In Mexico City, a separate payroll tax is levied on residents. In Dar es Salaam, there is a 10 percent income tax on interest earned by residents.

Sales taxes are typically levied at the retail level (Chicago or Los Angeles). However, in Buenos Aires a gross receipts sales tax is added on the national VAT. Similarly, in Rio de Janeiro and São Paulo there is a gross receipts tax on services. Under "excise taxes," the international practice includes general excise taxes with levies on the usual variety of excisable commodities, but also on specific goods only, such as alcoholic beverages (Frankfurt) or gasoline (e.g., Istanbul and Lima), or specific services such as electricity (e.g., Cape Town, Delhi, and Jakarta) and phone services (Chicago). Green taxes are pollution charges taking many forms, including carbon emission taxes or taxes on businesses that generate pollution.[34] For example, in Seoul the tax is paid by any business "exploiting natural resources." In some cases, the green tax is just an excise, as is the case with Istanbul, where the "environmental sanitation tax" is a sales tax on gasoline.

Many cities, especially in developed countries, have also been assigned the motor "vehicle tax." For example, in the cases of Barcelona, Budapest, Istanbul, and Madrid, city governments tax the ownership of vehicles by residents based on the value of the vehicle. In Toronto, the personal vehicle tax is a levy on residents of the city who own or lease a personal vehicle, paid when they renew their vehicle license plate validation. Tokyo charges a tax on the purchase of a vehicle, called the *automobile acquisition tax*. Seoul charges an automobile tax paid by owners of cars based on their use and their capacity. Shanghai, Guanzhou, and Beijing all levy the local level vehicle and vassal utilization tax, which is a tax based on the use of vehicles. A number of metropolitan areas levy a variety of "transportation taxes," with the proceeds earmarked for the development of transportation infrastructure; for example, Chicago levies a tax on taxi operators based on each cab and its capacity, and in Jakarta it takes on the form of a public transportation tax.

There are some other miscellaneous taxes, many of which have been assigned to urban centers around the world. These are taxes that generally offer a good tax handle and that can at times be interpreted as benefit charges, although they generally do not represent much revenue. For example, "financial taxes" take different forms; in Lagos this is a withholding tax on interest generated by savings accounts, but in New York City this is an extra business (profit) tax on banks operating

---

[34] Special taxes on businesses that generate pollution can be difficult to implement. For example, a local cap-and-trade policy is very unlikely to work since an origin-based tax would be anticompetitive and a destination-based tax would be impossible to implement.

within the city. New York also charges an additional 2 percent profit tax on insurance companies operating in the city. Istanbul has a tax on fire insurance premiums. "Gambling taxes" also take different forms: in New York the tax is a percentage of winnings; in Lima, a percentage of the original bet; in Chicago, an off-track betting tax; and in Bangkok, a surcharge on top of the VAT being charged on horse-racing bets. "Construction taxes" can take the form of permits to build but also tax the costs of construction. "Hotel taxes" generally take the form of an added sales tax on the hotel bill. "Advertisement taxes" and "amusement taxes" are charged on the use of sign boards and the like and on admission to amusement parks, respectively. "Natural resource taxes" are charged on extraction activities, such as quarries. "Inheritance taxes" are applied in Chinese cities and in Paris, and the "stamp tax" and "slaughter tax" are also applied in Chinese cities.

On the list of "possibly bad choices" of local taxes, the assignment of the corporate income tax at the local level is rare. Moscow is allowed to use a surtax on the national corporate income tax in its role as a regional government as opposed to a city government. In the cases of Tokyo, Lisbon, Geneva, and St. Louis, the city governments also have a surcharge on the central corporate income tax. The assignment of the VAT at the local level is even rarer. Three cities, Bangkok, Moscow, and Seoul, have their own surtax on the national VAT.

Overall, the survey of actual practice in the sample of cities shows a wider use of "good choice" taxes in developed countries than in developing countries. The reason that more developing countries do not use good choices of local taxes, such as individual income taxes, business taxes, or even vehicle taxes, has a lot to do with political economy issues. Most important seems to be the reluctance of the central authorities to share or cohabitate productive and elastic tax bases with subnational governments. Even though there are some issues with administrative capacity, this seems to be less valid for large urban centers and cities, where that capacity is likely to be present.[35] And in any case, piggybacking on central taxes or allowing for the central administration of local taxes can generally overcome capacity issues related to administration and enforcement.

Information on tax structure is scarce, and whatever is available is challenging to summarize in any reasonable way.[36] Information on actual collections for the surveyed cities can be even harder to collect. Table 8.3 presents tax structures for nine cities for the most recent year available. Note that even the reporting of taxes for these cities does not coincide in all cases with a strict definition of own taxes. Nevertheless, even a small cross section of cities shows considerable diversity in the number and relative importance of local taxes being used. The tax structures differ in the level of diversification of tax sources. For example, Chicago relies on a dozen different tax sources, each yielding some sizable revenues. By comparison, Lima relies only on two own-tax sources: property taxes and vehicle taxes. The property tax is important in cities like Barcelona or Delhi, but it is not as important in Tokyo, Buenos Aires, or Beijing. The individual income tax is the most important tax source

---

[35] But note also that there is a marked reluctance everywhere, in both developing and developed countries, for using asymmetric tax assignments, for example, by providing large cities with additional tax sources over those assigned to all local governments regardless of size and capacity.

[36] These data are not shown here, for space reasons, but are available from the author on request.

TABLE 8.3

Distribution of tax revenues for select cities, for the most recent year available (percent)

Tax	Barcelona (2009)	Beijing (2009)	Buenos Aires (2007)	Cape Town (2009)	Chicago (2009)	Delhi (2010)	Lima (2010)	São Paulo (2010)	Tokyo (2008)
Property tax	64.72	8.11	8.97	31.82	39.34	88.79	58.75	38.16	18.95
Sales tax	11.80	39.32			8.45			53.86	
Vehicle tax	8.58	0.57	8.72				22.58		2.01
Construction tax	2.88	3.72							
Resource tax									
VAT share	12.02	9.39	78.47						
State income tax share					8.18				
State sales tax share					9.62				
Individual income tax		9.29						6.56	42.36
Corporate income tax		22.49							23.92
Stamp tax		1.68	3.84						
Deed tax		5.39							
Utilities tax				68.18	8.32	11.20			
Transportation tax					3.98				
Advertisement tax						0.01			
Amusement tax					3.31				
Excise tax					2.70		8.25		5.60
Gambling tax							7.90		
Hotel tax					2.03				
Gasoline tax					6.67				
Telecommunication tax					5.96				
Other tax					1.03		2.52	1.42	7.15

SOURCE: Compiled by the authors from various data sources listed in the references.

in Tokyo, whereas for São Paulo the sales tax represents more than half of all tax revenues.

In the end, what score should be given to the actual practice in tax assignments in the group of large cities surveyed in this chapter? Table 8.4 attempts this, indicating the high, medium, and low potential of each tax in supporting a set of desirable characteristics, such as revenue potential, ability to fit the benefit principle, and nonexportability.[37] With some caveats, the scores presented in table 8.4 can work as a guideline for policy makers interested in identifying desirable traits in a long list of potential taxes that are used in the international practice to provide large cities with tax autonomy. Those taxes dubbed "good choices" expectedly tend to score higher, with more of the desirable properties. But it is obvious from table 8.4 that there are no perfect choices. The caveats in reading table 8.4 include, first, the fact that not all sales taxes, income taxes, or business taxes assigned at the local level are created equal. Better and, indeed, worse choices can be made for tax structure within each of those categories, and those choices need to be an important part of the selection process. The scores provided in table 8.4 are those that would correspond with the more desirable structures of each tax. The second important caveat is that there is no scientific way to assign the scores; rather, they represent one out of several possible interpretations.

SUMMARY AND CONCLUSIONS

Effective fiscal decentralization requires meaningful levels of revenue autonomy at the subnational level. Efficient spending decisions at the local level require that decision makers face the true marginal cost of funds. Besides providing revenue sufficiency, tax autonomy brings political accountability and higher fiscal responsibility (hard budget constraints) at the subnational level.

This chapter has focused on the current theory and practice of nonproperty tax assignments to local urban governments in developing and developed countries. The good news is that examples of best practices with economically attractive tax sources other than the property tax are not scarce and that providing adequate revenue autonomy is not a complex issue since it involves simply the power to set tax rates along with the availability of adequate tax handles. The bad news is that a large number of urban governments in developing countries, and also in many developed countries, have failed to adopt those best practices and continue to struggle with adequately financing their growing expenditure needs.

Meaningful subnational revenue autonomy typically requires the cohabitation of productive tax bases with the central government and discretion to set tax rates for taxes selected from a closed list. Subnational administration of subnational taxes can be desirable to enhance accountability, but some flexibility is desirable to allow centralized tax administration to take advantage of economies of scale in management and information.

---

[37] The list of desirable and relevant characteristics is by no means limited to those in table 8.4. For example, to get revenue assignments right, it may be important to pay close attention to the "starting points," including the tax culture, history, and the fiscal architecture of the country.

TABLE 8.4

Advantages and disadvantages of observed local taxes (excluding property taxes)

Tax	Revenue potential	Buoyancy-elasticity potential	Mobility of tax base	Potential efficiency costs	Sensitivity to cycles	Adaptability to the benefit principle	Even distribution of tax base
Good choices							
Business tax	M		M/H	M/H	H		L
Individual income and payroll taxes	H	H	L/M	M/H*	M/H	H	L
Sales tax (excluding gross receipts taxes)	H	H	L	L/M	M/H	M/H	H
Vehicle tax	L/M	M	L/M	L	L	M	M/H
Construction tax	M	M/H	L	M/H	H	M/H	M
Transportation tax	L	L/M	L	M	L/M	M/H	L
Excise taxes							
Alcohol tax	L	M/H	L	L	M	M	H
Electricity tax	L/M	H	L	L/M	M	H	M/H
General excise tax	L/M	M/H	M/H	M/H	M	M/H	L
Gasoline tax	M	H	M/H	M	M/H	H	M/H
Green tax	L	M	L/M	L	M	M/H	L/M
Telecommunications tax	L/M	H	L	M	M	M/H	M
Possibly bad choices							
Corporate income tax	M/H	H	H	H	H	L	L
VAT	H	H	M	M	H	M/H	L
Miscellaneous							
Advertisement tax	L	M	L	L	M	M	L
Amusement tax	L	M	M	M	H	M/H	L
Financial tax	H		M	H	H		L
Gambling tax	L	H	H	L	M	L/M	L
Hotel tax	L	H	M	M	H	H	L
Insurance tax	L	M	L	M	L	M	L
Natural resource tax	L	H	L	M	M	M/H	L
Stamp tax	L/M		M	H	M		L
Inheritance/wealth tax	L	L	M/H	L	L	L	M

Abbreviations: H, high potential; M, medium potential; L, low potential.

*In the case of payroll (wage) taxes, the distortion effects will tend to be higher.

**If levied on the place of work, it may be exported to nonresidents. This is not inappropriate, if the tax reflect services provided to nonresidents, such as commuters.

SOURCE: Computations building on Inter-American Development Bank (2010) and Artana et al. (2011).

Few revenue sources fulfill all the desirable properties for local taxes reviewed in this chapter; a compromise is generally needed. There is ample consensus that user charges and fees are the most appropriate source of revenue for local governments, fitting almost perfectly within the benefit principle. Nevertheless, it is not generally feasible to finance all local services with user charges. Better choices of local taxes

Vertical equity/ fairness	Cost of administration (by subnational government)	Compliance costs	Potential for corruption	Acceptability		Exportability	Visibility/local accountability
				By politicians	By the private sector		
	M	M	L/M	M	L/M		M/H
H	H	M	M/H	H	L	L**	H
L	M	M/H	M/H	H	M	M	M/H
H	M	M	L	M/H	M	L	H
M/H	M	M	M/H	H	L/M	L	H
M	H	M/H	M	M	L	L	M
L/M	L	L	M	H	M/H	M	M/H
L/M	L	L	L	H	L	L	H
L/M	M	L	L	L/M	M/H	M	M
H	L	L	L	H	L/M	L/M	H
M	M/H	M	L/M	H	H	M	H
M/H	L	L	L	H	M	L	H
M/H	H	M/H	M/H	H	L/M	H	L
L/M	M/H	L/M	L/M	L/M	L/M	L/M	M
M	M/H	M	M/H	H	M/H	M	M
M	L	M	M	H	L	M	H
	L	L	L	H	L		L
M/H	L	L	H	H	M/H	M/H	M
M	L	M	L/M	H	L	H	L
M	L	L	L	H	L/M	L	M
M	M	L	M	H	L	H	H
	L	L	L	H	L		L
H	M	M	M/H	L	L	L	H

include property taxes and betterment levies, vehicle and transportation taxes, local business taxes, flat (piggyback) individual income taxes, and final sales and excise taxes. Undesirable choices include corporate income taxes and the VAT.

The international experience with revenue assignments shows great diversity of approaches. User charges and fees tend to represent significant shares of total revenues in the city budgets of developed countries but not in developing countries, which typically underutilize user charges and fees as a financing source.

On the list of "good choices" are numerous examples in developing and developed countries. However, the particular structure used in the application of these taxes can often fail to be a desirable one, for example, with the adoption of gross receipt cascading taxes or distorting payroll taxes. On the list of "possibly bad choices" of local taxes, the assignment of the corporate income tax at the local level is rare, as is also the assignment of the VAT. A few large cities have been assigned these two taxes because of their dual roles of regional and local governments.

Two puzzles remain in the practice of revenue assignments that require additional research. Although there is a role for historical factors such as colonial roots (the "dead hand of history," as examined by McLure 2001), it remains difficult to explain why inappropriate assignments and bad design have proved so difficult to reform over the years in so many countries. A separate puzzle has to do not with their design but their actual implementation. Often the revenue autonomy provided in the revenue assignments goes unused by the same subnational governments demanding additional funding from their central governments. Future research should pay closer attention to the political economy of revenue assignments.

REFERENCES

Arnott, Richard, and Ronald E. Grieson. 1981. Optimal fiscal policy for a state or local government. *Journal of Urban Economics* 9:23–48.

Artana, Daniel, Sebastian Auguste, Marcela Cristini, and Cinthya Moskovits. 2011. Subnational revenue mobilization in Latin America and Caribbean countries: The case of Argentina. Paper presented at the Inter-American Development Bank Conference on Subnational Revenue Mobilization in Latin America and Caribbean Countries, Washington, DC (May 2–3).

Bahl, Roy. 2011. Financing metropolitan areas. In *Local government finance: The challenges of the 21st century*, ed. United Cities and Local Governments. Cheltenham, U.K.: Edward Elgar.

Bahl, Roy, Eunice Heredia-Ortiz, Jorge Martinez-Vazquez, and Mark Rider. 2005. India: An assessment of the fiscal condition of the states and their relations with the union government. Working Paper No. 05–22. Atlanta: Andrew Young School of Policy Studies, Georgia State University.

Bahl, Roy, and Johannes F. Linn. 1992. *Urban public finance in developing countries*. Washington, DC: Oxford University Press.

Bahl, Roy, and Bayar Tumennasan. 2004. How should revenues from natural resources be shared in Indonesia? In *Reforming intergovernmental fiscal relations and the rebuilding of Indonesia—The "big bang" program and its economic consequences*, ed. James Alm, Jorge Martinez-Vazquez, and Sri Mulyani Indrawati. Cheltenham, U.K.: Edward Elgar.

Bird, Richard M. 2000a. CVAT, VIVAT, and dual VAT: Vertical "sharing" and interstate trade. *International Tax and Public Finance* 7(6):753–761.

———. 2000b. Rethinking subnational taxes: A new look at tax assignment. *Tax Notes International* 8:2069–2096.

———. 2003. A new look at local business taxes. *Tax Notes International* 30:695.

Bird, Richard M., Shahid J. Burki, and Guillermo E. Perry. 2000. Subnational revenues: Realities and prospects. In *Annual World Bank Conference on Development in Latin America and the Caribbean, 1999: Decentralization and accountability of the public sector: Proceedings of a conference held in Valdivia, Chile, June 20–22, 1999*, ed. Shahid J. Burki and Guillermo E. Perry, 319–336. Latin American and Caribbean Studies: Proceedings series. Washington, DC: World Bank.

Bird, Richard, and Robert Ebel, eds. 2007. *Fiscal fragmentation in decentralized countries: Subsidiarity, solidarity and asymmetry*. Cheltenham, U.K.: Edward Elgar.

Bird, Richard M., and Pierre-Pascal Gendron. 1998. Dual VAT and cross-border trade: Two problems, one solution? *International Tax and Public Finance* 5(3):429–442.

———, 2001. Vats in federal countries: International experience and emerging possibilities. *Bulletin for International Fiscal Documentation* 55(7):293–309.

Bird, Richard, and Enid Slack. 2004a. Fiscal aspects of metropolitan governance. ITP Paper No. 0401. Toronto: Joseph L. Rotman School of Management, University of Toronto.

———, eds. 2004b. *International handbook of land and property taxation.* London: Edward Elgar.

Bird, Richard M., Christine I. Wallich, and Gabor Peteri. 1995. Financing local government in Hungary. In *Decentralization of the socialist state: Intergovernmental finance in transition economies,* ed. Richard M. Bird, Robert D. Ebel, and Christine. I. Wallich. Washington, DC: World Bank.

Boadway, Robin. 1997. Tax assignment in the Canadian federal system. In *Reshaping fiscal federalism in Australia,* ed. Neil A. Warren, 61–90. Sidney: Australian Tax Foundation.

Boadway, Robin, Maurice Marchand, and Marianne Vigneault. 1998. The consequences of overlapping tax bases for redistribution and public spending in a federation. *Journal of Public Economics* 68(June):453–478.

Boadway, Robin, Sandra Roberts, and Anwar Shah. 1994. The reform of fiscal systems in developing and emerging market economies: A federalism perspective. World Bank Policy Research Working Paper No. 1259. Washington, DC: World Bank.

Bos, Dieter. 1987. Public sector pricing. In *Handbook of public economics,* vol. 2, ed. Alan J. Auerbach and Martin Feldstein, 129–211. London: New Holland.

Casanegra de Jantscher, Milka. 1990. Administering the VAT. In *Value added taxation in developing countries: A World Bank symposium,* ed. Malcom Gillis, Carl S. Shoup, and Gerardo P. Sicat, 171–179. Washington, DC: World Bank.

Dahlby, Bev. 1996. Fiscal externalities and the design of intergovernmental grants. *International Tax and Public Finance* 3:397–412.

———. 2008. *The marginal cost of public funds: Theory and applications.* Cambridge, MA: MIT Press.

———. 2009. The optimal taxation approach to intergovernmental grants. Working Paper No. 2009–2016. Edmonton: Department of Economics, University of Alberta.

Dahlby, Bev, and Leonard S. Wilson. 1996. Tax assignment and fiscal externalities in a federal state. In *Reforming fiscal federalism for global competition,* ed. Paul M. Boothe. Edmonton: University of Alberta Press.

———. 2003. Vertical fiscal externalities in a federation. *Journal of Public Economics* 87:917–930.

Dillinger, William. 1991. *Urban property tax reform.* Washington, DC: World Bank.

Ebel, Robert D., and Robert Taliercio. 2005. Subnational tax policy and administration in developing economies. *Tax Notes International* (March 7), 919–936.

Esteller-Moré, Alejandro. 2005. Is there a connection between the tax administration and the political power? *International Tax and Public Finance* 12(5):639–663.

Flowers, Marilyn R. 1988. Shared tax sources in a leviathan model of federalism. *Public Finance Quarterly* 16(1):67–77.

Fox, William F., and Enid Slack. 2010. Local public finance in North America. In *Local government finance: The challenges of the 21st century,* ed. United Cities and Local Governments. Cheltenham, U.K.: Edward Elgar.

Gordon, Roger H. 1983. An optimal taxation approach to fiscal federalism. *Quarterly Journal of Economics* 98(4):567–586.

Hayek, Friedrich A. 1945. The use of knowledge in society. *American Economic Review* 35(4):514–530.

Hettich, Walter, and Stanley Winer. 1984. A positive model of tax structure. *Journal of Public Economics* 24(1):67–87.

Inter-American Development Bank. 2010. Subnational revenue mobilization in Latin American and Caribbean countries. A Research Network Project. Paper No. RG-K1194. Washington, DC.

Keen, Michael. 1998. Vertical tax externalities in the theory of fiscal federalism. *IMF Staff Papers* 45:454–485.

———. 2000. VIVAT, VCAT and all that: New forms of value-added tax for federal systems. *Canadian Tax Journal* 48:409–424.

———. 2003. Tax reform in Italy. *Tax Notes International* (February 17):665–682.

Keen, Michael, and Stephen Smith. 1996. The future of the value added tax in the European Union. *Economic Policy* 23:375–411.

Lindahl, Erik R. 1919. *The justness of taxation*. Lund, Sweden: Univeristy of Lund.

Linn, Johannes F. 1983. *Cities in the developing world: Policies for their equitable and efficient growth*. Oxford: Oxford University Press.

Martinez-Vazquez, Jorge. 2008. Revenue assignments in the practice of fiscal federalism, fiscal federalism and political decentralization. In *Fiscal federalism and political decentralization*, ed. Nuria Bosh and Jose M. Duran. Cheltenham, U.K.: Edward Elgar.

Martinez-Vazquez, Jorge, Charles E. McLure Jr., and Francois Vaillancourt. 2006. Revenues and expenditures in an intergovernmental framework. In *Perspectives on fiscal federalism*, ed. Richard Bird and Francois Vaillancourt. Washington, DC: World Bank.

Martinez-Vazquez, Jorge, and Cristian Sepulveda. 2011. Toward a general theory of tax assignments. International Studies Program Working Paper No. 1122. Atlanta: Andrew Young School of Policy Studies, Georgia State University.

Martinez-Vazquez, Jorge, and Andrey Timofeev. 2005. Centralized and decentralized models of tax administration. International Studies Working Paper No. 05-2. Atlanta: Andrew Young School of Policy Studies, Georgia State University.

———. 2010. Choosing between centralized and decentralized models of tax administration. *International Journal of Public Administration* 33:601–619.

McLure, Charles E., Jr. 1996. The sharing of taxes on natural resources and the future of the Russian Federation. In *Russia and the challenge of fiscal federalism*, ed. Christine I. Wallich. Washington, DC: World Bank.

———. 1998. The tax assignment problem: Ends, means, and constraints. *Public Budgeting and Financial Management* 9(4):652–683.

———. 2000. Tax assignment and subnational fiscal autonomy. *Bulletin for International Fiscal Documentation* (December):626–635.

———. 2001. The tax assignment problem: Ruminations on how theory and practice depend on history. *National Tax Journal* 44(2):339–363.

———. 2006. The long shadow of history: Sovereignty, tax assignment, legislation, and judicial decisions on corporate income taxes in the U.S. and the E.U. In *Comparative fiscal federalism: Comparing the European court of justice and the U.S. Supreme Court's tax jurisprudence*, ed. Reuven S. Avi-Yonah, James R. Hines, and Michael Lang, 119–190. Deventer: Kluwer.

———. 2010. How to coordinate state and local sales taxes with a federal value-added tax. *Tax Law Review* 63(3):639–704.

Mikesell, John L. 2007. Developing options for the administration of local taxes: An international review. *Public Budgeting and Finance* 27(1):41–68.

Musgrave, Richard A. 1938. The voluntary exchange theory of public economy. *Quarterly Journal of Economics* 53(2):213–237.

———. 1959. *The theory of public finance*. New York: McGraw-Hill.

———. 1983. Who should tax, where, and what? In *Tax assignment in federal countries*, ed. Charles E. McLure Jr. Canberra: Centre for Research on Federal Financial Relations, Australian National University.

Norregard, John. 1997. Tax assignment. In *Fiscal federalism in theory and practice*, ed. Teresa Ter-Minassian, 49–72. Washington, DC: International Monetary Fund.

Oates, Wallace E. 1972. *Fiscal federalism*. New York: Harcourt Brace Jovanovich.

Rodden, Jonathon A., Gunnar Eskel, and Jennie Litvack. 2003. *Fiscal decentralization and the challenge of hard budget constraints*. Cambridge, MA: MIT Press.

Rubinfeld, Daniel L. 1983. Tax assignment and revenue sharing in the United States. In *Tax assignment in federal countries*, ed. Charles. E. McLure Jr. Canberra: Centre for Research on Federal Financial Relations, Australian National University.

Slemrod, Joel, and Shlomo Yitzhaki. 1996. The costs of taxation and the marginal efficiency cost of funds. *International Monetary Fund Staff Papers* 43(1):172–198.

Smart, Michael. 1998. Taxation and deadweight loss in a system of intergovernmental transfers. *Canadian Journal of Economics* 31(1):189–206.

Toma, Eugenia F., and Mark Toma. 1986. A congressional control model of treasury revenue collection. *Southern Economic Journal* 53(1):141.

Varsano, Ricardo. 1995. The tax treatment of interstate commerce: ICMS versus Shared ICMS. Texto par Discussao No. 382. Brasilia: Instituto de Pesquisa Economica Aplicade.

———. 1999. Subnational taxation and the treatment of interstate trade in Brazil: Problems and a proposed solution. Paper presented to the ABCD-LAC Conference, Valdivia, Chile (July).

Vehorn, Charles L., and Ehtisham Ahmad. 1997. Tax administration. In *Fiscal federalism in theory and practice*, ed. Teresa Ter-Minassian. Washington, DC: International Monetary Fund.

Weare, Christopher, and Lee S. Friedman. 1998. Public sector pricing: An institutional approach. In *Handbook of public finance*, ed. Fred Thompson and Mark T. Green. New York: Marcel Dekker.

Wildasin, David E. 1983. The welfare effects of intergovernmental grants in an economy with independent jurisdictions. *Journal of Urban Economics* 13(2):147–164.

———. 1989. Interjurisdictional capital mobility: Fiscal externality and a corrective subsidy. *Journal of Urban Economics* 25(2):193–212.

———. 1998. Factor mobility and redistributive policy: Local and international perspectives. In *Public finance in a changing world*, ed. Peter B. Sorensen. London: Macmillan.

Wilson, John Douglas. 1999. Theories of tax competition. *National Tax Journal* 52(2):269–304.

GRANT FINANCING OF METROPOLITAN AREAS

A Review of Principles and Worldwide Practices

ANWAR M. SHAH

9

The allure of metropolitan areas is irresistible for many people: the promise of good jobs, good homes, a good life, good times for the young and the young at heart, and dreams of a prosperous future for all. In an information age with a borderless world economy where economic success is more closely tied to competitive advantage than to hackneyed notions of comparative advantage, metropolitan governments are at the core of the future prosperity of a nation. And they can serve as a tool to overcome a lack of trust and restore confidence in government through their commitment to improve social and economic outcomes.

These great expectations, however, are critically linked to the fiscal health of metropolitan areas. Fiscal health is closely tied to the fiscal regimes available, in particular, taxing powers and other financing options, such as grant and bond financing (Bahl 2011; Bahl and Linn 1992; Bird and Slack 2004; Slack 2010; Chernik and Reschovsky 2006; Peterson and Annez 2007). This chapter is concerned with a critical aspect of this financing: higher-level fiscal transfers. While these transfers may not be the dominant source of revenues for a large number of metropolitan areas, they have a significant bearing on incentives and accountabilities and the associated impacts on fiscal health of metropolitan areas. The design of these transfers requires careful thought on special features of metropolitan areas that distinguish them from smaller local government entities.

Most metropolitan areas have large populations, typically in excess of 1 million. Mumbai, India, has a population of 21 million, and Istanbul, Turkey, has a population of 13 million. Metropolitan areas are larger and more compact areas with higher population densities than the rest of the nation. This compactness facilitates agglomeration economies, as well as making metropolitan areas centers of arts,

I am grateful to Roy Bahl, Harry Kitchen, Johannes Linn, Melville McMillan, Ernesto Revilla, and Deborah Wetzel for helpful comments on an earlier version of this chapter.

culture, and learning and sources of innovation, growth, and productivity. They also afford better transportation and communication facilities and an overall better quality of life. This leads to a larger concentration of specialized skills and wealth and, on the downside, higher incidences of crime and poverty.

Metro areas typically have much broader responsibilities than do smaller local governments. Beyond municipal services, these encompass health, welfare, and hub functions for national and international finance, trade, and economic links. Because of this, in some countries metro areas are treated as provinces/states. Examples include Canberra in Australia; Bangkok in Thailand; Beijing and Shanghai in China; Tokyo in Japan; Seoul and Busan in South Korea (KRILA 2009); Berlin, Bremen, and Hamburg in Germany; and Helsinki in Finland. Typically, metro areas have multiple local jurisdictions, and some have multiple tiers of local jurisdictions. Metropolitan areas also typically have a larger revenue base and greater tax autonomy and therefore greater potential for self-finance.

In view of this, the grant-financing needs of metro areas are very different from other local governments. If taxing powers are adequately decentralized, there may in fact be no need for grant financing of operating expenditures of metro areas, as demonstrated by Tokyo and Seoul. This, however, is not the case for most metropolitan areas: they lack autonomy in taxing powers and have limited access to dynamic, productive tax bases. Existing tax bases, especially property tax bases, are overtaxed to finance municipal and education services, for example, in the United States and Canada, leaving little room to grow. In the United States, this problem is compounded by limits on local revenues and unfunded mandates in environmental and social spending. In most developing countries, metro governments lack administrative and fiscal autonomy and act as wards of the state, which hampers their efforts to play a leadership role in local economic development. In these circumstances, grant financing can play an important role. However, grants must be tailored to specific circumstances of metro areas, especially their broader role in local, national, and international governance. Grants must also reflect an expanded array of responsibilities that come with serving as nodes of national and international connectivity, as well as the special needs of a knowledge-based local economy. Grant design also must incorporate incentives and accountability mechanisms to ensure responsible and accountable local governance.

This chapter provides a synthesis on conceptual underpinnings of this literature and a brief overview of practices based on a review of 41 metropolitan areas across the world. It must be noted at the outset that the assignment of responsibilities must underpin any design of a grant program (see McMillan 2008). With appropriate assignments or reassignments, it is possible to minimize the need for higher-level assistance for metropolitan areas. However, this chapter takes these assignments (or misassignments) in practice as a given and examines options in grant design to facilitate better functioning of metropolitan governance. An overall theme of this chapter is that grants can (and should) be properly designed in almost any institutional/organizational setting, even those that may not seem ideal.

This chapter is organized as follows. A typology of grant instruments and their rationale and relevance for metro areas are discussed first, followed by conceptual guidance on grant financing of metropolitan services. The chapter then outlines models of metropolitan governance in practice and draws implications for the design of higher-level transfers. It also discusses implications of existing institutional arrangements for developing a grant strategy for metropolitan financing. A review of worldwide practices in grant financing of metro areas follows, by type of metropolitan governance and by type of country, highlighting the divergence of practice from theory. The concluding section draws lessons from grant financing of metropolitan areas and develops an agenda for reform.

GRANT INSTRUMENTS, RATIONALE, AND RELEVANCE FOR METROPOLITAN AREAS

Instruments of intergovernmental finance have important bearings on efficiency, equity, and accountability in governance.

Tax Base Sharing, Tax Yield Sharing, and Revenue Sharing

Mechanisms to share the tax base (metropolitan areas levy supplementary taxes on national bases), tax yield, and revenue are customarily used to address fiscal gaps or mismatched revenue means and expenditure needs arising from constitutional assignment of taxes and expenditures to different levels of governments. Tax base sharing means that two or more levels of government levy rates on a common base. Tax base determination usually rests with the higher-level government, with lower orders of government levying supplementary rates on the same base. Typically, taxes are collected by just one level of government, in most countries the central government, with proceeds shared downward or upward depending on revenue collection arrangements. Metropolitan Bangkok levies a surcharge on central value added taxes (VATs); excise taxes; business taxes; and liquor, gambling, and horse racing license fees and taxes. Tax base sharing is quite common in Eastern Europe and East Asia but almost nonexistent in most developing countries in Asia and Africa.

A second method of addressing the vertical fiscal gap is tax yield sharing. Typically, the central government collects shared taxes and apportions prespecified shares on a tax-by-tax basis to jurisdictions of origin. Tax sharing contributes to collection efficiency but may introduce incentives for the government level that collects the taxes to give relatively less effort to those taxes that it has to share. Tax-by-tax sharing is quite common in developing countries. Metropolitan Jakarta receives a fixed share of personal income taxes (PITs), property taxes, and natural resource revenues collected by the central government in its jurisdiction.

A third method of addressing vertical fiscal gaps is revenue sharing, whereby one level of government has unconditional access to a specified share of revenues collected by another level. Typically, not all revenues of the higher-level government but only a specified set of revenue sources are subject to pooling, based on a formula. Revenue-sharing agreements typically specify how revenues are to be shared among national and lower-level governments, with complex criteria for allocation among lower-level governments, sometimes imposing conditions for the eligibility and use of funds. The latter limitations run counter to the underlying rationale of unconditionality. Revenue-sharing mechanisms are quite common in developing countries. They often address multiple objectives, such as bridging fiscal gaps, promoting fiscal equalization and regional development, and stimulating tax effort at lower levels. Metropolitan cities in India receive funds both from central and from state revenue-sharing mechanisms. Metropolitan areas in Brazil receive transfers from state revenue-sharing mechanisms for municipal governments, the so-called municipal participation funds.

Intergovernmental Grants

Intergovernmental transfers or grants can be broadly classified into two categories: general-purpose (unconditional) and specific-purpose (conditional or earmarked) transfers.

GENERAL-PURPOSE TRANSFERS

General-purpose transfers are provided as general budget support, with no strings attached. These transfers are typically mandated by law, but occasionally they may be of an ad hoc or discretionary nature. Such transfers are intended to preserve local autonomy and enhance interjurisdictional equity (equalization grants). General-purpose transfers are called *bloc transfers* when they are used to provide broad support in a general area of subnational expenditures (e.g., education) while allowing recipients discretion in allocating the funds among specific uses. General-purpose transfers simply augment the recipient's resources. Since the grant can be spent on any combination of public goods or services or used to provide tax relief to residents, general nonmatching assistance does not affect relative prices (Boadway and Shah 2007; 2009). Formula-based general-purpose transfers are very common in developing countries. For the purpose of allocating these grants, metropolitan areas are typically treated as any other local government, as is done by states in Brazil, India, and Pakistan and by the central government in Indonesia. In some countries, general-purpose transfers are provided as equalization grants that are intended to enable different local jurisdictions to achieve reasonably comparable levels of public services at reasonably comparable levels of local taxation. Metropolitan areas in Indonesia, Russia, Poland, and most Eastern European countries receive such transfers along with smaller local governments. Grouping metropolitan areas with smaller local governments leads to an understatement of fiscal needs and overstatement of fiscal capacity in metropolitan areas. For example, the Jakarta metropolitan area is rated as a "fiscal surplus" area according to the existing formula for local autonomy (equalization) grants. Of course, it is possible to design measurement criteria that would overcome this antimetro bias and at the same time make the allocation criteria simpler and more transparent (see Shah 2012a; Shah, Qibthiyyah, and Dita 2012).

SPECIFIC-PURPOSE TRANSFERS

Specific-purpose, or conditional, transfers are intended to provide incentives for governments to undertake specific programs or activities. These grants may be regular or mandatory in nature and can be either discretionary or ad hoc. Conditional transfers typically specify the type of expenditures that can be financed (input-based conditionality): capital expenditures, operating expenditures, or both. Conditional transfers may also require attainment of certain results in service delivery (output-based conditionality). Input-based conditionality is often intrusive and unproductive, whereas output-based conditionality can advance grantors' objectives while preserving local autonomy (Shah, 2007; 2009; 2010a).

Conditional nonmatching transfers provide a given level of funds without local matching, as long the funds are spent for a particular purpose. Such grants are best suited for subsidizing activities considered high priority by a higher-level government but low priority by local governments.

Conditional matching transfers require grant recipients to finance a specified percentage of expenditures using their own resources. Matching requirements can be either open-ended, meaning that the grantor matches whatever level of resources the recipient provides, or closed-ended, meaning that the grantor matches recipient funds only up to a prespecified limit.

Matching requirements encourage greater scrutiny and local ownership of grant-financed expenditures; closed-ended matching is helpful in ensuring that the grantor has some control over the costs of the transfer program. Matching requirements, however, represent a greater burden for a recipient jurisdiction with limited fiscal capacity. In view of this, it may be desirable to set matching rates in inverse proportion to the per capita fiscal capacity of the jurisdiction in order to allow poorer jurisdictions to participate in grant-financed programs. If an equalization program is in vogue, it should recognize the equalization element of the conditional grant program to ensure there is no "double" equalization.

Conditional open-ended matching grants are the most suitable vehicles to induce lower-level governments to increase spending on the assisted function. If the objective is simply to enhance the welfare of local residents, general-purpose non-matching transfers are preferable, because they preserve local autonomy. To ensure accountability for results, conditional nonmatching output-based transfers are preferable to other types of transfers. Output-based transfers respect local autonomy and budgetary flexibility while providing incentives and accountability mechanisms to improve service delivery performance.

Output-based grants create an incentive regime to promote the results-based accountability culture. Consider the case where the national government aims to improve access to education for the needy and poor, as well as enhance the quality of such education. A commonly practiced approach is to provide grants to government schools through conditional grants. These grants specify the type of expenditures eligible for grant financing, for example, books, computers, and teacher aids, and also financial reporting and audit requirements. Such input conditionality undermines budgetary autonomy and flexibility without providing any assurance regarding the achievement of results. Such input conditionality, in practice, is difficult to enforce because there may be significant opportunities for fungibility of funds. Experience has also demonstrated that there is no one-to-one link between increase in public spending and improvement in service delivery performance (see Huther, Roberts, and Shah 1997).

To bring about accountability for results, consider an alternate, output-based design of such grants. Under the alternate approach, national government allocates funds to local governments based on the school-age population. The local governments in turn pass these funds to both government and nongovernment providers based on school enrollments. Conditions for receipt of these grant funds for nongovernment providers are that they must admit students on merit and provide a tuition subsidy to students whose parents do not have sufficient means to afford such fees. Conditions for the continuation of funds for all providers will be to improve or, at the minimum, maintain baseline achievement scores on standardized tests, improve graduation rates, and reduce dropout rates. Lack of compliance with these conditions will invite public censure and, in the extreme case, a threat of discontinuation of funds with perpetual noncompliance. Meanwhile, reputation risks associated with poor performance may lead to reduced enrollments and associated reduction in grant funds. There are no conditions on the use of funds, and schools have full autonomy in the use of grant funds and retention of unused funds. Such grant financing would create an incentive environment for both government and nongovernment schools to compete and excel to retain students and establish reputations for quality education (Shah 2009).

In the final analysis, it is parental choice that determines available grant financing to each school. Such an environment is particularly important for government schools, where staff typically have lifelong appointments and financing is assured regardless of school performance. Budgetary flexibility and retention of savings would encourage innovation to deliver quality education. Thus, output-based grants preserve autonomy and encourage competition and innovation while bringing strict accountability for results to residents. This accountability regime is self-enforcing through consumer choice (parental choice in this example). Such a school financing regime is especially helpful in developing countries and poorer jurisdictions in industrial countries plagued with poor quality of teaching and worse teacher absenteeism or lack of access to education in rural areas. The incentive regime provided by results-based financing will create market mechanisms to overcome these deficiencies over time (Shah 2010a).

A similar example of such a grant in health care would allocate funds to local governments based on weighted population by age class, with higher weights for senior citizens (>65 years of age) and children (<5 years of age). The distribution by local government to providers would be based on patient use. Minimum standards of service and access to health care would be specified for the eligibility to receive such transfers. Specific-purpose transfers can also be used to promote interjurisdictional competition, public-private partnership, or other collaborative or competitive approaches to enhance public services delivery and access. To achieve these ends, grant payments can be made on the basis of achieving either preset benchmarks ("certification") or higher ranks in relative quantitatively measured performance ("tournaments") (see Zinnes 2009).

For metropolitan areas, output-based transfers are useful candidates for financing operating expenditures for education, health, public transit, and infrastructure. Capital grants would be useful financing tools for overcoming infrastructure deficiencies or setting national minimum standards in quality and access of infrastructure. Tournament-based grants would be useful tools to create a competition among metropolitan areas in improving slums or overcoming congestion and pollution.

Grant Objectives and the Choice of Grant Instruments: A Conceptual View

In concluding this section, it is useful to summarize the choice of grant instrument in meeting specific objectives. This taxonomy of grants by objective is not specific to grant financing of metropolitan areas but is broadly applicable (Boadway and Shah 2009; Shah 2007; 2009).

- Bridging vertical fiscal gaps: reassignment of responsibilities, tax decentralization, and tax abatement accompanied by tax base sharing would be preferred instruments. Tax-by-tax sharing and deficit grants are less desirable alternatives.
- Setting national minimum standards: output-based grants with conditions on service standards would be desirable. Conditional input-based grants are less desirable.
- Overcoming infrastructure deficiencies in establishing national minimum standards: conditional capital grants based on a planning view with matching rates that vary inversely with local fiscal capacity.
- Compensating benefit spillovers: matching grant with matching rate consistent with the spillover of benefits.
- Influencing local priorities that are in conflict with national priorities: open-ended matching grants.
- Promoting competition among local governments: project- or output-based grants using certification to meet prespecified standards or tournament-based approach to reward top performers.
- Interlocal equalization: fiscal capacity equalization with explicit standard using the Robin Hood approach where richer jurisdictions contribute to the pool and poorer jurisdictions receive financing from the pool.

FINANCING METROPOLITAN SERVICES AND THE ROLE OF GRANT FINANCE

The role of grant financing is closely linked to the service delivery responsibilities of each metropolitan area, because several metropolitan services are better financed through other tools, as discussed below. For the purpose of our discussion, metropolitan services are grouped together either as people-oriented services or as services to both people and property.

People-Oriented Services

- Primary and secondary education and public health: These are merit services that are redistributive in nature, and as a result, higher-level grant financing would be important to ensure national minimum standards. Operating expenditures for these services are best financed by surcharges on PITs and fees supplemented by output-based nonmatching grants. Capital expenditures could be financed by borrowing and/or matching capital grants.
- Welfare assistance: This service is again a strong candidate for grant finance if it is a local responsibility, because of the redistributive nature of this service. Local

governments that provide a generous package of welfare assistance from own-source revenues are likely to lose tax base, as happened in the early 1970s in New York City and more lately in St. Louis, Missouri (see Inman 2005).

- Parks, recreation, and libraries: These services are weak candidates for grant finance but good candidates for finance through residential property taxes, surcharges on PITs, and fees.
- Museums, sports and fitness facilities, and concert halls: These facilities are poor candidates for grant finance and instead are better financed locally perhaps through reserves, revenue bonds, or other forms of capital finance that ultimately are funded by fees, and surcharges on local real property taxes and PITs. However, if some of these facilities in metro areas are intended for preserving national heritage, holding global events (e.g., the Olympics), and developing national-caliber athletes and performers, then such facilities should receive at least some national funding.

Mixed People- and Property-Oriented Services

- Water, sewer, airports, and ports: Capital costs could be covered by borrowing financed by reserves, real property taxes, surcharges on PITs and corporate income taxes, frontage taxes, matching grants, and public-private partnerships. Operating costs could be recovered by user fees and franchises.
- Arterial roads and regional public transit: Higher-level grant assistance would be important to finance partially both capital and operating costs. Capital costs could be financed by matching capital grants, borrowing, frontage taxes, and reserves. Operating costs could be financed by fuel taxes, tolls, fines, general revenues, transit fees, congestion charges, and benefit spillover compensation by conditional matching grants.
- Local streets and roads, public transit, street lighting, and parking: These are purely local services and are not appropriate for grant finance.
- Fire protection and ambulance service: These services are best financed from general revenues.
- Police, courts, and prisons: To the extent that these services may have some national externality, these could be partially financed by grants.
- Garbage and solid waste disposal: These services are best financed by user charges/ fees and franchises.
- Local environmental protection and discouraging "sins" and "bads": These services are best financed by environmental charges, congestion tolls, and taxes on gambling, alcohol, and tobacco.
- General services: Grant financing is not appropriate; instead, these services should be financed by local general revenues.

The above list highlights the relevance of service delivery responsibilities in determining relevant grant structures. The following section looks at the relevance of the governance structure and taxing powers of the metropolitan area for grant finance.

MODELS OF METROPOLITAN GOVERNANCE AND IMPLICATIONS FOR HIGHER-LEVEL FISCAL TRANSFERS

Metropolitan areas could be broadly grouped into six areas based on the level of coordination or centralization of metropolitan governance.

Unitary Governance

Under this model, the metropolitan area has single unified ("unicity") or single-tier coordinated governance. Examples of this governance include Addis Ababa, Bern, London, Melbourne, Prague, Pretoria, Toronto, and Yogyakarta. Yogyakarta has a joint secretariat comprising heads of the municipality of Yogyakarta and the districts of Slemen and Bantul for harmonization of infrastructure development, with special emphasis on solid waste and waste water management. Such governance arrangements offer the potential for the metropolitan area to be largely self-financed if it is given adequate fiscal autonomy. Canberra, Australia, is unique in that it is a city-state with single-tier governance. It has an elected assembly based on proportional party representation. The assembly chooses the chief minister.

City States or Integrated State and Metropolitan Governance

These are typically provincial (state) cities having the status of both a state or province and a metropolitan city. Governance structure usually comprises two tiers, with the lower tier either (1) serving as a deconcentrated arm of the upper tier, although having a directly elected council to provide oversight on central administration at the district or ward level, as in Bangkok; or (2) having autonomy for some local/neighborhood services, as in Beijing, Tokyo, and Madrid. These jurisdictions, by virtue of having city-state status, have the potential to be largely self-financing. In addition, such governance arrangements internalize intrametropolitan spillovers. Examples of metropolitan areas having city-state status include Bangkok, Beijing, Berlin, Brussels, Busan, Istanbul, Madrid, Montreal, Seoul, Shanghai, Tirana, Tokyo, Warsaw, and Zagreb. Istanbul has a two-tier unified structure, with 73 lower-tier municipalities and the upper tier having the power to override or approve lower-tier decisions. Tirana, Albania, has two-tier coordinated governance, with the upper tier governed by the municipal council and directly elected mayor and 11 submunicipal units having directly elected councils and executive heads. Warsaw is treated as an urban county with 18 districts. Each district has a directly elected district council and district executive. The Warsaw capital region is governed by a directly elected Warsaw council and is responsible for metropolitan tasks. It coordinates these tasks through district offices. Zagreb, Croatia, has a two-tier governance structure, with the top tier comprising a joint council of the city and Zagreb County. The city and the county assembly elect two members each to the joint council, and the joint council is chaired on a rotating basis between the city mayor and the county governor.

Bangkok, Thailand, is a single-tier provincial city covering the entire Bangkok metro area. The Bangkok metropolitan area council comprises 57 councilors: one for each 100,000 people. The metropolitan area is divided into 18 districts, each with its own directly elected council to supervise metropolitan offices. The metropolitan chief executive is elected at large for a four-year term. The governor is assisted in executive functions by a centrally appointed civil servant: a permanent secretary. In Belgium, the Brussels capital region has a higher-tier region with an elected parliament and a centrally appointed government responsible for municipal laws and supervision and regional infrastructure, housing, and environment. The lower tier has directly elected councils responsible for education, health, police, and municipal services. Madrid, Spain, comprises the community of Madrid, which includes 179 municipalities, including the city of Madrid. The community of Madrid is responsible for regional infrastructure, education, and health, and at the lower tier, Madrid city and municipalities have elected councils, and mayors (with dual role as council chair and chief executive) are responsible for all municipal services. Montreal, Canada, comprises metropolitan cities of Montreal, Longueuil, and Laval and 63 municipalities. It has a two-tier governance structure with the upper tier, the so-called Montreal metropolitan community, responsible for coordination of a few select services. Seoul metropolitan area has an upper tier: Seoul metropolitan government with provincial status and 25 autonomous lower-tier municipalities (Rhee 2010). Tokyo metropolitan government has a prefecture or regional government status with twenty-three special wards, twenty-six cities, five towns, and eight villages performing lower-tier functions.

Horizontally Coordinated Mandatory Two-Tier Governance

Under this structure, both upper and lower tiers have well-defined independent responsibilities. Examples include Belgrade, Copenhagen, Macedonia, Serbia, and Skopje. Belgrade has a directly elected city mayor and assembly as the first/upper tier and 17 municipalities with a directly elected municipal assembly and municipal chair elected by each assembly as the second/lower tier. Skopje, Macedonia, has a similar governance structure, with the city as the first tier and 10 municipalities as the second tier. The Copenhagen metropolitan region has a directly elected regional council as the first tier responsible for intermunicipal coordination and health services and 45 municipalities delivering all local-municipal services, including education, at the second tier. Grant-financing needs of such governments would be limited to mass transit, social services financing, benefit-spillover compensation, and intrametropolitan equalization.

Horizontally Coordinated Voluntary Two-Tier Governance

Under this governance structure, metropolitan areas comprise multiple local jurisdictions that voluntarily cooperate with one another on select metrowide functions and deliver some services jointly through partnership agreements. Examples include Helsinki (24 municipalities) and Vancouver. In both cases, the upper tier represents a partnership arrangement among municipalities in the metropolitan area. Grant-financing needs of such areas are primarily for mass transit and social services and for intrametropolitan equalization.

Uncoordinated Two-Tier Governance

Under this governance structure, regional and local governments coexist with little formal coordination mechanisms either horizontally or vertically. Examples include Bucharest in Romania and Chisinau in Moldova. Bucharest has a directly elected autonomous but uncoordinated two-tier system, with the city's council and mayor serving as the top tier and six sectors (districts) serving as second-tier municipalities. Metropolitan Chisinau comprises the capital city of Chisinau and 18 territorial local government units, with each having independent legislative and administrative organs. The upper-tier municipality has a directly elected municipal council and general mayor and is responsible for metrowide regulation of land and residential property, coordination of social and economic development, civil and social protection, public order, and emergency regime and response. All other local functions are performed by the city and municipalities. These governance arrangements require separate and substantive needs for intergovernmental finance, including intrametroplitan equalization.

Uncoordinated/Fragmented Single-Tier Governance

Under this structure, several independent local jurisdictions sometimes belonging to different states and provinces deliver services in subareas with little coordination. Examples include Abuja, Cape Town, Chennai, Delhi, Hyderabad, Jakarta, Kolkata, Mexico City, Milan, Mumbai, Puna, and Washington, DC. The Mexico City metropolitan area comprises the capital Federal District, with sixteen districts (*delegaciones*), fifty-eight municipalities of the state of Mexico, and one municipality of the state of Hidalgo. These jurisdictions are uncoordinated, although a plethora of coordinating agencies/commissions and planning bodies exist. The Chennai metropolitan area in India comprises one municipal corporation (Chennai), eight municipalities, twenty-six town *panchayats*, and one cantonment board. These 36 governments are uncoordinated. Similarly, Delhi has three uncoordinated local governments: the Municipal Corporation of Delhi, New Delhi Municipal Corporation, and Delhi Cantonment Board (Sridhar et al. 2008b). The Jakarta metropolitan area comprises the city of Jakarta, three urban municipalities, and three rural municipalities (districts) belonging to three provinces: Jakarta, Banten, and West Java. Governance in the metropolitan area is a single-tier uncoordinated structure, although a central coordinating agency, the Badan Kerja Sama Pembangunan (BKSP), has been established that brings together all heads of provincial and local governments to promote task coordination. The Washington, DC, metropolitan area includes the District of Columbia, municipalities in the northern part of the state of Virginia, and parts of the state of Maryland (Boyd and Fauntroy 2002). Milan represents a special case: according to the 1990 law, it is supposed to have a two-tier structure, with the higher-tier metropolitan city having a provincial status and performing regional functions and lower-tier municipalities within the metro region performing municipal functions. However, it still operates as a single-tier uncoordinated metropolitan area with multiple jurisdictions, with little coordination among multiple local jurisdictions in the metro area. Such fragmented governance maximizes the need for higher-level financing.

The above descriptions suggest a stylized view of grant financing, taking into account the governance and finance models adopted for metropolitan areas. If the "finance follows functions" principle is adopted, then metropolitan areas should have significant taxing powers, such that their revenue means would be largely consistent with their expenditure needs, and the needs for higher-level transfers to metropolitan areas will be minimized. They would still need transfers or other compensatory arrangements to compensate for benefit spillovers to nonresidents for use of metro services. It would also be desirable to provide them with assistance in financing redistributive services, because local financing of such services erode their tax bases. For horizontally coordinated or fragmented metro governance, in addition, some grant mechanisms for intrametropolitan equalization would also have to be examined.

In the event that taxing powers are not commensurate with metropolitan responsibilities and a large vertical gap persists, a menu of tax decentralization and grant-financing options would have to be explored regardless of the governance structure. In addition, for horizontally coordinated or fragmented governance models, intrametropolitan equalization alternatives would have to be examined. Competitive grants also are important for improving metrowide performance through incentives for performance excellence.

ADDITIONAL CONSIDERATIONS IN DEVELOPING A GRANT STRATEGY FOR METRO AREAS

The implications of the metropolitan governance and finance models for grant design are critical elements for developing a grant strategy for metropolitan areas. Several additional issues in developing such a strategy also require discussion.

Autonomous Public Agencies for Service Delivery

Some metrowide services are delivered by autonomous public agencies run on commercial principles rather than by general government. Such practice is quite widespread for water, sanitation, gas, electricity, and toll roads. These arrangements should have no bearing on grant design, because the case for grant finance should be based on the objectives and results sought and should not be linked to the management paradigm for such services.

Functional, Overlapping, and Competing Jurisdictions

Under such arrangements jurisdictions are organized along functional lines but overlap geographically within the metropolitan areas. Individuals and communities express their preferences directly through initiatives and referenda (see Frey and Eichenberger 1995). The jurisdictions could have authority over their members and the power to raises taxes and fees to fulfill their tasks. The school communities of Zurich metropolitan areas and special districts and boards in North America follow this concept in practice. Output-based grants are a suitable tool to finance such jurisdictions (Boadway and Shah 2007; 2009; Shah 2009; 2010a).

Fragmentation of Metropolitan Governance Through Proliferation of Single-Purpose Jurisdictions

Special-purpose jurisdictions with access to tax finance are quite common in metropolitan areas in industrial countries. The most common example of such jurisdictions is school boards with access to supplementary rates on residential property tax base. Proliferation of these agencies leaves municipal services with inadequate finance because existing tax bases, especially property taxes, are overtaxed, with little or no room for revenue growth. These problems are sometimes further compounded by limits on raising local revenues and unfunded higher-level mandates in environmental and social spending, as has been the case for the U.S. metropolitan areas of San Francisco and Los Angeles. Declines in general-purpose or equalization transfers exasperate this problem. Matching conditions for specific-purpose transfers do not help, either. In designing a metropolitan grant strategy, these issues must be considered to ensure that metropolitan governments have adequate resources to deliver municipal services.

Contracting Out Metropolitan Services

Metropolitan governments may choose to deliver some services through contractual arrangements or through concessions or franchises. For some services, they could use multiple providers to achieve more efficient provision outcomes. In such circumstances, grant design must ensure that service quality and access to the poor are not compromised. Output-based grants are an ideal tool to have this assurance.

GRANT FINANCING OF METROPOLITAN AREAS: THE PRACTICE

A review of international practices on grant financing of metropolitan areas is constrained by the scant details available even for metro areas in industrial countries. The data limitations restricted our sample to 41 metropolitan areas worldwide. To capture the diversity of experiences, the sample was organized using two alternative classifications: by type of metropolitan governance and by the use of a four-tier typology of countries.

Type of Metropolitan Governance

UNITARY GOVERNANCE
Nine sample areas fall in this category, also referred to as single unified ("unicity") or single-tier coordinated governance. Contrary to expectations, grant financing is an important source of finance for most such metro areas, with the notable exception of Addis Ababa, Melbourne, and Pretoria, which are largely self-financed. Close behind these leaders are Toronto and Bern. London is an outlier, receiving more than 80 percent of funds from central grant finance. Tax sharing is dominant in this sample only for Prague. For the sample as a whole, 9.4 percent of financing comes from tax sharing, 16.4 percent from general-purpose or equalization transfers, and 13.7 percent from specific-purpose transfers, with the remaining 60.9 percent self-financed (see table 9.1). In this cluster, Prague relies significantly on

TABLE 9.1

Grant financing of unified and city-state metro areas (percentage of total revenues)

Metro area	Population (millions, most recent year)	Tax sharing (may include tax base sharing)	General-purpose transfers	Specific-purpose transfers	Total grants*	Total transfers**	Own-source revenues
Unitary metro areas (n=9)							
Addis Ababa	3.1				3.1	3.1	96.9
Bern	0.3				24.4	24.4	75.6
Canberra	0.3		27.8	14.6	42.4	42.4	57.6
London	7.2		25.6	53.0	80.6	80.6	19.4
Melbourne	3.5				14.2	14.2	85.8
Prague	2.3	40.4	NA	NA	19.3	59.7	40.3
Pretoria	2.0				9.9	9.9	90.1
Toronto	5.1			24.0	24.0	24.0	76.0
Yogyakarta	2.0		66.5	7.2	73.7	73.7	26.2
Average	2.9	4.5	16.4	13.7	32.4	36.9	63.1
Unified two-tier governance: city-state metro areas (n=14)							
Bangkok	2.5	24.0	7.0	20.0	27.0	51.0	49.0
Beijing	15.0	29.2	16.6	5.2	21.8	51.0	49.0
Berlin	3.4	39.1	18.3	21.9	40.2	79.3	20.7
Brussels	1.0	36.0	3.0	3.0	3.0	39.0	61.0
Busan	3.7	3.0	2.0	13.0	15.0	18.0	82.0
Istanbul	13.4	65.0	10.0	0.0	10.0	75.0	25.0
Madrid community	6.0	64.0		5.0	5.0	69.0	31.0
(city)	(3.1)				(39.0)	(39.0)	(71.0)
Montreal	3.4				24.0	24.0	76.0
Seoul	10.4	0.8			8.3	9.1	90.9
Shanghai	17.4	32.9	24.7	1.5	26.2	59.1	40.9
Tirana	0.6		8.5	17.9	26.4	26.4	73.6
Tokyo	13.0				5.7	5.7	94.3
Warsaw	1.7	40.0	NA	NA	14.0	54.0	46.0
Zagreb	0.8	67.7	0	0.1	0.1	67.8	32.2
Average	5.4	28.7	6.4	12.2	18.6	47.3	53.7

NA, not available or not applicable. *Total grants refers to general-purpose plus specific-purpose transfers. **Total transfers refers to tax sharing plus total grants.

SOURCES: Compiled by authors from various sources listed in the references, especially OECD (2001; 2003a; 2003b; 2004a; 2004b; 2004c; 2005a; 2005b; 2006a; 2006b; 2006c; 2007; 2008a; 2008b; 2009; 2010).

revenue sharing from PITs and VATs. Revenue sharing in the Czech Republic is by the number of inhabitants multiplied by the coefficient of the size category of municipality. Prague has the highest coefficient: 2.7611 (Kubatova and Pavel 2009). In this sample, Prague is the only metropolitan area receiving special treatment because of its size class. All other metro areas are treated similarly to other municipalities. Metropolitan London is an outlier in view of its predominant reliance on central transfers and having the most constrained access to own-source finances. It receives 25.6 percent from revenue-sharing transfers (the so-called revenue support plus redistributed nondomestic rate grant) and 55 percent as specific-purpose transfers, of which the police grant amounts to 5.3 percent and the area-based grant contributes 2.4 percent (Department for Communities and Local Government 2010).

UNIFIED OR INTEGRATED TWO-TIER GOVERNANCE: CITY-STATE METRO AREAS

Fourteen sample areas have this type of governance, with great diversity in central financing. Metro Istanbul is treated just like any other local government, with revenue sharing based on population and 5 percent of centrally collected revenues returned by origin (OECD 2008b). Tirana, Albania, receives central general-purpose transfers based on population (70 percent), area (15 percent), and urban services (15 percent for other local governments, 0 percent weight for Tirana). Corporate income tax sharing is mandated by law but not implemented because 80 percent of national revenues are collected in Tirana. Thus, in general, the general-purpose transfers discriminate against Tirana. It should be noted that Albania is among the handful of countries (Russia being another) that operates a competitive grant program. The program was initiated in 2006 with a pool as large as the general-purpose transfers and finances local capacity investment in education, health, water supply, and general municipal infrastructure. The criteria for allocation include expected impact on economic and social development and compliance with local/regional development priorities; impact on poverty reduction and improved access to basic services; projects promoting cooperation among local governments; projects with community participation and funding; funding for the local counterpart of foreign funding; and ongoing projects that have contractual obligations (Dhimitri, Ikonomi, and Dhuka 2009).

In Warsaw, the most prominent central transfer is for financing the metro subway system (Jefremienko and Wolksa 2007). Zagreb receives financing from a share of taxes on income (PIT and corporate), real estate transfers, and specific-purpose grants. Income tax proceeds are allocated to local government using the following criteria: by origin municipality or town share, 52 percent; county share, 15 percent; share of decentralized functions, 12 percent; share of decentralized function realignment. In addition, local government receives a supplementary allocation for decentralized functions: primary education, 3.1 percent; secondary education, 2.2 percent; social welfare centers, 0.5 percent; nursing homes, 1.7 percent; health care, 3.2 percent; and fire protection, 1.3 percent. The metro region also receives 60 percent of the proceeds of the real estate transfer tax derived from the region. General-purpose transfers are available to local governments with below-average fiscal capacity based on PIT. Zagreb is not eligible for these transfers.

The decentralized functions are financed through specific grants based on standard costs (Kopric et al. 2007).

In Bangkok, the metropolitan area receives tax sharing amounting to 5 percent of PIT, and 40 percent of revenues from natural resources and fisheries and teak wood are shared with provinces. One hundred percent of the metropolitan-area surcharges on central taxes, such as VAT, specific business tax, liquor tax, excise tax, liquor and gambling license fees, and gambling tax on horse races, are returned by origin. General-purpose transfers have two components: the VAT transfer and the general duty transfer. According to the Decentralization Act (1999), 18.5 percent of VAT revenues are allocated to local governments based on a formula that includes population, area, revenue, and budget needs. The metropolitan area received 5.8 percent of the total pool in 2008. With the general duty transfer, 5 percent of the total pool is set aside as deficit/expenditure need grants. Of the remaining 95 percent, 10 percent is allocated to the provinces, with 65 percent of that allocated on a per capita basis, and the remaining 35 percent is allocated on an equal per jurisdiction basis. Specific-purpose transfers mostly fulfill central mandates for health; education; public transit; school lunch; support for elderly care, AIDS patients, and disabled persons; social services; and water and environmental services (Shah et al. 2012).

The Brussels metropolitan region receives tax shares proportional to the yield of income taxes in the region. The region also receives equalization payments under the National Solidarity Intervention (INS) program, when income tax receipts per capita are below the national average (Wynsberghe 2009).

In the Madrid metro region, two regimes exist for central transfers for small versus large municipalities. For large municipalities with populations in excess of 75,000, the general grant consists of two parts: a tax share of central government taxes and a grant from the complementary fund. Tax shares are 1.7 percent of PIT, 1.8 percent of VAT, and 2 percent of excise revenues. PIT is allocated among municipalities based on taxes collected locally, and VAT and excise shares are distributed by consumption and population shares (OECD 2007).

Washington, DC, receives federal grant funds for Medicaid, community development, education, public welfare, and public safety (Gandhi et al., as cited in Slack and Chattopadhyay 2009).

For this sample, tax sharing is the most significant if not the predominant source of revenues for metros in European and East Asian countries. For the sample as a whole, tax sharing contributes 28.7 percent to metro revenues; general-purpose transfers, 6.4 percent; specific-purpose transfers, 12.2 percent; and 53.7 percent of financing is raised from own-source revenues. As provincial cities, most of the metros in this group benefit from greater access to self-finance, but given their greater responsibilities, only about half of their expenditures are self-financed. It is interesting that, in the sample countries, there is no special recognition of their metropolitan character. Only Spain accords limited recognition to this nature by grouping large urban municipalities together for grant financing. Competitive grant finance is practiced only in Tirana.

HORIZONTALLY COORDINATED MANDATORY TWO-TIER GOVERNANCE

Three sample jurisdictions fall into this category and vary significantly in their dependence on grant finance (see table 9.2). For Belgrade, Serbia, tax sharing from PITs by origin is the dominant source of revenue. In addition, it receives financing from formula-based general-purpose transfers. Equalization transfers are distributed to local governments with shared revenues per capita below the national average, so Belgrade does not qualify (Gliorijevic et al. 2007).

Tax sharing from PIT and VAT is the dominant source of revenues for Skopje, Macedonia. Three percent of the revenues from PIT and VAT are transferred to municipalities. Of the PIT pool, the city and its municipalities receive 10 percent. Of the VAT pool for municipalities, 12 percent goes to the city of Skopje (40 percent share) and its 10 municipalities (60 percent share) (Veljanovski 2009).

Copenhagen is primarily self-financed. Denmark has a separate horizontal equalization program for metropolitan areas, requiring richer jurisdictions to contribute to the pool, from which poorer jurisdictions receive assistance.

For this subgroup, tax sharing is the predominant source of central transfers, financing 30.5 percent of metro expenditures; general-purpose transfers, 7.2 percent; and specific-purpose transfers, 4.6 percent; 57.7 percent of financing is raised from local taxes and charges (see table 9.2). Copenhagen is unique in this subgroup for its participation in horizontal equalization among metro areas.

HORIZONTALLY COORDINATED VOLUNTARY TWO-TIER GOVERNANCE

Of the sample metro areas, only Helsinki falls into this category. Helsinki is primarily self-financed, and like Copenhagen, it contributes to a horizontal equalization program.

UNCOORDINATED TWO-TIER GOVERNANCE

Of the sample jurisdictions, Bucharest and Chisinau have uncoordinated two-tier governance structure. In Chisinau, own-source finance dominates, with some financing from PIT sharing and formula-based general-purpose transfers (Roscovan and Melnic 2009). Bucharest is primarily transfer financed, with the PIT and VAT as shared taxes. Metro districts receive 23.5 percent of PIT, and the general council receives 47.5 percent and an additional 11 percent for district equalization. VAT sharing is discretionary (past allocation indexed by inflation) and given as lump sum grants earmarked for salaries and social benefits. Specific-purpose grants are mostly capital grants for streets, rural infrastructure, and school rehabilitation (Lonita 2009).

For the subgroup, two-thirds of financing is received from transfers, mostly in the form of proceeds from shared taxes, and one-third from own-source revenues. There is no special treatment of metro areas in this group.

UNCOORDINATED/FRAGMENTED SINGLE-TIER GOVERNANCE

Twelve sample jurisdictions have a fragmented single-tier metro jurisdiction; that is, several local governments operate in a metro area without any formal coordination arrangements. There is wide variation in the role of central/state

TABLE 9.2

Grant financing under horizontally coordinated or fragmented metro governance (percentage of total revenues)

Metro area	Population (millions, most recent year)	Tax sharing (may include tax base sharing)	General-purpose transfers	Specific-purpose transfers	Total grants*	Total transfers**	Own-source revenues
Horizontally coordinated mandatory two-tier governance (n = 3)							
Belgrade	1.7	41.5	9.0	0.1	9.1	50.6	49.4
Copenhagen	2.4		7.0	10.0	17.0	17.0	83.0
Skopje	0.5	50.0	5.5	3.7	9.2	59.2	40.8
Average	1.5	30.5	7.2	4.6	11.8	42.3	57.7
Horizontally coordinated voluntary two-tier governance (n = 1)							
Helsinki	1.2				10.3	10.3	89.7
Uncoordinated two-tier governance (n = 2)							
Bucharest	2.0	60.0	7.6	15.4	23.0	83.0	17.0
Chisinau	0.7	24.0	15.0	5.0	20.0	44.0	56.0
Average	1.3	42.0	11.3	10.2	21.5	63.5	36.5
Uncoordinated/Fragmented single-tier governance (n = 12)							
Abuja	1.4		60.0		60.0	60.0	40.0
Cape Town	3.0		20.0		20.0	20.0	80.0
Chennai	6.3	24.0			10.0	34.0	66.0
Delhi	13.9	17.9			9.0	26.9	73.1
Hyderabad	4.1	25.0			15.0	40.0	60.0
Jakarta	18.9	46.3			0.0	46.3	53.7
Kolkata	15.0				58.4	58.4	41.6
Mexico	18.4		38.0	32.0	70.0	70.0	30.0
Milan	7.4				33.0	33.0	67.0
Mumbai	21.0				20.0	20.0	80.0
Pune	3.8				9.0	9.0	91.0
Washington, DC	5.0		12.0	14.0	26.0	26.0	74.0
Average	9.8	9.4			23.1	32.5	67.5

*Total grants refers to general-purpose plus specific-purpose transfers. **Total transfers refers to tax sharing plus total grants.

SOURCES: Compiled by authors from various sources listed in the references, especially OECD (2001; 2003a; 2003b; 2004a; 2004b; 2004c; 2005a; 2005b; 2006a; 2006b; 2006c; 2007; 2008a; 2008b; 2009; 2010).

transfers in financing metro expenditures, with the Mexico City metropolitan region having the highest dependency on these transfers, and Pune, India, the least. It should be noted, however, that Mexico delivers a wider range of local services than does Pune. Jakarta is noteworthy for receiving only financing from shared taxes.

In the Mexico City metropolitan region, there are wide variations in the sources of finance of various jurisdictions. The Mexico Federal District finances 37 percent of expenditures from general-purpose transfers and an additional 19 percent from specific-purpose transfers; 44 percent of expenditures are self-financed. The municipality from the state of Hidalgo receives 27 percent of financing from general-purpose transfers, and 67 percent from specific-purpose and other transfers, financing 6 percent from own-source revenues. The Mexico state municipality receives 39 percent of financing as general-purpose transfers and 35 percent as specific-purpose or other transfers; the remaining 26 percent is raised from own-source revenues (OECD 2004b).

Chennai, India, has access to state tax sharing from entertainment tax, motor vehicle tax, and stamp duty surcharge. In addition, it receives general-purpose transfers based on formula allocation using a population and deprivation index. It also receives specific-purpose transfers for education and road maintenance (Sridhar et al. 2008a; Bandyopadhyay and Rao 2009).

Hyderabad, India, receives a state per capita grant that varies from Rs4 (10 cents) in the metropolitan city of Hyderabad to Rs202 (US$5) for Alwal (Sridhar et al. 2008c).

Jakarta is a provincial city. It receives both the provincial and city share from central taxes. Provinces receive by origin 8 percent of PIT and 16 percent of property taxes, property transfer taxes, mining land rent, mining royalties, forestry license fees, and forestry royalties. Local governments receive by origin 12 percent of PIT, 64 percent of other taxes, and 32 percent of forestry royalties. Provinces receive by origin 3 percent of oil and 6 percent of natural gas revenues. Local governments receive by origin 6 percent of oil and 12 percent of natural gas revenues. It also receives compensation for public-sector wages. Just like any other small or large local government, it is also eligible to receive financing for its fiscal gap based on the difference in its revenues and fiscal needs, using population, per capita gross domestic product, a human development index, and a construction price index as need factors. However, Jakarta is considered to have a fiscal surplus and therefore receives no funds from the general-purpose gap-filling transfer. Local governments with below-average fiscal capacity are also eligible to receive specific-purpose transfers to meet education, health, infrastructure, and agriculture development needs. Again, Jakarta does not qualify (Shah 2012a).

Abuja, Nigeria, receives revenues from formula-based revenue-sharing transfers from a federal excess crude oil account, VAT, and sale of government properties (Elaigwu 2009).

Cape Town receives general-purpose formula-based transfers that incorporate such factors as proportion of relatively poor households, infrastructure deficiencies, and needs for a limited range of services (OECD 2008a; Steytler 2005).

Washington, DC, receives federal grant funds for Medicaid, community development, education, public welfare, and public safety (Gandhi et al. 2009).

No sample area receives special treatment for being a metropolitan area in this subgroup. For the subgroup as a whole, tax sharing finances about 10 percent of expenditures and grants, 23 percent; financing from the remaining 67 percent of expenditures comes from own-source revenues.

ALL METRO AREAS

There are significant across-group variations in own-source financing of metropolitan expenditures by type of metropolitan governance, with horizontally coordinated two-tier metro areas least dependent on higher-level transfers and metro areas with uncoordinated single-tier governance most dependent (see figure 9.1).

While this review has unearthed isolated examples of better practices in grant design (see box 9.1), an overall conclusion is that in designing transfers to finance metropolitan expenditures, almost all countries, industrial and developing alike, do not recognize the governance structure of metropolitan areas, their responsibilities, and their unique roles in national and global connectivity. The only exceptions are Denmark, Finland, and the Czech Republic. Although the composition of metropolitan finance differs significantly across different models of metropolitan governance, these differences could not be explained by the nature of the underlying governance structure.

FIGURE 9.1

Own-source financing of metropolitan expenditures by type of metro governance

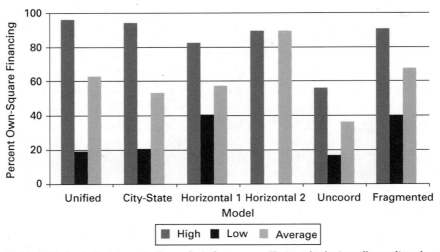

Models: Unified and city-state: vertically coordinated governance; Horizontal 1, horizontally coordinated mandatory two-tier governance; Horizontal 2, horizontally coordinated voluntary two-tier governance; Uncoord, uncoordinated two-tier governance; Fragmented, uncoordinated/fragmented single-tier governance.

BOX 9.1

Better practices in grant financing of metropolitan areas

Better practices in grant financing of metropolitan areas are hard to find. A few exceptions are noted below.

One Size Does Not Fit All

One size fit all approaches to grant allocation lead to much complexity in allocation criteria and yield inequitable results, for example in Indonesia (Shah 2012a). Most countries adopt a one size fits all approach in grant allocation to local governments. Prague is the only metropolitan area receiving special treatment due to its size class in a general purpose transfer (revenue sharing) program. The formula used for revenue sharing from PIT and VAT in the Czech Republic assigns a differential coefficient for redistribution depending upon the size class of the municipality with the highest weight assigned to Prague (Kubatova and Pavel 2009). Denmark, Sweden, and Finland represent even better examples as they adopt a "one size does not fit all" principle in their central transfers to local governments and group local governments by size class and type of municipality in grant determination (Shah 2012b). Under such an allocation system, metropolitan areas receive more equitable access to central finances.

Grants to Promote Competition Among Local Jurisdictions

These grants create incentives for greater cost efficiency and access in public service provision through inter-jurisdictional competition. Only in two countries, Albania and Russia, do grant programs have incentive provisions for greater inter-jurisdictional competition. Albania provides capital grants for social and physical infrastructure to municipalities that can demonstrate that their proposed projects would have greater potential impact on economic and social development and poverty reduction with improved access to basic services. Projects with higher level of own or external financing and inter-municipal cooperation are given priority in grant allocation (Dhimitri, Ikonomi, and Dhuka 2009). Russia through its Regional Fiscal Reform Fund established in 2007 provides competitive grants to local governments for achieving pre-specified reform objectives (see Zinnes 2009).

Output-Based Grant for School Finance

Output based grants provide incentives for results based accountability while preserving local autonomy. Output based grants are not practiced anywhere but grant design in a few countries does create incentives for competitive service provision by public and private providers and albeit indirectly for better performance. Bangkok metropolitan area public and private schools receive central grant financing based on school enrollments. Somewhat similar practices prevail in Brazil (also for health finance), Canada (also for health finance), Chile (through a voucher program), and Australia (Shah 2010a; 2010b). In none of these countries are grant allocations directly linked to service delivery performance, yet parental choices on school enrollments reward better performing schools in all these countries thereby introducing competition and bottom-up accountability for results as schools experiencing higher enrollments receive higher grant financing.

Intermetropolitan and Intrametropolitan Equalization

Interjurisdictional equalization serves to equalize per capita fiscal capacity and compensate for differential fiscal needs arising from inherent disabilities so that there is reasonably comparable access to public services at reasonably comparable tax burdens across local jurisdictions. For an equalization program based on the solidarity principle, rich jurisdictions contribute to the pool and poorer jurisdictions receive financing from the pool. It is desirable that there should be a separate such program by size class and type of local jurisdictions. Only Denmark and Finland have such programs for metropolitan areas as a class (Shah 2010b; 2012b).

Tax Rebates by Origin of Collection

Tax rebates by origin provide incentives for local economic development. China returns 25 percent of VAT by origin to its local governments, including Shanghai and Beijing (Shah and Shen 2007).

Typology of Countries

The sample of 41 metro areas were divided into four country groupings, as discussed below (see table 9.3).

METRO AREAS IN TYPE I COUNTRIES

These are highly urbanized middle-income countries with low to medium rates of expansion of metropolitan areas in a context of slow to medium economic growth performance (mostly Latin America, Europe and Central Asia, and Middle East and North Africa). A review of 10 metro areas was conducted: Belgrade, Bucharest, Chisinau, Istanbul, Mexico City, Prague, Skopje, Tirana, Warsaw, and Zagreb. The population range for this sample is from 600,000 in Tirana to 18.4 million in Mexico City. Metro areas in this sample, with the exception of Mexico City, have extensive local and metropolitan service responsibilities.

Tax-by-tax sharing, especially for income and value-added taxes, with prespecified central-local shares, dominates central-local transfers. General-purpose central-transfers are formula based, transparent, and predictable, typically embodying one-size-fits-all formulas that do not recognize special needs of metropolitan areas. Metro areas are at a disadvantage for general-purpose transfers but are assured reasonable financing due to return of a fixed proportion of tax yields from major taxes by origin. Overall central-transfers inclusive of tax sharing finance 59 percent of metro expenditures (see table 9.3).

METRO AREAS IN TYPE II COUNTRIES

These are low- to medium-urbanized middle-income countries with rapidly growing metropolises in the context of high economic growth (mostly Asia). A review of 12 sample metro areas was conducted: Bangkok, Beijing, Brazil metro areas as a group (Rezende and Garson 2006), Chennai, Delhi, Hyderabad, Jakarta, Kolkata, Mumbai, Pune, Shanghai, and Yogyakarta. This represents a diverse sample, with Yogyakarta, population 2 million, as the smallest metro area and Mumbai, population 21 million, as the largest. There is also great diversity in the metropolitan service responsibilities, with Beijing and Shanghai having the status of provincial governments and having responsibilities for a wide range of metropolitan services; Chennai, Delhi, Hyderabad, Kolkata, Mumbai, and Pune being responsible primarily for municipal services; and Bangkok (provincial status), Brazil metro areas, Jakarta, and Yogyakarta having an intermediate range of metropolitan responsibilities.

Tax sharing and tax base sharing dominate for metro areas with wider powers, such as Shanghai and Beijing, and also those with an intermediate range of powers, such as Bangkok, Jakarta, and Yogyakarta. Specific-purpose transfers have greater prominence in financing Brazil metro areas that have intermediate range of local service responsibilities. Formula-based, one-size-fits-all, general-purpose transfers dominate for metro areas with constrained powers such as Indian metro areas. On average, transfers finance 43.2 percent of expenditures in sample metro areas.

TABLE 9.3

Summary statistics on grant financing of metropolitan areas, by country typology

Country grouping	Sample metro areas	Range of local government responsibilities	Population range	Tax sharing (%)	General-purpose grants (%)	Specific-purpose grants (%)	Total grants (%)*	Total transfers (%)**	Own-source revenues (%)
Type I: highly urbanized middle-income countries with low- to medium-metro and economic growth rates	10	Wide	600,000 (Tirana) to 18,400,000 (Mexico city)	38.6	14.0	13.9	27.9	59.0	41.0
Type II: low- to medium-urbanized middle-income countries with high metro and economic growth rates	12	Narrow to wider	2,000,000 (Yogyakarta) to 21,000,000 (Mumbai)	25.2	19.7	9.7	29.4	43.2	56.8
Type III: low- to medium-urbanized low-income countries with high metro but low- to medium-economic growth rates	4	Narrow	1.4 m1,400,000, (Abuja) to 3,100,000 (Addis Ababa)	0	NA	NA	23.2	23.2	76.8
Type IV: industrial countries	15	Wider	340,000 (Canberra) to 13,000,000 (Tokyo)	8.9	13.2	21.4	25.4	34.3	65.7
ALL	41		340,000 (Canberra) to 21,000,000 (Mumbai)	18.2	15.6	15.0	26.5	39.9	60.1

NA, not available or not applicable. All transfer figures are simple averages of sample metro areas expressed are percentages of total revenues.

*Total grants refers to general-purpose plus specific-purpose transfers.

**Total transfers refers to tax sharing plus total grants.

SOURCES: Compiled by authors from various sources listed in the references, especially OECD (2001; 2003a; 2003b; 2004a; 2004b; 2004c; 2005a; 2005b; 2006a; 2006b; 2006c; 2007; 2008a; 2008b; 2009; 2010).

METRO AREAS IN TYPE III COUNTRIES

This grouping of countries includes low- to medium-urbanized low-income countries with high rates of metropolitan growth but low to medium rates of economic growth (mostly Africa) and comprises the four metro areas of Abuja, Addis Ababa, Cape Town, and Pretoria/Tshwane. Population for sample areas ranges from 1.4 million in Abuja to 3.1 million in Addis Ababa. These metro areas have a narrow range of metropolitan responsibilities. Formula-based revenue-sharing general-purpose transfers, with a uniform formula for all local governments, dominate. These formulas work to the disadvantage of metro areas. Grants on average finance 23.2 percent of metro expenditures. While local taxes finance most of the expenditures, taxing powers of local governments are highly constrained.

METRO AREAS IN TYPE IV COUNTRIES

This grouping includes industrial countries. The sample includes 16 metro areas: Berlin, Bern, Brussels, Busan, Canberra, Copenhagen, Helsinki, London, Madrid, Melbourne, Milan, Montreal, Seoul, Toronto, Tokyo, and Washington, DC. Population range for this sample is from a low of 340,000 in Canberra to 13 million in Tokyo.

There is also wide diversity in the range of metropolitan responsibilities, with Busan, Helsinki, Seoul, and Tokyo (all with provincial status) at the high end of the spectrum and London and Melbourne at the lower end, with the rest of the sample in between these ranges. Metro areas at the upper end of the spectrum are largely self-financing and at the lower end are primarily grant financed. An extreme example is London, which had central transfers finance 81 percent of its expenditures during 2008–2009. For the sample as a whole, specific-purpose transfers with input conditionality dominate higher-level financing. On average, central and state transfers finance 34.3 percent of metro expenditures.

ALL COUNTRIES

For the sample as a whole, there is great diversity in the range of metropolitan responsibilities shared by the metro areas, with Beijing, Busan, Copenhagen, Helsinki, Seoul, Shanghai, and Tokyo at the top of the totem pole and Melbourne and Indian metro areas such as Mumbai at the bottom end. For the sample average, tax sharing has a slight edge over general- and specific-purpose transfers. Nearly 40 percent of metro finances are from central transfers. Eight well-known metropolitan areas in our sample finance two-thirds of their expenditures from higher-level transfers, with Berlin, Bucharest, and London receiving about 80 percent of financing from such transfers (see figure 9.2).

CONCEPTUAL GUIDANCE VERSUS PRACTICE: NOTABLE POINTS OF DEPARTURE

Earlier sections highlighted conceptual considerations in the use of grant instruments. This was followed by a review of worldwide practices in grant financing of metropolitan areas. This section distills main points of departure of practice from the conceptual guidance.

FIGURE 9.2

Metro areas with more than 66 percent grant financing

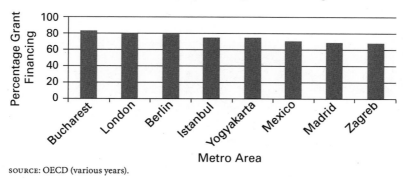

SOURCE: OECD (various years).

One Size Does Not Fit All. The practice contradicts this and most countries treat metro governments in generic formula used for grant allocation to all local governments. But this introduces inequities and inefficiencies, as metro government fiscal needs are measured on a yardstick that includes small towns with widely divergent fiscal capacities and needs. This introduces injustice for metro areas, as they have both above-average fiscal capacities and above-average needs, yet they are treated as if they have above-average fiscal capacity and average need. Fair treatment of metro areas requires a metro grant strategy that considers governance, finance, and special needs of metro areas.

The Nature of Metropolitan Services Considered in Designing Grants and Other Instruments of Finance. The practice provides no evidence of this. In fact, the practice even in industrial countries often contradicts this. For example, metropolitan areas in Canada, the United States, the United Kingdom, and a number of developing countries, including India, use property taxes and input-based conditional grants for school finance, whereas, as noted earlier, surcharges on PITs and output-based grants are more suitable for school finance. The United Kingdom and the United States also use specific-purpose grants for financing police protection in metro areas, yet general revenues are a more suitable instrument of police finance. Grant financing is relevant for financing a fraction of police expenditures that have externality for national security. Matching capital grants with matching rates that vary inversely with fiscal capacity for financing school, health, and transportation facilities are rarely practiced. Museums, sports and fitness facilities, and concert halls are poor candidates for grant finance unless they serve national objectives, yet grant financing of such facilities is widely practiced. Benefit spillover compensation is rarely available to metro areas.

Model of Metropolitan Governance and Finance Matters for Grant Finance. An earlier section highlighted how the models of metropolitan governance and finance matter for type and tools of grant financing. No new evidence was discovered that such considerations entered into designing grant financing of metro areas in practice. This neglect is unfortunate, because a holistic view of metropolitan financing and the tools required for grant financing is not possible without explicit consideration of governance and finance arrangements. For example, in horizontally coordinated and uncoordinated metro governance, there is a need for intrametro equalization and use of competitive grants for enhancing competition, the two tools that are rarely practiced. Output-based grants could also be used to facilitate functional, overlapping, and competing single-purpose jurisdictions giving residents greater voice, choice, and exit options. If metro governance is fragmented due to monopoly single-purpose jurisdictions with preferred access to tax finance, then more funds have to be directed to municipal finance through equalization grants. Output-based grants would also serve important tools in ensuring equitable access in the event services are contracted out.

Keep it simple. This principle is frequently ignored in practice, especially in designing revenue-sharing and equalization grants. Multiple factors that work at cross purposes are introduced, leading to lower transparency, equity, and efficiency of allocations.

Keep a singular focus. Most general-purpose grant programs have multiple objectives and, as a result, are unlikely to achieve any of the specified objectives. Having each grant instrument focus on a single objective would enhance chances of success.

Avoid input-based (or process-based) or ad hoc conditional grant programs. These types of programs undermine metropolitan autonomy, flexibility, fiscal efficiency, and fiscal equity objectives. Specific-purpose transfers available to metro areas are mostly input-control conditional grants. The only exceptions are school transfers available to metro areas in Brazil, Canada, Chile, Colombia, Denmark, Finland, Sweden, and Thailand and health transfers in Brazil, Denmark, Finland, and Canada (see box 9.1).

Introduce results-based finance to incentivize excellence in service delivery performance. Output-based transfers are rarely practiced but hold great promise for improving metropolitan government performance and accountability while preserving local autonomy (see box 9.1).

Introduce sunset clauses and review provisions. This is not practiced anywhere in grants to metropolitan areas.

LESSONS FROM INTERNATIONAL PRACTICE AND AN AGENDA FOR REFORM

A review of worldwide practices leads to the following summary of grant financing of metro areas. Metro areas have large economic bases and therefore little a priori need for grant financing, yet they have strong dependence on central transfers. This is because highly constrained fiscal autonomy is given to these areas in most countries, especially developing countries, with the notable exception of metro areas in China. Such a strong reliance on transfers undermines local autonomy and local accountability. Only Busan, Cape Town, Copenhagen, Helsinki, Melbourne, Mumbai, Pune, Seoul, and Tokyo stand out as being largely self-financed metro areas. Tax base sharing is practiced in only a few metro areas such as Bangkok, Seoul, and Tokyo. Tax-by-tax sharing is widely practiced. Such a practice is helpful in ensuring transparency and predictability of transfers, yet it creates incentives for central tax administrators to give less effort to those taxes that it has to share with metro areas.

General-purpose transfers are formula based, transparent, and predictable, yet they discriminate against metropolitan areas because they utilize a one-size-fits-all (common) formula for all local governments, large or small. Such formulas typically incorporate equal per jurisdiction components that discriminate against large metropolitan areas. Compactness is rarely rewarded, and higher needs of metro areas for transportation, education, health, culture, and welfare go unrecognized. Specific-purpose transfers are typically ad hoc project-based transfers with input conditionality. Such transfers typically address higher-level mandates with inadequate financing. In general, specific-purpose transfers are intrusive, reward grantsmanship, and distort local priorities. Egregious examples of specific-purpose capital transfers can be seen in Bangkok, where central financing for a section of above-ground metro was withdrawn, leaving poles that support no rails, and in Jakarta, where external financing of the metro was blocked by the central government after the local government had already initiated construction, leaving an eyesore in its wake.

Only a handful of examples of results-based intergovernmental finance and of tournament-based approaches to encourage interjurisdictional competition were discovered in grant financing of sample metropolitan areas (see box 9.1). Grants to compensate metro areas for benefit spillovers are also not practiced. Overall emphasis in grant financing of metro areas remains in dealing with vertical fiscal gaps or project-based specific-purpose grants.

To ensure that metropolitan areas can play their dual roles in improving economic and social outcomes for residents, it is important to strengthen their fiscal autonomy while enhancing their accountability to local residents. This would be possible if metro areas have access to a wide array of productive tax bases, including income, sales, and environmental taxes and charges. Given the special needs of metro areas, it would be best to give a separate and distinct treatment of these areas in grant financing. Results-based grant financing of social and transportation services and tournament-based approaches to encourage interjurisdictional competition need to be given serious consideration to ensure metropolitan autonomy while strengthening their citizen-based accountability. Incidentally, these reforms have less demanding data requirements than needed for traditional input-based conditional grants.

Overall, the practice of grant financing of metropolitan areas is at variance with the conceptual guidance in both industrial and developing countries. Such divergences represent important opportunities to reform metropolitan finances to enhance quality and access of metro services, as well as making metro governments more responsive and accountable to local residents in both developing and industrial countries.

REFERENCES

Bahl, Roy. 2011. Financing metropolitan areas. In *Local government finance: The challenges of the 21st century*, ed. United Cities and Local Governments. Cheltenham, U.K.: Edward Elgar.

Bahl, Roy, and Johannes Linn. 1992. *Urban public finance in developing countries*. New York: Oxford University Press.

Bandyopadhyay, Simanti, and M. Govinda Rao. 2009. Fiscal health of selected Indian cities. NIPFP, New Delhi, World Bank Working Paper Series. Washington, DC: World Bank.

Bird, Richard, and Enid Slack. 2004. Fiscal aspects of metropolitan governance. International Tax Program Paper No. 0401. Toronto: Rotman School, University of Toronto.

Boadway, Robin, and Anwar Shah, eds. 2007. *Intergovernmental fiscal transfers: Principles and the practice*. Washington, DC: World Bank.

———. 2009. *Fiscal federalism: Principles and practice of multi-order governance*. London: Cambridge University Press.

Boyd, Eugene, and Michael Fauntroy. 2002. Washington, DC and 10 other national capitals: Selected aspects of governmental structure. Washington, DC: Congressional Budget Office.

Chernick, Howard, and Andrew Reschovsky. 2006. Local public finance: Issues for metropolitan regions. In *Competitive cities in the global economy*, 417–432. OECD Territorial Reviews. Paris: Organisation for Economic Co-operation and Development.

Department for Communities and Local Governments. 2010. Local Government Financial Statistics No. 20 2010. London: U.K. Statistics Authority.

Dhimitri, Albana, Belinda Ikonomi, and Majlinda Dhuka. 2009. Financing metropolitan government: Tirana city. Working paper. Budapest: Open Society Institute.

Elaigwu, J. Isawa. 2009. Abuja, Nigeria. In *Finance and governance of capital cities in federal systems*, ed. Enid Slack and Rupak Chattopadhyay, 198–220. Kingston: McGill-Queens University Press.

Frey, Bruno, and Reiner Eichenberger. 1995. Competition among jurisdictions. In *The idea of competition among jurisdictions*, ed. Luder Gerken, 209–229. London: Macmillan.

Gandhi, Natwar, Yesim Yilmaz, Robertt Zahradnik, and Marcy Edwards. 2009. In *Finance and governance of capital cities in federal systems*, ed. Enid Slack and Rupak Chattopadhyay, 263–291. Kingston: McGill-Queens University Press.

Gligorijevic, Z., M. Ferencak, D. Savic, and V. Velovic. 2007. Financing metropolitan governments in transitional countries: Case study Belgrade. Unpublished document made available by the Town Planning Institute of Belgrade.

Hirt, Sonia. 2009. Begrade, Serbia. Cities 26: 293–303. www.elsevier.com/locate/cities

Huther, Jeff, Sandra Roberts, and Anwar Shah. 1997. *Public expenditure reform under adjustment lending. Lessons from World Bank experiences*. Washington, DC: World Bank.

Inman, Robert. 2005. Financing cities. NBER Working Paper No. 11203. Cambridge, MA: National Bureau of Economic Research.

Ionescu, Adrian, and Jozsef Hegedus. 2007. Financing capital governments in transitional countries. Working Paper. Warsaw: Project Warsaw, University of Warsaw.

Jefremienko, A., and C. Wolksa. 2007. Financing metropolitan governments in transitional countries: Case study of Warsaw. Working Paper. Warsaw: Project Warsaw, University of Warsaw.

Karpen, Ulrich. 2007. Metropolitan Regions in German Federation. In *Competition versus cooperation—German federalism in need of reform: A comparative perspective*, ed. Ralf Thomas Baus, Raoul Blindenbacher, and Ulrich Karpen, 245–262. Baden-Baden: Nomos Verlagsgesellschaft.

Kitchen, Harry. 2004. Local and metropolitan finance. Working paper. Peterborough, ONT: Trent University.

Kopric, Ivan, Anamarija Musa, Tereza Lugaric, and Tijana Vulcojicic. 2007. The city of Zagreb: Position and development in the Croatian governnace and public finance system. Working paper. Budapest: Open Society Institute.

Korean Research Institute of Local Administration (KRILA). 2009. Future of Korean local autonomy: New visions and challenges. Conference on Local Government in Korea, Seoul (September 4).

Kubatova, Kveta, and Jan Pavel. 2009. Financing capital governments in transitional countries: Czech Republic. Working Paper. Prague: University of Economics.

Kubler, Daniel. (2009). Bern, Switzerland. In *Finance and governance of capital cities in federal systems*, ed. Enid Slack and Rupak Chattopadhyay, 238–262. Kingston: McGill-Queens University Press.

Lonita, Sorin. 2009. Bucharest. Working paper. Budapest: Open Society Institute.

McMillan, Melville. 2008. A local perspective on fiscal federalism: Practices, experiences and lessons from industrial countries. In *Macro federalism and local finance*, ed. Anwar Shah, 245–290. Washington, DC: World Bank.

OECD. 2001. Cities for citizens: Improving metropolitan governance. Paris.

———. 2003a. Territorial review: Helsinki, Finland. Paris.

———. 2003b. Territorial review: Melbourne, Australia. Paris.

———. 2004a. Territorial review: Athens, Greece. Paris.

———. 2004b. Territorial review: Mexico City, Mexico. Paris.

———. 2004c. Territorial review: Montreal, Canada. Paris.

———. 2005a. Territorial review: Busan, Korea. Paris.

———. 2005b. Territorial review: Seoul, Korea. Paris.

———. 2006a. Territorial review: Milan, Italy. Paris.

———. 2006b. Territorial review: Stockholm, Sweden. Paris.

———. 2006c. Competitive cities in the global economy, territorial review. Paris.

———. 2007. Territorial review: Madrid, Spain. Paris.

———. 2008a. Territorial review: Cape Town, South Africa. Paris.

———. 2008b. Territorial review: Istanbul, Turkey. Paris.

———. 2009. Territorial review: Copenhagen, Denmark. Paris.

———. 2010. Territorial review: Toronto, Canada. Paris.

Peterson, George, and Patricia Annez, eds. 2007. *Financing cities*. Los Angeles: Sage.

Rezende, Fernando, and Sol Garson. 2006. Financing metropolitan areas in Brazil: Political, institutional and legal obstacles and emergence of new proposals for improving coordination. *Revista de Economia Contemporânea* 10(1):5–34.

Rhee, Se-Koo. 2010. Municipal finance of Seoul metropolitan government. Paper presented at the Seoul Development Institute, Seoul, Korea (May 31–June 3).

Roscovan, Mihai, and Doina Melnic. 2009. Financing capital governments in transitional countries: The case of Chisinau. Working Paper. Warsaw: Project Warsaw.

Shah, Anwar. 2007. A practitioner's guide to intergovernmental fiscal transfers. In *Intergovernmental fiscal transfers: Principles and the practice*, ed. Robin Boadway and Anwar Shah, 1–54. Washington, DC: World Bank.

———. 2009. Autonomy with accountability: The case for performance-oriented grants. In *General grants versus earmarked grants: Theory and practice. The Copenhagen Workshop, 2009*, ed. Junghun Kim, Jorgen Lotz, and Niels Jorgen Mau, 74–106. Copenhagen: Rosendahls Schultz Grafisk.

———. 2010a. Sponsoring a race to the top: The case for results-based intergovernmental finance for merit goods. Policy Research Working Paper No. 5172. Washington, DC: World Bank.

———. 2010b. Adapting to a changing world: Reflections on the reform of local governance for the next decade. In *Local public sector: A nordic perspective*, ed. Antti Moisio, 185–220. Helsinki: Office of the Prime Minister.

———. 2012a. Options for financing sub-national governments in Indonesia. In *Fiscal decentralization in Indonesia: A decade after the big bang*, ed. Ministry of Finance, 222–254. Jakarta: University of Indonesia Press.

———. 2012b. Public services and expenditure need equalization: Reflections on principles and worldwide comparative practices. World Bank Policy Research Working Paper Series No. WPS6006, World Bank, Washington, DC. (March).

Shah, Anwar, K. Nattaporn, Robert Boothe, and Shabih Mohib. 2012. *Local governance in Thailand*. Bangkok: World Bank.

Shah, Anwar, Riatu Qibthiyyah, and Astrid Dita. 2012. General-purpose central-provincial-local transfers (dau) in Indonesia: From gap filling to ensuring fair access to essential public services for all. Policy Research Working Paper No. 6075. Washington, DC: World Bank.

Shah, Anwar, and Chunli Shen. 2007. Fine tuning the intergovernmental transfer system to create a harmonious society and a level playing field for regional development. In *Public finance in China: Reform and growth for a harmonious society*, ed. Jiwei Lou and Shuilin Wang, 129–154. Washington, DC: World Bank.

Slack, Enid. 2010. Financing large cities and metropolitan areas. Working paper. Toronto: University of Toronto.

Slack, Enid. and Rupak Chattopadhyay, eds. 2009. *Finance and governance of capital cities in federal systems*. Kingston: McGill-Queens University Press.

Sridhar, Kala, and Simanti Bandyopadhyay. 2007. Improving the fiscal health of Indian cities: A pilot study of Pune. Unpublished paper. Washington, DC: World Bank.

Sridhar, Kala, Simanti Bandyopadhyay, and Satardu Sikdar. 2008a. Improving the fiscal health of Indian cities: A pilot study of Chennai. Unpublished paper. Washington, DC: World Bank.

———. 2008b. Improving the fiscal health of Indian cities: A pilot study of Delhi. Unpublished paper. Washington, DC: World Bank Institute.

———. 2008c. Improving the fiscal health of Indian cities: A pilot study of Hyerderabad. Unpublished paper. Washington, DC: World Bank.

Steytler, Nico, 2005. The place and role of local government in federal systems. Johannesburg: Konrad-Adenauer Stiftung.

Tokyo, Metropolitan Government. 2011. Overview of Tokyo. http://www.metro.tokyo.jp/English/profilre/overview05.html

Veljanovski, Aleksandra. 2009. The city of Skopje. Working paper. Budapest: Open Society Institute.

Wynsberghe, Caroline van. 2009. Brussels, Belgium. In *Finance and governance of capital cities in federal systems*, ed. Enid Slack and Rupak Chattopadhyay, 33–54. Kingston: McGill-Queens University Press.

Zinnes, Clifford. 2009. *Tournament approaches to policy reform. Making development assistance more effective*. Washington, DC: Brookings Institution.

Metropolitan Public Finances | 10

The Case of Mumbai

ABHAY PETHE

Conceptual-Contextual Background

Urban spaces in India are increasingly important (Mohan 2007). The future of India is significantly urban since globalization requires global city spaces.[1] This chapter is informed by the conviction that governance is key in considering issues related to both interurban and intraurban institutions and organizations and involves agents, agencies, and their interactions. Metropolitan government is an artificial, rather than organic, conceptual construct and should be considered as an emergent system, more complex than cities, generated by and generating interactions among many public and private organizations and civil society. Such evolving metropolitan governance in India resembles a "polycentric governance" system (see Pethe, Gandhi, and Tandel 2011; Pethe et al. 2012; Pethe, Tandel and Gandhi 2012).

Over the last few decades, India's pattern of urbanization has become distinctly top-heavy, as evidenced by the rapid growth of urban agglomerations and increased

The author acknowledges several persons for their help and support with the data and substantive insights. The author specifically thanks the officials of Mumbai Metropolitan Region Development Authority, Directorate of Economics and Statistics, Maharashtra Housing and Area Development Authority, Department of Municipal Administration, Mumbau Transformation Support Unit, and Maharashtra Economic Development Council, as well as Rakesh Mohan, Vidyadhar K. Phatak, Mala Lalvani, and Sunil Bhandare. Sahil Gandhi and Vaidehi Tandel, research assistants for this work, deserve a special word of appreciation. The author would also like to thank Sirus Libeiro for GIS assistance. The interactions with participants of the Conference organized by the Lincoln Institute of Land Policy and Brookings Institution on July 11–12, 2011 at Washington DC, as well as comments received via the mail, have improved the chapter.

[1] Some academics (see, e.g., Sassen 2010) believe we have reached a tipping point where cities and city-states are becoming more important economic categories than nation-states, which are becoming less important, if not redundant, because of global capital and technology.

numbers of cities with populations of 1 million or more (Kundu 2006).[2] The significant agglomeration economies arising from large metropolises feed into the economy in the form of higher economic efficiency and productivity growth (Mohan 2006).

The passage in India of the 73rd and 74th constitutional amendment acts (CAAs) in 1992–1993 was a significant reform addressing decentralization. It was meant to improve the management of local governments and to promote better public service delivery. The process of decentralization, however, remains far from satisfactory in the de facto sense and lacks true empowerment of urban local bodies (ULBs). Decentralization in major urban regions is further complicated by the strong presence of central and state governments, via their parastatals, in providing urban infrastructure.[3]

In an attempt to understand public finance in metropolitan regions, this chapter presents an analysis of the issues faced by one of the most important urban agglomerations in India: the Mumbai metropolitan region (MMR). Slack (2007, 15) terms the governance structure in Mumbai the "one-tier fragmented government model." It is important to recognize linkages with and participation of the central and state governments in the region. This direct participation can be attributed to the fact that the region contributes 70 percent of state-level and more than 11 percent of national-level tax revenues. The MMR may be characterized as the "goose that lays the golden egg," a strong economic engine that creates a stake for the higher levels of governments to remain invested in the region so that growth is sustained. However, given the set of problems the region faces in terms of inadequate infrastructure and poor livability, the extent of investments in the region by higher-level governments is not in sync with the level of return that accrues to them. This chapter highlights the structure of public finance and governance in MMR and considers problems and policy reform options.

FISCAL FEDERALISM IN INDIA: SETTING THE CONTEXT

India has been characterized as a union with centripetal bias. The 73rd and 74th CAAs implied that urban and rural local bodies will no longer be construed as mere creations of the state governments. The 74th CAA recognizes ULBs as the third tier in the Indian federal structure and entrusts them with a list of functions (in Schedule 12 of the CAA) and sources of revenues, in a de jure sense (see chapter 3).[4] ULBs are classified as municipal corporations and municipal councils based on the population criterion.

Apart from their own-source revenue handles, these ULBs were to be empowered through grants from the center and respective state governments, which may

---

[2]However, the 2011 census figures (Census of India 2011) actually show a decline in metropolitan city populations (although not in agglomerations) and the addition of more than a thousand new cities and towns.

[3]Parastatals are similar to state-owned enterprises and are headed by state/center-government-nominated CEOs.

[4]The de jure provisions have not led to de facto changes. The state governments continue to treat the ULBs as their own creations and exercise statutory control over most financial decisions. As an aside, the Reserve Bank of India categorizes the debt by ULBs as private debt (for details, see, e.g., Pethe, Mishra, and Rakhe 2009 and Pethe 2010 for further elaboration).

be tied or untied, as well as transfers that were formulated by the finance commissions. However, ULBs have remained small in size and unable to shoulder their expenditure responsibilities, primarily because of limited autonomy on the revenue and expenditure sides of the budget, and because of limited inflow in intergovernmental transfers. The importance of devolving the "three Fs," functions, finance, and functionaries (personnel), is not recognized in the de facto sense (see Pethe and Lalvani 2008).

The Indian tax system is set up with an asymmetry in the growth dividend that accrues in favor of the central government.[5] In contrast, states are constitutionally required to undertake many responsibilities, with implications for pressure on infrastructure provision and current expenditure budgets. These are effectively unfunded mandates. Further, reforms in the arena of fiscal operations, such as the central Fiscal Responsibility and Budget Management Act (2003) and related state-level fiscal responsibility legislation, severely constrain revenue expenditure capacity of the states, with consequent shrinkage of the discretionary fiscal space for the state.[6] In this situation, it is difficult to contemplate statutory devolution by states of untied grants to the ULBs (e.g., through the state finance commission awards), rendering them financially weak.

AN OVERVIEW OF THE MUMBAI METROPOLITAN REGION

The MMR, located on the western coast of India in the state of Maharashtra, extends over an area of 4,355 square kilometers, comprising 1,242 square kilometers of urban area, of which Greater Mumbai covers 437 square kilometers. With about one-tenth of the area compared with MMR, Greater Mumbai, defined by the jurisdiction of the Municipal Corporation of Greater Mumbai (MCGM), accommodates a population of around 12.5 million, which constitutes almost 60 percent of the total population of MMR. It is evident that Mumbai is a financial and commercial powerhouse and an overwhelmingly important economic center not just for the region or the state but, indeed, for the whole country (see Pethe 2005). Of the total outstanding credit in India, 27 percent is from Mumbai. The Bombay Stock Exchange and National Stock Exchange account for 80 percent of the value of all transactions in stock markets. The same order of magnitude is seen in annual merchant turnover and registration of mutual funds and foreign institutional investments. MMR's transport system handles some of the heaviest (local, national, and international) passenger and cargo traffic in India.[7] The city of Mumbai is packed with a density close to 30,000 persons per square kilometer.[8] The production structure of the local economy comprises 80 percent services, with implications for the

---

[5] This is especially important since incremental growth in the production structure of the Indian economy has been severely biased in favor of the service sector, which can be taxed only by the central government.

[6] While the Fiscal Responsibility and Budget Management Act and the state-level fiscal responsibility legislation are steps in the right direction, these have had unintended effects on expenditure autonomy of states. The concept of revenue expenditure/deficit needs to be revisited and refined.

[7] This importance is being challenged by the creation of the world-class airport at New Delhi.

[8] The actual density is much higher due to a floating population estimated at between 3 million and 5 million. This puts greater pressure on infrastructure. MMR represents the classic labor market, albeit employment here is largely informal in nature.

requisite skill sets for employability and livelihoods. The per capita income is double the average of the state and around three times the national average. MMR is thus a huge attractor for in-migration.[9]

Other than MCGM, corporations and councils in the region comprise 805 square kilometers. The total population of MMR was 18.8 million according to the 2001 census (Census of India 2001). The annual population growth rates have been approximately 1.9 percent and 2.7 percent for Mumbai and MMR, respectively, during the 1990s and 2000s, with migration, expectedly, playing a significant role. Thus, the population for MMR in fiscal year 2008–2009 is estimated to be approximately 22 million.[10] MMR accounted for 33.24 percent of gross state domestic product of Maharashtra and 4.34 percent of India's gross domestic product in 2008–2009.[11]

ULBs in Maharashtra are governed by the following four Acts, in addition to the 74th CAA: the Bombay Municipal Corporation Act (1888); the City of Nagpur Corporation Act (1948); the Bombay Provincial Municipal Corporations Act (1949); and the Maharashtra Municipal Councils, Nagar Panchayats and Industrial Townships Act (1965). The state is currently involved in a reconciliation exercise to create a single uniform Act governing all the ULBs in the state.

The currently existing eight municipal corporations and nine municipal councils in MMR are largely responsible for performing the 18 functions listed in the 12th Schedule of the 74th CAA, which include provision of public goods. The ULBs face severe budgetary constraints in successfully meeting these responsibilities.

Besides local governments, the state government also undertakes infrastructure investments through the numerous parastatals it has set up in MMR. These parastatals have been constituted to perform certain specific functions. Some of the most prominent state-level parastatals are the Mumbai Metropolitan Region Development Authority (MMRDA), which is a planning agency for MMR; the Maharashtra State Road Development Corporation under the Department of Public Works, which develops roads, bridges, and overpasses in MMR, as well as the rest of Maharashtra; and the Maharashtra Housing and Area Development Authority (MHADA) and Slum Rehabilitation Authority set up by the Department of Housing for providing affordable housing and slum rehabilitation. Several parastatals have also been set up by the central government, such as the Airport Authority of India and the different port trusts, railway boards, and others that are currently located in MMR.[12] The central government is also investing in MMR through

---

[9] According to the current exchange rate, US$1 equals 50 Indian rupees.

[10] Based on the provisional census estimates (2011), (Census of India 2011) the annual population growth rate from 2001 to 2011 was 3.57 percent, with a decadal growth rate of 42 percent. MMR's population in 2011 was approximately 26 million. With this growth rate, the population in MMR in fiscal year 2008–2009 would be around 24 million. These estimates seem to be on the lower side.

[11] In fiscal year 2000–2001, MMR's income was estimated to be Rs.787,377.8 million, which amounts to 86.84 percent of the total incomes of Mumbai, Raigad, and Thane taken together. MMR's income in the year 2008–2009 accounts for approximately 89.2 percent of the total income of the three districts and is estimated to be Rs.1,490,279.1 million. The proportion of MMR's income in the income of the three districts would increase over time because of the increasing pace of urbanization, influx of population in MMR, and other factors. MMR has been witnessing an average annual growth rate of about 8.34 percent from 2000–2001 to 2008–2009. Such a growth rate is expected to be accompanied by commensurate public and private investments in the region.

[12] The complete list of all parastatals can be found in the business plan for MMR by MMRDA and LEA International Ltd. (2007). One notices not just a lack of coordination among these different arms of government but that they frequently are involved in large numbers of time-consuming litigations.

centrally sponsored schemes, the most noteworthy being the Jawaharlal Nehru National Urban Renewal Mission (JnNURM).[13]

The Metropolitan Planning Committee (MPC) was set up following Article 243ZE of the 74th CAA in order to facilitate better coordination at the metropolitan level, creating a power conflict with MMRDA.[14] The MPC comprises elected representatives from all the ULBs and has the task of preparing a draft development plan for the metropolitan region (Joardar 2008). Besides public organizations, considerable investment is being made by the private sector in the region.

MMR is facing considerable problems in terms of proliferation of slums, lack of affordable housing, transport issues, poor quality of sanitation and drainage, and aged water supply and sewage systems. Further, the situation worsens farther from the city core. Thus, although a gamut of public and private organizations, as discussed previously, have been involved in financing infrastructure in the region, inadequate investments and inefficient delivery of public goods and services still exist. Analyzing the magnitude and trends of investment by these organizations would help estimate the extent of investment deficit in the region.

ULB FINANCES

The size of the urban local government in MMR, measured as percentage of revenue and capital expenditure to gross district domestic product, is estimated to be 5.59 percent of the local economy for the period from 2002–2003 to 2007–2008.[15] The size of MCGM for the same period was 6.61 percent of Mumbai's income, whereas the size of the other ULBs in MMR amounted to 3.35 percent of the economy of the rest of MMR (excluding Mumbai districts under MCGM). Investments made by ULBs in MMR from 2005–2006 to 2007–2008 comprised around 44.65 percent of total public investments in the same period.[16] It is important to recognize that Mumbai is a special case. Typically, local (city/town) government is quite small. The implication is that such small (and consequently weak) local governments are unable to play a comprehensive role in governance (as envisaged by the constitutional amendments related to decentralization), and civic administration of cities and towns.[17] The following sections analyze the expenditure and revenue

---

[13] Centrally sponsored schemes aim to attain certain socioeconomic objectives where the outcomes have been deemed unsatisfactory. These are introduced by ministries and departments in the central government and provide conditional grants to the state governments for implementing the schemes via state-level departments or parastatals. By definition, these deal with matters of importance for the citizens that appear in the concurrent constitutional list. Hence, there is an element of perceived encroachment of autonomy by the center on the domain of the states. For more on the nature of centrally sponsored schemes, see Pethe et al. (2010).

[14] The MPC was set up almost reluctantly and with considerable delay. The first couple of meetings that were held were largely unproductive (time spent in technical wrangles). How this will affect MMRDA's power and authority has yet to be determined.

[15] This is probably an overestimate since the tally of investments made by all the non-ULB public bodies, projects, and schemes is not complete.

[16] This is probably an overestimate since the tally of investments made by all the non-ULB public bodies, projects, and schemes is not complete.

[17] Data for most of the years since the 74th CAA (1992) was passed are incomplete and have been acquired from different data sources, leading to major issues of data reconciliation. Hence, here the analysis is limited to the five years between 2002–2003 and 2007–2008, which is sufficient to give an idea of the performance of decentralization in MMR, which has not changed drastically since that time. The work here is similar to that of Pethe and Lalvani (2007).

patterns of ULBs in MMR. Since MCGM overpowers the other ULBs in terms of its size, its finances are examined independently. The public finances of ULBs are analyzed by dividing them into three categories: MCGM, other municipal corporations (OMCs), and municipal councils (COs).[18]

Expenditure Patterns of ULBs in MMR

Examining expenditures can provide a rough idea of public goods and services provision by ULBs in MMR. The shares of MCGM, OMCs, and COs in MMR are given in figure 10.1, which shows that MCGM is indeed the largest ULB in the region: its share in the total expenditures made of all the ULBs in MMR amounted to more than 80 percent, while OMCs accounted for around 18 percent, and COs, around 2 percent. Not only is MCGM the dominant player, but also its proportionate role is increasing over time (even compared with OMCs).[19] It is well documented that, despite being inadequate, the magnitude and quality of public goods and services are far superior both to those elsewhere in India and to those in the places within MMR outside the administrative limits of MCGM (see MCGM 2009).

The expenditures of ULBs can be classified as revenue and capital expenditures. Revenue expenditures largely involve establishment and administration costs, as well as costs of operation and maintenance of assets. The range of functional responsibilities, as mentioned earlier, is given in the 12th Schedule of the Indian Constitution inserted after the 74th CAA. This comprises 18 functions that were to be transferred to the local bodies, along with the funds and functionaries. The list includes such items as primary education, health (in case of MCGM only; for other councils in MMR it is looked after by the state), street cleaning and lighting, water and sanitation, fire brigades, and museums and public libraries. The salaries of the employees involved in delivering these services are included in establishment costs. Capital expenditures involve asset creation expenditures. The breakdown of capital and revenue expenditures of MCGM, OMC, and CO in per capita terms is provided in table 10.1.

In per capita (real) terms, both capital and revenue expenditures have been increasing over the years for all categories. The proportion of revenue expenditure to total expenditure is much higher for MCGM than for OMC and CO.[20] This is indicative of the economies of scale not being realized in revenue expenditures, even considering that the capital investments are of a higher order and the quality of services are superior within the MCGM jurisdiction.

---

[18] The OMCs comprise six municipal corporations. The Vasai Virar Municipal Corporation, formed in November 2010, is not included in this category; however, the municipal councils that make up the new corporation have been incorporated in the CO category.

[19] MCGM is, in a way, a state within a state. The population of the city is more than that of 50 countries and 17 states in the Indian Union, and its aggregate revenue exceeds that of 16 of these states. Thus, when one discusses the size of the government and decentralization, it is important to keep in mind that while the size may appear satisfactory, as averages go, it hides the fact that ULBs other than MCGM are quite small and weak. Thus, the magnitude and quality of urban services suffer as one moves farther from the MMR core. For a comparison of MMRDA and MCGM, see Pethe, Gandhi, and Tandel (2011).

[20] The exception is in fiscal year 2007–2008, when the proportion of revenue to total expenditure for OMC was marginally higher than that for MCGM.

FIGURE 10.1

ULB expenditures as percentages of total MMR expenditures

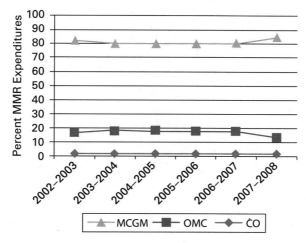

TABLE 10.1

Per capita expenditures in 1999–2000 prices (Rs.)

Fiscal year	MCGM		OMC		CO	
	Revenue	Capital	Revenue	Capital	Revenue	Capital
2002–2003	2810	523	1151	572	609	245
2003–2004	2852	551	1293	640	657	257
2004–2005	3169	485	1465	645	710	249
2005–2006	3009	791	1509	670	855	285
2006–2007	3426	1080	1538	971	1037	441
2007–2008	4569	1918	1588	1113	993	488

SOURCE: Calculations based on data from the Directorate of Municipal Administration.

An analysis of expenditures on different components of MCGM provides an overall picture of expenditure allocation (this is a reasonable proxy since this represents an overwhelming proportion of total expenditures). Table 10.2 shows a steady pattern headed in the "right" direction. Establishment expenditures constitute the largest share of revenue expenditures, albeit declining marginally. The question is whether enough is being spent by way of repairs, operations, and maintenance of public goods. Capital expenditures comprise two categories, mandatory public services (PS1) and mandatory plus merit goods (PS2).[21] The

---

[21] PS1 (public goods, category 1) comprises the mandatory services that must be delivered by the ULBs that are in the nature of pure public goods. PS2 (public goods, category 2) comprises extended services and includes goods in the PS1 category plus merit goods that can technically be privatized since their consumption can be excluded and no joint consumption is involved. PS2 shows a relatively large increase mainly due to water projects that involve greater costs because the water has to come from farther away. For details, see Karnik, Pethe, and Karmarkar (2006).

TABLE 10.2

Composition of MCGM expenditures

Expenditure	2002–2003	2003–2004	2004–2005	2005–2006	2006–2007	2007–2008
Capital Expenditure (% of total)	16	16	13	21	24	30
Establishment Expenditures (% of Revenue Expenditure)	55	54	50	59	48	43
PS1* (% of total)	11	9	5	8	15	15
PS2** (% of total)	14	14	11	16	19	24

*Public services, category 1: capital expenditures on core public services, such as drainage, sanitation, fire fighting, and others that must be provided by the public sector.

**Public services, category 2: capital expenditures on core public services plus some other merit goods, such as health, water, and sanitation.

SOURCE: Calculations based on data from the Directorate of Municipal Administration.

discrepancy between the share of PS2 and share of PS1 in total expenditure arises from the exclusion of some items vaguely titled "other expenditures," which is nontransparent.

Revenue Patterns of ULBs in MMR

OWN-SOURCE REVENUES

Revenues of ULBs in MMR constitute own-source revenues and external revenues. Own-source revenues are further classified into tax and nontax revenues. The most important taxes collected by ULBs are *octroi* (a tax levied on goods entering the jurisdiction of the local government by setting up various checkpoints) and property tax. Nontax revenues comprise the different user fees or charges levied on consumers of different public goods. The patterns of own-source revenues in per capita terms of ULBs in MMR from 2002–2003 to 2007–2008 are shown in table 10.3.

While both tax and nontax revenues have been increasing for the OMCs, nontax revenues of COs have been fluctuating. There has been a feeling (although not backed by much solid research) that much more improvement could be achieved in the nontax revenues by rationalizing charges. The predominant role of Mumbai (going back to the goose that lays the golden egg argument) and the high cost of living in Mumbai proper can be seen from the fact that, even in per capita terms, the tax burden is significantly higher in Mumbai than in other parts of MMR. Indeed, the ratio of tax to relevant gross domestic product works out to around 4.3 percent for Mumbai, compared with 2.16 percent for the rest of MMR.

To give a clear idea of the composition of revenues, a breakdown of own-source revenues by item for the OMCs is shown in table 10.4. Despite Mumbai being the entertainment capital of India, the entertainment tax collections are almost negligible, and in fiscal years 2002–2003 and 2005–2006 there was no revenue from this source, because the state government collects this tax and does not pass it on to the

TABLE 10.3
Per capita own-source revenue in 1999–2000 prices (Rs.)

Fiscal year	MCGM		OMC		CO	
	Own Tax	Own Nontax	Own Tax	Own Nontax	Own Tax	Own Nontax
2002–2003	2,236	1,060	1,102	426	412	221
2003–2004	2,317	1,031	1,233	528	451	203
2004–2005	2,478	1,149	1,348	514	415	128
2005–2006	2,691	1,210	1,534	570	520	168
2006–2007	3,260	1,308	1,675	645	583	231
2007–2008	3,390	1,689	1,898	795	631	176

SOURCE: Calculations based on data from the Directorate of Municipal Administration.

ULBs. Tax on "entertainment," as well as on "profession," from an economist's perspective is essentially a local tax (albeit not explicitly included in the 12th Schedule list of functions of ULBs), but neither is collected by the local governments (with only a small part of the latter being passed on by the state). Vehicle taxes, despite the exponential increase in numbers of vehicles, have remained constant over the years and are a negligible proportion of the total revenue incomes.[22] Although the share of user charges in own-source revenues is increasing, these charges are far from rationalized (see chapter 8), which is hampered by the political economy's aversion to charges.

Octroi commands a lion's share of own-source revenues for all municipal corporations, while the shares of property tax have been low. Below is a detailed discussion on octroi and property tax. First, however, buoyancies of the two tax sources for the period from 1995–1996 to 2007–2008 for MCGM and OMCs are provided in table 10.5.[23] The buoyancies have been estimated as the responsiveness of the revenues from the tax to changes in gross district domestic product for the series, in constant prices. The data have been acquired from different sources; hence, for data reconciliation, the buoyancies for three subperiods have been analyzed: 1995–1996 to 1999–2000, 2000–2001 to 2004–2005, and 2002–2003 to 2007–2008. Since these are computed on the basis of "actual accounts figures" rather than the estimated/budgeted figures, they include the effect of discretionary changes/actions by the enforcing officers and hence do not reflect the underlying rate structures.

Octroi tax, as a tax on entry of goods in a particular jurisdiction, is for various reasons recognized as an inefficient tax. It has been banned by all states in India other than Maharashtra, which has repealed octroi for all ULBs except municipal corporations (Rath 2009). The buoyancy of octroi for MCGM and OMC (except during 2000–2005) has exceeded 1 (table 10.5), and it comprises 45 percent of the

---

[22] Vehicle taxes are not included in table 10.4 because the data source does not explicitly include it. The findings given here on vehicle taxes are based on recent MCGM budgets. A related tax is collected and retained by the state government.

[23] Buoyancy of a tax is defined as the responsiveness of the tax to the changes in the tax base. This is an essential quality for determining the efficiency of the design of a tax.

TABLE 10.4

Breakdown of own-source revenue by item (percent)

Item	MCGM						OMC					
	2002–2003	2003–2004	2004–2005	2005–2006	2006–2007	2007–2008	2002–2003	2003–2004	2004–2005	2005–2006	2006–2007	2007–2008
Property tax	24	24	23	23	25	22	21	22	21	20	20	22
Entertainment	0	0.08	0.01	0	0.06	0.08	0	0	0	0	0	0
Octroi	44	45	45	46	46	45	51	48	51	53	52	49
Water charges	10	9	8	8	6	5	11	13	11	10	10	10
Fees/user charge	17	16	18	18	19	25	14	13	14	14	16	17
Sewerage	6	5	5	5	3	3	0	0	0	0	0	0
Any other	0	0	0	0	0	0	3	3	2	3	2	3

SOURCE: Calculations based on data from the Directorate of Municipal Administration.

TABLE 10.5

Buoyancy of octroi and property taxes

Government component	1995–1996 to 1999–2000	2000–2001 to 2004–2005	2002–2003 to 2007–2008
Buoyancy of octroi			
MCGM	1.45	1.47	1.66
OMC	1.34	0.806	1.49
Buoyancy of property tax			
MCGM	1.65	−0.17	0.96
OMC	2.62	0.15	0.99

SOURCE: Calculations based on data from the Directorate of Municipal Administration.

own-source revenues for MCGM and 50 percent for OMC (table 10.4), thus making octroi an important as well as buoyant revenue source. Thus, the repeal of octroi for corporations in MMR will not only strongly and negatively affect the revenues of corporations but also burden the state government, which has to compensate with an in-lieu grant, which would be of unmanageable magnitude. For both the octroi and property tax, the relevant laws stipulate some band or range setting of rates and base that is within the purview of ULBs. While there has been an in-principle consensus on abolishing the octroi and rationalization of property tax, unfortunately, action has been found wanting.

Property tax commands approximately 20–24 percent of own-source revenues for MCGM and OMC (table 10.4). This share of property tax has been unsatisfactory given the high land values of the region, especially in Mumbai district. Moreover, property tax buoyancies have been erratic. The period from 2000–2001 to 2004–2005, surprisingly, witnessed a buoyancy of property tax of 0.17 for MCGM and for OMCs, significantly less than 1, thus confirming that the property tax system in MMR, and more so in Mumbai, is suffering from some major flaws. The extant system of property tax is based on the rental value system. Rents in Mumbai city have been severely constrained under the Rent Control Act (1999), thus constraining the potential property tax revenues (see Karnik, Rath, and Sharma 2004; Pethe and Lalvani 2007).[24] However, there has been some increase, in absolute terms, in the property tax collection, largely due to (1) absence of rent control in the suburbs of Mumbai, where tremendous real estate growth has occurred since 2000; (2) better administration; and (3) a shift from residential to commercial use within the city. However, compared with estimated property tax collections, collection efficiency has been a mere 45 percent, leaving much room for further improvement. There is also the contentious issue of different arms of government paying the property tax, which in the case of MMR has led to protracted litigations. Although

---

[24]The Rent Control Act applies to a host of buildings predominantly in south and central Mumbai built more than 70 years ago. Many of them are "cessed" buildings that pay a cess, which is a fee paid to MHADA for repairs and maintenance. This is because the owners have no incentive or capacity to pay for repairs and maintenance, because they get very little return, since the rents on their buildings are frozen.

it is true that the ratios of property tax to gross domestic product are typically low (around 0.6 percent) for developing countries and even perhaps lower in India as a whole, in Mumbai the ratio is 1.4 percent, reflecting difficulty in increasing the burden through this recourse. It is clear that rationalization of property taxes should become a focus and will lead to major increases in revenues from this source, especially since the market property rates have been increasing monotonically.

The study by Karnik, Rath, and Sharma (2004) pointed out the benefits of moving to a capital-value-based system of property tax in Mumbai. However, Bahl and Linn (1992) noted that, for any change in the property tax system, it is crucial to weigh the trade-off between the transition costs involved in bringing about the change and the future benefits of a better system. While administrative costs involved in shifting to the capital-value-based system are indeed rather high (*Daily News and Analysis* 2011), the benefit of this shift is significant because it would ensure that the tax system adheres to the principle of "goodness of law."[25] Also, it is felt that reforms in the property tax system would provide a way to eliminate octroi.

It is clear from the above sections that the ratio of total revenues and expenditures is inversely related to the size of the ULB: for MCGM it is 95 percent; for OMCs, 93 percent; and for COs, 61 percent. Thus, even given the current inadequate expenditures (in terms of quality of provision of goods and service delivery), there is need for additional revenues. The thrust will have to be on devolution (untied grants) and additional (transfer of) revenue handles, as well as rationalization of user charges and extant taxes. There is very little scope for increasing tax rates, given that the citizens in Mumbai are already burdened by composite tax rates of 42 percent, which comprises taxes shared by center (25 percent) and state (13.6 percent), with ULB tax share being 3.4 percent (Prud'homme 2007).

GRANTS

Besides own-source revenues, the ULBs also receive grants from the state and central governments. In theory, awards by state finance commissions, regarding devolution of statutory untied grants from the state, should be implemented, leading to empowerment of ULBs and to improving the mismatch between expenditure assignments and revenue assignments. In practice, one sees only small ad hoc grants, and even the pass-through grants from the center are not administered efficiently, with the state governments taking undue shares in transferring the grants to the ULBs. In table 10.6, the intergovernmental grants, which include transfers from the central government as per the 11th and 12th Finance Commissions and grants-in-aid from the government of Maharashtra, are classified as "other revenues." Table 10.6 shows that the smaller the size of the ULBs, the greater their dependency of grants rather than on own-source revenues, with fiscal autonomy being the casualty. These flows create difficulty for planning because of the unpredictable and uncertain nature of these grants. Given the importance of grants in the finances of smaller ULBs, a more predictable formulaic basis for vertical sharing might be preferable (Pethe, Misra, and Rakhe 2009). Recognizing this, the 13th Finance Commission, a constitutionally recognized body set up to determine the sharing of

[25] For a report on the ramifications of the new property tax system, see *Times of India* (2011b).

TABLE 10.6
Other revenues as percentage of total revenue receipts

Fiscal year	MCGM	OMC	CO
2002–2003	2.45	8.49	34.59
2003–2004	2.31	2.69	39.67
2004–2005	2.32	3.73	43.42
2005–2006	2.38	2.98	40.39
2006–2007	3.24	4.39	42.54
2007–2008	2.27	4.88	25.51

SOURCE: Calculations based on data from the Directorate of Municipal Administration.

revenues from some sources between the center and the states, recommended that local bodies be transferred a percentage of the divisible pool fund.[26] This grant is subdivided into a basic and performance based component.

REVENUE EXPENDITURE, REVENUE RECEIPTS, AND BORROWING CAPACITY
Shares of revenue expenditures in revenue receipts, which show how much of the revenue receipts are used to fund revenue expenses, are given in table 10.7. OMCs and COs are far from having the capacity to spend or to leverage revenue surpluses for financing capital expenditure. Considering the functions to be undertaken by the ULBs in MMR and given the actual situation of extant level of public amenities, it appears that financial capacity to deliver public goods and services by them is inadequate. It must be mentioned that generally, even within the available leeway, the ULBs tend not to exploit the full revenue potential by undertaking sufficient tax effort. If ULBs are to meet the kind of capital expenditures that are essential for adequate provision of public goods and services they would have to resort to borrowing from banks, financial institutions, and capital markets. The potential for debt from the capital market remains unexploited by the ULBs. This could be attributed to the weak financial health of the ULBs, which affects their rating and hence the confidence of investors (Bagchi and Kundu 2003). Also, the reluctance of the state government to guarantee municipal bonds impedes many ULBs in borrowing (Rao and Bird 2010).

Table 10.8 provides an estimate of the borrowing capacity of the ULBs in MMR. The total amount that these ULBs would be able to raise is only Rs.66,040 million, which falls far short of the required capital investments that should be raised through borrowing to finance infrastructure. On average, ULBs in MMR borrow 3–4 percent of their total revenue receipts. Borrowings of ULBs in MMR on the higher side (4 percent) would amount to around Rs.4,400 million, which is less than one-tenth of the potential borrowing capacity. The actual borrowings are not only lower but also not autonomous in nature, because they must be approved by

---

[26] Although the 13th (central) Finance Commission seems to have recognized the local bodies formally as a third tier of government, the State Finance Commission's recommendations are not being accepted (for various reasons and compulsions), especially on the financial front, by the state governments. See Pethe, Karnik, and Karmarkar (2003) for details.

TABLE 10.7
Revenue expenditures as percentage of revenue receipts

Fiscal year	MCGM	OMC	CO
2002–2003	83	69	63
2003–2004	83	72	61
2004–2005	85	76	74
2005–2006	75	70	74
2006–2007	73	63	73
2007–2008	88	56	92

SOURCE: Calculations based on data from the Directorate of Municipal Administration.

TABLE 10.8
Borrowing capacity of ULBs, 2007–2008 (Rs. millions)*

Category	Revenue receipts	Revenue expenditure	Receipts minus expenditures	Net present value
MCGM	89,230	78,441	10,788	36,739
OMC	19,288	10,819	8,468	28,839
CO	1,613	1,477	136	463
Total	110,130	90,738	19,393	66,040

*Calculated as the annuity or net present value of 50 percent of the latest revenue account balance (revenue receipts minus revenue expenditures), presumed to repay debt over 15 years, at an assumed interest rate of 12 percent.
SOURCE: Calculations based on data from the Directorate of Municipal Administration.

the state government. MCGM, the largest corporation in terms of finances, has the largest borrowing capacity among ULBs in MMR, whereas COs have very little capacity to borrow. The borrowing capacity of ULBs urgently needs to be improved by undertaking reforms that will bolster their revenues. This is especially important since the ULBs, by definition, face a hard budget constraint.[27]

To begin with, ULBs should be duly and fairly assigned revenue handles and untied resources through formulaic and hence certain devolution. The other important source is via leveraging land, which is their biggest asset, although constitutionally "land" is a state subject. This has been attempted to some extent in MMR, mostly by parastatals, such as City and Industrial Development Corporation in Navi Mumbai (Phatak 2009) and MMRDA in Bandra Kurla Complex, but ULBs have so far not been able to extract the tremendous land values to bolster their finances. The use of development charges and betterment levies (that could be imposed despite land being a state subject) could be a viable means of self-financing smaller infrastructure projects. However, the use of such measures has to be preceded by reforms in land markets and transparent information systems. Accessing capital market

[27] The municipal acts require the ULBs to balance their budgets. Further, the absence of devolution and exposure to some borrowings/debt (even after approval) still being categorized as "private" exacerbate the situation.

(municipal bonds) or taking exposure to loans from financial institutions is yet another source. This would require that the ULBs' balance sheets be cleaned, especially those of smaller ULBs, and they need to be rated so that they present an acceptable risk for the banks and other financial institutions to take on exposure. One other way is for the weaker ULBs to come together with the stronger ones to form a virtual entity. This would call for innovation and modifications in the standard pooled fund bank models. This will help take care of the inclusive developmental mandate and avoid mere cherry-picking (for details, see Pethe and Lalvani 2006).

OTHER SOURCES OF INVESTMENTS IN MMR

One route to resolving the financing gap for MMR local governments is an increased direct role for central government, international agencies, parastatals, and private players. This, rather than devolution, seems to have been the strategy followed in MMR.

Jawaharlal Nehru National Urban Renewal Mission

Realizing the need to address the issues of haphazard urbanization, in 2005 the central government launched the largest ever nationwide scheme for urban infrastructure development, the Jawaharlal Nehru National Urban Renewal Mission (JnNURM). This scheme, in MMR, comprises approximately 13–15 percent of total public capital investments in the region. The scheme is aimed at providing funds to select cities to improve infrastructure and governance (the Submission for Urban Infrastructure and Governance) and to address problems of urban poverty (the Submission for Basic Services to the Urban Poor). Cities hoping to access funds from JnNURM for undertaking infrastructure programs had to undertake several governance reforms to becoming eligible for funds. Although it is true some of these reforms were not implemented quickly, there is no denying that pressure from the central government has forced the states to initiate the reforms listed. The infrastructure projects were to be funded (viability-gap-funding mode) in part by the center, state, and ULBs; however, the nodal agency was the nonelected developmental authority/parastatal (MMRDA). The share in total funding for MMR is 35 percent by the center, 15 percent by the government of Maharashtra, and 50 percent by the ULBs.

Only the stronger ULBs in the region, those of Mumbai and Thane, have been successful in releasing a significant proportion of their stipulated share. The performance of the government of Maharashtra in this regard has been poor. The process of financing is such that the ULBs first have to put up their share, followed by the state government. However, given the weak financial position of ULBs, they find it difficult to raise 50 percent of the project cost, and with the state government not fully releasing its share till the ULBs do so, the latter are unable to undertake the required infrastructure projects. Looking at the poor performance of MMR and other cities, the latest Ahluwalia Committee Report (2011) on Indian urban infrastructure and services recommends a new and improved JnNURM to apply the lessons learned from the experience for better outcomes.

International Donor Agencies

External assistance, through funding from international donor organizations, in big-ticket projects, as well as grassroots programs, is playing a crucial role in changing the face of MMR. This assistance has primarily been from large organizations, such as the World Bank and the Japan International Cooperation Agency (*Indian Express* 2011) on a project basis.

The most prominent (in terms of size and scope) among such externally funded projects has been the Mumbai Urban Transport Project set up under the auspices of the World Bank, Mumbai's biggest and most comprehensive project of improving transport management in the region. However, there have been inefficiencies in implementation and delays in loan repayments. The involvement of multiple public organizations in the project brought to the fore problems of cooperation and interorganizational conflict, which resulted in delays and cost escalations (*Indian Express* 2010; *Times of India* 2004).[28] The World Bank decided to suspend the loans for the project (Hindu Business Line 2006), albeit temporarily (*Daily News and Analysis* 2006). MMRDA has asked the World Bank for several extensions of their loan for the project (*Times of India* 2011a).

External aid agencies have also been working on slum-related projects in the region. For instance, the Slum Sanitation Program was funded by the World Bank in order to provide better sanitation facilities to slum inhabitants. The program was unique because of its participatory focus, with mandated participation by the slum dwellers through community-based organizations (CBOs) and nongovernmental organizations (NGOs). In fact, this was the World Bank's precondition for releasing funds (Sharma and Bhide 2005). While this program envisaged the participation of several CBOs and NGOs, in reality it ended up being managed by a single NGO, which had a good international reputation as well as political connections (McFarlane 2008; Sharma and Bhide 2005). The program did not meet expectations for outcomes, including unwillingness of slum inhabitants to participate in the program, absence of multiple NGOs (McFarlane 2008; Sharma and Bhide 2005), and failure to consider the power distribution among CBOs and local leaders and the divisive forces that split communities along ethnic, caste, religion, and economic lines (McFarlane 2008; Sharma and Bhide 2005).

The cases of the Mumbai Urban Transport Project and the Slum Sanitation Program are different: the former is a massive project at the metropolitan scale involving interactions among many public organizations, whereas the latter is a smaller program implemented at the grassroots level. Apart from a need for being better prepared (by the locals) for optimal utilization of international donors, the experience of both these projects points to the need for international donor organizations to understand the institutional environment in the country or region to which they lend support. One must recognize that international aid is a problem of collective action at multiple levels and requires a careful examination and understanding of

---

[28] It is not just the multiplicities per se but the fact that attempts to have the transportation infrastructure plans to be unified and integrated into the overall vision/plan have met with opposition. The reasons are not technical but rather political rent-seeking space contestations.

the linkages between different actors and the incentive structures for aid to be able to fulfill its desired objectives (Gibson et al. 2005).

Non-ULB Public Investments

As mentioned earlier, different departments of the government of Maharashtra, through state-owned parastatals, are seen to be making/leveraging investments in infrastructure in MMR. The magnitudes of investments made by some prominent parastatals are shown in table 10.9. A large proportion of the non-ULB public investments is routed through the MMRDA. For instance, MMRDA is responsible for the disbursements of the MMR Development Fund, the funds for the Mumbai Urban Transport Project, and the revolving funds for the Mumbai urban development projects and the Mega City Scheme. While other parastatals do not make significant capital expenditures on their own, they manage to leverage funds by various means in order to undertake large-scale infrastructure projects.

Leveraging the Investments via Public-Private Partnerships

Given the state of the finances of ULBs, investment via the classical mode of budgetary support is limited. The constraints arise from limits in technical and managerial capacities. Therefore, the public-private partnership (PPP) mode is increasingly perceived to overcome these limitations to rebalance the mix of investment sources and to create a demonstrable positive impact on the overall working and functioning of urban authorities. Indeed, urban authorities inevitably will have to progressively benchmark their existing and future augmentation of infrastructure services in a cost-effective and efficient way. Given their hard budget constraints, this could be possible by encouraging private participation in infrastructure provision since private corporations may be more efficient in terms of functioning. PPPs have been talked about but not really developed, largely because there is a trust deficit between the private and public agencies. Efficient execution of some major demonstrable projects would accelerate urban infrastructure development under the PPP framework.

TABLE 10.9

Non-ULB public investments in MMR, 1999–2000 prices (Rs. million)

Fiscal year	MIDC	MHADA	CIDCO	MMRDF	MUTP	MUDP-RF	MCS-RF
2005–2006	300	2,700	2,340	3,730	6,580	60	1,660
2006–2007	960	3,600	1,230	4,420	7,930	150	1,490
2007–2008	890	2,230	2,760	3,700	8,850	350	450
Total	2,150	8,530	6,320	11,850	23,360	560	3,600

Abbreviations: CIDCO, City Industrial Development Corporation; MCS-RF, Mega City Scheme revolving fund; MHADA, Maharashtra Housing and Area Development Authority; MIDC, Maharashtra Industrial Development Corporation; MMRDF, MMR Development Fund; MUDP-RF, Mumbai urban development projects revolving fund; MUTP, Mumbai Urban Transport Project.
SOURCE: Calculations based on data collected from MMRDA, CIDCO, MIDC, and MHADA.

In the last few years the MMRDA, the nodal development authority parastatal in MMR, has been involved in undertaking projects in the PPP mode.[29] This has largely been on a build-own-transfer basis and involves large projects related to metro corridors. Special-purpose funding vehicles have been set up, with the MMRDA involved via extending equity or debt to such special-purpose funding vehicle. The viability gaps in projects are identified, and almost all of this is funded through special assistance from the central government, with a debt:equity funding pattern of 70:30. The concessionaire period is typically around 30 years. There is also an enabling/facilitating type of PPP where no resources of the MMRDA are involved. Many more large-scale PPP projects are in the pipeline, not just by MMRDA but also by Maharashtra State Road Development Corporation and MHADA in the specific areas of road development and affordable housing.

For both international donors and PPPs, the contract is generally with the state or the central government. Except in the case of large municipal corporations, the lack of capacity to negotiate and undertake such contracts is the reason. This is being addressed through capacity building of smaller ULBs by setting up the Mumbai Urban Infrastructure Company Ltd., a special-purpose viability fund established with the help of multilateral agencies. In sum, although there is much potential in this mode of infrastructure finance, very little in concrete terms is seen in practice.

SNAPSHOT OF INVESTMENTS IN MMR

Prud'homme (2007) categorizes the key investments necessary to bolster growth as investments in productive capital, housing, and infrastructure. Public investments in MMR are carried out by the ULBs, the state government through parastatals, the leveraging effort through the PPPs, and the flows from the central government through plan and centrally sponsored schemes. This section examines the share of these public organizations in the total public investments in the region from 2005–2006 to 2007–2008. ULB investment in MMR during this period was around 45 percent of total public investments. Non-ULB public investments (including JnNURM investments) during this period were approximately 55 percent of total public investment in MMR. To gain perspective, note that total public investments are only around 12 percent of the total estimated investments (infrastructure and other) taking place in MMR from all the sources (private/ public/multilateral) as estimated by using growth and incremental capital output ratio figures.

---

[29]There are three major ongoing PPP projects. One is the Versova-Andheri-Ghatkopar metro corridor, which is 11.77 km and has 12 elevated stations. The special-purpose vehicle funding route is being used by Mumbai Metro One Private Ltd. at a cost of Rs.23,560 million. The viability gap fund is Rs.6,500 million, of which the Indian government has granted Rs.4,370 million. Another project is the Charkop-Bandra-Mankhurd metro corridor, 31.87 km with 27 elevated stations, being implemented by Mumbai Metro Transport Private Ltd. at the cost of Rs.82,500 million, with a viability gap fund of Rs.22,980 million, of which the Indian government has sanctioned Rs.15,320 million, with the rest to be borne by MMRDA and the state government. In another project, a total of 122 bus shelters were commissioned with a right to display for 10 years and a payment of stipulated yearly premium. Yet another project involves at least three large-scale solid waste management (regional landfill) facilities, which is a pioneering attempt to apply PPP on such a large scale.

The investment requirement may be seen from the MMR draft plan, the business plan that the state government had commissioned to MMRDA and LEA International Ltd. to actualize the Vision Mumbai document (Bombay First 2003). The report by MMRDA and LEA International Ltd. (2007) recommends a four-pronged approach to create a competitive, livable, bankable, and well-governed MMR. The plan articulates the role of each of the levels of government (local, metropolitan, state, and central). It estimates infrastructure investments to be Rs.2,565,400 million from 2005 to 2021. These include investment requirements for infrastructure at national, metropolitan, and local levels and also for land, real estate, and housing, which are taken together as a separate category. For the 2005–2021 period, investments for national-level infrastructure are estimated to be of the magnitude of Rs.288,370 million, and investments in power, Rs.545,210 million. Thus, the remaining investments, which are of the order of Rs.1,731,820 million, are to be carried out by the ULBs. It is further estimated that 25 percent of these investments have to be carried out by own-source revenues and by levying development charges, and 20 percent of the investments have to be raised through borrowings by the ULBs. The remaining investment requirement, according to the MMR business plan, is to be raised through intergovernmental transfers and private participation. On an annual basis, assuming an equal burden over all the years, the investments to be raised through own-source revenues, including development charges, and borrowings are Rs.26,957.02 million and Rs.21,337.23 million, respectively. Given the present tax handles and committed revenues of the ULBs, such additional investments seem quite impossible, especially for the smaller municipal corporations and the COs within MMR. The expenditures and resources for MMR for the years 2005–2006 to 2007–2008 are shown in table 10.10. The revenue and capital expenditures in MMR are 54 percent and 46 percent, respectively. The re-

TABLE 10.10

MMR balance sheet: Expenditures and revenue sources (percent)*

Item	For the years 2005–2006 to 2007–2008
Expenditure	
Revenue expenditure by the ULBs	53.97
Capital expenditure by ULBs, parastatals, and centrally sponsored schemes	46.03
Revenue sources	
ULB own-source revenue	68.27
ULB other revenues	2.49
ULB borrowings	3.78
State	19.38
Central	6.07

*Total expenditures are approximately Rs.290,000 million over the three years.

SOURCE: Calculations based on data from Department of Municipal Administration, MMRDA, CIDCO, Directorate of Economics and Statistics, Municipal Corporation of Greater Mumbai, and Maharashtra Industrial Development Corporation.

source flows are 68 percent from own-source revenues, with about 19 percent and 6 percent flowing from state and central government, respectively, and ULB borrowings at 4 percent. The total resources flowing in the region over a three-year period is Rs.290,000 million. If the ULBs are to meet the required additional investment as stated in the MMR business plan, they would have to double their existing capacity of own-source revenues and increase their borrowings severalfold.

Given the present capital investment of the government, the total public investment in the region comes to a small proportion of the total investment in the region. The residual investment of the total investment presumably comprises investment by the private sector in productive capital, as well as in infrastructure, and investment in housing and real estate sectors. The total envelope of direct investment comprises 88 percent from private sources (including multilateral agencies and international donors); of the remaining 12 percent of public investment, ULBs have a share of 45 percent and the parastatals, including JnNURM, 55 percent. This state of affairs has led to infrastructure bottlenecks in key sectors, thereby affecting livability and sustainable development in the region; the symptoms manifest as the chronic poverty, proliferation of slums, and poor-quality and inadequate basic amenities.

LAND GOVERNANCE, AFFORDABLE HOUSING, AND SLUMS IN MMR

Given that, on most socioeconomic parameters, MMR is doing better than the rest of the state (and many other parts of the country), it naturally continues to experience tremendous in-migration. Given, further, that the real estate prices are among the highest in the world (certainly in India), it also means that the incomes that informal livelihoods yield to such migrants are insufficient to afford them formal housing. Naturally, the biggest challenge facing MMR is the conspicuous presence of slums in its cities. That MMR is home to Dharavi, arguably the largest slum settlement in Asia, along with several large pockets of slums, indicates the gravity of the problem. The proportion of slum dwellers to total population and the spatial distribution of slums for the Mumbai district is shown in table 10.11. For the regional zone maps of Mumbai, see figure 10.2a and 10.2b. Mumbai's population has doubled since 1971; every other person living in Mumbai lives in slums.[30] Annez et al. (2010) show that the increase in slum population indicates the formal housing sector's lack of absorptive capacity. An underlying reason for the proliferation of slums is the natural and artificial (that is, policy induced) scarcity of land (Bertaud 2004), and the absence of affordable housing. Faulty regulation of land markets, speculation, rising incomes, and influx of population feed into the already huge demand pressure, and all of this along with asset bubbles leads to soaring property prices, making the already terrible situation worse. It is estimated that at the pres-

---

[30]The 2011 census figures show that the population in Greater Mumbai is stabilizing (Pethe et al. 2012) while the other parts of the region are growing. The greatest increase in population seems to be reported within MMR from the Thane district. There appears to be a "gentrification with a voluntary twist" under way (Pethe 2010, 3). Usually, gentrification has an element of direct coercion. Here, the point is that the extant incentives are such that people take rational actions in conformity with the incentive structure that result in a gentrification like outcome. There is an apparent element of voluntary behavior and hence we term it as gentrification with a voluntary twist.

TABLE 10.11

Zonal population growth and proportion of slums in Mumbai city (thousands)

Zone*	1971	1981	1991	2001	Percent population growth, 1971–2001	Slum dwellers as percentage of total population, 2001
Zone 1	1583.18	1487.34	1322.17	1377.58	−12.99	12.34
Zone 2	1487.2	1797.7	1852.74	1960.45	31.82	47.06
Zone 3	1097.32	1632.52	2041.42	2428.91	121.35	57.00
Zone 4	608.17	1225.65	1906.57	2703.42	344.52	51.35
Zone 5	589.88	999.79	1439.51	1867.12	216.53	78.51
Zone 6	604.83	1100.43	1363.52	1640.98	171.31	69.75
Total (decadal growth rate, %)	5970.58	8243.43 (38.07)	9925.93 (20.41)	11978.45 (20.67)	100.62	54.06

*For definition of zones, see figure 10.2.

SOURCES: Mumbai's population from 1971 to 1991, MMRDA (2003); population and slum population for 2001, Mumbai Human Development Report (2009).

ent property prices and income distribution, 94–95 percent of the population cannot afford a house in Mumbai (Gandhi 2012). Clearly, this calls for innovative solutions, including rental housing.

The proliferation of slums in the region brings to the fore fundamental issues of inequality, exclusion, and improper management of land and housing markets in metropolitan regions, and addressing these requires careful and deliberative policies. Over the years, several policies have been formulated but have undergone a transition reflecting the changing perceptions of the policy makers and international multilateral organizations related to slums and the role of public and private actors. The advent of privatization in India in the 1990s welcomed the involvement of private players in mitigating the problem of slums (O' Hare, Abbott, and Barke 1998). These private players are provided incentives in the form of transferable development rights by the government to participate in slum redevelopment (Nainan 2008). The use of transferable development rights has become widespread since it is the preferred mode of compensation by the government (because it is an off-budget tool) and can be sold to raise finances for projects. Thus, transferable development rights, which are essentially a planning tool, have been used as a financing tool. Apart from private actors, slum rehabilitation policies have also increasingly sought to involve NGOs and the communities living within the slums in the process of redevelopment.

The state government itself has continued to remain involved in slum redevelopment and provision of affordable housing to the poor. Apart from the MHADA, which has been providing affordable housing for decades, the government of Maharashtra assigned this role to two other parastatals: the Slum Rehabilitation Authority and the MMRDA. Both parastatals have the authority to generate and sell transferable development rights in the open market.

The plethora of policies and public and private actors involved in slum redevelopment and affordable housing provision have been unable to check the growth of

FIGURE 10.2a
Regional map of Mumbai

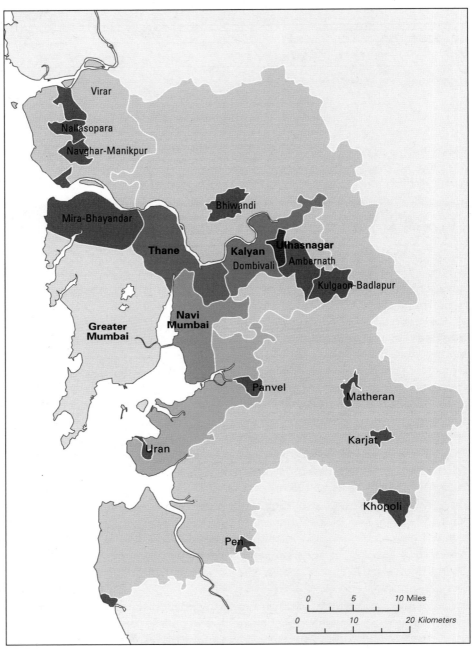

SOURCE: MMRDA (2003).

FIGURE 10.2b
Zonal map of Mumbai

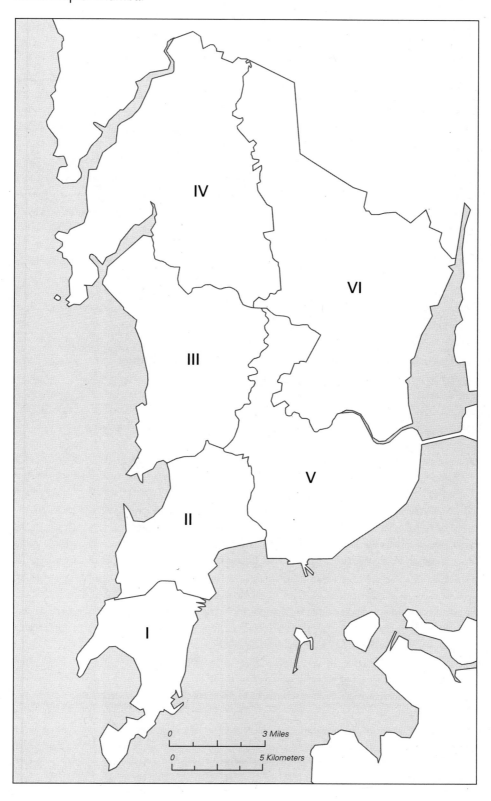

slums. Most of the policies have been myopic, with actual outcomes that differ greatly from intended outcomes. For example, rather than affecting the housing supply market, more houses are being built but fewer people are living in them. After thoroughly confounding the situation by transferable development rights and ad hoc Floor Space Index (also known as Floor Area Ratios) with premiums (shared between state and ULBs), there seems to be some rationalization through relaxation of Floor Space Index regime recently. The most recent policy pertaining to slums is the centrally sponsored scheme Rajiv Awas Yojana, which aims to make cities in India slum-free in five years. Given the performance of slum-related policies in the past, one does not hope for much success, unless the scheme's actors learn from the past and consider the informal institutions that affect incentives of different parties arising out of distortions in land and housing markets (Gandhi 2012). For Rajiv Awas Yojana to be successful, it should recognize Freire's "eight pillars" for the success of nationwide programs for slum upgrading (see chapter 14). Indeed, this holds for problems in MMR, which must be contextualized within the governance system in the region.

GOVERNANCE CONUNDRUM

It can be argued, especially regarding the performance of ULBs, the experience of land management, and the persistence of slums in MMR, that governance is key to ensuring that outcomes are socially efficient. Governance in MMR, being multi-level (vertical) and multiorganizational (horizontal) in nature, involves sharing of power (fiscal and functional) among the central, state, and local governments, as well as complex networks among various actors: ULBs and several task-specific state- and center-owned parastatals, not to mention the well-entrenched informal systems and actors.

The 74th CAA recognized local governments as a third tier of government, but as mentioned earlier, lack of implementation in terms of "three Fs," functions, finance, and functionaries (personnel), has led to weak local governments. In the case of MMR, this has led to severe incapacity, especially for the smaller ULBs, to undertake capital expenditures, resulting in infrastructure deficits in the region. The smaller ULBs in the region have become heavily dependent on large grants, which are devolved in an ad hoc manner, impeding the planning process of ULBs. The state and the center further impede the autonomy of the local bodies by carrying out enormous capital expenditures in MMR via their task-specific parastatals.

At the metropolitan level, the existence of fragmented local governments, along with multiple parastatals having overlapping jurisdictions, gives the governance system the appearance of a "polycentric governance system" endorsed by such scholars as McGinnis (1999a; 1999b; 2000), Ostrom (2010), and Ostrom, Tiebout, and Warren (1961). However, the governance system in MMR, although ostensibly polycentric, is far from being efficient (Pethe, Gandhi, and Tandel 2011). Barring MCGM and some municipal corporations, all other ULBs are too weak to perform even the basic functions expected of them, let alone engage in competition with one another or with the parastatals to provide public goods and services. Pethe, Gandhi, and Tandel (2011), in examining the case of MCGM and MMRDA, show that their relationship is characterized not by cooperation or competition but, rather, by destructive conflict and a power imbalance that favors the latter. For instance, the MMRDA does not pay property taxes that accrue to MCGM (*Indian Express* 1998). The vertical federal system affects the horizontal efficiency of the metropolitan system. These inefficiencies in the system have resulted in an increasing involvement of the civil society, which comes with its own set of issues (see Anjaria 2009; Zerah 2009).

The MPC is supposed to improve coordination and bring about cooperation among the various public bodies at the metropolitan level. However, having an empowered metropolitan-level body comprising elected members from the local governments may lead to inter-organizational conflicts. This seems to be the case for MMR, where the MPC has not been empowered because it would undermine the powers of both the state and the local governments. Thus, the absence of a system of institutions that ensures effective decentralization, process transparency (hence accountability), incentive compatibility, and citizen participation in the decision-making process renders the governance system in MMR inefficient and impedes potential growth and service delivery.

Conclusion

This chapter, by focusing on the situation in MMR, highlights the complexities that governments and policy makers in developing countries face in managing metropolitan regions. These regions require large investments in basic infrastructure if they are to attain sustainable growth rates. The analysis considered the political reality (fractured state within the federal set up), the state of decentralization or ineffective "home rule," and the conformity of policies with the "goodness of law" and incentive compatibility.

Although the situation in MMR is better than for other nonmetro ULBs in India, which suffer from chronic financial weakness, there is room for improvement even in the Mumbai region. Looking at the levels of spending on core public goods, it may be inferred that, for MMR as a whole, not enough is being spent on core public services. The reason for such low spending on public goods and services, especially by the small ULBs in MMR, can be attributed primarily to their weak financial position. Absence of buoyant revenue handles, excessive reliance on grants from the center and state governments, and inability to autonomously access capital markets have weakened their ability to fulfill their mandated functions.

This chapter indicates that public investments in the region originate from three important sources: ULBs, state government (via parastatals), and central government (via centrally sponsored schemes, e.g., JnNURM). However, capital expenditures of ULBs are rather low and far below those required to efficiently fulfill their mandated functions. Revenue handles with the ULBs are limited, and tax collections do not meet their potential. There is a need to reform the property tax system, which is the most important revenue handle with the ULBs, in order to bolster own-source revenues. The collections of user fees and charges are also low, pointing to a need for rationalization. There is tremendous dependence, especially by the weaker

ULBs, on grants received from the state and central government. These grants have been ad hoc in nature and are usually devolved with considerable delays. The weak fiscal situation of ULBs hampers their capacity to borrow funds from the capital markets.

While the performance of ULBs has been unsatisfactory, infrastructure investments in the region by centrally sponsored schemes, international donor agencies, parastatals, and private players (through PPPs) have been on the rise. Yet despite investment flows from the state and the center, the cumulative public investment in the region is not adequate to meet the backlog of investment and future demand in infrastructure. Hence, the higher-level governments do not recognize the full potential of rich dividends in the form of tax revenues that would accrue if they were to invest more in MMR. Poor land management policies are one of the most important reasons for manifestation of slums. Efficient land management will not only help mitigate the issue of slums but also be instrumental in improving the performance of the ULBs, which will help unlock tremendous land values to boost their revenues. Ultimately, it is clear that reform in governance systems is the key to ensuring better outcomes in terms of efficient delivery of public goods and services.

One of the chief stumbling blocks has to do with the huge data gaps, in both financial and physical terms (indeed, the latter makes it impossible to bring in a best practice like an outcome-based performance appraisal). The need to strengthen de facto decentralization in a meaningful sense is evident. At a more macro level, there is an urgent need to clarify jurisdiction of various authorities in both the horizontal and vertical sense, to creatively manage polycentricity.

Thus, during the 1990s and 2000s, there seems a long-awaited recognition that India's future is essentially urban. Despite de jure constitutional amendments, the reality vis-à-vis the management of the metros and city regions has not changed much. ULB investment and governmental structures in terms of revenues and expenditures, although clearly increased in absolute terms, has remained proportionately more or less the same since decentralization 20 years ago. This complex governance conundrum requires constant engagement and vigilance, as well as positive intent, angelic patience, and mature modesty toward realistic expectations.

This is a story of a metropolitan system that contributes hugely to the state, as well as to the nation as a whole. This "goose that lays the golden egg" is in need of serious attention. The issue is not really a conceptual matter as much as one of political will regarding implementation of uncluttered and sharply defined empowered subsystems that work cohesively. Thus, effective decentralization, attractive investment climate, and coordination among multiple agencies would help transform the MMR region into a people-friendly urban space.

REFERENCES

Ahluwalia Committee. 2011. Report on Indian urban infrastructure and services. National Institute of Urban Affairs. http://www.niua.org/projects/hpec/finalreport-hpec.pdf

Anjaria, Jonathan Shapiro. 2009. Guardians of the bourgeois city: Citizenship, public space and middle class activism in Mumbai. *City and Community* 8(4):391–406.

Annez, Patricia Clarke, Alain Bertaud, Bimal Patel, and Vidyadhar K. Phatak. 2010. Working with the market: Approach to reducing urban slums in India. Working Paper No. 5475. Washington, DC: World Bank.

Bagchi, Soumen, and Anirban Kundu. 2003. Development of municipal bond market in India: Issues concerning financing of urban infrastructure. *Economic and Political Weekly* 38(8):789–798.

Bahl, Roy W., and Johannes F. Linn. 1992. *Urban public finance in developing countries.* Oxford: Oxford University Press.

Baker, Judy, Rakhi Basu, Maureen Cropper, Somik Lall, and Akie Takeuchi. 2005. Urban poverty and transport: The case of Mumbai. Working Paper No. 3693. Washington, DC: World Bank.

Bertaud, Alain. 2004. Mumbai FSI conundrum: The perfect storm: The four factors restricting the construction of new floor space in Mumbai. http://alain-bertaud.com/AB_Files/AB _Mumbai_FSI_conundrum.pdf

Bombay First. 2003. *Vision Mumbai: Transforming Mumbai into a world-class city.* Mumbai: McKinsey & Company/Bombay First.

Census of India. 2001. Population Tables, Census of India.

———. 2011. Provisional Population Tables, Census of India.

Daily News and Analysis. 2006. World Bank resumes lending to MUTP. June 30. http://www .dnaindia.com/mumbai/report_world-bank-resumes-lending-to-mutp_1038719

———. 2011. Need more time for property tax bill: BMC. January 20. http://www.dnaindia.com /mumbai/report_need-more-time-for-property-tax-bill-bmc_1497136

Gandhi, Sahil. 2012. Economics of affordable housing in Indian cities: The case of Mumbai. *Environment and Urbanization Asia* 3(1):221–235.

Gibson, Clark, Krister Andersson, Elinor Ostrom, and Sujai Shivakumar. 2005. *The Samaritan's dilemma: The political economy of development aid.* Oxford: Oxford University Press.

Hindu Business Line. 2006. World Bank suspends aid to Mumbai project. *Hindu,* (March 2).

Indian Express. 1998. Hot property: Defaulters owe BMC 75 cr. (November 25).

———. 2010. MMRDA funds likely to dominate board meeting of Mumbai Rail Vikas Corporation. (December 31).

———. 2011. Bandra Metro line will need funds from Japan agency. (January 19).

Joardar, Souro. 2008. Urban governance in India: The case for a metropolitan planning committee. *Space* 13(1):69–85.

Karnik, Ajit, Abhay Pethe, and Dilip Karmarkar. 2006. Developing a quantitative framework for determining devolution of funds from the state government to local bodies. In *Local governments in India: Decentralization and beyond,* ed. Niraja Gopal Jayal, Amit Prakash, and Pradeep Sharma. New Delhi: Oxford University Press.

Karnik, Ajit, Anita Rath, and J. C. Sharma. 2004. Reforming property tax system: Simulated results for Mumbai city. *Economic and Political Weekly* 39(34):3818–3826.

Kundu, Amitabh. 2006. Trends and pattern of urbanization and their economic implications. In *India infrastructure report 2006 urban infrastructure.* New Delhi: Oxford University Press.

McFarlane, Colin. 2008. Sanitation in Mumbai's informal settlements: State, "slum" and infrastructure. *Environment and Planning* 40(1):88–107.

McGinnis, Michael, ed. 1999a. *Polycentric governance and development: Readings from the workshop in political theory and policy analysis.* Ann Arbor: University of Michigan Press.

———, ed. 1999b. *Polycentricity and local public economies: Readings from the workshop in political theory and policy analysis.* Ann Arbor: University of Michigan Press.

———, ed. 2000. *Polycentric games and institutions: Readings from the workshop in political theory and policy analysis.* Ann Arbor: University of Michigan Press.

MCGM. 2010. *Mumbai human development report 2009.* New Delhi: Oxford University Press. mhupa.gov.in/W_new/Mumbai%20HDR%20Complete.pdf

MMRDA. 2003. *Population and employment profile of Mumbai metropolitan region.* Mumbai: Mumbai Metropolitan Region Development Authority.

MMRDA and LEA International Ltd. 2007. *Business plan for Mumbai metropolitan region.* Draft Final Report. Mumbai.

Mohan, Rakesh. 2006. Managing metros. India Seminar. http://www.india-seminar.com/2006/557/557%20rakesh%20mohan.htm

———. 2007. Asia's urban century: Emerging trends. In *Land policies and their outcomes*, ed. Gregory K. Ingram and Yu-Hung Hong, 239–258. Cambridge, MA: Lincoln Institute of Land Policy.

Nainan, Navtej. 2008. Building boomers and fragmentation of space in Mumbai. *Economic and Political Weekly* 43(21):29–34.

O'Hare, Greg, Dina Abbot, and Michael Barke. 1998. A review of slum housing policies in Mumbai. *Cities* 15(4):269–283.

Ostrom, Elinor. 2010. Organizational economics: Applications to metropolitan governance. *Journal of Institutional Economics* 6(1):109–115.

Ostrom, Vincent, Charles Tiebout, and Robert Warren. 1961. The organization of government in metropolitan areas: A theoretical inquiry. *American Political Science Review* 55(4):831–842.

Pethe, Abhay. 2005. Mumbai: Fact file and budgetary analysis. New Delhi: Centre de Science Humaines.

———. 2010. Collusion, conflicts, informal systems and rent seeking: The great prototype Indian story of urban land management in Mumbai. Paper presented at Urban Design and Research Institute, Mumbai (December 10).

Pethe, Abhay, Sahil Gandhi, and Vaidehi Tandel. 2011. Assessing the Mumbai metropolitan region: A governance perspective. *Economic and Political Weekly* 46(26/27):187–195.

Pethe, Abhay, Sahil Gandhi, Vaidehi Tandel, and Sirus Libeiro. 2012a. Anatomy of ownership and management of public land in Mumbai: Setting an agenda using IAD framework. *Environment and Urbanization Asia* 3(1):203–220.

Pethe, Abhay, Ajit Karnik, and Dilip Karmarkar. 2003. Finances of urban local bodies in Maharashtra: A statistical profile. India Infrastructure Report. New Delhi: Oxford University Press.

Pethe, Abhay, and Mala Lalvani. 2006. Towards Economic Empowerment of ULBs in Maharashtra. *Economic and Political Weekly* 41:18–24.

———. 2007. A report on the local government finances: MMR region. Mumbai: Mumbai Transformation Support Unit.

———. 2008. Finances of panchayati raj institutions: A simple story but a messy plot. Working Paper No. 28. Mumbai: Vibhooti Shukla Centre, University of Mumbai.

Pethe, Abhay, Mala Lalvani, Manisha Karne, Sandhya Mahtre, Sahil Gandhi, and Surekha Kadam. 2010. Mid-term appraisal for Maharashtra. New Delhi: Planning Commission of India.

Pethe, Abhay, B. M. Mishra, and P. B. Rakhe. 2009. Strengthening decentralization—augmenting the consolidated fund of the states by the thirteenth finance commission: A normative approach. Issue 29 of DRG studies series. Mumbai: Department of Economic Analysis and Policy, Reserve Bank of India.

Pethe, Abhay, Ramakrishna Nallathiga, Sahil Gandhi, and Vaidehi Tandel. 2012. Economics of land use changes in Mumbai: Understanding the wedge between the de facto and de jure development. Working Paper No. 44. Mumbai: Vibhooti Shukla Centre Working Paper Series, University of Mumbai.

Pethe, Abhay, Vaidehi Tandel, and Sahil Gandhi. 2012. Understanding Issues Related to Polycentric Governance in the Mumbai Metropolitan Region. *Public Finance and Management* 12(3):182–203.

Phatak, Vidhyadhar K. 2009. Charges on land and development rights as a financing resource for urban development. In *India infrastructure report 2009: A critical resource for infrastructure*. New Delhi: Oxford University Press.

Prud'homme, Rémy. 2007. Seven notes on Mumbai's growth and how to finance it. www.rprudhomme.com/resources/2007+Seven+Notes+on+Mumbai+$28WB$29+.pdf

Rao, Govinda M., and Richard M. Bird. 2010. Urban governance and finance in India. Working Paper No. 2010–68. New Delhi: National Institute of Public Finance and Policy. (April).

Rath, Anita. 2009. Octroi—a tax in a time warp: What does its removal imply for greater Mumbai? *Economic and Political Weekly* 44(25):86–93.

Sassen, Saskia. 2010. The global city: Strategic sight, new frontier. In *Accumulation by dispossession, transformative cities in new global order*, ed. Swapna Banerjee-Guha. New Delhi: Sage.

Sharma, R. N., and Amita Bhide. 2005. World Bank funded slum sanitation programme in Mumbai: Participatory approach and lessons learnt. *Economic and Political Weekly* 40(17):1784–1789.

Slack, Enid. 2007. Managing the coordination of service delivery in metropolitan cities: The role of metropolitan governance. Policy Research Working Paper No. 4317. Washington, DC: World Bank.

Times of India. 2004. Differences between BMC, railways delay building of bridges. (March 21).

———. 2011a. MMRDA asks World Bank for 3rd loan extension. (February 1).

———. 2011b. New property tax to hit rentals in city. (September 21).

Zerah, Marie-Helene. 2009. Participatory governance in urban management and the shifting geometry of power in Mumbai. *Development and Change* 40(5):853–877.

Paying for Urbanization in China

Challenges of Municipal Finance in the Twenty-First Century

CHRISTINE P. WONG

11

China is urbanizing, and the pace is accelerating. The National Bureau of Statistics (NBS) reported a population of 1.34 billion at year end 2010, fully half of them living in cities (*CSY* 2011). Rapid urbanization is a recent phenomenon that was unleashed by the country's transition to a market economy (figure 11.1). Starting in the early 1980s, the dismantling of agricultural collectives freed rural labor to leave the land. Since then, rural-urban migration has steadily accelerated as government restrictions on population movement were eased, and plenty of jobs were created in cities by economic growth that has averaged more than 12 percent per annum in real terms since 1990.

The scale of China's urban transformation is unprecedented in human history. During the 1980s, urban population grew by 110 million; this accelerated to 157 million during the 1990s and 210 million during the first decade of the twenty-first century. Nationwide, the current urban population of 670 million is more than three times that in 1980, an increase of 480 million in just 30 years. The population of metropolitan Shanghai, China's largest city, grew from 16 million to 23 million between the 2000 and 2010 censuses, a 44 percent increase (Shanghai Statistical Yearbook 2011). During 2008–2011 alone, Beijing reportedly absorbed 500,000 new people each year (Green 2012).

Providing infrastructure and public services to accommodate urbanization of this scale and pace is a gargantuan task that would strain any government. In China, the challenge was all the more daunting as the ongoing process of transition from a planned economy to a market economy transformed virtually all aspects of social and economic organization and brought a catastrophic collapse in the government's revenue mechanisms that caused the budget to plunge from one-third of gross domestic product (GDP) in 1978 to a nadir of 11 percent before a new tax system began to restore fiscal health from the late 1990s onward (Wong and Bird 2008; World Bank 2002). The upturn in urbanization thus began in a difficult fiscal

FIGURE 11.1

Urbanization rates in China

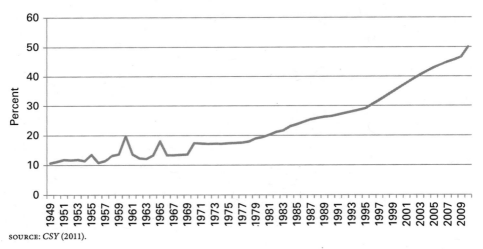

SOURCE: *CSY* (2011).

environment that worsened through the first two decades. The financial mechanisms and strategies for Chinese municipalities were forged in this harsh environment.

Despite this inauspicious start, China's spectacular economic growth performance over this period seems to provide prima facie evidence that the government has managed the urbanization process well enough. New cities have cropped up: the latest count shows 657 cities and nearly 20,000 towns, compared with 233 cities and 2,600 towns 30 years ago. Existing cities have expanded. City centers have been renovated and modernized, infrastructure has been built, and urban facilities appear to be keeping up with demand. Visitors to China typically fly into world-class airports and are whisked into town on multilane expressways. Cities and even modest county towns are crisscrossed by wide boulevards, and Chinese cities are setting world records in the pace at which subway lines are being built (National Development and Reform Commission and World Bank 2010).

In fact, a good deal of evidence points to an outstanding performance in providing growth-supporting infrastructural investments during this period. In 2010, for example, China was ranked 27th among 155 countries in the World Bank's Logistics Performance Index (LPI), a measure of a country's efficiency in moving goods to and from international markets. With an overall LPI score of 3.49, China is approaching the average of 3.55 for high-income countries, substantially outperforming its peer group of upper-middle-income countries (table 11.1).

The picture is more mixed on the provision of services. A 2006 survey of 5,000 households in five cities found citizens generally pleased with urban public services but worried about their high costs, with basic education per child taking up 10 percent of household income and per capita out-of-pocket payments for health care another 10 percent. The survey also found the provision and pricing of services to be highly regressive, with lower-income households receiving poorer-quality services but paying significantly larger shares of household income for them (Brixi 2009).

TABLE 11.1

Global logistics performance index scores, February 2010

LPI rank	Country	LPI score	Customs	Infrastructure	International shipments	Logistics competence	Tracking and tracing	Timeliness
27	**China**	**3.49**	**3.16**	**3.54**	**3.31**	**3.49**	**3.55**	**3.91**
	High-income countries	3.55	3.36	3.56	3.28	3.5	3.65	3.98
	Upper-middle-income countries	2.82	2.49	2.54	2.86	2.71	2.89	3.36
	Lower-middle-income countries	2.59	2.23	2.27	2.66	2.48	2.58	3.24
	Low-income countries	2.43	2.19	2.06	2.54	2.25	2.47	2.98

SOURCE: World Bank (2010).

How cities finance services for their growing populations and provide infrastructure for supporting the expanding economic base has an important impact on the nation's economic growth and well-being, yet surprisingly little is known about the finances of Chinese cities or, indeed, how municipalities have fared in the reforms of the economic system and public finances. There has been no study of municipal finance in China since 2000 (Asian Development Bank 2000; Wong 1997), although there is a small literature on urban infrastructure finance and, more recently, the role of land as a source of finance.[1]

In the large and vibrant literature on fiscal reform, the focus is overwhelmingly on central-local fiscal relations and the problems of rural public finance (Bahl 2011; Wong and Bird 2008; World Bank 2002; 2007a; 2007b). This lack of concern for municipal finance problems is best illustrated by the excellent, comprehensive treatment of the Chinese fiscal system written by senior officials in the Ministry of Finance (MOF) (Li 2006; 2010). In 648 pages, the topic of urbanization is written up as a box (taking up three-quarters of a page), in which the implications for public finance merited one sentence: "Following the acceleration of urbanization, government spending in the areas of public services and public basic infrastructure will increase significantly" (Li 2010, 119). This omission is all the more striking because, under China's decentralized fiscal system, the burden of financing this urban growth has been borne almost entirely by municipal governments.

This chapter attempts to fill this lacuna in the literature by describing and analyzing the financing of public services and infrastructure in municipalities in China. An examination of the practices of the past two decades makes it clear that municipal finance has evolved to rely overwhelmingly on extrabudgetary resources and borrowing, under a policy regime of benign neglect. The formal system of public

---

[1]On infrastructure, see Wu (2010; 2011), Mikesell et al. (2011), Honohan (2008), Gao (2007), and Su and Zhao (2007). On land, see Cao, Feng, and Tao (2008), Tao et al. (2010), and Guan and Peng (2011).

finance in China has made few accommodations for the needs of municipal finance. Except for a few favored cities in the rich coastal provinces, the formal system does not provide sufficient resources for cities to meet their responsibilities in service provision. Moreover, municipalities are prohibited from borrowing even for capital expenditures, making it difficult to finance infrastructure. Yet the remarkable growth and development of cities have proceeded because political leaders have been willing to tolerate a plethora of informal, backdoor solutions that enabled cities both to obtain the resources needed and to limit eligibility for benefits.

The chapter turns next to a brief discussion of China's urbanization trends and the administrative structure of Chinese cities. Discussion of municipal finance follows, focusing first on evolution of the formal fiscal system and then on extrabudgetary components. Financing of urban infrastructure and the emergence of local investment corporations then are discussed, and the chapter concludes with an analysis of the current system of municipal finance, noting both the achievements and accumulated macroeconomic risks of the strategy, and the adverse effects on welfare and distribution.

BACKGROUND AND CONTEXT: URBANIZING CHINA

In low-income countries, industrialization and economic growth are normally synonymous with urbanization, as labor is shifted out of agriculture. During the first decade of the People's Republic, China conformed to this "empirical regularity": as economic growth accelerated through the 1950s, people flooded into cities in search of higher-paying jobs in the new factories. Urban population grew by 69 million from 1950 to 1960, when the urbanization rate rose from 11.2 percent to 19.7 percent. This relationship was decisively broken in the early 1960s, though, when government policy turned antiurban.

It began from the failure of the Great Leap Forward, when the ambitious drive to reorganize agriculture in people's communes and produce steel from backyard furnaces collapsed and economic crisis ensued. To alleviate food shortages in the cities, the government forcibly returned millions of newly arrived migrants to their home villages in the early 1960s. In the wake of this traumatic episode, free population movements were abolished. A household registration (*hukou*) system that had been established in the 1950s was called into service. Through state control of grain and other key consumer goods and limiting rationing to those with urban hukou, the government was able to limit urban population growth.[2] For two decades thereafter, migration was strictly controlled, and industrialization continued without urbanization. During this period, urban growth stemmed only from natural population growth, minus an exodus of some 10–15 million youths who were sent to the villages for "reeducation" (Bernstein 1977). Even as industry grew from 28 percent of GDP in 1962 to 44 percent in 1980, the share of the population in urban areas remained below 20 percent (table 11.2).

---

[2]See Zhang (1983) on the workings of the hukou system. I am indebted to Andrew Watson for sharing this reference.

Against this background, the recent rapid urbanization can be seen partly as a catching-up process. Since the 1990s, urban population growth has outstripped total population growth, and the shift from rural to urban will continue even as China's total population growth is slowing (figure 11.2). Even at 50 percent, China is "underurbanized"; most countries at its income level have higher proportions of their population living in cities (Henderson 2009).

TABLE 11.2

China's urbanization and industrialization

Year	Urban population (millions)	Increase over past decade (millions)	Urbanization rate (percent)	Industry percentage of GDP*
1950	61.69			17.6
1960	130.73	69.04	19.7	28.3
1970	144.24	13.51	17.4	36.8
1980	191.4	47.16	19.4	43.9
1990	301.95	110.55	26.4	36.7
2000	459.06	157.11	36.2	40.4
2010	669.78	210.72	49.9	40.1

*The first two figures are from 1952 and 1962.

SOURCE: *CSY* (2007; 2011).

FIGURE 11.2

China's population growth by decade, 1950–2010 (in millions)

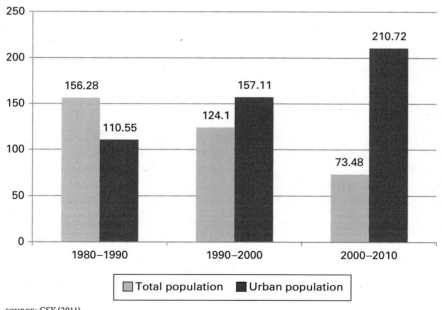

SOURCE: *CSY* (2011).

The Administrative Hierarchy of Urban Local Governments in China

China's intergovernmental fiscal system makes no distinction between urban and rural governments, and the assignment of revenues and expenditures is strictly according to their rank in the administrative hierarchy. Under this setup, the provincial capitals, which tend to be much larger, receive the same transfers and revenue-raising powers that other prefectural-level cities receive. The only concession to size is that larger cities are permitted a specified, higher rate than smaller ones for a few taxes, such as the urban maintenance and construction tax.

China is organized in an administrative structure with five levels of government. Under the central government, about 44,000 subnational governments (SNGs) are divided into four levels, nearly two-thirds of which are urban local governments (ULGs). Figures for year-end 2010 showed that the first level of SNG comprises twenty-two provinces and five autonomous regions organized for ethnic minorities, as well as four municipalities with provincial status: Beijing, Shanghai, Tianjin, and Chongqing. At the next level are 333 prefectural units, of which 50 are prefectures and 283 are cities. The fourth tier has 2,856 units, including 1,578 counties, 370 county-level cities, and 853 urban districts under the jurisdiction of prefectural-level cities. The bottom tier has 40,906 units that include 14,571 townships, 19,410 towns, and 6,923 urban "street offices" under the jurisdiction of county-level cities. This structure is presented in figure 11.3.[3]

China has more than 27,000 ULGs. Their distribution across the subnational levels is presented in table 11.3, which includes the category "provincial capital cities and line-item cities."[4] This category comprises 31 cities that have prefectural rank and are larger and more prosperous; fifteen of them have been informally given "deputy provincial level" status. Overall, the size distribution of cities is heavily concentrated at the low end, with nearly 40 percent of the urban population living in small county-level cities and towns ranging in size from 20,000 to 200,000–300,000. Some analysts have argued that Chinese cities are too small to take advantage of the agglomeration economies of urbanization (Chan, Henderson, and Tsui 2008; Henderson 2009). Table 11.4 presents the growth of ULGs by administrative rank for the period 1981–2010.

A Caveat on Population Data and City Size

The 2000 population census was the first time the government collected nation-wide information on migrants and included them in the urban population counts, alongside the registered, *hukou* population.[5] Before that, all members of the population were reported by birth place, regardless of where they were living at the time of reporting (Chan 2003). As a result, reported population trends did not reflect the

---

[3]In figure 11.3, districts and street offices are omitted because their populations are already included in the cities to which they are subordinated.

[4]"Line-item cities" was a category created in the late 1980s to confer a higher status on 14 cities destined for faster growth, to give them more direct access to central government resources without giving them full provincial status. After the tax sharing system reform in 1994, as a concession to the provinces, the number of line-item cities was reduced to five: Dalian, Qingdao, Ningbo, Xiamen, and Shenzhen.

[5]I am indebted to Kam Wing Chan for explaining some of the intricacies of population reporting.

FIGURE 11.3

Structure of government in China, 2010

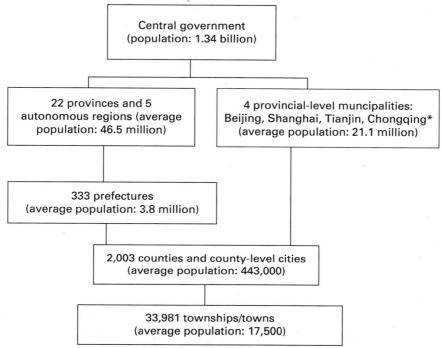

*None of the provincial-level municipalities have prefectural cities or county-level cities below them. Beijing has 2 counties, 142 towns, and 40 townships; Tianjin has 3 counties, 115 towns, and 20 townships; Shanghai has 1 county, 109 towns, and 2 townships; Chongqing has 21 counties, 587 towns, and 252 townships.
SOURCE: *CSY* (2011).

TABLE 11.3

Distribution of urban local governments by administrative rank and size, 2009

Governmental level	Number	Average population (millions)	Percentage of urban population
Provincial level	4	12.13	8
Provincial capitals and line-item cities*	31	3.06	15
Prefectural level	251	0.95	39
County level	367	NA	NA
Township level	19,322	NA	NA

NA, not applicable.
*Excluding Lhasa.
SOURCE: *CCSY* (2010).

TABLE 11.4

Growth of urban local governments by administrative rank, 1980–2010

| | Cities | | | | | |
Year	Provincial level	Prefectural level	County level	Total	Increase over past decade	Towns
1981	3	108	122	233	56	2,664*
1990	3	185	279	467	234	11,392
2000	4	259	400	663	196	19,692
2010	4	283	370	657	−6	19,410

*1982 figure.

SOURCES: Chan, Henderson, and Tsui (2008); *CSY* (1981; 1991; 2001; 2011); Chan and Hu (2003).

momentous geographic shifts that had begun nearly two decades earlier. Subsequent changes gradually brought the Chinese reporting methodology for urban populations closer to international norms (Chan 2009; Kamal-Chaoui, Leman, and Zhang 2009).

While the national data are improving, however, there is a tremendous amount of confusion in the citation of city-level statistics. This is partly due to Chinese terminology, which uses *shi* ("municipality") to refer interchangeably to either an administrative unit or a city, and the size difference is often huge. For example, the provincial-level municipality Chongqing has 21 rural counties, in addition to the municipal core. The whole administrative unit has a population of 33 million, only half of whom live in the urban, built-up core. Mistaking the two has led more than one Western reporter to proclaim Chongqing as the largest city in China and, indeed, the world (see Robinson 2011). Claims of China having hundreds of million-plus cities are likewise based on mistaking the administrative regions for municipalities. In Hebei province, the urbanization rate averages only 17 percent among its 11 prefectural-level units, so the municipalities are just one-sixth the size of the administrative regions (*CCSY* 2010).

Aside from the confusing terminology, city-level population data are "muddied" by the continued use of *hukou* population by many city officials, in contravention of the NBS's call, since 2001, to use actual population counts (*CCSY* 2001). Their motivation is simple: under pressure to boost per capita GDP and growth performance, it is tempting to use a lower population in the denominator.[6] The NBS appears to lack the clout to enforce reporting standards at subnational levels and contributes to the chaos by publishing conflicting population numbers.[7] Even though the subnational

---

[6] In 2000, for example, Shenzhen's per capita GDP was 133,305 yuan if counting only the hukou population but 23,759 yuan based on the actual population. Chan (2009) has found many instances of cities using lower than actual population figures and warns that "while national urban population figures are broadly accurate, individual city population numbers remain a statistical minefield" (25–26).

[7] For example, the population of Beijing was reported in the 2010 *China Statistics Yearbook* as 17.55 million and 14.92 million in 2009 for the administrative region and city proper, respectively. In 2010 *China City Statistics Yearbook*, also published by the NBS but based on city-level reporting, they were reported as 12.46 million and 11.75 million, respectively.

bureaus work under the guidance of the NBS, they are funded by SNGs at the same level and are required to report to local government before submitting their data upward through the statistical system.[8]

MUNICIPAL FINANCE: THE FISCAL SYSTEM

It is difficult to do a comprehensive study of municipal finance in China with information that is currently available to the public. One reason is that, at the national level, the Chinese statistical system does not distinguish between urban and rural regions. For public finance, for example, the data are disaggregated by administrative level, and prefectural-level cities cannot be separated out from rural prefectures, nor can the city districts be separated from their rural counties. More importantly, at present Chinese cities rely on extrabudgetary revenues for the bulk of their financing needs, and until recently little public information was available on these resources. This and the next section identify the components of finance available to municipal governments, assembling available information to analyze their structure and incentives, and draw some insights on how they work together.

Understanding how municipalities are financed starts with three facts. First, China assigns most expenditures to SNGs: municipal governments are responsible for providing and financing all vital services and infrastructure. Second, the intergovernment fiscal system is weak and is characterized by large vertical fiscal gaps at subnational levels, as well as large horizontal disparities. Third, to ensure that the economy continues to grow, the government has tolerated backdoor practices to permit SNGs to obtain the resources needed to finance expenditure responsibilities assigned by the intergovernmental fiscal system (IFS).

The Decentralized Fiscal System

In terms of budgetary expenditure percentages, China is one of the most decentralized countries in the world. In 2009, the central government accounted for just 20 percent of national budgetary expenditures. The rest were distributed among the four levels of SNG: 18 percent at the provincial level, 22 percent at the municipal (or prefectural) level, and 40 percent at the county and township level.[9] These high expenditure shares are caused by the assignment of many costly and vital responsibilities to lower-level governments. Under the current intergovernmental assignments, the county level is responsible for the provision of basic education, which, under Chinese law, is compulsory and free of charge for the first nine years. Counties are also responsible for the delivery of basic health care. Most unusual, governments at the prefectural and county levels are responsible for income maintenance functions: pensions, unemployment insurance, and social welfare. This is shown in table 11.5, where the counties accounted for most of the total national expenditures

---

[8]Schreyer and Holz (2005) provide a good summary of the Chinese statistical system and the problems of reform.

[9]Over the past decade the government has moved all major expenditure responsibilities upward from the township to the county level, including basic education, health, and social welfare. As a result, the township is no longer a significant level for budgetary purposes. For most purposes, it is more useful to aggregate county and township figures, as is done here.

TABLE 11.5

Distribution of budgetary expenditures by level of government, 2007
(percentage of total)

Government level	All budgetary expenditures	Education	Health	Social security and employment	Capital spending (2006)
Central	23.0	5.5	1.7	6.3	27.9
Provinces	17.7	15.0	17.2	24.9	18.5
Municipalities	22.2	18.8	26.2	27.7	28.8
Counties and townships	37.1	60.7	54.9	41.2	24.8

SOURCES: Calculated from MOF *China finance yearbook* (2008, 147); MOF *Compendium of local fiscal statistics* (2006; 2007).

on education and health, and municipal and county levels for the bulk of subsidies to social security in 2007. They are also responsible for the majority of capital spending on the budget.

These assignments were set in the 1980s, when fiscal decline had led to a series of reforms that decentralized the financing responsibilities to local governments. The assignments have remained largely unchanged in the intervening decades even as reforms were bringing large shifts in the composition of expenditures and recentralizing revenues to move more than 50 percent to the central government (Wong 1991; 2009). As a result, SNGs, both urban and rural, have faced large fiscal gaps.

What Do Cities Do? Growing Responsibilities and an Unresponsive Fiscal System

What cities do has changed dramatically since the late 1970s. Under the planned economy, economic development was the primary task, and the focus was on state-owned enterprises (SOEs) in industry. Data assembled for 1978 show that expenditures on economic development accounted for nearly 60 percent of SNG budgets, when capital construction, working capital, technological upgrading, geological prospecting, and the running costs of the departments of industry, transport, commerce, and agriculture are combined. Of these, the vast majority went to supporting SOEs. Through the transition, as SOEs were gradually weaned from budgetary support, direct expenditures on them declined. For a time, subsidies ballooned, absorbing 30 percent of total expenditures by the late 1980s as the government attempted to buffer both enterprises and households from the pain of price reform. Moreover, market reform led to competition and price adjustments that pushed many SOEs into financial difficulty and required loss subsidies, the same process that was causing the steep fiscal decline. As these burdens gradually receded, more resources were shifted to financing the day-to-day administration of government and providing public services.

The changing composition of local budgetary expenditures is shown in table 11.6. The percentages of SOE and development expenditures have declined substantially, and social expenditures have risen, as expected. However, development remains a

TABLE 11.6

Composition of budgetary expenditures (percentage of total, all SNGs)

Budget element	1978	1988	1998	2010
SOEs	55.7	28.1	19.6	NA
Development	57.5	21.7	24.3	35.6
Social	18.0	24.0	26.2	42.7
Administration	7.9	10.4	15.7	21.7
Subsidies	10.7	29.6	7.7	NA

NA, not applicable.

SOURCE: Data is drawn from *CSY*, various years, and regrouped by author's estimates.

large percentage of the budget: even in 2010 it was more than one-third of total expenditures, reflecting the growth- and investment-driven orientation of the Chinese economy and local governments.

During the 1980s and 1990s, the transition of the economy brought extraordinary pressure on municipal budgets. First, the ongoing fiscal decline had cut budgetary resources available to SNGs: it was 18 percent of GDP in 1978, 13 percent in 1988, and 8 percent in 1995 (Wong 2009). Cities were hard-hit as financial strains on SOEs translated into tax arrears and defaults in payment to suppliers and even workers.

In the meantime, the burdens of social expenditures increased, as market reforms necessitated a wholesale revamping of how social security was provided. Under the policy of full employment (job assignments) and lifetime tenure for workers, SOEs and collectively owned enterprises had provided jobs and social welfare. The pension systems were funded by the enterprises on a pay-as-you-go basis, with generous benefits: retirement at 55–60 years of age, and pensions set at 70–75 percent of the final wage and indexed to current wage levels (World Bank 1997). As reforms separated enterprises from government budgets, and as SOEs declined, the social security provisions quickly disintegrated. Many of the obligations were transferred onto municipal budgets, and new social welfare programs had to be set up to take their place. For municipal governments, these changes coincided with accelerating urbanization that brought ever more people into cities, for whom infrastructure and services had to be provided.

Yet the intergovernmental fiscal system seemed to take no notice of the plight of municipal governments. In the public discourse leading up to the tax sharing system (TSS) reform in 1994, no mention was made of municipal finance. All attention was focused on how to revive revenue collections, and especially on regaining central government control over the budget. The reform that was implemented revamped the tax system and tax administration, introducing a value-added tax (VAT) on manufactured products and a business tax on services. It created a new central tax service to collect central and shared taxes. The reform also fundamentally changed revenue sharing with SNGs and clawed back revenues to the center. In the process, the reform ignored the changing expenditure needs of local governments, urban and rural alike (Fock and Wong 2008; Wong 2007; Wong and Bird

2008; World Bank 2002).[10] Nor did the reform give SNGs any revenue autonomy, with all authority for tax policy retained at the center.

Moreover, through the period of declining budgetary resources, the central government's capacity and willingness to aid poor regions withered. From 1994 to 1997, intergovernment transfers fell to less than 1 percent of GDP nationwide. As a result, SNGs were essentially left on their own to finance their expenditure responsibilities, and both vertical and horizontal disparities in service provision widened (Wong 2009; Wong and Bird 2008).

REVENUE ASSIGNMENT UNDER THE FORMAL FISCAL SYSTEM

Under the TSS introduced in 1994, taxes are divided into central taxes, shared taxes, and "local" taxes. The initial intent of the TSS was to move away from the negotiated sharing of general revenues under the previous system, to one where revenues would be divided by tax assignment. Only a limited number of taxes would be shared, with uniform sharing rates across regions (see Li 2006; 2010; Wong and Bird 2008; World Bank 2002). At present four taxes are shared: the VAT, the corporate income tax (CIT), the personal income tax (PIT), and the securities trading tax. The broad outline of current assignment of taxes is presented in table 11.7.

However, the simplicity and objectivity intended in the TSS apply only at the central–provincial division; at lower levels the system is far more complex and murky. This is because the TSS specified only how taxes would be divided between the central and "local" governments and left it to the provinces to further divide among the four levels of SNG.[11] Given that SNGs have no authority to introduce new taxes or change the bases or rates of taxes, and with only a few revenue-rich taxes available, the system evolved to one where local taxes are extensively shared among SNGs.

Under the principal of territoriality, the province has little direct claim to taxes except through its authority, conferred by national policy, to set revenue-sharing rules with subprovincial governments. Provinces have exercised this authority to levy a "tax" on local taxes, taking significant percentages of the main taxes. Arrangements differ across provinces; a sample of sharing rates is presented in table 11.8.

At the next lower tier, prefectures can likewise take a percentage of the local taxes accruing to counties. Some examples from Liaoning are offered in table 11.9. In recent years, to help improve the fiscal status of counties, the government has called for removing prefectures from this hierarchical flow, under the policy of "provinces directly managing counties" (*shenguanxian*). Under the policy, now implemented in

---

[10] Public services in the rural sector had been provided by the people's communes under the planned economy. When communes were disbanded in the early 1980s, in most localities these services were left with neither an organizational nor a financial framework, and coverage was severely eroded through the 1990s (see Wong 2007; World Bank 2002).

[11] The Chinese administrative system works as a nested hierarchy, in which each level of government interacts with only the next level up or down. The central government directs only the provincial governments, provincial governments report to the central government above and direct the prefectural level below, and so on down the hierarchy. For some implications of this setup, see Wong (2009; 2011).

TABLE 11.7

Tax assignments in China

Central taxes	Shared taxes	Local taxes
Excise (consumption)	Value-added tax (75/25)	Business tax
Customs duties	Corporate income tax (60/40)	Property tax
Vehicle purchase tax	Personal income tax (60/40)	Urban land use tax
	Securities trading tax (97/3)	Vehicle use tax
		Vehicle license tax
		Ship tonnage tax
		Deed tax
		Stamp tax
		Urban maintenance and construction tax
		Land value-added tax
		Farmland occupation tax
		Resource tax

This is a simplified version; for more details and exceptions, see Wong and Bird (2008).

TABLE 11.8

Sharing rates by tax type between province and prefecture levels (percentage of local receipts)

Province, year	VAT	CIT	PIT	Business tax	Resource tax
Guangdong, 2011	NA	50/50	50/50	50/50	NA
Hebei, 2009	40/60	50/50	25/75	0/100	40/60
Hunan, 2010	25/75	30/70	30/70	25/75	25/75
Liaoning, 2004	40/60	50/50	37.5/62.5	30/70	NA
Shandong, 2003	NA	20/80	0/100	20/80	NA
Shanxi, 2003	NA	50/50	50/50	NA	NA

Abbreviations: CIT, corporate income tax; NA, not applicable; PIT, personal income tax; VAT, value-added tax.
SOURCE: Documents on implementing "provinces managing counties," and fieldwork in Liaoning in 2005–2006.

more than two-thirds of the provinces, counties would receive the same percentages as applied previously to prefectures in all the provinces listed in table 11.8.

The composition of revenues is shown in table 11.10 for different levels of government. Nationally, the VAT, applied to manufacturing, repair, and assembly activities, is the most important tax, accounting for 40 percent of total tax revenues. For SNGs, the business tax levied on services is the most important, producing one-third of tax revenues in aggregate. The urban maintenance and construction tax, levied as a surcharge on the VAT and business tax, is an important source of funding that is earmarked for use in building and maintenance of urban facilities. It accounts for 8 percent of tax revenues in prefectures and 7 percent in counties. Because of the extensive sharing of the main taxes among subnational levels, the same six taxes top the list of revenue sources for the province, prefecture, and

TABLE 11.9
Sharing rates between municipalities and their subordinate counties in Liaoning (percentage of local receipts)

Prefecture, year	Province	Prefecture	County
Anshan, 2003			
VAT	40	20	40
CIT	50	12.5	37.5
PIT	37.5	25	37.5
Business tax	30	30	40
Property tax	50	0	50
Panjin and Yingkou, 2004			
VAT	40	24	36
CIT	50	20	30
PIT	37.5	25	37.5
Business tax	30	28	42
Property tax	50	20	30

Abbreviations: CIT, corporate income tax; PIT, personal income tax; VAT, value-added tax.

SOURCE: Fieldwork visit September 2004 and background papers from Panjin and Yingkou in 2004.

TABLE 11.10
Composition of tax revenues at each administrative level, 2007 (percentage of total)

Tax	National (2010)	Province	Prefecture/ municipality	County
Business tax	13.9	39.2	31.1	31.7
VAT*	39.2	17.4	19.2	21.1
CIT	15.9	24.3	15.4	12.5
Deed tax	3.1	2.5	9.6	6.4
Urban maintenance and construction tax	2.3	2.2	7.8	7.1
PIT	6.0	10.1	5.8	5.3
Property tax		0.8	3.6	4.0
Land value-added tax	1.1	0.8	2.4	2.8
Urban land use tax	1.6	0.6	1.8	2.7
Stamp tax	1.2	1.1	1.8	1.9
Resource tax	1.3	1.0	0.7	1.7
Farmland occupation tax	0.5	0.1	0.4	1.9
Vehicle purchase tax	1.1	0.0	0.4	0.5
Tobacco tax	2.2	0.0	0.0	0.3

Abbreviations: CIT, corporate income tax; PIT, personal income tax; VAT, value-added tax.

The township level is omitted because since 2002/2003 its importance has been substantially downgraded and its responsibilities (and revenues) moved upward to the county level.

*The national VAT includes VAT and excise on imports.

SOURCE: MOF *Compendium of local fiscal statistics* (2007).

TABLE 11.11

Fiscal trends by tier of government (percentage of national total)

Category	1993	1998	2002	2006	2009
Revenues					
Central	22	50	55	53	52
Provincial	13	10	12	12	11
Prefecture/municipality	34	20	16	17	16
County + township	32	20	17	19	21
Expenditures					
Central	34	29	31	25	20
Provincial	11	19	20	18	18
Prefecture/municipality	29	24	21	23	22
County + township	27	28	29	34	40

SOURCES: MOF *Compendium of local fiscal statistics* (various years); Wong (1997).

county levels. The similarities in revenue composition are especially striking at the prefectural and county levels.

Taxes on land and real estate have grown increasingly important in Chinese cities. The deed tax, an ad valorem levy on turnover of land and property, is the fourth most productive tax at the prefectural and county levels. Combined with the property tax, the land VAT, and urban land use tax, the four taxes levied on land and real estate produced 17 percent of tax revenues at the prefectural level and 16 percent at the county level in 2007. The percentage of land-based taxes has grown even faster in recent years amidst the booming land and real estate markets.

This tax structure encourages a strong growth orientation in SNGs, given that the bulk of revenue comes from productive activities, and lacking taxing powers, the only way to increase local revenues is through economic growth. With the growth of land-related taxes, real estate development has come to rival industrialization as the growth targeted by local officials. Even with vigorous local economic growth, though, SNGs at the lower tiers are fighting an uphill battle in this top-down intergovernmental fiscal system.

National aggregate statistics show that municipalities have fared poorly in revenue sharing. Taking the prefectural level as a proxy (where more than 50 percent of the urban population reside), the fiscal trends in table 11.11 show municipalities losing significant percentages in both budgetary revenues and expenditures after the 1994 reform. Collectively, these municipalities had less than half of their percentage of national revenue in 2009 compared to 1993. Although grants from higher-level governments have become a significant revenue source since 1993, the municipalities' percentage of national expenditures (after transfers) fell by one-quarter while their percentage of the national population more than doubled.

Going Outside the Budget

Faced with growing expenditure needs and inadequate resources from the formal fiscal system, SNGs turned to extrabudgetary channels. Indeed, SNGs and government agencies were encouraged to find their own supplementary sources of revenue since the gradualist, incremental reform aimed to avoid creating pockets of resistance and instead implemented across-the-board cuts that affected even core services (Wong 2009). In the late 1990s, public service providers, including schools providing basic education, received on average only one-half of their operating revenues from the budget and had to find the rest through fees and "other incomes."[12] Even local police departments typically received only budgetary support for salaries and had to buy their uniforms, batons, and other equipment from revenues collected through fines and penalties (Bai 2004).

Extrabudgetary Revenues from Fees and Levies

The first recourse for government departments and public service providers was to levy fees, user charges, fines, and penalties under incentives that allowed the collecting agencies to use a part of the receipts for bonuses and topping-up salaries (Wong 2009; World Bank 2005). With these high-powered incentives, fees and other levies proliferated. In the aggregate, revenues from fees and levies totaled 8–10 percent of GDP in the late 1990s. SNGs were reportedly financing half or more of their expenditures from extrabudgetary funds (EBFs), and the proliferation of fees had become a bane of businesses and citizens alike (Wong 1998; 2001). In 1997, for example, McDonald's restaurants in Beijing were on average paying 31 fees that purportedly went to supporting not only the normal Beijing municipal services, but also air shelter repairs, river cleaning, public festival decoration, and Communist Party propaganda (World Bank 2000).

Since then, the government has taken a number of measures to curb the proliferation of fees and charges. The strategy was to clamp down on unauthorized fees and levies, bring administrative fees collected by government departments and agencies into the budget as much as possible, improve monitoring of revenues and expenditures of the major items of the EBFs, and gradually convert them to taxes.

The efforts have achieved some measure of success. Many fees have been abolished, including, most famously, all rural levies under the rural fee reform campaign that was implemented during 2001–2003. Administrative fees continued to grow but are now incorporated into budget accounting, though not unified budgeting. In 1996, the category "government fund" (GF) was created, and 13 of the largest fees and funds were put under GF, including the road maintenance fee, the vehicle purchase fee, the railroad construction fund, electric power fund, the Three Gorges Dam fund, and airport management fees and construction fund. GFs are subject to budget management, treated as "below the line" items, and reported annually in the budget reports.

---

[12] For details of how public service providers were funded, see World Bank (2005).

By removing some of the biggest sources of EBFs (e.g., the 13 funds accounted for more than one-fourth of the EBFs in 1997) and tightening authorization of new EBFs, the government has succeeded in whittling down what is reported in the formal category of "extrabudgetary funds," which fell to 3.4 percent of GDP in 2003. In 2010 the MOF stopped reporting EBFs altogether. Instead, the new budget classification reports tax revenues plus "nontax revenues" (NTRs), the replacement for EBFs, as the total "ordinary budget." In 2010 NTRs were approximately 100 billion yuan (1.7 percent of GDP), equal to 12 percent of the ordinary budget.

This "victory" is largely Pyrrhic, however, since the GF category, rather than being the transitional stage for bringing EBFs into the budget, has grown secularly, with the addition of some large and rapidly growing sources of revenue that are well outside of budgetary allocation. In 2010, it comprised more than 50 funds, with revenues of 3.7 trillion yuan (9.2 percent of GDP), compared to 7.4 trillion yuan in the ordinary budget (MOF 2011). Moreover, major sources of funding fall outside of the formal EBF/NTR and GF categories. For municipalities, the three biggest are land, the social security funds, and borrowing.

Land Transfer Revenues

Aside from charging user fees and imposing quasi taxes, monetizing state assets was another avenue for supplementing the budget, and land is the principal asset of municipal governments.[13] In addition to existing city land, the conversion of farmland into nonagricultural use provides municipal governments with revenues. The value of this revenue stream was greatly enhanced by the constitution and several amendments, which specify that only the state can undertake the conversion of farmland, conferring a monopoly on land conveyance on local governments. Moreover, the law also fixes the procurement price of farmland at a multiple of its historical agricultural output, thus ensuring that the bulk of the rising values of urban land accrue to local governments (Cao, Feng, and Tao 2008; Tao et al. 2010).

SNGs began to tap this rich source of revenue in the early 1990s (Guan and Peng 2011; Wong 1997). With accelerated urbanization boosting land values, this has grown to be a key source of extrabudgetary revenue for municipal governments. However, until recently there was little public information about the size of land transfer revenues since they accrue almost entirely to local governments, and the central government has struggled to gain access.[14] Moreover, until 2001, land transfers were mostly made by administrative allocation and negotiation, and the real value of the transactions was largely hidden. With the increased use of auctions, land transfers have become more transparent. The Ministry of Land Resources has published national and provincial data since 2001 (table 11.12). However, the data were incomplete: an audit conducted by the National Audit Office (NAO) of 11 municipalities, including Beijing, Tianjin, Chongqing, and Guangzhou, found that during 2004–2006 land transfer revenues were underreported by 71 percent (Fu

---

[13]The 1982 constitution specifies that urban land is owned by the state while rural land is owned by the collectives.

[14]Gaining information was made more difficult because, until recent years, the central government was continually asserting its right to share the revenue.

TABLE 11.12

Revenues from land transfer (billion yuan)

Year	Transaction volume	Net income
2001	129.59	
2002	241.58	
2003	542.13	179.91
2004	641.22	233.98
2005	588.38	218.97
2006	807.76	297.83
2007	1221.67	454.15
2008	1037.53	361.19
2009	1396.48	NA
2010	3010.89	NA

NA, not applicable.

2009 and 2010 data are from MOF 2011. The 2010 figure is the sum of four funds: income from the transfer of use rights for state-owned land, user charges for bringing new land under construction, the fund on profits of state-owned land, and receipts from agricultural land development (MOF 2011). This may be inconsistent with earlier figures reported by the Ministry of Land Resources. Income from land transfers alone was 2819.77 billion.

SOURCE: Ministry of Land Resources (2010).

2010). In 2007 the government designated land revenues as GF and required them to be remitted to the treasury and budget management. This seems to have improved reporting somewhat. The NAO found that for 2007–2008, the 11 municipalities underreported land transfer revenues by a much reduced 20 percent.

However, it is difficult to estimate the contribution of land revenues to municipal finance since they are partly used to compensate households for resettlement. Moreover, as shown in a later section, the importance of land revenues far exceeds their contribution to net income since it is also the main asset used by municipal governments as collateral for borrowing.

Social Security Funds

The social security funds (SSF) were created in 1996, with the introduction of insurance schemes for urban employees that provide coverage for pensions, work injury, unemployment, maternity, and health (see Hussain 2007; Wang 2005; Watson 2009). City-level pooling of pension obligations had begun in the 1980s, and this transfer was formalized in 1991, when the State Council introduced universal pooling of pension burdens and placed them at the city level, be they provincial, prefectural, or county-level cities.[15] Through the 1990s, the system was adjusted in several steps, creating the framework that exists today. The new system has moved the provision of pensions from defined benefits to a two-pillar system combining a

---

[15] State Council decision on pension insurance system reform for urban enterprise employees. June 1991. Cited in Chen (2009).

small social pension with individual accounts based on contributions made during the employee's work life (Dong and Ye 2003).

Under the new system, each city is responsible for collecting the employer and employee contributions to each scheme and managing the fiduciary responsibilities for the SSF. Although the basic framework is based on regulations issued by the central government, many details of the schemes are left to the discretion of the provincial and municipal governments (Hussain 2007). To minimize fiscal risks, cities were permitted to vary contribution rates and benefit levels, though some efforts have been made to harmonize them in recent years. At their inception, however, the SSFs were saddled with some unfunded liabilities when the pension scheme was obliged to accept the transfer of existing participants from the unfunded system, including retirees and employees who were approaching retirement, with no provisions for covering the costs. As a result, many pension pools are in deficit. One Chinese scholar estimated total deficits of all pension pools at 2.5 trillion yuan in 2005 and projected that it would grow to 6 trillion yuan in 30 years (Wang 2005).

Even though cities are the budget unit for social security, the SSFs are managed mainly by the Ministry of Human Resources and Social Security and its subnational counterparts outside the budget. The "social security and employment assistance" expenditure item in the budget comprises expenditures on social welfare, disaster relief, and fiscal subsidies to the SSF to cover shortfalls, while the main expenditures on social security are made under the SSF. Under China's decentralized statistical system, information on the SSF is reported by the ministry, separately from fiscal data.

With urbanization, an aging population, and with recent policies that have significantly expanded social safety net provisions, SSF expenditures have grown rapidly. Coverage has grown from just SOE pensions and an unemployment insurance program created in the 1980s, to include a pension program for residents who never held a formal sector job, as well as basic medical, work injury, and maternity insurance programs created in the 1990s. Since 1990, contributions to the SSF have grown from 1 percent of GDP to 4.7 percent in 2010, averaging an annual growth of 27 percent, scattered in the more than 2000 local SSF pools.

China's Fragmented Municipal Finance

The salient feature of these components of extrabudgetary finance is that information is scattered in different channels, and they are not always reported in full. Putting together all available information, figure 11.4 shows the "comprehensive budget," of all known resources mobilized for public expenditure excluding borrowing. Nationwide, the comprehensive budget has grown rapidly, from 27.2 percent of GDP in 2006 to 34.9 percent in 2010. Most of the growth came from land, a notoriously volatile revenue source. The ordinary budget (budget plus NTRs) also grew, from 18.9 percent to 20.9 percent, but its percentage was declining, to just 57 percent of the total in 2010. For SNGs, the composition is even more weighted toward nonbudgetary revenues: in 2010 the budget fell to less than 40 percent of the total (figure 11.5). Even with NTRs, the ordinary budget from own revenues is less than one-half of the comprehensive budget.

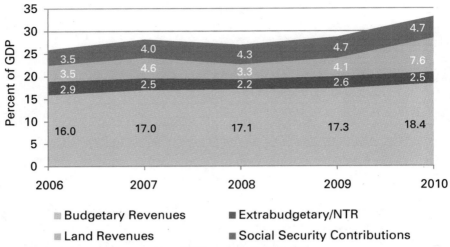

FIGURE 11.4
China's comprehensive budget (percent GDP)

■ Budgetary Revenues ■ Extrabudgetary/NTR
■ Land Revenues ■ Social Security Contributions

NOTE: EBF figures were used for 2006–2007, and NTRs were used for 2008–2010.
SOURCES: *CSY* (2010; 2011); MOF *China finance yearbook* (2010); Ministry of Land Resources (2010); MOF (2011).

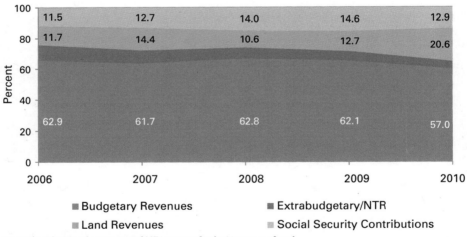

FIGURE 11.5
Composition of subnational revenues by source

■ Budgetary Revenues ■ Extrabudgetary/NTR
■ Land Revenues ■ Social Security Contributions

NOTE: The subnational percentage of SSF is assumed to be 90 percent of total.
SOURCES: *CSY* (2010; 2011); MOF *China finance yearbook* (2010); Ministry of Land Resources (2010); MOF (2011).

A composite picture of the comprehensive budgets of prefectural-level munici-palities is constructed in table 11.13, which includes transfers from higher-level governments. In this composite, land revenues exceed the size of the municipali-ties' ordinary budget revenues, though not when transfers are included. SSFs are almost 20 percent of the total, and this percentage can be expected to grow in the future.

Information on the different strands of revenue for Guangzhou, a prefectural-level city that is the provincial capital of prosperous Guangdong province, and Shanghai, a provincial-level city, is assembled in table 11.14. It is not surprising that these

TABLE 11.13

A composite picture of prefectural-level municipalities budget, 2010 (billion RMB)

Revenue source	All prefectural cities	Percentage of total
Ordinary budget revenues	1296.38	29.9
Gross transfers including tax rebates	504.65	11.6
Land revenues	1513.72	34.9
Government funds (excluding land)	174.82	4.0
Social security fund	847.04	19.5
Comprehensive budget	**4336.61**	**100.0**

The average population in 2009 was 1.16 million. The table is based on the following assumptions:

1. NTRs are used in place of EBFs to avoid double counting. Prefecture percentage is assumed to be 45 percent.
2. Prefectural percentage of budget revenues from 2009 is used for both own revenues and transfers.
3. Prefectural percentage of land revenues from 2004 is used and is assumed to be unchanged at 52 percent.
4. For all other components, 50 percent is used as the prefectural percentage. This is probably an underestimate.

SOURCE: Estimated from data used in figures 11.4 and 11.5.

TABLE 11.14

Revenue composition of Guangzhou and Shanghai, 2009 (billion RMB)

Revenue source	Guangzhou (percentage of total)	Shanghai (percentage of total)
Ordinary budget revenues	70.27 (35.5)	254.0 (49.4)
Gross transfers, including tax rebates	16.43 (8.3)	41.5 (8.1)
Land revenues	55.15 (27.9)	104.3 (20.3)
Government funds, excluding land	40.50 (20.5)	
Social security fund	15.36 (7.8)	114.3 (22.2)
Comprehensive budget	**197.70 (100)**	**514.13 (100)**
Population (million)	6.55	17.02
Per capita fiscal resources (thousand RMB)	30.20	30.21

SOURCES: CCSY (2010); MOF China finance yearbook (2009); Ministry of Human Resources and Social Security (2010); National Bureau of Statistics (2010b); Ministry of Land Resources (2010); National Bureau of Statistics (2010a); Shanghai Financial College (2010); Shanghai Statistical Yearbook (2010).

larger cities, with more diversified economic bases, draw a larger percentage of their revenues from taxes under the formal fiscal system. Even for them, land revenues form a significant part of revenues. In Shanghai, when direct and indirect taxes are included, land-based activities including real estate development have reportedly accounted for 35 percent of total revenues since 2006. In 2009 they accounted for fully 50 percent of the growth in revenues (Shanghai Financial College 2010, 6).

The SSF comprises nearly a quarter of revenues in Shanghai, and an even larger percentage of expenditures when direct budgetary expenditures are included. As one of the oldest industrial centers, Shanghai's SSF is burdened with huge "legacy" costs from the socialist system. In 2008, the municipality spent 12.14 billion yuan in fiscal subsidies to cover SSF arrears, absorbing 17–18 percent of budgetary expenditures (Shanghai Financial College 2010, 121). Because Shanghai also has the oldest population among Chinese cities, these subsidies can be expected to rise.

HOW DOES A MUNICIPAL BUDGET LOOK?

A typical municipal budget presentation includes budgetary information and some sketchy information on extrabudgetary revenues and expenditures (now called NTRs, in the "ordinary budget"). In the case of Jiangyin, a county-level city in prosperous Jiangsu province, the city statistical yearbook offers an unusually detailed disaggregation for EBFs that shows EBFs providing supplementary resources for funding many types of municipal expenditures (table 11.15).[16] Altogether, the EBFs were 941 million yuan in 2009, less than 10 percent of the size of the budget.

Jiangyin also had 1.6 billion yuan in SSF expenditures, as well as 2.9 billion yuan in GF expenditures, in addition to EBFs. Unfortunately, the yearbook does not provide the sources of GFs, so it is also not clear whether the figure includes land revenues, and no breakdown was provided on the uses of the SSF and GF.

The data for Jiangyin mirror the fragmented nature of the budget for municipalities overall, where management of the revenues is highly compartmentalized. The municipal budget allocates only revenues from the ordinary budget. All other revenues, from land, SSFs, and the different funds and fees that make up the EBF/NTRs and GFs, are allocated by the collecting agencies and departments. At the national level, there is no consolidated account of these resources. Even in a municipality, if such a consolidated account exists, it is not publicized and is not reported even to the people's congresses.[17]

The composition of expenditures from the ordinary budget accounts for SNGs, along with those for Guangzhou and Jiangyin, is presented in table 11.16. Data that are currently available do not permit a detailed breakdown of expenditures from the comprehensive budget, but we can assume that, overall, it is likely to tip the balance slightly toward social expenditures, and the trend will continue in that direction. SSFs are spent on social services, along with a majority of EBFs/NTRs,

---

[16] This is consistent with data from earlier studies showing that departmental expenditures often far exceed budget appropriations (World Bank 2002; 2005; 2007b).

[17] Guan and Peng (2011) note that land revenues are not reported to the people's congresses.

TABLE 11.15

Composition of fiscal expenditures in Jiangyin municipality, 2009 (million yuan)

Expenditure	Budgetary	Extrabudgetary	Social security fund	Government fund
General public services	1195.72	70.25		
Public safety	574.58	23.36		
Education	1681.03	323.48		
Science and technology	223.93	1.27		
Culture, sports, and media	99.67	16.97		
Social security and employment assistance	682.15	107.17		
Medical and health care	313.15	60.64		
Environmental protection	358.96	44.8		
Community affairs	2277.67	161.31		
Agriculture, forestry, and water conservancy	477.71	88.9		
Transportation	430.52	15.94		
Mining, power, and information industries	897.41			
Grain and material reserves	141.46			
Earthquake reconstruction assistance	140			
Other expenditures	662.79	26.83		
Total	10,169.83	940.92	1605.85	2900.1
Comprehensive budget	**15,616.7**			
Per capita (yuan)*	12,976			
Per capita, by component (yuan)*	8,450	782	1,334	2,410
Percentage of comprehensive budget	65.1%	6.0%	10.3%	18.6%

*The population of Jiangyin municipality in 2009 was 1.2 million.
SOURCE: *Jiangyin Municipal Statistical Bureau* (2010, 157).

TABLE 11.16

Composition of budgetary expenditures by broad category (percent)

Category	All SNGs 2010	Guangzhou 2009	Jiangyin 2009
Development	35.6	28.2	39.7
Social	42.7	41.2	35.1
Administration	21.7	30.5	25.2

All data are regrouped and recalculated on the same basis as table 11.6.
SOURCES: *CSY* (2011); National Bureau of Statistics (2010a); Jiangyin Municipal Statistical Bureau (2010).

assuming that the composition of expenditures in Jiangyin is broadly representative.[18] Land revenues are mostly earmarked for use in land preparation and urban infrastructure (i.e., 100 percent for development). Except for 2010, the sum of SSF and 60 percent of EBFs/NTRs has in the past few years been larger than land reve-

---

[18] The expenditures in Jiangyin are divided as 60 percent social and the rest for development and administration.

nues, tipping the balance toward social spending overall. However, this balance shifts sharply when we include borrowing.

Finally, a key feature of China's municipal finance is that a large portion of the urban population is excluded from urban services, most notably social welfare, social security, education, health care, and housing, and this is not reflected in the accounting of revenues and expenditures. These are the migrants who lack *hukou*, now estimated to be one-third of the total urban population (Miller 2012). This is likely part of the reason that China's urbanization has not spawned large slums, because migrants are discouraged from bringing their dependents to the cities with them.

INVESTMENT IN INFRASTRUCTURE

The provision of infrastructure is vital to supporting urbanization, and how to finance these investments is a central component of municipal finance. Under market reforms, public investment management has changed dramatically in China (Wong 2011). By far the most important was the rapid withdrawal of budgetary inputs to investment that was driven by fiscal decline. Except for a small spike under the fiscal stimulus programs in the late 1990s and again in 2008–2010, the percentage of budgetary inputs has remained below 5 percent of total investment since 1993 (table 11.17).[19] "Self-raised" funds have always been large and now finance more than three-quarters of the total. However, their composition is amorphous and ill-defined.

The second important change was that investment became decentralized. Figure 11.6 shows the SNG percentage of budgetary investment rising in line with the percentage of budgetary expenditures.[20] An additional aspect of the decentralization of investment responsibilities is that, just as higher-level governments were offloading them to SNGs, fiscally constrained SNGs often devolved the responsibilities to public institutions such as schools and hospitals and, likewise, encouraged them to find their own resources.

The authorities for investment decisions were also progressively devolved. Under the planned economy, investment projects went through a formal process of preparation that included feasibility studies, technical reviews, and appraisals before approval. Project approval authority was vested with the State Planning Commission (now renamed the National Development and Reform Commission [NDRC]) and its subnational counterparts, the DRCs. This was a key part of the macro coordination function performed by the NDRC, because project approval was a precondition for application for land, raw materials, and funding, including bank loans. Through the transition, project approval was progressively decentralized to lower-level governments. The decisive reform came in 2004, when the government limited the requirement for administrative approval to only projects financed by public funds and mega projects with investments exceeding a specified threshold

---

[19] For the 2008–2010 fiscal stimulus and its impact on public investment, see Wong (2011).

[20] In 2007 the MOF changed budget classification systems and stopped reporting capital spending separately from recurrent expenditures.

TABLE 11.17

Sources of finance for fixed investment (percentage of total)

Category	1982	1993	1995	2000	2003	2007	2009
Budget	22.7	3.7	3.5	6.8	4.8	3.9	5.1
Domestic credit	14.3	23.5	21.7	23.6	23.0	15.3	15.7
Foreign	4.9	7.3	13.1	5.8	4.5	3.4	1.8
Self-raised and other	58.1	65.5	61.7	63.8	67.6	77.4	77.4

Self-raised funds are a prefecture's or municipality's own receipts of enterprises or institutions. "Other" includes capital from bonds issued by enterprises or banks, levies, own capital of the administrative unit, and donations.

SOURCES: National Bureau of Statistics (2005), and *CSY* (2011).

FIGURE 11.6

Subnational percentages of budgetary expenditures and investment

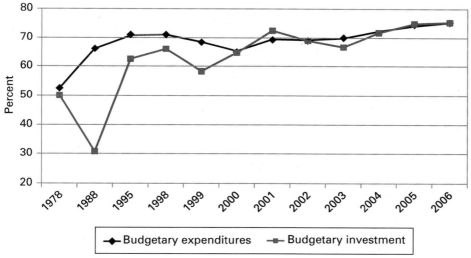

SOURCES: *CSY* (2011).

or in strategic sectors (State Council 2004; Wong 2011). Given the diversified funding of public investments and a lack of clear definition on what constituted "public funds," this decision was widely interpreted by SNGs to mean that only projects funded by the budget were required to go through the approval framework. The vast majority of public investment was considered exempted from 2004 onward, and the gatekeeper function of the NDRC and DRCs has been severely eroded.[21]

Just as there is no consolidated account of municipal budgets, there is no consolidated account of capital expenditures at the municipal level. In fact, it appears

---

[21]See Mikesell et al. (2011) for practices in Guangdong. In fieldwork conducted in December 2010, I learned that even in localities that retained administrative approval procedures, the exercise was largely pro forma, as approval was always granted if funding was assured.

TABLE 11.18

Investments by source and by sector, 2007

Sector	By source					By management jurisdiction	
	Budget	Loans	Foreign	Self-raised	Other	Central	Local
As percentage of total							
Social service facilities							
Education	12.3	12.9	0.6	66.2	8.1	10.2	89.8
Health	9.3	11.7	0.6	72.6	5.8	5.3	94.7
Infrastructure							
Urban water supply	11.1	20.3	3.7	58.1	6.8	1	99
Electricity	6	43.6	1	43.5	5.9	38.6	61.4
Transportation	13.5	33.3	1.5	43.2	8.4	24.4	75.6
Telecommunication	1.5	1.9	0.9	92.9	2.8	50.7	49.3
Infrastructural investment	**9.8**	**34.1**	**1.4**	**47.7**	**7**	**30.4**	**69.6**
All investments	**3.9**	**15.3**	**3.4**	**60.6**	**16.8**	**11.2**	**88.8**
As billions RMB yuan							
Infrastructure investment	216.9	756.6	30.9	1060.1	156.1	694.6	1587
All investment	585.7	2304.4	513.3	9137.3	2539.6	1316.5	10,429.9

SOURCE: Assembled from *CSY* (2008).

that there is no capital budget at any level of government (Mikesell et al. 2011; Wong 2011). Municipal governments finance infrastructural investments from budget appropriations, earmarked tax revenues (chiefly the urban maintenance and construction tax), extrabudgetary (now nontax) revenues, government funds, and land revenues, as well as policy loans from the state development banks.

The diversified and decentralized character of public investment is demonstrated in table 11.18, which shows that budgetary allocations are a minor percentage of investment funding, and they are only weakly tilted toward public infrastructure.[22] Even in the social sectors, the budget accounted for only 9–12 percent of investments, and the bulk of funding came from "self-raised" funds: user charges, fees, and other borrowing.

For urban infrastructure such as public utilities (water supply and drainage, sewerage, residential gas and heating, and public transport), parks, sanitation, and flood control, the Ministry of Construction (MOC) publishes a yearbook that provides more disaggregated data on urban construction and gives what looks to be a comprehensive accounting of funding sources and uses (tables 11.19 and 11.20). Unfortunately, the MOC coverage is incomplete, because it includes only activities of the urban construction departments. It does not include investments in housing, electricity, telecommunications, or ports, airports, and railways, nor does it include investments in social facilities such as sports stadiums, schools, clinics, and hospitals. But even for the subsectors that are included, the coverage appears to be

---

[22]Data from 2007 are chosen to avoid distortions introduced by the massive fiscal stimulus program implemented in 2008–2010.

TABLE 11.19

Sources of fiscal funds for urban maintenance and construction, 2008

Fund source	Billion yuan	Percentage
Central government allocation	7.56	1.3
Provincial government allocation	8.9	1.6
Municipal fiscal funds	**519.06**	**92.5**
Earmarked allocation	133.57	23.8
Urban maintenance and construction tax	74.43	13.3
Surcharge on urban utilities	8.96	1.6
Urban facilities charge on construction	33.18	5.9
User charges on urban facilities	26.33	4.7
• Bridge tolls	9.75	1.7
• Sewage treatment fee	12.32	2.2
• Garbage collection fees	2.31	0.4
• Waste water drainage fee	0.24	0.0
Receipts from land conveyance	210.54	37.5
Water charges	2.54	0.5
Asset income	1.63	0.3
Other income	28.4	5.1
Others	25.58	4.6
Total	561.10	

SOURCE: MOC (2009).

TABLE 11.20

Urban public infrastructure construction investment by sector, 2008

	Billion RMB	Percentage
Total investment	**736.82**	
Water	29.54	4.0
Gas	16.35	2.2
Central heating supply	26.97	3.7
Public transport	103.72	14.1
Roads and bridges	358.41	48.6
Waste water disposal	49.60	6.7
of which waste water treatment	26.47	3.6
Flood control	11.96	1.6
Parks and green space	64.98	8.8
Sanitation	22.20	3.0
of which garbage disposal	5.06	0.7
Others	53.08	7.2
New assets creation	415.45	56.4

SOURCE: MOC (2009).

incomplete. For example, for 2008 the MOC reported investments totaling RMB 29.54 billion in urban water supply and 16.35 billion in residential gas supply, while the NBS reported investments of 104.54 and 43.63 billion, respectively (*CSY 2009*, table 5–15; MOC 2009, table 4-1-2). On the funding side, while some land revenues go to funding urban maintenance and construction, most are usually reserved for larger-scale infrastructural projects undertaken by other departments (Mikesell et al. 2011).

The Emergence of Local Investment Corporations

One of the most important developments in municipal finance in China over the past two decades is the emergence of local investment corporations (LICs), which have been instrumental in helping SNGs achieve and maintain high levels of investment in infrastructure. Around the world, borrowing is widely used for public investments in infrastructure, and this method of financing is considered both efficient and fair (Bird 2005). In China, however, the 1994 Budget Law prohibits SNGs from borrowing without explicit permission from the State Council (Article 28).

To work around this constraint, starting in the 1980s SNGs, mostly at the prefectural and provincial levels, turned to the creation of special financial vehicles to undertake the task of raising funds for public investment. They were initially created as financially independent, single-purpose entities, often for the purpose of taking on loans from international financial institutions. Being financially independent restricted their scope to undertakings with the capacity for debt servicing, and these corporations were prevalent in the construction and operation of toll roads, power companies, water companies, and utilities.

A breakthrough came in 1992, when Shanghai created the first broad-based investment corporation to undertake investment in urban infrastructure, the General Corporation of Shanghai Municipal Property (SMPC), and gave it the mission to coordinate and provide for the construction of facilities such as water supply, sewerage, roads, and utility hookups. To finance these tasks, the corporation was assigned a variety of fiscal funds from the municipal budget and authorized to borrow (figure 11.7). Its creation allowed a quantum leap in financing for infrastructure to support urban renewal and expansion in Shanghai, raising it from the level of a few billion yuan per year prior to the creation of SMPC, to 17 billion and 38 billion in 1993 and 1994.[23] Investment in urban infrastructure totaled 540 billion yuan over the period 1998–2004 (Gao 2007), and the number of corporations of this type grew to 10 (Wu 2011).

Over time, the model spread to other municipalities. By the turn of the century, most cities had established LICs, and they came to play an increasingly key role in financing urbanization in many localities (Su and Zhao 2007). As they became more accepted, their separation from local public finances appears to have been relaxed, and SNGs began to guarantee many bank loans for LICs. Typically, the LICs raise and bundle bank loans and other financing, using a variety of municipal

---

[23] Investment in infrastructure was RMB 3.6, 4.8, and 6.1 in 1990, 1991, and 1992, respectively (SASS 1988).

FIGURE 11.7

General Corporation of Shanghai Municipal Property (SMPC)

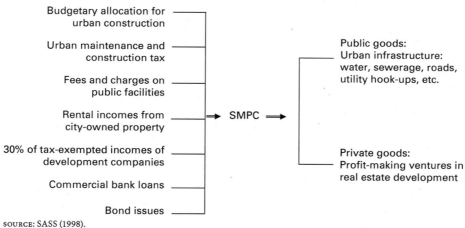

SOURCE: SASS (1998).

assets, including budgetary and off-budget revenues as equity and collateral. Increasingly, with urbanization bringing rising land values, land has become the principal asset backing LICs, and municipalities have pledged future receipts from land revenues as collateral for bank loans.[24]

Before 2009, even though LICs had by then accumulated 5 trillion yuan in bank loans, very little was known about them (National Audit Office 2011). The macroeconomic risks they pose came to light dramatically during the fiscal stimulus program, when they received their first official endorsement. In October 2008, the government announced a RMB 4 trillion stimulus program to combat contagion from the global financial crisis.[25] To ensure SNGs had sufficient funds to support the ambitious investment program, fiscal rules were relaxed, and SNGs were invited to borrow.[26] LICs went "viral": in 2009 alone they took on 3 trillion yuan in new loans, and in the first quarter of 2010 they took 40 percent of new credit nationwide (*Investors Bulletin* 2010; Wei 2010). It was only when the China Banking Regulatory Commission became concerned with the pace of lending to LICs that they discovered the near-complete absence of information about them. Previously they had existed in the interstices of China's mixed economy. They were never assigned a supervisory agency, and no one had asked for regular reporting of their activities.

Since mid-2009, the government has been engaged in a massive catching-up exercise in collecting information on LICs and their operations, culminating with a nationwide audit that took place during March–May 2011, involving

---

[24] The 2011 survey of LICs conducted by the National Audit Office (2011, 11) found that future land revenues were pledged as collateral for bank loans in 309 prefectures and 1,131 counties, equal to 93 percent and 56 percent of the those administrative units, respectively.

[25] For an analysis of how the fiscal stimulus program was implemented, see Wong (2011).

[26] In a joint document, the People's Bank of China and the China Banking Regulatory Commission (2009) called for "supporting localities with appropriate conditions to organize and build financial platforms, issue corporate debt and medium-term notes and other financial products, to broaden the channels of funding for providing counterpart funds for central government investment projects" (cited in Wei 2010, 2, my translation).

TABLE 11.21

TABLE 11.21

Local investment corporation debt, year-end 2010

Reporting agency	Number of LICs	LIC debt (trillion RMB)	Percentage of SNG revenue	Percentage of GDP
People's Bank of China	>10,000	<14.4	355	36
China Banking Regulatory Commission	9,828	9.1	224	23
National Audit Office	6,576	5	123	13

Abbreviations: GDP, gross domestic product; LIC, local investment corporation; SNG, subnational government.
SOURCES: *CSY* (2011); Zhang and Batson (2011).

41,000 staff from the NAO and their local subsidiaries (National Audit Office 2011). But even now the numbers are disputed as agencies disagree on what an LIC is (table 11.21).

Local Government Debt

While the LICs were the main vehicle for SNG borrowing, they were not alone. In its survey, the NAO had focused its mission on uncovering all debt guaranteed explicitly or implicitly by local governments. It found SNG liabilities totaling RMB 10.7 trillion at year-end 2010 (equal to 263 percent of their own revenues and 27 percent of GDP in 2010), of which LICs accounted for only half. Government departments accounted for a quarter, public service units (universities, schools, hospitals, research organizations, etc.) accounted for 18 percent, and "others" the rest. Almost 80 percent of the debt came from bank loans, 7 percent from bond issuance, and the rest from individuals and enterprises.

It seems the prohibition on local government borrowing was completely ineffective and served only to push it underground and out of the purview of the national authorities. All levels of SNG were involved, starting in the 1980s with the provinces. By the early 1990s, nearly all prefectures and counties were borrowing, and it had become a significant source of funding for SNGs, especially for infrastructure, but also other expenditures. In 2009 alone, at the peak of credit expansion under the stimulus program, SNGs borrowed as much as 4 trillion yuan, compared with their comprehensive revenues of 9.5 trillion.[27] While 2009 was an extreme year, the great boom in local building projects over the past 5–6 years, from new government districts, airports, subways, museum, and sports stadiums to new university campuses, suggests that funding has been readily available, much of it from borrowing.[28]

---

[27] The China Banking Regulatory Commission estimated that LICs took one-third of new credit in 2009, or 3.2 trillion yuan (*Investors Bulletin* 2010). Other local government entities presumably also took new debt during the year.

[28] A joint study found that in planning subway projects municipal officials generally worked without a financial plan and were confident that funds would be available. They also universally chose extremely large projects and underground options even though traffic volumes and building costs pointed to light rail as the superior option (National Development and Reform Commission and World Bank 2010).

The Soft Budget Constraint for Borrowing and Infrastructural Investment

In borrowing to finance infrastructure, China is following common practices in other parts of the world. Where it differs is in the unsupervised nature of the borrowing, not only by national authorities, but also, apparently, at the local level as well. In a trenchant critique, researchers in the NDRC Investment Research Institute described the current system of local investment finance as operating under "the three no's": no guiding framework, no limit, and no accountability (Wang, Gao, and He 2010). There is no overall framework that defines the scope of public investment. Municipalities often lack an investment plan that includes consideration of total debt levels. LICs often do not compile an assets and liabilities account, and they are so closely linked to SNGs that it is difficult to separate out and define their respective responsibilities. In China's immature financial system, banks are ill-equipped to provide the discipline expected from capital markets, especially when municipal finances are so complex and nontransparent. In any case, after more than 20 years of hypergrowth, there was a widespread belief that land values will always rise and that government can make good on guarantees.

REBUILDING MUNICIPAL FINANCE FOR THE TWENTY-FIRST CENTURY

Municipal finance in China today is the product of ad hoc, adaptive experimentation over the past three decades, a period during which the economy underwent three transitions: from a socialist planned economy to a market-oriented economy, from an agrarian society to an urban industrial society, and from being one of the world's poorest economies to a middle-income country. These transitions wreaked havoc on the preexisting social and economic organizations, and new ones had to be created. With the central government preoccupied with the fiscal crisis brought on by the decline of the state economy, municipalities were left on their own to cope with their changing environment.

In this maelstrom, municipal governments faced enormous pressures on two fronts: to provide a new social safety net to replace the one under the state economy, and to provide infrastructure to support the fast-unfolding economic growth and the migrants flooding in. They improvised. One tactic adopted was to limit eligibility for urban services to reduce the growth in demand for them, and the hukou system provided a convenient, fool-proof mechanism for excluding the new migrants.[29] The other was to go off-budget in search of resources, and SNGs displayed remarkable ingenuity in doing so.

This "model" of municipal finance, and especially many of its revenue mechanisms, had grown out of the extremely harsh fiscal environment that SNGs faced in the 1980s and 1990s, when mobilization of resources in support of growth was accepted as of paramount importance. The information examined in this chapter shows that municipal governments have overdelivered on this objective, mobiliz-

---

[29] This was noted in Kirkby (1985) and called "industrialization on the cheap."

ing off-budget resources to provide services and building massive amounts of infrastructure.

However, this laissez faire model of municipal finance has long outlived its usefulness, and the costs are piling up. In the twenty-first century, China is a global economic power, and its national objectives have shifted to a broader agenda that also calls for rebalancing the economic growth away from the high savings- and investment-driven growth to a more consumption-driven growth, and taking steps toward building a more inclusive "harmonious society" where citizens benefit more equally from China's economic miracle.[30] The dynamics of the current municipal finance system, where incentives for SNGs are lopsided in favor of developing off-budget revenues, are fundamentally at odds with this new agenda. The complex and opaque nature of the current municipal finances is also out of step with the government program to move toward transparency in the public sector and permit greater participation.

Moreover, the model is unsustainable. The most pressing immediate problem is that SNGs and their LICs have run up a mountain of debt that threatens to bring the banking sector grinding to a halt. The NAO reported that more than one-half of the 10.7 trillion yuan was due in 2011, 2012, and 2013. With the central government taking measures both to clamp down on new lending to LICs and to cool down the superheated housing price inflation, many SNGs have been unable to service their debt as land markets have slowed. Even in Beijing, for example, the Municipal Land Bureau reported that land lease revenues had slowed to a total of 25 billion yuan during the first five months of 2011, insufficient to cover the monthly interest cost of more than 10 billion yuan on the 250 billion yuan debt for the municipal land bank (*New Century* 2011). Nationwide, a mass default was avoided only when the government ordered banks in February 2012 to roll over their loans to LICs (Rabinovitch 2012). A more permanent bailout will likely have to be worked out step-by-step over the next few years.

Nor is the heavy reliance of municipal governments on one-off land lease sales sustainable. With leases running 40–70 years, urban land is virtually a nonrenewable resource, and in the more developed coastal cities it is already providing a declining portion of municipal revenues (Wang 2011).

As municipal finance evolved over the past 30 years, the patchwork of ad hoc responses left many issues unresolved, among them the coordination between levels of government coexisting within expanding metropolitan regions. Acute conflicts have arisen in China over the ownership of land, tax bases, and social assets, along with problems of coordinating infrastructure and service provision (Shanghai Financial College 2010). Accommodations are worked out on a case-by-case basis by the administrative units themselves, and little information is reported systematically about the arrangements. It may be more equitable and efficient to work out a national framework and provide guidance on best practices.

Finally, the decentralized financing has given rise to a two-tier society that keeps rural migrants permanently out of the mainstream of urban life. Although

---

[30]These goals have been repeated in official statements since 2003 and were embedded in the 11th Five Year Plan (2006–2010) and reiterated in the current 12th Five Year Plan.

their relative deprivation had been alleviated for the past three decades by the economic growth and job creation that brought rising incomes to the rural populace, the glaring unfairness is building social tensions and hindering investments in human development. The magnitude of the problem can be glimpsed in Shanghai, where the percentage of the nonhukou population staying for more than 6 months has grown from 20 percent of the total in 2000 to 39 percent in 2010 (Shanghai Statistical Yearbook 2011). Incorporating migrants into the provision urban services will require central government participation in financing them.

In the twenty-first century, China is an urban nation. Rebuilding the system of municipal finance must move to the top of the government's policy agenda. For a new system that can efficiently mobilize and manage fiscal and financial resources to deliver social welfare and infrastructure, municipal governments need access to more transparent and sustainable sources of finance from taxes, user charges, and grants. Greater revenue discretion, along with transparent and regulated access to credit, should help to harden their budget constraints. The first step toward rebuilding the system should be a rationalization of the intergovernmental fiscal system that assigns revenues and responsibilities in a way that is better aligned with the decentralized, increasingly mobile society that China has become.

REFERENCES

Asian Development Bank. 2000. *Managing urban change—strategic options for municipal governance and finance in China.* PRC:TA 2924—Study of Municipal Finance. Manila, Philippines: Asian Development Bank.

Bahl, Roy. 2011. Intergovernmental fiscal relations and local public finance: What is next on the reform agenda. In *China's local public finance in transition*, ed. Joyce Y. Man and Yu-Hung Hong. Cambridge, MA: Lincoln Institute of Land Policy.

Bai, Nansheng. 2004. A police story. Paper presented at the Conference on Rural Change in China, Peking University (July 5–6).

Bernstein, Thomas. 1977. *Up to the mountains and down to the villages: The transfer of youth from urban to rural China.* New Haven, CT: Yale University Press.

Bird, Richard. 2005. Getting it right: Financing urbanization in China. *Asia-Pacific Tax Bulletin* (March/April):107–117.

Brixi, Hana. 2009. China: Urban services and governance. World Bank Policy Research Working Paper 5030. Washington, DC: World Bank.

Cao, Guangzhong, Changchun Feng, and Ran Tao. 2008. Local "land finance" in China's urban expansion: Challenges and solutions. *China and World Economy* 16(2):19–30.

Chan, Kam Wing. 2003. Chinese Census 2000: New opportunities and challenges. *China Review* 3(2):1–12.

———. 2009. Measuring the urban million. *China Economic Quarterly* (March):21–26.

Chan, Kam Wing, Vernon Henderson, and Kai Yuen Tsui. 2008. Spatial dimensions of Chinese economic development. In *China's great transformation: Origins, mechanisms, and consequences of the post-reform economic boom*, ed. Thomas Rawski and Loren Brandt, 776–828. Cambridge, U.K.: Cambridge University Press.

Chan, Kam Wing, and Ying Hu. 2003. Urbanization in China in the 1990s: New definition, different series, and revised trends. *China Review* 3(2):49–71.

Chen, Shanzhe. 2009. Ministry of Human Resources and Social Security announces that provincial pooling will be implemented this year. *21st Century Economic Herald*, (February 20). http://www.sina.com.cn/china/hgjj/20090220/23505884229.html

Dong, Keyong, and Xiangfeng Ye. 2003. Social security system reform in China. *China Economic Review* 14:417–425.

Fock, Achim, and Christine Wong. 2008. Financing rural development for a harmonious society in China: Recent reforms in public finance and their prospects. World Bank Policy Research Working Paper No. 4693. Washington, DC: World Bank. (August).

Fu, Weigang. 2010. Why is there so much chaos on the use of land transfer revenues? *Dongfang Morning Post*, (April 25).

Gao, Guo Fu. 2007. Urban infrastructure investment and financing in Shanghai. In *Financing cities: Fiscal responsibility and urban infrastructure in Brazil, China, India, Poland and South Africa*, ed. George Peterson and Patricia Annez. Los Angeles: Sage.

Green, Stephen. 2012. Masterclass: China 2011, England 1890. On the Ground Working Paper. Hong Kong: Standard Chartered Bank. (January 4).

Guan, Qingyou, and Peng Mei. 2011. Land finance: The opiate. Unpublished manuscript.

Henderson, Vernon. 2009. Urbanization in China: Policy issues and options. http://www.cairncrossfund.org/download/十二五项目报告/Background%20Papers/Henderson%20-%20Final_Report_2009.11.10[Urbanization].pdf

Honohan, Patrick. 2008. Finance for urban centers. In *China urbanizes: Consequences, strategy and policy*, ed. Shahid Yusuf and Tony Saich. Washington, DC: World Bank.

Hussain, Athar. 2007. Social security in transition. In *Paying for progress in China: Public finance, human welfare and changing patterns of inequality*, ed. Vivienne Shue and Christine Wong. London: Routledge.

Investors Bulletin. 2010. A tight hoop should be put on local government financing platforms. (June 6). http://finance.ifeng.com/news/special/dfzwwj/20100606/2282325.shtml

Jiangyin Municipal Statistical Bureau. 2010. *Jiangyin Statistical Yearbook*. Beijing: China Statistics Press.

Kamal-Chaoui, Lamia, Edward Leman, and Rufei Zhang. 2009. Urban trends and policy in China. OECD Regional Development Working Paper 209/1. Paris: Organisation for Economic Co-operation and Development.

Kirkby, Richard. 1985. *Urbanization in China: Town and country in a developing economy 1949–2000 AD*. New York: Columbia University Press.

Li Ping, ed. 2006. *China: Intergovernmental fiscal relations* [in Chinese]. Beijing: Chinese Financial Economics Press.

———, ed. 2010. *A concise graphical depiction of the fiscal system* [in Chinese]. Beijing: Chinese Financial Economics Press.

Mikesell, John L., Jun Ma, Alfred Tat-kei Ho, and Meili Niu. 2011. Financing local public infrastructure: Guangdong province. In *China's local public finance in transition*, ed. Joyce Yanyun Man and Yu-Hung Hong. Cambridge, MA: Lincoln Institute of Land Policy.

Miller, Tom. 2012. At last, momentum for hukou reform. *GK Dragonomics*, (March 27).

MOC (Ministry of Construction). 2009. *Statistical yearbook of China's urban construction*. Beijing: China Planning Press.

MOF (Ministry of Finance). 2008. *China finance yearbook*. Beijing: China Financial and Economic Publishing House.

MOF (Ministry of Finance). Various years. *Compendium of local fiscal statistics* [difang caizheng tongji ziliao], ed. Budget Department and Treasury Department. Beijing: China Financial and Economic Publishing House.

———. 2011. Final accounts for the 2010 budget. Beijing: Ministry of Finance (July). http://yss.mof.gov.cn/2010juesuan/201107/t20110720_578448.html

Ministry of Human Resources and Social Security. 2010. *China labor statistical yearbook*. Beijing: China Statistics Press.

Ministry of Land Resources. 2010. *China statistical yearbook of land resources*. Beijing: Land Resources Press.

National Audit Office. 2011. *Local government debt audit results*. No. 35. Beijing: National Audit Office (June 27).

National Bureau of Statistics. Various years. *China city statistics yearbook*. Beijing: China Statistics Press. Cited as *CCSY* in text.

National Bureau of Statistics. Various years. *China statistics yearbook*. Beijing: China Statistics Press. Cited as *CSY* in text.

National Bureau of Statistics. 2010a. *Guangzhou statistical yearbook*. Beijing: China Statistics Press.

———. 2010b. *China population and employment statistical yearbook*. Beijing: China Statistics Press.

National Bureau of Statistics. 2005. *New China 55 years statistical compendium*. Beijing: China Statistics Press.

National Development and Reform Commission and World Bank. 2010. Urban rail development in China: Issues and options. World Bank Working Paper 55772. Washington, DC: World Bank. (January).

New Century. 2011. The heavy burden of land finance. Issue 25. (June 27).

People's Bank of China and China Banking Regulatory Commission. 2009. Some guiding opinions on further strengthening the adjustment of credit structures to promote the stable and relatively rapid growth of the national economy. (March 24).

Rabinovitch, Simon. 2012. *Financial Times*. (February 12).

Robinson, Eugene. 2011. China faces a series of daunting internal challenges. *Washington Post*, December 5. http://www.washingtonpost.com/opinions/china-faces-a-series-of-daunting -internal-challenges/2011/12/05/gIQAYx6qXO_story.html

SASS (Shanghai Academy of Social Sciences). 1988. Urban infrastructural investment and the "9-4" special funds and the Shanghai Longterm Facilities Company. Unpublished manuscript.

Schreyer, Paul, and Carsten Holz. 2005. Institutional arrangements for the production of statistics. In *Governance in China*. Paris: Organisation for Economic Co-operation and Development.

Shanghai Financial College, Institute of Urban Public Finance and Public Administration. 2010. *Urban public finance to promote the "two centre" construction of shanghai*. Beijing: Chinese Financial Economics Press.

Shanghai Statistical Yearbook (online). Various years. http://www.stats-sh.gov.cn/data/toTjnj .xhtml?y=2012

State Council. 2004. State council document on reform of investment institutions. Beijing: State Council of the People's Republic of China (July).

Su, Ming, and Quanhou Zhao. 2007. China: Fiscal framework and urban infrastructural finance. In *Financing cities: Fiscal responsibility and urban infrastructure in Brazil, China, India, Poland and South Africa*, ed. George Peterson and Patricia Annez. Los Angeles: Sage.

Tao, Ran, Fubing Su, Mingxing Liu, and Guangzhong Cao. 2010. Land leasing and local public finance in China's regional development: Evidence from prefecture-level cities. *Urban Studies* 47:2217–2236.

Wang, Dewen. 2005. China's urban and rural old age security system: Challenges and options. Working Paper Series No. 53. Beijing: Chinese Academy of Social Sciences. http://iple.cass .cn/file/dw17.pdf

Wang, Guangtao, ed. 2011. *The state of China's cities 2010/2011: Better city, better life*. Beijing: Foreign Languages Press.

Wang, Yuanjing, Gao Zhenhua, and He Yinzi. 2010. The challenge of local government fundraising and rebuilding the model—taking urban construction as an example [in Chinese]. *Economic Theory and Economic Management* 4:53–60.

Watson, Andrew. 2009. Social security for China's migrant workers—Providing for old age. *Journal of Current Chinese Affairs* 38(4):85–115.

Wei, Jianing. 2010. Causes and countermeasures of the risks of local government financing platforms. Unpublished manuscript.

Wong, Christine. 1991. Central-local relations in an era of fiscal decline: The paradox of fiscal decentralization in post-Mao China. *China Quarterly* 128(December):691–715.

———, ed. 1997. *Financing local government in the People's Republic of China*. Hong Kong: Oxford University Press.

———. 1998. Fiscal dualism in China: Gradualist reform and the growth of off-budget finance. In *Taxation in modern China*, ed. Donald Brean. New York: Routledge Press.

———. 2001. Converting fees into taxes: Reform of extrabudgetary funds and intergovernmental fiscal relations in China. In *Decentralization of the socialist state: Intergovernmental finance in transition economies*, ed. Richard Bird, Robert Ebel, and Christine Wallich. Beijing: Central Translation Press.

———. 2007. Can the retreat from equality be reversed? An assessment of redistributive fiscal policies from Deng Xiaoping to Wen Jiabao. In *Paying for progress in China: Public finance, human welfare and changing patterns of inequality*, ed. Vivienne Shue and Christine Wong. London: Routledge.

———. 2009. Rebuilding government for the twenty-first century: Can China incrementally reform the public sector? *China Quarterly* 200:929–952.

———. 2011. The fiscal stimulus program and problems of macroeconomic management in China. *OECD Journal on Budgeting* 2011(3):1–21.

———. 2012. Toward building a performance-oriented management system in China: The critical role of M&E and the long road ahead. World Bank Independent Evaluation Group ECD Working Paper Series No. 27. Washington, DC: World Bank. (September 1). www.worldbank .org/ieg/ecd

———. forthcoming. Can Humpty Dumpty be put together again? A review of public investment management in China. In *Investing to invest: Strengthening public investment management and global lessons*. Washington, DC: World Bank.

Wong, Christine, and Richard Bird. 2008. China's fiscal system: A work in progress. In *China's great transformation: Origins, mechanism, and consequences of the post-reform economic boom*, ed. Loren Brandt and Thomas Rawski. New York: Cambridge University Press.

World Bank. 1997. *China 2020: Old age security*. Washington, DC: World Bank.

———. 2000. *China: Managing public expenditures for better results*. Report No. 20342-CHA. Washington, DC: World Bank.

———. 2002. *China: National development and sub-national finance, a review of provincial expenditures*. Report No. 22951-CHA. Washington, DC: World Bank.

———. 2005. *China: Deepening public service unit reform to improve service delivery*. Washington, DC: World Bank.

———. 2007a. *China: Improving rural public finance for the harmonious society*. Report No. 41579-CN. Washington, DC: World Bank.

———. 2007b. *China: Public services for building the new socialist countryside*. Report No. 40221-CN. Washington, DC: World Bank.

———. 2010. Logistics Performance Index. http://web.worldbank.org/WBSITE/EXTERNAL /TOPICS/EXTTRANSPORT/EXTTLF/0,,contentMDK:21514122~menuPK:3875957 ~pagePK:210058~piPK:210062~theSitePK:515434,00.html

Wu, Weiping. 2010. Urban infrastructure financing and economic performance in China. *Urban Geography* 31(5):648–667.

———. 2011. Fiscal decentralization, infrastructure financing, and regional disparity. In *China's local public finance in transition*, ed. Joyce Yanyun Man and Yu-Hung Hong. Cambridge, MA: Lincoln Institute of Land Policy.

Zhang, Janet, and Andrew Batson. 2011. *DragonWeek*, (July 4).

Zhang, Qingwu. 1983. *Knowledge of household registration*. Beijing: Law Press.

Metropolitan Governance and Finance in São Paulo

12

DEBORAH L. WETZEL

With a population of 11.2 million residents, São Paulo is the largest city in Brazil, the largest city in the southern hemisphere, and the world's seventh largest city by population. The city is anchored to the São Paulo metropolitan region (SPMR), which with 20 million dwellers is among the five largest metropolitan areas in the world (Olinto 2011). The city is the capital of the state of São Paulo, the most populous Brazilian state, and exerts a strong influence in commerce, finance, the arts, and entertainment throughout Brazil and Latin America.

The SPMR was created in 1973, though São Paulo state had previously created administrative regional bodies in the late 1960s. The 1973 SPMR had 37 municipalities. An additional municipality was included in 1983, and another in 1991. Thus, the SPMR now comprises 39 municipalities, including the municipality of São Paulo (figure 12.1). As one of world's prominent metropolitan areas, São Paulo has undergone significant challenges and transformations. The city has experienced a decline in its manufacturing base, with significant implications for the incomes and living conditions for the people of the metropolitan area. As the SPMR seeks to reinvent itself, it must rely on metropolitan governance structures that provide little authority and coordination and on fiscal systems that are tied to the past and, at least for São Paulo municipality, take steps to address the city's increasing debt. Addressing key issues of effective planning, fiscal management, and delivery of services will be critical for the future of the SPMR, as will making use of the region's strong human resources and access to technical and research centers.

This chapter draws on a recent study carried out by the World Bank on the City of São Paulo. The author would like to thank Tom Kenyon and his team. See the references for further detail. The author would also like to thank Georges Darido and Leonardo Padovan for their support.

FIGURE 12.1

The São Paulo metropolitan region

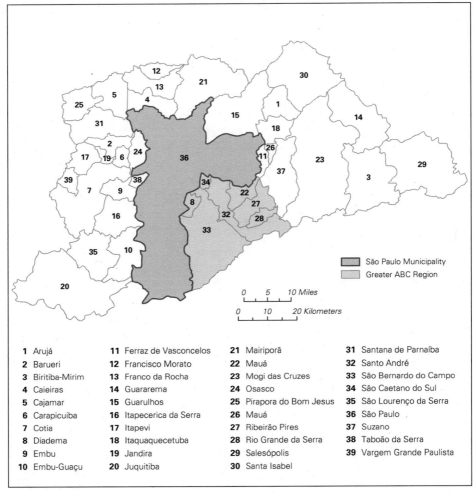

| | São Paulo Municipality |
| | Greater ABC Region |

1 Arujá	**11** Ferraz de Vasconcelos	**21** Mairiporã	**31** Santana de Parnaíba
2 Barueri	**12** Francisco Morato	**22** Mauá	**32** Santo André
3 Biritiba-Mirim	**13** Franco da Rocha	**23** Mogi das Cruzes	**33** São Bernardo do Campo
4 Caieiras	**14** Guararema	**24** Osasco	**34** São Caetano do Sul
5 Cajamar	**15** Guarulhos	**25** Pirapora do Bom Jesus	**35** São Lourenço da Serra
6 Carapicuiba	**16** Itapecerica da Serra	**26** Mauá	**36** São Paulo
7 Cotia	**17** Itapevi	**27** Ribeirão Pires	**37** Suzano
8 Diadema	**18** Itaquaquecetuba	**28** Rio Grande da Serra	**38** Taboão da Serra
9 Embu	**19** Jandira	**29** Salesópolis	**39** Vargem Grande Paulista
10 Embu-Guaçu	**20** Juquitiba	**30** Santa Isabel	

SOURCE: Adapted from Arretche (forthcoming).

This chapter looks at São Paulo's recent past to understand how metropolitan governance and finance have affected the development of this region and contributed to its challenges. After some background on the SPMR, its history, and recent economic changes, the chapter considers how metropolitan areas fit into the governance structures of Brazil and the impact this has had on the SPMR. A discussion of fiscal issues and management follows, with a snapshot of the SPMR as a whole and a discussion of fiscal data and expenditure management related specifically to São Paulo municipality. Then, after a look at some special financial tools that have been created to address specific needs, the chapter concludes with challenges going forward and thoughts regarding how they might be addressed.

TRANSFORMATION OF ECONOMIC ACTIVITY IN SÃO PAULO AND ITS IMPLICATIONS

In the early days of the Brazilian Republic in the late 1800s, São Paulo was a hub of the coffee economy, one of Brazil's main commodities during the period.[1] Strategically located between a main port (Santos) and the coffee plantations, São Paulo's location and the nature of coffee production laid the foundations for the future. Because coffee trees require about five years to yield a first crop (unlike sugar cane, which can be harvested within a year), production of coffee required greater financial capital over a longer period of time. Landowners moved closer to the state government in the municipality of São Paulo, which was the source of funding, and national and international banks clustered close to these prominent clients, thereby launching São Paulo's role as a financial center.

At the turn of the nineteenth century, the presence of financial capital, combined with significant immigration from both Europe and Japan and a location near a large port, made São Paolo an attractive base for manufacturing industry. Over the course of the twentieth century, changes in both domestic policy toward coffee and international markets, combined with an import substitution strategy, reinforced the focus of São Paulo as a center of manufacturing and finance (Biderman and Lopes 2011). High-, mid-, and low-tech manufacturing accounted for about 40 percent of São Paulo's economy in the late 1970s (figure 12.2). Efforts to stabilize the Brazilian economy under the Cruzado Plan stabilization program in 1986 and the opening of the economy in the late 1980s reduced the protection of the manufacturing sector and significantly shifted the underlying economic structure of the SPMR.

With the turn of the twenty-first century, São Paulo faces yet further demographic and economic shifts that suggest continued transformation. São Paulo's economy has become increasingly based on the tertiary sector, with an emphasis on services (figure 12.2). The presence of several universities and important research centers and think tanks, complemented by investment in science, technology, and innovation by the state of São Paulo, makes the metro region a desirable location for companies. At the same time, with the decline in the importance of manufacturing, there has been an increase in informal economic activity across the region, which leads to significant pressures in the provision of housing, infrastructure, and social services (Olinto 2011).

Deindustrialization of the SPMR's manufacturing base was also accompanied by significant shifts in the population. For some 30 years, the SPMR has experienced a shrinking of population at its central core and rapid population increase in lower-income districts in the suburban "belt" around São Paulo municipality. This reflects both an exodus from the center due to higher housing costs and the attraction of migrants from other parts of the country (figure 12.3).

Given the changes in economic activity and population shifts, average household per capita income in the SPMR has fluctuated during the 1980s, 1990s, and 2000s (figure 12.4). Per capita income in São Paulo increased quickly after the two major stabilization programs: the Cruzado Plan in 1986 and the Real Plan in 1994. In more

---

[1] Brazil was declared a republic in 1889.

FIGURE 12.2

Structural transformation in São Paulo

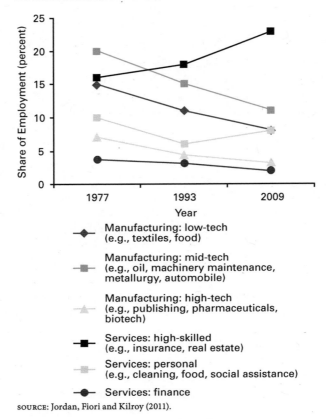

Manufacturing: low-tech
(e.g., textiles, food)

Manufacturing: mid-tech
(e.g., oil, machinery maintenance,
metallurgy, automobile)

Manufacturing: high-tech
(e.g., publishing, pharmaceuticals,
biotech)

Services: high-skilled
(e.g., insurance, real estate)

Services: personal
(e.g., cleaning, food, social assistance)

Services: finance

SOURCE: Jordan, Fiori and Kilroy (2011).

recent years, although incomes have grown in line with Brazil's overall growth, per capita incomes in the SPMR have not risen much beyond those of the early 1980s.

Average per capita incomes in the SPMR have changed relative to other metro areas in Brazil. Before 1989, SPMR household income per capita was higher than for other metro areas. Since that time, its position has steadily deteriorated. By 2009, SPMR's average per capita income was lower than that of the Federal District (Brasilia), Rio de Janeiro, and Porto Alegre.

Changes in economic activity and income per capita have also translated into sharp fluctuations in the poverty rate in the SPMR with peaks in 1984 and 1993 (figure 12.5). From 1981 to 2001, SPMR poverty rates were the lowest among metro areas in Brazil, but the rate increased significantly from 1996 to 2004, when it reached a third peak of 27 percent, higher than all other metropolitan areas. SPMR has yet to recover its place as the SPMR with the lowest poverty rates. However, the SPMR has always had less inequality than other Brazilian metro areas (figure 12.6). There was a significant increase in inequality from 1996 to 2002, the period when the economy was opened up and protection of the manufacturing sector was reduced. Inequality was reduced after 2002, following improvements in economic growth and employment and the expansion of social assistance programs.

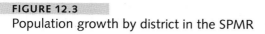

FIGURE 12.3

Population growth by district in the SPMR

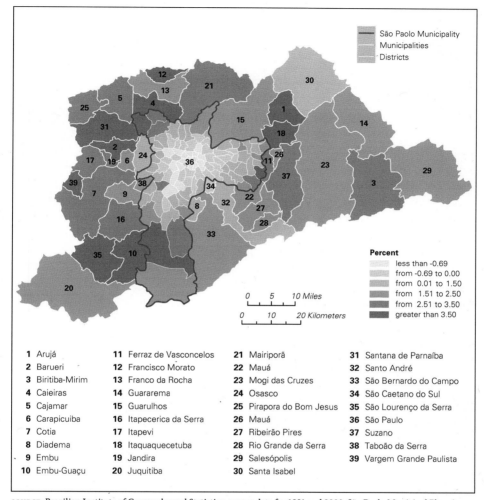

1	Arujá	11	Ferraz de Vasconcelos	21	Mairiporã	31	Santana de Parnaíba
2	Barueri	12	Francisco Morato	22	Mauá	32	Santo André
3	Biritiba-Mirim	13	Franco da Rocha	23	Mogi das Cruzes	33	São Bernardo do Campo
4	Caieiras	14	Guararema	24	Osasco	34	São Caetano do Sul
5	Cajamar	15	Guarulhos	25	Pirapora do Bom Jesus	35	São Lourenço da Serra
6	Carapicuiba	16	Itapecerica da Serra	26	Mauá	36	São Paulo
7	Cotia	17	Itapevi	27	Ribeirão Pires	37	Suzano
8	Diadema	18	Itaquaquecetuba	28	Rio Grande da Serra	38	Taboão da Serra
9	Embu	19	Jandira	29	Salesópolis	39	Vargem Grande Paulista
10	Embu-Guaçu	20	Juquitiba	30	Santa Isabel		

SOURCE: Brazilian Institute of Geography and Statistics, census data for 1991 and 2000, São Paulo Municipal Planning Secretariat.

The changes in the SPMR's economic base, combined with population shifts, have caused significant mismatches in land and labor markets (see World Bank 2012). The loss of industrial employment in the center of the SPMR has not been matched by new commercial activities. There is little overlap between growth in land use for commercial purposes and population growth. SPMR thus has large segments of population in places without jobs or access to transport.

Growth in the peripheral areas of the SPMR has also had negative environmental consequences.[2] Growth and illegal settlements threaten São Paulo's sources of drinking water, such as the Guarapiranga and Billings reservoirs. The withdrawal

---

[2]This and other points in this paragraph are drawn from World Bank (2012).

FIGURE 12.4

Per capita income in the SPMR and other metro areas (in constant 2009 reais)

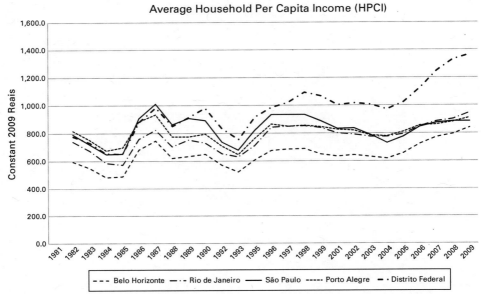

NOTE: In September 2012, one Brazilian real equaled US$0.49. From 2009 to 2012 this exchange rate fluctuated between US$0.40 and US$0.60.

SOURCE: Olinto (2011).

FIGURE 12.5

The evolution of poverty in the SPMR and other metro areas

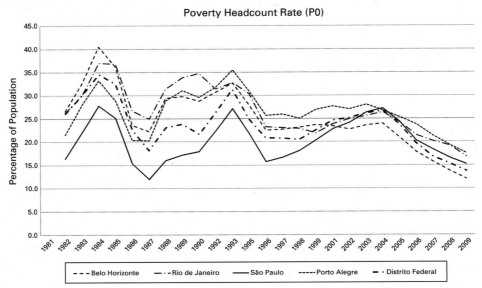

SOURCE: Olinto (2011).

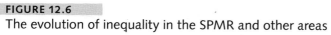

FIGURE 12.6

The evolution of inequality in the SPMR and other areas

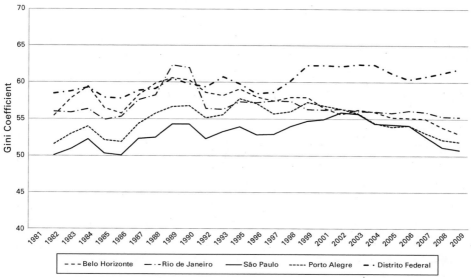

SOURCE: Olinto (2011).

of heavy industry has left vestiges of brownfield sites, some with leakage of toxic chemicals. Gaps in public transport infrastructure have also led to levels of road congestion that are among the highest in Latin America. São Paulo has the highest level of aggregate emissions of carbon dioxide, particulate matter, carbon monoxide, nitrous oxide, and sulfur dioxide from transport sources among Latin American cities.

This brief overview of the SPMR's economic transformation and its implications highlights a number of challenges. On a global level, São Paulo seeks to maintain or increase its relative weight as a global and regional center. With a gross domestic product in recent years of over US$200 billion, the SPMR has an economy comparable to small middle-income countries, such as Colombia or Malaysia, or city-states, such as Hong Kong and Singapore (see Jordan, Fiori, and Kilroy 2011). However, São Paulo's global position has been deteriorating relative to other rapidly growing cities in Latin America and in Asia.

A second challenge is that, within Brazil, other metropolitan areas, such as Belo Horizonte, the Federal District, Porto Alegre, Rio de Janeiro, and increasingly Recife and Salvador, have become attractive centers of growth and opportunity. As educational attainment at the secondary level has converged across the country, São Paulo has lost what was once a source of competitiveness. The commodity booms of the 2000s have also benefited other metropolitan areas more than São Paulo.

A third challenge is whether the ongoing structural transformation of the SPMR will be sufficient to drive higher levels of growth and competitiveness, as well as address spatial issues and the unfavorable trend in poverty. While growth in the service sector has compensated for the decline of manufacturing, continuous efforts to reinvent the economy are needed. These will also require immense investments in infrastructure to make growth and jobs accessible across the city, to address environmental issues, and to develop an attractive and livable metropolitan area for the twenty-first century.

These challenges place a premium on effective coordination, management, and fiscal health of the public entities that comprise SPMR, and particularly the city of São Paulo. The next sections consider these in turn.

METROPOLITAN GOVERNANCE IN BRAZIL AND SÃO PAULO

Article 25 of the Brazilian Federal Constitution of 1988 gives the states the right to create metropolitan governance structures. This was a shift from the 1967 constitution, which vested the authority to create metropolitan regions with the "Union," that is, the federal government. Paragraph 3 of Article 25 states, "The States may, by means of a supplementary law, establish metropolitan regions, urban agglomerations and micro regions, formed by the grouping of adjacent municipalities, in order to integrate the organization, the planning and the operation of public functions of interest." While giving states the authority to create such bodies, the constitution does not set any further requirements regarding structures or funding.

The 1988 constitution also established municipalities as full federation members with the same autonomy and sovereignty as the states. With this status, municipalities (of which there are more than 5,500 in Brazil) are not subordinated to states, or to any structures created by states, such as metropolitan areas.

The implications of these two aspects of the 1988 constitution for metropolitan authorities in Brazil are significant. While states have created metropolitan authorities or agencies, there are no formal mechanisms for funding or specific tools to implement metropolitan policies. As a result, such agencies have tended to focus on developing strategies and plans but have not had the teeth or mechanisms to support implementation of plans or policies (see Arretche forthcoming; Rezende and Garson 2006).

Given the autonomy of municipalities, any actions undertaken by a metropolitan agency must be specifically agreed to by all the municipalities involved. With the great spatial and economic differences across most metropolitan areas, coordination can be a challenge as incentives for joint action by municipalities may vary considerably. Veto points for moving forward on effective action multiply with the number of mayors and municipal councils involved. Political economy factors can also play an important role, for example, the political alignment, or lack thereof, of a state governor and the mayor of the core city of a metropolitan area can determine the ability to agree and move forward on metropolitan objectives.

While the federal level no longer has the right to create metropolitan areas, it does have an influence on how metro areas function through regulations that affect the ability of municipalities to work as a consortium. President Luiz Inácio Lula da Silva, early in his first term (2003–2007), created the Committee for Federative Articulation to help provide guidance on metropolitan policies. The committee consists of representatives of the union (federal) level and representatives of three nationwide municipal organizations (the Mayor's National Front, the

National Confederation of Municipalities, and the Brazilian Municipality Association) and the Forum of Metropolitan Entities. In 2005, the Consortia Law (law 11.107) was approved allowing consortia (of municipalities and otherwise) to take on a juridical status and thus allowing consortia to borrow and offer guarantees (see Arretche forthcoming). The law also allows consortia to exercise supervisory, regulatory, and planning roles.

After the approval of the 1988 constitution, 26 of Brazil's 27 states adopted constitutional articles at the state level establishing their metropolitan competencies, elaborating the criteria for metropolitan institutions, and typically including provisions for guaranteeing municipal and civil society involvement. Despite these constitutional articles, the need to find effective strategies for design and implementation of metropolitan plans, and reaching agreement with the municipalities of the metropolitan area on implementation of such plans remain key vulnerabilities.

Governance of the SPMR reflects the pressures and tensions that result from the 1988 constitution. Over time, a variety of government agencies have been created, but the ability of these agencies to play more than an advisory role has been limited. The role of planning and coordination was carried out by a state-level enterprise created in 1974: the Metropolitan Planning Enterprise for the Greater São Paulo Metropolitan Area. In 1994, Complementary Law 760/94 created the Development Council, composed of a representative of each municipality and state-level representatives.

SPMR transportation is overseen by the Metropolitan Enterprise for Urban Transportation and the São Paulo Company for Metropolitan Trains located under the secretary for metropolitan transportation. In May 2006, the governments of the state and municipalities in the SPMR signed an agreement creating the Integrated Transport Executive Committee as an executive board for the metropolitan transport system. The committee was designed as a tool to (1) strengthen partnership between the state and municipal transport secretariats; (2) align urban transport planning, administration, and oversight; (3) promote efficiency by setting operational standards and investment priorities; and (4) advocate an integrated vision of passenger accessibility through unified analysis and tariffs. In practice, the committee has functioned mostly as an ad hoc board of institutions generally lacking the capacity and continuity to analyze issues in detail or to drive a metropolitan agenda (see Darido 2011).

Interestingly, within the SPMR, subgroups of municipalities have formed various consortia to find cooperative solutions to address specific issues. In 1996, the "Baixada Santista" group of nine municipalities was formed to address issues related to the functioning of the Santos Port. In 2000, 19 cities established the Metropolitan Region of Campinas. The Greater ABC Chamber was created in 1997, building on the antecedents of the 1990s to bring mayoral, private-sector, and civil society groups together in seven municipalities (see figure 12.1) to address issues related to the automobile industry and watershed protection. The chamber and its associated forum have been a space for agreement and negotiation, reflecting that "bottom-up" coordination and activity can help to move metropolitan efforts forward.

In June 2011, the government of São Paulo state issued a new law (Complementary Law 1.139.2011) reorganizing the institutions of the SPMR. The law creates a variety of structures, building on those of the past:

- A development council for the metropolitan region (thereby legally ending the previous such councils from 1974 and 1994). The development council includes each mayor or his or her representative and representatives of the state that address issues of common interest. Two representatives from the Legislative Assembly are also included. The law emphasizes the importance of parity of municipalities and the state and of public meetings and consultations. Subjects for the council's deliberations include planning and land use; transport and the regional transport network; housing and sanitation; environment; economic development; social support; and sports and recreation.
- A consultative council, to elicit and present to the development council the proposals and views of civil society, the legislative branch at both the state and municipal levels, and the executive side of the state and municipal level. The consultative council will also be asked for views on key issues and proposals by the development council.
- Technical groups (*câmaras themáticas*) to pursue specific issues of interest to the SPMR.
- A regional enterprise, *entidade autarquia*, linked to the Secretariat of Metropolitan Development to organize, integrate, plan, and execute functions of common public interest to the SPMR, such as the regional transport network; housing and sanitation; and environmental issues. This enterprise will (1) collect revenues, whether shared or delegated or through charges and fees; (2) elaborate plans, programs, and projects of common interest, set goals for them, and oversee their execution; and (3) exercise other functions as needed and required by the law.
- A regional development fund, also linked to the Secretariat of Metropolitan Development. The resources of the fund will be overseen by six members, four representing the development council and two representing the regional enterprise, and will be administered by a formal financial entity. The functions of the fund are (1) to contribute financial and technical resources to address key metropolitan issues, as discussed above; (2) to undertake studies, analyses, and projects with the objective of improving municipal public services; and (3) to reduce social inequalities across the SPMR.

These new structures are clearly intended to bolster cooperation across the region and build mechanisms to address issues of common interest among the state and the SPMR municipalities. Over the years, many such structures have been created to support coordination and development across the SPMR, but with the limited funding and decision-making authority built into the constitution, they have not been able to do much more than provide an advisory role. Those that have been most successful have had a clear agenda (e.g., integrated transport) or have been able to bring together different stakeholders to solve specific issues (the Greater ABC Chamber). The effectiveness of these relatively new structures will be seen as time passes.

METROPOLITAN FINANCE

While the 1998 constitution gives states the right to create metropolitan institutions, it did not provide a specific mechanism for funding such institutions.[3] It does, however, give both the states and municipalities more autonomy in raising revenues and provides for a variety of transfers. Funding for metropolitan areas in Brazil is thus an amalgam of funding provided by the state-level and municipal governments. As the SPMR well demonstrates, coordination issues exacerbate the difficulties in funding effective public services and investment for the metropolitan areas.

With their autonomous status, municipalities in Brazil have a set of "own taxes" at their disposal:

- Tax on services, largely collected in cities with over 50,000 people.
- Tax on property and urban territory, the tax of greatest importance in medium-sized cities.
- Transfer tax on the sale of buildings.

Municipalities may also use betterment levies and charges for street lighting, business licenses, and other economic activities. These taxes become more important the smaller the size of the city.

Municipalities also receive a share of certain state taxes:

- 25 percent of the state value added tax: 75 percent of this amount is distributed by origin based on economic activity, and 25 percent to benefit the poor (based on state law).
- 50 percent of the vehicle tax.
- 22.5 percent of the tax on industrial products and the tax on federal profits, which form the Municipal Participation Fund. This fund is divided into two parts: 10 percent for municipalities that are capitals of states and 90 percent for other cities.
- 100 percent of profit taxes paid on city enterprises or foundations.
- 70 percent of tax in gold-related financial operations.
- 50 percent on rural territorial tax.

States and municipalities also benefit from transfers to fund specific activities, including education, health, social assistance, and investment, as well as a variety of discretionary transfers and, when relevant, royalties.

The Fiscal Responsibility Law, approved in 2000, also provides an important framework for management of state and municipal finance. The objective of this law was to regularize the planning, transparency, and accountability of subnational finances in order to prevent the budgetary overruns that had caused fiscal problems in the past. States and cities report annually to the national treasury on their fiscal status and alignment with the law's provisions. Key aspects of the Fiscal Responsibility Law include the following:

---

[3] This section draws heavily on Sakho (2011).

- Adoption of a broad definition of public debt, including short-term debt (annual debt operations), contingent liabilities, and counterpart funding.
- Prohibition of renegotiation of debt between different levels of government.
- Limits on total public debt (200 percent of current revenue), as well as limits on payments on debt repayment (13 percent of current revenue).
- Coherence between the annual budget law and the four-year pluriannual plan.
- Prohibition of new investment without evidence of ability to cover operational costs.
- Limitation of personnel expenditure to 60 percent of current revenues.

Aggregate fiscal accounts for all 39 municipalities of the SPMR are not available; however, Arretche (forthcoming) presents an overview of the distribution of revenues and expenditures of the SPMR in 2009. This provides a snapshot of the balance between the city of São Paulo and suburban São Paulo.

Table 12.1 shows that some two-thirds of SPMR revenues derive from the city of São Paulo, and one-third from the suburban parts of the SPMR; 44.5 percent of total operating revenue in the SPMR comes from own-source revenues, such as taxes and user fees. São Paulo city relies especially on service taxes and property taxes, while the suburban areas raise revenues mostly from property taxes, service taxes, and other own-source revenues. Intergovernmental transfers provide some 47.7 of revenues, with 19 percent from the federal government and 29 percent from the state. Intermunicipal transfers are effectively nonexistent.

Table 12.2 presents the distribution of spending within the SPMR for 2009. As with revenues, São Paulo city spending accounts for about two-thirds of metropoli-

TABLE 12.1

Distribution of operating revenues within the SPMR, 2009 (percent)

Revenue source	Central city	Suburban	SPMR
Taxes			
Property taxes	8.5	3.1	11.7
Property-related taxes	1.8	0.4	2.2
Income taxes	2.2	0.7	2.9
Service taxes	15.7	3.5	19.2
User fees	0.5	0.7	1.1
Other own-source revenue	3.8	3.7	7.4
Total own-source revenue	32.4	12.1	44.5
Intergovernmental transfers	26.9	20.8	47.7
Union transfers	9.9	9.1	18.9
State transfers	16.9	11.7	28.6
Intermunicipal transfers	0.2	0.0	0.2
Other transfers	9.7	4.3	14.0
Federal deductions	3.4	2.8	6.2
Total revenues	65.7	34.4	100.0

SOURCE: Data from Arretche (forthcoming).

TABLE 12.2

Distribution of operating expenditures within the SPMR, 2009 (percent)

Expenditure	Central city	Suburban	SPMR
General government	3.5	6.7	10.2
Transportation	4.9	0.7	5.6
Security	0.6	0.5	1.1
Police	0.4	0.3	0.7
Other security	0.2	0.2	0.4
Environment	0.6	0.3	0.9
Water	0.0	0.0	0.0
Sanitation	0.8	1.8	2.6
Education	14.5	8.3	22.8
Health	12.4	7.6	20.0
Social services	1.3	0.8	2.1
Pensions	10.4	1.6	12.0
Culture and recreation	1.1	0.6	1.7
Urban development and planning	7.4	3.4	10.8
Housing	1.4	0.6	2.0
Debt charges	6.5	0.6	7.1
Total expenditures	66.0	34.0	100.0

SOURCE: Data from Arretche (forthcoming).

tan spending, and suburban areas account for about one-third. As expected, given constitutional mandates, spending on education at 22.8 percent and on health at 20.0 percent are significant and are split between the city and suburban areas. Notably, spending on pensions at 10.8 percent and on general government at 10.2 percent are two significant spending items, with pensions mostly a city expenditure and general government expenditures more significant in suburban areas; 10.8 percent of SPMR spending in 2009 was on urban development and planning, and 7.1 percent on debt charges, mostly on the part of the city. Transport is about 5.6 of total SPMR spending, also largely carried out by the city. According to Arretche (forthcoming), neither the city nor suburban governments spend much on environment, water, and sanitation, which are covered by state enterprises or by the state government.

Given São Paulo municipality's weight in the spending of the SPMR and its overall magnitude as a city, it is of value to consider its fiscal policy and patterns in more detail over time. São Paulo's budget at R$20 billion in 2009 (about US$9 billion) is the largest of Brazilian cities, more than twice that of Rio de Janeiro and more than that of most states in Brazil. São Paulo is a leader in Brazil when it comes to fiscal innovation and reforms to improve tax efficiency, yet issues with expenditure management are leading to significant debt issues that will need to be addressed in the near future.

The government of São Paulo municipality has managed fiscal aggregates well in recent years through efforts at improving tax administration. Figure 12.7 shows fiscal balances from 2004 to 2010. Revenues have increased steadily in all years except 2009, the year most affected by the recent global crisis. The municipality has maintained its primary balance (i.e., the difference between current revenues and current spending) between 1.5 and 3.0 percent of municipal GDP.

Revenues and expenditures of the municipality have increased at a very rapid rate, as shown in table 12.3. The compound annual growth rate of current revenues was 9.7 percent in real (inflation-adjusted) terms from 2004 to 2010. Tax revenues were boosted by significant improvements in tax collection efforts, despite reductions in tax rates, particularly including garbage and public light contributions, and reductions in tax on property and urban territory and exemptions on service taxes to boost economic activity. Overall current spending grew at 9 percent, just under the rate of revenue collection, driven by expenditures in goods and services, which grew at 14.3 percent from 2004 to 2010. Interest payments averaged 10 percent of total current expenditures and increased 7 percent in real terms from 2004 to 2010.

Figure 12.8 shows the composition of revenues and expenditures for São Paulo municipality in 2010. Own-source revenues accounted for 44 percent of total revenues, with 24 percent coming from the tax on services, 14 percent from tax on property and urban territory, and 3 percent each from the transfer tax on the sale of buildings and the tax on city enterprises and foundations.

Transfers provided 41 percent of total revenue in 2010 and in general accounted for 40 percent of total revenues from 2004 to 2010. Transfer revenues (shared taxes) benefited from growing tax collections by the federal and state governments, from

FIGURE 12.7

Evolution of fiscal balances in São Paulo municipality, 2004–2010 (2010 R$ billions)

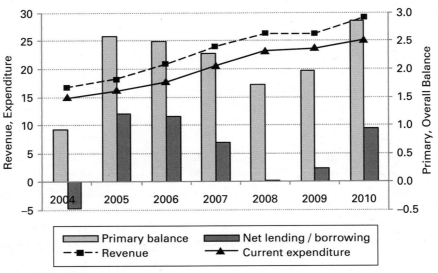

SOURCE: Sakho (2011).

TABLE 12.3

Current revenues and expenditures of São Paulo municipality, 2004–2010 (2010 R$ millions)

Unit: 2010	2004		2005		2006		2007		2008		2009		2010		2004–10
	Values	%	Values	%	Values	%	Values	%	Values	%	Values	%	Values	%	CAGR
Total revenue	**16,815**	100	**18,273**	100	**20,920**	100	**24,026**	100	**26,351**	100	**26,297**	100	**29,225**	100	9.7
Taxes	7,802	46	8,467	46	9,733	47	10,676	44	11,296	43	11,499	44	13,095	45	9.0
Social contributions	19	0	0	0	0	0	1,559	6	1,587	6	1,658	6	1,663	6	110.8
Transfers	7,247	43	7,391	40	8,299	40	8,808	37	9,939	38	10,384	39	11,842	41	8.5
Other current revenues	1,747	10	2,415	13	2,889	14	2,983	12	3,529	13	2,755	10	2,625	9	7.0
Current expenditure	**14,993**	100	**16,210**	100	**17,715**	100	**20,612**	100	**23,252**	100	**23,740**	100	**25,142**	100	9.0
Compensation of employees	4,663	31	5,297	33	6,617	37	6,589	32	7,137	31	7,188	30	7,475	30	8.2
Pensions	1,918	13	1,214	7	95	1	106	1	45	0	0	0	0	0	–100.0
Interest payments	1,531	10	1,810	11	1,940	11	2,183	11	2,347	10	2,145	9	2,293	9	7.0
Goods and services	6,880	46	7,889	49	9,063	51	11,734	57	13,723	59	14,407	61	15,374	61	14.3

SOURCE: Sakho (2011).

FIGURE 12.8

Composition of São Paulo municipality government revenue (A)
and expenditure (B), 2010

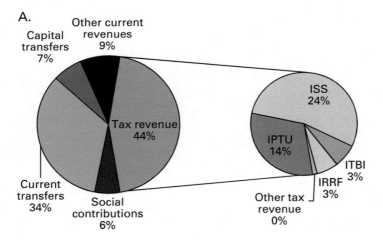

A.

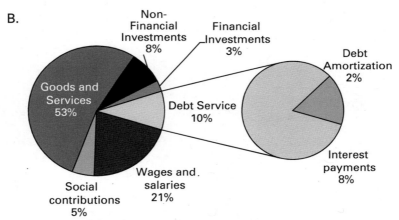

B.

Abbreviations: IPTU, Tax on property and urban territory; IRRF, Profit tax on city enterprises or
foundations; ISS, Tax on services; ITBI, Tax on transfer or sale of buildings.

SOURCE: Sakho (2011).

which municipalities receive a fixed share, as discussed above. In particular, the
municipality received a 33 percent increase in transfers from São Paulo state origi-
nating from the state value added tax. Capital transfers grew almost ninefold, on
the back of agreements (*convênios*), which marked the increase in public infrastructure investments that are part of Brazil's Growth Acceleration Program (Programa de Aceleração do Crescimento, PAC) launched in 2007. Capital transfers
from agreements are expected to continue to grow, as the second phase of the program (PAC-2) outlines further large public investment projects from 2011 to 2014.
Transfers from the Fund for Maintenance and Development of Basic Education
more than doubled in real terms, partly due to higher resource receipts for pre-

schools and increased enrollment rates. Yet transfer expenditures to the fund also rose over the period, due to increased earmarking of resources toward the education fund, with rising contribution shares since 2007. The municipality's contribution to the fund from its shared revenues from the state value added tax, tax on exported industrial products, and the Municipal Participation Fund rose gradually from 15 percent in 2007 to 20 percent in 2009 (table 12.4).

Figure 12.8 also shows the composition of total spending for São Paulo municipality in 2010. Expenditures on goods and services have been the main driver of current expenditure growth. Constitutionally mandated spending on education and health form one part of this spending, but other factors include the rise in external contracting of services to social organizations in areas such as garbage collection, cleaning, and health; subsidies to the transport company to compensate for the cost of the single tariff pass (*bilhete único*) losses; and transfers to indirect administration companies such as the municipal hospitals, as well as transfers to the pension funds. Employee compensation grew significantly in 2005 and 2006, leveling off thereafter. Interest payments grew over the period, except for 2009 because the limit imposed by the Fiscal Responsibility Law capped interest payments at 13 percent of net real revenue.

Investment has been modestly growing since 2006 and, despite a drop in 2009, recovered slightly in 2010 (figure 12.9). The municipality has maintained investment levels of 6–8 percent of net current revenues, which is quite modest given the investment needs of the city. Note that in 2010, 7 percent of the state government of São Paulo's total expenditures were spent on direct investment, and of this, about 49 percent of investments went to logistics and transport, which reflects road construction and maintenance, and 21 percent went to metropolitan transportation, mainly urban rail (São Paulo Company for Metropolitan Trains and the underground rail service at the SPMR) (Sakho 2011).

Most of São Paulo municipality's public debt stock (more than 90 percent, so-called intra limite debt) consists of debt renegotiated with the treasury through Provisional Measure 2185 in May 2000 (when the national treasury renegotiated most of the states' and large municipalities' debts). Through this agreement, the federal government took on São Paulo municipality's debt and directly repaid the financial institutions with federal government securities. The municipality's balance was refinanced into 360 monthly installments (30 years) indexed by a price index and an additional interest spread of 9 percent per year capitalized on a monthly basis. Provisional Measure 2185 also capped the value of monthly debt service installments paid by the municipality to the federal government at 13 percent of its revenue. If total debt service of the debt refinanced in 2000 and contracted since 2000 rises above 13 percent, the debt service amount exceeding 13 percent is recapitalized into the overall debt.

Despite these arrangements, São Paulo's municipality's net consolidated debt exceeds the limit set by the Fiscal Responsibility Law and has been growing in recent years. Net consolidated debt is defined as the totality of public debt contracts (internal and external), tax and social contributions installment debts, and debts due to judicial rulings (*precatórios*), net of certain financial asset deductions. Because of growing fiscal revenues and fiscal adjustments, the net consolidated

TABLE 12.4

Evolution of transfers to São Paulo municipality, 2004–2010 (2010 R$ millions)

	2004	2005	2006	2007	2008	2009	2010	CAGR 2004–2010 (%)
Transfers revenues	7,246,930	7,391,469	8,298,828	8,808,236	9,939,499	10,383,829	11,841,926	9
(As a share of total revenue)	43	40	40	37	38	39	41	
Current transfers	7,056,112	7,109,195	7,901,664	8,354,185	9,108,077	9,414,804	9,852,996	6
Federal and state transfers	5,846,783	5,865,841	6,479,482	6,721,706	7,001,276	6,996,162	7,273,545	4
SUS	1,119,461	892,544	1,054,257	1,057,124	1,003,781	1,134,179	1,037,525	−1
ICMS	3,203,280	3,267,754	3,530,173	3,693,585	4,045,539	3,896,993	4,272,594	5
IPVA	1,110,418	1,209,496	1,374,164	1,463,838	1,429,322	1,432,555	1,394,669	4
Other	413,624	496,048	520,888	507,160	522,634	532,434	568,757	5
Multigovernmental FUNDEB transfers	1,087,532	1,169,849	1,253,838	1,487,983	1,922,121	2,300,320	2,444,032	14
Convenios	118,975	62,471	143,479	109,408	125,721	72,370	85,870	−5
Private transfers	2,821	11,033	24,865	35,088	58,958	45,953	49,016	61
Capital transfers	190,818	282,274	397,164	454,052	831,422	969,025	1,988,930	48
Transfers expenses	**597,689**	**611,423**	**653,643**	**879,665**	**1,168,504**	**1,370,518**	**1,457,792**	**16**
Transfers to FUNDEB	597,689	611,423	653,643	879,665	1,168,504	1,370,518	1,457,792	16
Net transfers revenues from FUNDEB	*489,843*	*558,426*	*600,196*	*608,319*	*753,617*	*929,802*	*986,240*	*12*
Net transfers revenues	**6,649,241**	**6,780,046**	**7,645,186**	**7,928,572**	**8,770,995**	**9,013,311**	**10,384,135**	**8**
(As a share of total revenue)	40	47	45	39	37	36	36	

Abbreviations: CAGR, Compound Annual Growth Rate; FUNDEB, Fund for Maintenance and Development of Basic Education (O Fundo De Manutenção e Desenvolvimento de Educação Basico e de Valorização dos Profissionais da Educação); ICMS, State Value-Added Tax (Imposto Sobre Operações Relativas à Circulação Mercadorias); IPVA, Vehicle Tax (Imposto sobre a Propriedade de Veículos Automotores); SUS, Unified Health System (Systema Unifacado de Saúde).

SOURCE: Sakho (2011).

FIGURE 12.9

Evolution of capital expenditures in São Paulo municipality

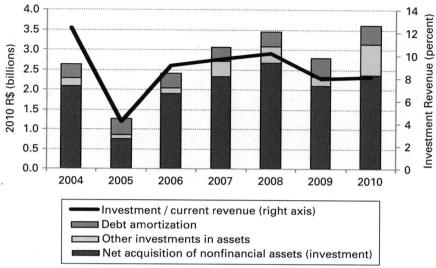

SOURCE: Sakho (2011).

debt-to-revenue ratio fell steeply from 246 percent in 2004 to 190 percent by 2007. Since 2007, however, the debt-to-revenue ratio has deteriorated. By the end of 2010, the municipality's net consolidated debt stock stood at 213 percent of net current revenue, above the 200 percent ceiling established by the Fiscal Responsibility Law.

Debt service has been growing modestly, driven recently by higher interest payments (figure 12.10). However, while debt service growth has been in line with the rise in revenues seen above, debt service obligations above the 13 percent ceiling have been contributing to growth of the debt stock.

PLANNING AND BUDGETING AND THEIR IMPLICATIONS FOR INVESTMENT

A key issue for São Paulo municipality, and for the SPMR as a whole, is the issue of planning and budgeting.[4] Budget management practices at the municipal and state level exacerbate the problems of coordination described above and make efficient use of resources to address key needs, especially investment needs, very difficult.

Planning

Taking São Paulo municipality as an example, table 12.5 shows four key planning instruments used by the city. The SP 2040 plan is currently under development by the Secretariat of Urban Development and is intended to develop a consensual long-term strategic view of the city, taking into account the spatial dimension. It is

---

[4] This section draws heavily on Clarke (2011).

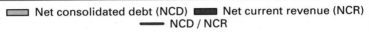

Evolution of São Paulo municipality's debt (A) and debt service (B)

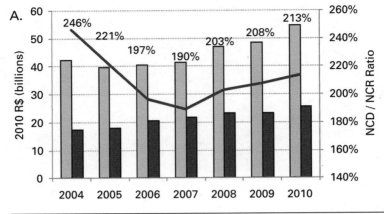

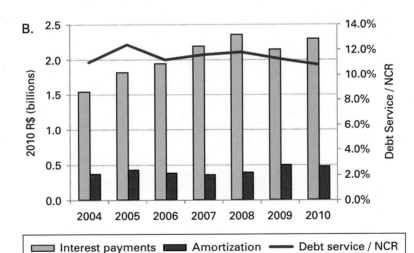

SOURCE: Sakho (2011).

being developed through extensive consultations, and the intention is that it should guide all other planning instruments. There are no specific fiscal or financial indicators.

The Strategic Directive Plan (PDE, Plano Diretor Estratégico) is also a comprehensive plan developed by the Secretariat of Urban Development that sets broad goals for São Paulo municipality; it defines, among other things, the city urban development policy, the overall scope of city sectoral public policies, and its urban-environmental plan. It was also elaborated in consultation with civil society. The PDE also calls for the formulation of regional plans, land zoning laws, transport, mobility, and housing plans. The annual investment program and annual budget

TABLE 12.5

São Paulo muncipality's planning instruments

Instrument	Time frame	Responsible agency	Objective
SP 2040: vision and long-term planning for the city of São Paulo	2012–2040	SMDU	States long-term development strategies for the city around five axis: social equilibrium promotion, sustainable urban development, mobility and accessibility, environmental improvement, and business opportunities
Strategic Directive Plan (PDE)	2002–2012	SMDU	States the strategy for urban development, including land and environmental zoning, over the ten-year period
Agenda 2012: city targets program	2009–2012	SEMPLA	Presents strategic actions, indicators, and targets for the city and its regional divisions and subdivisions aligned with electoral campaign promises for the three-year period
Pluriannual Plan (PPA)	2010–2013	SEMPLA	Sets directives, objectives, and targets, framing the budget allocation for the four-year period

Abbreviations: SEMPLA, Municipal Secretariat of Planning (Secretaria Municipal do Planejamento); SMDU, Secretariat of Urban Development (Secretaria Municipal de Desenvolvimento Urbano).
SOURCE: Clarke (2011).

laws are expected to incorporate the guidelines and priorities set forth by the PDE, but there are no formal mechanisms to ensure that this happens.

The Agenda 2012 is the result of a civil society initiative that amended the Organic Law of the Municipality to require the mayor to present a plan with strategic actions, indicators, and quantitative targets for each municipal district, in accordance with campaign promises and the PDE. The Agenda 2012 was developed by the secretary of planning and is structured around six axes: rights, sustainability, creativity, opportunities, efficiency, and inclusivity. Although there was no explicit cost information or a resource envelope to the agenda, the targets were set implicitly, taking funding constraints into consideration.

The fourth planning instrument at the center of government is the pluriannual plan (PPA, Plano Plurianual). Its focus is to establish directives, objectives, and targets, including on a regional and district basis, for the municipality and continuous program expenditures. It is a four-year plan developed in the first year of the mandate of a new government and extends into the first year of the mandate of the next government. It is probably best characterized as a detailed list of activities (particularly investments) to be carried out by the municipality. These activities have an expenditure provision attached both for the total and for the full four-year period, but these are indicative figures. The PPA in principle includes all municipal expenditures (including payroll and debt service) for the four-year period.

Each of these planning instruments attempts to express priorities and choices at a moment in time. However, none of them really constitutes a plan of action to be followed. The result is that each of the plans confers some authority on policy decisions, but in practice, their overlapping nature and lack of connection with the resources likely to be available mean that the real decisions are made, almost independently, in the preparation of the annual budget, and even more so during the process of execution of the annual budget. The patchwork of plans, which also include separately developed sectoral strategies, means that consistent priorities for the municipality are not being clearly defined.

In principle the Budget Guidelines Law (LDO, Lei de Diretrizes Orçamentárias) serves as the link between the PPA and Annual Budget Law. It takes from the PPA the current year targets and priorities. The LDO sets more specific rules for budget formulation and lays the ground for eventual changes in tax or spending based on changes in legislation. In compliance with the Fiscal Responsibility Law, it introduces fiscal targets for the current year and two additional years into the future and discusses fiscal risks and tax exemptions. Crucially, however, there is no mechanism for the outer year fiscal targets in the LDO to have any impact on the budgets in future years.

The final step of the planning process is the Annual Budget Law. The resources are allocated by programs and actions in each institution as well as by economic category (capital and current expenditures). The budget shows the resources allocated to each action and program in order to fulfill the current-year targets set by the LDO, in accordance with the PPA. However, since strategies are rarely costed, there are few mechanisms to ensure that the budget is allocated according to the resources needed to comply with the targets.

Budget Preparation

The budget preparation process starts in May with the issuance of budget instructions establishing the budget preparation calendar. The districts (*subprefeituras*) carry out public hearings, and subsequently, all budget units submit their budget proposals. Revenue forecasts are prepared at the same time by the Secretariat of Municipal Finance, so that budget requests can be reconciled with available resources. For the 2011 budget, the budget requests were about 40 percent higher than forecast resources, but they can be as high as double forecast revenues.

The budget allocations are made on an incremental basis. Based on historical spending patterns and ongoing contracts, the secretary of planning estimates the minimum amount of resources needed to guarantee the current provision of public services (recurrent expenditures) and other obligations, such as debt payments and judicial orders. Debt payments are defined for the budget process as the required legal minimum of 13 percent of net real revenue of the Fiscal Responsibility Law, not the amount required to ensure a downward ratio of debt to income. After taking into account the amount needed to pay for the recurrent expenditures and the total resource envelope estimated by Secretariat of Municipal Finance, provided all legal earmarks are complied with, the Secretariat of Planning derives the investment envelope, as a residual.

The choice of investment projects to be financed is somewhat ad hoc, involving consideration of whether they are foreseen in the Agenda 2012, if they have technical viability, and if they are ready for execution. Projects may still be included if they do not comply with these criteria but are often allocated only symbolic funding with the possibility of becoming eligible for further funding during the year. There is no formal costing system, and calculations of future recurrent expenditures from investment do not enter the formal budget process or affect the investment decisions. The provision for contingencies is very small.

Once the draft budget is prepared, it is submitted to the city council. The councilors can amend the budget to include new expenditures, with no limit on the number of amendments. However, for new spending to be introduced, amendments to cut expenditure in other areas or raise revenues are required. For the 2011 budget, more than 5,000 amendments were proposed, of which 1,415 were incorporated into the budget (see Clarke 2011).

Budget Execution

Once the budget is approved, the Secretariat of Municipal Finance issues an administrative regulation setting bimonthly forecasts of revenue in accordance to the revenue estimate in the budget, which sets spending limits for each budget unit. The regulation allows The Secretariats of Planning and Finance to freeze (*contingenciar*) resources (and corresponding expenditures) during budget execution. This is normally done at the beginning of the year. In 2010, R$1.8 billion of a R$26.8 billion budget (6.7 percent) was frozen, while in 2011 the freeze was more severe: R$5.6 billion out of R$35.6 billion (15.7 percent). The resource freeze arises from the inherent uncertainty regarding revenue collection and the need to fulfill the fiscal targets but also implies considerable uncertainty by budget units on the availability of resources. The allowances for expenditure are set by budget unit and revenue source, but the line secretariats can move resources from one unit to another. They can also unfreeze expenditures by offering to freeze other budget line items of an equivalent amount, as long as payroll and debt service expenditures are maintained. Requests for additional budget allocations must be submitted to the Secretariat of Planning during two periods of the year: April to August and October to November.

Frozen resources can be freed up throughout the year. The secretaries of planning and finance hold weekly meetings to evaluate revenue collection vis-à-vis the estimate and budget execution. Since a sizable amount of resources is frozen at the beginning of the year, since 2005 no additional resources have been frozen during the year. The executive can also alter the resources allocated to each program and action, up to the amount equivalent to 15 percent of all planned expenditures. However, the changes made within programs and within the same government agency and expenditure element are not counted within the 15 percent limit on budget reallocation.

The budget preparation and execution process of São Paulo municipality has particular implications. The first is that priorities are only very tenuously transmitted throughout the process, with few mechanisms in place to focus priorities and assure that they are addressed. The second implication is the very strong inertia in the whole process, with a focus on maintaining existing programs and structures. It is this aspect of the process that has led to the current situation of the municipality increasing debt, despite rapid growth of revenues. A third implication of the existing system is that it is fraught with uncertainty, which hinders any effective planning or coordination with other municipalities in the SPMR.

Table 12.6 shows the 2010 budget outcomes in São Paulo municipality at the level of major functions. For example, expenditure in environmental management was 44 percent lower than budgeted, while expenditure on transport was 37 percent higher than budgeted. Table 12.7 shows that these deviations in the transport budget did not occur only in 2010. From 2008 to 2010, major expenditures took place without having originally been budgeted or are budgeted and not spent. The fact that the deviations from the original budget can be so large and widespread implies that the budget process itself lacks credibility. The effect of this is that any focus on results or longer-term objectives for the city, and for the SPMR more broadly, becomes very difficult.

TABLE 12.6

Planned and executed 2010 budget for São Paulo municipality, by function (R$ millions)

Function	Budget	Revised	Actual	Deviation (%)
Total	27,898	29,209	26,952	−3
Education	6,253	6,214	5,540	−11
Health	5,399	5,444	4,911	−9
Pensions	4,051	4,139	4,004	−1
Special charges	2,755	3,169	3,135	14
Urban development	2,550	2,702	2,461	−3
Transport	1,707	2,402	2,346	37
Housing	1,041	991	900	−13
Social assistance	692	804	700	1
Legislature	579	543	476	−18
Administration	463	463	428	−8
Environmental management	424	279	239	−44
Sanitation	415	378	358	−14
Culture	362	376	311	−14
Public safety	302	306	254	−16
Sports and leisure	239	280	254	6
Communications	165	154	152	−8
Judicial	127	137	124	−3
Labor	118	116	78	−34
Energy	114	117	116	2
Trade and services	68	124	120	77
Other	73	70	46	−37

SOURCE: Data from Municipal Secretariat of Planning, São Paulo.

TABLE 12.7

Intrayear changes in São Paulo municipality's transport budget (R$ millions)

Expenditure	2008			2009			2010		
	Budget	Actual	Difference (%)	Budget	Actual	Difference (%)	Budget	Actual	Difference (%)
Total	1,512	1,847	22	1,836	1,875	2	1,707	2,346	37
Current expenditure	1,064	1,431	34	1,219	1,763	45	1,443	1,662	15
Roads	417	409	−2	429	477	11	561	548	−2
Urban Collectives	556	947	70	707	1,183	67	787	1,035	31
Capital expenditure	447	416	−7	617	111	−82	264	683	159
Railway		275	NA	218	50	−77	10	650	6,399
Roads	26	20	−22	93	18	−81	65	19	−70
Urban collectives	420	121	−71	305	43	−86	189	13	−93

NA, not available.

SOURCE: Data from Municipal Secretariat of Planning, São Paulo.

Investment Planning

Some of the biggest deviations in the budget occur in the area of investment expenditure. As noted, in the existing system, investment is treated as a residual item in the budget planning and execution process. Given that the future development of the city of São Paulo and the broader SPMR will depend upon the capacity to identify, finance, and complete appropriate investments in infrastructure, it is important to consider the processes by which investment is planned and executed.

There is no formal investment planning and screening process, and investment decisions are normally taken alongside other items of the budget. Currently investment proposals included in the Agenda 2012 or that are financed with earmarked funds, such as federal and state transfers, are prioritized, but these are also not immune from budget cuts if resources are seen to be inadequate. In addition to transfers from other levels of government, whose resources are directed to the investment projects, the other mechanism to raise funds to finance investments is a form of development bond (*certificado de potencial adicional de construção*, CEPAC), which also requires the resources to be spent in a specific city district or subregion.[5]

In practice, in line with broader metropolitan plans, the municipality has been prioritizing investments in housing and public transportation. The major investments are decided by the secretary of urban development together with the mayor, on the basis of technical information rather than an economic evaluation.

Other cities in the SPMR confront the same difficulties as São Paulo city in planning and budgeting, hindering coordination across the metropolitan area. Spending in the city of São Paulo constitutes some two-thirds of spending for the SPMR. The way in which it allocates resources and the efficiency with which they are used are thus critical for the ability of the SPMR to strengthen its competitiveness and meet the needs of the future. Current approaches to fiscal management have

---

[5] A CEPAC is a bond issued by the municipality that grants the holder specific development rights.

provided sustained increases in revenues and expenditures but do not seem to take into account increasing concerns about debt levels. The multiplicity of planning instruments in the city suggests that prioritization of spending is difficult and is often something that is imposed by other levels of government, either at the federal or the state level. The nature of the budget process also locks the city into incrementalism and uncertainty. While many state-of-the-art budget tools exist, it may be worth refocusing them on drawing down of the debt, creating space for investment, and improving the predictability of budget implementation as a foundation for both the city and the SPMR going forward.

Some Other Tools to Support Public Finances

São Paulo city has over the years developed some specific mechanisms to further urban development and raise revenue. Here a few are briefly described to demonstrate ways in which the city of São Paulo has pursued urban development in a constrained environment.[6]

Progressive Property Taxes

The city of São Paulo approved the use of a progressive property tax in July 2010. The objective was to create a tax instrument that would incentivize improved land uses for specific properties. The framework identifies underutilized or deteriorated properties and establishes a deadline for improvements. Owners failing to make such improvements would be charged staged increases in property tax assessments over time, which over a five-year period could increase up to 15 percent of the property value. If, after a specified deadline, the owner has failed to carry out the works stipulated by the authorities, the property can be expropriated in exchange for municipal bonds (CEPACs).

The law regulating the progressive property tax initially provided for application of the progressive tax to specific areas of the municipality: those with unbuilt or underbuilt land that would be suitable for housing and with existing infrastructure. To date, the municipal government has not notified owners in the areas where the instrument can be applied, so the instrument remains unused.

Enhanced Development Rights

Originally developed in the 1970s, the idea of enhanced development rights (*otorgo oneroso*) draws on the possibility of separating the "right to property" from the "right to build" with the aim that the city could charge for construction rights. The instrument was first approved and regulated in 1986 and was linked specifically to slum clearance programs. Originally, the enhanced development rights awarded the right to increase development densities for specific lots occupied by favelas (slums) in exchange for the responsibility of constructing social housing elsewhere in the city. By 1995, the requirement to build housing was removed from the legal framework, and

---

[6] This section draws from Samad (2011).

its attractiveness increased. From 1988 to 1998, enhanced development rights are estimated to have produced significant revenues for the municipal government.

The early use of this instrument was characterized by some complications that limited the impact of the program. First, accurately valuing and charging for enhanced development rights proved very difficult. Counterpart contributions were frequently underestimated. Second, revenues generated from the granting of developer rights were not consistently used for the intended purpose of social housing. Third, legal challenges were raised against the instrument, suggesting that the sale of exceptions to zoning was illegal, and these operations were declared unconstitutional in 1998.

A new enhanced development rights instrument was introduced in 2002 with the Strategic Master Plan. A series of decrees, laws, and government directives were produced providing detailed guidance on the procedures to be followed for approving applications and monitoring the amount of building potential actually "sold." A management structure was also developed linked to the Department of Building Approvals and the Department of Urban Planning in order to oversee use of the new instrument. From 2007 to 2009, an estimated US$200 million (R$408 million) was generated for the Municipal Urban Development Fund by enhanced development rights. This amount represented about 16 percent of total receipts and 20 percent of the amounts collected in property taxes in 2008.

Urban Operations

The Urban Operation is a legal tool of São Paulo city that can be used to designate areas for government-sponsored development projects, under which financiers/developers pay for development rights. Typical projects have supported the development and/or update of infrastructure, housing to replace slums, installing urban amenities in line with desired density, and protecting the environment, usually through a development consortium. Unlike the enhanced development rights, in which financial counterpart contributions are channeled into building housing outside the demarcated area, Urban Operation resources can be used only within the demarcated areas. The Urban Operation concept has been used for some time and with regulations set for each operation, with developers and financiers paying substantial sums for the enhanced building rights within the demarcated areas.

Ten urban operations are under way, five of which are implementing regulations. These operations include initiatives to revitalize old industrial and railway areas, as well as the building of highway links in the SPMR and addressing environmental issues (see box 12.1). They have proven to be an effective means to raise resources for the municipal development. At the end of 2010, these operations had generated significant resources with positive balances ranging from R$18 million to R$671 million.[7]

---

[7] Samad (2011) describes in details the specifics of four Urban Operations currently under way (Centro Urban, Água Branca, Faria Lima, and Água Espraiada).

BOX 12.1

São Paulo's proactive approach to environmental issues

Metropolitan areas typically suffer from a wide range of environmental issues: from high carbon dioxide emissions due to traffic congestions, to polluted water supplies, to declining biodiversity. São Paulo municipality, the heart of the SPMR, has taken a proactive approach to addressing these issues.

In 2009, São Paulo was the first city in Brazil to create a policy and guidelines for addressing climate change and a municipal committee to ensure that words were followed up with action. Emissions have already been reduced by 12 percent, and São Paulo plays a key role in the executive committee of the C40 Cities Climate Leadership Group and on the International Council for Local Environmental Initiatives (ICLEI).

On the mitigation side, São Paulo has already held three auctions of carbon credits, worth some $75.5 million reals (about US$38 million). The city has also developed a program of vehicle inspection and is moving to cleaner forms of transport, such as clean buses and bicycles, reducing the number of hospital internments and deaths in the city and saving on health costs.

On the adaptation side, the city government is creating many more parks and green spaces: 24 to date, with a goal of 100 by the end of 2012. The city is one of 21 cities in the world to take part in the Local Action for Biodiversity program of ICLEI, with the aim of bringing together issues related to urban biodiversity, poverty, and sustainable development.

Rethinking the urban space is also part of the plan to address environmental issues. Key urban operations are under way to restore rundown industrial areas and to address water and waste management. A multisectoral effort is under way to restore key watersheds in São Paulo city and in the broader metro area. The city has also created an environmental civil guard, with some 540 agents overseeing environmental measures and controls across the city. And the city has mapped areas that are highly vulnerable to risk, such as flooding or landslides, and it is including such concerns in the development of key infrastructure, including the construction of roads.

Although climate change and environmental sustainability pose enormous challenges, São Paulo demonstrates that local efforts and solutions can not only help to address these global issues but also make a more healthy, attractive, and desirable city in which to live.

SOURCE: São Paulo Research Foundation-FAPSEP (2012).

CEPACs

CEPAC is a bond issued by the municipality and sold in public auction that grants its holder the right to augment the construction area in excess of legislation or to construct buildings that deviate from the guidelines and use foreseen by the legislation. This right, however, can be exercised only within the perimeter of the respective Urban Operations, discussed previously. CEPACs are also used for paying suppliers or defraying compensation payments for expropriated properties needed to make way for urban interventions, subject to the agreement of all involved. The first CEPAC was issued in 2004, by means of the São Paulo Stock Exchange; R$30 million was raised (100,000 CEPACs with a face value of R$300).

Use of CEPACs requires providing security for investors, which involves monitoring of both the financial market and the progress being made in the Urban Operation. The Securities Commission has issued specific normative instructions (instruction 401/2003) covering the trading and distribution of CEPACs, ruling that no CEPAC can be issued without the issuing municipality seeking prior registration of the bonds in the commission. Considerable effort goes into developing the prospectus and in providing supplemental updates.

São Paulo city has been creative in developing instruments that specifically support urban and metropolitan development while providing a source of revenue. Other, smaller municipalities in the metro area may not have the projects or technical capacity required to use such instruments, but the innovations that have helped support São Paulo municipality's finances at the margin could potentially be deployed for the SPMR as a whole.

THE SPMR GOING FORWARD

The SPMR has seen much change over the decades and, as with all large metro areas, will continue to face pressures resulting from a growing population and economic transition. This brief review of governance and public finance in the SPMR highlights the growth and changes of the region over time and trends in public finance to address these changes. There are many issues to be addressed going forward, but two are especially important.

The first relates to finding effective mechanisms for coordination across the SPMR. As noted above, metropolitan areas are created at the state level, but each municipality has sovereignty and veto power over plans and programs to be implemented in its jurisdiction. This places a premium on creating mechanisms for coordination in which both the view of the state level and the views of the municipalities included in the metro area can be balanced. In the SPMR, the challenge is bringing together 39 different entities, with one much larger than the others, to make joint decisions and implement programs. Over the years, many such structures have been created to support coordination and development across the SPMR, but with the limited funding and decision-making authority built into the constitution, more often than not they have served only an advisory role. The new recently developed structures of the SPMR, including the development council, the consultative council, the technical groups, and the regional enterprise to support implementation of SPMR plans, allow for representation of all municipalities in the SPMR and may be able to play a more effective and concrete role than previous structures. However, the tension between the state and municipalities over who has ultimate decision-making authority and use of resources continues to be built into the system. Leadership can help to move the agenda forward, but finding solutions that work for all of the relevant municipalities will continue to be a challenge.

The second issue relates to effectively building investment priorities into the budget, which will continue to be a critical challenge. While amalgamated, detailed fiscal accounts for the SPMR are not available, the information that exists suggests that the municipalities of the SPMR do have at their disposal the tools to raise revenues, as well as significant transfers from higher levels of government. Given its size, São Paulo city is clearly the driver of the fiscal balances for the region as a whole. Given the economic and demographic changes in the SPMR, pressures for both social services and investment needs continue to grow. Many plans, programs, and strategies are created to address these needs, but which plan takes precedence and how they are linked to the actual resources available are never quite clear. Finally, in budget legislation, as well as in the budget process, critical investment spending is treated as a residual, subject to fluctuations in revenue collection. Uncertainty over the resources available for investment makes it extremely difficult to coordinate across two municipalities, much less 39, and creates a significant obstacle to meeting the immense investment needs of the SPMR.

São Paulo city has come up with innovative mechanisms to finance investment and urban renewal through urban operations and the issuance of bonds for enhanced development rights in specified areas. While these are useful, they are difficult to use for cross-jurisdictional purposes. A key priority for the metro region is to build investment priorities into the budget more effectively at all levels. Without this, it will be extremely difficult to undertake the investments necessary to economically, socially, and environmentally renew the SPMR so that it maintains it place on the global stage.

REFERENCES

Arretche, Marta. Forthcoming. Governance and finance in two Brazilian metropolitan areas. In *Governance and finance of large metropolitan areas in federal systems*, ed. Rupak Chattapadhyay and Enid Slack. Oxford: Oxford University Press.

Biderman, Ciro, and Marcos F. M. Lopez. 2011. The geographical dynamics of industry in metropolitan areas: Lessons for São Paulo. Background Paper to São Paulo City Study prepared by the World Bank. São Paulo: Center for Political and Economic Studies, Getulio Vargas Foundation.

Clarke, Roland. 2011. São Paulo city study. Annex 3: Public sector management. Washington, DC: World Bank. Draft.

Darido, Georges. 2011. São Paulo city study. Annex 5: Transport. Washington, DC: World Bank. Draft.

Jordan, Luke, Anita Fiori, and Austin Kilroy. 2011. São Paulo city study. Annex 1: Economic vocation. Washington, DC: World Bank. Draft.

Olinto, Pedro. 2011. São Paulo city study. Annex 7: Labor market outcomes. Washington, DC: World Bank. Draft.

Rezende, Fernando, and Sol Garson. 2006. Financing of metropolitan areas in Brazil: Political obstacles, institutional and new proposals to improve coordination. *Review of Contemporary Economics* 10(1):5–34.

Sakho, Seynabou. 2011. São Paulo city study. Annex 2: Fiscal policy. Washington, DC: World Bank. Draft.

Samad, Taimar. 2011. São Paulo city study. Annex 4: Urban development. Washington, DC: World Bank. Draft.

São Paulo Research Foundation. 2012. Presentation at the Workshop on Climate Change Programs, (August 23).

World Bank. 2012. São Paulo city study: Policy report. Washington, DC. Draft.

Metropolitan Infrastructure and Capital Finance 13

GREGORY K. INGRAM, ZHI LIU, AND KARIN L. BRANDT

Perceptions of the role of infrastructure in economic development and of the desired modes for providing infrastructure have evolved in the last two centuries at both the national and metropolitan levels. In the nineteenth and early twentieth century, much metropolitan infrastructure was privately provided. By the mid-twentieth century, infrastructure was viewed as the commanding heights of the economy, important for economic development but also subject to endemic market failures. Accordingly, public-sector involvement in infrastructure, advocated by both governments and development agencies, became the norm. Then in the 1980s and 1990s, concerns about government failure, poor performance of public infrastructure agencies, and large investment requirements heightened interest in the private provision and financing of infrastructure. Private participation in infrastructure (PPI) has since greatly expanded, doing well while falling short of the most optimistic expectations, with a more sector-focused and country-tailored approach evolving in recent years (Ingram and Fay 2008).

Infrastructure is not precisely defined, and it originally encompassed most social overhead capital. This chapter defines infrastructure to include energy (electricity and natural gas); telecommunications (fixed telephone lines, mobile phone service, and Internet connections); transportation (airports, railways, roads, and seaports); and water supply and sanitation (piped water and sewage collection and treatment). Many of these activities share technical features that require governmental regulation to improve outcomes, such as integrated networks and economies of

The authors acknowledge counsel and assistance from Wanli Fang, Om Prakash Agarwal, Arturo Ardila-Gomez, and Jorge Rebelo and helpful comments from Robert Buckley, Jeff Gutman, Anthony Pellegrini, and the volume editors.

scale that encourage natural monopolies, and economic features, such as externalities and attributes of public goods.[1]

Unfortunately, reliable data on infrastructure capital stocks are seldom available for urban versus rural areas or for metropolitan areas (Estache 2004), while national data are now reasonably ubiquitous. The analysis of infrastructure physical capital stocks reported here is based on country-level data available from the World Development Indicators database (World Bank 2011), including kilowatts of electricity-generating capacity, kilometers of paved roads, number of fixed telephone lines, number of mobile phone subscriptions, and share of households with access to safe water and adequate sanitation. Additional service quality data for roads and telecommunications are from the World Road Statistics (International Road Federation 2010) and the World Telecommunications Development Report (International Telecommunications Union 2010). The data for physical stocks across all sectors are for 2006, and complete data are available for 83 countries.

URBANIZATION AND INFRASTRUCTURE STOCKS

To explore the effect of urbanization and income on infrastructure, the relations across countries among infrastructure levels, urbanization levels, and income were examined by estimating the elasticities of national infrastructure stocks per capita with respect to the share of urban population and income per capita. In regressions of log infrastructure physical stocks per capita by sector on log purchasing power parity (PPP) gross domestic product (GDP) per capita, and urban population percentage, the coefficients are elasticities. The elasticities of infrastructure stocks with respect to urbanization are 0.01 or smaller, and only two of the six elasticity measures are statistically significant (table 13.1). This means that a doubling of urban population share would increase national infrastructure stocks by 1 percent or less. These findings indicate that a country's urbanization level has little relation with its amount of physical infrastructure stock.

The lack of relation between national infrastructure stocks and share of urban population at first seems surprising, but note that the estimated model holds income constant. Of course, income and urbanization are correlated (simple correlation of 0.60 in the sample used here), but urbanization varies widely in low-income countries (Fay and Opal 1999). In addition, two countervailing relations are likely to be at work. First, infrastructure's technical economies of scale mean that less physical stock per person is needed to provide infrastructure services as population density increases. Urban densities are much higher than rural densities, thus lowering urban infrastructure stock per capita. Second, in developing countries average urban incomes are typically higher than average rural incomes, and this would increase the demand for infrastructure services and for related urban infrastructure capital stock. These two effects may offset each other in the aggregate at the country level.

---

[1] This definition omits hospitals, schools, and government facilities, which do not utilize integrated networks and/or exhibit many economies of scale. It also excludes soft infrastructure such as governance, financial, social, and cultural assets and institutions that rely more on knowledge than on physical capital.

TABLE 13.1

Regressions of log per capita infrastructure measures on log PPP, income, and percentage of population urban

	Log electricity generation	Phone lines	Paved roads*	Mobile subscriptions	Access to sanitation	Access to water
Intercept	−5.11 (−8.37)	−5.38 (−8.68)	−7.9 (−10.07)	0.092** (0.17)	0.74** (1.87)	3.24 (19.35)
Log PPP income/capital	1.17 (13.02)	1.10 (12.04)	0.97 (8.44)	0.58 (7.08)	0.38 (6.50)	0.12 (4.88)
Percent urban	0.0096	0.004**	−0.0038**	0.014	0.0016**	0.0022**
	(2.15)	(0.88)	(−0.66)	(3.49)	(0.55)	(1.80)
N	83	83	83	83	83	83
R^2	0.85	0.81	0.63	0.73	0.56	0.52

Parentheses indicate t-ratios. Coefficients of PPP, income, and urban percentages are elasticities.

*The road length measure includes both intercity and urban roads.

**$p < 0.05$.

Similarly, Canning (1998) found that the impact of urbanization on infrastructure varies by sector: electricity and telephones increased with urbanization, while transport was not strongly related to urbanization. Other studies found that while population, per capita income, and population density are significant determinants of road length, urbanization is insignificant (Ingram and Liu 1999). Accordingly, this chapter develops investment projections at the national level. Metropolitan-level investment projections can be scaled from those, using metropolitan GDP or other appropriate measures.

Of course, even if detailed urban data were available, addressing infrastructure needs at the metropolitan level raises difficulties of definition in some sectors because infrastructure located outside of metropolitan boundaries can be integral to urban infrastructure services. In the power sector, metropolitan areas normally draw from a national or regional grid, and electricity-generating and distribution capacity are often located outside of urbanized areas. Metropolitan areas also have much transport capacity within their borders but benefit greatly from intercity transport located outside city boundaries. The same is true for telecommunications, where intercity capacity is an important component of urban telephone service. In these sectors, some attribution of the costs of infrastructure assets located outside of metropolitan areas would need to be made based on population or regional product, similar to the approach proposed here. Some other infrastructure sectors face less difficult metropolitan boundary issues. For example, mass rail transit, water supply, and sanitation networks are often essentially contained within metropolitan boundaries, and in many developing countries, reported national water and sanitation infrastructure levels include only urban data.

Turning to the relation between quantities of infrastructure facilities and income, the coefficients of table 13.1 for per capita income (elasticities of infrastructure with respect to PPP income) indicate that physical stocks of infrastructure and percentages of households served increase across countries at very different rates as PPP income grows. For example, when per capita PPP income doubles, electricity-generating capacity and phone lines more than double, road length almost doubles, and access to sanitation and water much less than doubles.

Because the quantity of infrastructure stocks by sector increases at different rates with income, the sectoral composition of infrastructure stock varies systematically across country income levels. Figure 13.1 shows the average composition of infrastructure stocks by value across country income groups (using World Bank [2011] country income categories). These shares by value are obtained by weighting the physical stocks by their unit costs (see table 13.2).

FIGURE 13.1

The sectoral mix of infrastructure varies with country income group

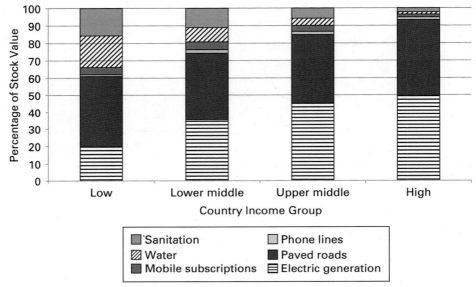

SOURCES: International Telecommunications Union (2010); World Bank (2011).

TABLE 13.2

Unit costs of infrastructure investment in 2010 and thereafter

Sector	Cost (US$)
Electricity generation	$1,900 per kilowatt of generating capacity, including network cost
Paved roads	$410,000 per kilometer of paved two-lane road
Phone lines	$261 per fixed line
Mobile subscriptions	$127 per subscriber
Water access	$400 per connected household
Sanitation access	$700 per connected household

SOURCE: Derived from Chatterton and Puerto (2005, table A1).

Figure 13.1 reveals that paved roads constitute a large share of the value of infrastructure stocks at all income levels and that electricity generation's share is large and grows rapidly, eventually exceeding the share of paved roads in upper-middle- and high-income countries. While the share of phone lines grows in middle-income countries, its base value is small relative to other sectors. Water and sanitation grow less rapidly than income, and their share of total infrastructure value decreases even as coverage expands. The surprise in figure 13.1 is mobile phone service. Fifteen years ago, this sector was virtually nonexistent in developing countries, and it has expanded dramatically, with coverage now much greater than for fixed telephone lines. While the elasticity for mobile subscriptions is less than 1 in table 13.1, it is the one infrastructure sector where the elasticity of expansion with income varies across income groups and where expansion of coverage has been driven more by cost reductions than by income growth. Since 2000, the investment required per mobile phone subscription has fallen more than 80 percent (Chatterton and Puerto 2005).

INVESTMENT PROJECTIONS

Based on countries' existing physical infrastructure stocks and the elasticity of stocks' growth with respect to national income, the magnitude of investment required is projected so that current infrastructure amounts in each sector increase in accordance with the estimated sectoral income elasticities. The results from one set of projections of annual investments, based on assumed economic growth rates of 5 percent in developing countries and 3 percent in high-income countries, are shown in table 13.3. This global projection is based on the sample of 83 countries (30 low-, 22 lower-middle-, and 21 upper-middle-income developing countries and 10 high-income countries) that have data for all infrastructure sectors. These projections are

TABLE 13.3

Investment and maintenance in infrastructure and national income

Country income group	Aggregate GDP, 2008 US$ (billion)	Assumed growth rate (%)	Infrastructure share					
			As percentage of national GDP			In 2008 US$ (billions)		
			Investment	Maintenance	Total	Investment	Maintenance	Total
Low	509.60	5	2.8	1.7	4.5	14.00	8.80	22.80
Lower middle	7,691.90	5	3.5	2.4	5.9	270.80	183.80	454.60
Upper middle	7,471.90	5	2.2	1.5	3.7	165.20	113.20	278.40
Developing total	15,673.40		2.8	2.0	4.8	450.00	305.80	755.80
High	42,041.40	3	0.8	0.9	1.7	332.80	363.70	696.40
Total	57,714.80		1.4	1.2	2.5	782.80	669.50	1452.20

SOURCE: GDP data from World Bank (2011).

what would be invested if past relations hold in the future; they are not normative projections from an optimization model showing what should be invested. Results have not been corrected for outliers or for countries with infrastructure deficits or surpluses.

The investment required as a percentage of GDP for the sampled countries in each income group to increase their infrastructure in line with estimated income elasticities was calculated, and this percentage was then applied to the total GDP of all countries in each income group. For example, the investment required for low-income countries in the sample to increase their infrastructure stocks as their incomes rise is calculated based on country physical stocks, the income elasticities in table 13.1, the unit costs in table 13.2, and the assumed growth rate. This amount was then transformed to a share of GDP for the 30 sampled low-income countries, and that GDP share was applied to the GDP total for all countries in the low-income group. The projections for new investment average 2.8 percent of GDP across all developing countries.

Maintenance, which averages 2.0 percent of GDP for developing countries, was calculated in a similar way based on annual maintenance costs that are: 2 percent of the replacement cost of electric power and paved roads, 3 percent for water and sanitation, and 8 percent for mobile and fixed-line telephone stocks (Fay and Yepes 2003). Projections for maintenance are also shown in table 13.3 using these general rules.

Reasonably growing lower-middle-income countries need about 5.9 percent of GDP per year for total infrastructure investment and maintenance, and upper-middle-income countries, 3.7 percent, with more required for investment than maintenance in all but high-income countries. The highest dollar amounts for investment and maintenance are projected for high-income countries ($696 billion), followed by lower-middle-income countries ($454 billion). Relative to high-income countries, developing countries taken together will require more annual investment and somewhat less maintenance. Financing will likely be needed for new investment in developing countries, while maintenance should be covered as an operating expense on an ongoing basis.

The projected shares and amounts provide an order-of-magnitude estimate of needed expenditures. These shares are generally similar to those formulated from 2000 to 2010 using a more disaggregated approach (Fay and Yepes 2003). These investment shares vary linearly with the assumed rate of economic growth and would be higher for faster-growing countries and lower for slower-growing ones. Given the lack of relation between the size of infrastructure stocks at the national level and urbanization, metropolitan estimates can be obtained by applying these GDP shares to the output of metropolitan areas.

Annual investment shares of metropolitan GDP are available for two special metropolitan areas, Hong Kong and Singapore, that had average economic growth rates from 2000 to 2010 of 4.4 percent and 5.9 percent, respectively. From 2007 to 2010, Hong Kong's infrastructure expenditure averaged 2.56 percent of its GDP, and Singapore's was 6.44 percent, indicating that higher growth rates are associated with higher infrastructure expenditures.

INFRASTRUCTURE SERVICE DELIVERY

The foregoing analysis of infrastructure capital stocks and investment assumes that economic growth increases the demand for infrastructure services and thereby the demand for additions to infrastructure capital. However, increasing the efficiency of use of existing infrastructure facilities may be an alternative means of increasing infrastructure services in many countries. The performance of infrastructure stocks in terms of delivering services efficiently varies widely across countries. Electricity losses range from 5 to 25 percent, faults per 100 phone lines range from 1 to 70, and unpaved roads range from 0 to 80 percent of all roads.

Because sectoral infrastructure stocks are highly correlated with income, it is not surprising that they are also highly correlated with one another within countries. For example, countries with ample paved roads also have large electricity-generating capacity. This high correlation of infrastructure stocks within countries is summarized in figure 13.2. However, infrastructure performance is not highly correlated with income, and the performance of infrastructure stocks (the quality of the services produced and the efficiency of production) has a much lower correlation within countries (figure 13.3). Moreover, both good and poor performance is observed across all country income levels. Inefficiency matters because increased efficiency reduces the need for investment in additional stocks.

FIGURE 13.2

Infrastructure stocks across sectors are highly correlated within countries

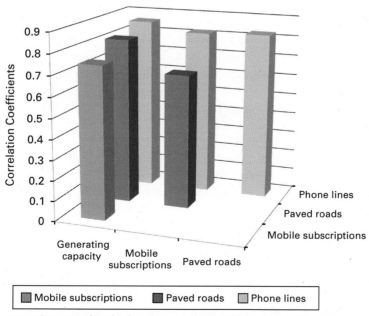

SOURCES: International Road Federation 2010; International Telecommunications Union (2010); World Bank (2011).

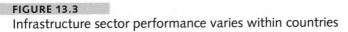

FIGURE 13.3

Infrastructure sector performance varies within countries

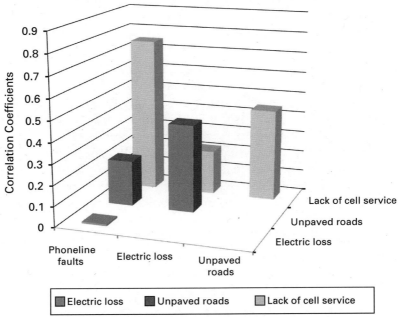

SOURCES: International Road Federation (2010); International Telecommunications Union (2010); World Bank (2011).

Many inefficiencies in infrastructure service provision have their roots in poor incentive frameworks, including soft budget constraints, large government subsidies, inadequate maintenance, and bureaucratic inefficiencies. Moreover, offering services below cost promotes overuse of services, a particular problem in electric power and water, where subsidized rates undermine end-user efficiency, stimulating demand for services and hence for investment. Latin America's electricity tariffs are about 75 percent of Organisation for Economic Co-operation and Development (OECD) tariff levels and do not cover full costs, while in other regions power tariffs range from one-third to half of OECD levels (Ingram and Fay 2008). Governments in sub-Saharan Africa already spend $4.1 billion a year (0.7 percent of GDP) on power and water subsidies that benefit mainly a small group of affluent customers (Foster and Briceño-Garmendia 2010). Obtaining sufficient infrastructure services involves not only investment in additional stocks but also improved management and service delivery from existing facilities.

Limited evidence from developing countries also shows that PPI has led to improved performance and efficiency. A comparison of performance by Gassner, Popov, and Pushak (2008) between utilities with private-sector participation and state-owned enterprises in the electricity and water distribution sectors in a number of countries found that private-sector participation resulted in improved quality of services, increased outputs, increased labor productivity, and an expanded capital base. Another study of electricity distribution companies in Latin America also found that privatization of ownership resulted in improved labor productivity, operating efficiency, and service quality (Andres, Foster, and Guasch 2006). Privatization of infrastructure service provision and competition among providers have improved service quality in telecommunications in many countries. Even in urban and suburban transport in some countries, privatization and competition have also improved public transit services and ridership (box 13.1).

CHANGING INTERNATIONAL SOURCES OF INVESTMENT FUNDS

While improving efficiency will help, most developing cities will require large new investments as their populations and economies grow. While some cities have been successful in financing urban infrastructure from traditional sources of local revenues (i.e., local tax revenues, user charges, and intergovernmental transfers), the revenue has often been modest and used mainly for local recurrent expenditures. Many developing cities not only have a small revenue base but also assume few responsibilities for the provision of municipal infrastructure.

Decentralization has enabled many cities to seek other sources of financing and modalities of infrastructure provision. Developing cities increasingly are successful in financing urban infrastructure through borrowing from commercial banks, issuing municipal bonds, imposing land development-related charges such as land concessions, and adopting public-private partnership financing. Development assistance and PPI grew dramatically in the last 20 years, providing metropolitan areas with much needed infrastructure finance.

BOX 13.1

Privatization and competition can improve efficiency: The case of Rio's subway and suburban rail

In 1997 the Rio de Janeiro state government privatized the city's subway and suburban rail systems that had been heavily subsidized to compensate for high deficits, insufficient management, and inadequate infrastructure. Concessions were awarded through a competitive bidding process to two private operators for subway operations and maintenance of the two systems, respectively, without operating subsidies. This move was part of a government effort to address the budgetary crisis of the mid-1990s. The two concessionaires significantly improved services, ridership, and financial performance with their improved management, cost control measures, and implementation of tariff integration agreements. One subway concessionaire, MetroRio, helped to expand the subway network by 62 percent in length, from 25.3 km to 40.9 km, and increased ridership by 71 percent, from 380,000 to 650,000 trips a day. In 2007 the government awarded MetroRio a 20-year concession renewable for an additional 20 years. The system is now sufficiently profitable, with a 1.6 cost recovery ratio. Prior to privatization of the suburban rail system, ridership had declined from 1.2 million trips a day in 1985 to 145,000 in 1998. After the privatization, ridership increased steadily to 530,000 trips per workday in 2010. Most remarkable, these subway and suburban rail performance and efficiency improvements were achieved without government operating subsidies during a period of slow metropolitan population growth, less than 1 percent a year.

SOURCES: Rebelo (1999); Gevert (2004); Briginshaw (2011).

Official Development Assistance and World Bank Trends

In recent decades, official development assistance (ODA) and lending from the World Bank's International Bank for Reconstruction and Development (IBRD), and International Development Association (IDA) commitments have continued to be an important source of infrastructure investment funds in developing countries.[2] ODA commitments for infrastructure recently reached $20 billion per year, an amount that is similar to the current infrastructure investment forecast for low-income countries in table 13.3. However, low-income countries receive only about 25 percent of total ODA, meaning that lower-middle- and upper-middle-income countries receive a majority of ODA. IBRD/IDA commitments for infrastructure trended down in the 1990s and then grew in the 2000s (see figures 13.4 and 13.5). The recent growth reflects the World Bank's increasing awareness of the impact of infrastructure service delivery on poverty reduction and economic development, embodied in the World Bank's Infrastructure Action Plan initiated in 2004. This engaged the International Finance Corporation (IFC) and the Multilateral Investments Guarantee Agency (MIGA). The subsequent Sustainable Infrastructure Action Plan aimed to scale up public-private partnership programs, including joint planning initiatives with IFC/IDA and MIGA/IDA projects in the Africa region from 2009 to 2011.

Figure 13.4 also shows that ODA and IBRD/IDA shares of lending commitments to infrastructure have followed different patterns. ODA's infrastructure share was fairly constant, around 15 percent, from 1980 to 1999, and then decreased to about 10 percent as commitments for infrastructure grew less rapidly than total ODA. The IBRD/IDA share declined from around 45 percent in 1980 to 16 percent in 1999 and then rebounded to above 40 percent in recent years.

PPI Trends

PPI in the form of direct investments, leases, and operating contracts revived in the late 1980s, grew dramatically in the 1990s, and became less regionally concentrated in the early 2000s. Figure 13.5 shows that the dollar value of PPI has been as volatile as ODA in relative terms (both varying by a factor of 2 in the past 15 years) while changing much more in absolute terms. PPI grew rapidly in the 1990s until the East Asian crisis of 1997, decreased, and then rebounded until the 2008 financial crisis. ODA commitments are not countercyclical but follow a pattern similar to that of PPI, with both peaking in the mid-1990s, bottoming in 2002, and rising again through 2008. The striking fact from figure 13.5 is that PPI commitments are nearly 10 times larger than ODA in 2007 for infrastructure and are now a major element of infrastructure finance. Its peak value of $160 billion is about 36 percent of the $436 billion new infrastructure investment forecast in table 13.3 for its primary recipients, lower-middle- and upper-middle-income countries. PPI and

---

[2] ODA encompasses concessional aid, so it includes IDA lending but not IBRD lending. IDA accounts for about 6–10 percent of total ODA. IBRD, IDA, IFC, and MIGA (mentioned later) are four of the five institutions that compose the World Bank Group.

FIGURE 13.4

Infrastructure share of ODA and IBRD/IDA commitments

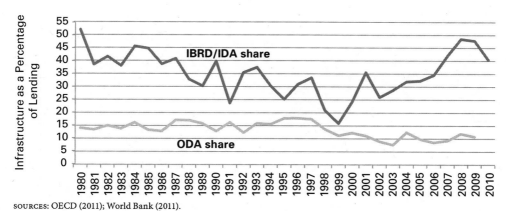

SOURCES: OECD (2011); World Bank (2011).

FIGURE 13.5

PPI is much larger than development assistance

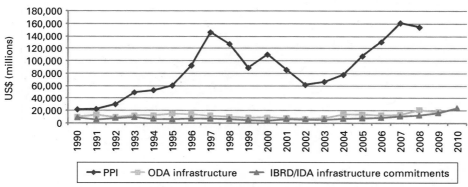

SOURCES: OECD (2011); World Bank (2011); World Bank and Public-Private Infrastructure Advisory Facility (2011).

development assistance to infrastructure together are now about 42 percent of the total new infrastructure investment forecast for all developing countries.

Although it follows a similar cyclical path over time as development assistance, the distribution of PPI across infrastructure sectors is very different from that of ODA and IBRD/IDA (figure 13.6). ODA and IBRD/IDA commitment shares are similar: both provide their largest support to transport and energy, substantial support to water and sanitation, and the least to telecom. In contrast, telecom is the largest recipient of PPI commitments, while water and sanitation receive the smallest share of total PPI. PPI in telecom is occurring across all country income groups, including low-income countries in Africa and elsewhere, with the bulk of PPI activity in mobile service.

Telecom has made the most progress toward privatization, and the number of state-owned telecom firms nearly halved from 150 in 1991 to 79 in 2003 (World Bank 2004). Many developing countries are passing up fixed telephone infrastructure for

FIGURE 13.6

International infrastructure investment varies by sectors and source, 1990–2008

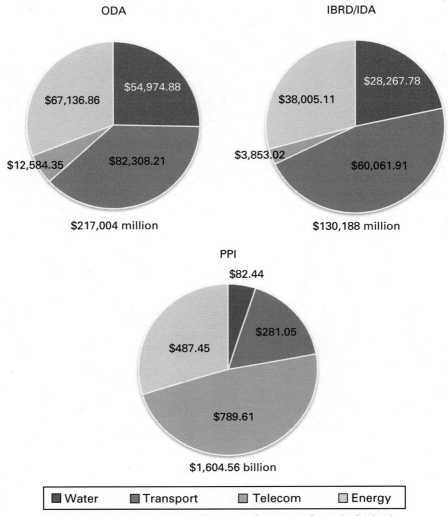

SOURCES: World Bank (2011); World Bank and Public-Private Infrastructure Advisory Facility (2011).

wireless service to reduce initial investment costs. The private sector's concentration in telecom and mobile service provision is attributed to the ease of cost recovery through direct user charges. Cost recovery is more difficult in other sectors, with water and sanitation the most challenging. As a result, there is little private investment in water and sanitation, and leasing with operating contracts is the common mode of private participation in those sectors.

In sectors other than telecom, PPI remains more concentrated among upper-middle- and lower-middle-income countries. About 80 percent of PPI in energy in the 2000s has been for electricity generation, predominately in upper-middle-income countries, where generation is being separated from distribution to enable competitive bidding for power-purchase contracts. Transport investment has also been more focused on upper-middle-income countries, and road projects have taken 45 percent of transport funds, the largest share. Investment in airports and railways increased but for only a small number of large projects, while investments for roads and seaports are more widely distributed. PPI in water and sanitation has been modest, with government investment still dominating. Activity has been mainly in lower-middle-income countries, and sewage treatment plants have received much of the investment. While activity in water and sanitation is a small share of PPI, because of the large size of PPI relative to ODA, the PPI funds involved have sometimes exceeded the dollar amounts of ODA flowing to this sector.

PPI has been spreading across more countries and regions, and its spread varies by sector, with telecom having the most ubiquitous private investment. The concentration of PPI among regions has been declining over time (see figure 13.7). In the 1990s, Latin America and East Asia received 96 percent of PPI funds. In the 2000s,

FIGURE 13.7

PPI is becoming less regionally concentrated: Investment percentage by region

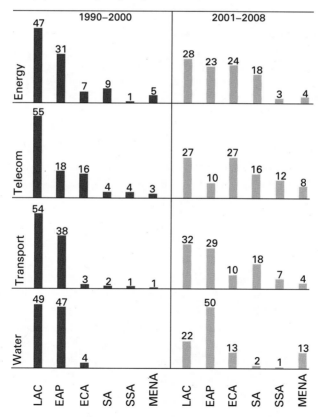

Abbreviations: EAP, East Asia and Pacific; ECA, Europe and Central Asia; LAC, Latin America and Caribbean; MENA, Middle East and North Africa; SA, South Asia; SSA, sub-Saharan Africa.

SOURCE: Adapted from World Bank and Public-Private Infrastructure Advisory Facility (2011).

TABLE 13.4

Top 10 PPI recipients among developing countries, 2001–2008

Country	Investment (billion 2008 US$)	Percentage of total
Brazil	111.9	13.3
India	110.2	13.1
Russia	74.7	8.9
China	57.2	6.8
Mexico	49.3	5.9
Turkey	32	3.8
Poland	24.8	2.9
Indonesia	22.9	2.7
Nigeria	22.2	2.6
South Africa	21.4	2.5
Total	526.7	62.5

SOURCES: World Bank and Public-Private Infrastructure Advisory Facility (2011); World Bank (2011).

these two regions have received 72 percent of PPI. Table 13.4 lists the top 10 countries receiving PPI funds in the 2000s. The top countries tend to be those with large economies and include upper-middle-, lower-middle-, and low-income countries.

Moving forward, countries once bypassed by PPI are likely to see increased PPI financing from other international banks or developing countries. The sub-Saharan Africa and Middle East and North Africa regions historically received the smallest amount of PPI. Infrastructure stocks are currently not keeping up with their rapid population growth, and needs are pressing, particularly in the water sector. In 2011 the IBRD, IFC, and the Islamic Development Bank responded by forming the Arab Financing Facility for Infrastructure to support public infrastructure services and public-private partnerships that follow conventional and Islamic-compliant financing. In addition, south-south flows of investment funds in infrastructure to sub-Saharan Africa are growing (box 13.2).

Recent Impediments to PPI

PPI has become increasingly popular in developing countries, largely because of fiscal constraints. In particular, developing cities typically have very limited fiscal space and modest local tax revenues to finance needed municipal infrastructure. Annez (2006) critiqued PPI's metropolitan performance for committing only 10 percent of its total infrastructure investment to urban areas, yet energy and telecommunications, the two largest PPI sectors that serve national and urban areas, were not included in that analysis.[3] PPI continues to spread across sectors and regions as developing cities are encouraged by the generally positive experience of

---

[3] Annez (2006) excluded all commitments from the energy and telecom sectors in urban-national calculations because of overlapping boundary issues. Physical infrastructure stocks can be located outside of the urban boundary yet provide service to urban areas. Together, telecom and energy comprise around 75 percent of total PPI commitments.

BOX 13.2

South-south infrastructure finance: Chinese investment in sub-Saharan African cities

South-south investment in sub-Saharan Africa is growing at a rate similar to that of ODA for infrastructure in the region. Investments from non-OECD Arab, Chinese, and Indian financiers reached $8.3 billion in 2006, surpassing ODA's $4.0 billion (figure 13.8). China plays the largest role among non-OECD infrastructure investors (figure 13.9). China's investment in sub-Saharan Africa's infrastructure grew from less than US$0.5 billion in 2002 to more than US$7 billion in 2006, China's official "Year of Africa." China's investment focuses predominately on power (hydropower) and transport (railroads), while PPI is in telecommunications and roads, and ODA in water and sanitation. China's investment is geographically targeted in oil-rich states, primarily Nigeria and Angola, but 35 countries have received Chinese infrastructure development finance.

The majority of Chinese infrastructure investment in sub-Saharan Africa is from the Export-Import Bank of China (92 percent), given as loans (50 percent) and export credit (44 percent). Only five percent of investment is classified as foreign direct investment, and 1 percent is given through grants. The Export-Import Bank's financing terms fall roughly between those of ODA and PPI. Chinese loans average a 3.1 percent interest rate, a 3.6-year grace period, and a 13.2-year term, whereas ODA creditors offer 1.7 percent, 7.7 years, and 32.9 years, respectively. The Export-Import Bank adapted an investment approach previously used by Western corporations in the early 2000s, commonly knows as the "Angola mode" or "resources for infrastructure," in which loan repayment terms are stipulated in resource-based transactions, most notably oil. For example, China invested $1,020 million in Angola to repair infrastructure (power, transport, information and communication technology, and water) that had been damaged during the civil war via an oil-backed loan enabling China to receive 10,000 barrels of oil per day (Foster et al. 2008). Much of the investment is in Luanda, Angola, where infrastructure is inadequate to serve the capital city's estimated 5 million residents. China invested more than US$61 million in the rehabilitation and extension of Luanda's electrical system alone from 2002 to 2006 and is now involved in the "new cities" expansion project to provide 1 million new homes and infrastructure services in surrounding suburban areas. The long-term impact of China's resources for infrastructure approach is unclear because so far there has been a lack of financial mechanisms or technology transfer to ensure future maintenance. Moreover, training and technology transfer during construction have been modest because China provides the workers for most projects.

SOURCES: Foster et al. (2008); World Bank and Public-Private Infrastructure Advisory Facility (2011); World Bank (2011).

improved performance of PPI projects in high-income countries such as the United Kingdom and Australia and more recent successful projects in developing countries.[4]

The results of PPI in the urban transport sector are mixed. Toll roads in metropolitan areas with established traffic generally perform well. But governments often face a dilemma when concessionaires demand toll increases to cover increased costs or when road users press the government to improve the condition or capacity of alternative routes.[5] PPI for urban rail projects has also emerged in the devel-

---

[4] For some recent assessments, see Arthur Anderson and Enterprise LSE (2000), Fitzgerald (2004), KPMG LLP (2007), National Audit Office (2003; 2007), and Partnerships U.K. (2006).

[5] For example, the Don Muang Airport Expressway in Bangkok, a toll road under a build-operate-transfer arrangement, ran into both problems in recent years.

FIGURE 13.8

China is a significant infrastructure financier in sub-Saharan Africa

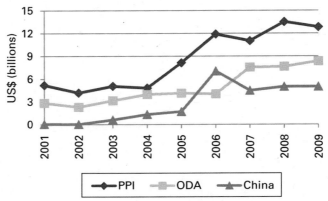

SOURCES: Foster et al. 2008; World Bank and Public-Private Infrastructure Advisory Facility (2011); World Bank (2011).

FIGURE 13.9

Non-OECD investors increase role in sub-Saharan Africa infrastructure

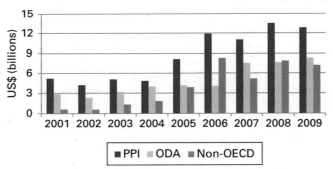

SOURCES: Foster et al. (2008); World Bank and Public-Private Infrastructure Advisory Facility (2011); World Bank (2011).

oping world since the 1990s. For example, seven contracts were awarded to build urban rail lines in Bangkok, Kuala Lumpur, and Manila. One of them, the Bangkok Elevated Road and Transit System (also known as the Hopewell Project), suffered severely from the 1997 financial crisis and was subsequently abandoned, but all other lines have been implemented and operate successfully. A detailed assessment of these lines concluded that despite various problems, these private investment projects were successful in delivering services to users and that the governments alone were unlikely able to build these lines in the same time frame (Allport 2005).

Despite various benefits of PPI, a number of impediments exist in the developing world. First, PPI projects are often carried out in an opportunistic rather than systematic way. Countries that are more successful in PPI are those with a clear policy and program, and some have even published model concession documents. India's national highway sector, for example, successfully attracted a large volume of private financing over the last eight years. Many of the privately financed highways are located in the metropolitan areas where traffic grows rapidly. The National Highway Authority of India (NHAI) website publishes guidelines for investment in the sector, the location of road sections suitable for PPI, and model concession documents (see Ministry of Road Transport and Highways 2012; NHAI 2012). The Ministry of Finance also issued guidelines for government financial support to PPI. All these send a clear signal to the market and lay a policy foundation for success.

Second, government institutional capacity remains weak in dealing with PPI. Without technical assistance from the multilateral development banks (agencies considered to be without vested interest by developing cities), most municipal governments would be reluctant to attempt PPI, and few have the financial resources needed for capacity building and upstream project preparation. To address the capacity issues, in recent years, more and more developing countries have chosen to establish public-private partnership units for facilitating and managing infrastructure investments (Public-Private Infrastructure Advisory Facility and World Bank 2007).

Third, the presence of various legal constraints is a major impediment. For example, Thailand's law does not allow arbitration for contract disputes between the government and a private firm. This essentially increases the perceived risk of PPI contracts in the eyes of private investors. Such a legal constraint has its historical roots in the public perception of government. In the developed world, a government that enters a business contract with the private sector is seen as an equal party along with the private firms in the business deals. However, in regions such as East Asia, the public generally considers the result of arbitration against the government as government failure, instead of the outcome of a dispute resolution in a business transaction. Mediation may be an alternative to arbitration. However, to date, there are few (if any) cases of mediation clauses being built in public-private partnership contracts.

The fourth impediment is more related to a lack of bankable projects and the generally poor business climate in the lowest-income countries (Leigland 2010). Despite significant shortfalls in access to infrastructure services, the lowest-income countries are much less successful in PPI investments than are middle-income countries. PPI activities are heavily constrained by thin markets, insufficient revenue streams, and lack of investment-grade credit ratings.

Finally, decentralization of revenues and investment responsibilities is also a significant complicating factor for PPI in many countries (Ingram and Fay 2008). Decentralization of decisions about infrastructure investments generally improves knowledge about local needs and priorities, but local municipalities often lack the technical expertise to implement projects or even oversee project implementation. It also may lead to policy incoherence between municipalities, particularly for water supply and sanitation. Decentralization often replaces a central client agency with many local client agencies, which increases transaction costs for private investors and exposes them to local client agencies with highly varying technical capabilities and financial capacities. China's decentralization experience highlights the disparity among municipalities in their ability to produce infrastructure finance due to changing central-local fiscal arrangements that distort revenue sharing (Wu 2010).

The Emergence of New Domestic Financing Instruments

New financing instruments and refined older instruments have evolved in response to lessons of experience and changes in the policies and regulatory frameworks of national governments. Today, the patterns of municipal financing for infrastructure investments vary significantly, and cities often use a mix of financing instruments for projects (box 13.3). In China, municipal governments assume major fiscal responsibilities for urban infrastructure development, while the national government limits its role to financing the key national infrastructure. In Thailand and Malaysia, national governments still play a major role in the financing and provision of urban infrastructure. Even so, Bangkok and Kuala Lumpur were successful in attracting sizable private financing for urban rail projects in the 1990s. Some middle-income countries, such as Mexico, Brazil, South Africa, India, and the Philippines, now have municipal bonds (Martell and Guess 2006). Long-term debt financing of local public infrastructure has existed in a number of countries for years, and efforts have emerged recently to strengthen local fiscal responsibility and reduce the risks of local debt crisis through laws and regulations (Liu and Webb 2011). Sales of public land or land use rights have also become a significant source of local infrastructure financing in China, Ethiopia, and India (Peterson 2006).

The key question is how developing metropolitan areas create sustainable sources of financing for capital investment. PPI is significant but also volatile; for example, investment levels dropped during financial crises in 1997 and 2008. It took several years for PPI to regain momentum after the 1997 financial crisis. The post-2008 slowdown in private infrastructure investment stems to a large degree from the accompanying disruption of financial markets. The 2008 crisis reduced the availability of private bank financing for project initiation and construction and also hindered the longer-term project-supported nonrecourse bond issues and senior debt that create necessary leverage for producing sufficient returns on project developers' equity investments (Leigland and Russell 2009). For example, many of Chile's bond investments in the transportation sector were downgraded, putting projects on hold, while sub-Saharan African countries report fewer lenders and higher interest rates from international banks.

Sources of local public funds gained importance amid the financial crisis and also with decentralization, which increased the need for large metropolitan areas to provide the funds required under public-private partnerships, to make public-sector investments, and to finance maintenance of publicly owned infrastructure assets. Property tax revenues, an important local revenue source in many OECD countries, contribute a relatively large share of subnational expenditures in developing countries (table 13.5). But the message is mixed on the property tax because subnational expenditures are a small share of government expenditures, indicating that decentralization is a work in progress in many developing countries. As a result,

BOX 13.3

Developing cities use a variety of financing instruments for urban rail

Urban rail systems are very expensive to build and operate, because construction costs per kilometer vary from US$50 million (for elevated light rail in an easy urban setting) to US$180 million (for underground heavy rail). Urban rail is often one of a city's largest investments, and its financing can be a major test of the city's ability to mobilize financial resources. Moreover, the operating cost recovery ratio of most of the world's urban rail systems is less than 1.0. This means that cities must subsidize operations and maintenance deficits, which pose the risk of becoming an enduring and growing financial burden.

Despite these impediments, an increasing number of developing cities have overcome the financial constraints to build and operate urban rail systems in the last 20 years. Brazil financed urban rail investments with a combination of financial resources from federal and state governments and multilateral development bank loans guaranteed by the federal government and the National Bank of Brazil. The Chilean national government financed Santiago's subway infrastructure, and the subway company financed the rolling stock and equipment with a guarantee from the national government. Bangkok built and operated an elevated light rail system under a build-operate-transfer (BOT) arrangement without government subsidies; the national government financed the civil works of the underground Blue Line with a Japan Bank for International Cooperation ODA loan, and a BOT concession financed the equipment and operations. Kuala Lumpur built three urban rail lines, each with varying BOT agreements and government guarantees for domestic debt; however, the government took control over operations after a few years when the rail lines faced financial difficulties.

More than 30 major Chinese cities have built or are currently planning and building urban rail lines. China's national government does not provide financial support for urban rail projects. Instead, cities use revenues from land concessions, commercial loans from the municipal government-owned local investment corporations, and local government surcharges and earmarked taxes to finance capital investments. New Delhi financed its metro system with equity capital from both central and local governments and soft loans from Japan Bank for International Cooperation. The Indian government introduced a scheme to fill the financing gap to the extent of 40 percent of the capital cost of infrastructure projects with public-private partnerships, and now its cities are initiating public-private metro projects in anticipation of obtaining central government financial support. Metropolitan areas are learning from one another as lessons from various financing schemes are transferred. Some cities are adapting the successful property-financed funding model (or codevelopment model) developed in Hong Kong, which provides a long-lasting revenue stream to support operations and maintenance.

SOURCES: Allport (2005); Briginshaw (2011); Gevert (2004); Rebelo (1999).

---

property tax revenues are a much smaller share of GDP in developing than in developed countries; hence, the potential of this local revenue source is yet to be realized.

The evolution of municipal financing in China during the 1990s and 2000s is perhaps one of the most striking and unique cases. During this period, China experienced rapid income growth and urbanization. GDP grew at an average rate of 10 percent a year, and the nation's share of urban population increased from 26 percent in 1990 to nearly 50 percent in 2010 (see chapter 11, figure 11.1). This is equivalent to rural-to-urban migration of 17 million people per year. Personal income growth and urbanization both create rapidly growing demands for quality and quantity of urban infrastructure services, well beyond levels that the conventional sources of municipal revenues could finance.

To accommodate this extraordinary growth in demand, most Chinese city governments have created local investment corporations (LICs) to manage and finance

TABLE 13.5

TABLE 13.5

Property tax performance in select country groups, 2000s

Country group	Government expenditure (percentage of GDP)	Subnational expenditure (percentage of government expenditures)	Property tax	
			Percentage of GDP	Percentage of subnational expenditures
OECD	42.3	32.7	2.12	12.40
Developing	24.6	13.0	0.60	18.37
Transitional	23.4	30.3	0.68	9.43

SOURCE: Bahl and Martinez-Vazquez (2008).

urban infrastructure development on behalf of the governments. Usually, the LICs are given some land parcels and/or municipality-owned, revenue-generating utility companies (e.g., water supply or gas supply) as initial corporate assets. LICs clarify to lenders what the assets are that back the loans and also protect firms from project-related liability. With these assets as collateral, LICs are able to borrow from China Development Bank and commercial banks. Many LICs are fiscally backed (they do not have stable revenue streams) and thus rely on municipal revenues to pay off debt services.

LICs provide an increasing share of infrastructure funding. They already account for 16 percent of domestic infrastructure finance demand in the East Asia/Pacific region. For example, the Suzhou Infrastructure Investment Company, established in 2001, manages the construction, financing, and operation of infrastructure projects. In this arrangement, the Suzhou city government plans its infrastructure, and the company is tasked with raising finance and developing the projects. Loan and project finance sources include the China Development Bank, local commercial banks, trust funds, build-operate-transfer arrangements, land sales revenue, and project revenue from user charges and fees. However, commercial bank lending to LICs formed by local governments in China has recently come under closer scrutiny. In June 2011, China's regulators planned a US$308–463 billion bailout (amounting to nearly 10 percent of annual GDP) for highly indebted local governments and their LICs (for a detailed account of LICs, see chapter 11).

In addition to financing through LICs, almost all Chinese cities rely on revenues from land concessions. City governments acquire rural land, service the land with basic infrastructure, and auction off the serviced land to real estate developers. In this way, the city governments capture the increased land values created by the infrastructure investment and change of land to urban use. This is one of the most comprehensive betterment levies currently in use.

Betterment levies that are less comprehensive than the practice in China have a long-standing history in many other cities. Bogotá has used betterment levies since the 1930s to finance infrastructure, including roads, water and sewer, and, more recently, sidewalks and public parks (Borrero et al. 2011). In the 1960s, betterment levies accounted for 16 percent of the total revenue in Bogotá; in Medellín, the share reached 45 percent. The levy is a flexible instrument whose revenue cannot exceed the cost of an infrastructure project. Bogotá's district administration takes into account taxpayers' capacities to pay the levy and the benefit produced by the project in quantitative and qualitative terms (e.g., travel savings, real estate value increases, and quality-of-life improvements).

Betterment levies based on land value increases related to mass rail transit (MRT) investments have been used in East Asia and are now spreading to other regions, a point illustrated in box 13.3. For example, MRT companies in Hong Kong and Tokyo have used revenues from the codevelopment of residential communities and commercial areas around new transit stations to help finance MRT projects. In Tokyo, nonfare revenue is 30–50 percent of total revenue for some MRT lines. In both cities, ongoing revenue from property management is becoming more important than profits from development projects and provides a sustainable income stream (Murakami 2012).

Several metropolitan areas around the world have been experimenting with the direct sale of municipal bonds on the national and international market. "Jozi bonds," developed in Johannesburg, are one variant on this theme. Johannesburg faced bankruptcy in the mid-1990s, with 4 million residents and a capital budget of less than $50 million. Most municipalities had recently incorporated poorly served townships within their borders, and this led to a decline of private bank lending to municipalities following the end of apartheid in 1994. The former townships lacked infrastructure services, particularly access to water and electricity, and the investment demands were straining the capacity of municipalities. Seeking new sources of financing, in 2004 the city of Johannesburg purchased a partial bond guarantee for 40 percent of the principal from the Development Bank of Southern Africa and the IFC (Ngobeni 2008). This improved the bond issues' Fitch rating to AA– and allowed for a doubling of the maturity to 12 years compared with nonguaranteed bonds. The Jozi bonds raised more than $22 million in their first month and expanded thereafter. Buyers must be South African residents to purchase the bonds, which are denominated in South African rand. The city of Johannesburg then offered Africa's first municipal bonds in 2007 with a return of about 10 percent a year.

After successfully issuing domestic bonds, in 2001 Bogotá became the first Colombian city to issue international bonds (Trelles Zabala 2004). The capital district of Santa Fe de Bogotá sold US$100 million in bonds with an interest rate of 9.5 percent and a five-year term for financing infrastructure projects. The bonds received global ratings by Fitch of BB+ and by Standard & Poor's of BB. The 2001 Bogotá bonds had no sovereign guarantee nor (as did the Jozi bonds) additional comfort or guarantees from governmental or international agencies.

India has been issuing municipal bonds; about 55 percent of the total of more than $200 million have tax-free status (Asian Development Bank 2008). Municipal bonds issued through private placement are not yet listed on the stock exchange. To reduce the risk and increase the marketability of these bonds, the India Securities Exchange Board is issuing guidelines to increase the transparency of issuances and to protect investors' interests. The political risks associated with these bonds is being reduced by taking steps to (1) require that the public operating agency is legally separated from the local government that is raising the revenue; (2) assure that tariffs will be adjusted to maintain a minimum debt service ratio; (3) include a clause to prohibit the government from building directly competing investments; and (4) include performance standards that allow the government to change management or call in the credit if standards are not met.

Municipal bonds are a more stable source of finance suitable for investments in urban infrastructure that are long-lived. Such bonds can also serve as a catalyst for reform in municipal financial management systems. However, low-income countries should not wait to implement municipal financial management system reform until the conditions are ripe for municipal bonds. Although a municipal bond market has not developed in China, the national government issued local bonds on behalf of select local governments and passed the proceeds to local governments under an on-lending arrangement. The receiving local governments are supposed to repay the national government. In case of default, the national government could hold a local government responsible by withholding part of the intergovernmental transfers such as local tax rebates and the local share of centrally collected tax revenues. This appears to be a practical option for long-term debt financing of local infrastructure before the conditions for a municipal bond market mature.

Funds from carbon credits, which are payments for activities that sequester carbon or reduce carbon emissions, also are evolving as sources of infrastructure finance. The World Bank is beginning to access future carbon credit cash flows to subsidize infrastructure projects by identifying infrastructure-related opportunities for reducing carbon emissions. In 2007, the Municipal Corporation of Greater Mumbai used carbon credits to finance the Gorai landfill closure and gas capture project (Bhardwaj and Inocentes 2011). The landfill operated from 1972 to 2008, taking in approximately 1,200 tons of solid waste daily, which imposed environmental and health threats on the nearby Gorai Creek and residential development. The Asian Development Bank provided financial assistance to the project through the certified emissions reductions (CERs) or generation of carbon credit funds. One CER amounts to a savings of one ton of carbon dioxide. Industrialized countries offset emissions they generate by purchasing the CERs from developing countries. Upon completion in 2010, the project became India's first clean development mechanism and its first landfill closure and gas capture project.

THE WAY FORWARD

The annual projected cost of infrastructure investment and maintenance needs in developing countries (US$755 billion) totals nearly 5 percent of the countries' aggregate GDP, with about 3 percent of GDP for investment in new capacity (US$450 billion) and nearly 2 percent for maintenance (US$305 billion). Because country infrastructure stocks seem unrelated to the level of urbanization, a country's urban share of this investment and maintenance is likely to be proportional to the country's urban share of its GDP, especially for energy and transport. This proportional relationship should be adjusted for location-specific preexisting stocks, specific needs, and infrastructure priorities. While the investment amounts are large, the most recent estimates of external funding commitments devoted to infrastructure in 2008 were, for ODA, US\$18 billion in 2009; IBRD/IDA, US\$23.7 billion in 2010, and PPI, US\$154.4 billion. Adjusting for double counting, these flows sum to roughly US\$190 billion, or about 42 percent of projected annual infrastructure investment. To fill the infrastructure finance gap, metropolitan areas should look internally to increase efficiency of existing infrastructure, define fiscal responsibilities, reduce subsidies, and set efficient tariffs, and they should look externally to draw in international investment.

Developing cities can assess the efficiency of service provision from existing stocks when reviewing the need for investment. Data are widely available for efficiency indicators such as the annual kilowatt hours produced per kilowatt of installed generating capacity or the loss of water from leakage and theft. Many cities, regardless of income level, can improve the efficiency of existing infrastructure stocks and services, because infrastructure performance is not strongly related to income. Much inefficiency is rooted in inadequate maintenance leading to sanitation system overflows, irrigation canal leakages, road deterioration, and power distribution loss. Investment in infrastructure maintenance is often underfunded, and providers must combine revenue from user charges and from public budgets to provide adequate maintenance. A reduction in road maintenance increases private vehicle user costs by much more than the maintenance savings. Repairing neglected roads is two to three times more costly than appropriate ongoing maintenance.

Defining metropolitan infrastructure investment responsibilities becomes increasingly important with fiscal decentralization, as some infrastructure stocks located beyond the metropolitan boundary support urban areas. In countries where funds for metropolitan level expenditures are mainly transferred from the central government, financing metropolitan level infrastructure investment raises few boundary or definitional difficulties because finance and debt service are either the direct or indirect responsibility of the central government. However, decentralization to the metropolitan level of the authority to raise revenues, allocate expenditures, and service debt reduces the responsibility of central governments for metropolitan finance in general and for the funding of infrastructure in particular. It also increases the importance of defining metropolitan fiscal responsibilities for infrastructure investment. Experience with decentralization highlights the importance of clarity and transparency in municipal financial planning, budgeting, programming, borrowing, and expenditures, as well as debt management.

Decentralization usually curtails the willingness of central governments to guarantee debts incurred by metropolitan areas to finance local infrastructure or other investments. This has created challenges for institutions like the World Bank, which requires its loans be guaranteed by the central government. Progress has been made in this area, with some metropolitan areas directly accessing international bond markets and some countries developing domestic municipal bond markets to finance infrastructure. However, if metropolitan areas have weak or ineffective restraints on borrowing, their direct or indirect indebtedness to domestic banks and to domestic and international bond holders can quickly become a problem. For example, excessive borrowing by LICs in China has recently led to a central government takeover of their indebtedness amounting to 10 percent of China's GDP.

Other internal approaches include pricing infrastructure services so that revenues cover costs. This promotes end-user efficiency and can substantially moderate demand. While subsidies are often defended on social welfare grounds, their beneficiaries are predominantly the nonpoor, who have access to regular services, while the poor are left with higher-cost, nonregular suppliers. Tank-truck-delivered water in favelas or slums that lack regular water service is the most notorious example of high-cost nonregular supply. Connection subsidies for services such as electricity and water (which favor the poor, because the rich are already connected) are a more effective means to increase access. Tariff schedules that do not cover full costs are common, with the weakest cost recovery in Africa and South Asia (Ingram and Fay 2008). The underlying demand is for infrastructure services, not physical stocks, and delivering higher flows of efficiently priced services from existing stocks can forestall or reduce the need to invest in additional capacity.

Metropolitan areas can look externally to draw in international investment, particularly PPI, which has increased from 2.5 times the size of ODA in 1990 to 7.4 times in 2008. While PPI mainly flows to middle-income countries, lower-income countries receive development assistance. ODA includes development assistance with at least a 25 percent grant element, and ODA commitments for infrastructure in 2008 are similar in size to the infrastructure investment projections for low-income countries. Unfortunately, only about a quarter of total ODA funds flowed to low-income countries in 2008, and data on the infrastructure share disbursed to low-income countries are not readily available. Some developing countries are beginning to make infrastructure investments in other developing countries, including low-income countries in sub-Saharan Africa, and these south-south flows are also likely to grow.

As metropolitan areas invest to fill the finance gap, they need to be aware of the relation between infrastructure investment and growth. As with national governments, metropolitan areas should invest in infrastructure capacity that supports their respective growth activity. The total investment projections (US$755 billion) for developing countries are aggregates for all countries across income groups and assume an average annual rate of economic growth of 5 percent. The investment projections vary directly with income growth, so countries that grow faster than average would need to devote a larger share of GDP to infrastructure investment. For example, if a lower-middle-income country growing at 5 percent per year was projected to spend 3.5 percent of GDP on infrastructure investment, such a country growing at 10 percent would have an infrastructure investment projection of 7 percent of GDP. Projections of maintenance expenditures are based on the size of existing stocks of infrastructure and do not vary directly with income growth rates.

Metropolitan infrastructure finance changed dramatically in the past 20 years. In addition to the enormous growth of PPI, several new (or renewed) financing options show particular promise, such as bond financing, south-south funding, and betterment levies based on increases in land values (often related to transport, water, or sanitation investments). While they require oversight, LICs that have well-defined assets can facilitate financing from banks and pension funds. Financing based on the sale of carbon credits also has promise, particularly in the energy and transport sectors. One area where more progress needs to be made is in reducing subsidies and setting service tariffs at a level that covers the cost of service. This has been achieved in mobile telecommunications, largely through user charges, but remains an elusive goal in most other infrastructure services. While external funding for infrastructure investment is substantial and growing, it does not now (and is unlikely in the future to) cover most of the financing requirements of developing countries and their metropolitan areas, so they will need to provide most of the infrastructure financing themselves. To this end, metropolitan areas need to learn from one another's experiences with infrastructure financing, efficiency improvements, and service delivery. International institutions have an important role in facilitating the required exchange of knowledge in these areas.

REFERENCES

Allport, Roger. 2005. Urban rail concessions: Experience in Bangkok, Kuala Lumpur and Manila. Transport Working Paper No. 2. China Sustainable Development Unit, East Asia and Pacific Region. Washington, DC: World Bank.

Andres, Luis, Vivien Foster, and José Luis Guasch. 2006. The impact of privatization on the performance of the infrastructure sector: The case of electricity distribution in Latin American countries. Policy Research Working Paper No. 3936. Washington, DC: World Bank.

Annez, Patricia. 2006. Urban infrastructure finance from private operators: What have we learned from recent experience? World Bank Policy Research Working Paper No. 4045. Washington, DC: World Bank.

Arthur Anderson and Enterprise LSE. 2000. Value for money drivers in the private finance initiatives. London: U.K. Treasury Taskforce.

Asian Development Bank. 2008. *Managing Asian cities.* Mandaluyong City.

Bahl, Roy, and Jorge Martinez-Vazquez. 2008. The determinants of revenue performance. In *Making the property tax work: Experiences in developing and transitional countries,* ed. Roy Bahl, Jorge Martinez-Vazquez, and Joan Youngman, 35–60. Cambridge, MA: Lincoln Institute of Land Policy.

Bahl, Roy, Jorge Martinez-Vazquez, and Joan Youngman, eds. 2008. *Making the property tax work: Experiences in developing and transitional countries.* Cambridge, MA: Lincoln Institute of Land Policy.

Bhardwaj, Nishant, and Daisy Inocentes. 2011. Carbon credits: Improving financing and sustainability of a landfill closure project. In *Knowledge showcase.* Asian Development Bank. http://www2.adb.org/documents/information/knowledge-showcase/gorai-landfill-closure.pdf

Borrero, Oscar, Esperanza Durán, Jorge Hernández, and Magda Montaña. 2011. Evaluating the practice of betterment levies in Colombia: The experience of Bogotá and Manizales. Working Paper. Cambridge, MA: Lincoln Institute of Land Policy.

Briginshaw, David. 2011. Brazil: A privatization model that works. *International Railway Journal* (July).

Canning, David. 1998. A database of world infrastructure stocks, 1950–1995. Policy Research Working Paper No. 1929. Washington, DC: World Bank.

Chatterton, Isabel, and Olga Susana Puerto. 2005. *Estimations of infrastructure investment needed in the South Asia region.* Washington, DC: World Bank.

Fay, Marianne, and Charlotte Opal. 1999. Urbanization without growth: A not-so-uncommon phenomenon. Policy Research Working Paper No. 2412. Washington, DC: World Bank (November).

Fay, Marianne, and Tito Yepes. 2003. Investing in infrastructure: What is needed from 2000 to 2010? Policy Research Working Paper No. 3102. Washington, DC: World Bank (July).

Fitzgerald, Peter. 2004. Review of partnerships: Victoria provided infrastructure. A report commissioned by the Department of Treasury and Finance, Government of Victoria (Australia). Melbourne, Victoria: Growth Solutions Group.

Foster, Viven, and Cecelia Briceño-Garmendia, eds. 2010. *Africa's infrastructure: A time for transformation.* Washington, DC: World Bank.

Foster, Vivien, William Butterfield, C. Chen, and Nataliya Pushak. 2008. *Building bridges: China's growing role as infrastructure financier for Africa.* Washington, DC: Public-Private Infrastructure Advisory Facility and World Bank.

Gassner, Katharina, Alexander Popov, and Nataliya Pushak. 2008, Does private sector participation improve performance in electricity and water distribution? Trends and Policy Options, No. 6, PPIAF. Washington DC: World Bank.

Gevert, Theodor. 2004. SuperVia unveils radical surface metro plan: Privatization and investment have revived Rio de Janeiro's once-ailing suburban rail network. *International Railway Journal* (August):41.

Ingram, Gregory, and Marianne Fay. 2008. Physical Infrastructure. In *International handbook of development economics*, ed. Amitava K. Dutt and Jaime Ros, 26, 301–315. Cheltenham, U.K.: Edward Elgar.

Ingram, Gregory, and Zhi Liu. 1999. Determinants of motorization and road provision. In *Essays in transportation economics and policy*, ed. Jose A. Gomez-Ibanez, William B. Tye, and Clifford Winston. Washington, DC: Brookings Institution.

International Road Federation. 2010. World road statistics. Geneva.

International Telecommunications Union. 2010. World telecommunications development report. Geneva.

KPMG LLP. 2007. Effectiveness of operational contracts in PFI. London.

Leigland, James. 2010. PPI in poor countries. *Gridlines* 51:1–4.

Leigland, James, and Henry Russell. 2009. Another lost decade? Effects of the financial crisis on project finance for infrastructure. *Gridlines* 48:1–4.

Liu, Lili, and Steven B. Webb. 2011. Laws for fiscal responsibility for subnational discipline: International experience. Policy Research Working Paper No. 5587. Washington, DC: World Bank.

Martell, Christine, and George M. Guess. 2006. Development of local government debt financing markets: Application of a market-based framework. *Public Budgeting and Finance* 26(1):88–119.

Ministry of Road Transport and Highways, Government of India. 2012. Guidelines for investment in road sector. www.nhai.org/Doc/15Nov12/Guidelines%20for%20Investment%20in%20Road%20Sector%20%28as%20on%2031%20October%202012%29.pdf

Murakami, Jin. 2012. Transit value capture: New town codevelopment models and land market updates in Tokyo and Hong Kong. In *Value capture and land policies*, ed. Gregory K. Ingram and Yu-Hung Hong, 285–320. Cambridge, MA: Lincoln Institute of Land Policy.

National Audit Office. 2003. PFI: Construction performance. London.

———. 2007. Benchmarking and market testing the ongoing services component of PFI projects. London.

Ngobeni, Jason. 2008. Asking the right questions: Johannesburg completes a groundbreaking municipal bond issue. *Gridlines* 33:1–4.

NHAI. 2012. Home page. www.nhai.org

OECD. 2011. Quick wizard for international development statistics. Paris.

Partnerships U.K. 2006. Report on operational PFI projects. London.

Peterson, George E. 2006. Land leasing and land sale as an infrastructure financing option. Policy Research Working Paper No. 4043. Washington, DC: World Bank.

Public-Private Infrastructure Advisory Facility and World Bank. 2007. *PPP units for infrastructure: Lessons for their design and use.* Washington, DC: Public-Private Infrastructure Advisory Facility and World Bank.

Rebelo, Jorge M. 1999. Rail and subway concessions in Rio de Janeiro: Designing contracts and bidding processes. *Viewpoint* 183:1–8.

Trelles Zabala, Rodrigo. 2004. Colombia. In *Subnational capital markets in developing countries*, ed. Maria Freire and John Petersen. Washington, DC: World Bank.

World Bank. 2004. *Global development finance: Harnessing cyclical gains for development.* Washington, DC.

———. 2011. World development indicators. Washington, DC.

World Bank and Public-Private Infrastructure Advisory Facility. 2011. Private participation in infrastructure (PPI) project database. Washington, DC.

Wu, Weiping. 2010. Urban infrastructure financing and economic performance in China. *Urban Geography* 31(5):648–667.

SLUM UPGRADING

14

MARIA E. FREIRE

With urbanization and its benefits, large flows of people have moved to cities, increasing the demand for shelter. Unfortunately, the formal market in developing countries rarely meets that demand for housing at affordable prices. Poor regulations, insufficient resources for infrastructure, and scarcity of serviced land often lead to high housing prices, patchy urban development, and exclusion of the urban poor, who have to settle in inadequate and informal places that lack basic amenities, minimal services, and housing security.

The word *slum* commonly describes the situation of people living in overcrowded quarters, without water and sanitation, and lacking title security. Rapid urban growth has outpaced the ability of urban authorities to provide for housing and health infrastructure in most metropolitan regions of developing countries. In Ho Chi Minh City in Vietnam, neither the government nor the private developers are able to provide the housing needed for 50,000 migrants per year. The resulting squatter and slum settlements now comprise 15 percent of housing in the city. In Dhaka, Bangladesh, only one-quarter of the population in the city is connected to the piped sewage system (McGee 2005). The outcome has been one of the highest rates of death from infectious diseases among Asian cities. In metro Manila, Philippines, and in Kuala Lumpur, Malaysia, the competitive demand for land in cities has led to the marginalization of the urban poor. In Greater Mumbai, India, 94–95 percent of the population cannot afford a house due to soaring property prices and speculation (see chapter 10).

The inability of city governments to plan and provide affordable housing is aggravated by the lack of coordination among different authorities that are in charge of economic development, urban planning, and land allocation. For example, in the Mumbai metropolitan region, multilevels of government, different protocols, and different cultures have undermined the success of many slum upgrading policies launched by the Mumbai metropolitan region (see chapter 10). Such coordination issues also exist in the São Paulo metropolitan region, as described later in this chapter.

Some countries, such as India, Brazil, and South Africa, have made great efforts to deal with the slum problem in a sustainable way. The complex Jawaharlal Nehru National Urban Renewal Mission program that includes Indian states and municipalities and the national housing program in Brazil (Minha Casa Minha Vida) are examples of this determination to deal with the lack of adequate shelter for the urban poor.

Yet progress has been slow. A recent review of the Society for the Promotion of Area Resource Centres (SPARC) program in India has identified some key obstacles to scaling up slum upgrading at both metropolitan and national levels (Merryl and Suri 2007). They include lack of areawide (metropolitan) strategies and planning for land use and slums; lack of community mobilization capacity; lack of participation of developers in low-income housing projects; lack of housing finance for low-income households; failure to leverage subsidies and household loans; and lack of participation of commercial banks in construction finance in slum projects. Add to this lack of commitment, good governance, and pragmatic approaches, and the result is a problem that will take decades to solve.

Slum upgrading policies should include three elements: provision of basic services and affordable infrastructure, improvement of shelter conditions, and security of land occupancy rights. From a policy viewpoint, this requires a combination of policies to lift income of slum dwellers and policies to improve the supply side of housing and land markets. Since cities in developing countries will continue to grow at a fast pace, urban authorities need to strengthen urban planning and metropolitan strategies to provide alternatives to slum formation. By making land available to the poor at affordable prices and ensuring the provision of housing, urban infrastructure, and transport services at the fringes of cities, metropolitan authorities could contribute to address the slum problem.

This chapter discusses the alternatives to finance slum upgrading at the scale of metropolitan areas and large cities. First, it examines the size of the problem as described by the U.N. Human Settlements Programme (UN-HABITAT), as well as the assumptions used to project the cost of providing a dwelling for everyone. Next is a review of the successive approaches to slum upgrading as implemented by donors and governments alike. The following section discusses the principles for slum upgrading finance and who should provide what in a municipal finance framework. It shows the potential that combinations of private, public, and external finance provide to committed communities. Five cases of slum upgrading policy are then reviewed, identifying the key elements that make them successful and whether these conditions can be replicable in other regions and large urban areas. The chapter concludes with key lessons from experience.

THE SIZE AND COST OF THE SLUM PROBLEM

The United Nations estimates that one-third of urban populations in developing countries, nearly one billion people, are living in slums (UN-HABITAT 2005). The

TABLE 14.1

Population living in slums

Region	Urban population as percentage of total population	Slum dwellers as percentage of urban population
World	47.7	31.6
Developed regions	75.5	6
Developing regions	40.9	43
Africa	44.9	60.9
Eastern Asia (excluding China)	36.5	42.1
South Asia	30	58
	75.8	31.9

SOURCE: Data from UN-HABITAT (2005).

largest proportion of the urban population living in slums is in the Africa region, followed closely by South Asia (table 14.1). The number of slum dwellers is projected to reach 1.4 billion by 2020 (Smolka and Larangeira 2008) and may well reach 2 billion by 2030, as a result of the urban "explosion" in sub-Saharan and South Asian countries and the lack of response from the formal markets for low-income shelter. Not all slum dwellers are at the extremes of poverty. One-fourth live on more than $2/day, suggesting that home deprivation is more than just a matter of income poverty (Baker and McCain 2009).

The cost of providing shelter to slum dwellers is hard to estimate. Slum upgrading is place specific, and unit costs vary greatly across cities. The U.N. Millennium Project estimates that, from 2005 to 2020, the upgrading needs of the 100 million slum dwellers (a target of Millennium Development Goal 11) will cost $67 billion during the 15 years. In addition, to provide new/alternative shelter for the 570 million new arrivals, another US$227 billion would be required. In total, the cost would reach US$294 billion (table 14.2). If one tried to expand the slum upgrading programs to the totality of 1 billion slum dwellers, the total cost would reach $897 billion, or about $60 billion a year. This is six times the total amount of investment currently being made in slum upgrading every year.

APPROACHES TO SLUM UPGRADING

The approach to slum upgrading has changed considerably from the 1950s to the 2000s. From the 1950s to the mid-1970s, many cities tried to deal with slums by keeping migrants from coming into town and bulldozing the shacks while providing public housing to relocate the slum dwellers (UN-HABITAT 2005). Following public outcry against those inhuman policies, other approaches emerged. Providing sites and services was one of them. Governments allocated land (with minimal infrastructure) to newcomers and encouraged them to construct their

TABLE 14.2

Investment requirements and potential sources of funding, 2005–2020

Target	Target population (million)	Cost per person (US$)		Cost 2005–2020	Overall cost, 2005–2020 US$ (billion)		
		Per year	Total, 2005–2020*		Donor contribution (US$)	Government contribution (US$)	Slum dwellers' contribution
1. Upgrading slums (Millennium Development Goal target)	100	45	670	67	23	37	7
2. Alternative shelter	570	27	400	227	78	126	22
3. Total	670	29	440	294	101	163	29
Per memoire							
4. Upgrading all slums	1,000	45	670	670			
5. Total (4 + 2)				897			

NOTE: The cost estimates are based on data from upgrading projects in Central America. A per capita cost of US$670 for slum upgrading and US$400 for alternative shelter includes investment in land titling, access to water, and sanitation and sewerage.

*Rounded numbers.

SOURCE: Data from U.N. Millennium Project (2005).

own dwellings. The approach was quite successful. In the 1970s and 1980s, the sites and services approach was tried in many countries across the globe: Botswana, Burkina Faso, El Salvador, Senegal, and Tanzania (Buckley and Kalarickal 2006). The global outcome was positive. Housing construction improved, and physical infrastructure was provided (Kessides 1997). Unfortunately, the sites were too far from the city, and the cost of infrastructure was too high for the cities concerned.

In situ upgrading then became the prevalent solution. This approach tried to improve the situation of the slum dwellers without necessarily moving them away. Early on, World Bank urban projects focused on access to water and sewage networks in slum areas. Many of these projects were demonstration activities and tried to show the potential of being replicated at a larger scale. Urban upgrading is still the predominant approach to deal with informal encroachments.

In the 1990s and 2000s, the approaches became more comprehensive, calling for an enabling approach: good policies, slum prevention, community participation, and engagement of the private sector. The role of the government shifted from provider to facilitator. Cities were expected to remove obstacles that blocked access to urban land, such as inflexible zoning and regulations. To stimulate demand, upfront subsidies looked appropriate, especially to leverage own savings or bank credit, and property rights became a high priority (Mayo 1991).

At present, one finds a wide range of policies that work together to provide affordable and adjustable housing solutions for the urban poor. The following are some examples.

- Community-driven programs: In these types of solutions, organized communities lead the design, financing, and implementation of upgrading programs. Examples include Bahia Alagados and Favela Bairro in Brazil and Dar es Salaam community urban improvement in Tanzania (see also table 14.3).
- National housing programs: This approach is best when there are massive needs for low-income housing. Morocco, Mexico, Tunisia, Brazil, and Chile have demonstrated that strong central institutions can achieve significant results, given adequate resources (UN-HABITAT 2005).
- Slum prevention: This approach has emerged as a priority, aiming for preventive planning and availability of sites (Cities Alliance 1999). This requires land at affordable prices and access to transportation and education to enhance economic opportunities. As cities expand, the relevant spatial unit has gone from the neighborhood to the metropolitan level.
- Private finance: Market-based housing finance has spread throughout the world (Buckley and Kalarickal 2006). For the poorest layers, the challenge is to leverage ongoing initiatives (microfinancing, savings and loans systems) and tap larger sources of capital finance.
- Land: Land markets and land policy are identified as major bottlenecks on the supply side. In the case of India, Annez et al. (2010) have shown the negative impact of land restrictions that have prevented millions of poor people in Mumbai from attaining affordable housing. Land also has the potential for urban

TABLE 14.3

Examples of community-based approaches to slum upgrading

Organization	Objectives	Features
Brazil: Goiania Federation for Tenants and Posseiros	Tenure security: public land occupied and tenure secured by appealing to rights of citizens to occupy unused land	Cover 100,000 former tenants. Efforts to get tenure security, covering 100,000 tenants, supported by a local grassroots organization
Malawi Homeless People's Federation	Land provision, flexible regulation	Since 2003 provided 760 plots for housing and housing construction loans for savings groups
Pakistan (Orangi)	Amenities provision: federations formed by slum dwellers	Covered about 100,000 households in Orangi and 300 locations in Pakistan, eliminating contractors and reducing standards to cover all costs
Thailand (national)	Amenities provision: subsidies and housing loans to community organizations formed by low-income slum households	Projects in 960 communities covering more than 50,000 households, with activities identified by each community
PRODEL (Nicaragua)	Amenities provision (cofinance small infrastructure projects)	Funds provided by nongovernmental organizations, local governments, and households, with 460 projects benefiting 60,000 households

SOURCE: Data from World Bank (2008).

finance in a wide range of countries and cities, from China to Latin America (Peterson 2009; Smolka and Larangeira 2008).

Financing Slum Upgrading: The Major Approaches

A Framework for Slum Improvement Finance

Slum upgrading programs are generally defined as a set of three activities: investment in infrastructure, improvement of shelter, and security of land tenure. In parallel, enabling policies such as land and housing markets, comprehensive metropolitan-wide planning, participation of the community, and improvement of household economic conditions are needed.

Financing slum upgrading is then equivalent to financing infrastructure, shelter, and land tenure, to which the usual framework of public finance can be applied, which postulates that public goods should be financed by public money and private

TABLE 14.4

Slum upgrading finance options

Services/programs	Characteristics	Financing	
		In theory	In practice
Basic services: trunk infrastructure	Public good	Public sector (with donor help), central and local	Donors, all levels of urban government, help from community organizations, federal and state funds
Basic services, individual connections	Private good	Households through tariffs	Subsidies, tariffs, community savings
Land titling	Private/public good	Private: purchase of title; public: land title programs	Public for large programs
Home improvement	Private good	Household savings	With help from up-front subsidies, microfinancing, community savings
Economic opportunities	Private good	Microfinance, community savings	Comprehensive upgrading programs
Home purchasing	Private good	Bank credit	With subsidies for those in need

goods by the beneficiary of those goods. Table 14.4 suggests a simple topology for how this might work.

LONG-TERM INFRASTRUCTURE

Start-up funding from the public sector seems to be essential. In most slum upgrading programs, federal and state funds finance trunk infrastructure. This can be helped by international grants, concessionary loans, budget resources, or commercial borrowing with government guarantees. Often, local governments fund the land preparation, connections, and supervision. Sometimes, cities form associations to finance large programs, as in Tamil Nadu, where the municipality association issued municipal bonds to finance slum improvements. In most cases, there are large financing gaps, and not all of the community can be served in a single program. The main problem is the low level of budget revenues in most cities of the developing world; in Nairobi, the per capita budget is US$7.0 per year; in Lagos, it is $2.3 (table 14.5). This is less than 5 percent of unit cost estimated by the United Nations (table 14.2).

SHORT-TERM OPERATION AND MAINTENANCE OF SERVICES

These should be covered by the users through adequate tariffs. Tariffs may need to be aligned to the purchasing power of the users. Cross-subsidization, public transfers, and social tariffs are often used to reach out to the poorest residents.

TABLE 14.5

Budget revenue per capita, 1998 (US$)

City	Budget per capita
Stockholm	5,450
Singapore	4,637
New York	3,609
Seattle	2,372
Dar es Salaam	11
Bujumbura	8
Nairobi	7
Phnom Penh	5
Lagos	2

SOURCE: Data from United Nations.

SHELTER IMPROVEMENTS AND LAND TENURE

These are private goods and should be financed by the beneficiaries. Nevertheless, low-income housing is a difficult sector. A large part of housing demand in developing countries comes from poor people, who are forced to spend 30–40 percent of their income on rent, compared with 19 percent in developed countries (ISTED 2005). Housing production is hindered by the very small incomes of the urban poor. Since the public sector cannot provide the required housing, and the formal sector does not find it profitable, most housing is produced by informal small developers in unplanned settlements. Accepting the concept of progressive housing, engaging informal developers, and reviewing the legislation that often pushes settlers to informality will help slum dwellers improve their shelter conditions.

Main Sources of Financing: Aid Donor Funding

Donor support plays a key role in urban upgrading. It provides cash for capital investment, as well as technical capacity and policy advice. Data from the World Bank and the Inter-American Development Bank, the two major donors, indicate that from 1992 to 2005, financial flows for slum upgrading and housing policy totaled US$11.7 billion (less than $1 billion a year): $6.7 billion from the World Bank and $5 billion from the Inter-American Development Bank (table 14.6). In both cases, lending for shelter shifted over time from small loans to large-scale policy-related programs, such as those in Brazil, Egypt, Mexico, and Poland (Buckley and Kalarickal 2006). Housing has also become a growing line of business for private-sector development. The International Finance Corporation (IFC), for example, has undertaken 45 investments in housing projects, and the Multilateral Investment Guarantee Agency (MIGA) has been offering guarantees in the housing sector.

The Inter-American Development Bank (IADB) has focused on housing voucher programs and urban upgrading. From 1993 to 2005, the IADB approved 29 housing loans totaling US$2.6 million and 36 slum upgrading projects worth US$3.2 billion. Upgrading represented almost half of the portfolio, followed by develop-

TABLE 14.6

World bank shelter loans, 1992–2005 (2001 US$ in millions)

Region	Slum upgrading	Sites and services	Housing policy	Housing finance	Disaster relief	Total	Percentage of total
Sub-Saharan Africa	42	16	2.5	17	2.9	81.3	1.2
East Asia	40.8	35.8	36.1	439.1	34	585.8	8.6
Europe and Central Asia	10.6	16.5	311	235	305	878.1	12.9
Latin America	129	0	657	1,585	397	2,773	40.8
Middle East and North Africa	94	358	48	290	550	1,341	19.7
South Asia	21	79	2.4	145	884	1,132	16.7
Total	337.4	505.3	1057	2711.1	2172.9	6791.2	100
Percentage of total	5	7.4	15.6	39.9	32	100	

SOURCE: Data from Shea (2008).

ment of long-term mortgage credit, up-front demand-side subsidies, or vouchers to individual households. The Asian Development Bank supports technical assistance to establish housing finance entities and mortgage systems. Examples include projects in Vietnam, Mongolia, India, and Indonesia (Shea 2008).

Among bilateral donors, the U.S. Agency for International Development (USAID), the Swedish International Development Agency (SIDA), the German Agency for International Cooperation (GIZ), and the Spanish Agency for International Cooperation (AECI) have significant programs in slum upgrading, with USAID being the largest. From 1960 to 1993, USAID funded housing programs with more than $110 million per year, mostly for low-income families. It also provided loan guarantees for housing in 44 countries. The Swedish SIDA, German GIZ and KfW Development Bank, and Spanish AECI have active programs focused on African cities, Central America, and select European countries. As a whole, less than 1 percent of the official development assistance finances upgrading.

Donors have also had a major impact in creating advocacy and financing agencies, such as Cities Alliance and the UN Slum Upgrading Facility. Both programs have been instrumental in raising awareness about the needs of the urban dwellers. Hundreds of cities have benefited from Cities Alliance assistance, including São Paulo, whose case is described later in this chapter.

From Land-Based Financing to Progressive Housing

LAND-BASED FINANCING

Urban land is a natural candidate to be taxed and to generate resources for shelter improvement. "Whenever the benefits of the project can be located within a certain benefit zone, it is economically efficient to finance infrastructure projects by using the increases in the value of land that results from them" (Peterson 2009, 4). Land sales, value capture via land sale, sale of development rights, and impact fees are the instruments most used by large cities, such as Mumbai and São Paulo (using the sale of development rights). Chinese cities, such as Shanghai, use land sale proceeds to finance most of their infrastructure needs in combination with capital market funds raised through special financial vehicles. In the case of São Paulo metro station projects, the proceeds of the auction of building permits were directly channeled to improve infrastructure of slums around the new metro station.

Other approaches try to curb speculative profits associated with the increase in land values due to greater demand for housing (Smolka and Larangeira 2008). In the case of two projects in Colombia, Nuevo Usme in Bogotá and Gonzalo Vallejo Macro-Pereira (Rojas 2010; Smolka and Larangeira 2008), the city government acquired land to develop serviced plots for low-income housing projects and to gain control over the form of land use. Participating landowners share in the land-value increments generated by large-scale development projects, although less than the market-increase in value.

In Porto Alegre, Brazil, the Social Urbanizer project uses the expertise of informal developers (Rojas 2010). A Social Urbanizer is a registered private real estate developer that helps the municipality develop areas for low-income housing. The city purchases land from a landowner and allows the Social Urbanizer to sell pieces of land and provide infrastructure incrementally, at standards below the rest of the city, provided the plots are offered at affordable prices. The model has several advantages. Households obtain legal plots at prices similar to those they would pay for illegal occupation, and the landowner is not subject to illegal occupations. The city government profits from the difference between the sale value of the plot and the price it paid the landowner. These profits help to finance infrastructure in the new settlements.

PROGRESSIVE HOUSING

The concept of progressive housing is particularly suited to low-income residents and to cities in rapid expansion. Under this approach, residents are allowed to legalize their land plots even before they are fully serviced often with the help of informal developers. The best-known cases are the land subdivision programs in El Salvador and Pakistan. Progressive subdivisions in El Salvador began in the 1960s and now serve 60 percent of the new low-income households, selling from 5,000 to 8,000 lots per year. Seventy private firms operate in this market. These firms work with landowners to subdivide the land and serve as financial intermediaries with the buyers of the plots to be developed. Thirty-five percent of the parcel is reserved for public spaces and infrastructure; the remaining is divided into lots of 150–250 square meters.

In Pakistan, Saiban, a nongovernmental organization (NGO) created in 1997, works in partnership with the government to formalize illegal developers. It purchases and subdivides the land on a grid plan consistent with city zoning regulations and sells the plots to informal settlers. Households make a down payment of 20–40 percent of the total price (about $175) and pay the remaining in monthly installments over eight years. The success of the program has inspired other commercial banks to offer financial products to low-income residents (Azfar and Rahman 2004).

Helping the Demand Side: Housing Microfinance

Low-income households rarely can afford a market-rate mortgage for a completed house.[1] Mortgage lending remains limited to upper- and middle-income households with steady and verifiable incomes. As a result, the main funding sources for low-income households to acquire housing, besides their own savings, have been supplier credit or neighborhood money lent at expensive terms (10–20 percent per month) or the financing described above under progressive housing. In this context, housing microfinance is an efficient method to help low-income households access credit. By borrowing small amounts of money, households can progressively upgrade their house.

Typically, housing microfinance comprises small loans (from $550 to $5,000) of limited maturity (from six months to three years), generally without collateral. In Peru, where microfinance has developed quickly, housing microfinance loans average $1,000, compared with the average subsidized mortgage loan of $30,000. Mibanco, the market leader in the financing sector, is Latin America's largest microfinance institution, with 70,000 active borrowers. Other microfinancing housing institutions include the Fundación Hábitat y Vivienda in Mexico; financial cooperatives (e.g., Federal Credit Union) in Guatemala; commercial banks involved with microfinance, such as the BancoSol in Bolivia; and specialized microfinance banks, such as Tameer Bank in Pakistan (Chiquier 2009; Ferguson 2008a; 2008b).

In South Africa, the Kuyasa Fund, a nonprofit microfinance institution based in Cape Town, has reached more than 2,700 clients with a total of US$1.8 million in housing loans. Grameen Bank in Bangladesh has delivered 600,000 housing loans since it was established. All these institutions show performance rates for their loans that exceed those of housing loans in the banking industry (Biswas 2003).

Sometimes housing microfinance is included as a component of neighborhood upgrading programs. In the case of the Local Development Program (PRODEL, Programa de Desarollo Local) in Nicaragua, small-scale community infrastructure projects are financed through small loans that range from $200 for housing improvement to $300–$1,500 for microenterprises. In 2003, more than 11,000 loans were given out for housing. The beneficiaries are low-income residents: 70 percent have a monthly income equivalent to $200 or less.

Collective Savings and Community Funds

While individual savings are generally small, collective savings have played an important role to link the poor and the financial institutions and provide funds for

---

[1] In only a few countries, such as Mexico or Malaysia, have mortgage lenders reached moderate-income households (Chiquier 2009).

improved housing and infrastructure. Mitlin (2007) stresses the significance of savings as a key source of shelter investment for low-income housing. In Pakistan, South Africa, and Namibia, infrastructure has been financed by community savings collected by the people through NGOs.

Community funds encourage savings by establishing and strengthening local savings groups that provide collective finance for shelter improvement. They also leverage resources from the national governments and from foreign donors and can contribute to infrastructure development (Mitlin and Muller 2004). Slum Dwellers International (SDI) is a good example of a network that incorporates savings and lending activities for shelter improvement. From 1995 to 2010, SDI has become an international movement with affiliates in more than 12 countries. It has helped millions of households to access land and improved housing with small grants. Other examples include Cambodia Urban Poor Development Fund, the Bann Mekong (secure housing) in Thailand, the Community Mortgage Program in the Philippines, PRODEL in Nicaragua, and the Jamii Bora Trust low-cost housing scheme in Kenya (UN-HABITAT 2005).

Community funds in India and Thailand have grown substantially with the help of the central government and foreign donors. The Community-Led Infrastructure Financing Facility (CLIFF) in India is a fund capitalized by donors that provides support for community-initiated housing and infrastructure projects that have the potential for scaling up. The facility works with the National Slum Dwellers Federation and other large community organizations to increase access of urban poor communities to commercial and public-sector finance for medium- to large-scale infrastructure and housing initiatives. It provides bridge loans, guarantees, and technical assistance (UN-HABITAT 2005).

Helping Demand: Housing Subsidies

Housing subsidies are used by many countries to help households purchase or repair their housing. Subsidies can be used to help beneficiaries overcome constraints in accessing housing finance, notably providing assistance with down payments and improving loan-to-value ratios. Hoik Smit (2009) uses the distribution of income in Mexico to illustrate the large percentage of people that cannot be served by the formal banking and would need specific support through, for example, targeted up-front subsidies.

In some countries, housing subsidies represent a considerable portion of their gross domestic product (GDP). In 2002, Algeria and Iran spent 4 percent of GDP in housing subsidies, the same amount spent on education and health (Buckley and Kalarickal 2006). In Chile, housing subsidies have had a major role in the strategy to extend formal housing to low-income groups (box 14.1). Minha Casa Minha Vida, the Brazil national housing program, follows a similar approach. This national housing fund receives contributions from the central government and from state and local governments to take care of infrastructure, while a wide program of subsidies helps residents make down payments or pay lower the average loan cost. In Mexico, the Habitat program is financed as part of the Urban Poverty Allevia-

BOX 14.1

Chile: A housing policy focused solely on up-front subsidies

Chile is often considered a pioneer in the design and implementation of housing subsidy programs in Latin America (OECD 2007). In the last 30 years, Chilean housing policies have focused on a demand-oriented system of up-front and targeted subsidies aimed to promote home ownership and reduce the housing deficit (Cummings and Di Pasquale 2002). In the 1980s, 1990s, and 2000s, more than 55 percent of the units built each year had some degree of housing subsidies. Public provision programs, which were the main channel to provide housing to first income quintile, have gradually been eliminated in favor of beneficiary-based subsidies (figure 14.1).

Until very recently, most programs favored the purchase of new units over existing ones, on the grounds that it would boost economic activity, increase employment, and ensure an increase in levels of home ownership.

That perception has now changed: since the end of 2006, second-hand units can be purchased through subsidized programs. In 2008 and 2009, 30 percent of the subsidies were used to purchase existing units.

This new strategy gives sellers the chance to move up the housing ladder, change neighborhood or city, or pursue other forms of investment with the product of the sale. It also provides the beneficiaries with more alternatives and adds value to a large portion of the housing stock that had been virtually absent from the real estate market.

FIGURE 14.1

Housing subsidies by delivery mechanism in Chile

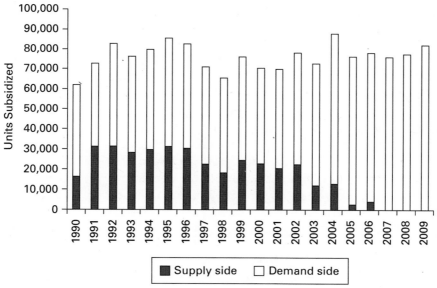

SOURCE: Data from Burgos (2010).

tion Program (Oportunidades) and includes a large component of housing subsidies. It operates on a territorial basis, focusing on the city blocks with the highest concentration of poor families. Operated by the Social Secretariat since 2007, Habitat has been successful at integrating different social and urban policies and targets them to the poorest city blocks.

Raising Other National Resources: Provident Funds

Provident funds are long-term savings schemes that operate through mandatory contributions (Chiquier 2009). They collect mandatory savings from private and public employees as a percentage of their salary. Emerging economies often use provident funds to solve the problem of lack of medium-term funds in the economy. Some provident funds have been critical in housing development, notably in Singapore, Brazil, Mexico, the Philippines, and Nigeria.

In Brazil, most low-income housing finance is funded by the FGTS (Fundo de Garantia do tempo de Servico), which operates as a provident fund. FGTS collects 8 percent from all formal private-sector workers. These savings are held in individual accounts from which workers can withdraw money for home purchases. Since 2005, FGTS has steadily refocused its target group on the lower-income groups, with 77 percent of its loans going to households with incomes less than five times the minimum wage. It has stopped financing the upper income class and is now implementing a system of up-front subsidies for low-income groups within the large National Housing Policy in Brazil (Chiquier 2009). INFONAVIT (Instituto Fondo Nacional de la Vivienda para los Trabajadores) in Mexico has a similar profile to help contributors to access housing loans. INFONAVIT provides 70 percent of the subsidized housing mortgage. Provident funds need careful management and rigorous accountability to ensure proper targeting.

Private-Sector Involvement and Financing

Slums provide a large potential market for private-sector investment (in addition to the informal developers and land dealers that help slum dwellers invade land) (Baker and McCain 2009).

Baker (2008) reports that poor people "at the bottom of the pyramid with incomes less than $3000 a year represent more than 4 billion people and more than $5 trillion in purchasing power." Much of these earnings are generated in the informal economy, which in many countries represent up to 40 percent of the GDP.

One of the drivers of this trend has been the idea that the "bottom of the pyramid" represents a large untapped market (see Prahalad and Hart 2002). HSBC and CitiGroup have been among the first large international banks to seek new partnerships in this area. In India, ICICI (Industrial Credit and Investment Corporation of India) is extending a wide range of financial services to the poor. In other cases, partnerships are being developed with local financial institutions. The Home Finance Company Bank of Ghana is working with CHF International to create low-income finance products including a home improvement finance product. Banks in Senegal have financed mortgages for low-income groups and public water supply.

Private firms also extend supplier credits (e.g., Patrimonio Hoy, the housing microfinance program of CEMEX Mexico) and mobilize capital through bond issues in the case of large metropolitan areas. FIRE-D, supported by USAID, helped the first and successful bond program (Moser 2006) issued by the Ahmedabad Municipal Corporation in 1998 to finance a citywide water and sanitation project that included the slum networking project Parivarta (Baker 2008). In 2005, eight municipalities around Bangalore (Bengaluru) created the Greater Bangalore Water and Sanitation Pooled Facility, a typical metropolitan structure that combined the commitments of the eight cities. USAID has also created finance facilities, such as the Community Water and Sanitation Facility, to help the municipality access commercial finance for slum infrastructure and service expansion projects (Baker et al. 2005).[2]

Alternative arrangements may include private-sector developers and private-sector financing. The Oshiwara II slum upgrading project in Mumbai used a public/private partnership comprising the organizing NGOs (Society for the Promotion of Area Resource Centres and NSDF), a private-sector bank that provided construction finance (ICICI), and a guarantee for the bank loan from USAID's Development Credit Authority (Merryl and Suri 2007). In São Paulo, some of the recent urban upgrading has been tied to the development of commercial areas around metro stations and funded by auctioning and trading similar construction rights (*solo criado*).

Output-based aid subsidies have been effective to get the private sector involved in particular projects, notably in extending water connection to slums. Disbursements are made against performance targets, such as the connection of a given number of new customers to the electrical grid or water distribution network. Private providers must provide their own finance up front (in most cases) to meet the performance targets. Output-based aid has been particularly effective in extending water connections to slums through one-time network extension and connection fee subsidies, as is being done in Manaus (Brazil), Jakarta, Manila, Mozambique, Surabaya (Indonesia), and Ethiopia (Baker and McCain 2009).

Progression of Finance Instrument Use

In sum, depending on technical capacity and budgetary resources, cities and metropolitan areas can use different combinations of instruments. Figure 14.2 summarizes how the sophistication of the instruments can grow with technical capacity and financial resources available to the policy maker. For poor and low-capacity cities, slum upgrading programs will probably be financed by grants and federal funds. Community initiatives (e.g., in Dar es Salaam, Nairobi, and Maputo) will be important assets as well. As technical capacity improves and more financial resources can be mobilized, slum upgrading can be financed by microfinancing schemes, community credit, or national provident funds. At the top of the ladder are national housing programs linked to financial sector and subsidy schemes that help urban dwellers to leverage their savings and purchase or rent affordable housing.

Learning from Concrete Cases

Preceding sections have reviewed various forms of slum improvement interventions and specific financing modalities employed in developing country cities. This

---

[2] Ahmedabad's four municipal bond issues raised $89.5 million from 1998 to 2006. The Greater Bangalore Facility raised more than $23 million with the assistance of a $780,000 partial credit guarantee from USAID, essentially mobilizing more than $29 in domestic capital for every dollar donated (Baker et al. 2005; Peterson 2009).

FIGURE 14.2

Sources of slum upgrading finance

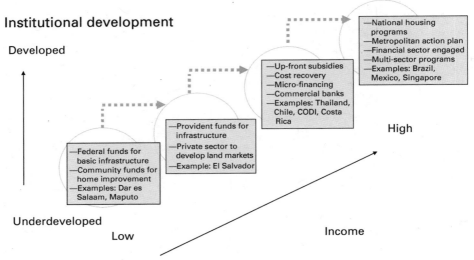

Abbreviation: CODI, Community Organizations Development Institute.
SOURCE: Data from World Bank and UN-HABITAT (1999).

section explores the experience in five concrete cases involving different approaches, each successful in its own way.

Singapore

The case of Singapore illustrates how institutions, basic services, and connectivity work together to produce an inclusive city (Hui and Wong 2004).[3] At independence in 1965, 70 percent of the population lived in overcrowded areas, and one-third squatted in squalid and unsanitary slums (*attap kampungs*) with primitive sanitation. Unemployment was at 14 percent, and half of the population was illiterate. Water-borne illnesses such as cholera and dysentery were a perennial problem, largely due to lack of an adequate potable water supply. Tuberculosis was common because of congested living conditions and low standards of hygiene.

Since the 1960s, Singapore has pursued a vision of "shelter for all" that provides affordable, adequate housing to the poor, especially the lower-income families. Public housing was identified as the primary mechanism for housing delivery, based on the idea that housing is one of the most basic needs and is a merit service: it should be provided regardless of the ability to pay, and because of the limited capacity of the private supply to meet the quantitative and qualitative housing demand.

To achieve this vision, Singapore launched a comprehensive public housing sector development plan, covering institutions, financing, allocation, and rentals.

---

[3]This chapter otherwise relies on Freire and Yuen (2004), Kallidaikurichi and Yuen (2010), and Wong, Yuen, and Goldblum (2008).

A law was passed regulating public housing delivery. As a result, within five years, 50,000 units of low-cost housing had been delivered. The building rate was 10 times faster than in the previous year. Forty years later, public housing is the predominant form of housing in Singapore: more than 85 percent of the population lives in publicly produced housing. A key factor that enabled such a large scale was the ownership of land; as in Hong Kong, more than half of the land in Singapore is state land, leased for 90 years to private owners.

The success of the Singapore large-scale upgrading was due to (1) good institutions, transparent governance, and commitment that led to a redevelopment of the center of the city; (2) steady financing streams fueled by a mandatory retirement provident fund; and (3) purchase of large portions of land. The success of Singapore also owes to strong political will combined with the technical and financial capacity to translate such will into urban plans sustained over a long time horizon.

Public housing estates were first developed in and around the central area, which reduced the dislocation of the households being resettled. Only incrementally did the public housing authority develop housing estates and new towns farther away from the city center. The first new town developed was located six to eight kilometers away. To compensate for the longer distance between their new homes and the city center, this new town was planned with a full range of neighborhood facilities and services, including public bus transport. Furthermore, the new town was located along highways connecting the town center to the city, thus facilitating relatively convenient and fast transportation to workplaces (Wong, Yuen, and Goldblum 2008). Eventually public housing spread throughout the city. All of the housing estates were connected to modern sanitation and sewage treatment works and to piped potable water and electricity. A solid waste management system was also provided. The public sector managed to buy more than two-thirds of the land in Singapore through the Land Amalgamation Act. This enabled development to occur without much speculation.

In the late 1960s, the city government introduced a financing system to help households buy public housing units through the use of a part of their mandatory retirement provident funds. The copayment scheme between state and homebuyers ensured financing for the housing program. In the beginning of the program, the homes built and bought were small. Over time, families moved to bigger apartments either because their wages increased or because children grew up and supplemented their parents' incomes. The proportion of residents living in smaller one- and two-room apartments declined to 5 percent in 2000, while those living in the larger four- and five-room apartments increased to more than 50 percent of public housing residents.

Hong Kong

Similarly to Singapore, Hong Kong is renowned for its extensive public housing program.[4] Since 1953, the Hong Kong government has supported public housing

---

[4]This section relies on Hui and Wong (2004).

development through the direct injection of capital and indirect subsidies of land. It has financed the construction of more than 1.3 million domestic units under public rental housing and various subsidized-ownership programs, which now accommodate about half of the population in Hong Kong.

In 1973, the new Hong Kong Housing Authority (HKHA) received the responsibility for the provision, allocation, and management of public housing. With the participation of the private sector, HKHA has moved from a highly subsidized institution to a self-financed institution, as announced in the long-term housing strategy prepared in 1987. Under this new financial system, subsidies and cost arrangements have significantly changed. Financial subsidies have been introduced in the form of a home purchase loan scheme. It offers low-interest down payment loans to eligible applicants to encourage them to purchase private-sector flats. In addition, the HKHA implemented various measures to ensure a more efficient control over subsidies, construction, and estate management.

Since 1997, the HKHA has been working to respond to the government's ambitions to increase the home ownership rate and speed up the allocation of public rental housing by building more public housing and increase the quotas of the housing purchase loan scheme. Although there is no new funding from the city government, the HKHA started selling housing purchase loan schemes to the Hong Kong Mortgage Corporation to obtain more funds for the home purchase loan scheme. Moreover, the private sector has increased its involvement in estate management and development of public housing. Still, more than 30 percent of Hong Kong residents live in public rental housing.

The HKHA's major sources of funding are an annual grant from the city government and recurrent income through selling and leasing its properties. The government largely supports the finance of public housing: it offers land, loans, and capital to the HKHA, which is responsible for planning and implementing the development of public housing. The HKHA is the largest landlord in Hong Kong. In 2001, it received $9.628 million from more than 660,000 rental flats totaling $9,528 million (Hong Kong Housing Authority 2000). However, public housing rents are set at a subsidized level. Since 1988, when the HKHA became a self-financing institution, it started to raise funds by investing in the housing ownership system and other commercial/industrial properties. Leasing spaces for commercial use, at near-market price, has been effective in financing the budget and helps offset the deficit from its rented sector. HKHA also announced the tenants purchase scheme in 1997, where tenants can buy their own flats.

Hong Kong's success reflects the management of urban land as a source of revenues for the city and the value of having an independent housing company, which administers the land occupation and derives its finance power from managing the sector. As in Singapore, it also reflects the benefits of city planning and management that is independent from any higher-level authority. However, the beneficiaries of subsidized housing in Singapore have more freedom in buying and selling their houses than in Hong Kong, where restrictions imposed on subsidized rental units hinder the free flow of the subsidized units in the housing market (Wong 2011).

Indonesia: The Kampung Improvement Program

The Kampung Improvement Program (KIP) of Jakarta, also known as the Muhammad Husni Thamrin program, is considered one of the best urban poverty programs in the world, primarily for two reasons. First, the cost per person of investment in slum upgrading is one of the lowest on record (ranging from US$118 in Jakarta to US$23 in smaller cities). Second, it combined centrally funded infrastructure with local and community participation. This resulted in rapid scaling up to more than 800 cities and towns, benefiting almost 30 million people since 1989 (Surjadi and Haryatiningsih 1998). Community-based organizations were fundamental to preserving the identity of the housing conditions across Jakarta's large metropolitan area and to adapting upgrading from site to site across such a large city. The secret to this success was the use of community-based organizations as project initiators, which could encourage active, innovative, and self-sustained communities to undertake urban upgrading with the resources that were available.

The KIP program was supported by four projects of the World Bank. The first two concentrated on physical improvements; the third included a social/economic dimension. During its peak performance in the 1970s, KIP was able to upgrade up to 2,000 hectares per year. KIP played a significant role in improving the quality of life of slum dwellers. "It improved infrastructure, paths, lighting, and housing. Land values increased; drainage helped reduce flooding; and good institutions were created. . . . Residents are better educated and healthier, household size declined, more residents are employed and have greater income, and women have taken jobs" (World Bank 1995).

KIP's success was rooted in three factors. The first was the political will of governments and the engagement of community. With the improvement and provision of affordable infrastructure, the communities were encouraged to renovate and build their houses with only a little help from the government. Second, there was good management. KIP was managed under a special, multidisciplinary unit, comprising well-trained staff providing a wide range of skills needed in slum upgrading. The staff working in the project unit received higher wages than the average public official, in line with a more intensive workload. Third, the project had financial and management support from the World Bank. This support was essential to scale up the project and implement it in large cities in Indonesia such as Bandung, Surabaya, and Semarang, using a combination of funding sources, including local and national governments and the World Bank.

While KIP had a tremendous impact on the lives of millions of people, sustainability issues emerged early on (Serageldin, Kim, and Wahba 2000) and have since materialized as a significant problem. KIP performance deteriorated over time as the maintenance costs increased and there was no budget to maintain communal works and infrastructure. In contrast to the Singapore and Hong Kong models of slum improvement and public housing development, the KIP had not adequately addressed the challenge of fiscal and financial sustainability.

Dar es Salaam: The Impact of Community Participation at the Metro Level

Dar es Salaam is a rapidly growing metropolitan area. It comprises three municipalities and a coordinating council, which has no authority over the other municipalities. All have very little budget. From 1948 to 2008, the population of the metropolitan area grew from 51,000 to 3.5 million. Lacking infrastructure, planning capacity, and resources, most of the new comers stayed in the fringes of the main city. In total, more than 80 percent reside in informal areas (Stren 2009). But contrary to the case in other slums, slum dwellers in Dar es Salaam have taken concrete steps to organize their communities and construct infrastructure or plea for better conditions and service delivery.

A positive aspect of Dar es Salaam is that most urban households enjoy relatively secure tenure. In 1983, all urban land was converted from freehold to government land with leasehold conditions. Subsequently, the government decided that all of those who occupy land can only be removed with an adequate compensation (Stren 2009).

In 1990, the World Bank financed a project to upgrade the poorest communities of the metro area in Dar es Salaam. The community was expected to help with project design and maintenance of the new facilities. The result has been encouraging. A recent assessment prepared by the World Bank (Stren 2009) concluded that the engagement of the community gave the population a great sense of ownership and provided incentives for the residents to contribute to the finance of the capital cost. Actually, each resident contributed about $22; in total, residents contributed 5 percent of the capital cost.

As part of the project design, the community helped in the prioritization process. Residents identified the 30 wards (out of 310) that would receive priority investments and contributed to preparation of the plans. To ensure comparability across wards, capital costs were set at $18,000 per hectare. The final version of the project was discussed with the communities.

The results have been remarkable. First, the project was a boost to the official approach that encourages slum dwellers (both house owners and tenants) to organize and obtain local services and infrastructure. Second, the project led to one of the most inclusive resettlement policies in Africa. The resettlement law was published in October 2008. It follows the guidelines and approaches of the World Bank resettlement policy (Stren 2009).

The case of Dar es Salaam shows how important it to have the participation of the community to identify priorities, raise funding, and supervise implementation of projects. Since most urban settlements in Dar es Salaam are informal, there are no income or consumption records and no way to prioritize the most needy. Using the community to help identify the families at risk was effective and accepted by the residents at large.

São Paulo: From Lack of Coordination to Improved Planning

The São Paulo metropolitan area, the largest city in Brazil with the most dynamic economy, has attracted a large number of migrants who settle in environmentally precarious areas. The SEAD Foundation estimates that one-third of São Paulo inhabitants live in slum and informal areas. Since the 1970s, the city has developed important programs to deal with the slum problems (from provision of public housing to rental solutions, upgrading, and generous subsidies), financed by multiple sources, including federal, state, municipal, and international finance. Nevertheless, lack of coordination across city programs and absence of coordination across metropolitan jurisdictions lessened the impact of the programs. At present, São Paulo has four agencies in charge of slum upgrading: Caixa Economica Federal, the official bank, the municipal housing secretary, the state housing secretariat, a housing cooperative, and several institutions in charge of managing funds, including the State Housing Fund. There is no metropolitan or citywide plan, and each agency has its own budget, programs, and clients.

The World Bank (2007) report on São Paulo suggests several low-income housing policy issues. First, the city policy is biased toward finished units (rather than basic units that can be completed by the residents over time) in an effort to relocate the people displaced from the catchment areas that provide most of the water to the city. No funds were allocated to encourage new low-income housing or progressive solutions, and the private sector has no particular role in the strategy. Second, the finished units are very expensive and require large subsidies to be affordable: from 70 percent to 90 percent of the unit cost. This leaves few resources to expand social housing programs. Third, the rental housing units built in 2005 are inhabited by households whose low earnings make it impossible for them to pay the rent that would finance maintenance of the units. Fourth, enforcement of land use restrictions is difficult for municipal authorities, and invasions of public land continue.

The authorities in São Paulo are aware of this situation and are making efforts to gather information on the types of slums and residents in the city, establish a database, and have information available to all actors in urban policy (Herling and França 2009). Given the number of institutions working in this area and the volume of resources, São Paulo should be able to upgrade the existing substandard housing stock while keeping pace with the new flows.

The positive experience with the development of a metropolitan program to improve urban settlements in two major water basins in São Paulo could serve as a model for doing so. The metropolitan region of São Paulo draws its water supply from environmentally protected suburban areas that have been occupied by informal settlements. To address this problem, the state government and the governments of nine municipalities in the São Paulo metropolitan region have implemented the Guarapiranga Basin Environmental Cleanup Program, aimed to restore the water quality of this watershed. The overall program, which was supported by a loan from the World Bank, includes five subprograms: installment of water and sewer services; waste collection and disposal; urban upgrading; environmental protection; and management of the basin by tripartite committees composed of representatives of the state and municipal governments and private citizens.

This new institutional arrangement allowed the integration of different agencies that work on land and upgrading. From 1993 to 2000, 87 settlements (favelas and informal subdivisions) were upgraded, benefiting 38,000 families. The main idea behind the program was to move from a narrowly focused water infrastructure project to a comprehensive slum upgrading program that would engage the residents in the process of protecting the quality of the water services. The second phase of the program began in 2008 with the inclusion of the sensitive water supply area near the Billings reservoir, with the goal of upgrading 81 settlements, favelas, and informal subdivisions by 2012 (Herling and França 2009).

As a result of this experience, São Paulo has combined social inclusiveness and environmental sustainability goals. The Municipal Housing Plan uses the 103 hydrographic subbasins as the unit of intervention for the entire municipality, recognizing the presence of informal land subdivisions and assuring that environmental and slum improvement go hand in hand throughout the city (França 2000). As part of the effort to improve city planning, São Paulo has obtained a grant from Cities Alliance to monitor the development of slums and informality in the city, to develop a statistical database and provide a better basis for future planning and interventions.

CONCLUSIONS: THE PILLARS OF SUCCESSFUL SCALING UP OF SLUM UPGRADING

Past experience suggests that success depends on several factors, notably the capacity of the urban government to finance infrastructure and deliver basic services and the capacity of the slum dwellers to mobilize resources to improve their dwellings. Experience has also shown that while small projects may be more successful and easier to implement, they cannot accommodate the needs of the rapidly growing urban population in many developing countries. To upgrade the current stock of slum dwellings and to prevent further slum development, integrated metropolitan planning should cover problems across urban and peri-urban areas and address multijurisdiction issues such as transport connectivity, water supply, and environmental cleanup in connection with slum upgrading. Table 14.7 provides a useful list of action items extracted from UN-HABITAT experience.

In addition, eight pillars for successful slum upgrading can be identified from the experiences reviewed in this chapter.

- Political will and good governance are key for successful upgrading. For many years, slum upgrading was small scale, neighborhood specific, and ad hoc. The creation of Cities Alliance and the work of international organizations (e.g., UN-HABITAT) have raised awareness concerning the need to scale up and design/implement nationwide comprehensive housing policies, with low-income housing at their core.
- It is critical to commit sufficient resources. UN-HABITAT estimates that $500 per year per capita is needed for effective slum upgrading. Unfortunately, in most of the developing world, city expenditures are a fraction of that amount. Scaling up slum upgrading will take time. To complement taxpayer resources, several countries have established national housing funds. Homeowner purchasing power can also be raised with a combination of up-front subsidies, microcredit, and access to housing finance.

TABLE 14.7

The do's of slum upgrading finance

Ensure that financing for slum upgrading is recognized as a priority within national development planning and infrastructure plans.

Encourage local and international banks and micro finance institutions to become active participants in financing upgrading as part of their core business. Guarantee and technical assistance will make a difference.

Build investment in slum upgrading on a firm foundation of community based savings and loan systems and local authority commitments to provide in-kind and monetary allocations on an annual basis.

Recognize that financing for slum upgrading requires a mix of short-, medium-, and long-term loans, integrating finance for building, infrastructure and livelihoods.

Provide mechanisms to blend municipal finance, cross subsidies and beneficiary contributions to ensure financial viability of upgrading projects and home improvement programs.

Develop a process for sharing risk analysis and planning for risk mitigation and management with all the key stakeholders.

Plan projects on a mixed-use basis with revenue generating elements such as saleable residential units and rentable commercial space in order to maximize financial viability.

Recognize that not everyone who lives in a slum is poor. Where an area upgrading strategy is to be implemented provision needs to be made for a range of income groups with steps taken to ensure that the poorest are not excluded.

Recognize that home ownership is not the solution to everyone's problems. Provision for the development of affordable rental property is an important component of financing slum upgrading.

Make the real cost of finance very clear so that people clearly understand the commitments they are making to loan repayment. Don't hide the real cost behind misleading promotional messages.

Where appropriate establish local upgrading finance facilities so that funding is locally available.

Ensure that subsidies are effectively targeted so that the benefits reach those for whom they are intended and build on the basis of long term engagement.

Explore options to use land allocation, readjustment and sharing methods to release finance for upgrading.

SOURCE: The UN-HABITAT Slum Upgrading Facility Newsletter (April 2009).

- A land policy framework must be established, and the strict land regulations and zoning that limit the supply of serviced land must be addressed. If land supply is inelastic, as is often the case, any increase in the purchasing power of the slum residents will only result in higher land prices, offsetting the impact of the subsidy policy.
- Connective infrastructure should enable the poor to have access to labor markets and to enhance the metropolitan labor market. Most urban upgrading packages include water, sanitation, and paved roads. Urban transportation is crucial to enable slum dwellers to access the labor market and connect with the formal economy.
- Participation of local communities will help assemble resources for basic infrastructure (as in Tanzania). Community participation is key to prioritize needs, identify recipients of assistance, raise communal funds needed for infrastructure, and ensure maintenance of new investment.

- Slum upgrading should include income generation components to enable households to finance their own shelter improvement and ensure the sustainability of the provision of basic services (Rojas 2010).
- Subsidies should be targeted to those who cannot afford to pay for housing improvement or services. Given the lack of data, information from the community and local government is crucial to identify individuals at risk.
- The influx of new settlers should be included in the plan. Because of the high costs involved with remedial strategies, preventing new slum formations has become the new mantra of urban planners. The best way to avoid slums is to ensure that land markets and solutions are available to all levels of income. This implies helping small credit and neighborhood schemes, microfinance, progressive housing, and small saving schemes (Rojas 2010).

Slum upgrading fails mostly because of a lack of realistic plans that take into account the financial and political constraints in providing affordable housing to the poor. In most cases, slum upgrading focuses on a small part of the population at risk, letting slums mushroom in other parts of the city. Investments in basic infrastructure are equally urgent, but preserving a share of city budget to extend basic services to slum areas is often an uphill battle. Even with political will, the mismatch between the needs of the increasing population and the lack of resources at the metropolitan level will lead to years of inadequate services and low living quality. The good news is that the accumulation of good experiences and the awareness that combinations of public, private, and community-based solutions can produce win-win outcomes for all stakeholders will lead to a concerted effort to improve the lives of the urban poor.

REFERENCES

Annez, Patricia, Alain Bertaud, B. Patel, and V. K. Phatak. 2010. Working with the market, approach to reducing urban slums in India. Washington, DC: World Bank. (November).

Azfar, Asad and Aun Rahman. 2004. Acumen fund and housing the urban poor. Available at http://www.acumenfund.org/uploads/assets/documents/saiban_study_9EHCYHWl.pdf

Baker, Judy. 2008. Urban poverty: A global view. Urban Paper No. 5. Washington, DC: World Bank. (June).

Baker, Judy, R. Basu, M. Cropper, S. Lall, and A. Takeuchi. 2005. Urban poverty and transport: The case of Mumbai. Policy Research Working Paper No. 3683. Washington, DC: World Bank.

Baker, Judy, and Kim McCain. 2009. Private sector initiatives in slum upgrading. Urban Paper No. 8. Washington, DC: World Bank.

Biswas, Smita. 2003. Housing is a productive asset, housing finance for self-employed women in India. *Small Enterprise Development* 14:1–49.

Buckley, Robert, and Jerry Kalarickal. 2006. Thirty years of world bank shelter lending: What have we learned? Washington, DC: World Bank.

Burgos, Slaven Antonio Razmilic. 2010. Property values, housing subsidies and incentives: Evidence from Chile's current housing policies. Master's thesis, MIT. http://dspace.mit .edu/bitstream/handle/1721.1/62112/708579235.pdf?sequence=1

Chiquier, Loic. 2009. *Housing finance.* Washington, DC: World Bank.

Cities Alliance. 1999. Cities Alliance for Cities Without Slums. Washington, DC.

Cummings, Jean, and Denise Di Pasquale. 2002. The spatial implications of housing policy in Chile. In *Chile: The political economy of urban development*, ed. Edward L. Glaeser and John R. Meyer. Cambridge, MA: Harvard University Press.

Ferguson, Bruce. 2008a. Market based models for land development for the low/moderate-income majority. *Global Urban Development* 4(2). http://www.globalurban.org/GUDMag08Vol4Iss2 /FergusonMarketBasedModels.htm

———. 2008b. A value chain framework for affordable housing in emerging countries. *Global Urban Development* 4(2). http://www.globalurban.org/GUDMag08Vol4Iss2/Ferguson ValueChain.htm

França, Elisabete. (2000). Guarapiranga: Urban and environmental recovery in the municipality of São Paulo. São Paulo: M. Carrilho Arquitetos.

Freire, Mila, and Belinda K. P. Yuen, eds. 2004. *Enhancing urban management in East Asia*. Aldershot, U.K.: Ashgate.

Herling, Tereza, and Elisabete França. 2009. *Social housing in São Paulo: Challenges and new management tools*. Washington, DC: Cities Alliance.

Hoik Smit, Marja. 2009. Housing subsidies. In *Housing financing*, ed. Loic Chiquier. Washington, DC: World Bank.

Hong Kong Housing Authority. 2001. Quality housing: Partnering for change. Annual Report on Enhancing Public Housing Quality. Available at http://www.housingauthority.gov.hk/eng /ha/ephq0001/pdf/ereport.pdf

Hui, Eddie C., and Francis Wong. 2004. The Hong Kong Housing Authority and its financial arrangement over the past 50 years. Hong Kong: Hong Kong Polytechnic University.

ISTED (Intitut des Sciences et des Etudes de Developpement). 2005. Emerging cities, keys to understanding and acting. www.villesendevenir.org

Kallidaikurichi, See, and Belinda Yuen. 2010. Developing living cities, from analysis to action. London: World Scientific Publishing Company.

Kessides, Christine. 1997. World Bank experience with the provision of infrastructure services for the urban poor: Preliminary identification and review of best practices. http://siteresources .worldbank.org/INTEMPOWERMENT/Resources/10142_urban.pdf

Mayo, Stephen. 1991. Housing policy and housing research: The view from the World Bank. *Housing Finance International* (December).

McGee, T. G. 2005. Urbanization takes on new dimensions in Asia's population giants. Population Reference Bureau. www.prb.org.

Merryl, Sally, and Ajay Suri. 2007. Low income shelter finance in slum upgrading. Washington, DC: Urban Institute.

Mitlin, Diana. 2007. The role of collective action and urban social movement in reducing chronic urban poverty. Working Paper No. 64. Manchester, U.K.: Chronic Poverty Research Centre.

Mitlin, Diana, and Anna Muller. 2004. Windhoek Namibia: Towards progressive urban land policies in South Africa. *International Development Policy Review* 26(2):167–186.

Moser, Caroline. 2006. Asset-based approaches to poverty reduction in a globalised context. Global Economy and Development Working Paper No. 01. Washington, DC: Brookings Institution.

Peterson, George. 2009. Unlocking land values to finance urban infrastructure. Washington, DC: World Bank.

Prahalad, C. K., and Stuart Hart. 2002. The fortune at the bottom of the pyramid. *Strategy +Business* 26:54–67.

Rojas, Eduardo. 2010. *Building cities, neighborhood upgrading and urban quality of life*. Washington, DC: Inter-American Development Bank.

Seetharam, Kalindakunri, and Belinda Yuen. 2010. Developing living cities: From analysis to action. London: World Scientific Publishing Company.

Serageldin, Mona, S. Kim, and Sahah Wahba. 2000. Decentralization and urban infrastructure management capacity. In *Third global report on human settlements*. UN-HABITAT.

Shea, Michael. 2008. Multilateral and bilateral funding of housing and slum upgrading development in developing countries. Washington, DC: International Housing Coalition.

Smolka, Martin, and Adriana Larangeira. 2008. Informality and poverty in Latin American urban policies. In *The new global frontier*, ed. Gordon McGranahan, George Martine, Mark Montgomery, and Rogelio Fernandez-Castilla. London: Earthscan.

Stren, Richard. 2009. Community infrastructure upgrading program case study: The case of Dar es Salaam. Washington, DC: World Bank.

Surjadi, Charles, and Darrundono Haryatiningsih. 1998. Review of Kampung Improvement Program Evaluation in Jakarta. Final Report for UNDP/World Bank Water and Sanitation Program by the Regional Water and Sanitation Group for East Asia and the Pacific. Jakarta: U.N. Development Programme/World Bank.

UN-HABITAT. 2005. Financing urban shelter: Global report on human settlements. London: Earthscan and UN-HABITAT.

U.N. Millennium Project. 2005. Investing in development. A practical guide to achieve the Millennium Development Goals. London: Earthscan.

Wong, Richard. 2011. Public policy in Hong Kong and China. Unpublished manuscript.

Wong, Tai-Chee, Belinda Yuen, and Charles Goldblum. 2008. Spatial planning for a sustainable Singapore [e-book]. Springer.

World Bank. 1993. Housing: Enabling markets to work. Washington, DC.

———. 1995. Kampung improvement programs. Impact Evaluation Report No. 14747. Indonesia Urban Projects. Washington, DC: World Bank (June 29).

———. 2007. São Paulo: Inputs for a sustainable competitive city strategy. Report No. 37324-BR. Washington, DC.

———. 2008. Reshaping economic geography. World Development Report. Washington, DC.

———. 2010. Africa's infrastructure a time for transformation. Washington, DC.

World Bank and UN-HABITAT. 1999. Cities alliance for cities without slums: Action plan for moving slum upgrading to scale. http://web.mit.edu/urbanupgrading/sponsor/ActionPlan .pdf

EXTERNAL ASSISTANCE FOR URBAN FINANCE DEVELOPMENT

15

Needs, Strategies, and Implementation

HOMI KHARAS AND JOHANNES F. LINN

The World Development Report (World Bank 2009b) describes cities as vital to economic growth. In successful countries, cities provide scale economies, efficiencies in logistics, and, in the provision of public services, dense labor markets that foster training and skills acquisition, innovation and creativity, diversification of production, lower environmental footprint through densification, and, ultimately, greater freedom for the individuals who live there. However, cities do not provide these benefits automatically or for free. City management is a complex undertaking of institutional development and governance; planning, partnerships, and consultations with the myriad stakeholders within cities; and considerable amounts of financing. Absent this, cities can generate problems as easily as benefits (see chapter 2).

The 2009 World Development Report also describes the billion slum dwellers in the developing world's cities. The international aid community has long recognized the pervasive effects of poverty, illiteracy, and mortality in slums and established a specific target as part of the U.N. Millennium Development Goals (MDGs): "By 2020, to have achieved a significant improvement in the lives of 100 million slum dwellers" (United Nations, n.d.). However, the U.N. Millennium Indicators monitoring site (United Nations 2012) shows that there are 100 million more slum dwellers than in 1990, as rapid urbanization offsets modest progress in improving the lives of those already in cities. The problem is especially severe and growing rapidly in Africa. A 2005 report of the Commission for Africa, chaired by Tony Blair, identified urbanization as the second most important challenge facing Africans, after the HIV/AIDS pandemic. The reasons are clear: sub-Saharan Africa has a staggering 71 percent of its urban population in slums, so business as usual is unacceptable (Commission for Africa 2005).

There is widespread agreement about the need for action in response to these opportunities and challenges. There is advocacy on the modalities through which assistance can be made: policy support and investments. There are now measurable targets at the global level, and a number of international organizations are dedicated solely to promoting urban development.[1] However, there is a sense in the development community that urban development has a low priority for donors, that funding is declining, that strategies are not acted upon, and that new approaches are needed even as it would seem obvious that external assistance should play a central role in urban development. The very fact that slum upgrading is included in the MDGs (along with other indicators that must be addressed at a spatial level, e.g., education, health, and poverty) shows that there is broad recognition that urban development issues can be resolved only by a combination of national and international policies if countries are to attain the speed and efficiency of urban improvements that are needed to meet the MDG targets.

Among the national and local policies that will be critical for meeting the needs of the rapidly growing areas in developing countries are those that determine the effective mobilization of financial resources for urban service provision, their efficient and equitable allocation to urban development priorities, and their effective management. International assistance can and should, therefore, not only aim to help meet the immediate funding needs but also contribute to improve the urban financial resource mobilization and management capacity.

This chapter addresses two sets of questions: (1) what is known about the amounts of aid that support urban development in developing countries relative to financing needs, and what needs to be done to assure accurate data to assess the amounts and trends of these flows; and (2) what is known about the strategic objectives and operational approaches followed by aid donors regarding urban development, especially regarding urban finance improvements, and about the effectiveness of the aid flows to urban areas in terms of their impacts in improving urban service provision and in raising the capacity to improve urban finance mobilization and management.

AID FOR URBAN DEVELOPMENT: PATTERNS, TRENDS, AND DATA ISSUES

This section reviews external assistance for urban development by assessing the need for urban assistance and by documenting trends in aid going into urban projects and programs. The section closes with a brief discussion of the determinants of urban aid as a share of total aid. Unfortunately, the analysis is constrained by the limited information available on the amount of support donors give specifically for urban or metropolitan city development.

Financing Needs

Urban financing needs are difficult to assess. Although there is no globally accepted figure for the level of overall investment requirements to make cities work well, ballpark estimates are available from various sources. The Zedillo report of the

---

[1] The U.N. Human Settlements Programme (UN-HABITAT) and Cities Alliance are among the most prominent.

U.N. High-Level Panel on Financing for Development (2001) estimates that additional resources of $4 billion per year would be required to achieve the MDG target of a significant improvement in the lives of 100 million slum dwellers by 2020.

The Asian Development Bank (AsDB), based on its experience with slum upgrading projects in Asia, estimates that $1,520 would be required per household in a slum to upgrade water supply ($400), sanitation ($700), solid waste management ($120), and the physical environment ($300) (AsDB 2006).[2] Applying this estimate globally implies a cost of $3.4 billion per year.[3]

However, dealing with existing slum dwellers does not take into account new migrants who continue to pour into urban slums. The global slum population is considered to be more than 1 billion people; thus, assuming that the growth of slum dwellers is the same as the rate of urbanization (2.2 percent per year), there would be an increase of 20 million slum dwellers per year from now to 2020. Added to the desired reduction of 10 million slum dwellers a year to meet the MDG target, this means that around $5 billion per year is needed just for slum improvements.

In addition to reducing the number of slum dwellers, urbanization requires achieving efficiency in the management of the growth of cities. In fact, financing requirements for city infrastructure projects are considerably greater than those required for slum upgrading. The AsDB (2006) estimates that its member countries' cities need $60 billion per year to function effectively, of which about half is currently met from all sources, public and private, domestic and international. Applying these estimates globally indicates urban public investment of about $120 billion per year. Of course, most of this must come from each country's own resources, but a significant fraction is needed from external assistance.

External Financial Resources for Urban Development

Finding a comprehensive measure of official development assistance (ODA) for urban development is difficult. Locational tags indicating whether a project is urban or rural are not used systematically while recording aid data. For example, if one adds up all projects labeled as either urban or rural in the ODA database of the Organisation for Economic Co-operation and Development's Development Assistance Committee, the total only amounts to 9 percent of all projects. This cannot be the case in practice but probably reflects the ambiguity in defining what constitutes urban aid. It remains unclear whether investment in a city school should be classified as an "urban" or an "education" investment. Currently, other themes, such as gender or climate change, which cut across different areas, use markers to identify if the project has the theme of "principal target," "significant target," or "not targeted," but this is not the case for urban or rural projects. As a first step toward measuring urban aid, it would be useful for all donors to apply a meaningful urban marker system. Absent that, it will remain difficult to assess the trends in urban foreign assistance and the gaps between resources and needs.

---

[2] These are expenditures required to convert a household from a slum dwelling to a nonslum dwelling.
[3] This is calculated taking the average household size as five and setting a goal of eliminating 100 million slum dwellers over nine years.

With this caveat, it is nonetheless possible to make some estimates for urban aid commitments. Following the methodology in Kharas, Chandy, and Hermias (2010), a series of ODA for urban projects was developed using the AidData web portal (AidData 2011), which provides access to information on all ODA and non-concessional loans of multilateral agencies like the World Bank and the AsDB (Findley et al. 2009). AidData aggregates data from multiple sources and provides a searchable database of global aid flows and projects. AidData allows for multiple sector and activity codes per project (unlike Development Assistance Committee data), so even if a project is largely sectoral (e.g., wastewater), it will show up as an urban project if there is a component with urban objectives, such as urban policy, planning, and management. This is often the case for urban projects where specific investments are used as the entry point for a broader discussion of urban policy issues with city officials. As explained below, loans, grants, and credits are identified that expressly target "explicit" and "implicit" urban objectives.

Explicit urban projects are all those that are coded with one or more of the following three purpose codes: urban development and management; low-cost housing; or housing policy and administration management. In 2008, ODA commitments from bilateral and multilateral sources that were marked with these purpose codes were $2.14 billion (figure 15.1). They represented approximately 1.2 percent of the $176 billion total ODA and nonconcessional loans committed that year (figure 15.2). The value of explicit urban commitments has not changed significantly over the last 14 years when measured in constant dollars. In fact, the level of commitments in 2008 was almost exactly the same as in 1995. Temporary spikes in

FIGURE 15.1

Urban aid commitments, 1995–2008

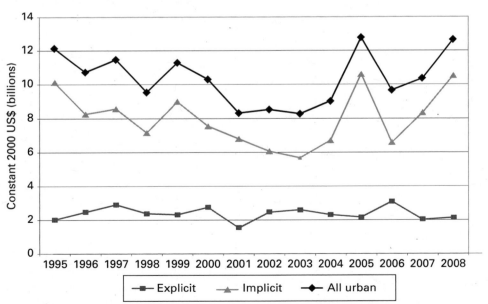

SOURCE: Data from AidData (2011).

FIGURE 15.2

Urban aid commitments as percentage of total aid, 1995–2008

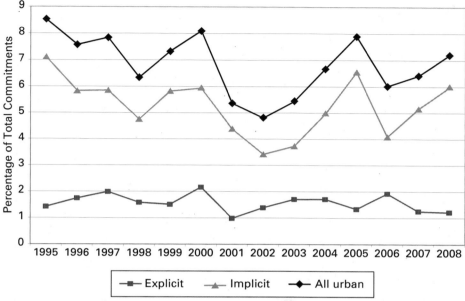

SOURCE: Data from AidData (2011).

1997, 2000, and 2006 were quickly reversed, suggesting that a few large projects may have been approved in these years, followed by a return to normal-size projects.

Implicit urban projects are imputed by searching all project titles, as well as their long and short descriptions, for a set of keywords that might indicate they have an urban purpose, even if not explicitly stated in the purpose code. Keywords include "urban," "city," "cities," "slum," "slums," "municipal," and "metropolitan," as well as a list of city names. The list of cities was drawn from the Economist Intelligence Unit's cost of living database (http://www.worldwidecostofliving.com/asp /wcol_WCOLHome.asp). It includes 76 developing country cities, including many capital cities. Implicit urban projects exclude explicit urban projects, so the total amount of foreign assistance for urban objectives is obtained by summing the two series. In 2008, there was $10.5 billion of external assistance in implicit urban projects from bilateral and multilateral sources, and about $12.6 billion in total urban assistance (figure 15.1). That is about 10 percent of global funding needs tentatively identified above.

Although over the last 10 years there is a slight upward trend in total urban aid, overall the amounts going toward urban development are small compared with needs. Expressed as a share of total bilateral and multilateral support, urban aid is on a flat to moderately declining trend, amounting to about 7 percent of total aid in recent years (figure 15.2). It would appear that other sectors have been more effective in gaining donor attention and funding support. The intention of the MDG slum reduction target, to focus the international community on global urban issues,

FIGURE 15.3

Urban aid commitments by donor, 1995–2008

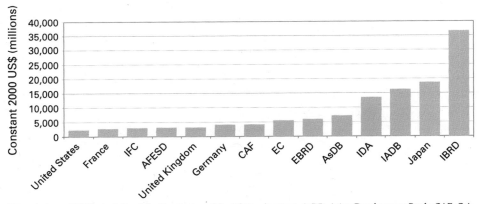

Abbreviations, AFESD, Arab Fund for Economic and Social Development; AsDB, Asian Development Bank; CAF, Caja Andino de Fomento; EBRD, European Bank for Reconstruction and Development; EC, European Commission; IADB, Inter-American Development Bank; IBRD, International Bank for Reconstruction and Development (World Bank); IDA, International Development Association (World Bank); IFC, International Finance Corporation.
SOURCE: Data from AidData (2011).

does not seem to have had an impact on increasing urban aid. As figure 15.1 reveals, urban aid may have actually fallen in 2001, just after the MDGs were adopted, and only after 2004 did they start to recover. Thus, it seems that urban aid has flatlined (see also Stren 2007).

In contrast to many other aid activities, urban aid is relatively concentrated and hence does not have the same kind of large coordination costs that are seen in other thematic areas, such as health and education.[4] While 44 donors have nonnegligible urban programs (i.e., they have committed more than $100 million to urban projects since 1995), only 22 have commitments of more than $1 billion each, and the top four donors accounted for 57.8 percent of all commitments. Multilateral agencies seem most oriented toward urban development; all of the top eight donors except Japan are multilateral agencies (figure 15.3). The World Bank is by far the largest donor to urban projects, with both the International Bank for Reconstruction and Development ($36 billion in commitments) and International Development Association ($13 billion) having significant programs.

Under what circumstances do countries receive a high share of urban aid? To answer this question, the share of urban aid in total aid was regressed on a number of country and donor characteristics. Based on figure 15.3, countries with a high share of multilateral aid are expected to also have a relatively high share of urban aid because multilaterals appear to have large urban programs. The urban share of the total population gives an indicator of the need for urban aid. Also included is a variable on government effectiveness, a summary indicator taken from the World Bank's Worldwide Governance Indicators, capturing perceptions of the quality of

---

[4] However, this does not preclude scattered and uncoordinated activities, for example, in Bangladesh (see box 15.2).

a country's bureaucracy. Finally, a variable on aid dependency is included, defined as the ratio of aid to the recipient country gross domestic product. Regional dummies complete the model.

Table 15.1 shows the results of an ordinary least squares regression on the determinants of the share of urban aid in total commitments from 1995 to 2008, covering 98 recipient countries. The results from this regression suggest that the share of urban aid received by a recipient country depends positively on the share of multilateral aid in total aid, recipient government effectiveness, and total aid levels. In contrast, the need for urban aid, proxied by the urban share of the population, is insignificant. Strikingly, sub-Saharan Africa systematically receives less urban aid than do other regions, perhaps because the African Development Bank has not been active in urban lending.

The top four recipients of urban aid from 1995 and 2008 are dynamic, middle-income emerging-market economies: China, Brazil, India, and Mexico (figure 15.4). Together, they account for 30 percent of total urban commitments to all recipient countries from 1995 to 2008.

Urban aid suffers from the micro-macro paradox in the evaluation of its impact, with successful micro-level interventions (see below for evaluation evidence) but limited impact on aggregate compared with the scale of the urban challenge and the size of urban financing needs. A more comprehensive and reliable recording of aid data is necessary to assess the support of urbanization through aid flows and to persuade donors to increase the level of their support. Indicators need to be developed to measure results for urban development at the city level, which can be aggregated for the country. Lack of documented results hampers the flow of external assistance to urban development. At the same time, donors must improve their reporting to the Development Assistance Committee, using urban markers and other ways of identifying urban interventions, in order to support urban projects.

TABLE 15.1

Regression results for urban aid, 1995–2008*

Share	Urban aid/total aid [log (standard error); $n=98$]
Multilateral share of total aid (log)	0.206** (0.101)
Urban share of population (log)	0.00674 (0.268)
Government effectiveness	0.577*** (0.206)
Total aid/initial GDP (log)	0.267** (0.105)
Europe and Central Asia	−0.363 (0.439)
Latin America and Caribbean	0.339 (0.403)
Middle East and North Africa	0.175 (0.433)
South Asia	0.349 (0.597)
Sub-Saharan Africa	−0.909** (0.403)

*$R^2 = 0.250$.
**$p \leq 0.05$.
***$p < 0.01$.
SOURCE: Calculations based on AidData (2011).

FIGURE 15.4

Urban aid commitments by recipient, 1995–2008

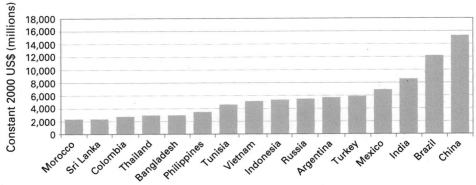

SOURCE: Data from AidData (2011).

APPROACHES TO URBAN FINANCE AND LESSONS FROM EXPERIENCE BY SELECT AID AGENCIES

This section summarizes the guidance provided by donor strategy documents and compares it with the lessons from actual experience as reflected in donors' project and program evaluation documents. Eleven strategy documents for seven donor agencies were reviewed.[5] They all share an overriding concern that urban local government capacity, accountability, and resources are generally very weak and in urgent need of strengthening if they are to be able to respond to rapid urbanization and severe urban physical and social infrastructure gaps. All strategy documents assign international development assistance an important role in helping to improve urban finance conditions as a key element for improving the performance of cities. None of them, however, focus specifically on metropolitan cities and how to assist them.

An examination of implementation showed no systematic assessment of experiences that donors had with their support for urban finance improvements. However, a sizable number of evaluations and reviews by three donor agencies for select areas of engagement and for some specific projects were analyzed. For the World Bank, three meta-evaluations are available (on municipal development projects [MDPs], projects in support of decentralization, and transport projects) and two reviews (on urban investment funds and lending for urban shelter).[6] In addition, eight recent evaluation reports are available for 18 urban projects in eight countries. For the AsDB, one meta-evaluation on urban development projects and seven evaluation reports of urban development programs in six countries are available.

---

[5] These strategy documents are African Development Bank (2010), AsDB (2008a; 2008b; 2009a), Cities Alliance (2006), Dirie (2005), EBRD (2004), International Housing Coalition (2009), USAID (2011), and World Bank (2002; 2009a).

[6] *Evaluations* are formal assessments by independent evaluation offices of aid donors, such as the Independent Evaluation Group (IEG) of the World Bank, that apply a standard evaluation and performance rating methodology. *Reviews* are assessments by experts (generally staff from or consultants working for the aid agency) that do not follow a standard evaluation methodology and do not apply formal performance ratings.

For the European Bank for Reconstruction and Development (EBRD), a review of the implementation of its municipal and environmental infrastructure operations policy is available, carried out by the EBRD evaluation department.

The strength of these evaluations and reviews is that they offer a broadly representative overview of the experience on the ground and on a comparative basis relative to other interventions by the same aid agency, as well as others. The evaluations, however, also have significant limitations: (1) even though the focus is on the most recent of the available evaluation documents (from 2006 to 2011), many of the projects that they review were initiated 10 or more years ago; (2) they do not cover experiences after the evaluation was completed; (3) few focus in-depth on urban finance interventions; (4) few focus on the experience with donor support to specific metropolitan areas; (5) only very few evaluations involve controlled experiments, and none of them allows for a statistical test of significance of the findings; and, (6) different standards of evaluation across institutions are likely, and possibly biases among the evaluators.

Nonetheless, the information contained in these evaluations and reviews is of great value in providing insights into what donors have actually done and how this compares with the donor strategies, what has been the degree of success of their interventions, and what have been key constraints and lessons from their engagement. The universe of the urban projects and programs evaluated and reviewed is indeed large, and the total amount of lending (about US$6 billion) is a significant fraction of the annual total annual ODA tracked in figure 15.1 (table 15.2).

The evaluations and reviews note that urban projects generally performed well, and in some cases better than the average project for the institution concerned over the period under review. For the World Bank's MDPs (reviewed in IEG 2009), 74 percent of completed projects were rated satisfactory, compared with 77 percent for all World Bank projects during the same period. MDPs performed best in Latin America and the Caribbean (86 percent satisfactory), above average in sub-Saharan Africa (75 percent), and worst in South Asia (43 percent). "Wholesale" projects (85 percent satisfactory) performed better than "retail" projects (67 percent). Annez, Huet, and Peterson (2008) found that municipal development fund (MDF) projects have done better on average than all World Bank projects and much better than World Bank credit-line projects. Buckley and Kalarickal (2006) noted that shelter projects were among the more successful of World Bank project areas, while the World Bank's Independent Evaluation Group (IEG 2007b) found that the performance of urban transport projects has been lower than average for transport projects from 1995 to 2005.

AsDB's and EBRD's urban projects generally performed equal to or better than projects in other sectors (AsDB 2006; EBRD 2010). Project performance assessments for AsDB find that single-city projects are performing substantially better than multicity programs. This is a striking difference from the World Bank's experience. AsDB (2006) ascribes the higher success rate of single-city projects to their simpler project design and institutional setup compared with multicity programs. One explanation for this difference between the experiences of AsDB and the World Bank might be that AsDB's single-city projects tended to involve fewer and less ambitious policy and institutional objectives than its multicity projects or the

TABLE 15.2

Key features of urban project evaluations and reviews

Evaluation/review (source)	Period	Number of projects	Amount of lending (annual average, billion US$)	Performance* (percent rated at least satisfactory)
World Bank municipal development projects (IEG 2009)	1998–2008	190	14.5 (1.3)	74
World Bank MDF projects (Annez, Huet, and Peterson 2008)	Mid-1970s to 2006	NA	11 (0.4)	63
World Bank decentralization projects (IEG 2008b)	1990–2007	NA	22 (2.8)	NA
World Bank urban shelter projects (Buckley and Kalarickal 2006)	Mid-1970s to 2005	NA	16 (0.5)	83
World Bank urban transport projects (IEG 2007b)	1995–2005	78	NA	78
AsDB urban sector projects (AsDB 2006)	1999–2005	88	4 (0.4)	81
EBRD municipal and environmental infrastructure operations (2010)	1993–2009	202	4.5 (0.3)	61

*Ratings are not strictly comparable across evaluations because of different performance criteria applied and different time periods of review. In the case of the World Bank, project performance overall increased substantially from the 1970s to the 2000s. As a result, ratings for longer time periods are likely to be biased downward, compared with ratings for more recent periods.

World Bank's retail projects. Another explanation could be that AsDB's evaluations give less weight to policy and institutional factors than do those of the World Bank.[7] More generally, AsDB (2006) notes that capacity-building and institutional development objectives were less frequently met than were overall project objectives.[8]

The remainder of this section reviews and contrasts the donors' strategic approaches and actual implementation experiences in seven areas of urban finance:

---

[7] For example, in the case of AsDB's loan to Vientiane, the evaluation concluded that the project was successful even though the project's "decentralized urban governance initiative was *partly relevant, ineffective, inefficient, and unlikely* to be sustainable" (AsDB 2010a, iv; italics in the original).

[8] AsDB project completion reports rate only 65 percent of projects successful in terms of their capacity building impact and only 50 percent in terms of institutional development.

decentralization; urban governments' own-source revenue mobilization; intergovernmental transfers; private finance; financial management and planning; partnerships and donor coordination; and scaling up.

Decentralization

Decentralization of governmental authority from the national to the local level is an important prerequisite for the effective development of urban government. Most of the urban strategy policy statements take the desirability and process of decentralizing responsibility and authority to lower levels of government as a given and, in effect, consider only how the capacity of urban governments to deliver improved services can be strengthened. The strategy report by the EBRD is an exception: it specifically postulates decentralization as a core objective, along with commercialization and environmental improvement (EBRD 2004). The report cites standard textbook arguments for decentralization, including better reflection of local preferences in public service provision and greater rationality and accountability in the use of public resources. However, with its principal focus on how to commercialize urban service delivery (including rational investment, cost-covering tariffs, independent management, and transparent and competitive procurement), even this strategy report does not address any of the complexities of design and implementation of decentralization reforms at the national or provincial level, which typically constrain the ability of local governments to improve their performance and the ability of aid organizations to support urban governments in their endeavors.

Only one recent evaluation assessed the results and quality of donor support for decentralization: the World Bank's evaluation of decentralization program funding in 20 countries from 1990 to 2007 (IEG 2008b).[9] World Bank support was provided mostly in the form of loans involving general budget support for national policy and institutional reforms. These operations generally do not deal specifically with urban fiscal and governance issues, nor do they focus on metro cities in particular, but they approach the decentralization challenge as an issue of nationwide policy and institutional reform. For its assessment, IEG considered four major areas of World Bank intervention: reform of intergovernmental relations; increase in own-source revenues of subnational governments; improved debt management; and enhanced administrative capacity and accountability.

According to the evaluation, the overall results of bank support were closely aligned with two factors: whether the governments had clearly identified their decentralization objectives and whether bank support was aligned with those objectives. The evaluation found that, for most countries, World Bank support had modest or negligible impact.[10] The report notes that, generally, the bank did not push for decentralization but assisted those countries that had identified

---

[9]No evaluations for other agencies address decentralization issues specifically, except that EBRD (2010) notes that policy dialogue in support of decentralization was an important component of EBRD municipal and environmental infrastructure operations.

[10]Interestingly, two of the high-impact cases involve postconflict countries, a fact that is not further addressed in IEG (2008b).

decentralization as a goal. In countries where the bank did push decentralization, such as Tunisia and Morocco, this had little effect (Annez, Huet, and Peterson 2008).

Results of World Bank support were generally better in the areas of helping countries developing suitable legal frameworks for decentralization and intergovernmental relations, creating transparent central governmental transfers, and improving public financial management at the subnational level. Areas of weak results included clarification of expenditure responsibilities, mobilization of own-source revenues at the local level, and introduction of citizens' oversight.

The evaluation report further notes that, overall, World Bank support was of mixed quality but did improve in more recent years. Principal weaknesses included variable quality of preparatory analyses of the decentralization challenge; weak understanding of the political economy; limited support for capacity building, especially at the subnational level; weak monitoring and evaluation (M&E), focused on process and outputs rather than outcomes; insufficient cooperation and coordination with other external donors; and lack of consistency in approach by different Bank organizational units supporting decentralization in a particular country.

The evaluation concludes with six recommendations for action: careful up-front analysis and development of an implementation plan; design of a comprehensive decentralization package involving fiscal, administrative, and governance reforms; selective support by the World Bank for parts of the overall package, with complementary engagement by other development donors; support for capacity building; a complementary mix of development policy loan and project loan support; and engagement for the long term.

Own-Source Revenues

All urban strategy documents agree that, in the wake of recent decentralization efforts in the developing world, local governments in general, and city governments in particular, have ended up with expanded expenditure responsibilities but that these have not been matched by sufficient increases in revenue authority. In addition, they note that local governments have not effectively used the revenue authority that they were given. Improving local revenue authority and effort is therefore a major, albeit difficult, thrust for official development agencies. Specifically, the Commonwealth Local Government Forum calls for the empowerment of local governments to raise their own resources in tandem with decentralization (Dirie 2005). The International Housing Coalition (2009) argues that they should be given more revenue authority, and the World Bank (2009a) urban strategy proposes to support local revenue-raising capacity and incentives for greater local revenue effort. The U.S. Agency for International Development (USAID 2011) supports improvements in cadastral services and municipal finance databases, while the Cities Alliance guidelines recommend greater reliance on cities' assets (especially land) and user fees (Cities Alliance 2006). EBRD (2004) focuses on cost recovery as part of its pursuit of commercialization of urban services but does not address the issue of the overall strengthening of the local revenue base. The World Bank's (2002) urban transport strategy sees room for greater use of congestion pricing, fuel and other motor vehicle taxation, and higher tariffs on public transport.

The most comprehensive evaluation of the impact of donor projects on own-source revenue performance of urban governments can be found in a special study conducted by the World Bank's IEG (2009). The MDPs covered typically three substantive areas: one-third of projects included support for municipal planning, about half provided support for municipal finance, and all of them financed investments in improved municipal services. The projects generally did not involve reform of the intergovernmental fiscal and transfer system. In the area of own-source revenue mobilization, MDPs typically involved improvements in tax records, cadastres, and revenue collection. More than two-thirds of the projects had only modest results in this area. According to the evaluation, successful revenue mobilization efforts were found where municipalities had clear incentives, particularly where project funding for service investments was conditioned on revenue improvements.[11] On the other hand, where high-level government grants were readily available as alternative sources of finance, own-source revenue effort lagged.

In the case of three World Bank MDPs separately evaluated by IEG (2006a) in Indonesia, no significant improvements in local revenues were observed, leading to serious problems with the funding of operations and maintenance expenses for the infrastructure supported by the project, and hence the sustainability of the project investments. In the case of two urban water supply projects, technical assistance for improved revenue mobilization was evaluated as moderately successful in terms of improved revenue performance, but there remained severe weaknesses in municipal revenue-raising capacity, which undermined the sustainability of the program (IEG 2006c). More generally, a review of individual urban project evaluations by IEG shows a notable lack of attention to the issue of own-source revenue generation, which is surprising in view of the importance of assuring an adequate municipal revenue base if loans are to be repaid and investments are to be sustainable.

In 2006 the Independent Evaluation Department of the AsDB in 2006 published a special evaluation study of AsDB support for urban development, which under the heading of capacity building and institutional development assessed AsDB's support for improvements in urban financial resource management, including water tariff revisions, improvement in billing and collection from computerization, increased collection of taxes, private-sector participation in projects, and management information systems.[12] It rated the performance of AsDB-funded urban projects poorly on capacity building and institutional development, and especially on financial and revenue-generating capacity of municipalities, explaining the low sustainability ratings of AsDB's urban development projects.

This link between poor revenue-raising capacity and low project sustainability is painfully obvious in all the country-specific evaluations of AsDB's urban projects that were reviewed. In particular, the urban projects in Karnataka, India (AsDB 2007); Indonesia (AsDB 2009b); Manila, Philippines (AsDB 2008c); and

---

[11] This was the case with the World Bank's Kazan Municipal Development Loan (IEG 2008a).

[12] In 2006 the Independent Evaluation Department was still called the Department of Operations Evaluation. For simplicity, AsDB's evaluation unit is consistently referred to as the Independent Evaluation Department here.

Vietnam (AsDB 2009d) had problems with own-revenue generation and hence with the financing of operations and maintenance, and project evaluation reports stress the importance of enhancing financing capacity. Among the key constraints listed are unwillingness or inability of municipal governments to raise and collect local service charges and taxes and inadequate attention by AsDB to the political and capacity constraints in designing and implementing these projects.

EBRD (2010) also notes the importance of own-source revenue mobilization for program sustainability but observes that municipal projects supported by EBRD often have found it difficult to raise urban service tariffs, a key objective under EBRD's commercialization strategy, to cost-covering levels, especially in the less advanced transition economies in Eastern Europe and Central Asia. Key reasons for this lack of progress are affordability concerns and lack of political will among the local authorities.

Borrowing

To facilitate the development of private urban finance and municipal access to financial markets, the donor strategies call for the development of appropriate legal and regulatory frameworks and for improving cities' credit worthiness, supported by structured debt instruments and credit enhancements, including guarantees from official agencies such as the U.S. Overseas Private Investment Corporation (International Housing Coalition 2009).[13] The World Bank strategy envisages increased activity by the World Bank Group's Subnational Finance Program, under which the International Finance Corporation, with World Bank technical support, provides funding on market terms to subnational governments for infrastructure investment and to facilitate access to private financial markets.[14] AsDB (2008b) argues that a "cluster" approach to urban development, under which cities that form natural economic clusters in a specified region cooperate in the planning and implementation of urban service provision, also facilitates the establishment of creditworthy entities that can access private finance more readily than individual cities. The Commonwealth Local Government Forum cites successful examples of private sourcing of urban finance with the municipal bond initiative in Ahmedabad, India, and the South African Municipal Infrastructure Investment Unit as examples of successful efforts to attract private financing (Dirie 2005).[15] AsDB notes that Korean municipalities have already issued bonds and considers it likely that China, India, Pakistan, and the Philippines will be able to issue municipal bonds in the near future (AsDB 2008b).

We found no systematic assessment of donor support for developing municipal access to credit markets. The World Bank's evaluation of MDPs (IEG 2009) offers some insight in its review of eight projects that supported municipalities in gaining access to credit markets, none of them in sub-Saharan Africa and East Asia. Six of

---

[13] It is noteworthy, though, that the strategies generally do not establish a clear link between the need to improve the cities' own-source revenue-raising capacity and the establishment of their credit worthiness.

[14] For more information on this program, see International Finance Corporation (2012).

[15] The South African Municipal Infrastructure Investment Unit is funded by the South African government and a small grant by USAID. It in turn provides grants to local governments to assist in meeting the costs of the preparation of public-private partnership projects for urban infrastructure.

these eight initiatives were judged successful. They involved support for municipal debt management, for establishing municipal credit facilities, for developing credit-rating systems, and for general improvements of municipal credit worthiness.[16] They found that easy access to central government grants was a disincentive for municipalities seeking credit.

Another source of information on the effectiveness of support for municipal credit mechanisms can be found in Annez, Huet, and Peterson (2008), who assess the experience of the World Bank with its support for MDFs.[17] As noted above, MDFs are institutional mechanisms for national governments to channel funding, both their own and those of external donors, to a multitude of municipalities in support of municipal, and especially urban, development. These funds can be provided as loans, grants, or a combination of both and are often supplemented with technical assistance for the strengthening of municipal institutional capacity, including financial management, planning, and resource mobilization.

According to Annez, Huet, and Peterson (2008), the credit model of MDFs works best in countries with a relatively well-developed financial sector and relatively strong municipal capacities. It was applied successfully in Latin America, with the La Financiera del Desarrollo Territorial S.A. (FINDETER) program in Colombia the most outstanding success (box 15.1). However, the state-level MDF introduced in a Brazilian project ran into difficulties due to poor design and legal limits on municipal borrowing (IEG 2006c).

Annez, Huet, and Peterson (2008) identify a number of challenges that need to be addressed by donors in the preparation of MDF credit operations:

- Municipalities should not bear unhedged foreign exchange risk; alternatives include the central government assuming such risk or hedging through facilities offered by institutions such as the World Bank.
- Donors should not burden MDF operations with policy conditionality aiming to reform the financial system; this is better handled through complementary development policy loans.
- New MDF institutions may be the preferred approach, but working through existing financial institutions should also be considered.
- MDF operations need to be realistic in their assessment of municipal creditworthiness, municipal loan demand, and willingness of banks to take on municipal credit risk.
- Municipal loan demand may be limited by uncompetitive MDF terms relative for commercial loan terms, by the availability of intergovernmental grants, by legal constraints on municipalities' ability to take on debt, or simply by their reluctance to do so. The ready availability of grants from higher-level government also discouraged some municipalities from taking up the MDF credits.

---

[16] IEG (2009) notes especially the successful examples of the MDFs in Colombia; Tamil Nadu, India; and Georgia.

[17] Annez, Huet, and Peterson (2008) refer to MDFs as "urban investment funds."

BOX 15.1

Municipal credit in Colombia: FINDETER

A particular success story is FINDETER in Colombia. The World Bank's support for Colombia's decentralization process during the 1990s included two municipal development loans for US$60 million and US$75 million, respectively. Key objectives of these two projects were to improve municipal service provision and develop a municipal credit market. The first project, approved in 1991, supported the creation of FINDETER, an organization set up specifically to rediscount long-term commercial bank loans to municipalities. Commercial banks took on municipal credit risk, but the rediscounting mechanism allowed them to offer twelve-year maturities instead of the usual five-year maturities. The second project, approved in 1998, whose preparation involved a systematic review of the experience with the first project, provided additional support for continued and scaled up operations of FINDETER.

The evaluation (IEG 2006b) assessed the performance of the two projects as satisfactory. The overall results included (1) a successfully functioning intermediary MDF (see below); (2) the development of local credit-rating institutions; (3) improved municipal creditworthiness; (4) improved fiscal performance of the municipal sector based on improved cadastral services and local revenue collection; and (5) improved municipal services.

The evaluation report notes a few challenges:

- The quality and timeliness of cadastral services remained mixed, and revenue performance of municipalities was not uniformly positive.
- The reluctance of some municipalities to incur debt limited loan demand.
- The government expanded FINDETER's mandate to include administration of central-local matching grants; this risked undermining FINDETER's strong record as an intermediary of commercial credit.
- While the first loan was cofinanced by the World Bank and Inter-American Development Bank (IADB), this was not repeated for the second loan; instead, two parallel loans were set up in order to facilitate procurement (due to the different procurement practices of the two development banks).

SOURCE: IEG (2006b).

The AsDB's review of its urban projects and MDPs does not report on any experience with support for municipal debt management, borrowing, or bond market development. However, AsDB's Indonesia urban project evaluations mention the reluctance of municipalities to borrow as a constraint to the implementation of AsDB's projects (AsDB 2009b; 2010b). AsDB (2008a) also concludes that MDFs, while helpful as a channeling mechanism for intergovernmental transfers, have not been effective in supporting access to private capital markets.

EBRD reports that private cofinancing of municipal projects from local or foreign banks was limited because of lack of interest among the banks, in part due to their lack of familiarity with municipal financing (EBRD 2010).

Intergovernmental Transfers

The strategy documents recognize that most cities today depend heavily on transfers from higher-level government but found the transfer mechanisms unpredictable and poorly structured in terms of the support and incentives they provide. The general recommendation is that transfers should be a combination of (1) untied grants, linked to reliable national revenue sources (e.g., the value added tax or sales tax); and (2) performance-based grants, which provide incentives for predetermined and monitored output of urban services (possibly involving municipal contracts with higher-level government). The World Bank (2009a, 9) urban strategy puts it as follows: "Performance benchmarks may include such items as timely preparation of budgets and financial reports, greater citizen participation in setting budget priorities, better maintenance of infrastructure assets, and measurable improvement in local service quality or coverage. Local governments that perform well or meet the contractual standard are rewarded with additional grant funds. Poor performers in principle should be penalized by a reduction in transfers."[18]

USAID stresses the importance of fair, timely, predictable, and transparent transfer systems. AsDB (2008a) notes that MDFs, which are institutions set up to channel transfers to municipalities, combined with performance monitoring and technical assistance, can be effective in assuring appropriate delivery and use of the transfers.

Despite the fact that the aid agencies' urban strategies recognize the importance of well-designed intergovernmental transfer mechanisms for effective urban finance, urban loan programs and their evaluations generally have not focused on transfers, and evaluations make few references to transfers.[19]

The only exception found was the review of MDFs by Annez, Huet, and Peterson (2008). While MDFs in middle-income countries have served as conduits for credit to municipalities, the more prevalent role for MDFs in low-income countries, or countries with weak financial market institutions, is to serve as conduits for national grants transferred to municipalities. Annez, Huet, and Peterson (2008) noted that the Senegal MDF project was highly successful. The MDF was introduced as part of a far-reaching reform of the intergovernmental grant system. It involved the improvement in financial management, in revenue mobilization, and in operations and maintenance by the local governments. Municipal contracts were successfully used. Other donors followed suit in supporting this approach as it reached national scale.

Annez, Huet, and Peterson (2008) also cite successful MDF World Bank projects in the Indian state of Tamil Nadu, where they involved the provision of grants (along with loans), as well as MDF projects elsewhere in South Asia and in sub-Saharan Africa, which principally involved grant-based MDFs. A common feature of grant-based MDF projects was the application of performance targets and/or municipal contracts, which municipalities had to meet or abide by if they wanted to remain eligible for grants. Annez, Huet, and Peterson (2008) note that performance grants and municipal contracts will not work well if governments are reluctant to cut off grants when commitments are not met.

---

[18] The qualifier "in principle" in the last sentence implies a recognition that higher-level authorities may in practice find it difficult to penalize local governments for nonperformance, which of course will undermine the very purpose and likely effectiveness of the performance-based grant approach. This is precisely what evaluations of World Bank projects demonstrated was a problem with performance conditions.

[19] The World Bank addressed transfer systems in the loan programs supporting decentralization but, as noted above, without an explicit focus on urban or metro city governments.

Private Participation in Urban Services

All strategies argue that cities increasingly need to rely on private engagement in urban services and on private sources of funding. AsDB in particular stresses this point for Asia, noting that while private finance has so far not been used to a significant extent, the large savings pool, deepening bond markets, and improved regulation of national financial systems provide a basis for proactively exploring increased reliance on private finance for urban services (AsDB 2008a). EBRD (2004, 4) sees commercialization both as a major instrument and as an outcome of greater private-sector participation in the form of "management contracts, concessions, outsourcing, 'Build, Operate, Transfer' (BOT) contracts and privatization." Perhaps more surprising, the African Development Bank also looks to private finance to play a greater role in urban finance in Africa. The AsDB urban transport strategy document argues that public-private partnerships can be valuable but often involve large financial or in-kind commitments by the municipal authorities and therefore need to be entered into with great care.

While private-sector engagement in urban service provision and finance was a strategic goal for all major agencies, the implementation record is at best mixed. Among 24 World Bank MDPs for which detailed reviews were carried out, only seven projects supported municipalities in seeking access to private investment, and only two of them showed success. According to the evaluation, key constraints were lack of municipal expertise for contract design and management, constraints on municipal tariffs, and the realities and perceptions of political risk and regulatory uncertainty (IEG 2009).

Similarly, AsDB did not promote significant engagement by the private sector.[20] In the cases where it did pursue private engagement (especially in urban water supply programs), it was with mixed success. Where governments provided favorable financial conditions for private investment (e.g., in Manila), private investors were able to operate and provide improved water services (AsDB 2008c), but where there were constraints on tariff setting and collection, private participation did not succeed (e.g., in Indonesia; AsDB 2010b).

EBRD, which pursued the private-sector participation option in the most systematic manner among the three multilateral agencies, also experienced difficulties, due to the complexity of the process of engagement, limitations of capacity in the municipalities to manage private-sector engagement, and lack of political commitment. Overambitious expectations on the part of EBRD staff added to difficulties, as goals of private participation were set at levels difficult to achieve in practice (EBRD 2010).

Financial Management and Planning

All strategies stress the importance of improved urban management and planning, including financial management and planning. The World Bank strategy focuses

---

[20] "In general, AsDB did not succeed in developing large numbers of public-private partnerships or in catalyzing large private sector investments in urban infrastructure. AsDB's work with the private sector to provide urban infrastructure remained sporadic—confined to some housing finance and a few infrastructure investments in city expressways (Bangkok Second Stage Expressway in 1990 and 1994 and the Manila North Tollway) and water supply (Chengdu Water Supply Project and Lyonnaise Viet Nam Water Company) (AsDB 2006, 18).

on four general elements in improved management: professional development; benchmarking performance; community engagement; and application of information and communication technology (World Bank 2009a). These overlap substantially with the priorities for capacity development and institutional strengthening proposed by AsDB (2008a). Both the African Development Bank and the World Bank highlight the importance of demand-side governance improvements, with enhanced accountability through transparent, participatory planning and budgeting mechanisms. The USAID (2011) notes that it supports improved results-oriented budgetary processes and the strengthening of financial management, with special attention to the role of customer surveys and technology.

Three specific institutional mechanisms for improved financial planning and management deserve mentioning:

- City development strategies were developed as a tool for urban planning under the auspices of the Cities Alliance and are recommended as useful tools by the International Housing Coalition and the World Bank. Cities Alliance (2006) specifically stipulates that financial planning should be an explicit part of city development strategies.
- Urban transport funds are a tool recommended by the World Bank (2002) and by AsDB (2009a) as a way to bundle financial resources for metropolitan-wide transport infrastructure investments and as means to attract private financing.
- Municipal development funds, as noted above, are instruments to channel national and foreign funds to municipalities, combined with technical assistance, as well as monitoring of utilization of funds. The AsDB urban strategy highlights the usefulness of MDFs as a mechanism for channeling central government transfers to municipalities but does not recommend them as an instrument for supporting municipalities' efforts to gain greater access to private capital markets. The World Bank's urban strategy makes no reference to such mechanisms (World Bank 2009a), even though Annez, Huet, and Peterson (2008) had recommended that the World Bank, which had reduced its support for this instrument, revive its use in its urban projects.

However, evaluation reports of urban projects devote remarkably little attention to assessing the extent and effectiveness of support provided for strengthening the financial management and planning of the municipalities that are supported. The evaluation of the World Bank's MDPs is the single exception (IEG 2009). It notes that in the area of financial management, MDPs typically involved support for the computerization and integration of municipal accounts, as well as training of financial staff. These efforts generally yielded good results. The report further notes that support for municipal planning, including investment planning, was unduly limited and that MDPs did not draw on the city development strategies instrument even though this is one of the two key pillars of the Cities Alliance, to which the World Bank belongs. The evaluation of EBRD projects notes the need for strong management and timely and accurate data collection to inform municipal decision making. It also stresses the importance of providing technical assistance and training for municipal staff in management and leadership, procurement, and infrastructure program implementation. No mention is made of capacity building in financial management and planning (EBRD 2010).

Specific aspects of MDFs as they relate to the design of credit and grant facilities channeled through such funds are addressed above. There remains the question of whether MDFs are a good institutional framework for supporting municipal finance development and capacity building. The alternative is to work with established ministerial units, which in principle can provide similar services as the MDFs. Based on their review of decades of support by the World Bank for MDFs, Annez, Huet, and Peterson (2008) concluded that the overall performance of MDF operations has been successful and that the World Bank should reinvigorate its support for this institutional approach, while making allowance for the diverse needs and capacities of different municipalities, and should, accordingly, tailor the provision of loans and grants. They further advise that project design and conditionality should remain simple and flexible in response to changing circumstances, to complement MDF project loans with development policy loans for broader policy reform, to apply effective results measurement to inform project design and scaling up, and to allow for financial support from other donors.

The overall evaluation of AsDB's urban operations does not comment on the experience with MDFs (AsDB 2006). But the AsDB's evaluation of donor support for urban development in Bangladesh highlights that the World Bank financed the newly set up Bangladesh MDF, while AsDB and other donors provided support to the existing Department of Local Government Engineering. The limited staff capacity of the Bangladesh MDF, its unfavorable cost sharing and repayment requirements, and the high quality of the department limited the effectiveness of the Bangladesh MDF and led the World Bank to reconsider its support (AsDB 2009c). EBRD (2010) reported on the development of an MDF approach in Bulgaria (and parallel initiatives in Romania and Serbia) but did not evaluate the performance of these initiatives.

Partnerships and Donor Coordination

All donor strategies stress the importance of approaching the urban development challenges by forming partnerships with local communities, local and national governments, the private sector, and civil society organizations. They bring together the many urban stakeholders across countries, cities, and agencies to share experience and best practice, often with the support and active engagement of key donors, especially the multilateral development banks and select bilateral official donors.

The strategies in general pay little attention to the issue of donor fragmentation and need for coordination of donor intervention in the urban sector and in specific cities.[21] It is symptomatic of this lack of attention that none of the reports mentions

---

[21] Exceptions are International Housing Coalition (2009) and EBRD (2004). The fact that principal donors have not systematically supported the development of strategic planning instruments at the city level (e.g., the previously mentioned city development strategies) likely contributed to the lack of focus on partnerships and coordination among donors.

the principles of effective aid endorsed by the Paris Declaration and Accra Agenda for Action, such as sectorwide approaches.[22]

In general, evaluation reports devote little or no attention to the issue of whether and how donors pursued partnerships and donor coordination. One notable exception is an evaluation carried out for AsDB of urban projects in Bangladesh, which covers the operations of four donor agencies (AsDB 2009c).[23] It notes that donor fragmentation has been a serious issue in the urban sector in Bangladesh and that until recently coordination among the principal donors, especially AsDB and the World Bank, was limited (box 15.2). It recommends that the donor community develop a phased program approach for decentralization, improved local revenue authority and capacity, and stronger human resource management at the local level. EBRD (2010) mentions partnerships with other donors in the context of grant cofinancing and policy advice. Grant cofinancing is important for EBRD programs in the poorer countries where fiscal and affordability constraints make it impossible for EBRD-financed projects to function without grant financing, which EBRD generally does not provide.[24] Policy advice also at times requires that EBRD cooperate with other donors. Unfortunately, the evaluation does not assess the effectiveness of EBRD's partnership engagement even though the bank's policy paper stressed the importance of partnerships, as noted earlier (EBRD 2010).

Scaling Up for Greater Impact

One of the key questions that donors should address in their urban sector strategies, and more generally, is how to ensure that the interventions they support not only involve one-off, small, or pilot projects but also are designed to support a longer-term strategy under which successful interventions are systematically scaled up.[25] The World Bank urban strategy stresses the importance of scaling up from local to national impact and promises to support programmatic approaches with strong policy and institutional content (World Bank 2009a). Similarly, AsDB (2008a, 272–273) notes that "the project-by-project approach to infrastructure and services investment has not worked" and calls for "road maps" for long-term engagement by national and local governments, as well as donors, moving from a "shotgun, scattered approach" to "focused support to improved city management." While this is encouraging, a more systematic focus on scaling up is likely needed in the way donors support urban development, including the development of urban financing instruments and institutions.[26]

Among the urban program and project evaluations, EBRD (2010) is the most explicit in its consideration of scaling up. This evaluation report specifically asks whether it is preferable to do freestanding projects in each country or "building an

---

[22]Sectorwide approaches are vehicles to pool donor resources in support of government-led sector strategies and are increasingly used by donors and governments in the education and health sectors.

[23]AsDB (2006) notes that one-quarter of all AsDB urban projects from 1999 to 2006 were cofinanced with other donors, which represented an increase from 1993 to 1999.

[24]EBRD (2010) does not mention the potential issues of sustainability and scalability of grant-financed projects.

[25]For a general statement of the need for scaling up, a framework for approaching the scaling up challenge, and a review of experience, see Hartmann and Linn (2008).

[26]For a general discussion of the experience with scaling up of development interventions and a framework for the analysis of scaling up, see Hartmann and Linn (2008).

BOX 15.2

Evaluation of donor support for urban development in Bangladesh

In 2005 AsDB, the U.K. Department for International Development, the Japanese government, and the World Bank prepared a joint country assistance strategy for Bangladesh. One of the outcomes of this strategy was the preparation of an evaluation of the urban programs of the four agencies, carried out by the AsDB's Independent Evaluation Department with the support of the evaluation departments of the other three donors (AsDB 2009c). From 2001 to 2008, these four donors approved 22 projects for $920 million in Bangladesh (more than half of this by AsDB), while other aid agencies (including the Canadian International Development Agency, the Danish development cooperation DANIDA, Italy, The Netherlands, the U.N. Children's Fund, and the U.N. Development Programme) contributed $239 million. Donors concentrated most of their support on the secondary cities during this period, because of difficulties with implementing projects in the country's largest cities, Dhaka and Chittagong, during the 1990s. Only late in the 2000s did AsDB and the World Bank resume support for these cities.

AsDB (2009c, i) notes that donor presence in the urban sector in Bangladesh was "very scattered" and with "incomplete coverage," especially if one takes into account the smaller donor agencies and nongovernmental organizations and that much of the assistance is not channeled through government agencies but implemented directly by donor and nongovernmental organizations' project implementation units. In the case of the water supply and sanitation, a sector donor coordination process was relatively well established, with an active local consultation group for water supply and sanitation counting 30 members. The four principal donors initiated a partnership framework for water supply and sanitation in 2007. It led to the preparation of a substantial water pipeline and sanitation projects in Dhaka and Chittagong. (The Department for International Development eventually did not sign onto the framework due to a shift in priorities.) The local consultation group for urban development did not function as well, due to low attendance, disagreements between the AsDB and the World Bank, absence of an agreed sector strategy, and lack of government engagement. DANIDA, one of the smaller donor agencies, tried to initiate a sectorwide approach for donors, but this did not take off.

Overall, the evaluation concludes "that external agencies do not seem to work hard to address the Paris Declaration commitment to 'avoid, to the maximum extent possible, creating dedicated structures for day-to-day management and implementation of aid-financed projects and programs'. Similarly, the agencies seem to have lost track of the ambition to 'Implement, where feasible, common arrangements at country level for planning, funding (e.g., joint financial arrangements), disbursement, monitoring, evaluating and reporting to government on donor activities and aid flows. Increased use of program-based aid modalities can contribute to this effort'" (AsDB 2009c, 33).

The evaluation recommends a phased programmatic approach for all donors in the urban sector, in support of an agreed urban sector strategy; explicit division of labor among donors, supported by a dedicated and donor-funded urban sector implementation agency; and a long-term commitment of donor funding, including for operation and maintenance requirements. The report mentions the need for attention to urban finance issues (in particular, water and sanitation tariffs) and recommends that municipal accountability be enhanced by making donor loans and grants conditional on the local revenue potential of urban subprojects to achieve greater cost recovery, but it does not provide any detailed analysis or recommendations.

SOURCE: AsDB (2009c).

expertise and doing many similar projects in several countries to obtain a synergistic effect" (EBRD 2010, 1). And while it does not provide an unequivocal answer, it does consider various aspects of the issue, including its recommendation that EBRD develop systematic case studies of "demonstration projects," based on effective project monitoring, and the recommendation that EBRD assist in the preparation of investment programs for individual cities, which could then serve as a framework for sequential projects funded by EBRD. The report cites the case of a sequence of water supply projects in Tajikistan, where EBRD first funded a project in the provincial city of Khujand in 2004 in support of improvements in and commercialization of the water services in the city. Since the project was judged to have been successful, it was followed up with a second project in Khujand and was used as a model for the preparation of two other EBRD water projects in Tajikistan covering, respectively, three cities in the south of the country and seven cities in the north and east. Other donors, such as the World Bank, have looked toward the EBRD experience as a guide, and the local gas and electricity companies in Khujand have been applying the lessons from the approach to commercialization of the water company (EBRD 2010).[27]

None of the other evaluations reviewed addresses whether the donor agency followed a systematic approach to assure appropriate follow-up of successful projects in the form of replication or scaling up of successful intervention, either through sequential projects funded by the donor himself or in partnership with others, or by appropriate hand-offs to other actors, whether government, private entity, or external donor.

Perhaps the most striking example of a lack of consideration of this issue is the case of the World Bank's evaluation of its MDPs. Although IEG (2009) covers many countries in which the World Bank funded more than one successive MDP, it does not comment on whether the multiple projects systematically built on one another in terms of coverage, institutional design, and lessons learned.[28] The absence of effective M&E gives rise to the inference that this was not the case. Similarly, most project-specific evaluations of multiple World Bank urban projects in specific countries give no indication that there was any serious longer-term planning and learning from one project to the next.[29] The one exception is the evaluation of the two FINDETER projects in Colombia in IEG (2006b), where the World Bank's second project was clearly a follow-on project of the first, even though M&E was again assessed as weak.

AsDB evaluations similarly do not address the question of scaling up, although AsDB (2006) flags the fact that AsDB failed to develop longer-term relations with specific cities, as recommended in its urban sector strategy.

One important indication of whether an effective scaling up approach is followed by aid agencies is the quality of the M&E in project design and implementation. If M&E is weak, the basis for judging whether a project is achieving its goals is weak or absent, and learning, which is a critical input into an effective scaling up process, cannot take place. The World Bank's evaluation of its MDPs concluded that M&E was generally weak. Only four of the twenty-four detailed project case

---

[27] EBRD (2010) goes one important step further in commenting on the internal processes and incentives within the organization. It notes that the internal review and approval process discourages repeat projects within a given country and that the performance bonuses for project officers, which are set according to the number of projects approved, encourage the development of projects that cover one city at a time rather than multiple cities.

[28] IEG (2009) covers 43 countries with more than one MDP and 25 countries with more than two MDPs. In the case of China, the report lists 23 MDPs.

[29] For examples of the lack of long-term sectoral planning and learning see IEG (2007a) for three MDPs in China, IEG (2006a) for three MDPs in Indonesia, and IEG (2006c) for two MDPs in Brazil.

studies carried out for this evaluation showed effective M&E.[30] Lack of focus on appropriate results metrics and lack of interest by the municipal authorities were the most common sources of difficulty. Most individual World Bank urban project evaluations reviewed also reported a weakness of M&E.[31] In the case of AsDB, the overall evaluation of urban programs does not comment on the quality of M&E (AsDB 2006), but two of the AsDB urban projects evaluations (Indonesia and Vietnam) highlight limited or poor M&E, and in the case of Indonesia the failure to learn the lessons from earlier AsDB operations was noted (AsDB 2009b; 2009d). EBRD (2010) does not comment on the quality of M&E.

CONCLUSIONS

The assessment of the available aggregate information on financing needs and aid flows for urban development presented in this chapter allows the following conclusions.

- Donors' urban strategies generally focus on the right issues and approaches to urban finance policy, but there is a glaring disconnect between the strategies and their implementation on the ground in all the areas of urban finance policy that were reviewed.
- Current aid flows to urban areas are undersized relative to needs, and they have been stagnant over time, despite updated strategies of select donors who seek to give greater prominence to urban development issues. Sub-Saharan Africa is underserved in terms of urban aid, although for the World Bank's MDPs, African project performance is above the average of urban projects worldwide.
- Urban aid suffers from the same micro-macro paradox as other forms of aid: individual urban development projects have been found to be satisfactory or successful in proportions similar to or better than projects in other sectors, but in practice, urban projects have not been deliberately sequenced so they would build on one another. On the contrary, the available evidence points to a lack of a systematic approach to replication and scaling up of successful urban development interventions due to pervasive weaknesses in M&E and lack of effective learning.
- The ability and willingness of municipal governments to raise their own-source revenue have been weak, and donor support for targeted improvements in local revenue capacity has been limited or has had limited impact; similarly, other forms of finance, such as intergovernmental transfers and local borrowing, have not received adequate attention. Intergovernmental transfers generally have been outside the purview of donor-supported urban development projects and even interfered with the implementation of credit-based urban development programs. In practice, few donor-supported initiatives can be found in judicious development of municipal borrowing practices, although some innovations have been suc-

---

[30] According to IEG (2009), this problem was already identified in IEG (2004) evaluating the World Bank's urban portfolio, in IEG (2010) for four projects in Mexico, and in IEG (2007c) for a project in Bangladesh.

[31] For examples of the lack of M&E, see IEG (2007a) for three projects in China, IEG (2006a) for three projects in Indonesia, and IEG (2006c) for two projects in Brazil.

cessful in developing responsible debt management, municipal credit ratings, and the successful issuance of municipal bonds.

- Evaluations of urban programs are a potentially useful but apparently underutilized source of learning for donors. Particularly problematic in the evaluations is the lack of systematic focus on whether sequential projects in a particular country are part of a longer-term urban development strategy for the country and building systematically on the experience of the preceding projects.

Given these trends, it appears unlikely that urban development assistance will receive the kind of attention from donors that would seem to be justified by need and by successful past experiences with shelter, slum upgrading, and low-income housing. Furthermore, donors do not focus on the specific opportunities and challenges of large metropolitan areas in developing countries, missing one of the most important strategic challenges of development.

If donors paid more attention to the implementation of their urban development strategies, improved urban financial management and planning, partnership development, donor coordination and division of labor, wholesale (multiple-city) approaches, sustainability, and scaling up of the programs they support, they could have far greater impact on urban development.

The design and implementation of the financing aspects of urban development projects and programs are key success factors for the impact, sustainability, and scalability of urban development programs funded by external donors. In this, MDFs seem to be good options for channeling credit to well-managed small- and medium-size municipalities. Urban development policy and investment loans could be effectively pooled by multiple donors to support urban/city investment strategies, possibly in the form of sectorwide approaches. Foreign exchange risk could be hedged or removed from municipal responsibilities.

There is no substitute for high-quality prior analysis of urban development, institutional, and financial challenges. Political stakeholder analysis is critical, as practice has shown that financial project conditions often are not fulfilled because of political opposition, rather than technical design. If donors neglect the urban finance dimension in design, implementation, and evaluation, they will likely be less successful in assisting countries to respond effectively to the great opportunities and challenges of rapid urbanization.

REFERENCES

African Development Bank. 2010. The bank group's urban development strategy: Transforming Africa's cities and towns into engines of economic growth and social development. Tunis: African Development Bank.

AidData. 2011. AidData 2.0 [database]. www.aiddata.org

Annez, Patricia Clarke, Gwenaelle Huet, and George E. Peterson. 2008. Lessons for the urban century: Decentralized infrastructure finance in the World Bank. Washington, DC: World Bank.

AsDB. 2006. Special evaluation study on urban sector strategy and operations. Manila.

———. 2007. India: Karnataka urban infrastructure development project. Performance Evaluation Report. Manila.

——. 2008a. *Managing Asian cities: Asia's urban challenge and how to respond.* Manila.

——. 2008b. *City cluster development: Toward an urban-led development strategy for Asia.* Urban Development Series. Manila.

——. 2008c. ADB assistance to water supply services in metro Manila. Evaluation Study. Manila.

——. 2009a. *Changing course: A new paradigm for sustainable urban transport.* Urban Development Series. Manila.

——. 2009b. Indonesia: Metropolitan Bogor, Tangerang, and Bekasi urban development sector project. Performance Evaluation Report. Manila.

——. 2009c. Sector assistance program evaluation for the urban sector and water supply and sanitation in Bangladesh: An exploratory evaluation of the programs of ADB and other aid agencies. Manila.

——. 2009d. Sector assistance program evaluation on urban services and water supply and sanitation in Vietnam. Manila.

——. 2010a. Lao People's Democratic Republic: Vientiane urban infrastructure and services project. Performance Evaluation Report. Manila.

——. 2010b. Indonesia: Has the multi-sector approach been effective for urban services assistance? Evaluation Study. Manila.

Buckley, Robert M., and Jerry Kalarickal. 2006. *Directions in development: Infrastructure. Thirty years of world bank shelter lending: What have we learned?* Washington, DC: World Bank.

Cities Alliance. 2006. *Guide to city development strategies: Improving urban performance.* Washington, DC.

Commission for Africa. 2005. Our common interest. http://www.commissionforafrica.info/2005-report

Dirie, Ilias. 2005. Municipal finance: Innovative resourcing for municipal infrastructure and service provision. Coventry, U.K.: Commonwealth Local Government Forum.

EBRD. 2004. Municipal and environmental infrastructure operations policy. London.

——. 2010. Municipal and environmental infrastructure operations policy review. Special Study. London.

Findley, Michael G., Darren Hawkins, Robert L. Hicks, Daniel L. Nielson, Bradley C. Parks, Ryan M. Powers, J. Timmons Roberts, Michael J. Tierney, and Sven Wilson. 2009. AidData: Tracking development finance. Paper presented at the PLAID Data Vetting Workshop, Washington, DC (September).

Hartmann, Arntraud, and Johannes Linn. 2008. Scaling up: A framework and lessons for development effectiveness from literature and practice. Wolfensohn Center Working Paper No. 4. Washington, DC: Brookings Institution.

IEG. 2004. Improving the lives of the poor through investment in cities: An update on the performance of the World Bank's urban portfolio. Washington, DC: World Bank.

IEG. 2006a. Second East Java urban development project; Bali infrastructure project; municipal innovations project. Project Performance Assessment Report. Washington, DC.

——. 2006b. Municipal development project; urban infrastructure services development project. Project Performance Assessment Report. Washington, DC.

——. 2006c. Ceara urban development and water resources project; Ceara water resources management pilot project. Project Performance Assessment Report. Washington, DC.

——. 2007a. Tianjin urban development and environment project, Zhejiang multicities development project, Shanghai environment project. Project Performance Assessment Report. Washington, DC.

——. 2007b. *A decade of action in transport: An evaluation of World Bank assistance to the transport sector, 1995–2005.* Washington, DC.

——. 2007c. Dhaka urban transport project. Project Performance Assessment Report. Washington, DC.

——. 2008a. Kazan municipal development loan. Project Performance Assessment Report. Washington, DC.

———. 2008b. Decentralization in client countries: An evaluation of World Bank support, 1990–2007. Washington, DC.

———. 2009. Improving municipal management for cities to succeed. Washington, DC.

———. 2010. FOVI restructuring project; affordable housing and urban poverty sector adjustment loan; second affordable housing and urban poverty reduction development policy loan; third affordable housing and urban poverty reduction development policy loan. Project Performance Assessment Report. Washington, DC.

International Finance Corporation. 2012. Subnational finance. www.ifc.org/subnationalfinance

International Housing Coalition. 2009. *The challenge of an urban world: An opportunity for U.S. foreign assistance*. Washington, DC.

Kharas, Homi, Laurence Chandy, and Joshua Hermias. 2010. External assistance for urban development: A scoping study for further research. Wolfensohn Center for Development Working Paper No. 14. Washington, DC: Brookings Institution.

Stren, Richard. 2007. International assistance for cities in developing countries: Do we still need it? In *Global urban poverty: Setting the agenda,* ed. Allison M. Garland, Mejgan Massoumi, and Blair A. Ruble. Comparative Urban Studies Project. Washington, DC: Woodrow Wilson International Center for Scholars.

U.N. High-Level Panel on Financing for Development. 2001. Report of the high-level panel on financing for development. New York: United Nations.

United Nations. n.d. United Nations Millennium Development Goals. Goal 7: Ensure Environmental Stability. http://www.un.org/millenniumgoals/environ.shtml

———. 2012. Millennium Development Goals indicators. mdgs.un.org/unsd/mdg/Data.aspx

USAID. 2011. Programming considerations of urban finance. www.makingcitieswork.org/urban -theme/programming-considerations-urban-finance

World Bank. 2002. *Cities on the move: A World Bank urban transport strategy review*. Washington, DC.

———. 2009a. Systems of cities: Harnessing the potential of urbanization for growth and poverty alleviation. The World Bank urban and local government strategy. Washington, DC.

———. 2009b. World development report 2009: Reshaping economic geography. Washington, DC.

CONTRIBUTORS

Editors

ROY W. BAHL
Regents Professor of Economics
Georgia State University

JOHANNES F. LINN
Senior Resident Fellow, Emerging
   Markets Forum
Nonresident Senior Fellow, Brookings
   Institution

DEBORAH L. WETZEL
Country Director for Brazil
World Bank

Authors

RICHARD M. BIRD
Professor Emeritus
University of Toronto

KARIN L. BRANDT
Research Analyst and Program
   Administrator
Lincoln Institute of Land Policy

RIËL C. D. FRANZSEN
Professor, African Tax Institute
University of Pretoria

MARIA E. FREIRE
Senior Consultant
World Bank

Professional Lecturer
Johns Hopkins University

GREGORY K. INGRAM
President and CEO
Lincoln Institute of Land Policy

DOUGLAS H. KEARE
Former Visiting Fellow
Lincoln Institute of Land Policy

HOMI KHARAS
Senior Fellow and Deputy Director
Brookings Institution

ZHI LIU
Lead Infrastructure Specialist, East Asia
   and Pacific Region
World Bank

JORGE MARTINEZ-VAZQUEZ
Regents Professor of Economics
Georgia State University

WILLIAM J. MCCLUSKEY
Research Reader, School of the Built
   Environment
University of Ulster

ABHAY PETHE
Professor, Department of Economics
University of Mumbai

ANWAR M. SHAH
Consultant/Adviser
World Bank

ENID SLACK
Director, Institute of Municipal Finance
    and Governance, Munk School of
    Global Affairs
University of Toronto

PAUL SMOKE
Professor, Wagner Graduate School of
    Public Service
New York University

INDER SUD
John O. Rankin Professor of
    International Affairs, Elliott School
    of International Affairs
George Washington University

CHRISTINE P. WONG
Senior Research Fellow and Chair,
    Chinese Studies
University of Oxford

SERDAR YILMAZ
Senior Economist
World Bank

SHAHID YUSUF
Chief Economist, The Growth Dialogue
George Washington University

INDEX

ABOUT THE LINCOLN INSTITUTE OF LAND POLICY

The Lincoln Institute of Land Policy is a private operating foundation whose mission is to improve the quality of public debate and decisions in the areas of land policy and land-related taxation in the United States and around the world. The Institute's goals are to integrate theory and practice to better shape land policy and to provide a nonpartisan forum for discussion of the multidisciplinary forces that influence public policy. This focus on land derives from the Institute's founding objective—to address the links between land policy and social and economic progress—that was identified and analyzed by political economist and author Henry George.

The work of the Institute is organized in three departments: Valuation and Taxation, Planning and Urban Form, and International Studies, which includes programs on Latin America and China. We seek to inform decision making through education, research, policy evaluation, demonstration projects, and the dissemination of information through our publications, Web site, and other media. Our programs bring together scholars, practitioners, public officials, policy makers, journalists, and citizens in a collegial learning environment. The Institute does not take a particular point of view, but rather serves as a catalyst to facilitate analysis and discussion of land use and taxation issues—to make a difference today and to help policy makers plan for tomorrow.

The Lincoln Institute of Land Policy is an equal opportunity institution.

LINCOLN INSTITUTE
OF LAND POLICY

113 Brattle Street
Cambridge, MA 02138-3400 USA

Phone: 1-617-661-3016 or 1-800-526-3873
Fax: 1-617-661-7235 or 1-800-526-3944
E-mail: help@lincolninst.edu
Web: www.lincolninst.edu